DEFINING AND MEASURING SUSTAINABILITY
The Biogeophysical Foundations

Edited by
Mohan Munasinghe
and
Walter Shearer

Distributed for the United Nations University
by
The World Bank
Washington, D.C.

Library of Congress Cataloging-in-Publication Data

Defining and measuring sustainability : the biogeophysical foundations
/ edited by Mohan Munasinghe, Walter Shearer.
     p.   cm.
    Includes bibliographical references.
    ISBN 0-8213-3134-5
     1. Sustainable development. 2. Natural resources—Management.
3. Sustainable development—Case studies.   I. Munasinghe, Mohan,
1945–   . II. Shearer, Walter.
HC79.E5D442   1995
333.7—dc20

95-2865
CIP

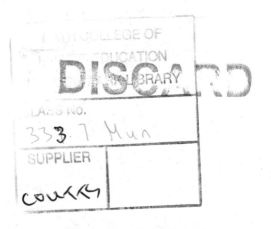

Contents

Foreword

The *Report of the World Commission on Environment and Development*, also known as the Brundtland Commission, has directed the attention of the international development community and the ecologically concerned to the goal of sustainable development. This goal was the focus in June 1992 of the United Nations Conference on Environment and Development, which resulted in the Rio Declaration, Agenda 21, and the UN Commission on Sustainable Development.

The true significance of this term presents difficulties because it involves two concepts that may appear incompatible at first sight: sustainability and development. Some have come to associate various aspects of development with destruction and degradation of the environment, while for others sustainability connotes economic stagnation. If the goal of sustainable development is to be achieved, a rethinking and reorganization of some widely-used concepts of development will be needed, as well as a rethinking of the views that equate sustainability exclusively with protecting flora and fauna.

Before a new paradigm for development emerges, a better scientific understanding of the requirements for sustainability is essential. We must be able to compare development and sustainability at different times and in different places to ensure that both are being achieved. To carry this out, clear definitions and practical measuring scales are required. The concept of development has been studied in great detail, and its definition, measurement scales, and the problems of the indicators in current use have been debated at length. However, comparatively little effort has been devoted to how sustainability is to be defined and measured.

As an international community of scholars working on the problems of human survival, development, and welfare, the United Nations University (UNU) was established, with its headquarters in Tokyo, Japan, to bring the best minds to bear on global problems of this nature. The World Bank has been pursuing the basic goals of development and poverty eradication for five decades. It was for this reason that we were pleased when the other sponsoring organizations agreed to join us in assembling a group of outstanding scientists in an International Conference on the Definition and Measurement of Sustainability: the Biological and Physical Foundations, held at the World Bank in June 1992. The primary goal of the conference was to explore the prospects of establishing a scientifically rigorous definition and set of measures for sustainability.

The sustainability of human economies in social, economic, and environmental terms requires the continuous and uninterrupted production of a minimum amount of natural biological products for food. In addition, we have come to rely heavily on a wide variety of organic products for medicines, fibre, energy, and construction materials. Thus, the net primary production generated by photosynthesis is a major pillar that sustains human beings as well as almost all other forms of life on Earth. Maintaining biological productivity is a key to sustainability.

A major problem that we are now facing for having neglected this cardinal principle emerged in the 1980s when it was estimated that a significant proportion of the net primary production of all terrestrial ecosystems was being diverted directly or indirectly to human use. With the anticipated doubling of the human population by 2050 and the urgent need for development, if present patterns of consumption persist, humanity will soon face the problems arising from diverting for its own use an ever increasing and unsustainably high volume of natural resources. In the face of such over-exploitation, the quality of the environment and of human life is likely to decline rapidly, accompanied by widespread suffering.

The factors necessary for the maintenance of biological production include fertility or nutrient availability, energy, adequate moisture, proper substrates, subcritical levels of toxic substances, and an adequate and genetically varied stock of biological organisms. Such factors form the biogeophysical foundation of sustainability. Only through biogeophysical measurements can the status and trends of natural and managed ecosystems be established and the true effectiveness of sustainable management practices be assessed.

The tasks before the conference participants were difficult ones—to make significant progress in: (a) agreeing on a scientific definition of biogeophysical sustainability; (b) providing the biogeophysical framework to complement the social and economic dimensions of an overall measure for sustainability; and (c) recommending indicators and biogeophysical measures for monitoring and predicting the sustainability of the major managed ecosystems.

The participants were presented with an even greater and more important challenge—to recommend, after careful consideration, a scientifically sound and practical set of indices of biogeophysical sustainability. The ecological equivalent of the system of national accounts and the gross national product employed in economics would be of immense use in identifying overstressed regions, comparing management practices, and monitoring the effects of policy decisions. To be practical, such indices would have to be based on data that can be readily and frequently obtained and be applicable to regions with landscape, national and continental dimensions. Yet the indices would have to be transparent enough for policymakers and citizens alike to comprehend their fundamental significance in the same way that people intuitively understand the meaning of the GNP. Thus, it appears that these measurements would somehow *have to* reflect net primary productivity, biological diversity, and perhaps other factors integrated over a mosaic of different ecosystems. Recent work on environmental indicators at the World Bank and elsewhere underlines the formidable problems of defining, measuring, analyzing, and interpreting such indicators.

This volume, which presents the highlights of the conference, shows that the participants have indeed taken a major step forward toward realizing the tasks set before them. At the same time, the ten conference recommendations indicate the formidable problems that still remain in attempting to agree on a practical scientific definition of and set of measures for sustainability. The volume contains a wealth of thought, discussion, and debate that will have to be taken into account in the final formulation of the practical definition and set of measures. For taking time from their important responsibilities to focus for a few days on this important aspect of sustainable development, the United Nations University and the World Bank extend their appreciation to all the distinguished participants who took part.

As this volume is the result of a cooperative effort, we would like to conclude by thanking all the co-sponsors and collaborators listed in the acknowledgments who made the conference successful and this publication possible.

Heitor Gurgulino de Souza
Rector, United Nations University
Tokyo

Ismail Serageldin
Vice President
Environmentally Sustainable Development
The World Bank, Washington, D.C.

Acknowledgments

As this volume is the result of a collaborative effort, a special debt of gratitude is owed to the following co-sponsors who made the conference and this publication possible:

- the United States Environmental Protection Agency's Environmental Monitoring and Assessment Program and, in particular, Dan McKenzie, who generously supported the conference;

- the Smithsonian Institution and especially Assistant Secretary Thomas Lovejoy for his contribution to the scientific organization and leadership of the conference;

- the East-West Center in Honolulu, where the first planning meeting for the conference was held and which also played a role in supporting the conference, and especially Richard Carpenter, without whose experience, insight, and perseverance the conference could not have achieved so much;

- the Ecological Society of America and its Sustainable Biosphere Initiative, and in particular its former president, Jane Lubchenco, as well as Jim Gosz and Stephanie Cirillo, for valuable support and assistance in convening the conference; and

- the governments of Norway and Sweden for partial financial support.

Sincere appreciation is extended to all the distinguished participants who took part in the conference for taking time from their important responsibilities to focus for a few days on this important aspect of sustainable development.

Gratitude is also extended to Courtesy Associates, particularly to Stacey Sickels, whose assistance was crucial to the professional way in which the conference was managed.

The editors extend a special note of thanks to the authors of the valuable contributions that made this volume possible and who cooperated so agreeably during the editing process, and to Adelaida Schwab for expertly shepherding the manuscript, to Maria Theresa Camilleri for diligently assembling the manuscript and transcribing the discussions, to Ramon Ray for preparing the graphics, and to Elizabeth Forsyth, Didier Godat, Connie Eysenck, and Stephanie Gerard for invaluable assistance during the editing and production process.

Contributors

Authors

Darwin W. Anderson is with the Department of Soil Science at the University of Saskatchewan, Saskatoon, Saskatchewan, Canada.

Meinrat O. Andreae is director of the Biogeochemistry Department of the Max Planck Institute for Chemistry, Mainz, Germany.

Peter B. Bayley is with the Illinois Natural Survey in Champaign, Illinois.

Gordon Beanlands is associate professor in the School for Resource and Environmental Studies at Dalhousie University in Halifax, Nova Scotia, Canada.

Stephen A. Bocking is assistant professor in the Department of Environment and Resource Studies at Trent University in Peterborough, Ontario, Canada.

Enríque H. Bucher is with the Centro de Zoología Aplicada of the Universidad de Córdoba in Córdoba, Argentina.

C. Lee Campbell is with the Department of Plant Pathology (USDA Air Quality) at North Carolina State University in Raleigh, North Carolina.

Richard A. Carpenter is a consultant who was formerly with the East-West Center of the Environment and Policy Institute in Honolulu, Hawaii.

Juan Carlos Castilla is a full professor in the Facultad de Ciencias Biológicas (Ecologia) at the Universidad Católica de Chile, in Santiago, Chile.

Gretchen C. Daily is the Winslow and Heinz Foundation Postdoctoral Fellow jointly at the Energy and Resources Group of the University of California in Berkeley, California and the Center for Conservation Biology at Stanford University in Stanford, California.

V. H. Dale is with the Environmental Sciences Division at the Oak Ridge National Laboratory in Oak Ridge, Tennessee.

Christopher F. D'Elia is provost, University of Maryland Biotechnology Institute in College Park, Maryland.

Robert E. Dickinson is a professor in the Institute of Atmospheric Physics at the University of Arizona in Tucson, Arizona.

Paul R. Ehrlich is the Bing Professor of Population Studies at Stanford University in Stanford, California.

Jerry F. Franklin is with the College of Forest Resources at the University of Washington in Seattle, Washington.

Eduardo R. Fuentes is with the Global Environment Facility unit of UNDP in New York.

Keechichiro Fuwa is Professor Emeritus of the University of Tokyo and President of the Society of Environmental Science in Tokyo, Japan.

R. H. Gardner is with the Environmental Sciences Division at the Oak Ridge National Laboratory in Oak Ridge, Tennessee.

R. Graham is with the Environmental Sciences Division at the Oak Ridge National Laboratory in Oak Ridge, Tennessee.

Walter W. Heck is with the USDA's Agricultural Research Service in Raleigh, North Carolina.

H. Francis Henderson is retired from the Fisheries Division of the United Nations Food and Agriculture Organization in Rome, Italy.

Dana L. Hoag is a professor in the Department of Agricultural Economics at North Carolina State University in Raleigh, North Carolina.

xiii

John P. Holdren is the Class of 1935 Professor of Energy at the University of California, Berkeley, and visiting distinguished scholar at the Woods Hole Research Center in Woods Hole, Massachusetts.

C. S. Holling holds the Arthur R. Marshall, Jr. chair in ecological sciences at the University of Florida in Gainesville, Florida.

C. T. Hunsaker is with the Environmental Sciences Division at the Oak Ridge National Laboratory in Oak Ridge, Tennessee.

D. Jones is with the Energy Division of the Oak Ridge National Laboratory in Oak Ridge, Tennessee.

J.M. Klopatek is a professor in the Biology Department at Arizona State University, Tempe, Arizona.

Richard L. Knight is associate professor in the Department of Fishery and Wildlife Biology at Colorado State University in Fort Collins, Colorado.

Sharad Lele is at the Harvard Institute for International Development in Cambridge, Mass.

Simon A. Levin is the George M. Moffett Professor of Biology in the Department of Ecology and Evolutionary Biology at Princeton University in Princeton, New Jersey.

Jane Lubchenco is professor of zoology at Oregon State University in Corvallis, Oregon.

Walter J. Lusigi is a senior ecologist in the Environmentally Sustainable Development Division of the Africa Technical Department, World Bank.

Jeffrey A. McNeely is chief conservation officer of the World Conservation Union (IUCN) in Gland, Switzerland.

Luiz Antonio Martinelli is with the Centre for Nuclear Energy in Agriculture (CENA) at the University of Sao Paulo, in Piracicaba, Brazil.

S. R. Morton is senior principal research scientist at the Centre for Arid Zone Research in Alice Springs, N.T., Australia.

Mohan Munasinghe is division chief for Environmental Policy and Research at the World Bank.

Michael J. Munster is with the Agrosystem Resource Group of the Environmental Monitoring and Assessment Program in Raleigh, North Carolina.

Deborah A. Neher is a professor in the Department of Plant Pathology at North Carolina State University in Raleigh, North Carolina.

R. V. O'Neill is with the Environmental Sciences Division at the Oak Ridge National Laboratory in Oak Ridge, Tennessee.

Ian J. Payton is with the Forest Research Institute in Christ Church, New Zealand.

Charles H. Peterson is with the Institute of Marine Sciences at the University of North Carolina in Chapel Hill, North Carolina.

Geoffrey Pickup is a program leader in the Division of Wildlife and Ecology at the Centre for Arid Zone Research in Alice Springs, N.T., Australia.

Donald L. Plucknett is a consultant in international agricultural research and a former scientific adviser with the Consultative Group on International Agricultural Research at the World Bank.

H. Ronald Pulliam is professor and director of the Institute of Ecology at the University of Georgia in Athens, Georgia.

P. S. Ramakrishnan is professor of ecology and dean of the School of Environmental Sciences at Jawaharlal Nehru University in New Delhi, India.

Kent H. Redford is associate professor and director of the Program for Studies in Tropical Conservation in the Center for Latin American Studies at the University of Florida in Gainesville, Florida.

Henry A. Regier is professor of environmental studies and zoology at the University of Toronto's Ramsay Wright Laboratories in Toronto, Ontario, Canada.

Jeffrey Edward Richey is with the School of Oceanography at the University of Washington in Seattle, Washington.

Paul G. Risser, a botany specialist, is the President of Miami University in Oxford, Ohio.

John G. Robinson is vice president for international conservation of the Wildlife Conservation Society in New York.

Eneas Salati is with the Fundação Brasileira para Desenvolvimento Sustentável in Rio de Janeiro, Brazil.

R. Maria Saleth is with the M.S. Swaminathan Research Foundation in Madras, India.

Walter Shearer is the Advisor on New and Renewable Sources of Energy at the United Nations University office in New York.

Kenneth Sherman is chief of the Branch of Ecosystems Dynamics of the Northeast Fisheries Science Center in Narragansett, Rhode Island, and adjunct professor of oceanography at the University of Rhode Island in Kingston, Rhode Island.

Nigel J. H. Smith is a professor of geography at the University of Florida in Gainesville, Florida, and a former long-term consultant for the World Bank.

Aprilani Soegiarto is Deputy Chairman for Natural Sciences at Lembaga Ilmu Pengetahuan Indonesia (Indonesian Institute of Sciences) in Jakarta, Indonesia.

Lee M. Talbot is an environmental consultant at the World Bank.

Jose G. Tundisi is a professor at the Centre for Water Resources and Applied Ecology at the University of Sao Paulo in San Carlos, Brazil.

M. G. Turner is with the Environmental Sciences Division at the Oak Ridge National Laboratory in Oak Ridge, Tennessee.

Reynaldo Luiz Victoria is with the Department of Physics and Meteorology at the Escola Superior de Agricultura "Luis de Queiroz" in Piracicaba, Brazil.

Peter M. Vitousek is a professor in the Department of Biological Sciences at Stanford University in Stanford, California.

Other Participants

Stephanie Cirillio is Program Assistant at the Sustainable Biosphere Initiative in Washington, D.C.

Ronald Carrol is with Sustainable Agriculture and Natural Resource Management (USAID) at the University of Georgia in Athens, Georgia.

Ned Cyr is with the National Oceanic and Atmospheric Administration in Washington, D.C.

Della Dennis is with the Sustainable Biosphere Initiative in Washington, D.C.

Jerrold Dodd is at the University of Wyoming's Range Management Department in Laramie, Wyoming.

Jerry Filbin is with the United States Environmental Protection Agency in Washington, D.C.

Steven Gasteyer is with the Committee on Agricultural Sustainability for Developing Countries in Washington, D.C.

Jerome Glenn is Executive Director for the American Council for the United Nations University in Washington, D.C.

Robert Goodland is Environmental Assessment Advisor at the World Bank

James Gosz is Director of the Division of Environmental Biology at the National Science Foundation in Washington, D.C.

Judy Gradwohl is Director of the Office of Environmental Awareness at the Smithsonian Institution in Washington, D.C.

Heitor Gurgulino de Souza is Rector of the United Nations University in Tokyo, Japan.

Richard Haeuber is with the Sustainable Biosphere Initiative in Washington, D.C.

Carole Hamilton is with the U.S. Bureau of Land Management in Washington, D.C.

Gary Hartshorn is with the World Wildlife Fund in Washington, D.C.

Eric Hyman is with Appropriate Technology International in Washington, D.C.

Peter R. Jutro is with the United States Environmental Protection Agency in Washington, D.C.

Thomas Lovejoy is Assistant Secretary for External Affairs at the Smithsonian Institution in Washington, D.C.

Elizabeth McCance is with the Office of Environmental Awareness at the Smithsonian Institution in Washington, D.C.

Dan McKenzie is with the U.S. Environmental Protection Agency's Environmental Monitoring and Assessment Program at Research Triangle Park, North Carolina.

James McNair is with the Academy of Natural Sciences, Washington, D.C.

Katy Moran is with the Office for External Affairs at the Smithsonian Institution in Washington, D.C.

Henri Nsanjama is with the World Wildlife Fund in Washington, D.C.

Gordon Orians is a professor in the Department of Zoology at the University of Washington in Seattle, Washington.

Marissa Perrone is with the Office of the U.S. Trade Representative, Washington, D.C.

Kathryn Saterson is Director of the Biodiversity Support Program at the World Wildlife Fund in Washington, D.C.

Ingrid Schultz is with the Environmental Protection Agency's Environmental Statistics Initiative in Washington, DC.

Roger Soles is with the U.S. Man and Biosphere Program at the Department of State in Washington, D.C.

Silvia Tognetti is with the National Academy of Sciences in Washington, DC.

Dan Tunstall is with the World Resources Institute in Washington, D.C.

Susan Ware is an Internation Affairs Specialist at the National Oceanic and Atmospheric Administration in Washington, D.C.

Naomi Weisman is with Technology Resources, Inc. in Laurel, Maryland.

An Introduction to the Definition and Measurement of Biogeophysical Sustainability

Mohan Munasinghe and Walter Shearer

This volume is based on papers prepared for the International Conference on the Definition and Measurement of Sustainability: The Biophysical Foundations, which was convened at the World Bank in Washington, D.C. from June 22 to 25, 1992.

The conference was conceived as an exercise to advance thinking on the biogeophysical foundations for defining and measuring sustainability and to provide useful policy considerations for the international development community. In addition to the formal papers and written responses in the volume, this introductory chapter is an attempt to describe the general context in which the conference took place and to capture the highlights and salient points of the many papers presented and the discussions that transpired. The papers themselves have been updated and revised in light of the conference deliberations and subsequent developments.

Origins of the conference

The motivation for the conference derives from the age-old concern about humanity's impact on the environment and the ultimate carrying capacity of the earth. Many thinkers, from Thomas Robert Malthus onwards, have expressed concern about the material limits to the magnitude of human consumption and the support system required for its sustenance. Others, most notably the so-called technological optimists, have argued that scientific progress and the increasing efficiency of resource use would help overcome this problem. This debate naturally led to the idea of sustainability and a search for ways to measure and monitor it. One example of the importance of such indicators emerged in 1986 when Peter Vitousek, Paul and Anne Ehrlich, and R.A. Matson (in their well-known article in *BioScience*) estimated that the organic matter equivalent to about 40 percent of the net primary production of all terrestrial ecosystems was being diverted directly or indirectly for human use. Thus, if the global population were to triple while production and consumption patterns remained the same, humanity would be faced with trying to co-opt for human use more than the total global net annual production of organic matter. This in turn would rapidly lead to diminishing production because of a reduction of the resource base. In this context, it appears that net primary production offers one basis for understanding the limits of sustainability, as well as some hope for developing from among all the variables a set of indicators (and perhaps an index) of one fundamental aspect of sustainability—its biogeophysical component.

In 1987 the *Report of the World Commission on Environment and Development* (the Brundtland Commission) and the popular version, *Our Common Future*, proposed the concept of sustainable development. The adoption of this idea by the international development community and its promotion as the theme of the UN Conference on Environment and Development (the Rio Conference) in 1992 further inspired an attempt to define and measure sustainability. *The basic challenge presented by sustainable development is in finding ways to define, measure, and operationalize it.* The purpose of the conference was to contribute toward the development of a practical way of measuring movement, if any, toward greater sustainability.

As defined by the Brundtland Commission, sustainable development must meet the needs of the present without compromising the ability of future generations to meet their own needs. This implies using resources today without limiting the options for succeeding generations; of necessity, this must involve environment and natural resources as well as social dimensions. However, this relatively new and attractive concept is impossible to satisfy in literal terms because, on the one hand, the current generation has to continue altering the biosphere in order to develop, and on the other hand, each time a history-dependent system such as an ecosystem is modified, future options change as well. This makes consideration of such impacts one of the most important issues in sustainable development. Therefore, a compromise is required between current uses and future options. Furthermore, it is important that sustainable development be understood not as decreeing a subsistence economy for Third World countries, nor as freezing landscapes in a particular configuration, but as conscious development within bounds determined through the best scientific evidence.

Such discussions must avoid confusing the terms sustainable development and sustainability. The former is about promoting development and ensuring that it is sustained. It involves two seemingly incompatible concepts: sustainability and development. Sustainability means maintenance or even improvement, without degradation, over the very long term. After decades of research, intervention, and observation, profound scrutiny of many aspects of development is occurring. However, the current state of understanding regarding sustainability is poor, and it is this concept that needs the urgent attention of the intellectual community.

In preparing for the 1992 meeting, it was recognized that sustainability involves complex interactions—biogeophysical, economic, social, cultural, and political—and that sustaining the global life-support system is a prerequisite for sustaining human societies. This is why defining and measuring the biogeophysical foundations of sustainability became the theme of the conference. It is also important to point out to the reader that during the conference and in preparing the chapters in this volume, the term "biophysical" was used. Subsequently it was decided that to avoid possible confusion with biophysics, a traditional and well-established subdiscipline of physics, the term used in the title of the present publication and throughout this introduction would be "biogeophysical." Although it has some drawbacks, the new term is recommended for future use when referring to the natural life-support system, the comprehensive study of which relies on the disciplines of biology, geology, chemistry, and physics. Therefore, for the sake of consistency, "biogeophysical" should be read in place of "biophysical" wherever it is encountered in the remainder of the text.

Organization of this volume

The contributions to this volume are arranged along the lines of the conference. Part A covers the major issues that affect all ecosystems in relation to biogeophysical sustainability. The issues treated by experts include key concepts and terminology, spatial and temporal scales, limits to the sustainable use of resources, cumulative effects, source/sink modeling of landscapes, and atmosphere and climate. Several chapters are accompanied by reviews from other participants. In view of the key role played by the overview papers, we elaborate on them briefly. The first chapter, by Holdren, Daily and Ehrlich, lays out the issues and concept of sustainability, sets a specific time frame of 500–1,000 years for evaluating sustainability, and notes that the crucial change rate is about ten percent per century.

The contribution by Munasinghe and McNeely provides three approaches to looking at sustainability: the economic, that is, growth and development; the environmental and natural resource; and the social and cultural. It compares the policy relationships of these three approaches and points out the challenges for the world in seeking to integrate them with sustainability. Because the challenges are great, the authors emphasize the need to clarify the issues not only for decisionmakers but for the public who must enact the appropriate changes.

The third contribution, by Vitousek and Lubchenco, brings to the fore three major issues for the elucidation of sustainability: the issue of global processes that can sometimes manifest themselves as global change; the idea of biological diversity; and the land-use issue, which becomes global by aggregation but can be important both locally and regionally.

Holling contributes a persuasive chapter on adaptive systems and furnishes an eloquent discussion of paradoxes—not only the paradox of sustainability and development, but also the paradox that all systems, no matter which ones are examined, appear to be governed primarily by a small number of key variables. Although these variables have different time scales, they aggregate into clusters, which provides an indication that the systems are hierarchical, have a definite structure, and should be accessible by examining key variables. The author also looks at the notion of policy changes and management strategies, noting that in many cases management appears to be quite clear and productive at the outset but, over time, becomes essentially dysfunctional if not pathological.

Beanlands' chapter takes on the difficult challenge of addressing cumulative impacts, pointing out that there are indeed some relationships between sustainable development and cumulative impacts but that they are difficult to measure and generally still beyond the reach of science. Most of these cumulative impacts are slow changes on the order of 1–3 percent, however, and the challenge is to find thresholds that become critical and to use them to drive decisions and management actions.

Pulliam's contribution looks at source-sink modeling, focusing primarily on ecosystem stability measured in terms of productivity, diversity, stability, and adaptability. Using these models, the author extends these interpretations to the landscape level, in this way providing models for predicting population behaviour in terms of heterogeneous landscapes. The author then proposes some management strategies at this level on the basis of the monitoring of a single species.

In the seventh chapter, Levin raises several important points, including the value of focusing on flexibility rather than on constancy, the need in terms of species and populations to focus on processes for the persistence of those species' survival and extinction, their spread in variability, and the importance of spatial and temporal relationships between disturbances and those population processes. Sustainability means different things at different scales, and the issue is how to aggregate measurements in the absence of a correct level of aggregation.

Andreae and Dickinson assess changes in the chemical and physical climate in light of the changing composition of the atmosphere in relation to sustainability. The increasing concentration of greenhouse gases in the atmosphere, the weakening ozone shield, increased local and regional pollution, and the decreasing capability of the atmosphere to oxidize biogenic and anthropogenic emissions are symptoms of progressive and unsustainable deterioration of the life-support system provided by the global atmosphere. The authors point out that because of multiple sources and sinks for many gases and aerosols, an effort to reduce one source can lead to increased emissions of the same or another gas from a different source.

The final chapter of Part A, from O'Neill and others, considers biogeophysical sustainability at the landscape and regional levels. It emphasizes that landscape ecology is important because most threats to sustainability involve changes in land use at large scales. The authors indicate that the combination of remote sensing, geographic information systems, and landscape theory offers a framework for defining a significant number of new indicators that are practical and interpretable. However, they warn that continued progress involves difficult new areas of research.

Part B contains reports of locations on the planet where the environment and society's reactions have been studied in great depth by specialists. These locations include a rocky intertidal marine coast in Chile, the Chesapeake Bay in North America, arid zones in Australia, high-altitude forests in Asia, and large marine ecosystems and fisheries.

Part C offers a series of reports on a variety of managed ecosystems for which leading scientists provide their expert opinion on the current status of biogeophysical indicators of sustainability. These reports cover agriculture, rangelands, fisheries, forests, wildlife, and natural areas and water resources in the tropical and temperate zones. Reviews of several of these reports immediately follow the principal contributions.

Below we review the main points that emerged during the conference.

Dimensions of sustainability

Before considering the matter of defining and measuring biogeophysical sustainability, the participants wrestled with the concern that something important might be lost in trying to define the biogeophysical aspects of sustainability independent of its human and social dimensions.

Concern was voiced that sustainability appears to be essentially a social construct, and one way to determine the contribution of biologists, ecologists, and geoscientists to the biogeophysical basis of human life is to understand where social issues come into play. First, it was proposed that social issues become important when determining what is to be sustained, for how long, and in what manner, whether sustaining refers only to nondecreasing average production or to resilience and adaptability, who is to benefit from what is being sustained, and how the benefits will be distributed. It was suggested that these determinations can be made only in the social arena, with the setting of the objectives or attributes of sustainability emerging from a sociopolitical process.

Second, it was suggested that social issues come into play when trying to understand why unsustainable practices and behaviour are so frequently observed among shortsighted people who thus undermine the ecological basis of their own lives or the lives of future generations. These considerations are extremely complex and involve individual behaviour and social and political structures and organizations. Such information is helpful in developing policies that would change unsustainable practices and promote the maintenance of the ecological basis of human life. It was also observed that with social and political aspects determining the objectives of sustainability, there is bound to be conflict among these objectives. Under such circumstances it was suggested that the task of the scientist is to provide information to help people choose among conflicting objectives by assessing the trade-offs among these objectives and the consequences of their application. This information would be particularly important where the trade-offs and consequences behave nonlinearly. This view suggests that having recognized such concerns, it should be easier to deal with sustainability without always having to address the social and cultural issues.

A pragmatic and policy-oriented concern was expressed in support of this view—focusing on developing one index or a set of indicators of sustainability runs the risk of aggregating together many distinct elements and thereby failing to understand the human causes and mechanisms of unsustainable management. It is expected that examination of what is known about sustainability in all its different aspects—such as renewable resources, nonrenewable resources, ecosystem services, and biological diversity—will reveal that these elements are distinct in the way they absorb impacts from their use and in what they contribute to human well-being. Keeping them separate, not insisting that they be mixed into one single indicator, and focusing instead on understanding why in specific cases there is unsustainable use of a particular resource, ecosystem service, or biological diversity might actually contribute to understanding (and thereby obviating) the social causes of environmentally unsustainable practices. Although sustainability is largely a natural state of affairs, unsustainability is the result of social actions, and, therefore, reducing these impacts involves a social process. Thus, it would seem that if the goal of devising an index or set of indicators of sustainability is to

provide a way of identifying unsustainable practices, more understanding of the human causes would be valuable in this endeavour.

Response to this view was that development and use of an index or set of indicators do not replace the need for disaggregated information and better understanding of the social causes of unsustainable practices. In fact, both approaches are needed and have complementary applications. The index is valuable for its monitoring and predictive powers, whereas more detailed studies and more understanding of human management practices are useful for developing and implementing policies to reduce unsustainable practices.

A somewhat different view presented at the conference is that beyond such matters as whether there is sufficient generation of financial resources to ensure economic sustainability, whether there is appropriate social organization and sufficient motivation for social sustainability, or whether there is sufficient power or collective will for political sustainability, what is sustainable and unsustainable is ultimately a biogeophysical, and not a social, matter. For example, it is a social decision to choose a land-use pattern from among several options, but the sustainability of each pattern will be determined by whether the biogeophysical conditions can be sustained when the land is used. The only exception to this would appear to be in deciding to accept something less than indefinite sustainability and adopt a particular time frame, or in defining the spatial area to be sustained. Otherwise the concern raised about social issues does not appear to require consideration in dealing with biogeophysical sustainability. Assuming a very long time horizon for sustainability, no new social issue appears. Similarly, the manner in which an ecosystem is sustained is not relevant as long as sustainability actually occurs. And the concerns about who is to benefit and how the benefits will be distributed are not relevant because sustainability can occur even if no one benefits at all. According to this view, the reasons for unsustainable practices and how they can be changed belong to the social and political realm and are irrelevant to defining and measuring biogeophysical sustainability. Those holding this view insist that sustainability in fact is the very simple concept of maintaining natural resource stocks and that it should not be unnecessarily complicated by encumbering it with social features and desired expectations. This would make it possible to identify a small number of indicators for describing biogeophysical sustainability that would not be socially and culturally sensitive and thus applicable in any location.

A simple analogy elucidates this position. To keep the world running, if one could control it, the first requirement would be to keep the biogeophysical system and its cycles working and to do so with maximum biological diversity. These are the constraints that human beings must respect. Only then is it possible to deal with the constellation of social and human concerns.

This approach is admittedly somewhat purist and reductionist in that the biogeophysical foundations of sustainability are to be studied first and largely independent of the economic, social, cultural, and political aspects. The argument is often made that, because the term biosphere traditionally includes only animals, plants, bacteria, and their life-support system, to the exclusion of human beings, environmental problems have developed because some human societies conceive of people as removed from the natural unity of life and placed in opposition to the rest of the biosphere. Thus, a cogent criticism of this approach is that it could further add to the environmental problems caused by many people's feeling of detachment from, even superiority to, the environment and biosphere.

In summary, the final synthesis emerging from the conference places the biosphere first as the necessary basis for human life and activity. Moreover, there appears to be justification for this approach because of: (a) the extreme complexity of sustainability; (b) the fact that human life and all human activities rely on a biogeophysical foundation that existed prior to (and therefore can be viewed as independent of) human existence but that can be perturbed and even radically altered by human activity; and (c) the serious commitment to include in the approach those occasions where human (social and cultural) dimensions do necessarily enter into considerations of biogeophysical sustainability. This is particularly so in the case of defining the temporal and spatial boundaries for the ecosystems to be sustained. Therefore, this approach requires that care be taken to (i) consider the human dimensions where appropriate and (ii) accept a commitment to undertake the subsequent task of integrating the biogeophysical foundations with the economic, social, cultural, and political aspects that will lead to the development of a complete picture of sustainability and ultimately of sustainable development.

An innovative model was proposed for viewing this broader picture of sustainability, employing an equilateral triangle with the ecological, economic, and sociocultural objectives of sustainability at its apexes (see Munasinghe 1993, and Munasinghe and McNeely this volume). This offers an elegant way of reflecting the compromises that have to be made in developing policy options and making decisions. There may be some "win-win" policies that allow all of these objectives to be addressed simultaneously, even though the conceptual approach cannot integrate the three objectives explicit. For example, there are more than a billion people without access to safe drinking water and sanitation. From an economic point of view, providing safe drinking water is one of the most cost-effective projects that can be undertaken because incidence of disease is reduced and, thus, productivity increased along with economic benefits. From an ecological and environmental point of view, it is also desirable because water quality is improved, and waste material that pollutes water courses is reduced. From a social point of view, such a project primarily assists the poor, thereby reducing social tensions and improving social sustainability.

The problem is that beyond such simple indicators there are necessary trade-offs between objectives—which is where the sustainable development triangle becomes important. In addition, the triangle directs attention to the capacity to adapt and take advantage of new kinds of opportunities such as come with the inevitable change in environmental conditions. It is because of such changes that analytical tools need to be developed that try to reconcile the conceptual tensions. The task of the scientific community is to develop analytical tools and indicators and to offer policy options to the decisionmakers. This involves taking complex concepts and models, boiling them down to the simplest idea possible to illustrate the extent of current understanding of the problem, and providing a set of policy options to the decisionmakers.

However, the conference participants were also reminded that individual human beings are a significant and critically important factor in sustaining their environment. Their involvement begins in their homes (which they would not pollute), spreads to their neighborhoods, and extends to their region. In eventually developing a sense of identity with their region, individuals can put pressure on politicians. Thus, communicating directly with citizens can often be as important, if not more so, than communicating with politicians.

Concepts of sustainability

A convenient, if not comprehensive, taxonomy of views regarding sustainability evolved in the course of discussions. First, the "input-output" view assumes that the internal dynamics of the ecosystem are more or less in a steady state—that is, they are not degrading over time. Beyond that, the primary focus is on inputs and outputs and whether they are sustainable.

Second, the related "state" definition requires simply that a sustainable ecosystem be one in which a state can be maintained indefinitely. The "capital" or "stock" view requires the maintenance of natural capital or stock at or above current levels and, thus, that the products of the ecosystem be used at a rate within that ecosystem's capacity for renewal. Sustainability is thereby ensured by living off the income rather than the ecological capital. The "ecosystem-characteristics-not-degrading-through-time" view requires the perpetuation of the character and natural processes of the ecosystem and indefinite maintenance of its integrity (productivity, diversity, stability, and adaptability) without degrading the integrity of other ecosystems.

Finally, there is the "potential throughput" view, emphasizing the use of resources within the capacity of those resources to renew themselves. According to this view, sustainability is defined on the basis of maintenance of potential, so that ecosystems can provide the same quantity and quality of goods and services as in the past. Potential is emphasized rather than stocks, biomass, or energy levels. To maintain this potential, which amounts to future options, there are two areas of concern: the degradation of the physical productive capabilities of the land and water and the loss of genetic diversity. This might mean sacrificing 90 percent of the stocks of a species while maintaining a viable population of that species so that in the future a society could rebuild the habitat for that species. Thus, maintaining stocks or energy levels is not as important as retaining the productive abilities of the land, specifically of the soil and the biotic components. Obviously, waste production can be tolerated only within the capacity of the system to assimilate those wastes. This basis for sustainability permits many alternative sustainable systems that involve various mixes of goods and services.

Definition of sustainability

Important considerations that were identified for developing a definition of sustainability are:

- the number of variables it contains
- ease in measuring these variables
- its capacity for generalization
- its applicability to different situations, and
- the flexibility it allows.

A definition should not attempt to freeze the current state but instead should define the boundaries within which there can be flexibility—because allowance must be made for the evolution of some components of the system. Such flexibility could be permitted within an input-output scheme, which would not require explicit adherence to a particular cultural or sociological framework but would allow any scheme to operate within certain biogeophysical bounds. Thus, definitions of sustainability might differ in terms of how they specify borders, envelopes, or states. The capacity for generalization refers to transsystem or translandscape measurements, whereas flexibility refers to conditions within systems. Flexibility can exist within the system in terms of cultural and social structures as long as the biogeophysical requirements are met. Space is another important variable that ranges from plots through landscapes, ecosystems, regions, nations, and continents to the entire biosphere.

The conference participants strove for a definition of biogeophysical sustainability that would be broad and general, all encompassing, not particularly controversial, and not inherently value-laden:

"Biogeophysical sustainability is the maintenance and/or improvement of the integrity of the life-support system on Earth. Sustaining the biosphere with adequate provisions for maximizing future options includes providing for human economic and social improvement for current and future human generations within a framework of cultural diversity while: (a) making adequate provisions for the maintenance of biological diversity and (b) maintaining the biogeochemical integrity of the biosphere by conservation and proper use of its air, water and land resources. Achieving these goals requires planning and action at local, regional and global scales and specifying short- and long-term objectives that allow for the transition to sustainability."

This definition contains an element of vagueness because it refers to integrity, a term not further defined or explained. It also recognizes that some options might be closed by attempts to achieve sustainability that allow for an improvement in human well-being. Furthermore, the participants were unable to resolve the philosophical issue of whether sustainability can be defined, in its simplest and purest form, independent of sustaining human welfare.

In considering time scales, it was felt important to include in the definition a consideration of a transition phase during which there might be some unsustainable practices, eventually leading to a state that could be sustainable indefinitely. The general feeling was that somewhere on the order of 50 to 100 years was a reasonable length for the transition phase but that this would be dependent on the resources and social and cultural considerations of each society. This transition period would be characterized by economic growth in the developing countries, stabilization of the world population, and the use of available nonrenewable resources to capitalize the establishment of a state that could be sustained.

However, the choices made and activities undertaken during the transition period would constrain the kind of state that can be maintained indefinitely thereafter. Obviously, while drawing down on renewable and nonrenewable stocks during the transition period in order to build an infrastructure that allows for a sustainable state at the end, some guidance would be needed to indicate whether the goals were actually being achieved during this period. It is important that during the transition, the capacity to renew is not lost. Species that are lost or soils that are degraded to the point where forests will not regrow, determine the location of the relevant boundaries.

Ecological capital

The concept of ecological capital was examined as a basis for better defining sustainability. However, ecological capital itself proved difficult to define. It was observed that in any attempt at a definition, it is insufficient to simply focus on the local scale, that is on stocks of trees or fishes, for example. Consideration of ecological capital requires a look at much broader scales and an understanding of ecosystems and the interaction among ecosystems in much broader terms than a local scale allows because of the complex feedbacks that occur on regional and global levels. This is an example of the differences that exist between ecological systems and economic systems, for which there is rarely a good one-to-one match.

Furthermore, an important difference in perception was found in the developing world and in the industrialized world in defining ecological capital. Ecological capital in the developing world is largely centered on how to provide enough food, fodder, and fuelwood for the sustenance of the community. Thus, there is an urgent need to expand economic activity, and the kind of criteria that would be required to measure the sustainability of these activities would be very different. In contrast, in the industrialized world the need is to scale back some economic activities in order to decrease their impact on the environment; therefore, the definition of ecological capital and the measurements of it that might be used globally are likely to differ. Developing a unified definition of ecological capital requires the reconciliation of these differences.

One approach to defining ecological capital is to try to link the concept to risk aversion and, particularly, to culturally-specific definitions of ecological capital. Various components contribute to ecological capital—air, soil, forests, and biological diversity. Two important characteristics are how renewable they are and, if degraded, how long it would take to recover them. From this perspective, the most important element is biological diversity because it probably requires the longest recovery time once lost. From the point of view of risk, there is another way in which the elements can be ordered. Take, for example, air, the stratospheric ozone shield, soil, and biological diversity as four of the components of ecological capital. Air has the shortest-term impact because the effects from its pollution will be noticed quickly. Stratospheric ozone depletion has a somewhat longer-term impact—that is, cancer rates will rise and food productivity will decline over a longer time period than people can survive without good air to breathe. The consequences of soil degradation will appear over an even longer period of time because soil deteriorates slowly. Finally, biological diversity will take the longest to show ill effects—for example, in terms of undiscovered chemicals and pharmaceutical products.

Therefore, in one system of ranking, biological diversity is the most important element because it takes the longest to recover (perhaps never), whereas in the other system it is the least important in terms of short-term impact. Risk modeling (used in studies of economics and behavioral ecology) and analysis of risk aversion explore the way people respond to risk and can help determine whether they are risk prone or averse. Cultural and social factors may strongly influence the outcome.

The foregoing examples complicate attempts to aggregate diverse ecological components into a single index. Thus, the risk-averse strategy of some cultures would dictate that most concern be given to the shorter-term results: air quality, water quality, and the stratospheric ozone shield, whereas the longer-term impacts associated with loss of soil and biological diversity would not receive as much weight in the aggregated index. Conversely, if the concern of the culture is about the long-term consequences and the time it takes for recovery, the components will be weighted differently. One of the major difficulties in trying to develop an aggregated index that covers all these components arises from the difference in these culture-specific approaches.

An important problem noted by conference participants was how to go about determining an acceptable level of environmental damage, which in turn implies a carrying capacity. The concept of maximum sustainable use invites the notion of maximum survivable abuse. One way the acceptability of damage could be determined is by identifying the point at which an increase in the activity in question produces greater marginal cost than marginal benefits. This rather satisfying theoretical definition is, unfortunately, difficult to implement in practice because of measurement problems. This would not be the case if all of the damages and all of the benefits could be quantified in commensurable units, say in monetary units. In practice this becomes a political decision having to do with people's values and preferences about the risks and uncertainty of future costs versus the shorter-term benefits they are offered from the expanded activity in question. It may be argued that society will generally prove to be risk averse and will want to leave itself some margin of error.

However, concern was expressed that in considering the concepts of stocks, flows, and ecological capital, there is a danger that such simple analogies do not adequately reflect the real complexity of ecosystems. It would appear that ecological processes, species interactions, and geological processes, all at different time scales, cannot be reduced to the simple metaphors of stocks, flows, and interest rates. Such metaphors cannot capture the differences and the very dramatic changes that can occur, depending on the level at which activities are directed. Thus, one proposal at the conference rejected the notion of stocks, flows, and ecological capital as a useful paradigm for approaching the biogeophysical foundations of sustainability.

In a similar vein, concern was expressed about the metaphor of ecosystem health. Although scientists are expected to develop an index, like temperature, which tells a lot about ecosystems, it was pointed out that the analogy with health is not entirely correct. There is a major difference between a tightly coupled system like the human body and an ecological system much more loosely coupled. Such differences must be reflected in the health construct used for ecological systems. No doubt the metaphor is inevitable and inescapable, and although scientists prefer to use the term integrity, the public will continue to refer to ecosystems as healthy or unhealthy. Therefore, scientists must make a special effort to educate the public about the real significance of the analogy between human and ecological health.

Indicators

The management of the global life-support system has been compared to piloting an airplane without instruments. Basically, humanity does not have a complete set of indicators (instruments) or monitors of the global life-support system, and this situation will prevail for some time. This shortcoming constitutes one of the major challenges for those trying to develop indicators of biogeophysical sustainability. Another problem that was noted at the conference involves scale, which complicates enormously any attempt to develop sustainability indicators. Thus, as a practical matter, indicators are needed that are useful over different time and space scales and for different levels, from the community to the biome. This requires a test set of indicators.

In looking for an organizing principle for measuring biogeophysical sustainability, three levels of activity can be identified. The first level involves determining measurements of sustainability. It appears unlikely that a set of universal measurements to cover freshwater lakes, marine fisheries, grasslands, and mountain tops can be found. By defining the basis for measuring and determining biogeophysical sustainability at the ecosystem or landscape level, the relevant measurements can then be aggregated into indicators at the second level. Therefore, it is important to assemble a generic list of indicators of biogeophysical sustainability to serve as a checklist for determining the correct ground for each of the ecosystems. Specific measurements must then be identified for each indicator. However, it is important to identify the status of this generic list of indicators at the regional and global levels, and this requires a composite index, which is the third level.

In summary, the three levels must be developed separately, but they are intimately interlinked. The first two levels, which are straightforward from a biogeophysical point of view, involve selecting indicators and trends that are applicable to specific systems at different spatial and temporal scales in different parts of the world. The third level, involving the development of an index (rather like GNP) for the biogeophysical health of the globe, requires the assembling of the indicators and their trends into some type of index that takes into account how those trends actually make an impact on human welfare. The ultimate goal might be to assemble all the pieces into an even broader index that will reflect all the elements (including economic, social, and political) of sustainability that determine long-term human welfare.

To avoid the slow process of identifying and reaching agreement on the relevant measurements of biogeophysical sustainability for the first level and later aggregating them into indicators for the second level, an attempt was made at the conference to "leap frog" by starting with the development of the second level, based on the practical requirements of policy analysts and decisionmakers. Thus, the participants prepared a selection of parameters from which candidate indicators could be developed to monitor and predict biogeophysical sustainability (see table). The parameters are as follows:

- landscape composition and patterns
- production of goods and services
- biological diversity
- water quality and quantity
- soil properties
- energy and nutrient flows
- atmospheric composition, and
- climate.

From an operational point of view, this list represents a checklist or framework. For each item listed, specific variables and an associated range of acceptable values must be identified, as well as a way of measuring each by an inexpensive technique. Moreover, measurements or values are needed for the different ecosystems. Because the indicators relevant to biogeophysical sustainability will be different for each ecosystem type, it was decided to assemble the results into a matrix with the relevant indicators given for each parameter category. Such a matrix, from which specific measurements could be derived, would have the added advantage of providing a framework with which to identify any important overlooked components for specific managed ecosystems. Using the Delphi technique, with contributions solicited from participants over a period that extended well beyond the actual conference, a unified list of candidate indicators of biogeophysical sustainability evolved for the following eight managed and natural ecosystems:

- agriculture
- forests
- rangelands
- wildlife and wild lands
- freshwater fisheries
- wetlands and ground water
- coastal resources, and
- marine fisheries.

In addition, the following human dimensions were considered to have an important impact on biogeophysical sustainability:
- human influences (such as land-use change or subsidies to landscapes—for example, fertilizer)
- human demography, and
- human well-being.

It was considered important to complement these results with a list of issues that should be considered when developing a set of indicators of biogeophysical sustainability. This list covers:

- scale (local, national, regional, global)
- purpose and use of the indicators (policy or broad resource allocation, specific management), and
- values (health, ecology, rules-of-thumb are to be used to specify the boundaries of sustainability.

Each selected parameter covers a number of issues that may not be immediately obvious in name or in ways that link it to other parameters. Therefore, some discussion appears to be warranted concerning the intended coverage of each parameter and the types of measurements that might be considered.

Landscape composition and pattern is intended to include topography, geology and substrate conditions in combination with soil properties. It requires periodic measurement of the various types of ecosystems in a landscape and the kinds of changes taking place. Such measurements give an indication of whether the system is sustainable and in what way the system is undergoing changes in terms of species composition, invasion of species, and degradation.

One indicator included under *production of goods and services* is land productivity, which is an indicator of the biogeophysical health. Productivity decline signals that something is wrong in the system. However, if the aim is to maintain productivity, it may be too late to wait for productivity to drop. Thus, predictive indicators are essential for measuring productivity. Furthermore, it should be borne in mind that measuring net primary productivity for forest, marine, and some other ecosystems turns out to be a challenging task that is only rarely accomplished. When considering a mosaic landscape containing many ecosystems, urban areas would likely be included. Of course, although they have negative values for productivity, they are important regions that cover a great part of the world and thus should not be overlooked.

Biological diversity is an important parameter. It is sometimes possible to identify in a natural ecosystem a few key species that likely reflect the system's overall biological diversity. Much biological diversity is available in managed systems, such as agriculture, in traditional societies. Therefore, the biodiversity indicator should reflect the biological diversity that is available in managed systems as well.

If the landscape is part of a watershed, an important indicator of *water quality* would involve the measurement of suspended particles and chemicals that are lost to the stream or river.

Among the important indicators of *soil properties* are soil fertility changes—physical as well as chemical. Comparative measurements can be made from time to time between managed ecosystems and natural ecosystems. This would add to better understanding of the kinds of subsidies,

such as fertilizers, that are being provided to the managed ecosystems and how the managed systems can be designed to replicate the internal controls that govern natural ecosystems. Thus, comparative measurements of soil fertility status (both in physical and chemical terms) between managed ecosystems and natural ecosystems would be appropriate indicators of the sustainability of the system.

Energy and nutrient flows should include the flow of materials, including both toxic and hazardous materials. This is one way to handle toxic materials and hazardous wastes, although they could also appear throughout the list under such parameters as *water quality and quantity, atmospheric composition,* and *soil properties.* By subsuming pollutants and toxic materials in this way, there is no need to add a specific parameter for pollution. Furthermore, *energy and nutrient flows* could include an energy input/output ratio that would indirectly reflect CO_2 emissions. This parameter should also cover the kinds of subsidies that go into managed ecosystems in terms of economics as well as energy.

The *climate* parameter should reflect the agriculture–climate interaction at the regional level. Agriculture, especially through its influence on the hydrological cycle through land-use change, has an influence on regional climate. If that interaction leads to a decrease in hydrological recycling—as it easily can for land uses that go from rainforest at one extreme to degraded agricultural land at the other—the associated decrease in rainfall or water retention capability can change the temperature cycles. This can lead to a costly loss of resources.

Though not definitive, and despite needing some refinement and precision, the proposed indicators constitute a significant step forward. And although this set does not introduce any new indicators or measurements, its novelty rests in the selection process. The conference participants were confident that this set of indicators is valid for scales from one hectare to the entire globe. They were confident that it could be based on measurements that use time-tested techniques and whose significance is well understood.

The set of indicators proposed for temperate rangeland (see Risser, this volume) was established as the model for other ecosystems. This set consists of five meaningful indicators that specify the health of the rangeland. The indicators for the different parameters (which are italicized, with the appropriate thresholds in parenthesis) are:

- *landscape composition*: range condition rating (good to excellent)
- *aboveground primary production*: peak standing crop (>300 g/m^2)
- *plant species diversity*: e$^{H'}$ (>5.0)
- *soil properties*: soil organic carbon content in top 20 cm of soil (> 3-5 kg/m^2), and
- *nutrient flows*: nitrogen content of vegetation (0.6% on a dry weight basis).

This set of indicators can be used to identify the biogeophysical sustainability of temperate range-land ecosystems. A sixth indicator would reflect the scale of the loss of habitat. For this, a surrogate indicator might be a change in the number of bird species, which are very sensitive to changes in the extent and juxtaposition of rangeland areas. Of course, rangeland ecosystems have much more temporal variability than other habitats, and thus temporal scale dynamics are important for understanding the variation and the applicability of different indicators. In particular, the measurement of the size of the soil organic carbon pool has some universality as an integrative indicator of the general health of rangelands.

This was viewed as an excellent example of the type of sets of indicators that should be developed for all other ecosystems. Based on the kinds of conditions to be maintained, it is expected that there is enough experience and expertise in the ecological community to assemble a set of indicators such as this for all ecosystems. Nevertheless, some participants held the view that although good indicators of biogeophysical sustainability can be proposed, developing practical measurements for them can be quite a difficult task.

It was noted that *World Resources Report* already publishes statistics for a number of important global indicators, six or eight of which appear to be good trend spotters. These include atmospheric CO_2 concentration, stratospheric ozone concentration, temporal changes in soil fertility, biological diversity loss, and changes in natural habitat.

Integrative indicators are important because they provide greater information and are often more sensitive to the interaction among variables and to critical thresholds than are single-variable indicators. Such integrative indicators are themselves good candidates for components of an index of biogeophysical sustainability. Important examples of individual indicators with significant integrative characteristics were also identified.

The first example concerns the biogeophysical basis of sustaining tropical water resources using the model of the Amazon region, which is representative of what an intact hydrological cycle ought to be. The goal is to monitor the integrity of the hydrological cycle for the relevant time and space scales. Because of the need to consider biological diversity, and due to the extremely tight coupling between hydrology and ecosystems, the central issue of the biogeophysical basis for maintaining integrity should be considered in some detail in the development of a useful indicator. Thus, from the point of view of the water cycle in the Amazon and its interaction with the vegetation, the efficiency of the water cycle can be expressed as the river discharge per unit basin area divided by the precipitation ratio. Both the precipitation and the run-off or discharge have the advantage of being measurable. On the basis of the accepted view that in the Amazon basin roughly 50 percent of the precipitation is derived from recycled water, the precipitation ratio becomes 0.5. An increase in this ratio would indicate that more of the precipitation is going to run-off and that there is less recycling, giving straightforward implications for the energy and water balances and for the vegetation. In this tropical forest environment the ecological niches are very fine. Two or three Celsius degrees of change can mean the difference between life and death for that system, as opposed to a fifty-degree change (for example, seasonal variations) in a temperate or boreal coniferous forest. But other factors can change the discharge rate per unit basin area, and to distinguish among them requires additional parameters—such as those based on the stable isotopic composition of the water involved. Taking the ^{18}O concentration of the rainwater normalized for area and time, changes in the recycling rate could be easily monitored.

This is an example of a physical indicator that contains a great deal of information about the ecosystem, and it demonstrates the need for making a trade-off between comprehensiveness and scrutability. It is illustrative of the type of indicator needed across a range of ecosystems and conditions that incorporates as much of the important information as possible into one or two numbers readily displayed and understood.

There may be instances where a particular set of indicators is intelligible to the lay public and also has scientific utility. One such example is the use of the lake trout as an multivariable indicator of the state of the Lake Superior ecosystem in

North America. The population of lake trout has been proposed as an indicator that captures much information about the state of integrity of the lake basin. A particular population level has been identified that indicates a high state of integrity of the lake ecosystem. Thus, this indicator not only integrates a variety of components but also is a piecemeal indicator for the different types of stress on the ecosystem. For example, it can be inferred from the trout population dynamics whether the lakes are being overfished; from the number of scars on the skin of adult fish whether the sea lamprey is being controlled; from the concentration of contaminants in the flesh whether the contaminant loadings are being controlled; and from the relative health of different stocks of lake trout whether their spawning grounds are free of silt. Thus, the well-being of the lake trout population is itself an integrative indicator of the ecosystem. The point is not that this alone is a sufficient indicator of the sustainability of the Lake Superior ecosystem but that it includes both the qualities sought in an indicator—that is, scientific validity and communicative facility to the general public.

A number of other interesting indicators with integrative capabilities were also discussed at the conference, but their significance would require more study before they could be included in the list of indicators. They include: (a) ecosystem integrity; (b) production efficiency, which relates to energy input versus output as well as soil and biological sinks and reservoirs; and (c) a comparison of human versus natural flows of energy and materials. This last would be an attempt to deal with the scale of human activity in terms of rates of mobilization of energy, soil, rock, and such elements as mercury, cadmium, sulfur, nitrogen, and phosphorous.

Practical considerations for applying indicators

Mention should be made of some of the concerns raised about the results, particularly as regards indicators. First, it can be expected that indicators and measurements will not be exactly the same, nor will they measure exactly the same thing for different natural or managed ecosystem, including urban ecosystems. Also, much effort is still required to select indicators that are the most operational but of sufficient generality to ensure global validity.

Another concern is the relevant spatial scale on which the measurements are to be made for each of the indicators. The issue of averaging over time is relevant. All natural and managed ecosystems are characterized by fluctuations on various time scales. It is important to ascertain the magnitude of fluctuations that is tolerable—that is, before they start threatening the sustainability of the ecosystem. Of course, an imposed constraint that accepts no changes is not likely to be acceptable to most societies. In many cases, any human activity of a particular kind will produce a change. Thus, the argument is not whether there is going to be a change, but how big a change is tolerable.

A number of other useful contributions to the development of indicators were also made, some of which are summarized here.

- *Off-site effects and subsidies.* Under any given definition of the geographical scale of interest, it is possible to imagine a situation where within a boundary everything is fine while adverse external impacts occur outside the boundary. One of the primary differences between the situations faced by the Sahelian pastoralist with impoverished soil and the Saskatchewan farmer on the rich plains of Canada is the inputs that the industrial world relies on to mask the degradation of soils. Thus, a useful indicator of sustainability is the size of the inputs used to mask the loss of resilience of these systems. A problem with output measurements is that it is often possible to maintain high yields for a long time, although nutrients and energy have to be imported from some other ecosystem. Therefore, space and time boundaries of the system to be sustained must be defined at the outset. Then for a predefined ecological management unit, primary production, biological diversity, and natural rates of recycling become important indicators within that unit.

- *Appropriate degree of aggregation in indicators.* For example, with regard to atmospheric composition, it must be decided whether it is the individual atmospheric components or the net effect or the greenhouse potential of all of them together that is important when looking at greenhouse gases.

- *Distribution of values.* When looking for measured values, it is sometimes not the mean value over a region or an area that should be sought, but rather the cumulative distribution function of values, including the tails of the distribution.

- *Butterfly effect.* If there can be large effects from small causes (analogous to the butterfly effect of chaos theory), one of the implications is that there are some uses of certain ecosystems that simply must be foregone. Thus, requiring biogeophysical sustainability implies forbidding some kinds of uses in some places because large adverse effects may follow.

- *Surrogates.* Surrogates can be used to monitor diversity. A great deal of the diversity of forest systems consists of invertebrates, microbial organisms, and fungal organisms that are not easily monitored. However, such conditions as structure and stage of development of a forest may indicate that at least the habitat conditions exist for those kinds of organisms.

- *Urban areas.* Urban environments, with their rapid growth, the consumptive lifestyles of their inhabitants, and dependence on external support systems, might be seen at first as offering one of the better ways of preserving biological diversity—typically by concentrating the population in urban areas and taking them out of direct conflict with the natural ecosystems elsewhere. However, further reflection shows that people who live in cities actually consume much more than people in the countryside. Furthermore, the evidence of past civilizations shows that urban consumption patterns are often not sustainable and ultimately begin to exceed the carrying capacity of the surrounding countryside (for the prevailing technology). Thus, moving people to cities may be just a short-term expedient unless there is a transition to long-term sustainable adaptation.

Next steps

The conference demonstrated that although there is a focus on specific ecosystem types or specific locations, it is not possible to reach a general consensus on what should be measured. Thus, it is necessary to get down to specifics for each given ecosystem, for which more specific indicators and measurements must be produced based on the above considerations.

Therefore, the next logical step is to hand over to specialist groups the task of deciding which specific measurements should be used for each indicator in the matrix. It will be necessary to identify—for each indicator and in the context of each region or ecosystem—the following:

- the appropriate spatial scale for the averaging, integration, or aggregation of the indicator

- the appropriate averaging time

- the level of fluctuations consistent with current notions of sustainability

- the magnitude of secular trends in the variables that are consistent with these notions of sustainability, and

- the needed or appropriate degree of aggregation of the particular indicator; for example, regarding energy flows, whether net primary productivity (NPP) is sufficient or whether information about energy flows at every trophic level is required).

Once this step has been achieved, there are two not necessarily incompatible directions in which to apply the selected indicators. Although the health of the biosphere and of individual ecosystems is important, the sustainability concept suggests the need to introduce an accounting principle. The idea is to produce a system of measurements that would be general enough to permit discussion of indicators of sustainability within a framework of global environmental accounting. The global accounting needs become obvious because of the complications created by too many indicators for different regions. Using a business analogy, the balance sheet at the end of the year shows whether the operation was sustainable (profitable) or unsustainable (unprofitable). This requires the ability to convert all the assets of the ecosystem (business) to a common unit so that accounting principles can be applied. It was suggested that the most important accounting principle would be production—generally the harvest, which is readily convertible to monetary terms, since there are markets. Two other aspects of importance are biological diversity and ecosystem processes and functions.

This set of indicators provides an opportunity for integrating several of them into a general index that would cover broader scales. Therefore, another approach would involve developing within each of the parameters a very specific, and probably region-specific, list of measurements to see if these could have a universal value. If so, further research would show the way to assemble these individual indicators into one or more indices aggregated across temporal and spatial scales.

The basic task is to determine what to do with the information obtained from specific indicators and how the indicators can be used constructivelym to emphasize the concerns of sustainability. In doing this there must be some trade-off between comprehensiveness, on the one hand, and simplicity, scrutability, and usability on the other. Obviously the number of indicators can be amplified ad infinitum, thus inviting the danger of making an index complicated. It is harder to assess the relative importance of different indicators—in particular, the ones that capture most of the properties considered important without adding so much complexity to the indicator that it approaches the degree of complexity of the real world.

In addition to reducing the number of indicators by careful selection, another technique that can simplify the process of formulating an indicator, and thus an index, is to simply establish a norm and divide the actual measurement by that norm. This produces a dimensionless indicator or index that becomes a common measure because it is always a comparison. The measurement of a base year or a healthy ecosystem could be selected as the norm, and departures from it could be monitored.

It was pointed out at the conference that the indicators fall into three broad groups: chemical, biological and physical. The chemical indicators are among the parameters for water quality and atmospheric composition, although such indicators would fall with the physical indicators. The biological indicators involve the biological diversity parameters at different levels. Finally, there is a set of physical indicators in terms of energy balance and land-use change as well as the quantitative aspects of some of the chemical and biological indicators. This method of organization might be of use in the development of an aggregate index of sustainability.

Toward policy considerations

The conference participants felt that the most up-to-date and perhaps the best general statement of what policymakers perceive as their requirements were in the documents that came out of the Rio Conference, namely Agenda 21 and the Rio Declaration. These provide an organizing principle for addressing sustainability because they spell out the existing policy commitments and agreements as well as the scientific goals and products needed to support those commitments. Further scientific requirements can also be derived from the goals and policies expressed therein.

However, it was suggested that for developing indices of sustainability, it is necessary to go beyond the above-mentioned documents and consider the manner in which they would be used. The policy challenge is frequently related to information that policymakers feel they need to make appropriate decisions. Discussions about declining biological diversity or a change in hydrological pattern in the Amazon basin do not usually draw the attention of policymakers. However, polic makers do want to know the consequence of such changes and how they effect the sustainability of natural resource systems that support people and life. Providing such information requires an ambitious agenda that will probably test the current state of knowledge.

Recommendations

The conference participants made the following ten general recommendations:

1. More work is needed to refine the definitions and propose the indicators for biogeophysical sustainability. The emphasis must be on starting at the smaller scales because it is not possible to synthesize results that have not been obtained at the scale of the individual unit.

2. For the purposes of communication, a very simple index is urgently needed—one that would permit and facilitate communication between biologists, sociologists, and economists. It is anticipated that the formulation of such an index will require an interdisciplinary effort. Such an index, or elements of such an index, might include atmospheric CO_2 concentration, atmospheric methane concentration, atmospheric oxygen concentration, net primary productivity, or biological diversity. Such an index should be useful over many scales, populations, and different types of ecosystem.

3. As the distinction between temperate and tropical agriculture is more one of measurement and knowledge about the ecosystem than of actual biogeophysical differences, many of the measurements made in temperate agriculture systems could be useful in tropical agricultural systems. This has not happened yet because

agricultural systems are much more diverse in the tropical areas as a result of a much greater number of crops, cropping sequences, and cultural diversity. Thus, obtaining relevant indicators becomes much more difficult, and it is necessary to concentrate research and data gathering activities on obtaining the information that will be needed for indicators of sustainability.

4. For natural ecosystems more knowledge is needed about the driving forces that keep those ecosystems in equilibrium, the natural processes involved, and the location of critical thresholds. These last are important because if they are exceeded they can lead to discontinuity—that is, a rapid transition to new states with very different conditions. To predict this, indicators are needed that can monitor the proximity of the threshold. Priority should probably be given to those phenomena that lead to major and dramatic shifts. Thus, it is important to be aware of the factors that reflect the maintenance of the current state. It would also be valuable to know how change to a better state might be achieved. For managed ecosystems there should be a similar list of critical thresholds and critical capacities. It would be helpful to identify the driving forces that have led to collapses or major changes in the past. Thus, a series of case studies dealing with these shifts and critical thresholds should be conducted.

5. Ecosystems are high-order nonlinear systems. Much valuable information might be derived from a study of ecosystems, using the techniques from physics, for example. Finding equivalencies between known physical systems and ecological systems could be a practical prospect. Physicists have learned that it is not always possible to predict the new state to which a nonlinear system will shift after a transition. But they have managed to begin predicting whether there will be a state transition and when it will occur, on the basis of signs that manifest themselves as the state-transition threshold is approached. This is an important area for exploration in ecology.

6. The significance of large system change is still uncertain, as when all indicators start changing in the "wrong direction." This is a topic on which much more research in needed.

7. Integrating information is difficult and challenging aspect of many disciplines of science. Even remote sensing is limited to a definite scale because of its limited resolution. Thus, landscape imagery provides a scale-dependent pattern for different composites or mosaics. Research needs to be conducted on the best use of information, its interpretation, and its aggregation to the larger scales. Such larger scales have smoothed and reduced variances. Although this is sometimes real, it often is an artifact of the aggregation process. Since averaging throws out a lot of information, there is a need to develop decision-based rules for aggregating information so as to maintain the information base present at small scales after extrapolation to larger scales. In some cases, where linear averaging is not adequate, fractals can be used to maintain information as scale is increased. This would be a valuable tool in developing the definitive set of indicators of biogeophysical sustainability.

8. There appears to be a need to assess the state of the science of sustainability to determine, for example, how well sustainability can be predicted, measured, and understood. There are perhaps a dozen myths about sustainability that can be, and have been, invoked. The time appears right for an independent review.

9. There must be a reorientation and refocus of research in the ecological sciences. With limited human and financial resources and most of the funds not being used on research that directly addresses local sustainability, the most important recommendation is that the research base and research funding be reoriented to focus on important questions about sustainability.

10. To better deal with all of this, a new discipline dubbed "econology" is proposed. Econology goes beyond combining the two older disciplines of ecology and economics and requires research that brings more externalities into this approach. Such research is also needed to overcome the automatic constraint inherent in dealing with steady-state models.

In addition, the participants proposed the follow-up activity to create high-level global indices of biogeophysical sustainability. The process begins by developing specific sets of indicators for a series of ecosystems of different types and in different parts of the globe. This would involve convening a series of working groups, with each one focusing on a particular ecosystem to develop the indicators and associated measurements of biogeophysical sustainability. Undertaking this task for a representative series of ecosystems, natural and managed, that can thus provide the foundation for work on one or several indices of biogeophysical sustainability is required for getting down to more detailed scales. This should be followed by a meeting of representatives from each group to work out the commonalities among the sets of indicators and the formulation of one or several indices of sustainability.

References

Munasinghe, Mohan. 1993. *Environmental Economics and Sustainable Development*, Washington , D.C.: The World Bank.

Vitousek, Peter, Paul Ehrlich, Anne Ehrlich, and R.A. Matson. 1986. "Human Appropriations of the Products of Photosynthesis." *BioScience* 36: 368–73.

Proposed indicators of biogeophysical sustainability

PARAMETER	ECOSYSTEMS							
	AGRICULTURE	FORESTS	RANGELANDS	WILDLIFE/WILDLANDS	FRESHWATER FISHERIES	WETLANDS/GROUNDWATER	COASTAL RESOURCES	MARINE FISHERIES
Landscape Composition and Patterns	Field size and mix Land-use conversion rate	Spatial variation of vegetation types Patchiness (gaps) Land-use conversion rate	Grazing gradients	Spatial variation of vegetation types Habitat patchiness (gaps) Corridors Land-use conversion rate	Spawning and nursery habitats Pool structure Corridors	Riparian vegetation Spatial variation of aquatic systems	Spatial variation of ecosystem types (incl. reefs, mangroves) Patchiness (gaps) Spawning and nursery habitats	Spawning and nursery habitats
Production of Goods and Services	Crop productivity (output/input) Crop genetic reserves	Wood and non-timber product yield	Stocking density Foliage crop productivity	Game hunting yield Population dynamics of wildlife	Total catch Catch composition (size and species) Catch per unit effort	Water withdrawal	Fishing yield Wood and non-timber vegetation product yield	Total catch Catch composition (size and species) Catch per unit effort
Biological Diversity	Species richness and diversity of indicator groups Population size of keystone species Crop diversity Soil and pest organism diversity	Species richness and diversity of indicator groups Population size of keystone species	Species richness and diversity of indicator groups Population size of keystone species	Species richness and diversity of indicator groups Population size of keystone species	Species richness and diversity of indicator groups Population size of keystone species	Species richness and diversity of indicator groups	Species richness and diversity of indicator groups	Species richness and diversity of indicator groups Population size of keystone species
Water Quality and Quantity	Salinity Seasonality Pollutant concentrations	Seasonality Evapotranspiration fluxes Pollutant concentrations Base flow	Precipitation pattern Pollutant concentrations	Seasonality	Seasonality Dissolved oxygen concentration Nitrogen (ammonium) concentration pH and eutrophication Pollutant concentrations	Seasonality (incl. flood plain inundation) Eutrophication Pollutant concentrations	Seasonality (incl. river discharge) Eutrophication Salinity Nutrient concentration Pollutant concentration	Seasonality Nutrient (plankton) concentrations Pollutant concentrations
Soil Properties	Organic carbon content Nutrient content Cation exchange capacity Erosion rate	Nutrient content	Salinity Organic carbon content Nutrient content	Soil type Organic carbon content Nutrient content	Substrate condition Metal ion and other pollutant concentrations	Erosivity Sediment delivery	Sediment delivery Pollutant concentration	
Energy and Nutrient Flows	Parent rock nutrient mobilization Nutrient (fertilizer) input fluxes Energy efficiency and quality	Primary productivity Nutrient mobilization	Nutrient mobilization	Nutrient mobilization	Primary productivity Progressive changes Bioaccumulation of pollutants		Primary productivity Nutrient fluxes	Primary productivity Bioaccumulation of pollutants
Atmospheric Composition	Acid precipitation UV-B irradiation Tropospheric ozone concentration Carbon dioxide concentration	Acid precipitation UV-B irradiation Tropospheric ozone concentration Carbon dioxide concentration	Acid precipitation UV-B irradiation Tropospheric ozone concentration	Acid precipitation UV-B irradiation Tropospheric ozone concentration	Acid precipitation UV-B irradiation	Acid precipitation Deposition of pollutants	Deposition of pollutants UV-B irradiation Tropospheric ozone concentration	UV-B irradiation
Climate	Temperature mean and variability Precipitation mean and variability	Temperature mean and variability Precipitation mean and variability	Temperature mean and variability Precipitation mean and variability	Temperature mean and variability Precipitation mean and variability	Temperature mean and variability Precipitation mean and variability	Precipitation mean and variability	Temperature mean and variability Precipitation mean and variability	Temperature mean and variability

Part A

Background Papers

1

The Meaning of Sustainability: Biogeophysical Aspects

John P. Holdren, Gretchen C. Daily, and Paul R. Ehrlich

This paper benefited greatly from interactions with R. Cicerone, A. Coale, T. Dietz, P. Gleick, R. Healy, R. Lenski, M. McDonnell, J. Lubchenco, T. Malone, B. McCay, N. Myers, D. Pimentel, G. Rabb, D. Skole, and M. Soule (U.S. National Academy of Sciences Planning Group for a study on ecological effects of human activities); Partha Dasgupta (Cambridge University); A. Ehrlich (Department of Biological Sciences, Stanford University); W. Falcon, L. Goulder, and R. Naylor (Institute for International Studies, Stanford University); R. Howarth, A. Kinzig, S. Lele, and R. Norgaard (Energy and Resources Group, University of California at Berkeley); G. Woodwell, R. Houghton, R. Ramakrishna, J. Amthor, and E. Davidson (Woods Hole Research Center); and M. Weitzman (Department of Economics, Harvard University). The responsibility for errors and infelicities, however, rests solely with the authors. Our work on this topic was supported in part by grants from the Winslow and Heinz Foundations. J. Holdren also gratefully acknowledges the hospitality of the Woods Hole Research Center during a 1992 sabbatical in which much of his part of this work was done.

A sustainable process or condition is one that can be maintained indefinitely without progressive diminution of valued qualities inside or outside the system in which the process operates or the condition prevails. (We exclude from consideration, in applying this definition, the depletion of available energy from the sun on a time scale of several billion years!)[1] Such a definition may be logically appealing, but it is hardly sufficient for addressing the meaning of sustainability in the context of practical choices about how to maintain or improve the well-being of humans on this planet.[2] What kinds of processes and conditions need to be sustained in the interest of maintaining or improving well-being? What are the sources and dimensions of the main threats to the sustainability of these? What places should be investigated and what should be measured to find out? Can sustainability be made compatible with—or traded off against—other desiderata relating to policy choices? (Consider, for example, sustainable development versus rapid development).

The proposition that particular human practices would prove unsustainable has cropped up in literature going all the way back to the ancient Greeks and somewhat more frequently and sweepingly in the two hundred years since the work of Malthus, above all in the period since World War II.[3] Only in the past five years, however, has sustainability become a catchword capable of capturing the attention not only of environmental scientists and activists but also of (some) mainstream economists, other social scientists, and policymakers.

This enhanced salience presumably resulted from a suite of coincident factors. For one, the world community is no longer transfixed by the Cold War. A second factor is the reluctant appreciation of the severity of the debt crisis in the developing world. A third is the substantial advancement in scientific understanding of the magnitude and consequences of ongoing global environmental transformations, including the depletion of stratospheric ozone, the buildup of greenhouse gases, and the destruction of biodiversity. Also very important has been the attention given to the notion of sustainable development in the report of the World Commission on Environment and Development (WCED 1987, also known as "the Brundtland report") and the avalanche of related studies that has followed.

Notwithstanding the extraordinary growth of the "sustainability" literature in the past few years (an unsustainable process, to be sure!), much of the analysis and discussion of this topic remains mired in terminological and conceptual ambiguities, as well as in disagreements about facts and practical implications.[4] These problems arise in part because the sustainability of the human enterprise in the broadest sense depends on technological, economic, political, and cultural factors as well as on environmental ones and in part because practitioners in the different relevant fields see different parts of the picture, typically think in terms of different time scales, and often use the same words to mean different things.

It is therefore appropriate, even though this introductory chapter and the conference of which it was originally a part are supposed to focus on the biogeophysical aspects of sustainability, to begin by locating the biogeophysical aspects within the context of the wider debate about what sustainability means and implies. We then address, in turn, some problems with defining biogeophysical sustainability in practical terms, the connection between biogeophysical sustainability and related concepts such as carrying capacity and the distinction between renewable and nonrenewable resources, the state of knowledge and debate about the character and origins of threats to biogeophysical sustainability, and some implications of the current state of knowledge and ignorance of these matters. We undertake all of this with a pronounced emphasis on the global level of analysis, leaving to the chapters that follow the task of addressing the character and measure of sustainability in particular regions and ecosystems.

Biogeophysical sustainability in context

Much of the current salience of concepts of sustainability has come from a wide-ranging international discussion about sustainable development, which has been defined variously as, for example:

- Meeting the needs of the present without compromising the ability of future generations to meet their own needs (WCED 1987)

- Improving the quality of human life while living within the carrying capacity of supporting ecosystems (IUCN 1991)

- Economic growth that provides fairness and opportunity for all the world's people, not just the privileged few, without further destroying the world's finite natural resources and carrying capacity (Pronk and Haq 1992).

These definitions have the appeal of appearing to reconcile the concerns of diverse constituencies—above all the development and environmental communities (Lele 1991)—but they raise at least as many questions as they answer. Is it possible to meet the needs of the present without compromising the capacity of future generations to meet their needs? How does one define needs anyway? What determines carrying capacity, and how does it vary from place to place and over time? What is the relation between economic growth and development? What constitutes fairness? Let us sketch out tentative answers to some of these broad questions—since those answers will partly shape our understanding of the environmental issues we want to address shortly in more detail—starting with the meaning of development. We think development ought to be understood to mean progress toward alleviating the main ills that undermine human well-being. These ills are outlined in table 1-1 in terms of perverse conditions, driving forces, and underlying human frailties. (The problems at each of these levels are themselves diversely and often tightly interconnected.) The development process is then seen to entail improving the perverse circumstances by altering the driving forces, which in turn requires overcoming, to some extent, the underlying frailties. Sustainable development then means accomplishing this in ways that do not compromise the capacity to maintain the improved conditions indefinitely.

Development by this definition should by no means be considered synonymous with economic growth, since growth by itself does not assure progress toward alleviating any of the indicated ills. (Economic growth may be a necessary condition for alleviating some of them, but it is certainly not a sufficient condition.) Note also that we have placed sustainable in front of development to mean not that the development is of a form that can be continued indefinitely but rather that the choice of processes and end states for development are compatible with maintaining the improved conditions indefinitely. Under this sort of interpretation, even the much-maligned

Table 1-1: Ills That Development Must Address

Condition	Meaning
Perverse conditions	
Poverty	1.1 billion—20 percent—of the 5.5 billion people on the planet live in absolute poverty and perhaps 2 billion people do not receive a sufficiently nutritious diet to alleviate disease
Impoverishment of environement	Disruption and erosion of environmental conditions and processes on which the well-being of those 5.5 billion people depend even more directly than on economic conditions and processes
Possibility of war	Civil, international, global, nuclear, or conventional wars manifest in the more than 100 instances of organized armed conflict since World War II, nearly all of them in the south, with a total loss of life in the tens of millions
Oppression of human rights	In forms beyond the three already listed, which deny human beings their dignity, liberty, personal security, and possibilities for shaping their own destinies
Wastage of human potential	Resulting from all of the foregoing and the despair and apathy that accompany them and from the loss of cultural diversity (Ehrlich 1980)
Driving forces	
Excessive population growth	Where excessive means growth that closes more options than it opens (Holdren 1973), a condition now prevailing almost everywhere
Maldistribution of consumption and investment	Where the maldistribution is of three kinds: between rich and and investment poor as the beneficiaries of both consumption and investment, between military and civilian forms of consumption and investment, and between the two activities themselves, that is, between too much consumption and too little investment
Misuse of technology	Which occurs in forms both intentional (as in weapons of mass destruction) and inadvertent (as in the side effects of a broad spectrum of herbicides and pesticides)
Corruption and mismanagement	Which are pervasive in industrial and developing countries
Powerlessness of the victims	Who lack the knowledge and the resources but above all the political power to change the conditions that afflict them
Underlying human frailties	
Greed, selfishness, intolerance, and shortsightedness	Which collectively have been elevated by conservative political doctrine and practice (above all in the United States in 1980–92) to the status of a credo
Ignorance, stupidity, apathy, and denial	The first consisting of lack of exposure to information, the second of lack of capacity to absorb it, and the third and fourth of having the information but lacking the conviction or optimism or fortitude to act on it

term sustainable growth need not be an oxymoron; it can be taken simply to mean growth in forms—and to end points—compatible with sustainability of the improved conditions it helps bring about.

If improvements in the human condition are to be not only achieved but also sustained, all of the ills will need to be addressed; this is so because failure to address any one of them can eventually undermine the progress made on all the others.

As the human enterprise expands, interdependencies mediated through the world economy, the global environmental commons, and international political and military relations link and intensify the threats posed by each of these ills. Thus the requirements for sustainability include not only the environmental factors to which we will shortly turn in detail but also military, political, and economic ones. The minimum requirements in each of these categories are presented in table 1-2.

Table 1-2: Requirements for Sustainable Improvements in Well-being

Area and requirement	Rationale
Military	
No weapons of mass destruction	No one can be secure as long as these exist anywhere, and as long as any country insists on retaining them, others will have an incentive to acquire them
Limited capabilities of national military forces	Security would be served by attaining a condition in which no nation's military forces were strong enough to threaten the existence of other states; this can be facilitated by "defense dominance," in which national forces are structured to be much stronger in defense than in offense. If stronger peacekeeping forces are needed, they should be placed under international control
Political	
Self-determination	Smaller political units should coalesce into or be absorbed by larger ones only by mutual consent, based on mutual advantage
Participation/empowerment	Societies are not stable—and hence not sustainable—unless their citizens have an effective voice in decisions that affect their lives
The rule of law	The rule of the strongest, the most devious, or the most unscrupulous is a prescription for perverse and destabilizing forms of competition
Guarantees for human rights	Majority rule does not include the privilege of abusing minorities; sustainability requires respect for cultural diversity as well as biotic diversity
Economic	
Reduced disparities within and between countries	The large gaps between rich and poor that characterize income distribution within and between countries today are incompatible with social stability and with cooperative approaches to achieving environmental sustainability
Internalization of environmental costs	Economic markets will lead to overconsumption of environmental resources and ultimately to unsustainability if these resources are not priced or are underpriced
Assignment of property rights to future generations	This approach seems essential to avoid the outcome in which high discount rates of economic actors allow actions that undermine long-term sustainability to appear economically attractive (Howarth and Norgaard 1990)
Environmental	
Preservation of the environmental basis of present and future well-being	What this requirement consists of and the way it might be attained are the topics of the rest of this chapter

With that wider array of considerations as context, we now take a closer look at the environmental dimensions of sustainability that are the main focus of this volume.

Definitions of environmental sustainability

The environmental aspect of sustainability has been the subject of a rich literature, albeit only recently with the term sustainability appearing explicitly.[5] As with the concept of sustainable development, however, the definitions of environmental sustainability to be found in the literature recent enough to use that term are often circular or unsatisfying in other ways. Consider the following capsule definitions:

- Sustainability refers to a process or state that can be maintained indefinitely (IUCN 1991)
- Natural resources must be used in ways that do not create ecological debts by overexploiting the carrying and productive capacity of the Earth (Pronk and Haq 1992)
- A minimum necessary condition for sustainability is the maintenance of the total natural capital stock at or above the current level (Costanza 1991).

The first statement is essentially a dictionary definition of sustainability; it tells us only what we already knew sustainability to mean. The second statement introduces the interesting term "ecological debt" to describe an element of unsustainability, but the elaboration in terms of overexploiting carrying capacity and productive capacity is not much help, insofar as it merely transfers the definitional burden to over-exploitation and carrying capacity. The third statement offers an actual specification of at least one element of sustainability, but there is still buried within it a definitional problem: How is "total natural stock" to be defined and measured? Assuming this hurdle can be overcome, the further question will surely arise: What is inviolable about the current level? Can environmental scientists give a good answer? We shall return to this issue below.

Of course, all serious writers on environmental sustainability go beyond the sorts of capsule definitions cited above and elaborate what sustainability might entail and require (see, for example, boxes 1-1 and 1-2). The 1980 World Conservation Strategy of the International Union for the Conservation of Nature, the United Nations Environment Program, and the World Wildlife Fund (IUCN 1980) concludes, for example, that sustainability requires "maintenance of essential ecological processes and life-support systems; preservation of genetic diversity; and sustainable utilization of species and resources." This three-part prescription seems to consist of different facets of the same thing: preservation of genetic diversity and sustainable use are essential to maintain essential ecological processes and life support systems.

Box 1-1: Definition and Measurement of Sustainability: The Biophysical Foundations
Keiichiro Fuwa

Environmental issues have become so popular that politicians around the world no longer need to be persuaded of their importance. Natural scientists have been using the word sustainability for a fairly long time, and recently social scientists as well as politicians have started to use it quite frequently. However, it has yet to be defined clearly.

Recommendations have been made for the definition of measurements and indicators of sustainability. Although by no means final, the following working definition of biophysical sustainability is satisfactory for the time being: *Biophysical sustainability means maintaining or improving the integrity of the life support system of Earth.* Sustaining the biosphere with adequate provisions for maximizing future options includes enabling current and future generations to achieve economic and social improvement within a framework of cultural diversity while maintaining (a) biological diversity and (b) the biogeochemical integrity of the biosphere by means of conservation and proper use of air, water, and land resources. Achieving these goals requires planning and action at local, regional, and global levels and specifying short- and long-term objectives that allow for the transition to sustainability.

Biophysical refers not only to biology and physics but also to geology and chemistry. This is expressed in the definition, particularly through mention of biogeochemical integrity. Natural science has become so interdisciplinary that it is often confusing; nevertheless physics, chemistry, geology, and biology remain the most basic disciplines. Biogeophysicochemistry expresses them all in one word, albeit an exceptionally long one.

Defining terms such as sustainability and sustainable development with reference to the global environment is, to my mind, complicated by the fact that humanity has been considered special and separate from other animals and plants. This has not always been the case. The Earth is divided into three spheres: atmosphere, hydrosphere, and lithosphere. The biosphere was added later as the fourth sphere but, unlike the others, includes those parts of the atmosphere, hydrosphere, and lithosphere in which life exists. Plants and animals are, of course, part of the biosphere, but more importantly, humans are included as just one species of animal and are not treated specially. In recent years, particularly when serious environmental problems were recognized, human activity was so intense and pervasive that it came to be considered—for example, by the Man and the Biosphere Programme—as separate from the activity of other forms of life.

Biophysical sustainability must, therefore, mean the sustainability of the biosphere minus humanity. Humanity's role has to be considered separately as economic or social sustainability. Likewise, sustainable development should mean both sustainability of the biophysical medium or environment and sustainability of human development, with the latter sustaining the former.

Box 1-2. Coming to Grips with the Biogeophysical Issues in a Social Construct, or How to Talk about Sustainability without Being a Social Scientist
Sharad Lele

> "You cannot talk about sustainability without talking about people, about politics, about power and control."
>
> Comment by a sociologist at a seminar on sustainability
> University of California, Berkeley, 1988

> "Sustainability is maintaining the ecological basis of economic well-being, so any discussion of sustainability must incorporate economic considerations."
>
> World Bank economist

Comments such as these threaten to create a gridlock in our discussions of the biophysical foundations of environmental sustainability. But we are clearly not (and probably nobody is) capable of conducting such an all-encompassing discussion. How then do we discuss the biophysical foundations of environmental sustainability, however defined? Social, political, and cultural issues come into play in a number of ways at two critical stages in any discussion of environmental sustainability.

Stage 1. In deciding,
- What is to be sustained? That is, what relative ranking is to be given to, say, current resource productivity, productive potential, or genetic diversity?
- What attributes, or combinations of attributes, of a particular system are to be maintained nondecreasing: average productivity, stability, resilience, or adaptability?
- Over what time scale is this sustenance desired?
- Who is to benefit? If a tradeoff is necessary between current and future consumption and well-being, or between the well-being of one community and that of another, who is to decide and how?
- Should it be economic value of any resource flow or stock that is maintained non-decreasing, or should it be the physical quantity of that flow?

Stage 2. In understanding,
- Why is there environmental unsustainability, however defined, in the world today?
- How would one achieve or move toward whatever notion of an environmentally sustainable society that is decided on in stage 1?

Stage 1 requires an explication of differing individual and cultural values, preferences, as well as beliefs about and approaches to a highly uncertain and unknowable future and then the resolution of such differences through some social process. Stage 2 requires an understanding of the complex array of social, political, and cultural factors in today's world that lead to environmentally unsustainable behavior.

The 1991 "Strategy for Sustainable Living" by the same triad of organizations (IUCN 1991) says that "sustainable use means use of an organism, ecosystem, or other renewable resource at a rate within its capacity for renewal." Operating within the capacity for renewal clearly is one of the key elements of sustainability, but this formulation does not deal with either nonrenewable resources or the possible off-site, out-of-ecosystem impacts through which exploitation of one resource within its capacity for renewal might adversely affect the renewability of other resources or the sustainability of other ecosystems.

The economist Herman Daly, who has been a pioneer in thinking systematically about these matters,[6] recently offered a more helpful three-part specification of the ingredients of sustainability (Daly 1991):

- Rates of use of renewable resources do not exceed regeneration rates
- Rates of use of nonrenewable resources do not exceed rates of development of renewable substitutes
- Rates of pollution emission do not exceed assimilative capacities of the environment.

Once this is clearly realized, it is easier to understand where our contributions as biophysicists and ecologists can be and ought to be in *informing* the process of reaching some societal consensus on the issues in stage 1. At the same time, we realize that, in our work, we have often made implicit decisions about the issues raised in Stage 1. We should therefore proceed as follows:

1. Clearly state the assumptions we are making about reality in a particular case, examine whether some assumptions are commonly shared, and determine the extent to which these may be justified. For instance, perhaps most ecologists believe that whatever is to be maintained nondecreasing in an ecosystem should be measured in physical, not economic, terms. This follows from their rejection of the belief commonly held and vigorously promoted by most economists: that technological change can continuously compensate for reduction in physical resource flows, thus preventing utility from decreasing.

2. Clearly state what value-based choices of objectives, of their ranking, of time horizons, and of users are being implicitly made in any particular case.

3. Identify a few scenarios corresponding to choices different from those that we might want to make.

Having done this, we can then proceed with our basic tasks:

4. Synthesize the current state of knowledge about the relationships between biophysical processes that affect different objectives at different temporal and spatial scales. That is, what intensity of harvesting under what technique of logging can be maintained in a tropical forest at a nondecreasing level for what time period? What would the implications of a nondecreasing resilience requirement be?

5. Identify a sparse set of indicators that best relate to each combination of objective, scale, and so forth and possibly identify threshold values for them. For instance, what would be the best indicator of stable harvests in the above-mentioned forest? What would be the indicator of resilience in the same system? What scales (spatial and temporal) may be most appropriate or sensible for measuring what attribute or type of sustainability?

6. Explore the ways in which the different scenarios interact; that is, the synergisms and contradictions among objectives, attributes, and indicators and between sustainability in general and other societal objectives. What are the tradeoffs between, say, maintaining timber productivity and maintaining biodiversity in a forest, or between average production and resilience? What are the tradeoffs between different levels of these attributes of sustainability and between the net yield or human well-being produced and the manner in which it is distributed within society?

If we are able to do this in a self-aware and socially sensitive manner, we will be able to overcome the paralysis of analysis and make a major contribution to the sustainability debate.

The first of these conditions, by being stated in the aggregate, partly addresses the problem of off-site impacts associated with the exploitation of individual renewable resources: the regeneration rates constraints presumably reflect cross-resource or cross-ecosystem impacts occurring within the overall pattern of resource exploitation.

The second condition, the rate of use of nonrenewable resources, offers a clever solution to the question of how any use of nonrenewable resources can be contemplated within a sustainability framework. Daly offers a detailed formulation on how to ensure that this condition is met, by earmarking part of the proceeds from the exploitation of nonrenewable resources for the development of renewable alternatives.

Daly's third condition, on rates of pollution emission, does not seem as satisfying. If assimilative capacity of the environment means the capacity to assimilate the pollution without any adverse effect on human health or welfare (including through diminution of ecosystem services), the difficulty is that there are many kinds of pollution for which the assimilative capacity, so defined, is probably zero (including, for example, ionizing radiation, chlorofluorocarbons, lead, and more). It does not seem to insist on no harm from pollution as a condition of sustainability; the question is rather what level of harm is tolerable on a steady-state basis, in exchange for the benefits of the activity that produces the harm.[7]

We would also add to Daly's three-part formulation that the first condition applies to resources for which substitution at the required scale is currently and foreseeably impossible (essential resources). It is useful to distinguish those from resources for which substitutes are currently or foreseeably available (substitutable resources). Renewable substitutable resources could be sustainably exhausted on the same basis as nonrenewable substitutable resources (Daily and Ehrlich 1992).

Biogeophysical sustainability in theory and practice

The two most important questions relating to a definition of biogeophysical sustainability are "What is to be sustained?" and "For how long?" It is useful to distinguish, with respect to these questions, between what one would like the answers to be in theory and what one might have to settle for in practice (see table 1-3).

Saying that what is to be sustained, in theory, is the magnitude and quality of benefit flows continuously derivable from the environment captures the idea that potential benefits are important, not merely the benefits that society happens to be deriving now. And, of course, saying that the time scale is forever takes the definition of sustainability seriously.

Alas, several practical problems intrude on the attractiveness of this theoretical approach. First, even the existing benefit flows from the environ-

ment—not to mention the potentially continuously derivable benefit flows—are partly unknown (indeed, partly unknowable) and also partly incommensurable. (Without commensurability, one is stuck with trying to sustain the individual, incommensurable benefit flows rather than—more sensibly—an aggregated total benefit flow within which tradeoffs among different types of benefits could be contemplated.)

Second, insisting that potential benefit flows remain constant over very long periods of time is problematic because environmental conditions and processes—climate, topography, the biota—are occurring all the time even in the absence of human interventions. The potential magnitudes of such changes over the very long term make the concept of forever essentially meaningless, at least in relation to the sustainability of conditions that humans of today care about.

Third, it is conceivable that technological improvements will permit well-being to be maintained despite diminished benefit flows from the environment. This argument is probably the one most heavily relied upon by those not convinced of the need to maintain the stream of environmental services undiminished. But attempts to substitute technology for diminishing or otherwise inadequate environmental services invariably entail monetary costs and often generate significant new environmental impacts. In some cases, these additional costs and impacts may more than offset the (presumed) benefits of the activities that necessitated augmentation of the natural environmental services in the first place; and even if it is supposed that this will not be the case, it strikes us as imprudent in the extreme to assume that suitable technology for replacing whatever environmental services are lost will become available in a timely manner and on the requisite scale.

Table 1-3: Biogeophysical Sustainability in Theory and Practice

What is to be sustained?	*For how long?*
In theory, the magnitude and quality of benefit flows that are continuously derivable from the environment	Forever
In practice, the magnitude and quality of stocks of environmental resources	Half-life of 500 to 1,000 years

In any case, in light of the difficulties of measuring actual and potential environmental benefit flows, and in light of the conceptual and practical problems of insisting on no degradation forever, it may be necessary in practice to settle for trying to sustain the magnitude and quality of environmental stocks. The time scale on which this ought to be ensured might be defined in practical terms by a resource or stock half-life of 500 to 1,000 years, a period much longer than current planning horizons, but much shorter than geologic time. A tentative rule for prudent practice, then, would be to *constrain the degradation of monitorable environmental stocks to not more than 10 percent per century*.

Note that degradation of 10 percent a century produces, strictly speaking (that is, with $Q = Q_0 \exp[-0.10t]$), a half-life of about 700 years for the resource. Degradation of 20 percent a century would mean a half-life of 350 years, leaving a quarter of the resource remaining after 700 years.

We focus on stocks in this prudent-practice approach, because that is what can most easily be measured (albeit still not all that easily). Although our approach is similar in this respect to the Costanza prescription quoted earlier, an important difference is the specification of a finite rate of degradation as opposed to insistence on maintaining the stocks at just their current level. This sidesteps slightly the argument with the economists and technologists over what is so special about the current levels; putting the argument in terms of degradation rates relies on the presumed circumstance that there is *some* degradation rate that is too high to be regarded as sustainable, even allowing for economic substitution and technological change.

Of course, it would not really be acceptable to run down environmental stocks at 10 percent a century indefinitely. The point is rather that a rate of 10 percent a century (which after all means about 0.1 percent a year) is slow enough to give society a reasonable chance of figuring out what this degradation is costing, which forms of degradation can be compensated for, how those forms can be stopped that cannot be compensated for or tolerated, and so on, before it is too late. At current degradation rates, by contrast, which are typically an order of magnitude or so higher (that is, in the range of 100 percent a century or more), natural services will be devastated before society even understands what is happening, let alone finds time to take evasive action on the needed scale.

Contrasting views about the sustainability of human activities

Given the above (or any other) definition of sustainability, some obvious questions present themselves:

- Are current practices for transforming natural resources into flows of economic goods and services sustainable according to the indicated definition? If not, in what respects and by what margins is sustainability violated?

- Can the larger flows of goods and services required to shrink the gap between rich and poor, or the still larger flows required to meet the needs of a doubled or tripled population, be delivered sustainably by expanding current practices or by using improved practices that are already known? Or would sustaining larger flows require improvements over the best practices now known?

To environmental scientists, the answer to the first question is clearly no. Current rates of degradation of essential resources are typically an order of magnitude too high (in the range of 100 percent a century or more) for them to qualify as sustainable. The margins by which sustainability is exceeded by various types and combinations of human activity are very difficult to ascertain, however. It follows from the first answer, in any case, that current practices could not possibly sustain even larger flows of goods and services, but whether best-known practices could do so requires further careful analysis.

Although environmental scientists would be in nearly unanimous agreement on the answers just given, many members of other academic disciplines and numerous policymakers would dispute not only these answers but also the relevance of the questions. It is worth looking more closely at the origins of these differences in viewpoint. They undoubtedly arise in part from ambiguities in and disagreements about the meaning of sustainability. A more important source of disagreement, however, are the differing assumptions, perceptions, and knowledge about (a) the importance of environmental conditions and processes in supporting human well-being, (b) the sensitivity of those conditions and processes to disruption, and (c) the character and amenability of society to remedy the anthropogenic impacts now threatening such disruption.

Confusion about the sensitivity of those conditions and processes to disruption is evident in the comment attributed to economist William Nordhaus that only 3 percent of gross national product (GNP) in the United States depends on the environment. In fact, the entire GNP in the U.S. depends, ultimately, on maintaining the biophysical requisites of sustainability. Furthermore, the importance of agriculture (the economic sector to which Nordhaus apparently was referring) is vastly underestimated by its present share of GNP.

The greatest disparities in interpretation of the relationships between the human enterprise and Earth's life support systems seem, in fact, to be those between ecologists and economists. Members of both groups tend to be highly self-selected and to differ in fundamental worldviews. Most ecologists have a passion for the natural world, where the existence of limits to growth and the consequences of exceeding those limits are apparent. Ecologists recognize that a unique combination of highly developed manual dexterity, language, and intelligence has allowed humanity to increase vastly the capacity of the planet to support *Homo sapiens* (Diamond 1991); nonetheless, they perceive humans as being ultimately subject to the same sorts of biophysical constraints that apply to other organisms.

Economists, in contrast, tend to receive little or no training in the physical and natural sciences (Colander and Klamer 1987). Few explore the natural world on their own, and few appreciate the extreme sensitivity of organisms—including those upon which humanity depends for food, materials, pharmaceuticals, and free ecosystem services—to seemingly small changes in environmental conditions. Most treat economic systems as though they were completely disconnected from the planet's basic life support systems. The narrow education and inclinations of economists in these respects are thus a major source of disagreements about sustainability.

Some of the responsibility for these continuing disagreements also rests, however, on the failure of ecologists and other environmental scientists to make a case for the importance of environmental conditions and processes and for the magnitude of anthropogenic threats to these, in terms understandable by and persuasive to others. This problem is partly a matter of too few environmental scientists having made the effort to articulate a coherent case, but also partly a matter of the great gaps in the environmental science itself. Nor has it helped that environmental scientists

are often as ignorant about economic principles, and their relevance to environmental protection, as economists are about ecological principles.

Approaching consensus about biogeophysical sustainability clearly will require more research, more communication across disciplines, and more education of the public and policymakers about a multitude of issues, notably:

- The character and dimensions of the ways environmental structure and function affect human well-being, including the identification of environmental services and the quantification of their magnitude and value.

- The ways human impacts imperil environmental services, involving identification of environmental systems at risk and the causes, extent, time scales, and degree of irreversibility of anthropogenic threats to these systems.

- The amenability of the threats to remedy, including potential improvements in technology and management, use of economic incentives to induce appropriate changes, and the social, political, and economic barriers to implementation of the remedies.

The causes and character of environmental damage

Understanding the amenability of the threats to remedy requires a closer look at the factors and trends that are at the root of the problem. An early approach to illuminate this issue was the "I = PAT" formula (Ehrlich and Holdren 1971, 1972):

(environmental) impact = population x consumption per person (affluence) x impact per consumption (technology).

Today, a bit of further disaggregation seems useful, so as not to confuse affluence with resource use (the two being separable by means of the inverse efficiency factor, resource use per economic activity) and so as to separate measures of what technology does to the environment (stress) from measures of actual damage, which depends not only on stress but on susceptibility (itself a function of cumulative damage from previous stresses, as well as other factors). Thus,

Damage = population x economic activity per person (affluence)

x resource use per economic activity (resources)
x stress on the environment per resource use
(technology)
x damage per stress (susceptibility)

Note that this expanded relation (like the previous I = PAT) is no more and no less than an identity. It is true by definition. People are free to argue about whether it is informative and useful—and we think it is—but to argue about whether it is right is foolishness.

Identities of this sort are instructive because they remind us that increases in population, affluence, and the ratio of environmental stress to economic activity (itself clearly a function of the composition of that activity and the technology with which it is accomplished) are multiplicative in their effect on damage, so that the impact of each factor is a matter not only of its own magnitude but also of the magnitudes of the others.[8] At the same time, such identities are deceptive, and above all deceptively simple, in that they fail to make explicit (a) the ways in which the variables on the right-hand side of the equation are not independent, (b) the ways in which institutions, beliefs, and values can influence all of the variables and the nature of the interactions among them, or (c) the ways in which the relative importance of the variables and the nature of the interactions among them vary with location and time.

With respect to the lack of independence of the variables, the magnitude and composition of economic activity per person, and their rates of change, are likely to depend in complicated ways on the magnitude and composition of the population and their rates of change. The nature of the technology used to generate economic activity (and thus the kind and magnitude of stresses exerted on the environment by that technology per unit of economic activity) will depend on the magnitude and composition of all economic activity (hence on population and economic activity per person) as well as on their rates of change. The damage to ecosystem services per unit of imposed environmental stress—a form of dose-response relation—will generally be a function both of the magnitude and composition of the stress and of their rates of change.

With respect to the role of institutions, beliefs, and values, it is clear, on reflection, that these underlie as well as modulate changes in population, economic activity per person, and the technological variables through which the combination of population and per capita activity exert stresses on ecosystems; and of course it is largely through institutions (economic, political, legal, and so on), through beliefs and values, and through changes in these that damage feeds back to population, economic activity, and technology.

The relative importance of the different causative and modulating factors and the nature and intensity of their interactions clearly vary drastically with the social and ecological contexts, hence with location as well as with time. The situation is further complicated by the wide array of mechanisms by which phenomena in one location and time—be these phenomena demographic, economic, technological, ecological, political, cultural, or other—propagate to and influence other locations and times.

Beyond these elaborations about the various contributing factors, it is important to be clear about what we mean by damage. Damage means reduced length or quality of life for the present generation or future generations. Damage may result from short-term alteration of environmental conditions, long-term degradation of environmental capital, and costs of attempts to avoid reductions in length and quality of life with compensating technological and social interventions.

This is of course an explicitly and self-consciously anthropocentric definition, consistent with the anthropocentric definitions of sustainable development that provide the context for this debate. The anthropocentric approach to environmental problems is not the only valid one, but (a) it is the one most likely to succeed in the policy arena and (b) the difficulties in agreeing on definitions, problems, and solutions are even greater if human well-being is not at the center of attention.

Of course, *any* economic activity will lead to *some* environmental damage except in cases where the susceptibility factor—damage per unit of stress—is zero. Such cases exist when environmental processes are capable of completely absorbing or buffering the imposed stress such that there is no short-term alteration of environmental conditions or long-term degradation of environmental capital of a magnitude sufficient to produce an impact on length or quality of life for any members of the present or future generations of humans. But would many types and levels of economic activity in real-world conditions actually meet this condition?

The critical issue is to specify a level of damage that is acceptable to society. An economist might argue, for example, that we should not refrain

13

from activities that cause *any* damage, but only from those whose marginal costs (the sum of the internal costs plus the damages as here defined) exceed their marginal benefits. That is, if one could measure all of the costs and all of the benefits in a single currency (such as 1992 dollars), one would define the rational limit on the scale of any economic activity as the level at which the slopes of the cost and benefit curves were equal. Then maximum sustainable abuse (Daily and Ehrlich 1992) would mean the level of abuse (stress) that pushes the total marginal cost (slope of total cost curve) to just equal the total marginal benefit (slope of total benefit curve). Alas, there is no hope of quantifying and monetizing all the diverse kinds of damages associated with economic activity (even the damages occurring in the present, not to mention the problem of bringing future damages into our common currency, which requires agreeing on a discount rate).

In practice, then, cost-benefit-type approaches to determining maximum sustainable abuse are stuck with the problem of apples-and-oranges aggregation of qualitatively different damages, current and future damages, and damages and benefits. Additional daunting problems include dealing with stochasticity and establishing an appropriate margin of safety in the face of uncertainty. All these difficulties mean that tastes and preferences about the proper weighting of different categories become relevant and that the issue is political as much as technical. (A huge literature about risk perception and risk acceptance is relevant in some respects to these issues of maximum sustainable—or maximum tolerable or maximum prudent—abuse.)

Ignorance, knowledge, and uncertainty

As suggested earlier, the list of what is not known and what needs to be known in order to address "sustainability" with comprehensiveness and rigor is a very long one. Table 1-4 illustrates this point by presenting in abbreviated form the research agenda on ecological aspects of the issue that was developed recently as part of the Sustainable Biosphere Initiative of the Ecological Society of America (Lubchenco and others 1991). Another compact survey of research requirements related to sustainability is available in the agenda of the International Geosphere-Biosphere Programme of the International Council of Scientific Unions (ICSU 1992). The most important and demanding research sub-agenda of all may be one embedded in the environment-society elements of these lists: namely, the question of how to formulate and implement economic and social incentives for preserving the essential characteristics and functions of environmental systems.

At the same time, there is a great danger in falling into the scientist's trap of calling for more research without sufficiently emphasizing what we already know and the implications of that knowledge. We know for certain, for example, that:

- No form of material growth (including population growth) other than asymptotic growth, is sustainable;

- Many of the practices inadequately supporting today's population of 5.5 billion people are unsustainable; and

- At the sustainability limit, there will be a trade-off between population and energy-matter

Table 1-4: Research Needed in Ecological Science on Sustainability

Research area	Need
Ecological causes and consequences	Changes in climate. Changes in atmosphere, soil, and freshwater and marine chemistry.
Ecology of conservation and biodiversity	Global distribution of species and change factors. Biology of rare and declining species. Effects of global and regional change on diversity.
Strategies for sustainable ecological systems	Patterns and indicators of responses to stress. Guidelines and techniques for restoration. Theory for the management of ecological systems. Introduced species, pests, and pathogens. Integration of ecology with economics and other social sciences.

Source: Lubchenco and others 1991.

throughput per person, hence, ultimately, between economic activity per person and well-being per person.

This is enough to say quite a lot about what needs to be faced up to eventually (a world of zero net physical growth), what should be done now (change unsustainable practices, reduce excessive material consumption, slow down population growth), and what the penalty will be for postponing attention to population limitation (lower well-being per person).

Of course there are implications of what is not known as well as implications of what is known. The holes in society's knowledge should motivate development of strategies for minimizing the dangers associated with uncertainty. Any sensible prescription for dealing with the kinds of uncertainty we face will include adopting no-regrets strategies, buying insurance, and avoiding the biggest downside risks:

- No-regrets strategies entail taking steps that minimize vulnerability to the uncertain hazards while at the same time conferring benefits that make the steps worthwhile even if the uncertain hazards later turn out to be small.

- Insurance strategies entail paying to minimize vulnerability, but without expecting that other benefits (besides minimizing vulnerability) justify the investments; the payments beyond the expectation of other benefits are the premium, and the issue becomes how big an insurance premium should be paid.[9]

- Avoiding the biggest downside risks, finally, means trying to leave the biggest margin of safety against the hazards with the biggest negative consequences (largest areas and numbers of people affected, highest degrees of irreversibility), even if the probabilities of these downside outcomes are unknown or appear to be small.

There is, of course, much more to be said about the meaning and measurement of biogeophysical sustainability and about what human societies should be doing about it. But since this chapter is intended only to set the stage for the more detailed treatments to follow, we happily leave the rest to them.

Notes

1. A billion is 1,000 million.

2. Although concerns other than the maintenance or enhancement of human well-being can be posited as principles for guiding human behavior (see, for example, Ehrenfeld 1978), we shall accept for the purposes of this chapter that the perspective focuses on the well-being of humans.

3. Some landmarks in this early sustainability literature include Marsh 1864; Vogt 1948; Osborn 1948; Brown 1954; Carson 1962; Ehrlich 1968; Cloud 1969; SCEP 1970; and Meadows and others 1972.

4. A particularly helpful review calling attention to these difficulties is that by Lele 1991.

5. In addition to references cited in note 3 above, some major works include Ehrlich and Ehrlich 1970; Institute of Ecology 1971; Ehrlich and others 1977; CEQ 1980; IUCN 1980, 1991; Myers 1984; Mungall and McLaren 1990; Woodwell 1990; Turner and others 1991; Dooge and others 1992; Meadows and others 1992.

6. See, for example, Daly 1973, 1977, 1991; Daly and Cobb 1989.

7. Harm that would qualify as tolerable, in this context, could not be cumulative, else continuing additions to it would necessarily add up to unsustainable damage eventually. Thus, for example, a form and level of pollution that subtract a month from the life expectancy of the average member of the human population, or that reduce the net primary productivity of forests on the planet by 1 percent, might be deemed tolerable in exchange for very large benefits and would certainly be sustainable as long as the loss of life expectancy or reduction in productivity did not grow with time. Two of us have coined the term "maximum sustainable abuse" in the course of grappling with such ideas (Daily and Ehrlich 1992).

8. The following discussion was adapted from the unpublished report of a National Academy of Sciences study group, chaired by Holdren in 1991, on human impacts of ecosystems. See also the acknowledgments to this paper.

9. The idea of society's buying insurance is hardly unprecedented: much of the $300 billion a year that the U.S. spends on defense, for example, represents an insurance policy against contingencies considerably less likely to come about than are some of the environmental disasters one could mention.

References

Brown, Harrison. 1954. *The Challenge of Man's Future*. New York: Viking.

Carson, Rachel. 1962. *Silent Spring*. Boston: Houghton-Mifflin.

CEQ (Council on Environmental Quality). 1980. *The Global 2000 Report to the President*. With the U.S. Department of State. Washington, D.C.: U.S. Government Printing Office.

Cloud, Preston. 1969. *Resources and Man*. A study and recommendations by the Committee on Resources and Man of the Division of Earth Sciences, National Academy of Sciences, National Research Council, with the cooperation of the Division of Biology and Agriculture. San Francisco: W. H. Freeman.

Colander, D., and A. Klamer. 1987. "The Making of an Economist." *Economic Perspectives* 1, pp. 95–111.

Costanza, Robert, ed. 1991. *Ecological Economics: The Science and Management of Sustainability*. New York: Columbia University Press.

Daily, Gretchen C., and Paul R. Ehrlich. 1992. "Population, Sustainability, and Earth's Carrying Capacity." *BioScience* 42:10, pp. 761–71.

Daly, Herman E. 1977. *Steady-State Economics*. San Francisco: W. H. Freeman.

———. 1991. "Elements of Environmental Macroeconomics." In R. Costanza, ed., *Ecological Economics*. New York: Columbia University Press.

Daly, Herman E., ed. 1973. *Toward a Steady-State Economy*. San Francisco: W. H. Freeman.

Daly, Herman E., and J. B. Cobb, Jr. 1989. *For the Common Good: Redirecting the Economy toward Community, the Environment, and a Sustainable Future*. Boston: Beacon.

Diamond, Jared. 1991. *The Rise and Fall of the Third Chimpanzee*. London: Radius.

Dooge, J. C. I., G. T. Goodman, J. W. M. La Rivière, J. Marton-Lefèvre, T. O'Riordan, F. Praderie, and M. Brennan, eds. 1992. *An Agenda of Science for Environment and Development into the 21st Century*. Cambridge, England: Cambridge University Press.

Ehrenfeld, David. 1978. *The Arrogance of Humanism*. New York: Oxford University Press.

Ehrlich, Paul R. 1968. *The Population Bomb*. New York: Ballantine.

———. 1980. "Variety Is the Key to Life." *Technology Review* 82 (March-April), pp. 58–68.

Ehrlich, Paul R., and Anne H. Ehrlich. 1970. *Population, Resources, Environment*. San Francisco: W. H. Freeman.

Ehrlich, Paul R., Anne H. Ehrlich, and John P. Holdren. 1977. *Ecoscience: Population, Resources, Environment*. San Francisco: W. H. Freeman.

Ehrlich, Paul R., and John P. Holdren. 1971. "Impact of Population Growth." *Science* 171, pp. 1212–17.

———. 1972. "One-Dimensional Ecology." *Bulletin of the Atomic Scientists* 28:5 (May), pp. 16, 18–27.

Holdren, John P. 1973. "Population and the American Predicament." *Daedalus* (Fall), pp. 31–34.

Howarth, R. B., and R. B. Norgaard. 1990. "Intergenerational Resource Rights, Efficiency, and Social Optimality." *Land Economics* 66, pp. 1–11.

Institute of Ecology. 1971. *Man in the Living Environment*. Madison, Wisc.: Institute of Ecology.

ICSU (International Council of Scientific Unions). 1992. *Global Change: Reducing Uncertainties*. Stockholm: Royal Swedish Academy of Sciences, International Geosphere-Biosphere Programme.

IUCN (International Union for the Conservation of Nature). 1980. *World Conservation Strategy: Living Resource Conservation*. With the United Nations Environment Program and the World Wildlife Fund. Gland, Switzerland.

———. 1991. *Caring for the Earth: A Strategy for Sustainable Living*. With the United Nations Environment Program and the World Wildlife Fund. Gland, Switzerland.

Lele, Sharachchandra M. 1991. "Sustainable Development: A Critical Review." *World Development* 19:6, pp. 607–21.

Lubchenco, Jane, A. Olson, L. Brubaker, S. Carpenter, M. Holland, S. Hubbell, S. Levin, J. MacMahon, P. Matson, J. Melillo, H. Mooney, C. Peterson, H. Pulliam, L. Real, P. Regal, and P. Risser. 1991. "The Sustainable Biomass Initiative: An Ecological Research Agenda." *Ecology* 72, pp. 371–412.

Marsh, Gerge Perkins. 1864. *Man and Nature, or Physical Geography as Modified by Human Action*. Reprinted in 1965 by Cambridge, Mass.: Belknap Press of Harvard University Press.

Meadows, Donella H., Dennis L. Meadows, and Jorgen Randers. 1992. *Beyond the Limits*. Post Mills, Vt.: Chelsea Hills Publishing Co.

Meadows, Donella H., Dennis L. Meadows, Jorgen Randers, and W. W. Behrens III. 1972. *The Limits to Growth*. New York: Universe Books.

Mungall, Constance, and Digby J. McLaren, eds. 1990. *Planet under Stress*. New York: Oxford University Press.

Myers, Norman, ed. 1984. *GAIA: An Atlas of Planetary Management*. New York: Doubleday.

Osborn, Fairfield. 1948. *Our Plundered Planet*. Boston: Little, Brown & Co.

Pronk, Jan, and Mahbubul Haq. 1992. *Sustainable Development: From Concept to Action. The Hague Report*. New York: United Nations Development Program.

SCEP (Study of Critical Environmental Problems). 1970. *Man's Impact on the Global Environment*. Cambridge, Mass.: M.I.T. Press.

Turner, B. L., William C. Clark, Robert W. Kates, John F. Richards, Jessica T. Mathews, and William B. Meyer, eds. 1991. *The Earth as Transformed by Human Action*. Cambridge, England: Cambridge University Press.

Vogt, William. 1948. *Road to Survival*. New York: Sloane.

Woodwell, George M., ed. 1990. *The Earth in Transition: Patterns and Processes of Biotic Impoverishment*. New York: Cambridge University Press.

WCED (World Commission on Environment and Development). 1987. *Our Common Future*. Oxford, England: Oxford University Press.

Key Concepts and Terminology of Sustainable Development

Mohan Munasinghe and Jeffrey McNeely

The authors gratefully acknowledge assistance in preparing this chapter from Noreen Beg and Marten Jenkins, as well as useful inputs from Shelton Davis, Alfred Duda, John English, Genedy Golubev, Kenneth King, Alcira Kreimer, Anil Markandya, Ranjiva Munasinghe, Norman Myers, and Iona Sebastian.

The expression sustainable development was coined to demonstrate that economic growth and environmental protection can be compatible. Many definitions have been provided for this phrase (Pearce, Barbier, and Markandya 1989; Pezzey 1989). At the most basic level, dictionaries define the verb sustain as "to give support to, nourish, keep up/prolong," among others, and development as the improvement of human welfare and the quality of life. Development is therefore not entirely synonymous with economic growth, which focuses mainly on real incomes. A narrow definition of sustainable development would indicate that per capita income or well-being is constant or increasing over time. The wider concept of sustainable development is less precise and embraces a set of indicators of well-being (including income) that could be maintained or increase over time. The World Bank, in its *World Development Report 1992*, states that sustainable development means basing developmental and environmental policies on a comparison of costs and benefits and on careful economic analysis that will strengthen environmental protection and lead to rising and sustainable levels of welfare (World Bank 1992).

The practice of sustainable development involves making choices between alternatives. Any given development activity will inevitably advance some interests while prejudicing others. In order for informed choices to be made, economic, ecological, political, social, and cultural factors all need to be considered and presented to decisionmakers in an unambiguous (and unbiased) fashion. This is a formidable task, and this chapter attempts to make a small contribution to the debate.

Different disciplines place varying interpretations on the concept of sustainability. While economists emphasize the maintenance and improvement of the living standards of humans, ecologists and scientists have broadened the meaning to express concerns about preserving the adaptability and function of entire ecological and biophysical systems. At the same time, geographers and anthropologists have focused on the viability of social and cultural systems (Toman 1992).

Understanding sustainable development in turn requires that the competition for resources be placed in a historical context, in order to identify and describe the social and economic underpinnings of environmental degradation. By examining how underlying processes have evolved in the past, it becomes easier to understand the goals of various types of development activities and institutional arrangements.

A historical perspective

Throughout the course of human evolution, the populations that survived were by definition those that had a sustainable relationship with their environment; that is, unsustainable behavior led to displacement or extinction of the population or to a change in behavior. This does not mean that early human populations did not have significant ecological impacts or modify their environments to suit their needs better. Indeed, coincident with the first arrival of *Homo sapiens* in North America, some thirty-four genera of large mammals became extinct, and the first arrivals of humans into Australia, New Zealand, and Madagascar were accompanied by significant losses of species of large animals that were easily harvested by the new and sophisticated predator (Martin 1984). Presumably, hunters missed at least some of these easily hunted species once they were gone, while local cultures based on the harvesting of large mammals necessarily adopted other means of earning a living or themselves became extinct.

The unsustainable pressures of human activities on the environment greatly increased as the domestication of animals and the cultivation of crops became common. Thus traditional nomadic pastoralism is generally accepted as being more environmentally benign than agriculturalism, given that agriculture deliberately transforms nature and ecosystems by altering soils and growth patterns and through deforestation (Goudie 1990; Ponting 1990).

Boyden and Dovers (1992) describe how the human aptitude for culture gave rise to "technometabolism," involving new inputs and outputs of materials and energy through various kinds of technological processes. They outline the phases of this process. Phase 3, the early urban phase, led to several biologically and socially important changes, including the occupational and social stratification of human society, the institutionalization of warfare, and the increased role of contagious disease as a cause of mortality.

Ponting (1990) discusses how sociological changes acted as a catalyst for the first known large-scale anthropogenic disruptions to the biophysical environment. In Mesopotamia, the need for food surpluses to support a growing nonproducer class of bureaucrats and soldiers led to an intensive, irrigated agricultural system; the consequent waterlogging and salinization of the fields destroyed the basis for Sumerian society, around 2370 B.C. In the Indus Valley of India and the Mayan lowland tropical jungles of Mesoamerica, large-scale deforestation and the resultant soil erosion precipitated a similar collapse of society, caused by the inability of fragile ecosystems to support a massive, complex infrastructure. In a somewhat different manner, the demands of rapid population growth on the environment during the heyday of the Roman Empire led to long-term environmental decline in the Mediterranean (caused by deforestation and soil erosion from overgrazing). A similar picture comes from many, if not most, individual civilizations of the past (Darlington 1969). The process of civilization could be more broadly defined to include not only the rise and fall of individual societies but also their progressively increasing levels of organization and complexity. The future sustainability of this broader evolutionary process will depend on the ongoing search for paths of long-run sustainable development.

The increased demands that industrial countries place on natural resources, and growing poverty in developing nations, threaten the prospects for achieving a level of ecological sustainability while protecting human well-being. A major issue today is the highly resource-intensive per capita consumption in industrial nations, but population growth will also add to the pressure on natural resources in the future. Today humans use approximately 12,000 times as much energy (mainly in the form of fossil fuels) as they did 400 generations ago when farming was first introduced. Nearly 80 percent of this energy is used in industrial nations, which constitute only 25 percent of the world's population. The same imbalance is also seen in the per capita generation of waste between the two groups of countries. The great intensification of technometabolism in the industrial countries has resulted in the rapid increase of gaseous waste emitted into the atmosphere. In particular, scientists have noted an increase of 25 percent in the carbon dioxide content of the atmosphere since the preindustrial age (see table 2-1 and figure 2-1 for examples of carbon dioxide emissions by country and average annual consumption per capita of energy, metals, and so forth for selected countries).

The increase in greenhouse gases is expected to lead to an increase in the mean global temperature of from 2° to 5° over the next fifty years. Some scientists believe that global warming will result in a rise in sea level, an increased rate of deserti-

Table 2-1: Average Annual Consumption per Capita, Various Years

Product and year of data	World	Total	Canada	Germany	France	Italy	Japan	United Kingdom	United States
Energy (gigajoules)									
Total fossil fuels, 1989	54.71	190.32	270.95	160.98	94.98	106.56	109.80	142.11	282.93
Solids, 1989	18.71	53.13	44.65	74.41	14.48	10.01	26.96	47.94	80.15
Liquids, 1989	22.48	90.27	127.06	57.75	60.24	69.35	67.51	56.97	127.21
Gas, 1989	13.53	46.92	99.25	28.82	20.26	27.19	15.33	37.20	75.57
Metals (kilograms)									
Crude steel, 1989	153.20	489.09	529.72	563.08	312.77	486.71	757.64	304.00	411.44
Aluminum, refined, 1990	3.39	15.94	15.66	17.83	12.77	11.32	19.55	7.89	17.24
Copper, refined, 1990	2.04	9.54	6.95	13.29	8.46	8.24	12.76	5.52	8.54
Lead, refined, 1990	1.05	4.71	3.44	5.79	4.51	4.48	3.38	5.25	5.13
Nickel, refined, 1990	0.16	0.76	0.46	1.21	0.79	0.47	1.29	0.57	0.50
Tin, refined, 1990	0.04	0.19	0.11	0.28	0.15	0.11	0.28	0.18	0.15
Zinc, slab, 1990	1.32	4.93	4.75	6.85	5.03	4.69	6.59	3.29	3.95
Industrial materials (kilograms)									
Cement, 1983–85	197.72[a]	416.06	239.86	502.67[b]	376.17	670.11	550.66	242.85	327.23
Fertilizer, 1989–90	27.63	58.18	82.67	58.39	108.67	31.52	15.74	41.22	75.21
Forest products									
Roundwood (cubic meters) 1989	0.67	1.35	6.71	0.56	0.70	0.27	0.68	0.12	2.04
Paper and paperboard (kilograms), 1989	44.39	229.61	236.09	181.62	148.17	116.05	221.84	168.15	306.71

a. World consumption is assumed to be equal to world production.
b. Consumption in the Federal Republic of Germany plus production in the German Democratic Republic.

Figure 2-1: Cumulative Emissions of Carbon Dioxide from Fossil Fuels for Twenty-five Countries with the Highest Emissions, 1950–89

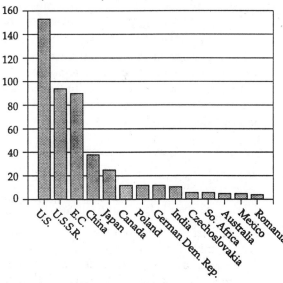

(billions of metric tons of carbon dioxide)

Note: The European Community comprises twelve countries: Belgium, Denmark, France, Federal Republic of Germany, Greece, Ireland, Italy, Luxembourg, the Netherlands, Portugal, Spain, and the United Kingdom.

Source: Unpublished data from the Carbon Dioxide Information Analysis Center and the Oak Ridge National Laboratory.

fication, and species extinction. Also, in the mid-1980s more than 85 percent of the chlorofluoro-carbons (CFCs) released into the atmosphere came from the industrial countries (see figure 2-2 for use of CFCs and halons by region in 1986). Under the best outcome of the Montreal Protocol, the concentration of CFCs in the stratosphere will increase to three times the present level in the next thirty years, resulting in increased ultraviolet radiation from the sun due to depletion of the ozone layer (Boyden and Dovers 1992). The consequences are likely to include greater incidence of skin cancer, cataracts, and so forth in humans as well as disruption of ecosystems due to the lethal effects of increased ultraviolet radiation on many organisms.

Poverty and environmental degradation

Any discussion of sustainable development would be meaningless without recognition of the close relationship between poverty and environmental

Figure 2-2: Current and Projected Use of Chlorofluorocarbons and Halons, by Region, 1986 and 2000

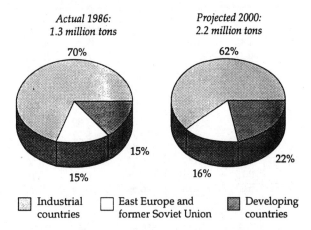

Actual 1986:
1.3 million tons

Projected 2000:
2.2 million tons

☐ Industrial countries   ☐ East Europe and former Soviet Union   ■ Developing countries

Source: Munasinghe and King 1992, pp.24–25.

degradation. It is clear that the poor suffer the consequences of environmental degradation most, especially since they are the most vulnerable and least able to avoid or mitigate the consequences.

The Hague Report (Pronk and Haq 1992) points out that the ratio of per capita incomes is 150:1 between the top and bottom 20th percentiles of the world population. It estimates that most poor people live in areas of high biodiversity and fragile ecosystems: 80 percent of Latin America, 60 percent of Asia, and 50 percent of Africa. Basically, the greatest proportion of the poor live in rural areas: 69 percent in Sub-Saharan Africa, 74 percent in South Asia, and 60 percent in Latin America (World Resources Institute 1992a). A contributing factor to poverty and environmental degradation is that rural areas lag behind urban areas in human development, with infant mortality in some countries 30 to 50 percent higher and malnutrition as much as 50 percent higher. The difficulties in determining the priorities of sustainable development are highlighted by the following statistics (World Bank 1992).

For land,

- The rate of soil degradation and desertification is increasing, mainly affecting the rural poor. Countries like Costa Rica, Malawi, Mali, and Mexico may be losing 0.5 to 1.5 percent of gross national product (GNP) annually in terms of farm productivity.

- Up to 20 metric hectares a year of primary tropical forests (about 1 percent of total) are being lost.

- In one of many examples, 5,000 Philippine villagers were killed by recent flooding caused in part by the presence of deforested hillsides.

For water,

- Approximately 1 billion people in the developing world are still without access to clean water for drinking and bathing.[1]

- About 1.7 billion must contend with inadequate sanitation facilities, resulting in 900 million cases of diarrheal diseases annually and 3 million deaths (mostly infant mortalities); another 500 million people suffer from trachoma, 200 million from schistosomiasis or bilharzia, and 900 million from hookworm.

For air,

- About 1.2 billion people live in urban areas in developing countries that do not meet World Health Organization standards on dust and smoke; it is estimated that the reduction of such pollutants would save 300,000 to 700,000 lives annually.

- Firewood, charcoal, and dung, the primary fuels of developing countries, endanger the health of 400 million to 700 million people (especially women and children) with health consequences equivalent to smoking several packs of cigarettes a day. Automobile emissions, primarily lead, also contribute to health problems related to air pollution.

- In the long term, even global warming is likely to have the most severe consequences for low-income countries and the poor, as they will be the least able to cope with the range of potential impacts.

In developing countries, rapid population growth, agricultural modernization, and inadequate land tenure systems are creating ever larger populations with little or no access to productive land. This results in rural to urban migration or the increased use of marginal lands. As more and more people exploit open-access resources in order to survive, the environment is further degraded. This degradation occurs through soil erosion, loss of soil fertility, desertification, deforestation, depleted fish and game stocks, loss of biodiversity and natural habitats, depletion of groundwater, pollution, siltation of rivers, and so on. The end result is a reduction in the carrying capacity and productivity of the land and a loss of absorptive carbon sinks, as in the Amazon. This has both intragenerational and intergenerational consequences, exacerbating existing poverty and threatening the economic prospects of future generations.

In developing countries, it is not so much the quality of life that is at risk because of environmental degradation, but life itself. Although economic growth is crucial, these poor nations must adopt models of development that are less material- and energy-intensive and more environmentally sound than in the past. The industrial countries can assist in this effort by facilitating the transfer of technology and financing environmentally sustainable projects in developing countries.

General ideas about sustainable development

Probably the best-known and most frequently quoted definition of sustainable development is provided in the Brundtland Report as "development that meets the needs of the present without compromising the ability of future generations to meet their own needs" (World Commission on Environment and Development 1987, p. 8). This definition is anthropocentric and based on the concept of intergenerational equity.

An economist's working definition of sustainable development could be "the maximization of net benefits of economic development, subject to maintaining the services from and quality of natural resources over time." This implies that renewable resources (especially scarce ones) should be used at rates less than or equal to the natural rate of regeneration and that the efficiency with which nonrenewable resources are used should be optimized, subject to how effectively technological progress can substitute for resources as they become scarce (Pearce and Turner 1990). To this could be added the requirement that waste be generated at rates less than or equal to the assimilative capacity of the environment (Barbier 1991).

Dasgupta and Mäler (1990) point out that a decline in resource stocks per se is not a reason for concern. They state that "whether or not policy should be directed at expanding environmental resource bases is something we should try and deduce from considerations of population change, intergenerational well-being, technological pos-

sibilities, environmental regeneration rates, and the existing resource base." Other researchers share the view that we can avoid the prospect of Malthusian scarcity by resource substitution and technological innovations (Toman 1992).

However, many also share the view that the scale of human pressure on natural systems is already well beyond a sustainable level (as discussed in Toman 1992). In the former Soviet Union, as Gerasimov (1974, as cited in Goudie 1990) has pointed out, up to the industrial revolution, "the natural environment taken as a whole was able, up to a point, to withstand anthropogenic disturbances, although there were also local irreversible changes. Since the industrial revolution, the general intensity of human impact on the environment has exceeded its potential for restoration in many large areas of the earth's surface, leading to irreversible changes not only on a local but also on a regional scale." Examples of human-induced environmental degradation are illustrated in figures 2-3 and 2-4, which provide examples of water degradation and the location and types of soil degradation.

Sustainability has also been defined as "a relationship between dynamic human economic systems and larger dynamic, but normally slower-changing ecological systems, in which (a) human life can continue indefinitely, (b) human individuals can flourish, [and] (c) human cultures can develop, but in which (d) effects of human activities remain within bounds, so as not to destroy the

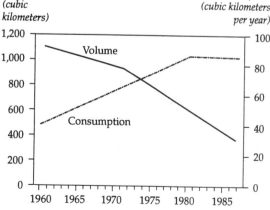

Figure 2-3: Consumption of Irrigation Water and Volume of the Aral Sea, 1960–87

Source: Micklin 1988.

Figure 2-4: Types of Soil Degradation, by Region

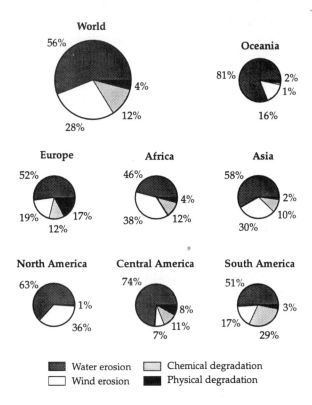

Note: Categories not shown for a region represent less than 1 percent.

Source: Oldeman, van Engelen, and Pulles 1990, fig 5.

Figure 2-5: The Ecological System

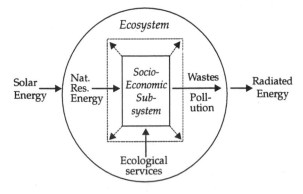

Note: The capacity of the ecosystem may become overloaded by the growing socioeconomic subsystem (the broken lines).

Source: Munasinghe 1993.

diversity, complexity, and function of the ecological life support system" (Costanza 1991; see figure 2-5).

Essentially, if economic growth is an increase in quantity, then logically it cannot be sustainable indefinitely on a planet with a finite amount of resources. Economic development, however, is an improvement in the quality of life and does not necessarily imply an increase in the quantity of resources consumed. In this context, measures such as the Overseas Development Council's Physical Quality of Life Indicator and the United Nations Development Program's Human Development Index have been proposed. Such qualitative rather than quantitative development may be sustainable and could become the desirable long-range goal of humanity.

Concepts and definitions of sustainable development

As indicated earlier, we might identify three broad approaches to sustainability, as shown in Figure 2-6. Economists relate sustainability to the preservation of the productive capital stock. Physical scientists relate sustainability to the resilience or integrity of biological and physical systems (Perrings 1991). A third view relates sustainability to a concern about the adaptability and preservation of diverse social and cultural systems (Toman 1992). This section provides a brief overview of each in turn.

Economic approach

The economic approach to sustainability originates in the Hicks-Lindahl definition of income as the maximum flow of benefits possible from a given set of assets, without compromising the flow of future benefits. This requires the preservation or increase of the base of assets over time. Solow (1986) describes the sustainability condition as follows: "A society that invests in reproducible capital, the competitive rents on its current extraction of exhaustible resources, will enjoy a consumption stream constant in time, . . . an appropriately defined stock of capital—including the initial endowment of resources—is being maintained intact, and . . . consumption can be interpreted as the interest on patrimony." (The constant stream of consumption is one interpretation of intergenerational equity.) As discussed

Figure 2–6: Approaches to Sustainable Development

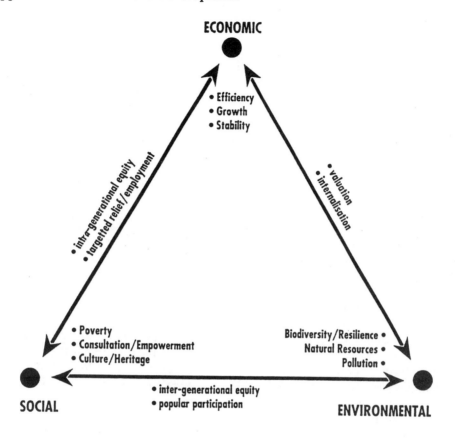

Source: Munasinghe 1993.

below, the measurement of a country's base of assets might be broadened to include natural capital, in addition to man-made capital and human-resource capital.

It has been argued that maintaining the stock of natural capital is not essential to the development of a sustainable economy, that technological change improves the efficiency of resource use, and that more productive man-made capital can be substituted for natural capital (electricity for fuelwood, fertilizers for manure, and so forth). Livestock can replace wild animals in the diet, without necessarily reducing species diversity (the Masai in the savannas of Africa are an example); modern pharmaceuticals can replace medicinal plants; and domesticated plants can replace harvests from the wild. However, there are certain caveats to this argument (Pearce and Turner 1990). According to the First Law of Thermodynamics, energy (and matter) cannot be created or destroyed. Therefore, man-made capital and natural capital are not independent: the latter is often needed to make the former. Second, natu-

ral capital fulfills life support functions that are not met by man-made capital (for example, the ozone layer). Finally, the neoclassical interpretation of substitutability between inputs cannot be easily applied to natural capital, given their multifunctionality and difficulties of physical quantification and economic valuation. For example, table 2-2 presents a table of nonmarket goods available from a forest ecosystem.

Cleveland (1991) points out that, while the neoclassical production model assumes that capital and labor are primary inputs to production (ignoring the substantial quantities of energy used in the process of harvesting resources itself), a biophysical model of the economic process assumes that capital and labor are intermediate inputs and that the underlying primary factors of production are low-entropy energy and matter. Cleveland re-analyzed the seminal work of Barnett and Morse on scarcity (1963) from a biophysical perspective and found that energy use increases with resource depletion, because lower-quality deposits require more energy to locate and upgrade.

25

Table 2-2: Environmental Functions of Forests

Source of materials and services	Sink for wastes	General and life support
Timber	Absorption of waste	Genetic pool
Fuelwood	Recycling nutrients	Climate regulation
Other business products	Watershed protection	Carbon fixing
Non-wood products	Protection of soil quality	Habitat for people, flora, and fauna
Genetic resource	and resistance to erosion	Aesthetic, cultural, and spiritual source
Recreation and tourism		Scientific data

Source: Munasinghe 1992a.

Additionally, natural and man-made capital are only substitutable to a limited extent. Natural capital is subject to irreversibilities. Natural capital can be depleted but not increased, if previous decrements have led to extinction (Pearce, Barbier, and Markandya 1989). Furthermore, the species of plants and animals driven to extinction may have provided significant but presently unknown benefits in the future. For example, a new chemical isolated from the back of the Ecuadorian poisonous frog *Epipedobates tricolor* is a painkiller 200 times as potent as morphine. Called "Epibatidine," it is a member of an entirely new class of alkaloids: an organo-chlorine compound, which is rarely found in animals. Thus important discoveries remain to be made in the natural world, provided that species are allowed to survive and evolve.

The issue of irreversibility is closely linked to the role of uncertainty. There is considerable scientific uncertainty about the adverse consequences of global warming. The chemistry of acid rain is still being developed. We do not completely understand how to relate the role of ocean currents to the determination of climate, and the ways in which stands of natural forest affect microclimates are still being researched. We are not even certain about the loss of assimilative capacity that could be sustainable. Even changes of 5 or 10 percent in the carrying capacity of the Earth can be viewed as having enormous social and political consequences on a global scale (Schneider 1990). Given such uncertainty about environmental benefits and costs, it becomes increasingly difficult to make tradeoff decisions between man-made capital and natural capital.

The issues of vulnerability and resilience also merit attention. In many developing countries, the margin of flexibility is so low between a sustainable and nonsustainable society that any external shocks could have severe economic and social consequences. Already, it is reported that 10 percent of the Earth's potentially fertile land has been turned into desert or wasteland, while a further 25 percent may be endangered. Each year, 8.5 million hectares are lost through erosion and siltation (Pronk and Haq 1992). Given such dire conditions, natural capital would probably be preferable to man-made capital, in the sense that it may reduce vulnerability and increase resilience (Pearce and Turner 1990). Self-reliance is an important related quality that should be maintained (Lovelock 1979).

A key concern in wishing to maintain a constant stock of capital is the essentially socio-ethical issue of intragenerational and intergenerational equity. The concept of intragenerational equity calls for a spatial universality requirement: the current highly skewed distribution of income and poverty is recognized as unacceptable. This concept is also linked to the issue of resilience. Intergenerational equity has a temporal universality requirement: the rights of future generations to an acceptable level of welfare must be protected.

Another consideration is that, when natural capital is destroyed, the habitats of other species are damaged. As scientists discover more complex interconnections in biophysical systems, which in turn underlie the productive basis of human society, then the preservation of whole ecosystems (natural capital) may be viewed in economic terms. An extreme version of this approach is centered around the so-called Gaia hypothesis, which states that the totality of life on Earth is responsible for controlling the temperature, chemical composition, oxidizing ability, and acidity of the Earth's atmosphere (Potvin 1992). In addition, there is the purely ethical issue of existence rights for other species.

It is clear that deciding what is the relevant stock of capital and how it should be measured depends on the substitutability in production, and indispensability, of the different components of capital: machines, technical knowledge, and renewable and nonrenewable resources (Pezzey 1989). The challenge for economists is to expand the analysis of resource values to consider the function and value of ecological systems, making greater use of ecological information, and to extend economic theory and analysis to examine more fully the implications of biophysical resource limits. Valuation techniques must be further developed, in particular to improve methodologies for assessing how future generations might value different attributes of natural environments. The technique of environmental accounting seeks to adjust the present system of national accounts and commonly used measures like gross domestic product (GDP), by explicitly considering degradation of environmental assets and expenditures to remove pollution (Lutz and Munasinghe 1991). One key question is how to distinguish between efficient allocation of resources and socially oriented concerns such as issues of intergenerational and intragenerational equity (Toman 1992).

The impact of trade on sustainable development is being examined more and more. Norgaard (1987) has pointed out that development occurring as a result of exchange has encouraged agricultural specialization, with the resultant reduction in the diversity of crops and supporting species. He also notes that, although neoclassical trade theory assumes that the factors of production are mobile, the environmental services provided by biodiversity, which give land its value, cannot freely shift from one product to another. McRobert (1988) observes that traditional economics research on trade policy does not account for hidden environmental externalities (through pollution and change in climate) that are implicit in the transportation of goods.

Biophysical approach

Sustainability from a biophysical perspective is linked to the idea that the dynamic processes of the natural environment can become unstable as a result of stresses imposed by human activity. Sustainability in this scenario refers to maintaining a system's stability, which implies limiting the stress to sustainable levels on ecosystems that are central to the stability of the global system (Perrings 1991). (This idea is related to the protection of the resilience of fragile ecosystems through the maintenance of natural capital.)

From a thermodynamics perspective, sustainability is related to the fact that in ecosystems where energy flows are open, the system tends to organize itself into stable or quasi-stable states, within the constraints imposed by its environment. In ecosystems where resource values are incompatible with that self-organization, the system will switch from one thermodynamic path to another, or from one self-organization to another (Perrings 1991). Threshold values exist for the diversity of species within an ecosystem. If any one population in an ecosystem falls below its critical threshold level, the self-organization of the whole is altered. The integrity of an ecosystem is measured by its ability to maintain its self-organization through the selection of an optimum operating point along the same thermodynamic path—that is, without undergoing the irreversible change that occurs from switching paths. Economic activity that imposes unsustainable levels of stress on the natural environment may generate negative feedback effects.

Using reasoning somewhat similar to the neoclassical argument for the substitutability of capital, Potvin (1992) states that, "at the end of a period during which depletable inventories are drawn down for use, if structural and chemical energy newly embodied in things of human design and manufacture exceeds the energy lost to reserves themselves, then exploitation of these inventories is consistent with ecosystem self-organization." This enables, for example, humanity to use a finite mineral and fossil inventory in order to generate a perpetual stream of income, assuming that society invested all the rents from the resource. If capital goods are acquired rapidly enough to make up for the continually declining use of resources, resources can continue to be used and reserves remain positive. A vital element of the Cobb-Douglas production function, $Q = K^\infty R^{1-\infty}$, is that each input is essential. If either capital stocks or resources are run down to zero, then output is zero (Hartwick and Olewiler 1986).

Ecological sustainability basically implies the preservation of biodiversity at a sustainable level. Biodiversity, a term that has entered widespread usage since the late 1980s, has arisen because other terms, such as "living natural resources" or "the living environment," were inadequate to deal with the complexities of conserving the living systems on which human welfare depends. This new approach involves local communities, scientists, indigenous peoples, and many parts of government working together to ensure that biological resources—land, forests, oceans, and so forth—are used in ways that are sustainable and contribute to intergenerational equity.

Biodiversity (as defined by the United Nations Environment Program, Intergovernmental Negotiating Committee for a Convention on Biological Diversity 1992) means "the genetic, taxonomic, and ecological variability among living organisms; this includes the variety and variability within species, between species, and of biotic components of ecosystems."

Conserving biodiversity is the foundation of sustainable development:

1. It supports current productive systems.

2. Future practical values and needs are unpredictable.

3. Our understanding of ecosystems is insufficient to be certain of the role and impact of removing any component (especially irreversible and catastrophic effects).

In addition, variety is inherently interesting and more attractive. For example, both high agricultural productivity and human health depend on the preservation of a diverse biota consisting of the estimated 10 million species of plants and animals that inhabit the planet. However, approximately 90 percent of the food for humans comes from just fifteen plant species and eight animal species (Pimentel and others 1992).

The continued productivity of agriculture and forestry depends on the preservation of biodiversity. Microbes fix nitrogen from the atmosphere for use by crops and forests: an estimated 90 million tons of nitrogen is fixed for use by agriculture worldwide with a value of almost $50 billion annually (Hardy and others 1975, as quoted in Pimental and others 1992). Cross-pollination is essential for crop reproduction in many cases. More than forty U.S. crops, valued at approximately $30 billion, require insect pollination for production (Robinson and others 1989, as quoted in Pimental and others 1992). Although an estimated $20 billion a year is spent on pesticides, parasites and predators in natural ecosystems are providing about five to ten times this amount of value in terms of natural pest control (Pimental and others 1992). When one considers that these are just a token sample of the benefits of preserving biodiversity, the importance of ecological sustainability is evident.

Any discussion of sustainability must examine the question of the sustainable use of renewable resources (especially biodiversity), in addition to the more easily quantifiable area of nonrenewable mineral resources. There is no direct relationship between the market value of biological resources and their prospects for preservation (Orians 1990). An example of this is deforestation caused by strip mining of coal. The extractive resource is valued more highly than the species that are being destroyed due to loss of habitat. Living organisms also differ from minerals in that they reproduce and can increase, whereas chemical resources may be converted into other forms of matter but do not generate more of their kind (Orians 1990).

Sustainable use implies gaining benefits from a resource on a continuing basis, either through direct consumption (such as logging or hunting) or through nonconsumptive means (for example, tourism). For use to be sustainable in the long term, consumption cannot exceed the natural increment. Acceptable levels of use are primarily a matter of judgment, based on reproductive rates, habitat condition, market demand, and so forth, but when the size of a stock is considered to have reached a level so low as to threaten the continued existence of the resource, then strict preservation may be the only available option.

Another issue to be considered in the discussion of sustainability is the definition of natural. This word is understood by most people to be that which is determined by wild nature and is often perceived as the opposite of human. In fact, naturalness is a relative term covering a range of human influences from the most pristine (for example, Antarctica, where no permanent human settlements are found, while major human influences are felt primarily through air pollution and the harvesting of resources from the surrounding seas) to the most human-influenced end of the ecological scale (for example, a primary man-made urban environment).

Similarly, nativeness is not really a definition but rather a descriptive continuum in time that ranges from the most ancient, continuous, species in an area (such as oaks in Europe or elephants in Africa) to the most recent immigrants into an area (such as starlings in Europe). The acacia trees that are so distinctive in the African savannas, for example, have been there less than 100 years and are the result of human introduction of a devastating exotic pathogen; just as they have become the defining characteristic of the African savanna for many people, so too will successful immigrants eventually become "natives" as natural selection creates new ecological communities.

To most early ecologists the natural ecosystem was the community that would be reached after a long period without large-scale disturbance (fire, wind storm, and so forth). This was the climax community, which would be in equilibrium, in which some parameter of interest (species composition, biomass, or net primary productivity) is roughly constant from year to year when averaged over the whole landscape or in which opposing processes are approximately balanced on a landscape scale. More recently, ecologists have learned that most areas are subject to various types of large-scale disturbance, including storms, fires, changes in climate, and outbreaks of pests. Therefore, in many areas it may be unrealistic to try to define the natural vegetation for a site; several communities could be the natural vegetation for any given site at any given time (Sprugel 1991).

As ecologists learn more about the history of ecosystems, it becomes increasingly obvious that although the general idea of trying to preserve vegetation in a natural state might be desirable, identifying a specific point in time as epitomizing the natural state is ill-advised. At any given moment, the vegetation of any area has some special characteristic that makes it different from another time that might equally well have been chosen. Therefore, sustainability does not necessarily imply maintaining some static natural state, but rather maintaining the resilience and capacity of the ecosystem to adapt to change.

Gomez-Pompa and Kaus (1992) have pointed out that many of the tree species now dominant in the mature vegetation of tropical areas were, and still are, the same species protected, spared, or planted in the land cleared for crops as part of the practice of shifting agriculture. The current composition of mature vegetation is therefore at least partly the legacy of past civilizations: the heritage of cultivated fields and managed forests abandoned hundreds of years ago.

One example of the complexity of sustainability issues is the now well-known perennial corn, *Zea diploperennis*, which is a secondary species that grows in abandoned cornfields. To protect the species, the slash and burn techniques of this form of traditional agriculture have to be continued to provide the habitat that it requires. Without all the human cultural practices that go with the habitat, the species will be lost forever. Yet this dimension of species maintenance has been neglected in our own tradition of natural resource management.

The general state of the physical environment is to a large extent determined by living organisms. For example, the presence of free oxygen in the environment is the result of biological photosynthesis, and living organisms play a major role in the biogeochemical cycles of such elements as sulfur, calcium, nitrogen, and phosphorus (Orians 1990). Limits on the sustainable use of physical processes in the environment are related to both additions and subtractions of materials. The most important mechanism whereby materials are removed from the environment is the alteration of ecosystems: deforestation, drainage of wetlands, and the conversion of diverse grasslands into degraded pastures. These activities decrease the size of the original habitat, altering the ratio between the habitat's edge (with altered microclimates) and interior, thereby resulting in higher rates of species extinction. Second, such activities increase distances between patches of habitat, thereby lowering recolonization rates of species (Orians 1990).

The spatial nature of additions and subtractions leading to overreach of a system's limits, depends on the general type of environment. In the atmosphere, for example, because of the lack of physical structure and the high rates of movement and mixing of the medium, most problems are global and regional rather than local (for example, global warming and acid rain). In contrast, the cumulative effects of human activities at the terrestrial level are primarily local, the most critical concern being alteration and fragmentation of the habitat (Orians 1990). Here, sustainability issues basically revolve around land (and water) management. When land is privately owned, land use management can become a complex issue. Furthermore, publicly held lands are just as difficult to manage due to the pressure that public interest groups exert on governments. Decisions about land use management tend to be made on small spatial scales, whereas the problems of habitat loss call for large-scale solutions. This is compounded by the fact that political boundaries do not coincide with ecological boundaries, rendering agreements on efficient land management solutions more difficult.

A very recent example of unsustainable use and the need for clear management responsibility and ownership is the caviar-producing sturgeon, which is rapidly becoming the latest victim of the collapse of the former Soviet Union. Over the past six months, four independent states and two autonomous regions have appeared around the Caspian Sea, which contains more than 90 percent of the world's sturgeon stocks. According to Dobbs (1992), "As a result, the tightly regulated caviar-producing cartel formed by the former Soviet Union and Iran has collapsed, leading to a free-for-all in which Russian poachers, Azerbaijani mafia bosses, and Turkmen bureaucrats muscle their way into the lucrative business." Already threatened by a string of ecological disasters in and around the Caspian Sea, sturgeon stocks may be completely depleted within three or four years. Prior to the collapse of the former Soviet Union, strict quotas were established by the Ministry of Fisheries, and a powerful inspectorate cracked down on poachers and dealers in illegal caviar. Sturgeon no longer swim up Azerbaijan's poisoned and dammed-up rivers, so local fishermen catch immature sturgeon in the Caspian Sea, a practice that will accelerate the demise of the fishery. Such a free-for-all may earn short-term profits for a few, at the cost of long-term welfare for many.

Sociocultural approach

Crucial, but often overlooked, factors in sustainable development are the social and cultural aspects. Ethical values, beliefs, and institutions develop within sociocultural systems to meet human needs. The world is in a period of very rapid change, when new institutions are being created to manage natural resources, based on socioethical values about the environment. Few countries, for example, had national parks departments until the 1960s, and most ministries of the environment were created after the Stockholm Conference in 1972. Many of these government decisions and structures were based on expectations of substantial budgets, but recent developments suggest the inevitability of severe cutbacks in government expenditure and the unsustainability of the original schemes.

Developing sustainable social and cultural practices to help manage renewable resources is one of the major challenges of the coming decade, as numerous models are attempted. One such model was laid out in *Caring for the Earth* (IUCN

1991). It was followed up in 1992 when United Nations Environment Program and International Union for the Conservation of Nature joined the World Resources Institute in publishing the *Global Biodiversity Strategy*, a document outlining the policies that need to be followed if biodiversity is to be conserved. Such an approach might be based on the following guidelines:

- Economic incentives for sustainability should be a foundation of resource management (including the correct pricing of resources and internalization of environmental costs).

- Policies and programs must be responsive to the needs of the people who live closest to the resources being managed.

- Policies and programs must be adapted to the specific characteristics of the resources being managed.

- Approaches must be flexible and able to adapt to changes.

Freeman (1991) shows that the economic value of resources depends in part on the management regime. Value is influenced not only by biological and economic factors but also by institutions that manage the resources and, ultimately, by values embedded in the underlying sociocultural matrix.

Economists may contend on theoretical grounds that environmental degradation *should* take place so long as the gains from the activities causing the degradation (such as clearing a forest for agriculture) are greater than the benefits of preserving the area in its existing form. The idea of an optimum stock of natural assets is based on this comparison of costs and benefits, but it assumes that the full forgone benefits of preserving the area in its original form (opportunity costs) can be assessed accurately and that the gains from the activities are also accurately estimated. Some economists question how well ecological processes—or capital flows such as contributions to geochemical cycles—can be captured by traditional cost-benefit analysis, suggesting instead that in the face of uncertainty, irreversibility, discontinuities, and catastrophic collapse of natural systems, conserving what remains could be a sound risk-averse strategy (Pearce, Barbier, and Markandya 1990).

A growing consensus in today's society is making it increasingly difficult for policymakers to ignore the issue of intragenerational equity. Large disparities of income—with the accompanying risk of wars, conflicts over diminishing resources, migrations, and other destabilizing effects—are clearly not socially desirable nor sustainable. The recent conflict in the Middle East (partly attributed to concerns over access to oil reserves) serves as a reminder of the enormous waste of resources and the potential for environmental disasters. In general, conflicts can affect numerous nations due to the flow of refugees and pollutants across boundaries. Trade, finance, communications, and ecological processes tie the world system into a tight web. The continuation of inequitable development is inherently unstable, as demonstrated by recent world events. The increasing access of the poor to radio and television has created new expectations that governments may not be able to meet with their present base of resources and unsustainable practices. This may result in social discord (and often an increasing rate of environmental degradation). One remedy is to convert "have-nots" into stakeholders and managers of open-access resources. This involves rebuilding institutions and social systems, as well as redistributing assets and income in some way.

Likewise, the issue of intergenerational equity needs to be addressed. One of the steps required to guarantee the continued presence of the human species would be to arrest the creation of intergenerational externality that results from the unsustainable management of renewable and nonrenewable resources. Future generations will have to bear the cost of any reduction in the flow of capital caused by the reduction or degradation of the present stock of renewable resources. Issues that surround the present use of natural resources—such as contamination of groundwater, modification of climate, disposal of radioactive waste, and harvesting of marine fisheries at the appropriate level—need to be considered while keeping the welfare of future generations in mind. This does not necessarily mean that we ignore today's problems of intragenerational equity in favor of future generations. For example, "If a particular project being considered maximizes the present value, but confers some unacceptably low or negative net benefits on future generations . . . current gains could be set aside as a trust fund. The interest would serve to balance the distribution of the net benefits among generations. Compensation does not necessarily have to be monetary—whatever the form, the compensation mechanism provides a way of sharing maximum net benefits among generations" (Tietenberg 1988).

For the same reasons that we seek to maintain biodiversity, we could also seek to preserve social and cultural diversity (especially in indigenous or tribal cultures). There may be hidden knowledge concerning, for example, cooperative modes of behavior, social stability, and so forth that could improve overall sustainability and efficiency of resource use (especially common property). In particular, ethnobotanists and agriculturalists have shown us that indigenous (or "primitive") cultures may have much to teach so-called modern societies about alternative medicinal and agricultural practices. In our haste to modernize, we may lose valuable information embedded in traditional cultures and value systems that could improve our understanding of practical steps to achieve greater sustainability. Finally, given the need to change the dominant paradigm in industrial nations (which emphasizes material-intensive growth), the diversity of human societies and cultures and their embedded wisdom could be used more effectively.

Since the industrial revolution, and especially in the past few generations or so, a fundamental ecological, economic, and cultural shift has occurred. The world's collection of highly diverse cultures adapted to local environmental conditions is now being replaced by a world culture characterized by high levels of material consumption. Economic growth based on the conversion of fossil fuels to energy greatly expanded international trade, and improved public health measures have spurred such a rapid expansion of human consumption that new approaches to resource management are urgently required. These approaches have overwhelmed the conservation measures of local communities, often bringing overexploitation and poverty to many rural communities and great wealth to cities and certain social classes.

Overexploitation is to be expected in times of very rapid cultural change, as traditional controls break down and humans learn to exploit resources in new ways. The movement of Europeans into the Americas is only one dramatic example of this process. Technological innovations—such as plantation agriculture or industrial logging—tend to favor exploitation of biological resources and the weakening of traditional approaches to conservation, especially when a technologically superior group moves into a region occupied by technically less-sophisticated groups. The dominant or invading society has the option of moving on to fresh resources when an area is exhausted and would derive no particular advantage from adopting the traditions of sustainable, conservative use practiced by the indigenous society. The dominant society is able to earn virtually all the cash benefits of the forest, while paying almost none of the long-term environmental costs imposed on the indigenous society.

At the same time, the subordinated groups lose any advantage from traditions of conservative use that might have been favored when they could exclude other groups from their territory. These traditions evolved when costs and benefits were internalized in the decisions made by communities. However, since the local people are now paying far higher environmental costs of resource degradation, their only rational response is to join the exploiters in trying to seek greater short-run benefits as well. Thus, traditional management systems that were effective for thousands of years have become obsolete in a few decades, replaced by systems of exploitation that may yield short-term profits for a few but impose long-term costs on many who are often poor.

Meredith (1992) points out that culture persists only where it meets, at the minimum, the biological needs of a community or where it fits the base of resources. It is therefore crucial that a certain adaptive capacity exist in the dynamic relations among resources. For example, technology transfer is better described as a stimulant to the development of local technology, since it can be adapted to a particular base of resources or culture but cannot be transplanted in any viable form.

One of the dominant economic needs in the world today is the earning of foreign exchange and expansion of international trade. Such forces have contributed to the more complete exploitation of biological resources. As an inevitable result, cultural diversity is also reduced, for two main reasons. First, a significant component of cultural diversity that enables people to earn a living from the local biological environment is becoming less functional, and second, subordinated groups begin to imitate the culture of the dominant group, thereby losing a major portion of their cultural uniqueness. As just one indicator of the loss of cultural diversity, about half of the world's 6,000 main languages are moribund and spoken only by middle-aged or elderly people.

Are all traditional systems doomed to failure, falling victim to state and private ownership? Or do traditional systems of community-based resource management still have something to contribute? Let us examine a few of the issues.

Development—action that alters the environment so that it caters more effectively to human needs—is essential if the world is to be free from poverty and squalor, but such development must be based on naturally regenerating resources that can meet our needs indefinitely and on prudent use of depletable resources.

Within the process of development, more room must be found for wild nature. The processes of wild nature renew the oxygen in the air, maintain the cycles of essential elements, sustain the fertility of the land, and regulate the flow of rivers. We turn to wild nature for new crops and new drugs as well as for the beauty that enriches life. Environmental protection and development are not opponents but are inseparably one, having interlinked ecological, economic, and cultural components.

The economic interdependence among nations is often viewed as basically desirable, and indeed the World Commission on Environment and Development has called for greatly expanded interdependence through enhanced flows of energy, trade, and finance. Each day several hundred billion dollars flow across national boundaries, because of stock market and trading transactions. This is twice as large as the GNP of Sub-Saharan Africa, for example. This global interdependence has brought very considerable material benefits to many parts of the world, greatly increasing per capita GNP worldwide. However, some observers have suggested that such interdependence—making the world a single global system—is one source of the global depletion of resources. As the distinguished ecologist Ray Dasmann pointed out over a decade ago, when we are all part of a single system connected by powerful economic forces, it becomes easier to overexploit one part of the global system because other parts will soon compensate for such overexploitation. The localized damage may not even be noticed until it is too late to do anything to avoid permanent degradation.

The system of trade now linking the entire globe, primarily for the benefit of urban populations, has led to great prosperity for those who have been able to benefit from the expanded productivity. However, it has often resulted in the devastation of local ecosystems, to the detriment of the local, and mainly poor, people who remain dependent on the now-depleted natural resources.

Social discrimination, cultural barriers, and exclusion from national political processes make indigenous people vulnerable and subject to exploitation. Many groups become dispossessed and marginalized, and their traditional practices disappear. They become the victims of what could justifiably be described as cultural extinction. The World Commission on Environment and Development (1987) has recognized this problem, stating that "it is a terrible irony that as formal development reaches more deeply into rain forests, deserts, and other isolated environments, it tends to destroy the only cultures that have proved able to thrive in these environments."

Various major impacts of exploiting the environment (such as the greenhouse effect and possible changes in climate) suggest the inevitability of profound changes in the way humans relate to the environment. The exact direction of these changes is unpredictable: the ecological practices of human communities could take any of a large number of forms in the coming years. One possibility would be a series of local adaptations to locally available resources, with distant resources being consumed only to the extent that such use is sustainable. In particular, correct economic valuation of natural resources (with the maximum practical internalization of environmental costs) would be needed to ensure efficient management of these assets. This need not necessarily mean a radical reduction in the quality of life, but social, economic, and environmental conditions will surely be fundamentally different than they are in today's consumer society and perhaps will come to resemble more and more the sustainable approaches of traditional cultures.

Cultural diversity, which is provided above all by the great variety of indigenous cultures in all parts of the world, contributes the human intellectual "gene pool," the basic raw material for adapting to the local environment. Indigenous people who live in intimate contact with their major resources could therefore provide practical knowledge to guide a shift to sustainable societies (at least in their own local context). The challenge is in applying this knowledge and, where appropriate, transferring associated techniques and thinking to resource management systems appropriate to today's circumstances. Finally, the sustainability of highly interconnected (but often diverse) modern societies will depend on how cultural pluralism is encouraged but also on whether it is managed effectively.

Reconciling different approaches to operationalize sustainable development

The primary goal of environmental management is to use resources better. Perrings (1991) states that "the optimal control problem involves the maximization (or minimization) of some index of performance as a function of a set of state variables and control inputs, subject to the constraint posed by the natural dynamic of those state variables." There is a clear correlation between this approach and the economic problem of maximizing welfare, and minimizing social cost, through the appropriation of environmental goods and services.

Perrings and others have demonstrated that the workability of the Hicks-Lindahl concept of sustainability in an economic sense is limited, because it is dependent on the controllability and (stochastic) predictability of the global system, an area of considerable uncertainty. Ecological sustainability, however, is more suitable for a control policy that does not depend on the controllability or stochastic predictability of the global system; it is able to assure the sustainability of uncontrollable systems subject to basic uncertainty by employing an ecological sustainability constraint (minimum safety standards). This constraint imposes direct restrictions on resource-using economic activities that will, in theory, protect the stability, integrity, and resilience of the environment.

Economic modeling allows us to study rigorously issues that are interrelated and global in scale. However, what such models omit (by choice and by current shortcomings in scientific understanding of environmental issues) may turn out, in retrospect, to be crucial to understanding a particular issue. Such models are therefore abstractions, albeit useful ones, that should always be tempered by judgment. One of the most promising approaches involves valuation of the environment and incorporation of such monetary measures into conventional economic decisionmaking. The strengths and limitations of economic approaches are explained below.

Economic approaches at the local or project level

Over the past few decades, economists have developed and presented several models that have attempted to reconcile traditional economic theory, on which decisions are currently made, with efficient natural resource management options that facilitate sustainable development. Environmental economic models that seek to incorporate ecological concerns into neoclassical macro- and micro-economic theory face difficulties. Complications arise because natural systems tend to cut across the decisionmaking structure of human society. For example, a forest ecosystem (like the Amazon) could span several countries and interact with many different economic sectors (such as energy, transport, and agriculture) within the country. Also, many externalities (for example, global warming, acid rain, or groundwater contamination) are not only difficult to measure in physical terms, but even more difficult to convert into monetary equivalents (to measure the willingness to pay of the parties affected by the externalities). Quite often the approach taken is to impose regulations and standards, expressed in physical measurements only, that try to eliminate the perceived external damages. However, this approach may not be effective, because no attempt is made to compare the costs of compliance with the real benefits provided (damages avoided). Furthermore, in many developing countries, the regulations and standards are established without a realistic implementation mechanism or appropriate institutional structures. At the same time, traditional regulations and standards are undermined through inappropriate state policies, resulting in a higher rate of environmental degradation.

With the adherence to a predetermined set of environmental limits (safe minimum standards), traditional decisionmaking procedures that rely on technoengineering, financial and economic analyses of projects and policies, or a multicriteria method may be used to manage natural resources in a sustainable manner. The primary role of such constraints is to ensure that the trajectory generated through the parametric optimization of an imperfectly controlled and imperfectly understood system does not also threaten global stability. In other words, ecological sustainability constraints can be thought of as precautionary constraints; the limits they impose on economic activity will depend on the local stability of the ecosystems involved and on the projected losses if these ecosystems become unstable due to the effects of economic activity. Intragenerational issues such as poverty also will continue to be given high priority in the sustainable development process. More generally, multicriteria tradeoffs will be required among economic efficiency, environmental degradation, and poverty reduction.

Cost-benefit analysis and valuation methods seek to estimate the monetary and nonmonetary costs and benefits of a given project in monetary terms. Unfortunately, they are not always successful. Thus when projects and policies and their impacts are to be embedded in a system of broader (national) objectives (for example, preservation of biodiversity)—some of which cannot be easily valued in monetary terms—multicriteria decisionmaking methods offer an alternative approach. These methods facilitate tradeoffs among different objectives. Often both cost-benefit and multicriteria analyses are used jointly in a complementary way.

Safe minimum standards

Concerns over intergenerational equity issues and recognition of the limitations of economic models that have tried to address environmental issues led to calls for the establishment of safe minimum standards, as formulated by Ciriacy-Wantrup and developed by Bishop (Norton and Ulanowicz 1991). Figure 2-7 illustrates the safe minimum standard for balancing natural resource tradeoffs and imperatives for preservation. Toman (1992) defines the safe minimum standard as a "socially determined dividing line between moral imperatives to preserve and enhance natural resource systems and the free play of resource tradeoffs." This requires the current generation to desist from actions that could result in environmental impacts with high-cost or irreversible damage. Examples of such resources include wetlands, the global climate, wilderness areas, Antarctica, and other areas with unique functional or even aesthetic values.

This approach differs from standard economic approaches that require valuations of resources and the use of economic incentives to achieve efficient resource allocation (see the discussion of ecological sustainability constraint as detailed by Perrings 1991). The method places greater significance on irreversible damage to the ecosystem as opposed to short-run economic sacrifices experienced as a result of measures to curb environmental impacts. The approach could be relatively equitable, if environmental safeguards are determined by judgments that reflect societal values. More specifically, a better understanding of the economic costs and benefits of environmental impacts would help to establish better safe minimum standards.

Figure 2–7: Safe Minimum Standard for Balancing Natural Resource Tradeoffs and Imperatives for Preservation

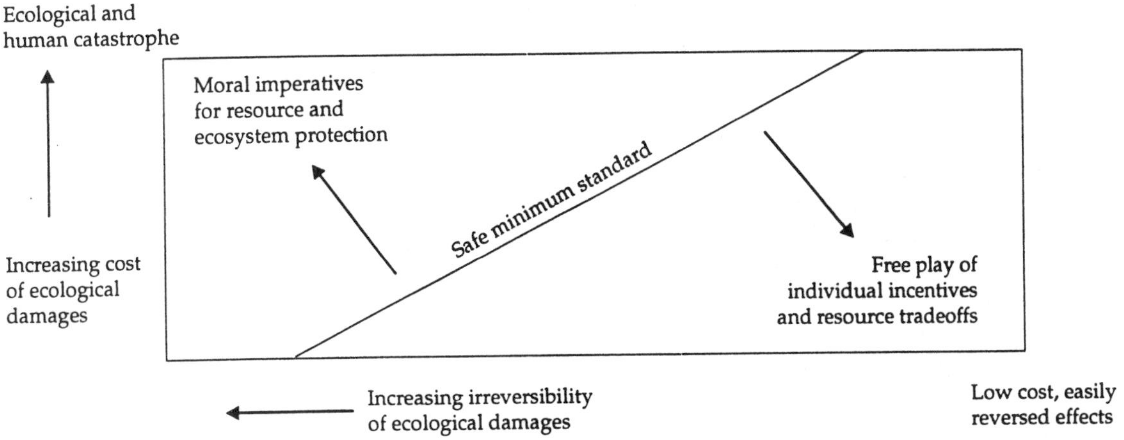

Source: Bryan Norton, Georgia Institute of Technology.

How such standards would be established and enforced, however, has been debated at length. The anticipated agreement on global warming will provide an opportunity to observe the applicability of the standards approach in a practical context. In view of the uncertainty underlying global warming models, the "precautionary principle" is invoked whereby relatively costless steps might be taken immediately as an insurance policy to avoid very large (but uncertain) costs in the future. Guidelines and objectives that might function as safe minimum standards are discussed in appendix 2-1, along with examples of international proposals for the implementation of sustainable resource management.

Valuation of environmental assets and impacts

Numerous questions concern different approaches to implementing sustainable development. One such question is the meaning of optimization (see Schneider 1990). Does optimization entail the maintenance of maximum biomass or the maintenance of maximum diversity of species? Does optimization mean the maintenance of stability for the longest period of time or the maintenance of maximum productivity of extant species? Since evolutionary change is a dynamic process, at what point is the optimum achieved?

This point and others will have to be dealt with as the process of implementation proceeds and our base of scientific knowledge expands. The role of ecologists and economists is to present the maximum possible information to the general public and to decisionmakers, so that costs and benefits are carefully weighed before a decision is made.

In order to establish a valid decisionmaking framework within which constraints could be determined, it is necessary to put a value on resources (Munasinghe 1992a, 1992b). Conceptually, the *total economic value* (TEV) of a resource consists of its (a) use value (UV) and (b) nonuse value (NUV). *Use values* may be broken down further into the direct use value (DUV), the indirect use value (IUV), and the option value (OV, potential use value). One needs to be careful not to double-count both the value of indirect supporting functions *and* the value of the resulting direct use (for a discussion and example of this, see Aylward and Barbier 1992). The categories of *nonuse value* are existence value (EV) and bequest value (BV). Therefore, we may write:

$$TEV = UV + NUV \text{ or}$$
$$TEV = (DUV + IUV + OV) + (EV + BV)$$

Figure 2-8 shows this disaggregation of TEV in schematic form.[2] Below each valuation concept, a short description of its meaning, and a few typical examples of the environmental resources underlying the perceived value are provided. Option

35

Figure 2–8: Components of Total Economic Value

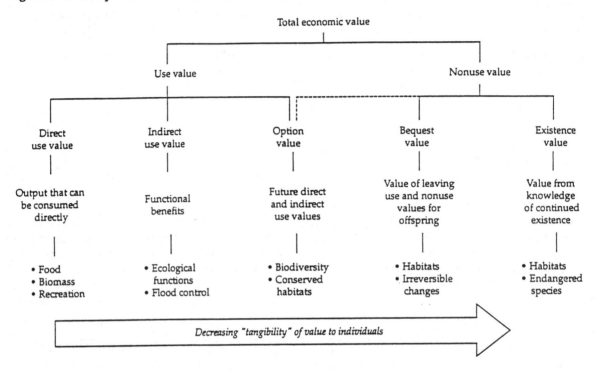

Source: Munasinghe 1992a.

values, bequest values, and existence values are shaded, to caution the analyst about some of the ambiguities associated with defining these concepts; as shown in the examples, they can spring from similar or identical resources, while their estimation could be interlinked also. However, these concepts of value are generally quite distinct. *Option value* is based on how much individuals are willing to pay today for the option of preserving the asset for future (personal) direct and indirect use. *Bequest value,* while excluding individuals' own use values, is the value that people derive from knowing that others (perhaps their own offspring) will be able to benefit from the resource in the future. Finally, *existence value* is the perceived value of the environmental asset unrelated either to current or to optional use, that is, simply because it exists (see, for example, Randall and Stoll 1983).

A variety of valuation techniques may be used to quantify these concepts of value. The basic concept of economic valuation underlying all these techniques is the willingness to pay of individuals for an environmental service or resource, that is, the area under the compensated or Hicksian demand curve (for an up-to-date exposition, see Braden and Kolstad 1991, chap. 2). As shown in

table 2-3, valuation methods can be categorized, on the one hand, according to which type of market they rely on and, on the other hand, by how they make use of actual or potential behavior. These valuation techniques and other issues relating to cost-benefit analysis are discussed in greater detail in appendix 2-2.

Only a small fraction of living species have direct economic importance in terms of commercial value. Other species are used for hunting and fishing, and some species such as the giant panda are valued for their aesthetic value alone. Economic techniques have been developed that place a monetary value on use and nonuse values for independent species. Orians (1990) suggests a tradeoff mechanism involving the use of "valued ecosystem components" (VECs). A VEC could be a single species of economic or aesthetic value, systems of interacting species, or an entire ecosystem. The theory and practice of the exploitation of single species is the most intensively studied aspect of applied ecology (Orians 1990). The determination of optimal harvesting rates can usually be accomplished if basic demographic requirements and habitat requirements are known. However, populations that have been seriously reduced in number may fall below a

Table 2-3: Taxonomy of Relevant Valuation Techniques

Basis	Conventional market	Implicit market	Constructed market
Based on actual behavior	Effect on production Effect on health Defensive or preventive cost	Travel cost Wage differences Property values Surrogate goods	Artificial market
Based on potential behavior	Replacement cost Shadow project		Contingent valuation

Source: Munasinghe 1993.

threshold of sustainability, which will not allow the population to regenerate to pre-exploitation levels. This is because the interactions among species can be altered to the extent that a new alternative stable state of the ecosystem is established in which the interrelationships are so altered as to make returning to the original state impossible (see Orians 1990; Perrings 1991). This is the case with commercial overfishing.

In some cases tradeoffs between different types of value must be assessed to determine sustainability of use. For example, dolphins caught in fish nets have a purely aesthetic value, but the tuna harvest has a purely economic value. Thus, relative weights would have to be assigned to the values in order to determine policy.

Managers of natural resources cannot ignore relationships between predator and prey or issues related to appropriate scale when they aim for sustained yields. For example, harvesting practices of balsam fir in New Brunswick have created age distributions and stand densities that are favorable for rapid growth of the spruce budworm population, which defoliates and kills trees on a massive scale. Managing and making decisions on scales that are too small does not allow for the maximum sustainable yield to be produced if conditions suitable for outbreaks of budworms persist (Orians 1990). Furthermore, one must not forget that interactions between predator and prey also have important evolutionary components affecting sustainability. For example, attempts to reduce populations of certain prey (such as insects that are pests) usually create mortality patterns that do not mimic the stochastic behavior of the target population, in particular with regard to prey genotypes. An example of this is the evolution in North America of agricultural pests better able to withstand a given mortality agent because farmers use pesticides at an

unsustainable rate. Therefore, the sustainable use of a control agent (whether it is a toxic chemical, a biological control agent, or a hunter) is the use at which the agent can continue to achieve its desired effect (Orians 1990).

Another instance where control agents may have a counterproductive effect is related to the mutualistic interactions between species. In cases where such interdependent relationships exist, sustainable use requires maintenance of such relationships. Thus, excessive use of pesticides on fruit trees is incompatible with pollination and, hence, the production of fruit.

Species richness—the sum total of species in an ecosystem—can be a VEC and is recognized as such in the U.S. Endangered Species Act, which states that maintaining species richness is a societal goal (Orians 1990). The protection of species richness can generally (theoretically) be achieved through efficient management of land use. But this is difficult because, as mentioned earlier, decisions about land use are usually made on a smaller scale than that which is required to maximize survival of the species. Moreover, protected areas only cover approximately 5 percent of the terrestrial landscape, while the demand for land continues to grow; it is unlikely that society will be prepared to preserve all species at the cost of alternative land uses.

According to the 1992 *World Resources Report*, cropland covers 11.2 percent (having grown 2.2 percent in a decade, while the world population increased 20 percent); permanent pasture covers 25 percent, having increased 0.1 percent in the last decade; and forest and woodland covers 31 percent, having increased 1.8 percent in a decade (World Resources Institute 1992b). "Other land" totals 32 percent, having increased 1 percent in the last decade, and wilderness areas cover 26 percent (including the 5 percent that is legally

37

protected). Many of these land uses are entirely consistent with the preservation of biodiversity, and the implied conflict between cropland and other uses is perhaps not really a struggle between agriculture and alternative uses. First, agricultural land also contains important biological diversity; second, many forest lands harbor significant biodiversity even when they are used primarily to produce timber; and third, most increases in agricultural productivity are, in any case, going to come from intensification rather than expansion onto marginal lands. Finally, as many ecologists have pointed out, the optimal use of areas not suitable for permanent agriculture is to ensure that sufficient land exists to enable considerable benefits to be earned for society, in terms of harvested goods, specific services (such as watershed protection and tourism), and more abstract services (such as conserving biodiversity and maintaining evolutionary potential). But if conflict over land use does occur, improved economic valuation and multicriteria analysis must be used to help decisionmakers determine which species are more highly valued, given a set of criteria deemed important.

A key consideration to keep in mind is that species may have divergent values for different groups, depending on income level and whether private or social costs and benefits are being assessed. For example, a living snow leopard may have high aesthetic value to individuals in an affluent society, even though they may never be able to see the animal. To an individual poacher surviving at subsistence level, however, the value of the pelt far outweighs social and ethical considerations. The solution to this dilemma is to enforce strict regulations to preserve such species, while providing poachers alternate and viable ways of generating income. Information campaigns to alert consumers to the true costs incurred by their purchases (potential extinction of the species) have also proven successful to a certain extent (Pearce 1991).

The methods described in appendix 2-2 seek to estimate costs and benefits of a given project in monetary terms. As previously stated, when projects or policies and their impacts are to be integrated into a system of broader (national) objectives, some of which cannot be easily quantified in monetary terms, multicriteria decisionmaking offers a supplementary approach that may facilitate the optimal choice among investment options or available policies.

Multicriteria analysis

In the multicriteria (or multiobjective) approach, desirable objectives need to be specified. These often exhibit a hierarchical structure. The highest level, representing the broad overall objectives (such as improving the quality of life), is often vaguely stated and therefore has limited operational function. Some of these, however, can be broken down into more operational lower-level objectives (such as increasing income), so that the extent to which the latter are met may be practically assessed. Sometimes only proxies are available (for example, if the objective is to enhance recreational opportunities, the attribute number of recreation days can be used). Although value judgments may be required to choose the proper attribute (especially if proxies are involved), in contrast to the single–criterion methodologies used in economic cost-benefit analysis, measurement does not have to be in monetary terms. More explicit recognition is given to the fact that a variety of concerns may be associated with planning decisions.

An intuitive understanding of the fundamentals of multiobjective decisionmaking can be provided by a two-dimensional graphical exposition such as that presented in figure 2-9. Assume that a project has two noncommensurable and conflicting objectives, Z_1 and Z_2. Assume further that alternative projects or solutions to the problem (*A*, *B*, and *C*) have been identified. Clearly, point

Figure 2–9: Pareto Optimal Curve and Isopreference Curves

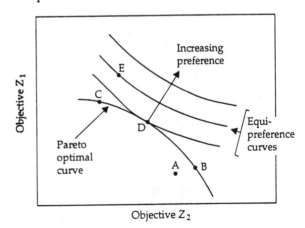

B is superior to (or dominates) A in terms of both Z_1 and Z_2. Thus, alternative A may be discarded. However, we cannot make such a simple choice between solutions B and C, since the former is better than the latter with respect to objective Z_2 but worse with respect to Z_1. In general, more points (or solutions) such as B and C may be identified to define the set of all nondominated feasible solution points that form a Pareto optimal curve (or curve of best options). This line is also called a transformation curve or efficient frontier.

For an unconstrained problem, further ranking of alternatives cannot be conducted without introducing value judgments. Specific information has to be elicited from the decisionmaker to determine the preferred solution. In its most complete form, such information may be summarized by a family of equi-preference curves that indicate the way in which the decisionmaker trades off one objective against the other. The preferred alternative is that which results in the greatest utility; that is, which occurs (for continuous decision variables as shown here) at the point of tangency D of the highest equi-preference curve, with the Pareto optimal curve. In this case, point E (on an even higher equi-preference curve) is not attainable.

Several multicriteria methods have been developed (for an introductory overview relevant to natural resource analysis, see Munasinghe 1993; for an extensive survey including references to about 150 applications, see Romero and Rehman 1987; for a shorter but more recent survey, see Petry 1990). Which practical method in particular is suitable to determine the best alternative available depends on the nature of the decision. For instance, interactive involvement of the decisionmaker has proved useful in the case of problems characterized by a large number of decision variables and complex causal interrelationships. Some objectives can be dealt with through direct optimization, while others require the satisfaction of a certain standard (such as a level of biological oxygen demand no lower than 5 milligrams per liter).

A recent applied research study in developing countries, performed by Meier and Munasinghe (1992), examines the practicality of using multiattribute decision analysis in the setting of a developing country. The study determined that the use of multiattribute scoring systems, in which nonprice attributes are accounted for separately, has limited validity. The applications (studied in developing and industrial countries) pay insufficient attention to key methodological requirements and are generally inconsistent. Problems also exist in the definition of attributes (for example, the environmental consequences of land use are not clearly expressed).

The authors suggest that it would be preferable to work with value or utility functions rather than purely physical scales for measuring attributes. Moreover, one of the most useful tools of multiattribute analysis is the tradeoff curve, which displays available options and their impacts in terms of two objectives.

Orians (1990) outlines a multicriteria approach to decisionmaking, whereby the sustainable use of a particular ecosystem is defined by how the different VECs are ranked and weighted. As VECs conflict, an optimal solution requires that how specific systems are used is balanced with patterns of how uses are allocated among different systems. Such values are not constant and can change significantly over time. As such, some nonsustainable development is unavoidable—it is, in fact, more likely to occur when rates of critical processes remain unknown, when boundaries between domains of a system's stability are not appreciated, or when ecosystem components are undervalued. Such nonsustainable development is also favored by short-term planning horizons, small spatial frames, and economic incentives for overuse. Such uncertainties and short-term perspectives call for a precautionary approach, in which allowance is made for the limitations of current knowledge, for risk, and for changing values. A principal cause of nonsustainable development is that private benefits accrued promote overexploitation at a high social cost. In such situations, the solution may lie in combining a set of regulations governing resource use with an alteration of economic incentives to internalize societal costs.

The major accomplishment of multiobjective decision models is that they allow for more accurate representation of decision problems, in the sense that several objectives can be accounted for. However, a key question concerns whose preferences are to be considered. The model only aids a single decisionmaker (or a homogeneous group). Various interested groups often assign different priorities to the respective objectives, and normally it may not be possible to determine a single best solution via the multiobjective model. Also, the mathematical framework imposes constraints on the ability to represent the planning problem effectively. Nonlinear, stochastic, and dynamic formulations can assist in better defining the problem but impose costs because of the complexity of formulating the problem and then solving the model (Cocklin 1989).

Nevertheless, in constructing the model, the analyst communicates information about the nature of the problem, specifying why factors are important and how they interact. Liebman (1976) observes that modeling is thinking made public and considers the transfer of knowledge to represent perhaps the most important contribution of modeling. With respect to the second point of criticism (diverse preferences), Liebman suggests that there is value in constructing models from differing perspectives and comparing the results.

Economic approaches at the macro level

As policymakers start to use some of the concepts of sustainable development, they have found that the traditional use of GNP as a macroeconomic indicator of growth does not guarantee environmentally benign growth. Thus economists have increasingly attempted to include a variety of natural resources in their calculations of national products and incomes. Current national accounting systems do not capture the value of natural resources adequately, and, therefore, development strategies that rely on standard income accounting techniques do not result in sustainable development. A significant first step in the implementation of sustainable development is to meld the traditional accounting techniques into a framework that permits the computation of measures such as an environmentally adjusted net domestic product (EDP) and an environmentally adjusted net income (ENI). Some of the effects of unsustainable development such as resource degradation, pollution, and poor waste-disposal practices, together with their repercussions on society, cannot be captured by market-based information and standard accounting techniques. Correction of three primary shortcomings of current accounting will move the implementation of sustainable resource management practices forward because the new approach stresses the long-run maximization of EDP. These shortcomings are (1) excluding natural and environmental resources from the balance sheets, (2) failing to record the depreciation of natural capital, and (3) excluding environmental damages while including clean-up costs in the national income.

There has been some discussion in the literature as to how user costs (revenues generated by nonrenewable resources) should be invested in an asset to produce a future stream of income equal to that which is lost through consumption. The more rigorous proponents of sustainable development would argue that the user cost should be reinvested in an asset that not only replaces income lost but also acts as a physical substitute for the nonrenewable resource. Regardless of which method is employed, the implementation of a user cost adjustment in national accounts would generally result in GNP being revised downward (Moseley 1992).

As previously stated, ecologists argue that the major threat to biodiversity is not direct human exploitation of species, but the alteration and destruction of habitat that result from changes in land use, urbanization, infrastructure development, discharge of various pollutants into the environment, and so forth. Human population growth is the most frequently cited cause of the anthropogenic stressors on the environment, but the stability of ecological systems—of which humans are an integral part and on which our continued existence depends—does not imply a certain equilibrium level of human population growth as some groups would advocate. However, the continued ability of Earth's ecosystems to maintain stability will depend on the level of stress to which they are subjected. Therefore, reductionists, in the interest of limiting the further degradation of physical and biological resource systems, need to work toward understanding and addressing the incentives that underlie human population trends. This will involve the accelerated implementation of projects that address rural poverty, health, education, land tenure, and the unequal distribution of income and assets that is prevalent in most developing countries. If policymakers and social scientists continue to believe that social ignorance and institutional irresponsibility are solely to blame for the current trend of world population growth, we will not come any closer to resolving the fundamental issues (Perrings, Folke, and Mäler 1992).

The successful implementation of sustainable development will require price reform (at the global level) of environmental resources for which effective markets can be created. Conducted in the name of self-sufficiency and national defense, government intervention, particularly in markets for agricultural products and other tradable natural resources such as timber and minerals, has driven prices at the national level below those ruling in the world market. This widens the gap between private and social value, which perpetuates unsustainable development at the local and global level. The reform (ideally, the elimination) of fiscal policies such as subsidies (for clearing land in agriculture and forestry, unsustainable systems of agricultural price support, and so forth) that encourage environmental degradation through the farming of marginal land should, one hopes, result in the more socially optimal and sustainable use of natural resources (Perrings, Folke, and Mäler 1992).

Some practical steps at global, regional, and local levels

The following is a more detailed set of guidelines and objectives that will move the world closer to its goal of sustainable resource management. These are by no means the only approach to sustainable practice, and individual approaches will depend on one's values, beliefs, and current and long-term goals. As previously stated, the United Nations Environment Program, International Union for the Conservation of Nature, World Wildlife Fund, and World Resources Institute have recently published lists of objectives and management regimes for responsible development and the protection of biodiversity; the following list includes some of their conclusions. As numerous scientists have pointed out, interactions among the different goals change as the scale of the system is extended from the local, to the regional, to the national level, and so forth. The behavior of more complex systems in such a hierarchy cannot be studied in isolation. The choice of sustainable development goals to be pursued will differ from level to level. The following breakdown is therefore presented in the form of global, regional, and national objectives (adapted from Holmberg 1992).

Global objectives

- Develop national and international policy frameworks to foster the sustainable use of natural resources and the maintenance of biodiversity.

- Design and adopt accounting systems that give appropriate economic value to natural resources and establish economic pricing based on the polluter-pays principle.

- Promote conservation action through international cooperation and national planning.

- Maintain representative examples of the full spectrum of ecosystems, biological communities, habitats, and their ecological processes.

- Increase scientific understanding of natural resources and apply that understanding to their more efficient management.

- Expand research into the biophysical resources as a basis for improving management.

- Develop indicators of social sustainability and incorporate them into overall indicators of sustainable development.

- Give full consideration to issues of cultural diversity when designing and implementing projects.

Regional and national objectives

- Implement management procedures at the landscape level in order to integrate human activities with conserving natural resources.

- Reduce economic incentives that promote the wasteful use of natural resources and establish prices that reflect full economic costs (including internalization of environmental impacts).

- Strengthen the management tools for conserving natural resources and apply them more broadly.

- Greatly strengthen the human and institutional capacity for conserving and using biodiversity sustainably, especially in developing countries, by using the full range of government agencies, nongovernmental organizations, and the private sector.

- Establish sufficient protected areas containing viable populations of the target species and design activities so that they take place primarily outside the protected areas.

- Maintain viable populations of the nation's native plants and animals, well distributed throughout their geographic range.

- Maintain genetic variability within and among populations of native species, to maintain their evolutionary potential.

41

Local objectives

- Promote awareness and understanding of the importance of natural resources and biodiversity among the public (especially urban dwellers), decisionmakers, and politicians.

- Implement policies, incentives, and conditions that will enable rural populations, including those living in and around protected areas, to continue using their natural resources in sustainable ways.

- Introduce conservative levels of harvesting biological resources, based on evaluation of the target species and continued monitoring to assess the impact of use.

- Establish management structures and legal frameworks—within the local communities whenever possible—with the capacity to control levels of use.

- Institute education programs that improve local-level management of natural resources.

Governments are already starting to follow and provide backing for some of these guidelines and management regimes. A new Green Fund—the Global Environment Facility—has been created under the management of the World Bank, United Nations Environment Program, and International Union for the Conservation of Nature and is channeling several hundred million dollars into biodiversity projects in developing countries. A new Biodiversity Convention, after several years of negotiation, was adopted at the Earth Summit in Rio de Janeiro, Brazil, in June 1992.

If we focus on the biodiversity issues, several agreements have been, or are in the process of being, completed at the international level. These include the Global Biodiversity Strategy, prepared by the World Resources Institute, the International Union for the Conservation of Nature, and the United Nations Environment Program, in consultation with the Food and Agriculture Organization and UNESCO (the United Nations Education, Scientific, and Cultural Organization); the Draft Convention on Biological Diversity currently being prepared by United Nations Environment Program; and the guidelines prepared by the Scientific and Technical Advisory Panel (STAP) for the Global Environmental Facility (GEF) regarding criteria for eligibility and priorities for selection of GEF projects (many of which are directly linked to the preservation of biodiversity). Details are provided in appendix 2-1.

Sustainability indicators

The development of sustainability indicators recognizes the need to monitor human impacts on the environment and also attempts to relate levels of human use to a reproducible indicator. Both the analytical definition and practical measurement of such indicators are complicated. It is conceptually easier to deal with sustainability indicators at larger levels of aggregation. The rest of this section briefly reviews broadly defined indicators, as an introduction to the topic.

Some recent attempts have been made to devise ways to measure and monitor sustainability. Shearer (1992) proposes a Biophysical Sustainability Index, on the basis that all life on Earth is sustained by the net primary biological production generated by photosynthesis. Moseley (1992) provides examples of sustainability indicators for five sectors: greenhouse gases, agriculture, freshwater resources, forestry, and energy.

Shearer observes that the factors necessary to maintain biological production include fertility or availability of nutrients, energy, adequate moisture, proper substrates, minimum level of toxic substances, and an adequate and genetically varied stock of biological organisms. He uses these facts to develop a Biophysical Sustainability Index (BSI), which he suggests can be used to monitor policy rather than to replace scientific measures of sustainability.

The Biophysical Sustainability Index is comprised of a net primary productivity factor, NPPF (which reflects more of the economic concerns) and a biological diversity factor, BDF (which represents the ecological aspects); such that,

$$BSI = NPPF \times BDF.$$

The NPPF is defined as the ratio of the annual net primary production, ANPP, of the region over a given year, y, to that of the same region over the previous year, $y-1$. The ANPP of a given year is defined as

$$ANPP = PPA + PPP - HPCP$$

where PPA is the primary production of annuals, PPP is the primary production of perennials, and HPCP is the harvested primary capital of perennials. The data needed to calculate the ANPP is obtainable through satellite imagery and aerial photography, using a geographic information system.

The BDF of a region is defined as the ratio of the current selected biological diversity, CSBD, of the region (the number of species of a set of taxa thriving in the region) to the natural selected biological diversity, NSBD, of the same region (the number of species of the same set of taxa thriving in the region prior to human intervention). The set of taxa selected is chosen on the basis of those that are regularly monitored, those that are reasonably well known, those that are mostly immobile (for ease of monitoring), and those that are conspicuous.

Essentially, the proposed BSI has the following form:

$$BSI = \frac{(ANPP_y / ANPP_{y-1})}{(CSBD / NSBD)}$$

Moseley (1992) presents a somewhat different approach to measuring sustainability, using the Brundtland Commission's definition of sustainable development as a guiding principle to examine five sectors—greenhouse gases, agriculture, freshwater resources, forestry, and energy—in terms of their potential as sustainability indicators at the national level.

GREENHOUSE GASES

Global sink capacity (for increased emissions due to human activity) is defined as the difference between the mass of anthropogenic gas emissions and the annual change in atmospheric mass of that gas. Moseley discusses different means of determining sink capacity rights on a national basis.

If population is the determinant, then nations that encourage population growth would be rewarded. Another method of apportionment would be allocation based on a country's relative land mass. However, since land has different levels of carrying capacity, this would also be an inequitable form of distribution. Apportionment based on 1989 levels of emissions would reward countries with

the highest level of emissions in that year. Moseley argues that the most equitable way of apportioning the sink would be through a combination of population and land area criteria.

The Intergovernmental Panel on Climate Change has devised a conceptual unit—the global warming potential—that allows for comparisons between different greenhouse gases based on their contribution to global warming. The figure is determined by integrating an expression for the removal rate times an expression for the infrared absorption potency of the gas. A global warming potential output quota is based on (1) a quota for the world derived from the sinks for CO_2 and methane and (2) a quota for individual countries dependent on the average of their percentage of world population and land mass. The difficulty inherent in this method is that it assumes a substitutability between the sinks of different greenhouse gases. However, unless threshold emission levels are reached, a certain amount of substitution at the abstract level is permissible.

AGRICULTURE

A viable indicator of sustainable agriculture is the preservation of the integrity of agricultural soils. A key measure of productivity that can be examined is the ratio of crop production to fertilizer consumption, which indicates how land responds to fertilizer subsidies over time. From a sustainability point of view, the ratio should remain constant or increase over time. Decreasing ratios point to (1) fertilizer use that has increased to the point of diminishing returns or (2) the insufficient replacement of organic matter through fertilizer inputs, leading to soil depletion. As shown in table 2-4, the ratio of crop production to fertilizer use has declined drastically over the last decade.

Table 2-4: Ratio of Crop Production to Fertilizer Use

Year	1980	1985	1986	1987	1988	Changes in irrigated land as a % of cropland between 1978 and 1988 (percent)
United States	27	43	43	42	33	0
Sweden	21	26	28	27	26	0
Japan	13	13	13	12	12	–5
Thailand	119	100	86	59	67	7
Nepal	169	87	73	84	74	19
Kenya	43	32	33	32	30	0
Mali	106	71	55	60	115	3
Mexico	43	35	31	30	30	1
Ecuador	55	61	47	51	42	2

Source: World Agricultural Trends and Indicators, 1970-88, USDA, 1989.

FRESHWATER RESOURCES

Moseley identifies two potential indicators of sustainability for freshwater reources. The first measures the level of human exploitation of freshwater resources (domestic and external river flows and groundwater generated from endogenous precipitation). A measure that better examines the sustainability of water use practices is to identify the percentage of population served by wastewater treatment facilities. Countries with high levels of water use should ideally have correspondingly high levels of wastewater treatment capacity. Although these are useful measures of sustainable practice, data for developing countries are not easily available.

FORESTRY

The concept of sustainable yield (the amount of a resource that can be harvested without reducing its long-term stock; see Pearce and Turner 1990) is more readily applicable to fisheries than forestry, because tree populations have a longer period of regeneration. However, environmental indicators for temperate forests have been prepared for member nations of the Organization for Economic Cooperation and Development (Moseley 1992). Annual harvest was compared to annual increment, in the form of a ratio. However, aggregate figures at the national level can be misleading. Although the United States is losing overall forest cover, annual increment is increasing because old forests are being replaced by younger ones with higher growth rates. Although the production of wood increases, wildlife habitats and recreational areas are lost as a consequence of this policy.

ENERGY

By examining consumption of commercial energy per constant U.S. dollar of GNP, the production of renewable energy and the exploitation of renewable resources, it is possible to observe if a country is moving towards sustainable use of energy (Moseley 1992). Measures to increase energy efficiency are another key indicator of sustainable use and are particularly important because they allow for economic growth while keeping the quantity of throughputs constant.

Conclusions

The dictionary definitions of the words sustain and develop suggest that the expression sustainable development may be generally interpreted to mean the maintenance or improvement of the quality of life on a continuing basis. There are three main interpretations of sustainability based on different disciplinary approaches: economic, ecological/biophysical, and sociocultural.

Historically, the rise and decline of past cultures may often be traced to unsustainable practices, especially degradation of some vital natural resource. Nevertheless, human society as a whole has increased in complexity and organization over the ages, and the future sustainability of this evolutionary process will depend on the search for paths of long-run sustainable development. In modern times, the pressure of human activities has caused environmental damage on a scale not experienced before. High levels of consumption per capita in some parts of the world are one reason.

The rapidly growing populations of the poorer countries will continue to add to the environmental burden as development proceeds, especially if the material- and pollution-intensive patterns of past growth (experienced by the industrial nations) continue to be followed. Poverty and environmental degradation are closely linked, because the majority of the global population who are poor also tend to be the most severely affected by pollution and the degradation of natural resources. Therefore, sustainable development suggests that future progress will have to focus more on the quality of human life and less on the quantity of resources consumed, although the two aspects are related, especially for low-income groups.

The economic approach to sustainability is based on the Hicks-Lindahl concept of the maximum flow of income that can be generated while at least maintaining (or increasing) the stock of assets (or capital) that yield these benefits. Problems of interpretation arise in identifying the kinds of capital to be maintained and their substitutability (man-made, natural, human resources, and so forth) as well as in valuing these assets, particularly ecological resources. The issues of uncertainty, irreversibility, and catastrophic collapse also pose difficulties.

The ecological view of sustainability focuses on the stability of the biophysical system. Of particular importance is the viability of subsystems (species, biotic components) that are critical to the global stability of the overall ecosystem. Protection of biological diversity is a key aspect.

Furthermore, natural systems may be interpreted to include all aspects of the biosphere (including primarily man-made environments like cities), with emphasis placed on preserving their resilience and dynamic ability to adapt to change, rather than conservation of some ideal static state.

The sociocultural concept of sustainability seeks to maintain the stability of social and cultural systems, including the reduction of destructive conflicts. Both intragenerational equity (especially elimination of poverty) and intergenerational equity (protection of the rights of future generations) are important elements of this approach. Preservation of cultural diversity across the globe, and the better use of knowledge concerning sustainable practices inherent in many indigenous communities, should be pursued. Modern society must encourage and harness pluralism and grass-roots participation in order to engender a more effective framework for making decisions.

Reconciling these concepts and operationalizing them as a means to achieve sustainable development are formidable tasks. The diversity of immediate needs and concerns, as well as long-term goals throughout the world, suggests that there is no universal right or wrong approach to sustainable development. To a village-level official in the developing world, sustainable development may mean, first and foremost, dealing with poverty and human misery through health and education services. Meanwhile, to a government regulator in an industrial country, it may mean protecting the physical environment from emissions of both greenhouse gases and other effluents that cause acid rain by developing the right economic incentives and monitoring compliance with point discharge regulations. The existence of diverse perceptions and the existing structure of decisionmaking do not readily allow for consensus building, and the variety of problems at the microlevel does not facilitate constructive synthesis at the level of macro policy.

One useful practical approach to sustainable development that may be more comprehensible to policymakers and the public might be to maximize net benefits of economic and social development, subject to maintaining the services from and quality of natural resources over time. This implies that renewable resources (especially scarce ones) should be used at rates less than or equal to the natural rate of regeneration and that the efficiency with which nonrenewable resources are used should be optimized, subject to substitut-

ability between resources and technological progress. Another requirement is that waste be generated at rates less than or equal to the assimilative capacity of the environment (to preserve resiliency) and that efforts be made to protect equity within and between generations. Finally, the implementation of sustainable development will require a pluralistic and consultative social framework that, inter alia, facilitates the exchange of information between dominant and hitherto disregarded groups—to identify less material- and pollution-intensive (qualitative rather than quantitative) paths for human progress.

In addition to the broad recommendations that would be helpful at the global, national, and local levels, certain specific short-term actions will meet all criteria simultaneously. For example, improvements in access to clean drinking water and sanitation will increase productivity (economic), reduce environmental pollution (ecological), and benefit the poor (social). In the medium and long term, other project and policy options will require tradeoffs among the different objectives. Better techniques of valuing the environmental and social impacts of human activities will help to improve decisionmaking. In certain cases, the safe minimum standards approach could be helpful, especially when uncertainty and irreversibility are involved. Multicriteria analysis is another supplementary technique to help policymakers make difficult tradeoffs.

Since approaching sustainable development from the perspective of only one discipline has significant shortcomings, it will be necessary for biologists, physical and social scientists, and economists to work together. This will permit decisionmakers and society to make better choices between alternative courses, based on the presentation of relevant and unbiased information. There is urgent need for continued research by multidisciplinary teams to improve our understanding of economic valuation, the functions of ecosystems, the flow of energy, and the dynamics of social systems. At the same time, society has to continue with its present evaluation of its fundamental values and to recognize and define the values that it seeks to promote through different types of development activities and institutional arrangements.

To conclude, even though public awareness of the relationship between the environment and development has greatly increased, and governments are now devoting considerable energy and resources to the issue, much more needs to be done. No country in the world uses its natural environment as well as it could and should. The natural and biophysical assets of the Earth are being wasted, partly because our economic systems value only what human societies have created. The recently concluded United Nations Conference on Environment and Development was an important watershed and fresh starting point that has generated much momentum. But do our leaders yet have the political courage and will to implement the solutions that are required? Are consumers in the north willing to curb their overuse of energy and emission of greenhouse gases that already overtax the resilience of the global atmospheric commons? Are they willing to alter the terms of trade and reverse economic flows, so that development in the south is stimulated rather than continually undermined? Will the south confront its own inadequacies in implementing programs to reduce poverty, internal income disparities, and population growth? Are governments everywhere willing to permit local communities to have greater influence in planning and managing their own resources, where doing so will reduce inequity, exploitation, and waste of natural resources? And are the leaders of the conservation movement willing to put human needs at the forefront of their concerns and to insist that while development must be sustainable, it must also be centered on people?

Notes

1. A billion is 1,000 million.
2. The various terms in the equation for TEV may be grouped in somewhat different ways for convenience; see, for example, Walsh, Loomis, and Gillman 1984. In order to measure willingness to pay for wilderness protection, they sought to separate (a future-oriented) *preservation value* from *recreational use value* (in current use). Accordingly, these authors defined preservation value (PV) as option value plus existence value plus bequest value, that is, PV = (OV + EV> + BV).
3. Work is ongoing to identify defensive expenditures. Such expenditures by firms are treated in the current System of National Accounts as intermediate costs and are therefore not part of value added or final output. Defensive expenditures by households and governments, in contrast, are treated as final expenditures and included in GDP. Present research seeks to address this and other issues and inconsistencies in the System of National Accounts (see Lutz and Munasinghe 1991).

Appendix 2-1. Current Strategies for Ensuring Biodiversity

Global biodiversity strategy (1992)

At the international level, the Global Biodiversity Strategy calls for conserving biodiversity through international cooperation, integrating biodiversity conservation with international economic policy, strengthening the international legal framework for conservation to complement the Convention on Biological Diversity, integrating biodiversity conservation constraints into development assistance, and increasing the funding for biodiversity conservation, with the development of innovative, decentralized, and accountable ways to raise funds and spend them effectively.

At the local level, the strategy recommends reform of land tenure systems and development of new resource management partnerships between government and local communities, creation of institutional conditions for bioregional conservation and development, provision of incentives to encourage the sustainable use of products and services from the wild for local benefits; and adequate use (with appropriate benefits provided) of local knowledge of genetic resources.

The strategy outlines appropriate actions to strengthen the tools and technologies of biodiversity conservation, including identifying national and international priorities for strengthening protected areas and enhancing their role in biodiversity conservation; enhancing the value and improving management plans for protected areas; strengthening the capacity to conserve species, populations, and genetic diversity in natural habitats; and strengthening off-site conservation facilities to conserve biodiversity, educate the public, and contribute to sustainable development.

The strategy explicitly recognizes the importance of increasing the appreciation and awareness of the value of biodiversity. It suggests that the dissemination of information by relevant institutions be encouraged and calls for the promotion of basic and applied research on biodiversity conservation as well as the development of human resources capacity for biodiversity conservation.

UNCED convention on biological diversity (1992)

Key elements of the convention of the United Nations Conference on Environment and Development are that each contracting party shall undertake the following:

- Develop national strategies (or adapt existing strategies) for the conservation and sustainable use of biological diversity and shall integrate concerns for biodiversity into relevant sectoral or cross-sectoral plans.
- Identify and monitor components of biological diversity over which it exercises sovereign rights.
- Promote the establishment and strengthening of national inventory, regulation, or management and control systems related to biological resources.
- Develop methodologies to undertake sampling and evaluation on a national basis of the components of biological diversity and the status of ecosystems.
- Establish a system of in-situ conservation for ecosystems and natural habitats.
- Adopt measures for the ex-situ conservation of components of biological diversity where providing in-situ facilities is impracticable or not feasible.
- Integrate consideration of the conservation and sustainable use of biological resources into national decisionmaking, adopt measures relating to the use of biological resources to avoid or minimize adverse impacts on biological diversity, protect and encourage customary use of biological resources in accordance with traditional cultural practices that are compatible with the requirements of sustainable use, and support local populations to develop and implement remedial action in degraded areas where biological diversity has been reduced.
- Take appropriate measures for the fair and equitable sharing of benefits derived from research, development, and use of biological and genetic resources between the sources of those resources and the persons who use them.
- Develop economic (including pricing) and social policies that act as incentives to conserve

biodiversity and the sustainable use of biological and genetic resources on private lands.

- Establish and maintain programs for scientific and technical education, training, and research in the identification, conservation, and sustainable use of biological diversity and its components; provide support in such areas to developing countries.

- Promote public education and awareness of biodiversity conservation and its importance.

- Introduce appropriate procedures for environmental assessments of proposed projects likely to have significant impacts on biological diversity.

- Establish global lists of biogeographic areas of importance and species threatened with extinction.

- Facilitate the transfer of technology and encourage participation in biotechnological research activities.

- Produce regularly updated world reports on biodiversity based on national assessments in all countries.

STAP guidelines (1991)

Projects eligible for GEF funding accomplish one or a combination of the following aims: the reduction of greenhouse gas emissions, the protection of biodiversity, the protection of international waters, and the reduction of depletion of the ozone layer. In terms of the protection of biodiversity, STAP suggests that GEF should support projects that are linked to the management and protection of various ecosystems—including in-situ as well as ex-situ conservation, where necessary, in protecting the biodiversity of species and of genetic material—and that GEF should support regions, ecosystems, and species that, for reasons of degradation of habitat, pressure, or threat of extinction, require immediate attention. STAP places priority on the allocation of resources for the protection of biodiversity as follows (and suggests that useful techniques and instruments to implement such programs include legislative techniques, tax policies, subsidy approaches, and land use planning):

- Comprehensive approach to an entire ecosystem throughout its area, including human populations, taking into account species richness, diversity, and degree of threat.

- Establishment and consolidation of protection areas.

- Promotion of sustainable use of biota.

- Education, training, and research.

- Inventories.

- Institution-strengthening, including the support of scientific communities and the development of national mechanisms to coordinate programs for the conservation and sustainable use of biodiversity.

- Public awareness programs.

Appendix 2-2.
Cost-Benefit Analysis

Given the importance of sustainable development, it is evident that environmental externalities should be incorporated into the framework of traditional cost-benefit analysis. The following section (mostly derived from Munasinghe 1993) summarizes ways to improve the integration of natural resource and environmental issues into economic analyses of projects and policies. The main emphasis is given to methods and approaches for valuing environmental effects, issues relating to the discount rate, and the problems raised by risk and uncertainty.

Valuation of environmental costs and benefits

The basic concepts involving both use and nonuse values of environmental assets were described in the main text. The various valuation techniques summarized in table 2-3 are discussed below in greater detail.

Direct effects valued on conventional markets

Methods considered in this section are based on how a change in environmental quality directly affects actual market-related production.

EFFECT ON PRODUCTION
An investment decision often has environmental impacts, which in turn affect the quantity, quality, or production costs of a range of productive outputs that may be valued readily in economic terms. In a case study on soil conservation in Lesotho, increased production from conserved land is estimated (Bojo 1991). In the valuation of a Peruvian rainforest, the values of different production schemes are compared (Peters and others 1989). Another example includes impacts on tropical wetlands (Barbier and others 1991).

EFFECT ON HEALTH
This approach is based on health impacts caused by pollution and environmental degradation. One practical measure that is relevant is the value of human output lost due to ill health or premature death. The loss of potential net earnings (called the human capital technique) is one proxy for foregone output, to which the costs of health care or prevention may be added (as a form of replacement/preventive expenditure). The above measure assumes that earnings reflect the value of marginal product and that medical treatment costs are well defined. The method also encounters difficulties when the cause-effect link between environmental quality and ill-health is unclear, or the sickness is chronic (that is, of long duration).

This technique seeks to avoid ethical controversies associated with valuing a single life, attempting instead to place a value on the statistical probability of ill-health or death (akin to the actuarial values used by life insurance companies). Moreover, governments and public health authorities routinely set priorities and allocate health expenditures that affect human well-being. This in turn provides a baseline for determining implicit values placed by society on various health risks.

DEFENSIVE OR PREVENTIVE COSTS
Often, costs may have been voluntarily incurred by communities or individuals to mitigate or undo the damage caused by an adverse environmental impact. For example, if the drinking water is polluted, extra filtration and/or purifying chemicals may need to be used. Then, such additional defensive or preventive expenditures (ex-post) could be taken as a minimum estimate of the benefits of mitigation. The assumption is that the benefits of avoided environmental degradation at least exceed the costs of avoidance. The advantage of the technique is that defensive or preventive outlays (already made) are easier to determine than the value of the original environmental damage. One weakness is that the defensive actions are sometimes decided upon quite arbitrarily with little reliance on market forces, so that the costs bear little relation to the potential environmental benefit. Recently, Harrington and others (1989) evaluated the economic damages of a waterborne disease outbreak, emphasizing that the valuation of averting behavior requires the establishment of a relationship between observable defensive expenditures, and non-observable willingness to pay.

Potential expenditure valued on conventional markets

This section summarizes techniques in which potential or future actions could be valued in conventional markets to provide a measure of environmental degradation, provided there is a high degree of certainty that such actions will be undertaken.

REPLACEMENT COST AND SHADOW PROJECT

If an environmental resource that has been impaired is likely to be replaced in the future by another asset that provides equivalent services, then the costs of replacement may be used as a proxy for the environmental damage. This is an ex-ante measure similar to the (ex-post) defensive costs approach. It may be argued that the benefits from the environmental resource should be at least as valuable as the replacement expenses. The replacement cost approach has been applied to protecting groundwater resources in the Philippines, by determining the cost of developing alternative water sources (Munasinghe 1990b).

A shadow project is usually designed specifically to offset the environmental damage caused by another project. The cost of the shadow project reflects an institutional judgment on the value of environmental assets that are thereby restored. The approach has been discussed in the context of project-level sustainability. The original project and shadow project together form a sustainable package that helps to maintain undiminished some vital stock of environmental resources. For example, if the original project was a dam that inundated some forest land, then the shadow project might involve the replanting of an equivalent area of forest elsewhere. Often, the equivalency criterion is hard to satisfy exactly—in the above example, the two tracts of forest may have the same volume of biomass, but could differ widely in terms of biodiversity.

Valuation using implicit (or surrogate) markets

Often, relevant market data are not available in directly usable form to value environmental resources. In many such cases, analysis of indirect market data (for example, using statistical and econometric methods) permits the valuation to be carried out implicitly. A variety of such surrogate market-based methods—including travel cost, the "hedonic" methods (property value and wage differential), and proxy goods—as well as their applicability under different circumstances, are described below.

TRAVEL COST

This method seeks to determine the demand for a recreational site (for example, number of vis-

its per year to a park), as a function of variables such as consumer income, price, and various socioeconomic characteristics. The price is usually the sum of observed cost elements like (a) entry price to the site; (b) costs of travelling to the site; and (c) foregone earnings or opportunity cost of time spent. The consumer surplus associated with the demand curve provides an estimate of the value of the recreational site in question. More sophisticated versions include comparisons (using regression analysis) across sites, where environmental quality is also included as a variable that affects demand (for a detailed survey, see Mendelsohn 1987). Until a few years ago, most applications of this technique were to be found in the market economies, but quite recently several examples have emerged involving developing world applications. The travel cost for domestic trips to a forest is estimated in a Costa Rica case study (Tobias and Mendelsohn 1991). In another study on the value of elephants in Kenya, the travel cost of tourists from Europe and North America is used to estimate consumer surplus (Brown and Henry 1989).

PROPERTY VALUE

In areas where relatively competitive markets exist for land, it is possible to decompose real estate prices into components attributable to different characteristics such as house and lot size, proximity to schools, shops and parks, etc. (Cropper and Oates 1992). To value an environmental variable like air or water quality, the method seeks to determine that component of the property value attributable to the relevant environmental variable. Thus, the marginal willing-to-pay (WTP) for improved local environmental quality is reflected in the increased price of housing in cleaner neighborhoods. This method has limited applicability in developing countries because it requires a well-functioning housing market as well as sophisticated information and tools of statistical analysis. Jimenez (1983) used this technique to explain changes in housing prices in a Manila slum area, upgraded partly due to water and sanitation service improvements.

WAGE DIFFERENCES

As in the case of property values, the wage differential method attempts to relate changes in an economic price variable (that is, the wage rate) to environmental conditions. The underlying assumption is that there is some component of the wage that is determined by the environmental pollution or hazard associated with the job or work site. The technique is relevant when competitive labor markets exist, where wages (that reflect the marginal product of labor) equilibrate the supply and demand for labor. One concern is that the approach relies on private valuations of health risks, rather than social ones. In this context, the level of information on occupational hazards must be high, for private individuals to make meaningful tradeoffs between health-risk and remuneration. Finally, the effects of all factors other than environment (for example, age, skill level, job responsibility) that might influence wages must be accounted for, to eliminate bias and isolate the impacts of environment.

PROXY MARKETED GOODS

This method is useful when an environmental good or service has no readily determined market value, but a close substitute exists that does have a competitively determined price. In such a case, the market price of the substitute may be used as a proxy for the value of the environmental resource. Barbier and others (1991) provide an example involving marketed and non-marketed fish substitutes.

Valuation using constructed markets

In cases where market information cannot be used directly or indirectly, market-like behavior needs to be deduced through construction or simulation. The methods summarized below depend on direct questions, surveys, or marketing experiments.

ARTIFICIAL MARKET

Such markets are constructed for experimental purposes, to determine consumer WTP for a good or service. For example, a home water purification kit might be marketed at various price levels, or access to a game reserve may be offered on the basis of different admission fees, thereby facilitating the respective estimation of values placed by individuals on water purity or on the use of a recreational facility.

CONTINGENT VALUATION

When relevant market behavior is not observable, the contingent valuation method (CVM) puts direct questions to individuals to determine how much they might be willing-to-pay (WTP) for an environmental resource, or how much

compensation they would be willing-to-accept (WTA) if they were deprived of the same resource. The contingent valuation method is more effective when the respondents are familiar with the environmental good or service (for example, water quality) and have adequate information on which to base their preferences. CVM is likely to be far less reliable when the object of the valuation exercise is a more abstract aspect, such as existence value.

Generally, declared WTA tends to be significantly greater than the corresponding WTP. This may be partly attributable to "strategic bias" where respondents feel they would be better off inflating the amounts they would receive rather than the sums to be paid out, if the hypothetical questions posed were somehow to become a reality in the future. In the case of poorer individuals, WTP may be limited by the ability-to-pay, whereas WTA is not. The questionnaires have to be carefully designed, implemented, and interpreted to overcome the above mentioned difficulties, as well as other types of bias (for details, see *The Energy Journal* 1988). Munasinghe (1990a) provides several early examples of the application of CVM to value the quality of electricity services in developing countries.

A review by Pearce and Markandya (1989) compared valuation estimates obtained from market-based techniques and CVM, using results from seven studies carried out in industrial nations. They found that the corresponding estimates overlapped within an accuracy range of plus or minus 60 percent. The conclusion is that CVM, cautiously and rigorously applied, could provide rough estimates of value that would be helpful in economic decisionmaking, especially when other valuation methods are unavailable. A case study using the CVM for estimating the value of elephants in Kenya (Brown and Henry 1989) shows that it is possible to achieve an understanding of the order of magnitude of the benefits through modest methods. Another study, on WTP for water services in southern Haiti, tests the CVM for different biases, indicating the limits of its reliability (Whittington and others 1990).

The discount rate

Economists typically use a forward-looking approach in which past (or sunk) costs and benefits are ignored, while a discount rate is applied to future costs and benefits to yield their present values. Standard criteria for cost-benefit analysis (CBA), such as the net present value (NPV) and internal rate of return (IRR) are derived in this way. The issue of choosing an appropriate discount rate has been discussed in the context of general CBA for many years (Dasgupta and others 1972, Harberger 1976, Little and Mirrlees 1974).

Two concepts mainly help to shape the discount (or interest) rate in a market economy. First, there is the rate of time preference of individuals, which determines how they compare present-day with future consumption. Second, there is the rate of return on capital, which determines how an investment (made by foregoing today's consumption) would yield a stream of future consumption (net of replacement). In an ideally functioning market the interest rate, which equilibrates savings and investment, also equals both the marginal rates of time preference and return on capital. In practice, government policy distortions and market failures lead to divergences between the rates of time preference and return on capital. Furthermore, the social rate of time preference may be less than the individual time preference rate, because long-lasting societies are likely to have a bigger stake in the more distant future than relatively short-lived individuals.

The long-term perspective required for sustainable development suggests that the discount rate might play a critical role in intertemporal decisions concerning the use of environmental resources. The rate of capital productivity is very high in many developing countries because of capital scarcity, and the rate of time preference also is elevated because of the urgency of satisfying immediate food needs rather than ensuring long-term food security (Pearce and Turner 1990). Projects with social costs occurring in the long term and net social benefits occurring in the near term will be favored by higher discount rates. Conversely, projects with benefits accruing in the long run will be less likely to be undertaken under high discount rates. Thus, some environmentalists have argued that discount rates should be lowered to facilitate environmentally sound projects meeting the CBA criteria. However, this would lead to more investment projects of all types, thereby possibly threatening fragile environmental resource bases. Norgaard (1991) argues that lowering discount rates can in fact worsen environmental degradation—by lowering the cost of capital and thereby lowering the cost of production, more is consumed in the near

term relative to the case where discount rates were higher. Further, using a very low discount rate to protect future generations is inequitable, since this would penalize the present generation and increase inequalities across time periods—especially when the present contains widespread poverty.

In order to facilitate such intergenerational transfers, one option is to impose a sustainability constraint, whereby current well-being is maximized without reducing the welfare of future generations below that of the current generation. In practice, this would entail monitoring and measurement of capital stocks (man-made, human, and natural), and a broad investment policy which seeks to ensure that compensating investments offset depreciation of existing assets (Pearce 1991). Theoretically, the aim would be to ensure that the overall stock of assets is preserved or enhanced for future generations, but practical application of this principle would be difficult.

Risk and uncertainty

Risk and uncertainty are an inherent part of economic decisions. Risk represents the likelihood of occurrence of an undesirable event such as an oil spill. In the case of uncertainty, the future outcome is basically unknown. Therefore, the risk of an event may be estimated by its probability of occurrence, whereas no such quantification is possible for uncertainty since the future is undefined. The risk probability and severity of damage could be used to determine an expected value of potential costs, which would be used in the CBA. However, the use of a single number (or expected value of risk) does not indicate the degree of variability or the range of probability values that might be expected. Additionally, it does not allow for individual perceptions of risk. The risk probability may be used to devise an insurance scheme to protect against the risk.

In the case of uncertainty, it is not possible to estimate the expected value of costs or insure against an unknown eventuality. The increasing scale of human activity, the complexity of environmental and ecological systems, and the lack of knowledge of how these systems might be affected, all emphasize the need to deal with uncertainty more explicitly. A cautious approach is the key to dealing with uncertainty. Global warming is an illustrative example. In the past, the greenhouse effect of CO_2 emissions was not known or recognized as a risk. At the present time, there is still considerable uncertainty about the future impacts of global warming, but given the large magnitude of potential consequences, caution is warranted.

The traditional and simple way of incorporating risk and uncertainty considerations in project level CBA has been through sensitivity analysis. Using optimistic and pessimistic values for different variables can indicate which variables will have the most pronounced effects on benefits and costs. We note that while sensitivity analysis need not reflect the probability of occurrence of the upper or lower values, it is useful for determining which variables are most important to the success or failure of a project (Dixon and others 1988). More sophisticated approaches to analyze risk and uncertainty are available (Braden and Kolstad 1991).

The issue of uncertainty plays an important role in environmental valuation and policy formulation. Option values and quasi-option values are based on the existence of uncertainty. Option value (OV) is essentially the "premium" that consumers are willing to pay to avoid the risk of not having something available in the future. The sign of option value depends upon the presence of supply and/or demand uncertainty, and on whether the consumer is risk averse or risk loving. Quasi-option value (QOV) is the value of preserving options for future use in the expectation that knowledge will grow over time. If a development takes place that causes irreversible environmental damage, the opportunity to gain knowledge through study of flora and fauna is lost. Increased benefits to be derived through future knowledge expansion (which is independent of exploitation) leads to a positive QOV. This suggests that the resource exploitation should be postponed until increased knowledge facilitates a more informed decision. If information growth depends on the use taking place, which is unlikely in an environmental context, then QOV is positive (negative) when the uncertainty applies to the benefits of preservation (exploitation) (Pearce and Turner 1990, Fisher and Hanemann 1987).

Bromley (1989) suggests that the way in which policymakers address uncertainties depends on their perception of the existing entitlement structure. The interests of the future are only protected by an entitlement structure that imposes a duty on current generations to consider the rights of future generations (or, as he terms them, "missing markets" because "future generations are unable to enter bids to protect their interests"). Without such a structure, decisionmakers may tend to ignore costs to future generations, and minimize costs to current generations at the expense of the future. If the entitlement structure is adjusted, the policymaker can then examine three policies to protect the interests of future generations: (1) mandated pollution abatement; (2) full compensation for future damages (for example, by taxation); and (3) an annuity to compensate the future for costs imposed in the present. In the face of uncertainty, the first option might be the most efficient.

Other important sources of uncertainty linked with environmental issues include uncertainty over land tenure (which leads to deforestation and unsustainable agricultural practices), and uncertainty of resource rights (which can accelerate the rate of depletion of a nonrenewable resource). Policymakers can address these issues by instituting land reforms, and by designing appropriate taxation policies that return rents to public sources rather than to private agents.

References

Aylward, B., and Edward Barbier. 1992. "Valuing Environmental Functions in Developing Countries." *Biodiversity and Conservation* 1, pp. 34–50.

Barbier, Edward. 1991. *Economics, Natural Resource Scarcity, and Development: Conventional and Alternative Views*. London: Earthscan Publications, Ltd.

Barbier, Edward, W. M. Adams, and K. Kimmage. 1991. "Economic Valuation of Wetland Benefits: The Hedejic-Jamiare Floodplain, Nigeria." LEEC Discussion Paper DP 91-02, April.

Barnett, Harold, and Chandler Morse. 1963. *Scarcity and Growth: The Economics of National Resource Availability*. Baltimore, Md.: Johns Hopkins University Press.

Botkin, D. B. 1990. *Discordant Harmonies: A New Ecology for the 21st Century*. New York: Oxford University Press.

Bojo, J. 1990. "Economic Analysis of Agricultural Development Projects. A Case Study from Lesotho". EFI Research Report, Stockholm: Stockholm School of Economics.

Boyden, S., and S. Dovers. 1992. "Natural Resource Consumption and Its Environmental Impacts in the Western World. Impacts of Increasing Per Capita Consumption." *Ambio* 21:1.

Braden, J. B., and C. D. Kolstad, eds.1991. *Measuring the Demand for Environmental Quality.* New York: Elsevier.

Bromley, Daniel W. 1989. "Property Relations and Economic Development: The Other Land Reform." *World Development* 17:6, pp. 867–77.

Brown Jr., G., and W. Henry. 1989. "The Economic Value of Elephants." London Environmental Economics Centre, *Discussion Paper* 89-12.

Cleveland, C. J. 1991. "Natural Resource Scarcity and Economic Growth Revisited: Economic and Biophysical Perspectives." In R. Costanza, ed., *Ecological Economics: The Science and Management of Sustainability.* New York: Columbia University Press.

Cocklin, C. 1989. "Mathematical Programming and Resources Planning I: The Limitations of Traditional Optimization." *Journal of Environmental Management* 28, pp. 127–41.

Costanza, R., ed. 1991a. *Ecological Economics: The Science and Management of Sustainability.* New York: Columbia University Press.

———. 1991b. "The Ecological Economics of Sustainability: Investing in Natural Capital." In R. Goodland and others, eds., *Environmentally Sustainable Economic Development: Building on Brundtland*, pp. 83–90. Paris: UNESCO.

Cropper, M. L., and W. E. Oates. 1992. "Environmental Economics: A Survey." *Journal of Economic Literature*, Vol. XXX (June), pp. 675–740.

Daly, Herman. 1990. "Towards Some Operational Principles of Sustainable Development." *Ecological Economics* 2:1, pp. 1–6.

Darlington, C. D. 1969. *The Evolution of Man and Society.* New York: Simon and Schuster.

Dasgupta, Partha, and Karl-Goran Mäler. 1990. *The Environment and Emerging Development Issues. Proceedings of the World Bank Annual Conference on Development Economics 1990*, pp. 101–29. Washington, D.C.: World Bank.

Dasgupta, P., S. Marglin, and A. K. Sen. 1972. *Guidelines for Project Evaluation.* UNIDO, New York.

Dixon, John, and others. 1988. *Economic Analysis of the Environmental Impacts of Development Projects.* London: Earthscan Publications, in association with the Asian Development Bank.

Dobbs, M. 1992. "Bootlegging Thrives, Sturgeon Flounder as Caviar Cartel Splits." *International Herald Tribune*, June.

Energy Journal. 1988. Special issue on Electricity Reliability, 9 (December).

Fisher, Anthony C., and W. Michael Hanemann. 1987. "Quasi Option Value: Some Misconceptions Dispelled." *Journal of Environmental Economics and Management* 14, pp. 183–90.

Freeman, A. Myrick. 1991. "Valuing Environmental Resources under Alternative Management Regimes." *Ecological Economics* 3, pp. 247–56.

Gomez-Pompa, A., and A. Kaus. 1992. "Taming the Wilderness Myth." *Bioscience* 42:4, pp. 271–79.

Goodland, R., H. Daly, S. L. Serafy, and B. von Droste, eds. 1991. *Environmentally Sustainable Economic Development: Building on Brundtland.* Paris: UNESCO.

Goudie, A. 1990. *The Human Impact on the Natural Environment.* 3d ed. Cambridge, Mass.: M.I.T. Press.

Grumbine, E. 1990. "Protected Biological Diversity through the Greater Ecosystem Concept." *Natural Areas Journal* 10:3, pp. 114–20.

Hanley, Nick D. 1989. "Valuing Rural Recreation Benefits: An Empirical Comparison of Two Approaches." *Journal of Agricultural Economics* 40:3 (September), pp. 361–74.

Harberger, A. C. 1976. *Project Evaluation: Collected Papers.* University of Chicago Press.

Harrington, W., A. J. Krupnick, and W. O. Spofford, Jr. 1989. "The Economic Losses of a Waterborne Disease Outbreak." *Journal of Urban Economics*, 25:1, pp. 116–37.

Hartwick, J. M., and N. D. Olewiler. 1986. *The Economics of Natural Resource Use.* New York: Harper and Row.

Hodgson, Gregor, and John Dixon. 1988. *Logging versus Fisheries and Tourism in Palawan.* Occasional Paper 7. Honolulu, Hawaii: East-West Environment and Policy Institute.

Holmberg, J. 1992. "Operationalizing Sustainable Development in the World Bank." World Bank, Washington, D.C. Draft.

Hyman, J. B., and C. Wernstedt. 1991. "The Role of Biological and Economic Analysis in the Listing of Endangered Species." *Resources* (Summer).

IUCN (International Union for the Conservation of Nature). 1991. *Caring for the Earth: A Strategy for Sustainable Living.* With the United Nations

Environment Program and the World Wildlife Fund. Gland, Switzerland.

Jimenez, E. 1983. "The Magnitude and Determinants of Home Improvement in Self-Help Housing: Manila's Tondo Project." *Land Economics* 59:1, pp. 70–83.

Lele, Sharad M. 1991. "Sustainable Development: A Critical Review." *World Development* 19:6, pp. 607–21.

Liebman, J. 1976. "Some Simple-Minded Observations on the Role of Optimization in Public Systems Decisionmaking." *Interfaces* 6, pp. 102–08.

Little, I. M. D. and J. A. Mirrlees. 1974. *Project Appraisal and Planning for Developing Countries.* Basic Books, New York.

Lovelock, J. E. 1979. *Gaia: A New Look at Life on Earth.* Oxford, England: Oxford University Press.

Lutz, Ernst, and Mohan Munasinghe. 1991. "Accounting for the Environment." *Finance and Development* 28 (March), pp. 19–21.

Martin, P. 1984. "Prehistoric Overkill: The Global Model." In P. Martin and R. Kline, eds., *Quaternary Extinctions: A Prehistoric Revolution,* pp. 354–403. Tucson: University of Arizona Press.

McRobert, D. 1988. "Questionable Faith." *Probe Post* 11:1.

Meier, P., and Mohan Munasinghe. 1993. *Incorporating Environmental Concerns into Power Sector Decision-making: A Case Study of Sri Lanka.* World Bank, Washington, D.C.

Mendelsohn, M. 1987. "Modelling the Demand for Outdoor Recreation." *Water Resources Research* 23:5, pp. 961–7.

Meredith, T. C. 1992. "Environmental Impact Assessment, Cultural Diversity, and Sustainable Rural Development." *Environmental Impact Assessment Review* 12:1/2 (March/June).

Micklin, Philip. 1988. "Desiccation of the Aral Sea: A Water Management Disaster of the Soviet Union." *Science* 241 (September 2), pp. 1170–76.

Mitchell, Robert C., and Richard T. Carson. 1989. *Using Surveys to Value Public Goods: The Contingent Valuation Method.* Washington, D.C.: Resources for the Future.

Moseley, W. 1992. "Measuring the Environmental Sustainability of Human Economies: Some Suggestions and Examples of Indicators at the National Level." Environment Department, World Bank, Washington, D.C. Draft.

Munasinghe, Mohan. 1990a. *Electric Power Economics.* London: Butterworths Press.

———. 1990b. "Managing Water Resources to Avoid Environmental Degradation." Environment Department Working Paper 41. World Bank, Washington, D.C.

———. 1992a. "Biodiversity Protection Policy: Environmental Valuation and Distribution Issues." *Ambio* 21:3, pp. 227–36.

———. 1992b. *Water Supply and Environmental Management.* Boulder, Colo.: Westview Press.

———. 1993. *Environmental Economics and Sustainable Development.* Washington, D.C.: World Bank.

Munasinghe, Mohan, and K. King. 1992. "Protecting the Ozone Layer." *Finance and Development* (June), pp. 24–25.

Nabhan, G. P., A. M. Rea, K. L. Hardt, E. Mellink, and C. F. Hutchinson. 1982. "Papago Influences on Habitat and Biotic Diversity: Quitovac Oasis Ethno-Ecology." *Journal of Ecology* 2, pp. 124–43.

Norgaard, R. B. 1991. "Sustainability as Intergenerational Equity." Asia Regional Series, Report IDP-97, World Bank, Washington D.C.

Norton, B., and R. Ulanowicz. 1991. "Scale and Biodiversity Policy: A Hierarchical Approach." *Ambio* 20:1, pp. 1–6.

Oldeman, L. R., V. W. P. van Engelen, and J. H. M. Pulles. 1990. "The Extent of Human-induced Soil Degradation." In L. R. Oldeman, R. T. A. Hakkeling, and W. G. Sombroek, eds., *World Map of the Status of Human-induced Soil Degradation: An Explanatory Note.* 2d ed. rev., annex 5. Wageningen, the Netherlands: International Soil Reference and Information Centre.

Orians, Gordon H. 1990. "Ecological Concepts of Sustainability." *Environment* 32:9 (November), pp. 10–15, 34–39.

Pearce, D. W. 1991. *Development and the Natural World.* World Bank, Washington D.C.

Pearce, David, Edward Barbier, and Anil Markandya. 1989. *Blueprint for a Green Economy.* London: Earthscan Publications.

———. 1990. *Sustainable Development: Economics and Environment in the Third World.* London: Edward Elgar, Ltd.

Pearce, David W., and Anil Markandya. 1989. *The Benefits of Environmental Policy: Monetary Valuation.* Paris: OECD.

Pearce, David W., and R. Kerry Turner. 1990. *Economics of Natural Resources and the Environ-*

ment. London: Harvester-Wheatsheaf.

Pearce, F. 1991. *Green Warriors: The People and the Politics behind the Environmental Revolution.* London: Bodley Head.

Perrings, Charles. 1991. *Ecological Sustainability and Environmental Control.* Centre for Resource and Environmental Studies, Australian National University.

Perrings, Charles, C. Folke, and Karl-Goran Mäler. 1992. "The Ecology and Economics of Biodiversity Loss: The Research Agenda." *Ambio* 21:3, pp. 201–11.

Peters, C. M., A. H. Gentry, and R. O. Mendelsohn. 1989. "Valuation of an Amazonian Rainforest." *Nature* 339 (June 29), pp. 655–56.

Petry, F. 1990. "Who Is Afraid of Choices? A Proposal for Multi-Criteria Analysis as a Tool for Decision-making Support in Development Planning." *Journal of International Development* 2, pp. 209–31.

Pezzey, John. 1989. "Economic Analysis of Sustainable Growth and Sustainable Development." Working Paper 15. Environment Department, World Bank, Washington, D.C. Processed.

Pimental, D., and others. 1992. "Observing Biological Diversity in Agricultural/Forestry Systems." *Bioscience* 42:5, pp. 354–62.

Pollan, M. 1990. "Only Man's Presence Can Save Nature." *Journal of Forestry* 88:7, pp. 24–33.

Ponting, C. 1990. "Historical Perspectives on Sustainable Development." *Environment* 32:9, pp. 4–9, 31–33.

Potvin, Joseph. 1992. "Classification and Appraisal Criteria for Conservation Investments." Global Environment Facility, World Bank, Washington, D.C. Draft.

Pronk, J., and M. Haq. 1992. *Sustainable Development: From Concept to Action. The Hague Report.* New York: United Nations Development Program.

Randall, Alan, and John Stoll. 1983. "Existence Value in a Total Valuation Framework." In *Managing Air Quality and Scenic Resources at National Parks and Wilderness Areas.* Boulder, Colo.: Westview Press.

Romero, C., and T. Rehman. 1987. "Natural Resource Management and the Use of Multiple Criteria Decision-making Techniques: A Review." *European Journal of Agricultural Economics* 14, pp. 61–89.

Schneider, S. 1990. "Debating Gaia." *Environment* 32:4, pp. 5–9, 29–32.

Shearer, W. 1992. "A Proposal for a Biophysical Sustainability Index." United Nations University, New York and Tokyo. Private communication.

Solow, Robert. 1986. "On the Intergenerational Allocation of Natural Resources." *Scandinavian Journal of Economics* 88:1, pp. 141–49.

Soule, M. E. 1991. "Conservation: Tactics for a Constant Crisis." *Science* 253, pp. 744–50.

Sprugel, D. G. 1991. "Disturbance, Equilibrium, and Environmental Variability: What Is 'Natural' Vegetation in a Changing Environment?" *Biological Conservation* 58, pp. 1–18.

Tietenberg, Thomas. 1988. *Environmental and Natural Resource Economics.* 2d ed. Glenview, Ill.: Scott Foresman and Company.

Tobias, D. and R. Mendelsohn. 1991. "Valuing Ecotourism in a Tropical Rain-Forest Reserve." *Ambio* 20:2, April.

Toman, M. A. 1992. "The Difficulty in Defining Sustainability." *Resources* (Winter), pp. 3–6.

United Nations Conference on Environment and Development. 1992. "Conservation of Biological Diversity." In *Agenda 21*, chap. 15. Rio de Janeiro.

Walsh, Richard G., John B. Loomis, and Richard A. Gillman. 1984. "Valuing Option, Existence, and Bequest Demands for Wilderness." *Land Economics* 60:1 (February), pp. 14–29.

Westman, W. E. 1977. "How Much Are Nature's Services Worth?" *Science* 197, pp. 960–64.

Whittington, D., J. Briscoe, X. Mu, and W. Barson. 1990. "Estimating the Willingness to Pay for Water Services in Developing Countries." *Economic Development and Cultural Change* 38:2.

World Bank. 1992. *World Development Report 1992: Development and the Environment.* New York: Oxford University Press.

World Commission on Environment and Development. 1987. *Our Common Future.* Oxford, England: Oxford University Press.

World Resources Institute. 1992a. *Global Biodiversity Strategy.* Washington, D.C.

———. 1992b. *World Resources Report.* New York: Oxford University Press.

Young, M. D. 1992. *Sustainable Investment and Resource Use: Equity, Environmental Integrity, and Economic Efficiency.* Paris: UNESCO; Carnforth: Parthenon Publishing Group.

3

Limits to Sustainable Use of Resources: From Local Effects to Global Change

Peter M. Vitousek and Jane Lubchenco

The term sustainable has undergone a rapid migration and radiation from its long-term home in forestry and fisheries into the wider ecological, agricultural, and development communities. In its previous habitat, the term referred to management strategies in which a small enough fraction of a resource (trees, fish) is harvested so that the stock of the resource is not diminished; growth in volume or population of the resource is sufficient to replace the amount harvested. In contrast, nonsustainable management strategies take a larger fraction of the resource, thereby diminishing the stock and (eventually) the amount harvested. In an economic analogy, the stock of a resource is equivalent to principal and its growth rate is equivalent to interest; use of interest alone is sustainable because it leaves the principal intact, but any higher rate of use diminishes principal.

The meaning of sustainable is clear as it applies to forestry and fisheries, although long-term success in managing either forests or fish in a sustainable way has been elusive (Ludwig, Hilborn, and Walters 1993). However, in its expanded niche as part of sustainable agriculture, sustainable development, and a sustainable biosphere, the term has taken on additional meanings. Where once only a single resource, the one being harvested, was considered, we are now concerned with the integrated and cumulative effects of human activities or management practices on a multitude of resources and processes, from the local to the global scale. Now, it is not only a question of whether humanity can harvest a resource without reducing its stock but also a question of whether humanity can use resources without at the same time changing regional and global systems in deleterious, uncontrolled, or unpredictable ways.

The evolution of the term sustainable can be illustrated straightforwardly with a set of examples. Consider first a region occupied by natural grassland ecosystems, say the mixed-grass prairie of central North America. Net primary production in the grassland is supported by nitrogen cycling from soil organic matter to grasses, often through animals, and back to soil organic matter; occasional fires accelerate this cycle briefly (Ojima 1987; Parton and others 1987). A small number of humans can use the region sustainably by harvesting grazing animals, if they do so at a low enough intensity to avoid depleting the stock of those animals.

Now consider the same region being used for pioneer agriculture. The prairie soil is plowed, crops are planted, and the prairie grasses are suppressed. Net primary productivity remains high for a time and in a form useful to humans, but it is now supported by net oxidation of soil organic matter and release of the organic nitrogen it contains (Bolin and others 1983). If this organic matter or nitrogen is not replaced, the system is not sustainable; it achieves its productivity only by depleting an essential resource, and sooner or later yields will fall and the agricultural systems will fail.

Pioneer agriculture of this sort can be made sustainable through shifting cultivation if enough land is available and if the human population using the land is small enough. In this system, humans practice agriculture for a short period of time on any given plot, then abandon that plot and use another, and so on until after some time they return to the first plot. Shifting cultivation can be sustained if the interval between visits to a given site is long enough for soil fertility (and other features of the land) to regenerate (Nye and Greenland 1960). However, such a system is highly vulnerable to any increase in population or economic pressure.

Finally, consider a modern agricultural system in the same area. Modern agriculture, of course, covers a multitude of practices, but common to most of them is the fact that net primary production of the crop is supported by inputs that humans control. For example, nitrogen from fertilizer generally becomes a relatively large source of nitrogen for crops. Is such a system sustainable? The question must now be asked on at least two scales: locally and regionally or globally. On the local scale, the answer depends on the particular agricultural practice examined, and it is arguable in many cases. Many observers are impressed with the increasing amount and variety of inputs required to maintain productivity and with concurrent rates of erosion, salinization, and other changes in soils. Many others are impressed that increasing inputs have led to some quite spectacular increases in yields and also that humans demonstrably are good at adapting land management to match many alterations in soils.

On a regional or global level, the case for the sustainability of many modern agricultural practices is not so debatable. Inputs to modern agricultural systems include energy from fossil fuels, fertilizer, pest control, weed control, and often irrigation water; outputs include alterations in the composition of the atmosphere and in regional air quality, changes in water quality and sometimes depletion of groundwater, and changes in biological diversity both within and outside the region. As widely practiced, such agricultural systems are not sustainable in that they cannot persist on a large scale without altering the region and indeed the Earth system as a whole.

Coral reefs provide a different example of the relationship between spatial scale and the sustainability of harvesting practices. Coral reefs are widely recognized as being among the most productive ecosystems on Earth (Crisp 1975; Lewis 1977). This productivity occurs despite the oligotrophic waters surrounding most reefs and is thought to be intimately dependent on the efficient recycling of nutrients within the reef community. Reefs are thus unlike many other coastal marine ecosystems, which depend primarily on nutrients from adjacent systems, for example, via upwelling or terrestrial runoff. The high incidence of symbiotic relationships between plants and animals on coral reefs is thought to reflect the advantage accrued to an efficient transfer of nutrients among these components.

Despite being very productive, however, reefs are highly susceptible to certain kinds of overexploitation (Birkeland 1992; Munro and Williams 1985; Russ 1985). Traditional, even heavy, subsistence fishing on coral reefs is usually sustainable, especially when nutrients, for example in the form of scraps and fecal material, are returned to the reef. These fishing practices appear to retain nutrients within the system. Large-scale export fisheries, however, have dramatically different effects. Not only do they remove more biomass, but they now transport biomass completely out of the system instead of recycling it. The result of this combined depletion of fish stocks and export of nutrients is an overfished and impoverished reef and thus an unsustainable fishery (Birkeland 1992).

As fish become scarce on these reefs, destructive methods of fishing are often employed to harvest the remaining fishes. Dynamiting is a common, if illegal, method. The resulting destruction of reefs leads to further impoverishment, now involving the stocks of other, nontarget species as well as destruction of the habitat itself. Practiced on a large scale, this cumulative impoverishment has consequences for the entire basin.

These two examples illustrate some of the ways in which our thinking about sustainability has changed. The scale of the area under consideration has increased as we appreciate the regional and global impacts of local practices. Inclusion of the larger scale often changes conclusions about the sustainability of a practice, as feedbacks at regional and global scales impose different limits than those of the more narrow local focus. To determine sustainability, one must consider not only the stock of a particular resource but also the process required to maintain those stocks, other populations, and other functions. Maintenance of these processes often involves larger scales and different constraints.

In this chapter, we focus on some of these integrated regional and global consequences of human activity, not on other (very important) questions, such as the extent to which high-input systems can be maintained in the long term on local scales or how much biomass and nutrients can be exported from a system before it collapses. We consider human activities to be nonsustainable to the extent that they alter features of the Earth system, such as the composition of the atmosphere and its capacity to process pollutants, the stability of the climate, the formation and maintenance of soil fertility, the ability of aquatic (freshwater and marine) systems to process and recycle nutrients, and above all the maintenance of the diversity of organisms that carry out many of these functions (Ehrlich and Mooney 1983). We first consider some human activities that have global consequences, then focus on human responses to these changes.

Human activity and global change

That the current level of human activity alters many features of the Earth system on regional and global scales is beyond dispute. Change in climate (for example, global warming!) receives a large amount of attention, but it is not the best documented, not currently the most important, and not the most permanent of the components of global change caused by humans.

The changing atmosphere

The atmosphere mixes more rapidly than the other great spheres of the Earth system (oceans and terrestrial ecosystems), and it is not surprising that global changes have been detected most readily in the atmosphere. Measurements of carbon dioxide concentrations have been carried out since 1957; during that time, concentrations have increased more than 10 percent, from 315 to over 355 parts per million, and the rate of increase has accelerated (Keeling and others 1989). Could this rapid increase result from a fortuitous interaction between our relatively brief record of measurements and a natural fluctuation in carbon dioxide concentrations? The answer is no, because measurements of carbon dioxide concentrations in air bubbles trapped in Greenland and Antarctic ice show that concentrations were stable near 280 parts per million for at least 1,000 years before the ongoing exponential increase began (Watson and others 1990).

There is no doubt that the ongoing increase is a by-product of human activity, primarily the combustion of fossil fuels and, secondarily, changes in land use. The amount of carbon released from the burning of fossil fuel is more than sufficient to account for the global increase (Schlesinger 1991). More convincingly, the relative atmospheric abundance of the carbon isotopes ^{13}C and ^{14}C have decreased over time in a pattern and magnitude that demonstrate that their concentrations are being diluted by carbon released from fossil fuel combustion (which is ^{14}C-free and ^{13}C-depleted) and to a lesser extent loss of terrestrial biomass (^{13}C-depleted; Siegenthaler and Oeschger 1987; Stuiver 1978).

This human-caused increase in carbon dioxide is already substantial (more than 25 percent of the initial value), and it is the major factor driving anthropogenic enhancement of the greenhouse effect. Moreover, increased concentrations of carbon dioxide are likely to affect terrestrial biota directly by increasing growth rates of some but not all plants and by increasing the amount but decreasing the quality of food available to many animals and decomposers (Bazzaz 1990; Mooney and others 1991). Elevated carbon dioxide could also have direct effects in marine ecosystems (Smith and Buddemeier 1992).

Anthropogenic increases in concentrations of a number of other stable gases also have been documented (Watson and others 1990). These include the industrially produced chlorofluorocarbons (CFCs), methane, and nitrous oxide. The increase in methane is believed to be due to a combination of agricultural activities (particularly the growing of paddy rice and the maintenance of domestic ruminants) and industrial processes (Cicerone and Oremland 1988). The reasons for increasing nitrous oxide are less certain but are believed to relate to changes in tropical land use and the massive alteration of the global nitrogen cycle brought about by intensive agriculture (Matson and Vitousek 1990; Vitousek and Matson, forthcoming).

All of these gases can enhance the greenhouse effect; in addition, CFCs and nitrous oxide break down in the stratosphere and cause a breakdown of stratospheric ozone. The ability of CFCs to affect stratospheric ozone was identified in 1974 (Molina and Rowland 1974), and their importance as an agent for global change was debated actively at that time. Nevertheless, everyone was surprised by the discovery of a springtime hole in the Antarctic ozone in the mid-1980s, though perhaps not by the subsequent proof that CFCs cause this depletion as a consequence of a previously unsuspected set of interactions (Prather and Watson 1990; Rowland 1989).

Not all of the human-caused changes to the atmosphere involve stable, globally distributed gases. Anthropogenic increases in concentrations of chemically reactive gases have led to decreased tropospheric concentrations of the hydroxyl radical, the major oxidizing agent in the atmosphere (Thompson 1992). The resulting decrease in the ability of the atmosphere to cleanse itself leads to an increased atmospheric lifetime, and hence increased concentration, of methane.

At the same time, a syndrome of elevated tropospheric ozone concentrations, acidic precipitation, and elevated nitrogen deposition occurs over most of the economically developed regions of the Earth (Crutzen and Zimmerman 1991; Logan 1985), and similar changes are now being observed seasonally in developing tropical regions (Fishman and others 1991; Keller and others 1991). High application rates of nitrogen fertilizer, intensive animal husbandry, and the production of nitrogen oxides and sulfur oxides by internal combustion engines and other industrial processes all contribute to these changes; biomass burning is the most important source in many developing tropical areas (Andreae and others 1988; Crutzen and Andreae 1990). Europe, where increases in agricultural production have been most impressive (and most heavily subsidized), is affected particularly severely by these by-products of human activity (Schulze 1989).

Changes in land use

Human-caused change in land use (land clearing, agricultural intensification, urbanization, and so forth) is currently the most consequential component of global change, and its effects are already with us. However, land use can be difficult to treat as a global change, because unlike the atmosphere or oceans, terrestrial ecosystems do not mix on any time scale that is relevant to human sustainability. Consequently, it is impossible to characterize global changes in land use by measurements in one or a few locations. Any global effect must be the sum of many changes to local ecosystems. In practice, change in land use alters enough local ecosystems substantially enough to contribute directly to increased concentrations of greenhouse gases (Watson and others 1990), to affect regional climate and atmospheric chemis-

try (Keller and others 1991; Shukla, Nobre, and Sellers 1990), to alter the chemistry of major river systems (Peierls and others 1991), and to be the most important cause of global change to coastal marine ecosystems and coral reefs (Howarth 1988; Smith and Buddemeier 1992). Nevertheless, its most important effect probably is simply to alter local systems; some types of major ecosystems have nearly disappeared (tall-grass prairie, tropical deciduous forest), and many others have been degraded or fragmented.

The global effects of changes in land use have been summarized in two ways: in terms of the amount of land altered by humanity and in terms of the fraction of terrestrial productivity that humanity controls. Turner and others (1990) have estimated that nearly half of the land surface of Earth has been transformed by human activity, in that it has been converted to cropland or to improved pastures or been desertified. Much of the rest of Earth has been affected through logging or extensive grazing on range lands but has not been transformed in character. Alternatively, Vitousek and others (1986) have calculated that nearly 40 percent of the terrestrial net primary productivity of Earth is now being used, dominated, or destroyed by human activity; again, much of the remainder is affected, although not overwhelmingly so.

These two estimates are in reasonably close agreement, and both imply that all of Earth's terrestrial ecosystems and an overwhelming majority (certainly more than 99 percent) of its species must persist on little more than half of the area they once occupied. To the extent that these natural systems, species, and populations provide goods or services that are essential to the sustainability of human systems, their shrunken base of operations must be a cause for concern.

Loss of biological diversity

The most permanent component of anthropogenic global change is the extinction of species and genetically distinct populations. Extinction is a natural phenomenon; under normal circumstances, an average species lasts perhaps 10 million years from appearance to extinction (Ehrlich and Wilson 1991). "Normal" conditions are punctuated by episodes of mass extinction, of which five are known in the past hundreds of millions of years.

Human activity is accelerating the process of extinction dramatically. Observations of well-studied groups such as birds, together with calculations of losses based on species per area and species per energy relationships (Wilson and Peter 1988), suggest that current rates of extinction are orders of magnitude above background rates. Most of the extinctions that have occurred to date have been caused by changes in land use, although biological invasions by exotic species have also played a significant role (D'Antonio and Vitousek 1992). Other components of global change are likely to contribute more and more in the next century.

If these human-caused extinctions continue, the next few decades will entrain a mass extinction of a magnitude greater than any since the Cretaceous-Tertiary boundary 65 million years ago. This loss of diversity is by far the least reversible component of global change. The greenhouse gases we are concerned with have atmospheric lifetimes lasting from a decade to a little more than a century; their concentrations could return to background levels in at most a few centuries if anthropogenic forcing were removed. Climate might be a little slower to respond due to buffering by the oceans; the restoration of soil fertility on severely degraded sites could take a millennium or two. In contrast, overall levels of species diversity (in terms of the number of species on Earth) might recover from a catastrophic mass extinction in a *million* years, and the loss of particular species and their genetic information would be permanent.

Human response to global change

There is no doubt that human activity causes global change and no mystery about the ultimate cause. The scale of human activity—the product of our population and our effect on the rest of the Earth system—has become large relative not just to that of other species but also to the flow of energy and materials on a global scale. Global effects on the atmosphere, on land use, and on other species are already clear; effects on climate and other components of the Earth system are coming. There are no serious arguments against these points. Where arguments exist, they concern how bad the changes will be and how soon they will occur. The specific arguments are: Do we need this species? Will that change in climate reduce our gross national product (GNP) significantly? More generally, while an informed and reasonable person must concede that the current levels of human impact on the Earth system are

degrading or altering the system in now-unpredictable ways (that is, the impact is not sustainable), many intelligent people argue that it is too soon to act because the changes are not yet to the point that they really matter to humanity. (Arguments that action is too expensive, that future technological advances will mitigate any problems, or that precipitate action in the face of uncertainty might be regretted later are subsets of this point of view.)

What is the point at which it really matters? How would we know if it had been approached or exceeded? We cannot answer these questions definitively for several reasons. First, for many components of global change, the level of uncertainty about the overall consequences of change is relatively high. We know that human activity alters soil fertility and water quality over large areas of Earth; we also know that human activity is causing a substantial increase in rates of population and species extinction. We know that extinction impoverishes the genetic library that supports agriculture and health care. However, the extent to which this loss of diversity itself affects aspects of how the ecosystem functions, such as the maintenance of soil fertility or water quality, is not known (Lawton and Brown 1993; Vitousek and Hooper 1993). Without this information, we cannot predict with any confidence how many (or which) species could be lost before ecosystem functions that support humanity are degraded by direct consequences of the loss of diversity. Both the Ecological Society of America (Lubchenco and others 1991) and the international Scientific Committee on Problems of the Environment (Schulze and Mooney 1993) have identified this as a high-priority area of research, but answers will not come quickly.

Second, there is every reason to believe that the Earth system will not respond gradually and evenly to global change. Rather, substantial lags, nonlinearities, thresholds, and interactions can be anticipated even if the human-caused forcing functions themselves vary gradually and continuously. The best current example of a nonlinear response to change is the Antarctic ozone hole. The effect of CFCs on ozone depletion had been identified, but no one predicted the rapid development of the ozone hole, which was discovered more or less by accident (Farman, Gardiner, and Shanklin 1985; Rowland 1989).

Climatic change in the past also involved significant thresholds and nonlinearities. The climatic oscillation between glacial and interglacial conditions (COHMAP Project 1988; Imbrie 1985) involves rapid changes superimposed on gradual changes in forcing functions; positive feedbacks based on ice cover, atmospheric carbon dioxide concentrations, and perhaps cloud condensation nuclei produced by marine phytoplankton all could contribute to the oscillation (Houghton, Jenkins, and Ephraums 1990). On a shorter time scale, there is evidence that patterns of ocean circulation can change quite rapidly from one quasi-stable state to another, driving very rapid, substantial, and relatively persistent changes in the global climate (Broecker 1987). Human forcing is now driving Earth's climatic system into conditions that differ from those at any time in the Pleistocene; it is unlikely that we will be able to use the past record to guess what surprises (nonlinearities, thresholds, and so forth) these new conditions will bring, but the past does tell us that some surprises are very likely.

Finally, environmental monitoring is now inadequate to pick up many likely changes in the global environment, including some of those that could affect humanity most directly. The measurements of atmospheric carbon dioxide that have been made over the past thirty-five years are tremendously useful; it is difficult to imagine where we would be without them. They demonstrate global change unambiguously. There have been a number of attempts to use such measurements further to determine the sources and sinks of carbon dioxide globally (see, for example, Tans, Fund, and Takahashi 1990), but the measurements are carried out in so few sites (and those sites are so removed from local sources of variation) that it is difficult to obtain information at a scale finer than an entire hemisphere.

Our ability to detect global change in land use is much worse, even though remote-sensing technology is available and appropriate to the task. Equally important, our knowledge of the distribution and changing patterns of Earth's biological diversity remains haphazard.

All of these concerns present impediments to our ability to analyze the effects of human-caused changes in the Earth system, and all of them can (and should) be addressed by research programs. Many are now being studied more or less systematically. This research will contribute to showing how the world works and how it is altered by human activity. It may identify some surprises in advance, and it can suggest areas where change is occurring particularly rapidly. However, it can never be enough to direct policy unambiguously. By the time we determine the significance of each species in a tropical rain forest in terms of its effect on ecosystem function, very likely more than half of these species will be extinct. We will never identify (in advance) all of the surprises that will occur as the Earth system changes, and monitoring will never be sufficient to detect early warning signs of all the important components of global change. Therefore, research should not be considered a substitute for action designed to reduce human impacts on the biosphere. Moreover, policies guiding this action must be based on the most current scientific understanding of these impacts and must recognize the inherent difficulty in making precise predictions about highly complex systems.

Indeed, our current knowledge about the scope, significance, and variety of global changes resulting from human activity should catalyze immediate action to reduce these impacts. Specifically, prompt, vigorous actions should be initiated to reduce the rate of growth of the human population, reduce the use of energy, reduce the consumption of resources, and implement policies and practices that are sustainable at local, regional, and global scales. None of these objectives is easy; each is essential.

Despite many uncertainties about how to achieve these objectives, it is imperative that new, more responsible policies and practices be implemented. Programs such as the Sustainable Biosphere Project of SCOPE (the Scientific Committee on Problems of the Environment) are designed to help identify options for a more sustainable use of resources. These options must be based on the recognition that sustainability must be evaluated at not only the local, but also the regional and global scales.

References

Andreae, M. O., E. V. Browell, M. Garstang, G. L. Gregory, and R. C. Harris. 1988. "Biomass Burning and Associated Haze Layers over Amazonia." *Journal of Geophysical Research* 93, pp. 1509–27.

Bazzaz, F. A. 1990. "The Response of Natural Ecosystems to Rising Global CO_2 Levels." *Annual Review of Ecological Systems* 21, pp. 167–96.

Birkeland, C. 1992. "Differences among Coastal Systems: The Controlling Influences of Nutrient Input and the Practical Implications for Management." In *Coastal Systems Studies and Sustainable Development*, Proceedings of the COMAR interregional scientific conference. UNESCO Technical Papers in Marine Science 64. Paris: UNESCO.

Bolin, B., P. J. Crutzen, P. M. Vitousek, R. G. Woodmansee, E. D. Goldberg, and R. B. Cook. 1983. "Interactions of Biogeochemical Cycles." In B. Bolin and R. B. Cook, eds., *The Biogeochemical Cycles and Their Interactions*, pp. 8–40. Chichester, England: John Wiley and Sons.

Broecker, W. S. 1987. "Unpleasant Surprises in the Greenhouse." *Nature* 328, pp. 123–26.

Cicerone, R. J., and R. Oremland. 1988. "Biogeochemical Aspects of Atmospheric Methane." *Global Biogeochemical Cycles* 2, pp. 299–327.

COHMAP Project. 1976. "Climatic Changes of the Last 18,000 Years: Observations and Model Simulations." *Science* 241, pp. 1043–52.

Crisp, D. J. 1975. "Secondary Productivity in the Sea." In D. E. Reichle, J. E. Franklin, and D. W. Goodall, eds., *Proceedings of a Symposium on Productivity of World Ecosystems*, pp. 71–89. Washington, D.C.: National Academy of Sciences.

Crutzen, P. J., and M. O. Andreae. 1990. "Biomass Burning in the Tropics: Impact on Atmospheric Chemistry and Biochemical Cycles." *Science* 250, pp. 1669–78.

Crutzen, P. J., and P. H. Zimmerman. 1991. "The Changing Photochemistry of the Atmosphere." *Tellus* 43, pp. 136–51.

D'Antonio, C. A., and P. M. Vitousek. 1992. "Biological Invasions by Exotic Grasses, the Grass-fire Cycle, and Global Change." *Annual Review of Ecology and Systematics* 23, pp. 63–87.

Ehrlich, Paul R., and H. A. Mooney. 1983. "Extinction, Substitution, and Ecosystem Services." *BioScience* 33, pp. 248–54.

Ehrlich, Paul R., and E. O. Wilson. 1991. "Biodiversity Studies: Science and Policy." *Science* 253, pp. 758–62.

Farman, J. C., B. G. Gardiner, and J. D. Shanklin. 1985. "Large Losses of Total Ozone in Antarctica Reveal Seasonal $C10_x/NO_x$ Interaction." *Nature* 315, pp. 207–10.

Fishman, J., K. Fakhruzzaman, B. Cros, and D. Nganga. 1991. "Identification of Widespread Pollution in the Southern Hemisphere Deduced from Satellite Analyses." *Science* 252, pp. 1693–96.

Howarth, R. W. 1988. "Nutrient Limitation of Primary Production in Marine Ecosystems." *Annual Review of Ecology and Systematics* 19, pp. 89–10.

Houghton, J. T., G. J. Jenkins, and J. J. Ephraums, eds. 1990. *Climate Change: The IPCC Scientific Assessment.* Cambridge, England: Cambridge University Press.

Imbrie, J. 1985. "A Theoretical Framework for the Pleistocene Ice Ages." *Journal of the Geological Society of London* 142, pp. 417–32.

Keeling, C. D., R. B. Bacastow, A. F. Carter, S. C. Piper, and T. P. Whorf. 1989. "A Three Dimensional Model for Atmospheric CO_2 Transport Based on Observed Winds. 1: Analysis of Observational Data." *Geophysical Monographs* 55, pp. 165–236.

Keller, M., D. J. Jacob, S. C. Wofsy, and R. C. Harris. 1991. "Effects of Tropical Deforestation on Global and Regional Atmospheric Chemistry." *Climatic Change* 19, pp. 145–58.

Lawton, J. H., and V. K. Brown. 1993. "Redundance in Ecosystems." In E.-D. Schulze and H. A. Mooney, eds., *Biodiversity and Ecosystem Function*, pp. 255–70. Berlin: Springer-Verlag.

Lewis, J. B. 1977. "Processes of Organic Production on Coral Reefs." *Biology Review* 52, pp. 305–47.

Logan, J. A. 1985. "Tropospheric Ozone: Seasonal Behavior, Trends, Anthropogenic Influence." *Journal of Geophysical Research* 90, pp. 10, 463–10, 482.

Lubchenco, J., A. M. Olson, L. B. Brubaker, S. R. Carpenter, M. M. Holland, S. P. Hubbell, S. A. Levin, J. A. MacMahon, P. A. Matson, J. M. Melillo, H. A. Mooney, C. H. Peterson, H. R. Pulliam, L. A. Real, P. J. Regal, and P. G. Risser. 1991. "The Sustainable Biosphere Initiative: An Ecological Research Agenda." *Ecology* 72:2, pp. 371–412.

Ludwig, D., R. Hilborn, and C. Walters. 1993. "Uncertainty, Resource Exploitation, and Conservation: Lessons from History." *Science* 260, pp. 17–18.

Matson, P. A., and P. M. Vitousek. 1990. "Ecosystem Approach to a Global Nitrous Oxide Budget." *BioScience* 40, pp. 667–72.

Molina, M. J., and F. S. Rowland. 1974. "Stratospheric Sink for Chlorofluoromethanes: Chlorine Atomic Catalysed Destruction of Ozone." *Nature* 249, pp. 810–12.

Mooney, H. A., B. C. Drake, R. J. Luxmoore, W. C. Oechel, and L. F. Pitelka. 1991. "Predicting Ecosystem Responses to Elevated CO_2 Concentrations." *BioScience* 41, pp. 96–104.

Munro, J. L., and D. M. Williams. 1985. "Assessment and Management of Coral Reef Fisheries: Biological, Environmental, and Socio-economic Aspects." *Proceedings of the Fifth International Coral Reef Congress, Tahiti*, vol. 4, pp. 543–81.

Nye, P. H., and D. J. Greenland. 1960. "The Soil under Shifting Cultivation." *Technical Communications* (Commonwealth Bureau of Soils, Farnham Royal, England) 51.

Ojima, D. S. 1987. "The Short-term and Long-term Effects of Burning on Tall-Grass Prairie Ecosystem Properties and Dynamics." Ph.D. diss., Colorado State University.

Parton, W. J., D. S. Schimel, C. V. Cole, and D. S. Ojima. 1987. "Analysis of Factors Controlling Soil Organic Matter Levels in Great Plains Grasslands." *Soil Science Society of America Journal* 51, pp. 1173–79.

Peierls, B. L., N. F. Caraco, M. L. Pace, and J. J. Cole. 1991. "Human Influence on River Nitrogen." *Nature* 350, pp. 386–87.

Prather, M. J., and R. T. Watson. 1990. "Stratospheric Ozone Depletion and Future Levels of Atmospheric Chlorine and Bromine." *Nature* 344, pp. 729–34.

Rowland, F. S. 1989. "Chlorofluorocarbons and the Depletion of Stratospheric Ozone." *American Science* 77, pp. 42–44.

Russ, G. 1985. "Effects of Protective Management on Coral Reef Fishes in the Central Philippines." *Proceedings of the Fifth International Coral Reef Congress, Tahiti*, vol. 4, pp. 219–24.

Schlesinger, W. H. 1991. *Biogeochemistry: An Analysis of Global Change*. San Diego, Calif.: Academic Press.

Schulze, E.-D. 1989. "Air Pollution and Forest Decline in a Spruce (*Picea abies*) Forest." *Science* 244, pp. 776–83.

Schulze, E.-D., and H. A. Mooney, eds. 1993. *Biodiversity and Ecosystem Function*. Berlin: Springer-Verlag.

Shukla, J., C. Nobre, and P. Sellers. 1990. "Amazonian Deforestation and Climate Change." *Science* 247, pp. 776–83.

Siegenthaler, U., and H. Oeschger. 1987. "Biospheric CO_2 Emissions during the Past 200 Years Reconstructed by Deconvolution of Ice Core Data." *Tellus* 39B, pp. 140–54.

Smith, S. V., and R. W. Buddemeier. 1992. "Global Change and Coral Reef Ecosystems." *Annual Review of Ecology and Systematics* 23, pp. 89–118.

Stuiver, M. 1978. "Atmospheric Carbon Dioxide and Carbon Reservoir Changes." *Science* 199, pp. 253–58.

Tans, P. O., I. Y. Fund, and T. Takahashi. 1990. "Observational Constraints on the Global Atmosphere CO_2 Budget." *Science* 247, pp. 1431–38.

Thompson, A. M. 1992. "The Oxidizing Capacity of the Earth's Atmosphere: Probable Past and Future Changes." *Science* 256, pp. 1157–64.

Turner, B. L. II, W. C. Clark, R. W. Kates, J. F. Richards, and J. T. Matthews. 1990. *The Earth as Transformed by Human Action*. Cambridge, England: Cambridge University Press.

Vitousek, Peter M., Paul R. Ehrlich, A. H. Ehrlich, and P. A. Matson. 1986. "Human Appropriation of the Products of Photosynthesis." *BioScience* 34:6, pp. 368–73.

Vitousek, Peter M., and D. U. Hooper. 1993. "Biological Diversity and Terrestrial Ecosystem Biogeochemistry." In E.-D. Schulze and H. A. Mooney, eds., *Biological Diversity and Ecosystem Function*, pp. 3–14. Berlin: Springer-Verlag.

Vitousek, Peter M., and P. A. Matson. Forthcoming. "Agriculture, the Global Nitrogen Cycle, and Trace Gas Flux." In R. Oremland, ed., *Biogeochemistry of Global Change: Radiative Trace Gases*. New York: Chapman & Hall.

Watson, R. T., H. Rodhe, H. Oeschger, and U. Siegenthaler. 1990. "Greenhouse Gases and Aerosols." In J. T. Houghton, G. J. Jenkins, and J. J. Ephraums, eds., *Climate Change: The IPCC Scientific Assessment*, pp. 1–40. Cambridge, England: Cambridge University Press.

Wilson, E. O., and F. M. Peter, eds. 1988. *Biodiversity*. Washington, D.C.: National Academy of Sciences.

4

Sustainability: The Cross-Scale Dimension

C. S. Holling

A new class of problems is challenging the ability to achieve sustainable development:

- *These problems are more and more frequently caused by slowly accumulated human influences on air, land, and oceans that trigger sudden changes that directly affect the health of people, the productivity of renewable resources, and the vitality of societies.*
- *The spatial span of connections is intensifying so that the problems are now fundamentally cross-scale in space as well as in time.*
- *The problems are essentially nonlinear in causation and discontinuous in both their spatial structure and temporal behavior.*
- *Both the ecological and social components of these problems have an evolutionary character.*

The problems are therefore not amenable to solutions based on knowledge of small parts of the whole nor on assumptions of constancy or stability of fundamental relationships: ecological, economic, or social. Such assumptions produce policies and science that contribute to a pathology of rigid and unseeing institutions, increasingly brittle natural systems, and public dependencies.

But recent advances in theory, method, and regional experience are leading to a truly cross-scale understanding and to the identification of the attributes of renewal capital that are the foundations for sustainable development in a world of surprises.

In the most fundamental sense, the renewal capital for nature is the physical structure of the environment that sustains and is controlled by the biota at all scales. For people, it is social trust and accessible knowledge.

The biophysical dimensions of sustainable development cannot be separated neatly from the economic or the social dimensions. To attempt to do so would encourage piecemeal strategies of investments that have failed to improve the status of people. Those strategies have invested in parts of the whole, typically investments in resource development, while ignoring the responses of nature and the adaptive traditions of people. The present recognition of the role of nature in issues of sustainability is certainly an advance, but not if that appreciation simply encourages a policy lurch away from narrow economic development and toward equally narrow environmental protec-

tion. Partial policies fail. Integrated policies may have a chance to succeed.

Lamentably, partial policies are more comfortably congruent with the disciplinary expertise that is an important foundation for education and research. But a biologist's or an ecologist's discipline-based design for sustainability cannot be trusted any more than an economist's or an engineer's. Doing so leads to a disciplinary and policy myopia that generates the very problems and conflicts that sustainable development is supposed to address.

I argue here, however, that practical ways are emerging to measure and invest in sustainable development that draw on a spectrum of disciplinary scholarship within a framework that leads to integrated understanding and integrated policies. This has become possible with recent advances in theory, method, and the sciences themselves and from regional experience in the restoration of ecosystems. This approach is leading to truly cross-scale understanding and to the identification of the attributes of renewal capital that are the foundations for sustainable development in a world of surprises.

In the most fundamental sense, the renewal capital for terrestrial nature is the physical architecture of the biophysical environment that sustains and is controlled by the biota at all scales. For people, it is social trust and accessible and usable knowledge.

A cross-scale journey

Metaphors can help clarify complex and apparently paradoxical notions such as sustainable development. Do ecosystems—their structure, function, and behavior—provide a useful metaphor? That depends on the scale of observation, both in time and space.

If I observe a 400-year-old, 1,000 hectare stand of Douglas fir trees in British Columbia from the perspective of my three-score years and 3 or 4 kilometers of easy walk, I see a true model of sustainability. The resource capital that measures that particular perspective of sustainability might be the standing biomass, just as the new generation of resource economists and accountants now propose.

If I view the stand from the perspective of the tree's lifetime, not mine, however, I see sustainability as perpetuation of a 400-year period of tree growth, which was initiated by a major disturbance covering at least 1,000 hectares. The resource capital allowing that period of growth might be measured by the nutrient-holding attributes of soil, not by the standing biomass.

If I extend time still further to several lifetimes of trees and expand my spatial perspective to a sub-continental scale, I realize that the originating disturbance events are periodic. Such disturbances are not intrusions from outside but are an inherent part of ecosystem succession. In the case of a stand on the storm-swept west coast of Vancouver Island, the disturbance could well be a windstorm capable of clear-cutting many hundreds of hectares as a normal process whenever

extremes of weather intersect with increasing vulnerability of the stand as trees become mature. For different tree species, in different regions of the boreal forest, the natural disturbance might be an outbreak of insects or a forest fire. Sustainability at that scale can be seen as the maintenance of successional cycles of stand-level boom-and-bust to produce a perpetuating mosaic of stands of trees of different ages, each stand covering 100 to 1,000 hectares. The resource capital responsible for maintaining that pattern is the set of biotic and abiotic processes that perpetuate the dynamic mosaic. It can be measured by physical attributes of vegetation patterns and by climate.

By this time, and at this geographic extent, I am describing a good part of the present unlogged, unmanaged, high-latitude forest of North America, Europe, or Asia. Now I am at a scale where there are groups of ecosystems of coniferous and mixed forests and of lakes, bogs, and wetlands. They aggregate to form the boreal forest biome whose existence is itself a passing and transient thing, which emerged in its present form perhaps 8,000 years ago following the retreat of the ice sheets. Pollen records demonstrate that the aggregation of tree species following the retreat of the ice sheets was a highly individualistic process depending on an individual species' response to weather, unique dispersal properties, and distance to the source of seeds. The processes defining the system at this scale now include geophysical cycles that are responsible for rhythms of glaciation, erosion, and land movement.

I could go on in this journey in time and space and only stop when I encounter the whole universe and the big bang of its origin. Or I could proceed into smaller scales from the starting point of a stand of 400-year-old trees and pose questions of persistence of patches within which plants compete for water, nutrients, and light, then persistence of plants within those patches, persistence of branches, persistence of leaves and needles, and so on. Each set of questions would provide a different perspective on sustainability and a different way to measure it.

I am not dwelling on these different scale-dependent perspectives in order to claim that sustainability is so relative as to be meaningless. Rather, I do so to illustrate that a universal feature occurs at all these scales, from needle to planet. Each description is a cycle of birth, growth, death, and renewal. What sustains such cycles? Oddly, the processes of death and renewal rather than those of birth and growth lie at the heart of sustainability. That is where we need to search for measures of sustainability: measures of disturbance and of the capacity to renew after disturbance. Consider the succession of ecosystems.

Ecosystem function

Over the last decade, the literature on ecosystems has led to major revisions in the original Clementsian view of succession. That initial view was one of a highly ordered sequence of species assemblages moving toward a sustained climax whose characteristics are determined by climate and edaphic conditions. This revision comes from extensive comparative field studies (West, Shugart, and Botkin 1981), from critical experimental manipulations of watersheds (Bormann and Likens 1981; Vitousek and Matson 1984), from paleoecological reconstructions (Davis 1986; Delcourt, Delcourt, and Webb 1983), and from studies that link models of systems and field research (West, Shugart, and Botkin 1981).

The revisions include four principal points. First, the species that invade after disturbance and during succession can be highly variable and determined by chance events. Second, both early and late successional species can be present continuously. Third, large and small disturbances triggered by events like fire, wind, and herbivores are an inherent part of the internal dynamics and in many cases set the timing of successional cycles. Fourth, some disturbances can carry the ecosystem into quite different stability domains: for example, mixed grass and tree savannas turn into shrub-dominated semi-deserts (Walker 1981); that is, more than one climax state is possible.

In summary, therefore, the notion of a sustained climax is a useful but essentially static and incomplete equilibrium view. The combination of these advances in understanding ecosystems by studying population systems has led to one version of a synthesis that emphasizes four primary stages in an ecosystem's cycle (Holling 1986).

The traditional view is that succession of an ecosystem is controlled by two functions: exploitation, in which rapid colonization of recently disturbed areas is emphasized, and conservation, in which slow accumulation and storage of energy and material is emphasized. But the revisions in understanding indicate that two additional functions are needed (see figure 4-1). One is that of release, or creative destruction, a term

borrowed from the economist Schumpeter (as reviewed in Elliott 1980), in which the tightly bound accumulation of biomass and nutrients becomes increasingly fragile (overconnected in systems terms) until it is suddenly released by agents such as forest fires, insect pests, or intense pulses of grazing. The second is one of reorganization, in which soil processes of mobilization and immobilization minimize nutrient loss and reorganize nutrients to become available for the next phase of exploitation.

During this cycle, biological time flows unevenly. The progression in the ecosystem's cycle proceeds from the exploitation phase (box 1 of figure 4-1) slowly to conservation (box 2), very rapidly to release (box 3), rapidly to reorganization (box 4), and rapidly back to exploitation. During the slow sequence from exploitation to conservation, connectedness and stability increase, and a capital of nutrients and biomass is slowly accumulated. That capital becomes more and more tightly bound, preventing other competitors from using it until the system eventually becomes so overconnected that rapid change is triggered. The agents of disturbance might be wind, fire, disease, insect outbreak, or a combination of these. The stored capital is then suddenly released, and the tight organization is lost to allow the released capital to be reorganized and the cycle to begin again.

Figure 4-1: Flow of Events between Four Ecosystem Functions

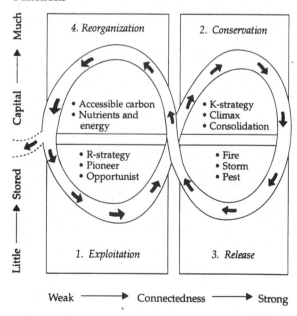

The arrows show the speed of that flow in the cycle: arrows close to each other indicate a rapidly changing situation, and arrows far from each other indicate a slowly changing situation. The cycle reflects changes in two attributes: (1) the Y axis, which is the amount of accumulated capital (nutrients, carbon) stored in variables that are the dominant keystone variables at the moment, and (2) the X axis, which is the degree of connectedness among variables. The exit from the cycle, shown at the left of the figure, indicates the stage at which a flip is most likely to lead into a less or more productive and organized system, that is, devolution or evolution as revolution!

That pattern is discontinuous and is dependent on the existence of changing multi-stable states that trigger and organize the release and reorganization functions. Instabilities and chaotic behavior trigger the release phase, which then proceeds in the reorganization phase, where stability begins to be reestablished. In short, chaos emerges from order, and order emerges from chaos! Resilience and recovery are determined by the fast release and reorganization sequence, whereas stability and productivity are determined by the slow exploitation and conservation sequence.

Moreover, there is a nested set of such cycles, each with its own range of scales. In the typical boreal forest, for example, fresh needles cycle yearly, the crown of foliage cycles with a decadal period, and trees, gaps, and stands cycle at periods of close to a century or longer. The result is a hierarchy in which each level has its own distinct spatial and temporal attributes (see figure 4-2).

Dynamics of hierarchies

A critical feature of such hierarchies is the asymmetric interactions between levels (Allen and Starr 1982; O'Neill and others 1986). In particular, the larger, slower levels maintain constraints within which faster levels operate. In that sense, therefore, slower levels control faster ones. If that were the only asymmetry, however, it would be impossible for organisms to exert control over slower environmental variables. Many geologists criticize the Gaia theory on these grounds (Lovelock 1988): How could slow geomorphic processes possibly be affected by fast biological ones? However, it is not broadly recognized that the birth, growth, death, and renewal cycle, shown in figure 4-1, transforms hierarchies from fixed static structures to dynamic entities whose levels are vulnerable to small disturbances at certain critical times in the cycle (Holling 1992). That represents a transient but important bottom-up asymmetry.

There are two key states in which slower and larger levels in ecosystems become briefly vulnerable to dramatic transformation because of small events and fast processes. One is when the system becomes overconnected and brittle as it slowly moves toward maturity (box 2 of figure 4-1). At this stage, relations among the plant species are tightly competitive. From an equilibrium perspective, the system is highly stable (that is, return times are fast in the face of small disturbances), but from a resilience perspective (see, for example, Holling 1987), the domain over which stabilizing forces can operate becomes increasingly small. Brittleness comes from such a loss of resilience. Hence the system becomes an accident waiting to happen. In the boreal forest, for example, the accident might be a contagious fire that becomes increasingly likely as the amount, extent, and flammability of fuel accumulate. Or it could be an outbreak of insects that spreads as increasing amounts of foliage both increase food and habitat for defoliating insects and decrease the efficiency with which their vertebrate predators search for them (Holling 1988).

Figure 4–2: Hierarchies of Space and Time for Forests and Atmospheres

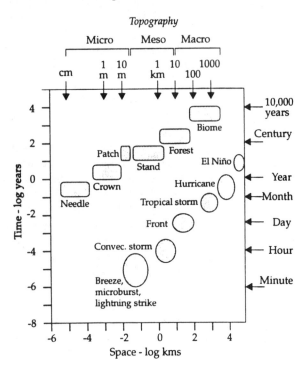

Small and fast variables can also dominate slow and large ones at the stage of reorganization (box 4 of figure 4-1). At this stage, the system is underconnected, with weak organization and weak regulation. As a consequence, this is the stage most affected by probabilistic events that allow a diversity of entrained species, as well as exotic invaders, to become established. On the one hand, it is the stage most vulnerable to erosion and to the loss of accumulated capital. On the other hand, it is the stage from which jumps to unexpectedly different and more productive systems are possible. At this stage, instability comes from the loss of regulation rather than the brittleness of reduced resilience.

The degree to which small, fast events influence larger, slower ones is critically dependent on the accumulation, cycling, and conservation of accumulated capital. And that in turn depends on the meso-scale disturbance processes. Human management of renewable resources or impacts of macroscale phenomena, such as change in climate, can release a pattern of disturbance that destroys large amounts of accumulated renewal capital over large areas. If too much capital is destroyed over too large an area, the system can flip into a qualitatively different stable state that persists unless there is explicit rehabilitation through management. As an example, that is why grazing at sustained, extensive, but moderate levels can transform productive savannas into less-productive systems dominated by woody shrubs (Walker and others 1969). Or why successful efforts at controlling forest fires can lead to so much accumulated fuel over such a large area that the inevitable runaway fire destroys accumulated soil and the capacity of trees to regenerate.

The question for issues of human transformation from the scale of fields to that of the planet, therefore, is how much change it takes to release disturbances whose intensity and extent are so great that the renewal capital is destroyed to the point where regeneration of plants is seriously compromised. Thus, two sets of questions need to be addressed in order to assess the sustainability of development. First, how much disturbance will be generated, for how long, and over what areas? Second, how much renewal capital is destroyed, for how long, and over what areas?

That still leaves open the question of what specific kinds of renewal capital are the measure of sustainability. Is it the number of trees as the new resource economists suggest? But why should trees be the only future permitted? Is it the struc-

ture of soils that, if retained, allows a number of different kinds of ecosystem to flourish, with trees or not? Is it the mosaic of architectural features that maintains the diversity of habitats and species? I cannot comfortably answer these questions, but I can identify a direction in which to search for the answers.

Two puzzles of sustainability

Recently, I resolved two difficult puzzles that had emerged during a review of some twenty-three examples of managed ecosystems (Holling 1986). Those examples fell into four classes: forest insect, forest fire, savanna grazing, and aquatic harvesting. One puzzle seemed to be a paradox of the organization of ecosystems. The other seemed to be a paradox of the management of ecosystems. Both have turned out to be the consequence of the natural workings of any complex, evolving system.

The first paradox suggested that the great diversity of life in ecosystems is traceable to the function of a small set of variables, each operating at a qualitatively different speed from the others. The second suggested that any attempt to manage ecological variables inexorably leads to more brittle ecosystems, more rigid management institutions, and more dependent societies. I shall deal with each in turn.

The ecosystem organization puzzle

How could the great diversity within ecosystems possibly be traced to the function of a small number of variables? The models that were developed and tested for these examples certainly generated complex behavior in space and time. Moreover, those complexities could be traced to the actions and interactions of only three to four sets of variables and associated processes, each of which operated at distinctly different speeds. The speeds were therefore discontinuously distributed and differed from their neighbors often by as much as an order of magnitude. A summary of the critical structuring variables and their speeds are presented in table 4-1. For the models, at least, this structure organizes the time and space behavior of variables into a small number of cycles, presumably abstracted from a larger set that continues at smaller and larger scales than the range selected.

But are those features simply the consequence of the way modelers make decisions rather than the results of an ecosystem's organization? This uneasy feeling that such conclusions can be a figment of the way we think, rather than of the way ecosystems function, led to a series of tests using field data to challenge the hypothesis that ecosystem dynamics are organized around the operation of a small number of nested cycles, each driven by a few dominant variables.

The critical argument is that, if there are, in fact, only a few structuring processes, their imprint should be expressed on most variables. That is, time-series data for fires, intensity of seeding, number of insects, flow of water—indeed any variable for which long-term, yearly records are available—should show periodicities that cluster around a few dominant ones. In the case of the eastern maritime boreal forest of North America, for example, those periodicities were predicted to be three to five years, ten to fifteen years, thirty-five to forty years, and more than eighty years. Similarly, a few dominant spatial "footprint" sizes should be associated with one of the cycles of disturbance and renewal in the nested set of such cycles. Finally, the animals living in specific landscapes should demonstrate the existence of this lumpy architecture by showing gaps in the distribution of their sizes and gaps in the scales at which decisions are made for location of region, foraging area, habitat, nests, protection, and food.

All the evidence we have so far confirms just those hypotheses for boreal forests, for boreal region prairies, for pelagic ecosystems (Holling 1992), and for the Everglades of Florida (Gunderson 1992). Various alternative hypotheses based on developmental, historical, or trophic arguments were disproved in the fine traditions of Popperian science, leaving only the world-is-lumpy hypothesis as resisting disproof.

Therefore, there is strong evidence for the following conclusions:

(1) A small number of plant, animal, and abiotic processes structure biomes over scales from days and centimeters to millennia and thousands of kilometers. Individual plant and biogeochemical processes dominate at fine, fast scales; animal and abiotic processes of meso-scale disturbance dominate at intermediate scales; and geomorphological ones dominate at coarse, slow scales.

(2) These structuring processes produce a landscape that has lumpy geometry and lumpy temporal frequencies or periodicities. That is, the physical architecture and the speed of variables are organized into distinct clusters or quanta, each of which is controlled by one small set of structuring processes. These processes organize behavior as a nested hierarchy of cycles of slow production and growth alternating with fast disturbance and renewal (as shown in figure 4-1).

(3) Each quantum is contained to a particular range of scales in space and time and has its own distinct architecture of object sizes, distance between objects, and fractal dimension within that range.

(4) All of the many remaining variables, other than those involved in the structuring processes, become entrained by the critical structuring variables, so that the great diversity of species in ecosystems can be traced to the function of a small set of variables and the niches they provide. The structuring processes are the ones that both form structure and are affected by that structure. These structuring variables are, therefore, where the priority should be placed in investing to protect biodiversity.

(5) The discontinuities that produce the lumpy structure of vegetated landscapes impose discontinuities on the behavior and morphology of animals. For example, gaps in the distri-

Table 4-1: Key Variables and Speeds in Five Groups of Managed Ecosystems

System	Fast	Intermediate	Slow
Forest insect	Insect, needles	Foliage crown	Trees
Forest fire	Intensity	Fuel	Trees
Savanna	Annual grasses	Perennial grasses	Shrubs
Aquatic	Phytoplankton	Zooplankton	Fish

Source: The key references are McNamee, McLeod, and Holling 1981 for forest insects; Holling 1980 for forest fires; Walker and others 1969 for annual grasses; and Steele 1985 for phytoplankton.

bution of body mass of resident species of animals correlate with scale-dependent discontinuities in the geometry of vegetated landscapes. Thus these gaps, and the body mass clumps they define, become a way to develop a rapid bioassay of ecosystem structures and of human impacts on that structure. This opens the way to develop a comparative ecology across scales that might provide the same power for generalization that came when physiology became comparative rather than species specific.

(6) Conversely, changes in landscape structure at defined ranges of scale caused by land use practice or by changes in climate will have predictable impacts on the community structure of animals (that is, animals of some body masses can disappear if an ecosystem's structure at a predictable range of scale is changed). Therefore predicted (using models) or observed (using remote imagery) impacts of changing climate or land use on vegetation can also be used to infer the impacts on the diversity of animal communities.

The lessons for both sustainable development and biodiversity are clear: focus should be placed on the structuring variables that control the lumpy geometry and lumpy time dynamics. They are the ones that set the stage upon which other variables play out their own dramas. That is, the health and viability of the physical and temporal infrastructure of biomes at all scales are what sustains the theater; given that, the actors will look after themselves!

The ecosystem management puzzle

An even more surprising and puzzling feature emerged in the comparison of the twenty-three examples. All the examples were associated with management of a resource where the very success of management seemed to set the condition for collapse. Is there some general property of unsustainability that is touched in these examples, or is the observation simply the result of cases selected because of an unconscious attraction to catastrophic visions? Again, some independent tests were necessary.

Each of the examples represented policies of management whose goal was to control a target variable in order to achieve social objectives, typically maintaining or stimulating employment and

economic activity. In the case of management of eastern North American spruce and fir forests, the target was an anticipated outbreak of a defoliating insect, the spruce budworm (Clark and others 1979); for the forests of the Sierra Nevada Mountains, the target was forest fires (Holling 1980); for the savannas of South Africa, the target was the grazing of cattle (Walker and others 1969); for the salmon of the Pacific northwest coast, the target was salmon populations (Walters 1986).

In each case the goal was to control the variability of the target: insects and fire at low levels, cattle grazing at intermediate stocking densities, and salmon at high populations. The level desired was different in each situation, but the common feature was to reduce variability of a target whose normal fluctuations imposed problems and periodic crises for pulp mill employment, recreation, farming incomes, or fishermen's catch.

The typical response to threats of fire or pestilence, flood, or drought is to narrow the purpose, focus on it exclusively, and solve that problem as so defined. Modern engineering, technological, economic, and administrative experience can deal well with such narrowly defined problems. And in each example, the goal was successfully achieved: insects were controlled with insecticide; the frequency and extent of fires were reduced with fire detection and suppression techniques; cattle grazing was managed with modern rangeland practice; and salmon populations were augmented with hatchery production.

At the same time, however, elements of the system were slowly changing. First, reducing the variability of the ecological target produced a slow change in the spatial heterogeneity of the ecosystem. Forest architecture became more contiguous over landscape scales, so that if defoliating insects or fire were released, the outbreaks could cover larger areas with more intensive impacts than before management. Rangeland gradually lost drought-resistant grasses because of a shift in competition with more productive but more drought-sensitive grasses. If drought occurred, the consequences were therefore more extensive, more extreme, and more persistent: grasslands turned irreversibly into shrub-dominated semi-deserts. Wild populations of salmon in the many streams along the coast gradually became extinct because fishing pressure increased in response to the increased populations achieved by enhancement. That left the fishing industry precariously dependent on a few hatcheries whose productivity declined with time.

In short, the success in controlling an ecological variable that normally fluctuated led to more spatially homogenized ecosystems over landscape scales. It led to systems more likely to flip into a persistent degraded state, triggered by disturbances that previously could be absorbed. Management successfully froze each system in the conservation stage of the cycle of growth and production, disturbance, and renewal (box 2 of figure 4-1), thereby making each system a larger and larger accident waiting to happen.

Those changes in the ecosystems could be managed if it were not for concomitant changes in two other elements of the interrelationships: in the management institution(s) and in the people in the society who reaped the benefits or endured the costs. Because of the initial success, in each case the management agencies shifted their objectives from the original social and ecological ones to the laudable objective of improving operational efficiency of the agency itself: spraying insects, fighting fires, producing beef, and releasing hatchery fish with as much efficiency and with the least cost possible. Efforts to monitor the ecosystem for surprises rather than for product therefore withered in competition with internal organizational needs, and research funds were shifted to more operational purposes. Why monitor or study a success? Thus the gradual reduction of resilience of the ecosystems was unseen by any but maverick and suspect academics!

Success brought changes in the society, as well. Dependencies developed for continuing, sustained flow of the food or fiber that no longer fluctuated as it once had. More investments therefore logically flowed to expanding pulp mills, recreational facilities, cattle ranches, and fishing technology. That is the development side of the equation, and its expansion can be rightly applauded. Improving the efficiency of agencies should also be applauded. But if, at the same time, the ecosystem from which resources are garnered becomes more and more brittle, more and more sensitive to large-scale transformation, then the efficient but myopic agency and the productive but dependent industry simply become part of the source of crisis and decision gridlock.

So there is the paradox: success in managing a target variable for sustained production of food or fiber apparently leads to an ultimate pathology of more brittle and vulnerable ecosystems, more rigid and unresponsive management agencies, and more dependent societies. That seems to confirm one opinion that sustainable development is an oxymoron.

But something seems to be inherently wrong with that conclusion, implying, as it does, that the only solution is a radical return of humanity to being "children of nature." The argument is based on two critical points. One is that reduced variability of ecosystems inevitably leads to reduced resilience and increased vulnerability. The second is that there is, in principle, no different way for agencies and people to manage and benefit from the development of resources.

Again some independent evidence is needed. Are there counter examples? Oddly, nature itself provides counter examples of tightly regulated yet viable systems in the many cases of physiological homeostasis. Consider temperature regulation of endotherms (warm-blooded animals), for example, which represents a system where internal body temperature is not only tightly regulated within a narrow band, but at an average temperature perilously close to lethal. Moreover, the costs of achieving that regulation require ten times the energy for metabolism than is required by an ectotherm. That would seem to be a recipe for disaster, and a very inefficient one at that. Yet evolution somehow led to the extraordinary success of the animals having such an adaptation: the birds and mammals.

In order to test the generality of the hypothesis of variability loss/resilience loss, I have been collecting data from the physiological literature on the viable temperature range of the internal body for organisms exposed to different classes of variability. The data are organized into three groups ranging from terrestrial ectotherms (cold-blooded animals) exposed to the greatest variability of temperature from unbuffered ambient conditions, to aquatic endotherms exposed to an intermediate level of variability because of the moderating attributes of water, to endotherms that regulate temperature within a narrow band. As predicted, the viable range of internal body temperature decreases from about 40°C for the most variable group to about 30°C for the intermediate, to 20°C for the tightly regulated endotherms. Resilience, in this case the range of temperatures that separates life from death, clearly does contract as experience with variability is reduced. Therefore, reducing the variability of living systems from organisms to ecosystems inevitably leads to loss of resilience.

But that seems to leave an even starker paradox of control inevitably leading to collapse. But, in fact, endothermy does persist and therefore serves as a revealing metaphor for sustainable development. This metaphor contains two features that were not evident in my earlier descriptions of examples of resource management.

First, the kind of regulation is different. Five different mechanisms, from evaporative cooling to the generation of metabolic heat, control the temperature of endotherms. Each mechanism is not notably efficient by itself. Each operates over a somewhat different range of conditions and with different efficiencies of response. It is this overlapping "soft" redundancy that seems to characterize biological regulation of all kinds. It is not notably efficient or elegant in the engineering sense, but it is robust and continually sensitive to changes in internal body temperature. That is quite unlike the examples of regulation by management where goals of operational efficiency gradually isolate the regulating agency from the things it is regulating.

Second, endothermy is a true innovation that explosively released opportunity for the organisms evolving it. Maintaining high body temperature—short of death—allows the greatest range of external activity for an animal. Speed and stamina increase, and activity can be maintained at both high and low external temperatures. A range of habitats forbidden to an endotherm is open to an ectotherm. The evolutionary consequence of temperature regulation was suddenly to open opportunity for dramatic organizational change and the adaptive radiation of new life-forms. Variability was therefore not eliminated. It was reduced and transferred from the animal's internal environment to its external one, as a consequence of the continual probes of the whole animal for opportunity and change. Hence the price of reducing internal resilience and maintaining high metabolic levels was more than offset by that creation of evolutionary opportunity.

Surely the release of human opportunity is at the heart of sustainable development! It requires flexible, diverse, and redundant regulation, monitoring that leads to corrective responses, and experimental probing of the continually changing reality of the external world. Those are the features of adaptive environmental and resource management (Holling 1978; Walters 1986). Those are the features missing in the descriptions of traditional, piecemeal, exploitive resource management and its ultimate pathology.

In fact, that is what eventually happened in at least one of the examples quoted. In New Brunswick, the intensifying gridlock in forest management, combined with slowly accumulated and communicated understanding of the integrated nature of the ecological, industrial, and social interrelationships, led to an abrupt transformation of policy whose attributes became much like those just described (Baskerville, forthcoming). It is a policy that functions for a whole region by transforming and monitoring the smaller-scale stand architecture of the landscape and by focusing the productive capacities of industry.

There is even the suspicion, in these examples of regional resource management, that institutions and society themselves achieve periodic advances in understanding and learning through the same four-box cycle of growth and production, release, and renewal that shapes the spatial and temporal dynamics of ecosystems. But each proceeds at its own pace and in its own space, and that creates extraordinary conflicts when ecosystems, institutions, and societies function on scales that are extremely mismatched. If the scale of all three becomes more congruent, it is likely that the inevitable bursts of human learning can proceed with less conflict and more creativity.

Conclusions

This chapter has used metaphors and paradoxes to provide some insight into what sustainable development is and what measures its properties. The ecosystem metaphor led to the conclusion that there is a cycle of slow growth and production that triggers fast disturbance and renewal. The slow growth and production phase accumulates natural capital. It is analogous to the processes of what we call development.

The fast disturbance and renewal phase releases bound and constrained capital and reorganizes it to reestablish the ecosystem cycle. It is analogous to the conditions of what we call sustainability, and it is the phase where diversity is maintained. Therefore sustainability is measured by some attributes of disturbance and renewal, and development is measured by some attributes of growth and production.

A paradox helps clarify the specific attributes that determine sustainability of an ecosystem. The paradox is that a few simple processes seem to generate the great complexity and diversity within ecosystems. Ecosystems are hierarchically structured into a number of levels. Relatively few processes determine this structure, and each imposes distinct frequencies in space and time on the ecosystem over different ranges of scale. They entrain all other variables.

Hence both sustainability and biodiversity are determined by the structuring variables of disturbance and renewal that control the lumpy geometry and lumpy time dynamics. To use another metaphor, they set the stage on which other variables play out their own dramas. The health and viability of the physical and temporal infrastructure of biomes at all scales sustain the theater; given that, the actors will look after themselves!

A second paradox suggests that many existing examples of management of renewable resources have led inexorably to more brittle ecosystems, more rigid management institutions, and more dependent societies. Its resolution comes from another biological metaphor of regulation: that of homeostatic regulation of body temperature in endotherms. Indeed, successful control of variability there does reduce resilience within the system regulated. But, unlike the pathology of management noted, the regulation responds to internal change and is robust. It transfers internal variability externally to release opportunity for probing, creative opportunities.

The release of human opportunity is at the heart of sustainable development! It requires flexible, diverse, and redundant regulation, monitoring that leads to corrective responses, and experimental probing of the continually changing reality of the external world.

Finally, sustainable development is not an ecological problem nor a social problem nor an economic problem. It is an integrated feature of all three. Effective investments in sustainable development simultaneously retain and encourage the adaptive capabilities of people, of business (enterprises), and of nature. The effectiveness of those adaptive capabilities can turn the same unexpected event (for example, drought, change in price, shifts in market) into an opportunity for one system or a crisis for another. Those adaptive capacities depend on processes that permit renewal in society, economies, and ecosystems. For nature, it is the structure of the biosphere; for businesses and people, it is usable knowledge; and for society as a whole, it is trust.

We may postulate that investments to increase productivity are only viable if all these sources of renewal capacity are maintained or enhanced. Temporary erosion of these might be bearable so long as recovery is made within the critical time unit of half a human generation (note the relation to intergenerational equity and freedoms of choice). But continued erosion of any one ultimately reaches the point where it cannot be re-versed by normal, internal recovery. That state is the condition defined as poverty, a condition of inability to cope.

References

Allen, T. F. H., and T. B. Starr. 1982. *Hierarchy: Perspectives for Ecological Complexity*. Chicago, Ill.: University of Chicago Press.

Baskerville, G. L. Forthcoming. "The Forestry Problem." In L. H. Gunderson, C. S. Holling, and S. S. Light, eds., *Barriers and Bridges for the Renewal of Regional Ecosystems*.

Bormann, F. H., and G. E. Likens. 1981. *Patterns and Process in a Forested Ecosystem*. New York: Springer-Verlag.

Clark, W. C., and others. 1979. "Lessons for Ecological Policy Design: A Case Study of Ecosystem Management." *Ecological Modelling* 7, pp. 1–53.

Davis, M. B. 1986. "Climatic Instability, Time Lags, and Community Disequilibrium." In J. Diamond and T. Case, eds., *Community Ecology*, pp. 269–85. New York: Harper and Row.

Delcourt, H. R., P. A. Delcourt, and T. I. Webb. 1983. "Dynamic Plant Ecology: The Spectrum of Vegetational Change in Space and Time." *Quaternary Science Reviews* 1, pp. 153–75.

Elliott, J. E. 1980. "Marx and Schumpeter on Capitalism's Creative Destruction: A Comparative Restatement." *Quarterly Journal of Economics* 95, pp. 46–58.

Gunderson, L. H. 1992. "Spatial and Temporal Hierarchies in the Everglades Ecosystem with Implications for Water Management." Ph.D. diss., University of Florida, Gainesville, Fla.

Holling, C. S. 1980. "Forest Insects, Forest Fires, and Resilience." In H. Mooney, J. M. Bonnicksen, N. L. Christensen, J. E. Lotan, and W. A. Reiners, eds., *Fire Regimes and Ecosystem Properties*. General Technical Report WO-26. Washington, D.C.: U.S. Department of Agriculture Forest Service.

———. 1986. "Resilience of Ecosystems: Local Surprise and Global Change." In W. C. Clark and R. E. Munn, eds., *Sustainable Development of the Biosphere*, pp. 292–317. Cambridge, England: Cambridge University Press.

———. 1987. "Simplifying the Complex: The Paradigms of Ecological Function and Structure." *European Journal of Operational Research* 30, pp. 139–46.

———. 1988. "Temperate Forest Insect Outbreaks, Tropical Deforestation, and Migratory Birds." *Memoirs of the Entomological Society of Canada* 146, pp. 21–32.

———. 1992. "Cross-scale Morphology, Geometry, and Dynamics of Ecosystems." *Ecological Monographs* 62:4, pp. 447–502.

Holling, C. S., ed. 1978. *Adaptive Environmental Assessment and Management.* London: John Wiley and Sons.

Lovelock, J. 1988. *The Ages of Gaia.* New York: W. W. Norton and Co.

McNamee, P. J., J. M. McLeod, and C. S. Holling. 1981. "The Structure and Behavior of Defoliating Insect/Forest Systems." *Research in Population Ecology* 23, pp. 280–98.

O'Neill, R. V., D. L. DeAngelis, J. B. Waide, and T. F. H. Allen. 1986. *A Hierarchical Concept of Ecosystems.* Princeton, N.J.: Princeton University Press.

Steele, J. H. 1985. "A Comparison of Terrestrial and Marine Systems." *Nature* 313, pp. 355–58.

Vitousek, Peter M., and P. A. Matson. 1984. "Mechanisms of Nitrogen Retention in Forest Ecosystems: A Field Experiment." *Science* 225, pp. 51–52.

Walker, B. H. 1981. "Is Succession a Viable Concept in African Savanna Ecosystems?" In D. C. West, H. H. Shugart, and D. B. Botkin, eds., *Forest Succession: Concepts and Application*, pp. 431–47. New York: Springer-Verlag.

Walker, B. H., D. Ludwig, C. S. Holling, and R. M. Peterman. 1969. "Stability of Semi-arid Savanna Grazing Systems." *Journal of Ecology* 69, pp. 473–98.

Walters, C. J. 1986. *Adaptive Management of Renewable Resources.* New York: McGraw Hill.

West, D. C., H. H. Shugart, and D. B. Botkin. 1981. *Forest Succession: Concepts and Application.* New York: Springer-Verlag.

5

Cumulative Effects and Sustainable Development

Gordon Beanlands

Preventing the slow, persistent, and cumulative degradation of natural systems resulting from human activity is the ultimate environmental challenge facing society. Although a concise definition is open to debate, the term cumulative effects is generally considered to refer to the long-term accumulation of residual environmental changes resulting from all previous developmental actions. Conceptually it is easier to consider cumulative effects as a second-order set of problems, or a problem syndrome.

The problem of cumulative effects has been recognized for many years and is, explicitly or implicitly, at the root of most concepts of environmental conservation, protection, and management. For example, according to Orians (1986, p. 2), "Management of renewable resources is basically cumulative effects management." Over the last ten to fifteen years, however, the problem of cumulative effects has become a major focus of attention for applied natural scientists, environmental managers, and policymakers. This attention has been reflected in a number of scientific and management conferences devoted specifically to the problems of cumulative effects (CEARC and National Research Council 1986; Conservation Foundation 1990; Estevez and others 1986; Williamson, Armour, and Johnston 1985).

The number of publications on cumulative effects has also grown rapidly, increasing from less than five papers a year between 1975 and 1980 to an average of twenty-four a year between 1985 and 1988 (Williamson and Hamilton 1989). Several bibliographies on cumulative effects have been published recently, containing in excess of 150 references (Davies 1991; Delcan Corporation 1988; Williamson and Hamilton 1989).

This increased attention is related in part to publicity given to rates of loss or deterioration of resources of the global commons. For example, the general public has a better understanding of how multiple human activities, spread over space and time, have resulted in cumulative problems of change in climate, ozone depletion, acid rain, groundwater contamination, species extinction, and habitat fragmentation.

More and more of the professional community is realizing that the cumulative aspects of the more serious environmental problems account for the difficulty in developing viable solutions. For example, two informal surveys of the most pressing problems of cumulative effects facing society resulted in the following lists:

Williamson, Armor, and Johnston (1985)

- Multiple small hydro dams
- Flood control projects
- Coastal wetlands development
- Wetlands drainage
- Hazardous waste disposal
- Nutrient loading (estuaries)
- Dredging of waterways
- Urbanization of farmland
- Air pollution and acid rain
- Eutrophication of lakes
- Nonpoint soil erosion

Peterson and others (1987)

- Acidic precipitation
- Urban air quality
- Bioaccumulation of toxins
- Climatic change
- Spread of infrastructure
- Loss and fragmentation of habitat
- Erosion and degradation of soil
- Agricultural chemicals
- Loss and degradation of groundwater
- Changes in freshwater
- Increased harvest rates

This increased awareness of cumulative environmental effects on the part of the general public and professional communities has been reflected in a growing number of statutes requiring the assessment of cumulative effects. For example, a recent survey of federal laws in the United States discovered that the terms cumulative impacts or cumulative effects appear seventeen times in ten statutes, and the term cumulative impacts appears in sixty-one sets of regulations (Conservation Foundation 1990). In addition, the recently passed Canadian Environmental Assessment Act requires that cumulative effects be considered in various stages of the environmental review process including screening, comprehensive study, assessment, and mitigation (Canadian House of Commons 1992).

Not surprisingly, consideration of the ultimate implications of cumulative environmental changes at the global level was among the factors that led the World Commission on Environment and Development to promote the concept of sustainable development (WCED 1987). In other words, the challenge of sustainable development includes arresting or reversing the cumulative depletion and degradation of the natural systems on which current and future generations depend. On a world scale, cumulative effects and sustainable development are inextricably linked, reflecting the mega environmental problem and the mega environmental solution, respectively.

This chapter highlights the evolution of the concept and practice of cumulative effects as a specific subset of environmental change and draws comparisons with the policymaking and decisionmaking implications related to sustainable development.

Definitions, concepts, and approaches

Numerous attempts have been made to define cumulative effects or impacts. One of the earliest and most influential definitions was developed in 1978 by the U.S. Council on Environmental Quality (CEQ 1978, 40 C.F.R., sect. 1508.7) under regulations made pursuant to the National Environmental Policy Act:

> The impact on the environment which results from the incremental impact of the action when added to other past, present, and reasonably foreseeable future actions regardless of what agency (Federal or non-Federal) or person undertakes such actions. Cumulative impacts can result from individually minor but collectively significant actions taking place over a period of time.

Clark (1986, p. 114) offered the following commentary on cumulative impact assessment, which incorporates a working definition of cumulative effects:

> Cumulative impact assessment examines the consequences of multiple sources of environmental disturbance that impinge on the same valued environmental component. The characteristic "multiple" nature of the sources of cumulative impacts may arise in three ways: the same kind of source recurs sufficiently frequently through time, the same kind of source recurs sufficiently densely through space, different kinds of sources impose similar consequences on a valued environmental component.

Peterson and others (1987, p. 5) considered cumulative effects to occur when "at least one of two circumstances prevails: persistent addition of material, a force, or an effect from a single source at a rate greater than can be dissipated; or compounding effects as a result of the coming together of two or more materials, forces, or effects, which individually may not be cumulative."

Perhaps the most succinct definition of cumulative effects is offered by the Canadian Environmental Assessment Research Council (CEARC 1988, p. 2):

> Cumulative effects occur when impacts on the natural and social environments take place so frequently in time or so densely in

space that the effects of individual "insults" cannot be assimilated, or the impacts of one activity combine with those of another in a synergistic manner.

Individually, these impacts may not be qualitatively different from environmental effects associated with single-project developments, but collectively they often require different kinds of research and management approaches if they are to be dealt with effectively.

These definitions, and others, require that cumulative changes be interpreted within specified time, space, and organizational scales. It is the expanded nature of these scales that separates cumulative effects from the more limited time periods and geographical boundaries used in addressing the effects of single projects. Critical scientific and management factors must be taken into account to ensure that cumulative effects are considered within the appropriate context of time and space. For example, ecological time lags may require that cumulative effects be monitored over extended periods, while jurisdictional boundaries may be the priority concern from a management perspective.

In general, these considerations support the adoption of an approach to managing cumulative effects based on at least a regional level (watershed, municipality, and so forth) and extending over a period of years. Therefore, although scientists may be tempted to study the cumulative changes over time in well-bounded ecosystems (lakes, wetlands, estuaries), managing the multiple sources of stress on those systems effectively requires a much broader geographic coverage. This need to link the scientific and management aspects in efforts to resolve the problems of cumulative effects was the major theme of an international symposium held in 1986 (CEARC and National Research Council 1986).

Perhaps the complexity inherent in the concept of cumulative effects has been responsible for the proliferation of methodologies, techniques, and approaches developed to address the issues involved. Some of these are merely extensions of techniques to assess environmental impact developed to meet legislative requirements. In other cases, it is often difficult to distinguish methods for identifying, evaluating, and managing cumulative effects from the basic principles involved in regional planning, river basin planning, and integrated resource management. Such overlap is

symptomatic of the continuum in environmental planning, which extends from project-based impact assessments, to policy and program assessments, to cumulative effects assessment, to regional planning, to sustainable development.

A review of two recent bibliographies on cumulative effects (Davies 1991; Williamson and Hamilton 1989) indicated that 20 to 30 percent of the publications listed offered some form of guidance (procedure, approach, handbook, framework, technique, methodology, or model) on conducting cumulative effects assessments. The general utility of such guidance, however, may be open to question. For example, Granholm and others (1987), after screening more than ninety methods, concluded that most were good at describing problems but performed poorly when it came to analysis and evaluation.

Nevertheless, the scientific and management communities have developed and tested a number of approaches designed specifically to increase our understanding of and ability to manage cumulative effects. These initiatives can be grouped according to whether they are (a) generic in focus, (b) driven by regulatory requirements, or (c) in response to threatened or vulnerable resources.

Generic focus

Bain and others (1986) propose a general methodology for evaluating the cumulative effects of multiple human developments. It consists of three phases: analysis, evaluation, and documentation. A unique aspect of this approach is its use of a computer screening process in the evaluation phase to compare and select developmental configurations.

Sonntag and others (1986) have developed an analytical framework for assessing cumulative impacts. The framework involves determining the interactions between three main components: activities (classified according to project characteristics), system structure and process (the nature of the receiving system), and cumulative impacts (determined through a step-wise analysis).

Lane and others (1988) present a comprehensive framework for assessing cumulative effects. It begins with a decision tree to distinguish among four types of cumulative effects. This is followed by characterization of the type of causality involved. The entire process is guided by a sequential series of activities.

Regulatory focus

Under contract to the U.S. Army Corps of Engineers, INTASA Inc. developed a six-step procedure for assessing the regional cumulative impacts of developing hydropower. The procedure is based on the use of indexes that require few new data, are easily calculated, and can be used for comparisons between regions. The procedure has been applied to a number of river basins (INTASA Inc. 1981).

The U.S. Federal Energy Regulatory Commission has proposed a cluster impact assessment procedure for assessing the cumulative impacts of multiple small-scale hydroelectric developments on a single watershed (Emery 1986). The cumulative effects resulting from project clustering are first examined through sub-basin disaggregation and then dispersed across sub-basins using linear algebra and principles of information theory.

An analysis of potential cumulative effects is required before any oil or gas resources may be developed on wet tundra on the Alaskan North Slope. In response to this requirement, the U.S. Fish and Wildlife Service has developed a method using an integrated geobotanical and historical disturbance map for predicting and evaluating cumulative impacts. This method is based on a landscape approach and uses maps produced by the oil industry for operational purposes (Walker and others 1986).

Focus on vulnerable resources

Under an agreement with the U.S. Environmental Protection Agency, the U.S. Fish and Wildlife Service conducted a series of workshops on bottomland hardwood wetlands that produced a methodology for assessing cumulative impact (Gosselink and Lee 1988). The methodology applies the landscape approach of island biogeography to the fragmentation and loss of habitat. The key hypothesis is that individual features are not as important as the overall pattern in the formulation of conservation measures.

Weaver, Escano, and Winn (1987) describe a cumulative effects assessment model for application in the management of grizzly bears. It is designed to quantify individual and collective effects of various land uses and activities in space and time and to provide managers with an analytical tool for evaluating alternative decisions relative to the conservation of grizzly bears.

Even this brief sample shows that the methodology for assessing cumulative effects has a short history, both in its development and in its implementation. Federal government agencies, driven by the need to meet regulations, have been responsible for most of the supportive research and trial applications. It is a complex topic that crosses over numerous fields of study in the natural, social, and managerial sciences, and its boundaries are difficult to set. For this reason, substantive progress in a practical sense has been slow.

Bodies of water, particularly wetlands, act as natural collection and disposal systems; in the words of Preston and Bedard (1988, p. 577), they "can be viewed as a series of flow-through reaction vessels." It is perhaps for this reason, along with the fact that they are relatively easy to bound, that they have been the predominant focus of attention for cumulative effects assessment. Such is the case from regulatory, management, and scientific perspectives. In fact, the professional *Journal of Environmental Management* devoted an entire issue (vol. 12, 1988) to all aspects of cumulative impacts on wetland ecosystems. Thus, the evolution of our concepts and the growth of our empirical evidence concerning this complex phenomenon are largely based on the study of rivers, lakes, wetlands, and estuaries. Since terrestrial systems are more heterogeneous, and arguably more vulnerable to direct human intervention, the experience with water ecosystems may not be directly transferable.

Based on this brief overview, some parallels can be drawn between cumulative effects and sustainable development. First, they both lack precise definitions, which has resulted in much confusion over basic objectives and operating paradigms. Second, in both cases, researchers and managers need to think laterally, across a number of disciplines, in order to gain a comprehensive understanding of the concepts involved, which few are trained to do. Third, in both cases it is difficult to establish practical operational boundaries, with the result that managers are overwhelmed by the sense that "everything is connected to everything else." Finally, for both cumulative effects and sustainable development, our intuitive understanding of the concepts involved is much more advanced than our ability to apply that knowledge in a meaningful and practical manner.

Cumulative effects: A specific type of change

Why is change associated with cumulative effects different than other types of environmental change? There are two main reasons: the direction and rate of change. First, all environmental variables, whether physical or biological, change naturally over time but tend to fluctuate within some long-term envelope of stability. In other words, they appear to be in some form of dynamic equilibrium. In the case of cumulative effects, however, the implication is that change in the variable of concern is unidirectional and that no counterbalancing forces are at play. It may be, of course, that the observed change is merely a small part of a very long natural cycle, which is the counter argument to the assertion of global warming. In other cases, however, such as the increasing acidity of precipitation and the gradual accumulation of toxic chemicals in groundwater aquifers, the changes are clearly induced by humans.

Implicit in the concern over the unidirectional change of cumulative effects is that the variable in question is moving in relation to some norm, limit, standard, or threshold value. If there is no stated or implied threshold, then monitoring the change is of academic interest only, in the sense that it will not precipitate any concern. In the context of cumulative effects, it is not necessary that thresholds be established, or even known,

only that they be perceived to exist. Such is the case, for example, with the gradual depletion of the ozone layer, where experts cannot give a quantitative threshold of concern but are worried about the health implications of a continuing decline.

The focus of attention in studies of cumulative effects appears to be split between recording gradual changes and deciding on appropriate thresholds. In cases where thresholds are not a concern, there seems to be an interest in recording cumulative effects for some future reference. An example of this archival approach is the recent report on the state of the environment in Canada (Canadian Ministry of Supply and Services 1991). This large volume consists almost exclusively of graphs and tables, with explanatory text, depicting cumulative changes in a wide variety of environmental and natural resources. Examples include concentrations of mercury in fish, breeding populations of ducks on the western prairies, growth rates for maple trees, concentrations of various pollutants in air, concentrations of nitrite and nitrate in the Great Lakes, abundance of harbor seals, global mean surface air temperatures, and global emissions of carbon dioxide from the burning of fossil fuels (see figures 5-1 through 5-8). In all of these cases, a gradual but clearly established trend is evident over a period of at least ten years or more and, in some cases, decades.

Figure 5–1: Average Mercury Concentrations in Walleye Collected from Lake St. Claire, Canada, 1970–89

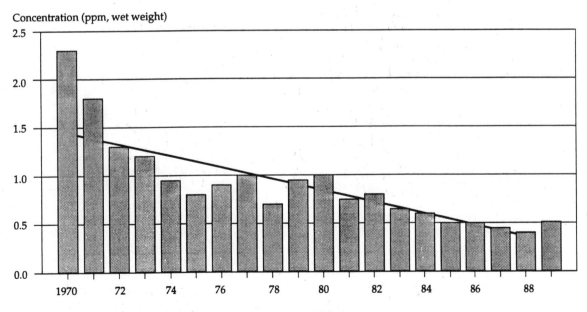

Concentration (ppm, wet weight)

Source: Canadian Ministry of Supply and Services 1991, p. 21-15.

Figure 5–2: Trends in the Size of Breeding Populations of Mallard and Northern Pintail in Western Canada, 1966–89

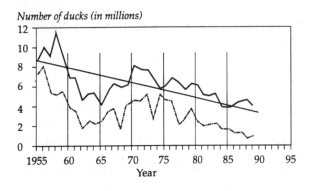

Number of ducks (in millions)
12
10
8
6
4
2
0
1955
60
65
70
75
80
85
90
95
Year
Northern Pintail
Mallard

Source: Canadian Ministry of Supply and Services 1991, p.6–18.

Figure 5–3: Growth of Sugar Maples in Areas of High, Moderate, and Low Levels of Atmospheric Pollution, 1900–90

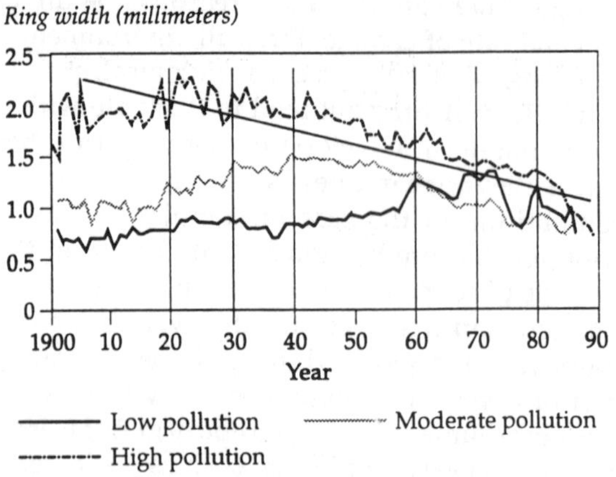

Ring width (millimeters)
2.5
2.0
1.5
1.0
0.5
0
1900
10
20
30
40
50
60
70
80
90
Year
Low pollution
Moderate pollution
High pollution

Source: Canadian Ministry of Supply and Services 1991, p. 24–11.

Figure 5–4: Trends in Canada's Air Quality, 1974–89

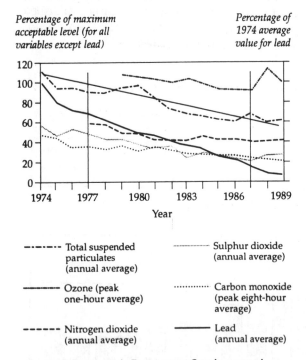

Percentage of maximum acceptable level (for all variables except lead)
Percentage of 1974 average value for lead
120
100
80
60
40
20
0
1974
1977
1980
1983
1986
1989
Year
Total suspended particulates (annual average)
Sulphur dioxide (annual average)
Ozone (peak one-hour average)
Carbon monoxide (peak eight-hour average)
Nitrogen dioxide (annual average)
Lead (annual average)

Source: T. Furmanczyk, Environment Canada, personal communication.

Figure 5–5: Abundance of Harbor Seals in British Columbia, Canada,1973–86

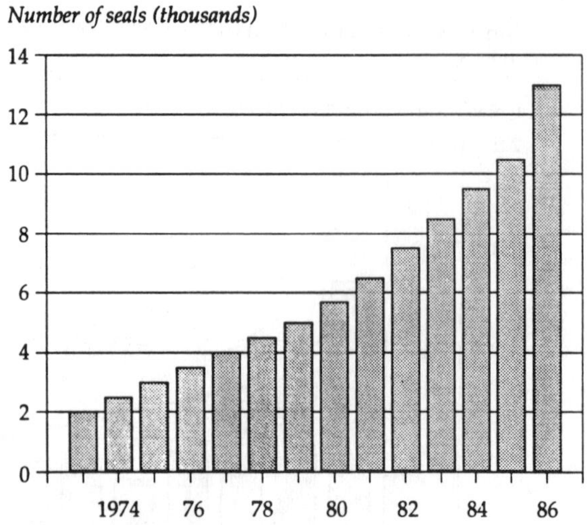

Number of seals (thousands)
14
12
10
8
6
4
2
0
1974
76
78
80
82
84
86

Source: Canadian Ministry of Supply and Services 1991, p. 8-17.

Figure 5–6: Concentrations of Nitrate and Nitrate in Parts per Billion e in the Open Waters of the Great Lakes, 1970–88

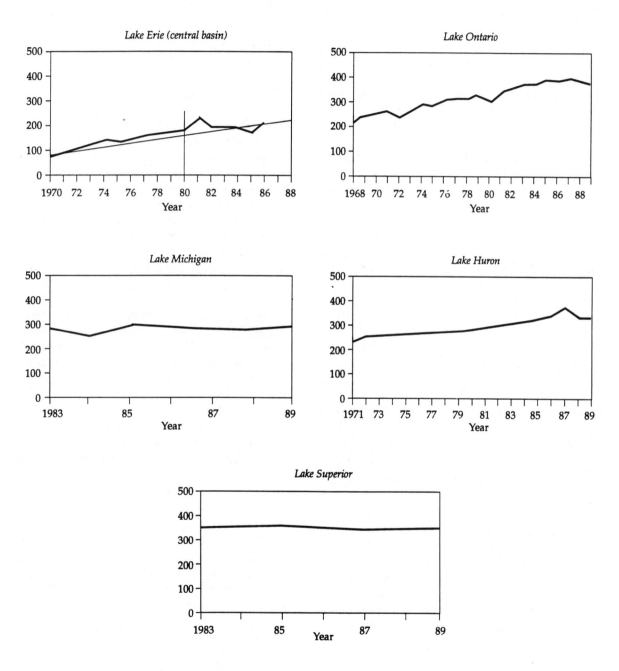

Source: Provided by Dave Dolan, International Joint Commission, Windsor.

Figure 5–7: Variation of Global Mean Surface Air Temperature in Canada, 1861–89

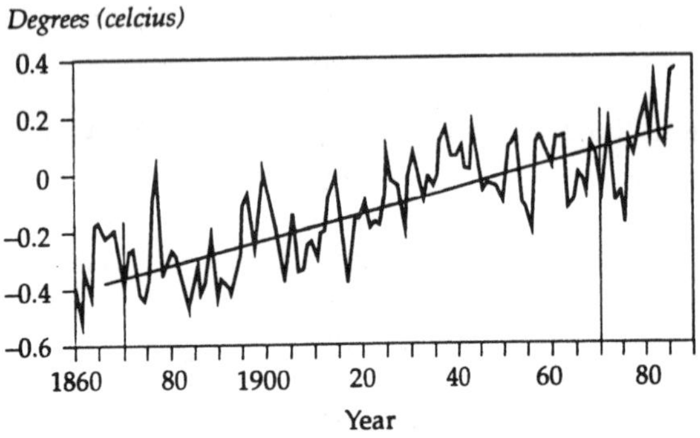

Degrees (celcius)

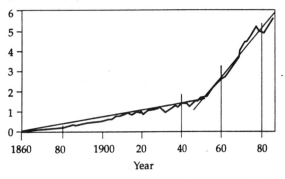

Source: Canadian Ministry of Supply and Services 1991, p. 22–12.

Figure 5–8: Global Emissions of Carbon Dioxide from the Burning of Fossil Fuels, 1860–1988

Emissions (billions of tonnes of carbon per year)

Source: Canadian Ministry of Supply and Services 1991, p. 2–21.

The second characteristic that distinguishes cumulative effects from other types of environmental variability is the rate of change. The term implies a slow rate, but how slow is slow? A cursory examination of the trends in the graphs of the Canadian *State of the Environment Report* (Canadian Ministry of Supply and Services 1991) provides some clues. In almost all cases, a fitted trend line represents an annual change of between 1 and 3 percent. This reference rate seems to apply equally as well to cumulative changes in human activities, for example, trends in air emissions, as it does to cumulative effects in natural variables. Such a rate of change appears to be readily observable—measurable—but not of a sufficient magnitude to warrant immediate corrective action, especially in situations where (a) thresh-

olds have not been established or (b) current levels are well separated from threshold values.

The Canadian publication gives examples of both positive cumulative effects, such as decreasing levels of pollution, and negative cumulative effects, such as declining populations of certain species. The reference rate of change of 1 to 3 percent a year appears to be valid in both situations. In other words, it may take as long for systems to recover following the removal of stressors as to be degraded following the onset of the stressors. Recovery is also a cumulative effect.

The decisionmaking dimension

The success of all approaches to environmental protection and management ultimately depends on the degree to which they influence relevant decisionmakers. The management of cumulative effects is no different. Cumulative effects lead to procrastination in decisionmaking. Since the rate of change is small and constant, there is a high degree of ambivalence as to exactly when corrective action is warranted. In general, the point at which decisions are taken—the decision flash point—is influenced by three main factors. The first is the nearness of the cumulative variable to a predetermined or implied threshold. As the variable approaches the threshold, the probability of remedial action being undertaken increases.

The experience with declining populations of Atlantic salmon in eastern Canada is an illustrative example. During the 1950s and 1960s spawning populations of Atlantic salmon in many rivers in eastern Canada exhibited a slow but constant decline. The change was the result of the cumulative effects of hydroelectric developments on the rivers, destruction of spawning habitat, widespread water pollution, and overfishing on the ocean feeding grounds. The declining trend had been known and monitored for many years by fisheries biologists, but no action had been taken to conserve the remaining stocks.

By the mid-1970s, the situation had, in the minds of some officials, become quite critical. A graph was prepared showing the cumulative decline in all east coast spawning stocks over the time period for which data were available. When the minister responsible for making a decision was shown that the extrapolated trend line indicated a likelihood that local populations would be totally extinct within a couple of decades, he was motivated to take action. In other words, in the mind of the key decisionmaker, the difference between the cumulative effects variable (salmon population) and the threshold (extinction of local populations) had been reduced to a point where intervention was required.

In this case the reluctance to take action was related to the political and financial costs involved. The initial decision eventually resulted in the government buying back salmon fishing licenses from hundreds of commercial fishermen at a cost of millions of dollars, as well as initiating a multi-faceted and long-term salmon enhancement program. To date, the populations have shown signs of recovery, but at a slower rate than expected by the scientists. This example illustrates the comprehensiveness of mitigation measures that are often required to reverse trends resulting from cumulative effects problems. It also demonstrates the need to make decisions at the highest levels of authority since the actions necessary to correct cumulative effects problems often require politically sensitive negotiations. In this case the scientists had been aware of the cumulative decline for some time but lacked the authority to make the required decisions.

The second factor influencing the decision point is related to the length of time between observations of trends. Repetitive readings over short periods of time reveal only small changes that may lead to a certain degree of complacency and acceptance. Infrequent measurements of the same variable that show relatively large incremental changes are more likely to have a shock value.

The third factor related to decisionmaking in the context of cumulative effects has to do with the rate of change of the variable in question. It was noted above that annual rates of change between 1 and 3 percent seem to be common to many trends that represent cumulative impacts. It was also postulated that, depending on threshold levels, such rates have a low probability of precipitating immediate corrective action. This raises the question as to whether there is, in a general sense, a rate of cumulative environmental change beyond which immediate concern is more likely to be generated.

Figure 5-8 provides some clues to answer this question. Before 1950 the average annual rate of increase in carbon dioxide emissions from the burning of fossil fuels was approximately 3 percent. As a result of increased industrialization following the end of World War II, the annual rate

of carbon dioxide emissions increased to approximately 5 percent. The continuation of this post-war rate raised concerns among atmospheric scientists that have led to international negotiations at the political level aimed at reducing the rate of carbon dioxide emissions on a global basis. Undoubtedly, the absolute concentration of carbon dioxide in the atmosphere—a quantitative threshold—influenced these developments; however, the abrupt change in the cumulative rate of change was probably also a contributing factor. In this case, an increase in the annual rate of change from 3 to 5 percent was sufficient to raise concerns and lead to action.

Comparing cumulative effects and sustainable development

As indicated, the management of cumulative effects and sustainable development share a number of similarities and linkages. These can be discussed under two headings: concepts and practice.

Concepts

Neither cumulative effects or sustainable development is well defined. Both are subject to vague meanings and disagreements among professionals over the nature and scope of the intended problematic. This lack of definition is both a strength and a weakness. In spite of the vagueness of the terms, both evoke an intuitive understanding of the complexity of the issues involved. Since they represent higher orders of aggregation of cause-and-effect relationships, they are conceptually robust enough to be applied to a wide variety of societal problems. Both concepts are inherently interdisciplinary in nature, which reflects the reality of dealing with the complex linkages among environmental, economic, cultural, and political issues.

It can be argued that both terms represent obverse intellectual traps. The term cumulative effects is an intuitively obvious way to state a problem, but it does not pose equally tractable solutions. The term sustainable development, in contrast, represents an intuitively obvious solution without providing insights into the fundamental nature of the problems. The former captures the essence of the ultimate environmental problem, and the latter promotes the formulation of the ultimate social solution.

Both concepts are firmly rooted in expanded scales of time, space, and organization. At the global level, they pose similar challenges for management and control. Many of the basic problems being addressed by sustainable development, such as climatic change, ozone depletion, loss of biodiversity, and accumulation of toxins, are examples of cumulative effects operating on a world scale. At this level of aggregation, both approaches have identical scale, boundary, and threshold characteristics and define problems and solutions in a similar way. The notion of intergenerational equity is germane to the definition of sustainable development but does not appear in the literature on cumulative effects. Yet the focus of study is on historical trends that often span more than one human generation. It is possible, therefore, to define the objective of cumulative effects management as ensuring that the variable of concern remains within its natural envelope of stability between generations. When stated in this way, the similarity between the two concepts is clearly evident.

Practice

So far, the concepts behind sustainable development and cumulative effects management have proven difficult to translate into practice. The expanded scales of time and space that underlie the concepts do not generally match the jurisdictional mandates of existing institutions. Even more important, the organizational and decisionmaking infrastructure required to manage and control human activities effectively at such scales has yet to be developed.

The legislative requirement to consider cumulative effects in many development applications has spurred scientific and management studies on this topic. Progress, however, is slow and experience is limited to controlling cumulative changes in relatively small and well-defined ecosystems or management units.

Most of the current effort going into sustainable development is intellectual in nature, focusing on refining concepts, definitions, and terminology. The first operational experiments will likely revolve around attempts to integrate environmental, economic, and social considerations in policy formulation. These are complex issues, and it will be some time before tangible results are available for review.

In the meantime, our experience in working at larger scales is limited to planning regions, watersheds, and coastal zones. These can be considered as rudimentary experiments in managing development at expanded scales of space and organization, although they usually lack the longer-term, strategic, intergenerational aspects of sustainable development and cumulative effects management. Given the complexity and comprehensiveness of the two approaches, it is not surprising that our record on implementation is so limited.

References

Bain, M. B., J. S. Irving, R. D. Olson, E. A. Stull, and G. W. Witmer. 1986. "Cumulative Impact Assessment: Evaluating the Environmental Effects of Multiple Human Developments." ANL/EES-TM-309. Argonne National Laboratory, Argonne, Ill.

CEARC (Canadian Environmental Assessment Research Council). 1988. "The Assessment of Cumulative Effects: A Research Prospectus." Ottawa, Canada.

CEARC and National Research Council. 1986. *Cumulative Environmental Effects: A Binational Perspective.* Proceedings of a workshop co-sponsored by the Canadian Environmental Assessment Research Council and the National Research Council, Ottawa, Canada.

Canadian House of Commons. 1992. "Bill C-13, an Act to Establish a Federal Environmental Assessment Process Passed on March 19, 1992." Ottawa, Canada.

Canadian Ministry of Supply and Services. 1991. *The State of Canada's Environment.* Ottawa: Government of Canada.

CEQ (Council on Environmental Quality). 1978. "Regulations under the U.S. National Environmental Policy Act." Washington, D.C.

Clark, William C. 1986. "The Cumulative Impacts of Human Activities on the Atmosphere." In *Cumulative Environmental Effects: A Binational Perspective.* Proceedings of a workshop co-sponsored by the Canadian Environmental Assessment Research Council and the National Research Council. Ottawa, Canada.

Conservation Foundation. 1990. *Making Decisions on Cumulative Impacts.* Proceedings of a conference co-sponsored by the Council on Environmental Quality, the U.S. Environmental Protection Agency, and the National Science Foundation, Washington, D.C., June.

Davies, Katherine. 1991. "Cumulative Environmental Effects: A Compendium." Report prepared for the Federal Environmental Assessment Review Office, March.

Delcan Corporation. 1988. "Annotated Literature Review of Cumulative and Incremental Environmental Impact." Prepared for Natural Resources Branch, Canadian Parks Service, Ottawa, Canada, August.

Emery, R. M. 1986. "Impact Interaction Potential: A Basin-wide Algorithm for Assessing Cumulative Impacts from Hydropower Projects." *Journal of Environmental Management* 23, pp. 341–60.

Estevez, E. D., J. Miller, J. Morris, and R. Mannan. 1986. *Managing Cumulative Effects in Florida Wetlands.* Proceedings of a conference, held in Sarasota, Florida, October 1985. New College Environmental Studies Program Publication 37. Madison, Wisc.: Omni Press.

Gosselink, J. G., and L. C. Lee. 1988. "Cumulative Impact Assessment Principles," In J. A. Kusler, M. L. Quammen, and G. Brooks, eds., *Proceedings of the National Wetland Symposium: Mitigation of Impacts and Losses*, pp. 196–203. Technical Report 3. Association of State Wetland Managers, Chester, VT.

Granholm, S. L., E. Gerstler, R. R. Everitt, D. P. Bedard, and E. C. Vlachos. 1987. "Issues, Methods, and Institutional Processes for Assessing Cumulative Biological Impacts." Prepared for Pacific Gas and Electric Company, San Ramon, Calif.

INTASA Inc. 1981. "National Hydroelectric Power Resources Study: Environmental Assessment." Prepared for the U.S. Army Corps of Engineers, Institute for Water Resources, Ft. Belvoir, VA., contract DACW72-80-C-002.

Lane, P. A., R. R. Wallace, R. L. Johnson, and D. Bernard. 1988. "Reference Guide to Cumulative Effects Assessment in Canada." P. Lane and Associates, Ltd., Halifax, Canada, October.

Orians, Gordon H. 1986. "Cumulative Effects: Setting the Stage." In *Cumulative Environmental Effects: A Binational Perspective.* Proceedings of a workshop co-sponsored by the Canadian Environmental Assessment Research Council and the National Research Council, Ottawa, Canada.

Peterson, E. B., Y. H. Chan, N. M. Peterson, G. A. Constable, R. B. Caton, C. S. Davis, R. R. Wallace, and G. A. Yarranton. 1987. "Cumulative Effects Assessment in Canada: An Agenda for Action and Research." Background paper prepared for the Canadian Environmental Assessment Research Council, Victoria, Canada.

Preston, E. M., and B. C. Bedard. 1988. "Evaluating Cumulative Effects on Wetland Functions: A Conceptual Overview and Generic Framework." *Journal of Environmental Management*, 12, pp. 561–64.

Sonntag, N. C., R. R. Everitt, L. Rattie, C. P. Wolf, J. Truett, A. Dorcey, and C. S. Holling. 1986. "Cumulative Impact Assessment: Review of State-of-the-Art and Research Recommendations." Environmental and Social Systems Analysts, Ltd., Vancouver, Canada.

Walker, D. A., P. J. Webber, M. D. Walker, N. D. Lederer, R. H. Meehen, and E. A. Nordstrand. 1986. "Use of Geobotanical Maps and Automated Mapping Techniques to Examine Cumulative Impacts in the Prudhoe Bay Oil Field, Alaska." *Environmental Conservation* 13, pp. 149–60.

Weaver, J. L., R. E. F. Escano, and D. S. Winn. 1987. "A Framework for Assessing Cumulative Effects on Grizzly Bears." *Transcripts of the North American Wildlife Natural Resource Conference* 52, pp. 364–76.

Williamson, Samuel C., C. L. Armour, and R. L. Johnston. 1985. "Preparing a FWS Cumulative Impacts Program: January 1985 Workshop Proceedings." Biological Report 85(11.2). U.S. Fish and Wildlife Services, Washington, D.C.

Williamson, Samuel C., and Karen Hamilton. 1989. "Annotated Bibliography of Ecological Cumulative Impacts Assessment." Biological Report 89(1). U.S. Fish and Wildlife Service, Washington, D.C.

WCED (World Commission on Environment and Development). 1987. *Our Common Future.* United Nations, World Commission on Environment and Development. Oxford, England: Oxford University Press.

Managing Landscapes for Sustainable Biodiversity

H. Ronald Pulliam

Many of the ideas presented in this chapter were developed and discussed by participants in a weekly meeting of students and postdoctoral associates working with me. I am particularly grateful to John (Barny) Dunning, Jianquo Liu, David J. Stewart, Brent Danielson, Scott Pearson, and Brian Watts for sharing their data, ideas, and criticisms. Portions of the research discussed here were supported by the National Science Foundation, the Department of Energy, and the U.S. Forest Service.

Most animal and plant species live not just in nature preserves but also in the matrix of managed, human-dominated ecosystems in which such preserves are embedded. In the long run, preservation of biological diversity will depend at least as much on how we manage the matrix as on how much land we set aside in preserves. Accordingly, a great challenge for sustainable development is designing and managing landscapes to balance the needs of economic development and the preservation of biological diversity.

The traditional approach to preserving biological diversity has been to set aside nature preserves in which neither economic development nor resource extraction is allowed. Important as this approach has been to the preservation of some species, biological diversity cannot be preserved solely by setting aside such preserves (Hansen and others 1991; Liu 1992; Wilcove 1989) because (1) the area of such preserves is too small, (2) the rapid increase in human population and the subsequent pressure for other uses of the land make it doubtful that much more land can be set aside, and (3) species in preserves are greatly affected by the changes in land use and other human activities in the landscapes surrounding them.

This chapter explores how ecological theory can be employed in schemes to preserve biological diversity while permitting sustainable eco-

nomic development. It considers first how population models incorporating habitat-specific demography can be used to predict how single-species populations might respond to changes in land use. An example is then given where a management plan developed primarily over concern for an endangered species leads to the possibility that other species might also become threatened or endangered. A discussion of problems associated with managing for a single endangered species leads to a consideration of how changes in land use might influence patterns of biological diversity in general. Finally, the chapter concludes with a discussion of using ecological models to explore how land management plans might simultaneously influence economic (market) profits, biological diversity, and other aspects of environmental quality.

Landscapes of suitable patches

All organisms live in heterogeneous environments. Individuals of the same species living in relatively close proximity to one another may experience totally different physical and biotic environments to the extent that some may be able to survive and reproduce while others cannot. At spatial scales substantially larger than what one individual experiences, the landscape experienced by a population represents a mosaic of good and bad places for the species. The growth, or lack thereof, of the population is determined not only by the quality of the individual microsites occupied but also by the spatial and temporal distribution of suitable and unsuitable microsites or patches of habitat.

A field or woodlot that is a single patch of relatively uniform quality for a bird or mammal may, at the same time, be a mosaic of patches of quite different quality for individual nematodes or shrubs. For any species, the landscape containing a population may be mapped as a mosaic of suitable and unsuitable patches. Each map is specific to the habitat requirements of one species and must be done at a scale appropriate to that organism. In general, the scale must be fine enough to resolve the areas occupied by individuals over significant portions of their lifetimes.

In order to map the patches of suitable habitat for a particular species, one must have a set of criteria for drawing the habitat boundaries. Following Elton (1949) and Andrewartha and Birch (1984), ecologists choose a habitat boundary to have "certain homogeneity with respect to the sort of environments it might provide for animals" (Andrewartha and Birch 1984, p. 223). In managed landscapes, drawing habitat boundaries is usually simplified by the strong contrasts between habitats with different management histories. For example, a pine plantation is clearly discernible from a neighboring old field or deciduous woodlot. In landscapes less dominated by human activities, habitat boundaries are often "softer" and more arbitrary.

Suitable sites for a particular species may often be distributed as isolated patches embedded in a matrix of unsuitable habitats. Spatially explicit models, developed to predict population trends, require that suitable habitat be distinguished from unsuitable habitat so that all suitable sites can be located on a map. To illustrate how this can be done, figure 6-1 shows suitable habitat for Bachman's sparrow on a 5,000-hectare tract at the Savannah River Site, a U.S. Department of Energy facility near Aiken, South Carolina. Dunning and Watts (1990) have shown that this species requires a dense layer of grasses and forbs in the first meter above ground and an open understory (2 to 4 meters above ground). At the Savannah River Site, both old-growth pine stands that are frequently burned and very young pine stands have the appropriate vegetative structure and are

therefore suitable breeding sites for this species. Hardwood stands and pine stands between five and eighty years of age are not suitable for Bachman's sparrows, because their understory or canopy vegetation is too dense and does not permit sufficient light to reach the forest floor. Figure 6-1 shows the actual distribution of suitable sites on the study area in 1990. Based on the known history of land use of the area and the proposed management plan for the site, the probable distribution of suitable sites can be reconstructed for the past or projected into the future.

Several of the factors that influence the location of suitable habitat for Bachman's sparrow are quite general in that they influence the location of habitat for many terrestrial species. Factors like soil type, topography, and vegetative cover all give information on the suitability of a site for a particular species, and all of these factors can be readily mapped. For Bachman's sparrow, soil type and topography influence the rate at which seedling trees grow and, therefore, the ages of pine stands that have vegetation profiles suitable for the sparrow. In addition, time since disturbance, successional status, and management history may provide additional information on the suitability of a site. For Bachman's sparrow, the age since planting of a young stand and the time since the last understory fire in an old stand both provide valuable information on suitability of the stand.

The combination of factors determining suitability of the site is different for every species. Such information alone is not enough to determine unambiguously the presence or absence of a species, but it can usually be used to categorize habitats as suitable or unsuitable and in some cases to assign a probability of occupation. As discussed below, a map based on information about the amount and location of suitable sites under existing or proposed patterns of land use can be an invaluable tool for species management.

Habitat-specific demography: Sources and sinks

The previous discussion of distribution does not differentiate among habitats of different quality except inasmuch as they might be suitable or unsuitable for a given species. What do we mean by suitable habitat? Might a species occur in unsuitable habitat?

Figure 6-1: Distribution of Suitable Breeding Habitat for Bachman's Sparrow in 1990 on a 5,000-Hectare Tract at the Savannah River Site

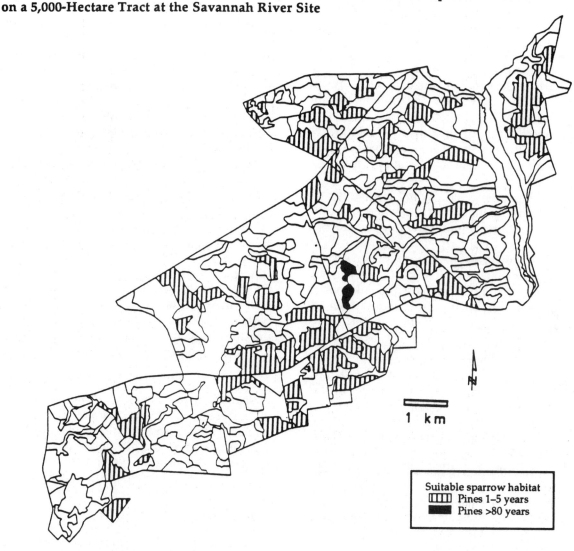

Suitable sparrow habitat
⊞ Pines 1–5 years
■ Pines >80 years

1 km

Note: Bachman's sparrow breeds both in older-growth pine forests and young clear-cuts but not in middle-aged pine stands.

Following Pulliam (1988), consider a population that has n_T individuals in the late spring just prior to the reproductive season. If none of the adults dies during reproduction, and each adult produces an average of b offspring, then at the end of the breeding season there will be $n_T + bn_T$ individuals. Furthermore, if adults survive the nonbreeding season with probability P_A and juveniles survive with probability P_J, then at the end of the year there will be $P_A n_T + P_J bn_T$ individuals. The finite rate of increase for the population (defined as $l = P_A + bP_J$) gives the number of individuals at the beginning of year $T + 1$ per individual at the beginning of year T.

The finite rate of increase can vary from year to year as the survival rates and reproductive rates vary. The geometric mean of the rates for a sequence of years characterizes the mean growth rate of the population over that time. If the long-term mean l is less than 1.0, the population will decline, and if it exceeds 1.0, the population will grow. Obviously, the population cannot grow forever, so for a population that does not go extinct or become infinitely abundant, the long-term l must be close to 1.0.

The finite rate of increase can also be used to describe spatial variation in growth rates. In this case, we refer to the habitat-specific rate of increase and calculate l based on the birth and death rates that apply in a specific habitat or patch of habitat alone. This concept of habitat-specific growth rate is complicated by dispersal. If each habitat or patch of habitat is isolated from all others, then the value of l calculated for any one habitat is the growth rate experienced by the population in that habitat. However, if habitats are connected, the population growth rate is given by the weighted average across all habitats, that is, different parts of the population are growing at different rates.

Some habitats are clearly more suitable than others. Consider the simple case where two habitats are of different quality and migration occurs between them. Habitat 1 is the better habitat, called the source, and here reproduction exceeds mortality, so that the habitat-specific growth rate, l_1, is greater than 1.0. In habitat 2, the sink, mortality exceeds reproduction, so l_2 is less than 1.0. Assume that the subpopulation in the source habitat grows at the l_1 until it reaches a population (n_1^*), which represents the maximum number of breeding individuals that can be accommodated in the source habitat. Once the source has reached the maximum number of breeding individuals, there are $l_1 n_1^*$ individuals at the end of each nonbreeding season; of this total only n_1^* can remain to breed, and the remaining $n_1^*(l_1 - 1)$ must emigrate from the source habitat into the sink habitat.

In this example, the sink subpopulation would soon disappear in the absence of any immigration, because at the end of each year there would be fewer individuals than there were at the beginning. However, with the steady immigration of $n_1^*(l_1 - 1)$ individuals from the source habitat, the sink population will grow to an equilibrium population of

$$n_2^* = n_1^*(l_1 - 1) / (1 - l_2).$$

Note that $l_1 - 1$ is the per capita reproductive surplus in the source habitat, and $1 - l_2$ is the per capita reproductive deficit in the sink habitat. Clearly, if the reproductive surplus in the source is much larger than the reproductive deficit in the sink, the sink habitat will contain far more individuals than the source habitat, even though the sink subpopulation depends on emigration from the source for its very existence. In other words, most of the individuals in a local population may exist in habitat unsuitable for them (Pulliam 1988).

Spatially explicit models

Most population models are conceptual models that do not attempt to incorporate the complexities of real landscapes. As Levins (1966) has pointed out, general models are often neither precise nor realistic. One of the general themes of both conservation biology and landscape ecology is that details, such as the geometry of habitat patches in a landscape, can influence population trends and extinction probabilities. Population models that are not spatially explicit make very unrealistic assumptions about the dispersal behavior of individuals and do not reflect the complexity of real landscapes. Whereas such models are useful for gaining general insights into population dynamics, they are poorly suited for managing particular species on particular landscapes. On the other hand, spatially explicit models are well suited for incorporating realistic details of particular species and landscapes, but, because they are so specific, the conclusions reached cannot always be generalized to other species and landscapes.

Mobile Animal Population—or MAP—is a class of spatially explicit population simulation models that accounts for the actual spatial locations of habitat patches and simulates habitat-specific demography and the dispersal behavior of organisms. The original version of the model, BACHMAP, was developed to simulate the abundance and distribution of Bachman's sparrow in managed pine plantations at the Savannah River Site. The model is, however, flexible and can be adapted to a variety of animal species on any landscape, either hypothetical or real.

MAP can be linked to a geographic information system description of a real landscape (Liu 1992). The model has mostly been run on landscapes ranging from 1,000 to 5,000 hectares but can be adapted to larger or smaller landscapes. The model represents a landscape as a grid of cells, each of which is the size of an individual territory of the species being simulated (2.5 hectares for Bachman's sparrow). Clusters of adjacent cells represent the size and location of forest tracts in the landscape; these tracts are assumed to be relatively uniform in their suitability for the species of interest. MAP models contain subroutines that specify forest management practices, succession, and, in some cases, the growth rates of tree species. Thus, the model can depict the structure of the current landscape and project the landscape's structure in the future based on a management plan specifying a harvest and replanting schedule. Other management activities such as thinning or burning stands, which might influence suitability of the stand, can be easily incorporated into the model.

Bachman's sparrows breed in pine stands that have a dense ground layer of grasses and forbs and an open understory (Dunning and Watts 1990). In managed pine plantations of the southeast, these conditions occur in very young pine stands (less than five years after planting) and in very old stands (more than eighty years old). Middle-age stands (between six and seventy-nine years old) have dense understories, which shade out the ground-layer forbs and grasses that provide food and nesting sites to the species.

MAP models simulate structure and change of the landscape and explicitly incorporate dispersal behavior. Dispersal is assumed to occur in the spring just before reproduction. If an adult female dies and leaves surviving female offspring, then one of those offspring inherits the natal territory. Juveniles that do not inherit their natal territory disperse in search of unoccupied, suitable breeding sites. On each move to a new site, the dispersing female faces a fixed risk of mortality, so the probability of dying while dispersing is higher when there are fewer suitable sites or more of the suitable sites are already occupied.

BACHMAP has been parameterized based on field studies of Bachman's sparrows and similar species (Dunning and Watts 1990; Haggerty 1986). Pulliam, Dunning, and Liu (1992) provide a detailed discussion of how these parameters were determined and provide the results of an extensive sensitivity analysis. By running the model with various combinations of parameters from the set of feasible ranges for each parameter, they conclude that the population dynamics of the species is more sensitive to variation in demographic variables than to variation in variables describing dispersal behavior. Changes in adult and juvenile survivorship have especially large impacts on population size and probability of extinction. Accordingly, current field efforts to obtain better parameter values are focusing on these parameters.

MAP and other spatially explicit models provide land managers with a new tool for predicting how management plans and changes in land use may affect species of concern. A few such models are sufficiently well developed and parameterized so that they can be used immediately. For most species, however, the relevant parameters are not known, and several years of concentrated fieldwork would be required to determine them.

Managing for diversity

Managing an ecosystem may be directed at a single species or at multiple species. Each approach addresses different concerns and faces different challenges.

Problems with single-species approach

Managing an ecosystem for a single endangered or threatened species may lead to the decline of populations of other species and, in some cases, may lead to additional species becoming threatened or endangered themselves. A case in point is the many salmonid species in rivers of the northwestern United States. These species and subspecies, many of which are rare and threatened with extinction, have substantially different habitat requirements, and changes in management that improve habitat for one species may worsen habitat for another.

In some cases, vast tracts of land may be managed primarily for a single species, as is the case for the spotted owl (*Strix occidentalis*) in the northwestern United States. Such circumstances naturally result in conflict between economic and conservation goals and may result in conflict between the needs of the target species and those of many other species. A somewhat similar example exists in the southeastern United States, where the red-cockaded woodpecker (*Picoides burealis*) is a species of major concern in managed pine forest. This species requires large tracts of older-growth stands of longleaf and other pine species. Management for the red-cockaded woodpecker interferes with the ability of humans to achieve high economic return from harvesting the pines and, as discussed below, may also result in the decline of other species of concern.

The Savannah River Site (SRS) is a 770-square-kilometer reserve consisting mostly of managed pine forest in the uplands and hardwoods in the bottomlands along the Savannah River and other major streams. Natural resource management is part of the mission of the SRS, and forest lands on the site are managed by the U.S. Forest Service. Silvicultural practices at the site over the past forty years have resulted in a mosaic of even-aged pine stands mostly ranging from 10 to 100 hectares in size. As part of a long-term forest management program, the Savannah River Forest Station has developed the "Savannah River Site Wildlife, Fisheries, and Botany Operation Plan" (SRFS 1992). One of the primary objectives of this plan is to maintain a viable population of the red-cockaded woodpecker.

The operations plan considers the habitat requirements of a variety of rare plant and animal species, including the red-cockaded woodpecker. The approach is to identify management indicators, which are plant and animal species and plant communities chosen for management emphasis and monitoring. The plan identifies about sixty such management units, the great majority of which are vertebrate or plant species. For each unit, a minimum objective is set, which for most species is a minimum number of individuals or breeding pairs to be maintained at the site.

The operations plan proposes a major change in the management strategy for SRS forest over the next fifty years. It calls for a shift from pine rotations of 30 to 40 years to 80 to 100 years, in order to increase the number of older-growth pine stands of the sort favored by the red-cockaded woodpecker. Liu (1992) and Liu, Dunning, and Pulliam (forthcoming) have used a MAP model to simulate the long-term impact of this proposed change on the viability of Bachman's sparrow. For the entire SRS, the management objective is to maintain 1,100 breeding pairs of sparrows (SRFS 1992). Our simulations have been run on a 5,924-hectare portion of the site for which we have a detailed geographic information system giving vegetative cover and history of land use. Extrapolating down from the objective of 1,100 pairs for the entire SRS gives a management objective of 115 pairs for the 5,924-hectare study site.

BACHMAP was linked to this geographic information system to project future patterns of land use under the proposed operations plan and to simulate the impact of the changes in land use on Bachman's sparrow. Figure 6-2 shows the predicted population trends for Bachman's sparrow for two harvest strategies. There are currently about 65 breeding pairs of the sparrow on this 5,924-hectare area (Dunning, unpublished data). If the proposed operations plan is employed, the population size of Bachman's sparrow is predicted to decline to 20 to 30 breeding pairs around the year 2000 and then to increase slowly and reach the minimum management objective of 115 pairs sometime after the year 2030.

Based on replicated simulations and sensitivity analysis, Bachman's sparrow does not appear to be in danger of local extinction due to the proposed management plan, but, nonetheless, over the short-term, it will probably decline significantly from its current level. The

point is simply that managing primarily for one endangered species can potentially threaten others. This is not meant to be a criticism of the SRS Wildlife, Fisheries, and Botany Operations Plan. In many ways, with its multispecies approach and emphasis on habitat management, the operations plan is a model approach. It could be improved, however, by incorporating quantitative predictors of population trends as the one discussed here. The basic problem is that such quantitative tools are in their infancy, and management plans cannot wait for such models to be sufficiently parameterized and validated. Over the next decade, such models can be expected to develop rapidly and become useful tools for resource managers. Management plans such as the SRS Wildlife, Fisheries, and Botany Operations Plan should remain flexible tools that are capable of making mid-course corrections as predictive tools are further developed and refined.

Figure 6–2: Predicted Population Trends for Bachman's Sparrow over the Next Fifty Years Based on Two Alternative Management Plans

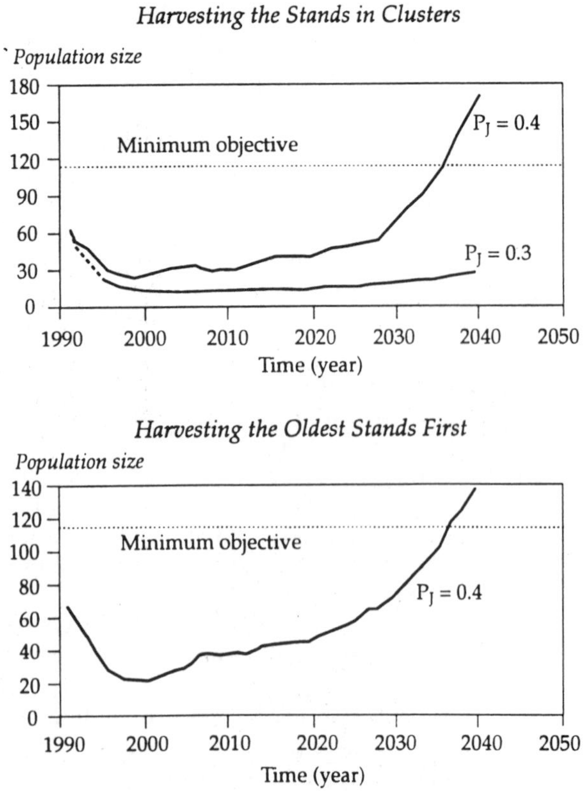

Harvesting the Stands in Clusters

Harvesting the Oldest Stands First

Note: In both cases, the sparrow populations decline to a low level before gradually increasing to the minimum objective size. The parameter P_J refers to the survival probability of juvenile sparrows. If the lower value (0.3) is assumed, the sparrow population never recovers to its original level.

Fragmentation and species diversity

The theory of island biogeography has been applied to habitat fragments created by deforestation (Diamond 1975; Wilson and Willis 1975), and despite warnings to the contrary (Margules, Higgs, and Rafe 1982) may still provide the best general guide to the preservation of biological diversity in habitat fragments. The number of species (S) on an island is approximately related to island area (A) by the "species-area" equation $S = cA^z$, where c is an empirically determined constant that varies among taxa and z is a constant, usually in the range of 0.25 to 0.35. The application of the theory of island biogeography in general, and this equation in particular, assumes that the area surrounding a habitat fragment is truly unsuitable to the species in question, as would be water surrounding an oceanic island. Furthermore, the equation is an equilibrium relationship that is only reached after many of the original species have become extinct (see Brown 1978; Kadmon and Pulliam 1994).

Forest fragments in heterogeneous landscapes are very different from oceanic islands in that the surrounding matrix may be uninhabitable for some species, but suitable for others. This may be particularly true in human-dominated landscapes where natural areas are embedded in a complex matrix of habitat types, some of which are suitable for some of the species in the natural area. Figure 6-3 illustrates this point with three hypothetical bird species occupying a forest fragment and some of the habitats in the surrounding landscape. Species A inhabits the forest understory and adjacent old-field habitats that have similar ground cover, but species A does not inhabit the mowed ground layer in residential areas. Species B occurs only in the forest since the mid-story vegetation it requires is not found in either the residential areas or old fields. Species C, a canopy species, does well in the forest habitat and the surrounding residential areas, which also have mature forest trees, but this species does not inhabit old fields. In this example, the effective

Figure 6-3: Response of Different Species to Deforestation

Note: Different species may respond very differently to deforestation. Species B is a specialist on old-growth forest, and when 90 percent of the forest is lost, 90 percent of the habitat for this species is lost. Species A and C, however, can also thrive in other habitats in the human-dominated landscape surrounding the forest preserve. Accordingly, the effective deforestation is less for these species.

degree of forest fragmentation is different for each species. For species B, the forest fragment constitutes an island of suitable habitat. The island is larger for species A and C, but the island for species A is different from that for species C.

The species-area equation has been used to predict the consequences of habitat fragmentation. According to the relationship between species and area in the equation, the percentage of the original species remaining after a loss of suitable habitat should be $(A_R / A_0)^z$, where A_R is the area remaining and A_0 is the original area available. Thus, with $z = 0.3$, a loss of 50 percent of the original habitat should result in a loss of about 20 percent of the original species, and a 90 percent loss of habitat should result in a loss of about 50 percent of the species.

The species-area curve has been used to try to predict the consequences of widespread deforestation in the Amazonian Basin and other parts of the world undergoing rapid changes in land use. Primary forests have long since been lost in other parts of the world, however, with apparently far less loss of species than predicted by the simple application of the species-area curve. For example, more than 90 percent of the forests of eastern United States have been logged or otherwise cleared, but far less than 50 percent of the native biota has been lost. There are at least three reasons for this discrepancy. First, extinction across a large area may require decades or even centuries to proceed to completion. Accordingly, many species currently considered threatened and endangered may be evidence of a gradual process of extinction still under way. Second, the extinction of some species has been prevented by direct intervention of humans, sometimes at very great cost. Third, even after most of the forest has been cut, much of the resulting secondary growth, managed forests, and other human-dominated habitat may provide suitable habitat for many species. In other words, the effective loss of forest for many species may have been far less than 90 percent.

To evaluate the potential of human-dominated habitat to buffer the impact of deforestation on species loss, consider the following example meant to represent the situation for forest birds in the eastern United States. Suppose 90 percent of the original forest is cut, but that most of the original forest inhabitants can use some portion of the human-dominated matrix surrounding the remaining old-growth forests. In other words, only a fraction of the species originally inhabiting the forest are so specialized that they can not find suitable habitat in the surrounding second growth and managed habitats. If, for example, 90 percent of the forest species can use 50 percent of the managed landscape plus the 10 percent of remaining forest, then only about 14 percent, $1 - (0.6)^{0.3}$, of these species would be lost. If half of the remaining 10 percent of forest specialist species were doomed to extinction, the total loss of species would be about 18 percent, instead of the 50 percent predicted by a 90 percent loss of habitat.

Economic considerations

Landscape models of the sort discussed in this chapter can be used to explore how land use and land management practices influence both biological diversity and economic revenues. For example, the MAP models, which predict patterns of species abundance and biological diversity, require information on patterns of land use and forest management practices such as frequency of burning, length of rotation, and size of stand, all of which have an important impact on economic revenue (see box 6-1 for indicators of sustainability at the landscape level).

ECOLECON is a spatially explicit, object-oriented model that simulates the population dynamics of animals and economic performance based on forest landscape management practices (Liu 1992; Liu, Cubbage, and Pulliam, forthcoming). ECOLECON incorporates a MAP model with detailed information about species-specific use of habitat and demography with a forest growth and yield model containing economic information about management costs and timber prices. Given current parameters, the model simulates the growth rates of loblolly pines based on information about density of planting and type of soil and calculates yield of pulpwood—chip and saw—and sawtimber, depending on the length of rotation chosen. Net income is based on yield, the prices of pulp and timber, and the costs of forest regeneration and maintenance, plus property tax and administrative costs.

ECOLECON predicts the impact of land use and management decisions on animal populations while calculating net income, net present value, and land expectation value. The parameters of the biological portion of ECOLECON are presently set for predicting the abundance and distribution of Bachman's sparrow on managed pine plantations. Liu (1992) and Liu, Cubbage,

Box 6-1. Indicators of Sustainability at the Landscape Level
Sharad Lele

The following are some of the indicators of sustainability that need to be addressed at the landscape level:

• *Changes in land use.* One of the major factors affecting sustainability is change in the pattern and level of land use. Therefore, monitoring changes in overall patterns of land use is essential. This involves periodic assessment of changes in the amount, distribution, and size of different types of patches (land uses) in the landscape, including both human-created and natural or semi-natural types. From this assessment, functional changes in the landscape can be inferred, assuming that there is basic understanding of conditions and processes within the patch types and an understanding of patch by patch interactions (that is, edge effects). Changes in conditions within a patch type—successional changes in composition and structure—should also be a part of this assessment.

• *Biodiversity.* Some periodic assessment of biodiversity is important. This could take a variety of forms but certainly should include attention to population levels of indicator species essential to the ecosystem's health. In addition, protocols can be developed to assess overall levels of diversity based on the occurrence of various patch types or structural features within the landscape. A basic assumption is that many elements of diversity are to be found in managed landscapes and not simply within natural areas; this must be considered in any monitoring program and in any effort to develop inferences about various management alternatives.

• *System inputs and losses.* Assuming that the basic landscape unit is a watershed or drainage basin, system inputs and losses should be assessed on that basis. Natural inputs would be expected to be primarily through the atmosphere; hence, they would need to be addressed in any monitoring program. System losses are probably best assessed in the river that drains the landscape. This requires hydrologic monitoring and a program of sampling and measuring particulate and dissolved materials leaving the watershed, for example, chemical species and particulate soil materials and sediments and chemicals, including nutrients.

• *Soil properties.* Given the fundamental importance of soils in the production of food and fiber, some program for periodically assessing soil conditions—amount or depth, physical properties (macroporosity), chemical conditions (level of nutrients and organic matter), and biology (diversity of soil microflora and fauna)—should be conducted. Emphasis should be on conditions in patch types heavily managed for commodities, but periodic comparisons with natural systems as baselines are also essential. A part of the assessment should also be the periodic analysis of soil subsidies being used to maintain fertility, such as levels of fertilization.

• *Economic and energy balance.* Periodically, some measure(s) of economic (including energy) inputs to and outputs from the drainage system are desirable. In economic terms, this would be an economic input-output analysis.

• *Human condition.* Some monitoring of the human population and its status needs to be conducted; perhaps this should be done at the regional rather than the landscape level. In any case, some measures of the human condition are appropriate in order to determine whether it is stable, declining, or improving. Various measures are possible, including health status, caloric intake, levels of satisfaction, income, and morbidity.

and Pulliam (forthcoming) show that whereas land expectation value is usually maximized with short rotations (approximately twenty years), sparrow populations are largest with rotations more than eighty years in length. Factors such as size of stand, fragmentation of forest, and amount and location of mature pine stands in the landscape all influence economic revenues as well as size of the animal population and probability of extinction. Whereas no management plan maximizes both economic profit and population size, some management schemes result in both relatively high net income and bird populations that, while intermediate in size, are nonetheless sufficient to make extinction very unlikely.

We are currently developing versions of ECOLECON and related models to predict population sizes and extinction probabilities for selected bird, mammal, amphiban, and invertebrate species and to predict trends in biological diversity in general. We are also working on ways to expand the model to include forests other than mono-specific stands of pines. Finally, we plan to expand the economic portion of the model to include other extractive and recreational land uses. We now have a working model that can be used in an adaptive management framework to help forest managers choose landscape management schemes that yield reasonable economic revenues without threatening plant and animal species of concern to management. Although our models to date are specific to species and conditions in the southeastern United States, the approach is quite general and could be a useful tool for managers in other locations wishing to balance economic and ecological goals.

Sustainable landscape management

Maintenance of biological diversity is only one aspect of sustainable management of landscapes. For example, landscapes can be characterized as sustainable only if the nutrient losses of their component parts (forests, agricultural fields, and so forth) are balanced by nutrient inputs. Furthermore, sustainability implies that the management of one habitat or one landscape is not done at the expense of another. Thus, the agricultural productivity of one landscape cannot be said to be sustainable if that productivity is had at the expense of the nutrients of another system or, for that matter, at the expense of supplies of fossil fuels. Also, a landscape cannot be viewed as sustainable if it exports (leaks) toxic materials that degrade other systems. For example, forest or agricultural productivity in one landscape is not sustainable if it requires the use of pesticides that are transported to adjacent landscapes or into groundwater.

The necessity to consider how management of one habitat or landscape influences neighboring habitats or landscapes suggests a hierarchical approach to sustainable systems. According to this approach, components of a subsystem are said to be sustainable only if the practices within the subsystem can be maintained indefinitely without degrading other subsystems or the larger system of which they are a part. For example, an agricultural field must be managed so as not to degrade either the soil within the field, on which its own productivity depends, or the integrity of adjacent subsystems (such as biodiversity of forest reserves or quality of groundwater). The agricultural field must also be managed so as to preserve the integrity of the larger human ecosystem of which it is a part, including the economic security of the humans who manage the system.

Maintaining biological diversity must thus be viewed in the context of managing the integrity of human-dominated landscapes and the regional economic systems on which they depend. This approach will require integrating models of bio-logical diversity with models of agricultural and forest management, and even these must be viewed as subsystems to be integrated into larger models of global economic and Earth system trends.

References

Andrewartha, H. G., and L. C. Birch. 1984. *The Ecological Web.* Chicago, Ill.: University of Chicago Press.

Brown, J. H. 1978. "The Theory of Insular Biogeography and the Distribution of Boreal Birds and Mammals." *Great Basin Naturalist Memoirs* 2, pp. 209–27.

Diamond, J. M. 1975. "The Island Dilemma: Lessons of Modern Biogeographic Studies for the Design of Nature Preserves." *Biological Conservation* 7, pp. 129–46.

Dunning, John B., and B. D. Watts. 1990. "Regional Differences in Habitat Occupancy by Bachman's Sparrow." *The Auk* 107, pp. 463–72.

Elton, C. 1949. "Population Interspersion: An Essay on Animal Community Patterns." *Journal of Ecology* 37, pp. 1–23.

Haggerty, T. M. 1986. "Reproductive Ecology of Bachman's Sparrow (*Aimophila aestivalis*) in Central Arkansas." Ph.D. diss., University of Arkansas, Fayetteville.

Hansen, A. J., T. A. Spies, F. J. Swanson, and J. L. Ohmann. 1991. "Conserving Biodiversity in Managed Forests: Lessons from Natural Forests." *BioScience* 41, pp. 382–92.

Kadmon, R., and H. Ronald Pulliam. 1994. "Island Biogeography: Effect of Geographical Isolation on Species Composition." *Ecology* 74, pp. 977–81.

Levins, R. 1966. "Strategy of Model Building in Population Biology." *American Scientist* 54, pp. 421–31.

Liu, Jianquo. 1992. "ECOLECON: A Spatially Explicit Model for Ecological Economics of Species Conservation in Complex Forest Landscapes." Ph.D. diss., University of Georgia, Athens.

Liu, Jianquo, F. Cubbage, and H. Ronald Pulliam. Forthcoming. "Ecological and Economic Effects of Forest Landscape Structure and Rotation Length: Simulation Studies Using ECOLECON." *Ecological Economics.*

Liu, Jianquo, John B. Dunning, and H. Ronald Pulliam. Forthcoming. "A Spatially Explicit Model of Animal Population Dynamics on a Changing Landscape: The Bachman's Sparrow at the Savannah River Site." *Conservation Biology.*

Margules, C., A. J. Higgs, and R. W. Rafe. 1982. "Modern Biogeographic Theory: Are There Any Lessons for Nature Reserve Design?" *Biological Conservation* 24, pp. 115–28.

Pulliam, H. Ronald. 1988. "Sources, Sinks, and Population Regulation." *The American Naturalist* 132, pp. 652–61.

Pulliam, H. Ronald, John B. Dunning, Jr., and Jianquo Liu. 1992. "Population Dynamics in a Complex Landscape: A Case Study." *Ecological Applica-tions* 2, pp. 165–77.

(SRFS) Savannah River Forest Station. 1992. "Savannah River Site Wildlife, Fisheries, and Botany Operations Plan." Savannah River Forest Station, Forest Service, U.S. Department of Agriculture.

Wilcove, D. S. 1989. "Protecting Biodiversity in Multiple-use Lands: Lessons from the U.S. Forest Service." *Trends in Ecology and Evolution* 4, pp. 385–88.

Wilson, E. O., and E. O. Willis. 1975. "Applied Biogeography: The Design of Nature Preserves." In M. L. Cody and J. M. Diamond, eds., *Ecology and Evolution of Communities*, pp. 522–34. Cambridge, Mass.: Belknap Press.

Comments

Eduardo R. Fuentes

I will make my comments from the perspective of a biologist who is interested in landscapes and is living in a developing country. Ronald Pulliam's very attractive presentation addresses the question of sustainable development and biodiversity at the landscape level, with particular emphasis on metapopulations, sources, and sinks. In my comments, I refer to sustainable development from the perspective of developing countries and then address some emerging questions concerning landscape development, metapopulations, sources, and sinks.

Sustainable development

Sustainable development has been defined as using resources today without affecting the options for future generations. This is a relatively new and attractive concept. However, it is a criterion that is almost impossible to satisfy, because, on the one hand, the current generation must necessarily continue altering the biosphere to develop and, on the other, frequently when a history-dependent system, such an ecosystem or the biosphere, is modified, there are changes in future options. A compromise is therefore called upon between today's uses and future options. In the future, other, new options will be available, but if they cannot be specified now, they should not concern the present analyses.

For developing countries that will have to continue changing their landscapes in the future, this is a very important point. For them at least, sustainable development should not be understood as freezing the landscape at a particular configuration, but rather as continuous development within a set of restrictions associated with the maintenance of as many future options as possible.

For example, it would not be culturally sustainable to attempt to freeze growth in Latin America or in a country like Chile, where about 40 percent of the people are below the poverty line. In such countries, land uses are expected to change, and our definitions should consider those changes. The question, then, is what defines the appropriate set of restrictions that

would maintain as many future options as possible and still allow for current developments.

Because ecological systems are very complex and we understand them only to a very limited extent and because we need freedom for human creativity, I suggest that rather than attempting to define what is sustainable, we should concentrate on what we perceive as not sustainable and as clearly and unnecessarily eliminating future options. Finding the bounds of what does not seem sustainable *today* if continued indefinitely is more realistic than attempting to specify conditions for sustainable situations. Defining these bounds could be somewhat easier and more coherent with the necessary freedom and the inherent changes of a market economy than attempting to specify, and later plan, the exact future use of land for each particular region. Therefore, rather than thinking of ideal landscapes with a rigidly stable physiognomy, we might think of the maximum stresses that various subsystems can tolerate and still maintain some future options. Perhaps one of the most important consequences of present discussions on sustainable development will be the greater scope that environmental impact assessments could have in the future if they consider not only current consequences but also reductions in future options.

With all the limitations of our current knowledge, at least five different axes can be used to define a five-dimensional envelope that indicates where serious consequences for future options begin.

Development must consider the fate of the two most nonrenewable resources: soils (with all their internal complexity) and biodiversity (in its widest meaning). Hence development schemes ought to consider maintaining these variables within accepted standards and monitor their changes. Development must also consider changes in climate, since climate defines the basic scenario for all organisms and human activities. Overall temperatures might be increasing, and rainfall patterns might also change in the near future. Change in climate should be a prime target when considering, assessing, and monitoring development. Human population and especially per capita impacts should also be considered. It is of the highest interest to quantify and monitor these impacts. The globalization of the economy is likely to pose difficulties for our attempts to evaluate the per capita impact of people in the large consumption centers in the world. A final and crucial bound for sustainable development concerns pollution and the accumulation of toxic and radioactive materials, which will eventually make life on earth impossible. Within the rather extreme bounds imposed by the limits of physiologically tolerable contamination, additional frames could deal with different levels of quality of life. Monitoring sustainable development should also involve the amounts of materials and residues accumulated in the different compartments of the planet and how our well-being depends on the state of those deposits. These five dimensions can be used to define a hypervolume that determines bounds for landscape transformations without unnecessarily limiting future options.

Several questions can be posed at this point. Should each stage be sustainable or should only end states be? Should we attempt to manage landscapes so that all states can be reversed? What is the appropriate spatial scale in each case? Should all or a few areas in the globe move within the five-dimensional envelope? Another question pertains to the particular system that should be aimed at. A landscape, for example covered with forests, can be used at any of N different levels (states) depending on energy and material inputs from surrounding areas. At one extreme are quasi-pristine states; at the other are various types of agricultural fields. All of them could be sustainable, and most involve some kind of compromise with future options. The greater the transformation and the greater the transformed area, the lesser the options for the future. The question is what inputs are needed and from where they will be obtained so that the process in the area can be considered sustainable.

The area considered in sustainable development as well as the transformations allowed are very important, because phenomena are different at different scales. For example, the area in which to express the phenomenon of altitudinal bird migration is different from the area in which to observe the dynamics of sustainable tree gaps, or the area in which to observe the life cycle of salmons. Maintaining a spatially or functionally restricted version of a system, which naturally needs more area or a higher amplitude of oscillations for its expression than the area we can afford to maintain, involves energy and material inputs and can be very costly and be nonsustainable in the long run.

Sources and sinks

Sources and sinks are part of systems in which there is heterogeneity, for example, landscapes. In general, if portions (patches) of the landscape have different potentials, there will be flows, sources, and sinks. The examples given in the chapter by Pulliam are examples of a particular case in which the potentials relate to habitats with different relative population densities.

However, in a landscape there are several kinds of heterogeneities, generating different types of sources and sinks:

- Water moving along the slopes of a watershed from the source areas distributed throughout it or in a portion of it and sinking by percolation or through the lower end of it

- Sediments behaving roughly parallel to water

- Individuals of a particular species, including beneficial (resource species) such as many coastal marine species (see, for example, Roughgarden and others 1988), wildlife species (Lande 1988; Poiani and Fuentes 1989; Roughgarden and Fuentes 1977), as well as pest species, as in the Norte Chico of Chile (Fuentes and Campusano 1985), all responding to permanent or sporadic habitat gradients and constituting sources and sinks of different kinds

- Sets of species, as in colonization events following natural disturbance of complex forest ecosystems (Veblen, Schlegel, and Oltremari 1983), competing fugitive species (Bengtson 1991), predator-prey systems requiring different patches (as in Huffaker's 1958 famous experiment with mites and oranges).

For individuals both of the same and of different species, the question of sources and sinks involves habitat quality with its intraspecific and interspecific connotations and specificities. Consequently, different population processes are likely to have different areas of importance. The previous example with the ranges for the altitudinal migration of birds, the salmon cycle, and the tree-phase dynamics illustrates this point well. In all these cases, the area involved and its heterogeneity is crucial if the system is to be maintained, but the areas themselves are different or at most overlap only partially.

Within species, numbers as well as composition within a given area vary within years, between years, between decades, between centuries.

Sustainable use implies that some species will be "lost" anyway. What species composition should concern us when thinking of the sustainable development of a given area?

More generally, if spatial heterogeneity and therefore geophysical as well as population sources and sinks are as common as they seem to be, their disruption should be an important concern when defining the bounds for sustainable development. However, if the relevant areas for the various geophysical and population processes overlap only partially, there are difficult choices to be made. Which of these partially overlapping areas should be preserved? Obviously, all areas cannot be preserved if we want to develop the land, and necessarily some source-sink systems will have to be altered. Research on sources and sinks should therefore not only describe these systems but also consider the consequences of transforming and even deleting some of them.

References

Bengtson, J. 1991. "Interspecific Competition in Metapopulations." *Biological Journal of the Linnean Society* 42, pp. 219–37.

Fuentes, Eduardo, and C. Campusano. 1985. "Pest Outbreaks and Rainfall in the Semiarid Region of Chile." *Journal of Arid Environments* 8, pp. 67–72.

Huffaker, C. B. 1958. "Experimental Studies on Predation: Dispersion Factors and Predator-Prey Oscillations." *Hilgardia* 27, pp. 343–83.

Lande, R. 1988. "Genetics and Demography in Biological Conservation." *Science* 241, pp. 1455–60.

Poiani, A., and E. R. Fuentes. 1989. "Preferences of Native Rodents for Shrub Clumps of Various Sizes and Compositions: Implications for the Structure of the Chilean Matorral." *Redia* 72, pp. 133–48.

Roughgarden, J., and Eduardo R. Fuentes. 1977. "The Environmental Determinants of Size in Solitary Populations of West Indian Anolis Lizards." *Oikos* 29, pp. 44–51.

Roughgarden J., S. Gaines, and H. Possingham. 1988. "Recruitment Dynamics in Complex Life Cycles." *Science* 241, pp. 1460–66.

Veblen, T. T., F. M. Schlegel, and J. V. Oltremari. 1983. "Temperate Broadleaf Evergreen Forests of South America." In J. D. Ovington, ed., *Ecosystems of the World*, vol. 10: *Temperate Broad Leaved Evergreen Forests*. New York, N.Y.: Elsevier.

7

Scale and Sustainability: A Population and Community Perspective

Simon A. Levin

It is a pleasure to acknowledge support of the National Science Foundation, the Andrew W. Mellon Foundation, the U.S. Department of Energy, the National Aeronautics and Space Administration, the U.S. Environmental Protection Agency, McIntire-Stennis, and Hatch. Most important, I thank Colleen Martin for her indispensable help with this chapter and for ten years of collegial interaction. The invitation to construct this chapter came just as I was completing the manuscript, "The Problem of Pattern and Scale in Ecology," which was published by the Ecological Society of America (Levin 1992a). This chapter covers much of the same material and summarizes the appropriate points presented in the Ecology paper. Parts are reproduced with permission of the Ecological Society of America.

Understanding the problem of sustainability requires understanding the scale of natural space and time of population dynamics and how the pattern of habitat on various scales influences survival of a population. It is often argued that a fluctuating population, because it is, at times, smaller than a stable population of the same mean size, faces higher probabilities of extinction and genetic bottlenecks that are associated with low population size. But neither the notion of fluctuation nor even that of size makes sense without reference to the spatial and temporal scales of interest; an understanding of how variability is associated with area and time period is thus fundamental to defining and effecting sustainability.

Achieving sustainability requires characterizing the natural patterns of variability within an ecosystem or landscape and understanding what biotic and abiotic processes are essential for their maintenance. Understanding patterns in terms of the processes that produce them is the essence of science and the key to developing principles for management. Without an understanding of mechanisms, each new stress on each new system must be evaluated de novo, without any scientific basis for extrapolation; such understanding provides the foundation for understanding and management.

Addressing the problem of scale also has fundamental applied importance. Global and regional changes in biological diversity, in the distribution of greenhouse gases and pollutants, and in climate all have origins in and consequences for fine-scale phenomena. The general circulation models that provide the basis for predicting climate operate on spatial and temporal scales many orders of magnitude greater than the scales at which most ecological studies are carried out (Hansen and others 1987; Schneider 1989); satellite imagery and other means of remote sensing provide spatial information somewhere in between the two, overlapping both. General circulation models and remote-sensing techniques also must lump functional ecological classes, sometimes into very crude assemblages (such as the "big leaf" to represent regional vegetation), suppressing considerable ecological detail. To develop the predictive models that are needed for management, or simply to allow us to respond to change, we must learn how to connect the disparate scales of interest of scientists studying these problems at different levels.

The capability to make these connections across scales is fundamental to developing strategies for sustainability. Any management strategy involves intervention, and intervention is perturbation. An understanding of how a population, a community, or an ecosystem will respond to perturbation must involve some understanding of what mechanisms construct that system and mediate the patterns it exhibits on diverse scales of space, time, and organizational complexity.

Indeed, even the determination of management objectives requires us to select scales of interest. What system components are of primary interest? Are individual species to be maintained, or should the focus be on functional groupings? Microbial decomposition must be maintained, but do we care about the preservation of every species within the microbial community? The benthic community performs critical functions for the system, but many of these can be protected even if the species composition of the community is altered.

Similar considerations apply to the management of multispecies fisheries, at least to the extent that consumer preferences can be shifted from one species to another. Terrestrial communities provide other examples; the value of a forest, for example, will be measured differently by different individuals. If a forest is viewed solely as a source of fiber, the relevant measures of performance will differ from those that would be guided by a recognition of the forest as wilderness, or as critical habitat for its denizens, or as mediator of climate. Once again, scale and perspective are critical.

In general, there is no single way to measure the functioning of an ecosystem or its ecological or human value. One must impose some selective filter on the infinity of possible measures of a system's performance and decide which features are most representative. This applies not only to the level of functional detail but also to the spatial and temporal scales of interest. Thus, it is essential to understand how the perspective associated with a particular choice of scales biases the view of a system and how to extrapolate from one scale to another.

To achieve these objectives, we must understand how information is transferred from fine scales to broad scales, and vice versa. We must learn how to aggregate and simplify, retaining essential information without getting bogged down in unnecessary detail. The essence of modeling is, in fact, to facilitate the acquisition of this understanding by abstracting and incorporating just enough detail to produce observed patterns.

The reference to particular scales of interest emphasizes a fundamental point: there is no single correct scale on which to describe populations or ecosystems (Allen and Starr 1982; Greig-Smith 1964; Meentenmeyer and Box 1987; Steele 1978, 1989; Wiens 1989). Indeed, the forces governing the history of the evolution of life, shaped by competitive pressures and co-evolutionary interactions, are such that each species observes the environment on its own unique suite of scales of space and time (see, for example, Wiens 1976).

When we observe the environment, we necessarily do so on only a limited range of scales; therefore, our perception of events provides us with only a low-dimensional slice of a high-dimensional cake. In some cases, the scales of observation may be chosen deliberately to elucidate key features of the natural system; more often, the scales are imposed on us by our perceptual capabilities or by technological or logistical constraints (Steele 1978). In particular, the observed variability of the system depends on the scale of description (Haury, McGowan, and Wiebe 1978; Stommel 1963).

In describing natural phenomena, we mimic evolution by averaging over uncertainty. At very fine spatial and temporal scales, stochastic phenomena (or deterministically driven chaos) may make the systems of interest unpredictable. Thus we focus attention on larger spatial regions, longer time scales, or statistical ensembles, for which macroscopic statistical behaviors are more regular. This is the principal technique of scientific inquiry: by changing the scale of description, we move from unpredictable, unrepeatable individual cases to collections of cases whose behavior is regular enough to allow generalizations to be made. In so doing, we trade the loss of detail or heterogeneity within a group for the gain of predictability; we thereby extract and abstract those fine-scale features that have relevance for the phenomena observed on other scales. The implications for sustainability are profound. In preservation, we must not become embroiled in the details of how a system functions. We must determine its essential features and assure that these are maintained. Those essential features cannot be defined without reference to a set of external valuations of the system. Science can illuminate a decision making process, but it cannot substitute for it.

The concepts of scale and pattern are ineluctably intertwined (Hutchinson 1953). The description of pattern is the description of variation, and the quantification of variation requires the determination of scales. Thus, the identification of pattern is an entrée into the identification of scales (Denman and Powell 1984; Powell 1989).

Our efforts to develop theories of how ecosystems or communities are organized must revolve around attempts to discover patterns that can be quantified within systems and compared across systems. Thus, considerable attention has been directed to techniques for describing ecological or population patterns (Burrough 1981; Gardner and others 1987; Milne 1988; Sokal, Jacquez, and Wooten 1989; Sugihara, Grenfell, and May 1990). Once patterns are detected and described, we can seek to discover the determinants of pattern and the mechanisms that generate and maintain those patterns. With an understanding of mechanisms, one has predictive capacity that is impossible with correlations alone.

The problem of ecological pattern is inseparable from the problem of the generation and maintenance of diversity (Levin 1981). Not only is the heterogeneity of the environment often essential to the coexistence of species, but the very description of the spatial and temporal distributions of species describes patterns of diversity. Thus, understanding pattern, its causes, and its consequences is central to understanding evolutionary processes such as speciation as well as ecological processes such as succession, community development, and the spread and persistence of species.

Mosaics and fragmented environments

A fundamental challenge in achieving sustainability is to cope with the fragmented environments that human activity has imposed on the landscape. Not only are natural systems mosaics of patches in various stages of successional development, but the broader landscape itself is a patchwork of urban, agricultural, natural, and other pieces. This landscape is thus the result of a process that has defied sensible regional and global patterns, satisfying limited local or exploitative objectives without thought to the sustainability of the whole enterprise. Generally, the problem of sustainability has been avoided by viewing the exploited areas as being open systems and drawing heavily on other systems and

other areas, indeed other nations, to provide the life support services that have been eliminated locally. That may work well on local scales, and less well but adequately on broader scales, but it cannot go on indefinitely, and ultimately each region must be made as closed and self-sufficient as possible for sustainability to be achieved. It is well understood that larger systems are less open than smaller ones, because of elementary geometric principles. As the developing nations begin to achieve equity in terms of the drain they place on the environment, there will be no place left to turn for sustenance. We must understand how to manage these fragmented systems, on scales from the forest to the biosphere.

The view of systems as mosaics of islands has taken a number of interesting directions. The concept of patch dynamics (Levin and Paine 1974; Paine and Levin 1981; Pickett and White 1985; Watt 1947) has become a popular theme in both the terrestrial and marine literatures and has led to new views of community structure. Metapopulation models, in which systems are viewed as composed of interacting populations of local demes, have been shown to be of importance in conservation biology (Armstrong 1988; Burkey 1989; Fahrig and Paloheimo 1988a, 1988b; Gilpin and Hanski 1991; Nuernberger 1991), evolutionary theory (Levene 1953), and epidemiology (Levin and Pimentel 1981) and have become the focus of considerable theoretical effort (for example, Nee and May 1992), especially the role that the structure of the metapopulation plays in facilitating the coexistence of species.

Food webs

One of the most natural ways to describe a community or an ecosystem is in terms of the trophic relationships among species and the tangled web that results (Elton 1958; Levin, Levin, and Paine 1977; Odum 1983; Paine 1966, 1980). Considerable theoretical interest has been directed to regularities that can be detected in the topological structure of such webs (Cohen 1977, 1989; Pimm 1982; Sugihara 1982; Yodzis 1989). This seems all the more remarkable because such patterns seem to hold true regardless of the criteria used to define the elements of a web or the criteria for deciding that a link exists between two species (but see Cohen 1989; Schoener 1989). Indeed, there clearly is no unequivocal way to characterize a web. Is a taxonomic subdivision most appropriate, or would a functional one serve better? Should subdivision stop at the species level, consider different demographic classes, be partitioned according to genotype, and so forth? However a class were defined, one could partition it further according to various kinds of criteria, reducing variability within a class while sacrificing the predictability that can be achieved for larger assemblages. This is the same kind of problem confronted when one deals with spatial and temporal scale, but with added layers of complexity.

Global change in climate and ecological models

Global changes in climate and in the concentrations of greenhouse gases will have major effects on the vegetational patterns at local and regional scales (Clark 1985; MacArthur 1972); in turn, changes that occur at very fine scales, such as alterations in rates of stomatal opening and closing, ultimately will have impacts at much broader scales (Jarvis and McNaughton 1986). General circulation models, which form the basis of predictions of climate, operate on scales of hundreds of kilometers on a side, treating as homogeneous all of the ecological detail within (Schneider 1989; Hansen and others 1987). On the other hand, most ecological studies are carried out on scales of meters or tens of meters (Kareiva and Anderson 1988), and even ecosystem studies are at scales several orders of magnitude less than those relevant to general circulation models. Thus, a fundamental problem in relating the large-scale predictions of the climate models to processes at the scale of ecological information is to understand how information is transferred across scales (Jarvis and McNaughton 1986; Levin 1993).

To address this problem, both statistical and correlational studies are needed, as is modeling designed to elucidate mechanisms. A useful place to begin is the quantification of spatial and temporal variability as a function of scale (see, for example, Kratz, Frost, and Magnuson 1987; McGowan 1990). Long temporal and spatial series can be used to examine similar patterns in the variation of climate and components of the ecosystem; where scales of variation match, there is at least the basis for investigating mechanistic relationships. An example is the continuous plankton recorder surveys of the North Atlantic, which

have provided data on spatial variations in the distributions of phytoplankton and zooplankton over half a century (see, for example, Colebrook 1982; McGowan 1990). The evidence from these studies has been that large spatial and temporal scales show the greatest variations and that these correlate well with large-scale variations in climate (Dickson and others 1988; McGowan 1990). The approach taken (Radach 1984) is first to ask how much of the variation can be explained by variation in the physical environment and then to look to autonomous biological factors to account for the balance. This mode of attack perhaps requires scrutiny, given the possibility that intrinsic biotic factors might account for some variation in climate. Only mechanistic approaches that examine the effects of scale can address this puzzle.

Ågren and others (1991) review models of the linkage of production and decomposition and discuss the linkages of process at different scales. The problem of scaling from the leaf to the ecosystem and beyond fundamentally challenges predictions of the effects of global change (Ehleringer and Field 1993; Norman 1980). Ågren and others (1991) point out that ecosystem models that operate at only one level of integration are not likely to incorporate mechanisms properly and that it is essential to develop methods for integrating from finer scales; this reiterates the central theme of this chapter. A related problem is the need to connect processes operating at different levels of integration, as for example, the linkages between grassland biogeochemistry and atmospheric processes (Parton and others 1989; Schimel and others 1990).

It is worth noting (Holling, personal communication) that separating climatic and biotic influences on changing patterns of ecosystem can be extremely problematic. Extrinsic influences can trigger qualitative changes in the dynamics of the system (Levin 1978); cases in point may involve fires or outbreaks that are triggered by a change in climate but show very little correlation with it (for example, Holling 1992b).

Pattern and scale

The critical environmental problem facing society today is sustainability: the maintenance of our natural and managed systems so that they will be available, in roughly the form we found them or better, for later generations. To achieve sustainability, however, it is helpful if not essential to know what it is. What are the properties of these systems that we most wish to sustain? Indeed, does sustainability mean preservation as is, or does it incorporate the natural patterns of change and growth that occur and are perceived differently at different spatial, temporal, and organizational scales?

Only one answer is possible to the last question. Change and renewal are essential features of any system, and attempts to suppress such change can undermine sustainability. Modern views of optimal strategies for managing forest fires are evidence of this principle, and Holling's emphasis on resilience and flexibility must guide informed practice (Holling 1986). Yet the rate of change and variation will differ with the spatial and temporal scales of interest and with the way in which components are aggregated in one's view of the system. Unless we can identify a single spatial, temporal, and organizational scale of interest, we must ask how a system's properties change with perceptual scale. And in any case, to achieve sustainability, we must understand how the patterns described at one scale of interest are influenced by events, both natural and anthropogenic, that are taking place on other scales.

The question of identifying which aspects of a system must be preserved is more problematic, because it cannot be answered without reference to how society values and wishes to use the system. Ecosystems perform diverse services to humans by serving as sources of food and fiber, as mediators of environmental quality, and as places to recreate. Decisions to dedicate segments of the landscape to particular functions are personal or societal decisions, rather than scientific ones, though decisions about land use fundamentally affect global sustainability. Explicitly recognizing the role that external valuation plays in measuring the health or capital of an ecosystem is a first step toward achieving sustainability. Balancing those decisions in ways that maintain the global good is our greatest challenge.

Two fundamental and interconnected themes in ecology are the development and maintenance of spatial and temporal pattern and the consequences of that pattern for the dynamics of populations and ecosystems. Central to these questions is the issue of how the scale of observation influences the description of pattern; each individual and each species experiences the environment on a unique range of scales and thus responds to variability individualistically. Thus, no description of the variability and predictability of the environment makes sense without reference to the particular range of scales that are relevant to the organisms or processes being examined.

Such issues are most clear for spatial and temporal scales but apply as well to organizational complexity. The recognition in marine fisheries that total yield in multispecies fisheries remains fairly constant over long periods of time, though the composition of species may change dramatically (May 1984), is a consequence of broadening the scale of description. Similarly, a claim that microbial communities are stable to perturbations, such as the introduction of genetically engineered organisms, results from the application of a taxonomically broad filter, perhaps because only a fraction of the microbial community can be identified. In ecosystems research, one is likely to be concerned with a functional guild of microorganisms that perform a particular service to the ecosystem and to use functional redundancy to explain why ignoring changes within a guild is acceptable. This is the key to scaling and interrelating phenomena at different scales: knowing what fine detail is relevant at the higher levels and what is noise.

There are several stages in the examination of the problem of pattern and scale. First, one must have measures to describe pattern (Gardner and others 1987; Milne 1988), so that criteria can be established for relating that pattern to its causes and consequences. Cross-correlational analyses can provide initial suggestions as to mechanisms but may miss emergent phenomena that arise from the collective behavior of smaller-scale processes. Theoretical investigations of the various mechanisms through which pattern can arise provide a catalog of possibilities and may suggest relevant experiments to distinguish among hypothesized mechanisms.

All ecological systems exhibit heterogeneity and patchiness on a broad range of scales, and this patchiness is fundamental to population dynamics (Levin 1974; Roughgarden 1976), community organization and stability (Holling 1986; Kareiva 1987), and element cycling (Bormann and Likens 1979). Patchiness is a concept that cuts across terrestrial and marine systems and provides a common ground for population biologists and ecosystem scientists. Patchiness, and the role of humans in fragmenting habitats, is key to the persistence of rare species and the spread of pest species. The level of species diversity represents a balance between regional processes, such as dispersal and species formation, and local processes, such as biotic interactions and stochasticity (Ricklefs 1987).

Spatial pattern and patchiness have many consequences for the biota. Patchiness in the distribution of resources is fundamental to the way organisms exploit their environment (Mangel and Clark 1986; Pulliam 1989; Schoener 1971; Wiens 1976). Environmental heterogeneity provides a diversity of resources that can lead to coexistence among competitors that could not coexist in homogenous environments (Horn and MacArthur 1972; Levin 1970, 1974); but the problem of how to count the number of resources is vexing. Trivially, no environment is completely homogeneous. But how different must resources be to support different species? This question, which has been central in community ecology (MacArthur 1970; May and MacArthur 1972; Whittaker and Levin 1977), goes to the heart of the problem of scale. Species can subdivide the environment spatially, concentrating on different parts of the same plant (Broadhead and Wapshere 1966), different layers of vegetation (MacArthur, Recher, and Cody 1966), or different microenvironments; or they can subdivide it temporally, partitioning a successional gradient (Levin and Paine 1974) or a seasonal one. Thus, resource partitioning can result in temporally constant, spatially nonuniform patterns, or spatially constant, temporally nonuniform ones, or spatiotemporal mosaics (Levin and Paine 1974; Paine and Levin 1981; Tilman 1988; Whittaker and Levin 1977).

All of this reinforces the recognition that there is no single correct scale at which to view ecosystems; the individualistic nature of responses to environment means that what we call a community or ecosystem is really just an arbitrary subdivision of a continuous gradation of local species assemblages (Whittaker 1975). It also carries important implications for predicting how the biota will respond to global change and other stresses. Communities are not well-integrated units that move en masse. They are collections of organisms and species that respond individualistically to temporal variation, as they do to spatial variation. This is also true, of course, of the evolutionary responses of populations. Thus, if predictable patterns may be observed in what we define as communities and ecosystems, they have arisen through the individualistic ecological and evolu-

tionary responses of their components, rather than some higher-level evolution at the ecosystem level, Gaia notwithstanding (Lovelock 1972; see also Schneider and Boston 1991 for a wide range of views).

That there is no single correct scale or level at which to describe a system does not mean that all scales serve equally well or that there are not scaling laws. This is the major lesson of the theory of fractals (Mandelbrot 1977; Milne 1988; Sugihara and May 1990). The power of methods of spatial statistics—such as fractals, nested quadrat analysis (Greig-Smith 1964; Oosting 1956), semivariograms or correlograms (Burrough 1981, 1983a, 1983b; Sokal, Jacquez, and Wooten 1989; Sokal and Oden 1978), or spectral analysis (Chatfield 1984)—or of allometry (Brown and Nicoletto 1991; Calder 1984; Harvey and Pagel 1991; Platt 1985) is their capability to describe how patterns change across scales. Thus, such methods have been used in ecology to quantify change in soils and in ecosystem properties at the level of subfields (Robertson and others 1988) or landscapes (Krummel and others 1987) and in marine systems to quantify the distribution of physical factors, primary producers, and consumers (Haury, McGowan, and Wiebe 1978; Levin, Morin, and Powell 1989; Steele 1978, 1991; Weber, El-Sayed, and Hampton 1986).

The simple statistical description of patterns is a starting point, but correlations are no substitute for mechanistic understanding (Lehman 1986). Modeling can play a powerful role in suggesting possible mechanisms and experiments, in exploring the possible consequences of individual factors that cannot be easily separated experimentally, and in relating fine-scale data to broad-scale patterns.

Because there is no single scale at which ecosystems should be described, there is no single scale at which models should be constructed. Methods from statistics and dynamical systems theory can play an important part in helping to determine the dimensionality of underlying mechanisms and of appropriate models (Schaffer 1981; Schaffer and Kot 1985; Sugihara, Grenfell, and May 1990; Takens 1981). We need to have available a suite of models of different levels of complexity and to understand the consequences of suppressing or incorporating detail. Models that are insufficiently detailed may ignore critical internal heterogeneity, such as that which is responsible for maintaining species diversity (Holling 1986); it is clear, for example, that the broad brush of the general circulation models ignores detail that is relevant for understanding biotic influences on climatic systems, and vice versa. On the other hand, overly detailed models provide little understanding of what the essential forces are, have more parameters and functional forms to estimate than the available data justify, admit multiple basins of attraction, and are more prone to erratic dynamics that hamper prediction and parameter estimation. Just as we would not seek to build a model of human behavior by describing what every cell is doing, we cannot expect to model the dynamics of ecosystems by accounting for every individual, or for every species (Ludwig, Jones, and Holling 1978). We must determine what levels of aggregation and simplification are appropriate for the problem at hand.

In an extremely instructive study, Ludwig and Walters (1985) have shown clearly that in some cases aggregated models can serve as better management tools than highly detailed models, even when the data used to fit the parameters of the model have been generated by the detailed model; in retrospect, this should accord well with intuition. The problem of aggregation and simplification is to determine the minimal level of detail that is sufficient to the task (Levin 1992b; Rastetter and others 1992).

Conclusions

Classical ecological models (Scudo and Ziegler 1978) treated communities as closed, integrated, deterministic, and homogeneous. Such models are simplifications of real systems and provide a place to begin analysis. However, each of these assumptions must be relaxed if we are to understand the factors governing the diversity and dynamics of ecosystems. Virtually every population will exhibit patchiness and variability on a range of spatial and temporal scales, so that the definition of commonness or rarity is a matter of scale (Schoener 1987). Virtually every ecosystem exhibits patchiness and variability on a range of spatial, temporal, and organizational scales, substantial interaction with other systems, and significant influence of local stochastic events. These phenomena are critical for the maintenance of most species, which are locally ephemeral and competitively inferior and which depend on the continual local renewal of resources and mechanisms such as dispersal to find those opportunities. Fragmentation, local disturbance, and vari-

ability also can have major consequences for patterns of nutrient cycling (Bormann and Likens 1979), persistence (Pimm and Gilpin 1989), and patterns of the spread of introduced species (Durrett 1988; Mooney and Drake 1986). The key is to separate the components of variability into those that inhibit persistence and coexistence, those that promote them, and those that are noise (Chesson 1986).

To address such phenomena, we must find ways to quantify patterns of variability in space and time, to understand how patterns change with scale (for example, Steele 1978, 1989; Dagan 1986), and to understand the causes and consequences of pattern (Levin 1989; Wiens 1989). This is a daunting task that must involve remote sensing, spatial statistics, and other methods to quantify pattern at broad scales; theoretical work to suggest mechanisms and explore relationships; and experimental work, carried out both at fine scales and through whole-system manipulations, to test hypotheses. Together, these can provide insights as to how information is transferred across scales and, hence, how to simplify and aggregate models.

The problem of relating phenomena across scales is the central problem in biology and in all of science. Cross-scale studies are critical to complement more traditional studies carried out on narrow single scales of space, time, and organizational complexity (Holling 1992a; Levin 1988, 1989; Meentenmeyer and Box 1987; Steele 1978, 1989), just as measures of $\int$-diversity are needed to complement within-community measures of å-diversity (Whittaker 1975). By addressing this challenge, using the insights gained from similar studies in other sciences and the unique approaches that must be developed for ecological systems, we can enhance greatly our understanding of the dynamics of ecosystems and develop the theoretical basis necessary to manage them.

References

Ågren, G. I., R. E. McMurtrie, W. J. Parton, J. Pastor, and H. H. Shugart. 1991. "State-of-the-Art of Models of Production-Decomposition Linkages in Conifer and Grassland Ecosystems." *Ecological Applications* 1, pp. 118–38.

Allen, T. F. H., and T. B. Starr. 1982. *Hierarchy: Perspectives for Ecological Diversity*. Chicago, Ill.: University of Chicago Press.

Armstrong, R. A. 1988. "The Effects of Disturbance Patch Size on Species Coexistence." *Journal of Theoretical Biology* 133, pp. 169–84.

Bormann, F. H., and G. E. Likens. 1979. *Pattern and Process in a Forested Ecosystem.* New York: Springer-Verlag.

Broadhead, E., and A. J. Wapshere. 1966. "*Mesopsocus* Populations on Larch in England: The Distribution and Dynamics of Two Closely Related Coexisting Species of Psocoptera Sharing the Same Food Resource." *Ecological Monographs* 36, pp. 328–83.

Brown, J. H., and P. F. Nicoletto. 1991. "Spatial Scaling of Species Composition: Body Masses of North American Land Mammals." *American Naturalist* 138, pp. 1478–512.

Burkey, T. V. 1989. "Extinction in Nature Reserves: The Effect of Fragmentation and the Importance of Migration between Reserve Fragments." *Oikos* 55, pp. 75–81.

Burrough, P. A. 1981. "Fractal Dimensions of Landscapes and Other Environmental Data." *Nature* 294, pp. 240–42.

———. 1983a. "Multiscale Sources of Spatial Variation in Soil. I: The Application of Fractal Concepts to Nested Levels of Soil Variation." *Journal of Soil Science* 34, pp. 577–97.

———. 1983b. "Multiscale Sources of Spatial Variation in Soil. II: A Non-Brownian Fractal Model and Its Applications in Soil Survey." *Journal of Soil Science* 34, pp. 599–620.

Calder, W. A. III. 1984. *Size, Function, and Life History.* Cambridge, Mass.: Harvard University Press.

Chatfield, C. 1984. *The Analysis of Time Series: An Introduction.* 3d ed. London, England: Chapman and Hall.

Chesson, P. 1986. "Environmental Variation and the Coexistence of Species." In J. Diamond and T. J. Case, eds., *Community Ecology*, pp. 240–56. New York: Harper and Row.

Clark, W. C. 1985. "Scales of Climate Impacts." *Climatic Change* 7, pp. 5–27.

Cohen, J. E. 1977. "Ratio of Prey to Predators in Community Food Webs." *Nature* 270, pp. 165–77.

———. 1989. "Food Webs and Community Structure." In J. Roughgarden, R. M. May, and Simon Levin, eds., *Perspectives in Theoretical Ecology*, pp. 181–202. Princeton, N.J.: Princeton University Press.

Colebrook, J. M. 1982. "Continuous Plankton Records: Seasonal Variations in the Distribution and Abundance of Plankton in the North Atlantic Ocean and the North Sea (*Calanus finmarchicus*)." *Journal of Plankton Research* 4, pp. 435–62.

Dagan, G. 1986. "Statistical Theory of Groundwater Flow and Transport: Pore to Laboratory, Laboratory to Formation, and Formation to Regional Scale." *Water Resources Research* 22, pp. 120S–134S.

Denman, K. L., and T. M. Powell. 1984. "Effects of Physical Processes on Planktonic Ecosystems in the Coastal Ocean." *Oceanography and Marine Biology Annual Review* 22, pp. 125–68.

Dickson, R. R., P. M. Kelly, J. M. Colebrook, W. S. Wooster, and D. H. Cushing. 1988. "North Winds and Production in the Eastern North Atlantic." *Journal of Plankton Research* 10, pp. 151–69.

Durrett, R. 1988. "Crabgrass, Measles, and Gypsy Moths: An Introduction to Interacting Particle Systems." *Mathematical Intelligencer* 10, pp. 37–47.

Ehleringer, J., and C. Field, eds. 1993. *Scaling Physiological Processes: Leaf to Globe.* San Diego, Calif.: Academic Press.

Elton, C. S. 1958. *The Ecology of Invasions by Animals and Plants.* London: Methuen.

Fahrig, L., and J. Paloheimo. 1988a. "Determinants of Local Population Size in Patchy Habitat." *Theoretical Population Biology* 34, pp. 194–213.

———. 1988b. "Effect of Spatial Arrangement of Habitat Patches on Local Population Size." *Ecology* 69, pp. 468–75.

Gardner, R. H., B. T. Milne, M. G. Turner, and R. V. O'Neill. 1987. "Neutral Models for the Analysis of Broad Landscape Pattern." *Landscape Ecology* 1, pp. 19–28.

Gilpin, M. E., and I. Hanski, eds. 1991. *Metapopulation Dynamics.* London: Academic Press.

Greig-Smith, P. 1964. *Quantitative Plant Ecology.* 2d ed. London: Butterworths.

Hansen, J., I. Fung, A. Lacis, S. Lebedeff, D. Rind, B. Ruedy, G. Russell, and P. Stone. 1987. "Prediction of Near-term Climate Evolution: What Can We Tell Decision-makers Now?" In *Preparing for Climate Change*, pp. 35–47. Proceedings of the first North American conference on preparing for climate changes, October 27–29. Washington, D.C.: Government Institutes, Inc.

Harvey, P. H., and M. D. Pagel. 1991. *The Comparative Method in Evolutionary Biology.* Oxford, England: Oxford University Press.

Haury, L. R., J. A. McGowan, and P. H. Wiebe. 1978. "Patterns and Processes in the Time-space Scales of Plankton Distributions." In J. H. Steele, ed., *Spatial Pattern in Plankton Communities*, pp. 277–327. New York: Plenum.

Holling, C. S. 1986. "The Resilience of Terrestrial Ecosystems: Local Surprise and Global Change." In W. C. Clark and R. E. Munn, eds., *Sustainable Development of the Biosphere*, pp. 292–317. Cambridge, England: Cambridge University Press.

———. 1992a. "Cross-scale Morphology, Geometry, and Dynamics of Ecosystems." *Ecological Monographs* 62:4, pp. 447–502.

———. 1992b. "The Role of Forest Insects in Structuring the Boreal Landscape." In H. H. Shugart, ed., *A Systems Analysis of the Global Boreal Forest*, pp. 170–91. Cambridge, England: Cambridge University Press.

Horn, H. S., and R. H. MacArthur. 1972. "Competition among Fugitive Species in a Harlequin Environment." *Ecology* 53, pp. 749–52.

Hutchinson, G. E. 1953. "The Concept of Pattern in Ecology." *Proceedings of the National Academy of Sciences* 105, pp. 1–12.

Jarvis, P. G., and K. G. McNaughton. 1986. "Stomatal Control of Transpiration: Scaling up from Leaf to Region." *Advances in Ecological Research* 15, pp. 1–49.

Kareiva, P. M. 1987. "Habitat Fragmentation and the Stability of Predator-Prey Interactions." *Nature* 321, pp. 388–91.

Kareiva, P., and M. Anderson. 1988. "Spatial Aspects of Species Interactions: The Wedding of Models and Experiments." In Alan Hastings, ed., *Community Ecology*, pp. 35–50. Lecture Notes in Biomathematics 77. Berlin: Springer-Verlag.

Kratz, T. K., T. M. Frost, and J. J. Magnuson. 1987. "Inferences from Spatial and Temporal Variability in Ecosystems: Long-term Zooplankton Data from Lakes." *American Naturalist* 129, pp. 830–46.

Krummel, J. R., R. H. Gardner, G. Sugihara, R. V. O'Neill, and P. R. Coleman. 1987. "Landscape Patterns in a Disturbed Environment." *Oikos* 48, pp. 321–24.

Lehman, J. T. 1986. "The Goal of Understanding in Limnology." *Limnology and Oceanography* 31, pp. 1160–66.

Levene, H. 1953. "Genetic Equilibrium When More than One Ecological Niche Is Available." *American Naturalist* 87, pp. 331–33.

Levin, Simon A. 1970. "Community Equilibria and Stability, and an Extension of the Competitive Exclusion Principle." *American Naturalist* 104, pp. 413–23.

———. 1974. "Dispersion and Population Interactions." *American Naturalist* 108, pp. 207–28.

———. 1978. "Pattern Formation in Ecological Communities." In J. H. Steele, ed., *Spatial Pattern in Plankton Communities*, pp. 433–66. New York: Plenum.

———. 1981. "Mechanisms for the Generation and Maintenance of Diversity." In R. W. Hiorns and D. Cooke, eds., *The Mathematical Theory of the Dynamics of Biological Populations*, pp. 173–94. London: Academic Press.

———. 1988. "Pattern, Scale, and Variability: An Ecological Perspective." In A. Hastings, ed., *Community Ecology*, pp. 1–12. Lecture Notes in Biomathematics 77. Heidelberg: Springer-Verlag.

———. 1989. "Challenges in the Development of a Theory of Community and Ecosystem Structure and Function." In J. Roughgarden, R. M. May, and Simon A. Levin, eds., *Perspectives in Ecological Theory*, pp. 242–55. Princeton, N.J.: Princeton University Press.

———. 1992a. "The Problem of Pattern and Scale in Ecology." *Ecology* 73:6, pp. 1943–67.

———. 1992b. "The Problem of Relevant Detail." In S. Busenberg and M. Martelli, eds., *Differential Equations Models in Biology, Epidemiology, and Ecology, Proceedings, Claremont 1990*, pp. 9–15. Lecture Notes in Biomathematics 92. Berlin: Springer-Verlag.

———. 1993. "Concepts of Scale at the Local Level." In J. R. Ehleringer and C. B. Field, eds., *Scaling Physiological Processes: Leaf to Globe*, pp. 7–19. San Diego, Calif.: Academic Press.

Levin, Simon A., J. E. Levin, and R. T. Paine. 1977. "Snowy Owl Predation on Short-eared Owls." *The Condor* 79, p. 395.

Levin, Simon A., A. Morin, and T. H. Powell. 1989. "Patterns and Processes in the Distribution and Dynamics of Antarctic Krill." In *Scientific Committee for the Conservation of Antarctic Marine Living Resources: Selected Scientific Papers, Part 1*, pp. 281–99. SC-CAMLR-SSP/5. Hobart, Australia: Committee for the Conservation of Antarctic Marine Living Resources.

Levin, Simon A., and R. T. Paine. 1974. "Disturbance, Patch Formation, and Community Structure." *Proceedings of the National Academy of Sciences* 71, pp. 2744–47.

Levin, Simon A., and D. Pimentel. 1981. "Selection of Intermediate Rates of Increase in Parasite-host Systems." *American Naturalist* 117, pp. 308–15.

Lovelock, J. E. 1972. "Gaia as Seen through the Atmosphere." *Atmospheric Environment* 6, pp. 579–80.

Ludwig, D., D. D. Jones, and C. S. Holling. 1978. "Qualitative Analysis of Insect Outbreak Systems: The Spruce Budworm and Forest." *Journal of Animal Ecology* 44, pp. 315–32.

Ludwig, D., and C. J. Walters. 1985. "Are Age-structured Models Appropriate for Catch-Effort Data?" *Canadian Journal of Fisheries and Aquatic Sciences* 42, pp. 1066–72.

MacArthur, R. H. 1970. "Species Packing and Competitive Equilibrium among Many Species." *Theoretical Population Biology* 1, pp. 1–11.

———. 1972. *Geographical Ecology.* New York: Harper and Row.

MacArthur, R. H., H. Recher, and M. Cody. 1966. "On the Relation between Habitat Selection and Species Diversity." *American Naturalist* 100, pp. 319–32.

Mandelbrot, B. B. 1977. *Fractals: Form, Chance, and Dimension.* San Francisco, Calif.: Freeman.

Mangel, M., and C. W. Clark. 1986. "Towards a Unified Foraging Theory." *Ecology* 67, pp. 1127–38.

May, R. M., ed. 1984. *Exploitation of Marine Communities.* Berlin: Springer-Verlag.

May, R. M., and R. H. MacArthur. 1972. "Niche Overlap as a Function of Environmental Variability." *Proceedings of the National Academy of Sciences* 69, pp. 1109–13.

McGowan, J. A. 1990. "Climate and Change in Oceanic Ecosystems: The Value of Time-Series Data." *Trends in Ecology and Evolution* 5, pp. 293–99.

Meentenmeyer, V., and E. O. Box. 1987. "Scale Effects in Landscape Studies." In M. G. Turner, ed., *Landscape Heterogeneity and Disturbance,* pp. 15–34. New York: Springer-Verlag.

Milne, B. T. 1988. "Measuring the Fractal Geometry of Landscapes." *Applied Mathematics and Computation* 27, pp. 67–79.

Mooney, H. A., and J. A. Drake. 1986. *Ecology of Biological Invasions of North America and Hawaii.* New York: Springer-Verlag.

Nee, S., and R. M. May. 1992. "Dynamics of Metapopulations: Habitat Destruction and Competitive Coexistence." *Journal of Animal Ecology* 61:1, pp. 37–40.

Norman, J. M. 1980. "Interfacing Leaf and Canopy Light Interception Models." In J. D. Hesketh and J. W. Jones, eds., *Predicting Photosynthesis for Ecosystem Models.* Vol. 2, pp. 49–67. Boca Raton, Fla.: CRC.

Nuernberger, B. D. 1991. "Population Structure of *Dineutus assimilis* in a Patchy Environment: Dispersal, Gene Flow, and Persistence." Ph.D. diss., Cornell University, Ithaca, N.Y.

Odum, H. 1983. *Systems Ecology: An Introduction.* New York: John Wiley.

Oosting, H. J. 1956. *The Study of Plant Communities.* 2d ed. San Francisco, CA: W. H. Freeman.

Paine, R. T. 1966. "Food Web Complexity and Species Diversity." *American Naturalist* 100, pp. 65–75.

———. 1980. "Food Webs: Linkage, Interaction Strength and Community Infrastructure. The Third Tansley Lecture." *Journal of Animal Ecology* 49, pp. 667–85.

Paine, R. T., and Simon A. Levin. 1981. "Intertidal Landscapes: Disturbance and the Dynamics of Pattern." *Ecological Monographs* 51:2, pp. 145–78.

Parton, W. J., C. V. Cole, J. W. B. Stewart, D. S. Ojima, and D. S. Schimel. 1989. "Simulating Regional Patterns of Soil C, N, and P Dynamics in the U.S. Central Grassland Region." In L. Bergstrom and M. Clarholm, eds., *Ecology of Arable Land,* pp. 99–108. Dordrecht, the Netherlands: Kluwer Academic.

Pickett, S. T. A., and P. S. White, eds. 1985. *The Ecology of Natural Disturbance and Patch Dynamics.* Orlando, Fla.: Academic Press.

Pimm, S. L. 1982. *Food Webs.* Population and Community Biology Series. New York: Chapman and Hall.

Pimm, S. L., and M. E. Gilpin. 1989. "Theoretical Issues in Conservation Biology." In J. Roughgarden, R. M. May, and Simon A. Levin, eds., *Perspectives in Theoretical Ecology,* pp. 287–305. Princeton, N.J.: Princeton University Press.

Platt, T. 1985. "Structure of the Marine Ecosystem: Its Allometric Basis." In R. E. Ulanowicz and T. Platt, eds., "Ecosystem Theory for Biological Oceanography." *Canadian Bulletin of Fisheries and Aquatic Sciences* 213, pp. 55–75.

Powell, T. M. 1989. "Physical and Biological Scales of Variability in Lakes, Estuaries, and the Coastal Ocean." In J. Roughgarden, R. M. May, and Simon A. Levin, eds., *Perspectives in Theoretical Ecology*, pp. 157–80. Princeton, N.J.: Princeton University Press.

Pulliam, H. Ronald. 1989. "Individual Behavior and the Procurement of Essential Resources." In J. Roughgarden, R. M. May, and Simon A. Levin, eds., *Perspectives in Theoretical Ecology*, pp. 25–38. Princeton, N.J.: Princeton University Press.

Radach, G. 1984. "Variations in the Plankton in Relation to Climate." *Rapports et Proces-Verbaux des Réunions* (Conseil International pour l'Exploration de la Mer) 185, pp. 234–54.

Rastetter, E. B., A. W. King, B. J. Cosby, G. M. Hornberger, R. V. O'Neill, and J. E. Hobbie. 1992. "Aggregating Fine-scale Ecological Knowledge to Model Coarser-scale Attributes of Ecosystems." *Ecological Applications* 2, pp. 55–70.

Ricklefs, R. E. 1987. "Community Diversity: Relative Roles of Local and Regional Processes." *Science* 235, pp. 167–71.

Robertson, G. P., M. A. Huston, F. C. Evans, and J. M. Tiedje. 1988. "Spatial Patterns in a Successional Plant Community: Patterns of Nitrogen Availability." *Ecology* 69, pp. 1517–24.

Roughgarden, J. 1976. "Influence of Competition on Patchiness in a Random Environment." *Theoretical Population Biology* 14, pp. 185–203.

Schaffer, W. M. 1981. "Ecological Abstraction: The Consequences of Reduced Dimensionality in Ecological Models." *Ecological Monographs* 51, pp. 383–401.

Schaffer, W. M., and M. Kot. 1985. "Nearly One-Dimensional Dynamics in an Epidemic." *Journal of Theoretical Biology* 112, pp. 403–27.

Schimel, D. S., W. J. Parton, T. G. F. Kittel, D. S. Ojima, and C. V. Cole. 1990. "Grassland Biogeochemistry: Links to Atmospheric Processes." *Climate Change* 17, pp. 13–25.

Schneider, S. H. 1989. "The Greenhouse Effect: Science and Policy." *Science* 243, pp. 771–81.

Schneider, S. H., and P. J. Boston, eds. 1991. *Scientists on Gaia*. Cambridge, Mass.: M.I.T. Press.

Schoener, T. W. 1971. "Theory of Feeding Strategies." *Annual Review of Ecology and Systematics* 2, pp. 369–404.

———. 1987. "The Geographical Distribution of Rarity." *Oecologia* (Berlin) 74, pp. 161–73.

———. 1989. "Food Webs from the Small to the Large." *Ecology* 70, pp. 1559–89.

Scudo, F. M., and J. R. Ziegler. 1978. *The Golden Age of Theoretical Ecology: 1923–1940*. Lecture Notes in Biomathematics 22. Berlin: Springer-Verlag.

Sokal, R. R., and N. L. Oden. 1978. "Spatial Autocorrelation in Biology 2: Some Biological Implications and Four Examples of Evolutionary and Ecological Interest." *Biological Journal of the Linnean Society* 10, pp. 229–49.

Sokal, R. R., G. M. Jacquez, and M. C. Wooten. 1989. "Spatial Autocorrelation Analysis of Migration and Selection." *Genetics* 121, pp. 845–56.

Steele, J. H. 1978. "Some Comments on Plankton Patches." In J. H. Steele, ed., *Spatial Pattern in Plankton Communities*, pp. 1–20. New York: Plenum.

———. 1989. "Discussion: Scale and Coupling in Ecological Systems." In J. Roughgarden, R. M. May, and Simon A. Levin, eds., *Perspectives in Theoretical Ecology*, pp. 177–80. Princeton, N.J.: Princeton University Press.

———. 1991. "Can Ecological Theory Cross the Land-Sea Boundary?" *Journal of Theoretical Biology* 153, pp. 425–36.

Stommel, H. 1963. "Varieties of Oceanographic Experience." *Science* 139, pp. 572–76.

Sugihara, G. 1982. "Niche Hierarchy: Structure, Organization, and Assembly in Natural Communities." Ph.D. diss., Princeton University, Princeton, N.J.

Sugihara, G., B. Grenfell, and R. M. May. 1990. "Distinguishing Error from Chaos in Ecological Time Series." *Philosophical Transactions of the Royal Society of London Bulletin* 330, pp. 235–51.

Sugihara, G., and R. M. May. 1990. "Applications of Fractals in Ecology." *Trends in Ecology and Evolution* 5, pp. 79–86.

Takens, F. 1981. "Detecting Strange Attractors in Turbulence." In D. A. Rand and L. S. Young, eds., *Dynamical Systems and Turbulence: Warwick 1980*, pp. 366–81. Lecture Notes in Mathematics 898. Berlin: Springer-Verlag.

Tilman, D. 1988. *Plant Strategies and the Dynamics and Structure of Plant Communities.* Princeton, N.J.: Princeton University Press.

Watt, A. S. 1947. "Pattern and Process in the Plant Community." *Journal of Ecology* 35, pp. 1–22.

Weber, L. H., S. Z. El-Sayed, and I. Hampton. 1986. "The Variance Spectra of Phytoplankton, Krill, and Water Temperature in the Antarctic Ocean South of Africa." *Deep-Sea Research* 33, pp. 1327–43.

Whittaker, R. H. 1975. *Communities and Ecosystems.* New York: Macmillan.

Whittaker, R. H., and S. A. Levin. 1977. "The Role of Mosaic Phenomena in Natural Communities." *Theoretical Population Biology* 12, pp. 117–39.

Wiens, J. A. 1976. "Population Responses to Patchy Environments." *Annual Review of Ecology and Systematics* 7, pp. 81–120.

———. 1989. "Spatial Scaling in Ecology." *Functional Ecology* 3, pp. 385–97.

Yodzis, P. 1989. *Introduction to Theoretical Ecology.* New York: Harper and Row.

Comments

Charles H. Peterson

I wish to acknowledge support from the National Science Foundation and the State of North Carolina for support under projects of the Cooperative Institute of Fisheries Oceanography and to thank W. Ellington, M. E. Hay, H. Lenihan, and F. Micheli for their comments on the manuscript.

Simon Levin in his 1992 MacArthur award lecture printed in *Ecology* (Levin 1992) and again in his contribution to this volume provides irrefutable justification for the need to design, conduct, and integrate analyses of ecological problems on multiple spatial and temporal scales. This mandate to environmental scientists is as necessary and as compelling in the study of sustainability of resource use as it is in the study of any basic problem in ecology. The fundamental nature, durability, and articulate expression of the wisdom and advice provided by Levin in these contributions are likely to ensure their longevity as conceptual roadmaps guiding the strategies of ecological problem solving for some long time into the future.

I see a continuing, unfulfilled need for an analogous contribution in the social sciences on the implications of scale to our ability to achieve sustainable use of our planet's natural resources. There is a serious danger implicit in the recent publicity over sustainable development and the role of ecological science in achieving sustainability. The danger is that unrealistic expectations of what ecology and natural sciences might provide may deflect attention away from the need to address the social science context and the core social problem that requires us even to question sustainability: the unchecked growth of the human population.

Reliance on some unspecified, future technological innovation has long been used as an excuse for failing to use resources in a sustainable fashion. Although Malthus (1806) may have failed to predict accurately the time scale on which resources would limit growth of the human population, the principle of ultimate resource limitation on which he built his argu-

ments drives the push for sustainable development today. Recent calculations suggest that humans now use and co-opt something like 40 percent of the present net global terrestrial productivity (Vitousek and others 1986). Even in the absence of further human population growth, the economies of many populous countries are expanding, thus ensuring further exploitation of global production. The human population of the globe is perilously close to its sustainable limit today. No false sense of security over the power of ecology to design strategies for sustainable use can be allowed to deflect attention from attempts to solve the human population crisis.

Although Levin's essays on the role of scale in ecology and in achieving sustainability of resource use follow the optimistic prescription set forth by the Ecological Society of America's Sustainable Biosphere Initiative (Lubchenco and others 1991), it is important to temper this enthusiasm with a corresponding analysis of how the spatial and temporal scales of human societies constrain and otherwise affect the implementation of advice from natural science on sustainable resource use. The ecological problems of human use of resources do not differ intrinsically from the ecological challenges posed by the exploitation of other species in natural ecosystems. What is different is the need to recognize explicitly the implications of human social scales in achieving sustainability.

Some ecologists (for example, Ehrlich 1968; Hardin 1993; Murdoch 1980) have devoted substantial effort to addressing the important connection between natural and social sciences in dealing with the problems of human population and resource exploitation. Nevertheless, need still exists for an introspective and integrative overview of the role of scale in interactions between natural and social science, analogous to what Levin has done here for natural science alone. The political, social, and economic landscapes of the human societies on Earth provide the practical, realistic framework in which sustainability must be implemented. In the absence of a sophisticated understanding of the interactions between social scales of human populations and scales of impacts on the natural resources on which they rely, the work of ecologists on sustainability of resource use will be of little practical value.

References

Ehrlich, Paul R. 1968. *The Population Bomb.* New York: Ballantine.

Hardin, G. 1993. *Living within Limits: Ecology, Economics, and Population Taboos.* New York: Oxford University Press.

Levin, Simon A. 1992. "The Pattern of Pattern and Scale in Ecology." *Ecology* 73, pp. 1943–67.

Lubchenco, J., A. M. Olson, L. B. Brubaker, S. R. Carpenter, M. M. Holland, S. P. Hubbell, Simon A. Levin, J. A. McMahon, P. A. Matson, J. M. Melillo, H. A. Mooney, C. H. Peterson, H. Ronald Pulliam, L. A. Real, P. J. Regal, and P. G. Risser. 1991. "The Sustainable Biosphere Initiative: An Ecological Research Agenda." *Ecology* 72, pp. 371–442.

Malthus, T. R. 1806. "An Essay on the Principle of Population." 3rd ed. London: J. Johson Publishers.

Murdoch, W. W. 1980. *The Poverty of Nations: Population, Hunger, and Development.* Baltimore, Md.: Johns Hopkins University Press.

Vitousek, P. M., P. R. Ehrlich, A. H. Ehrlich, and P. A. Matson. 1986. "Human Appropriation of the Products of Photosynthesis. *Bioscience* 36, pp. 368–73.

8

Sustainability and the Changing Atmosphere: Assessing Changes in Chemical and Physical Climate

Meinrat O. Andreae and Robert E. Dickinson

The atmosphere maintains life on Earth through its physical weather and climate system and through the effects of its chemical composition. In a broad sense, there is no question but that these systems are naturally sustainable; they will keep operating, no matter what. Life has been present on Earth for 4 billion years, and it seems highly likely that it will, in some form, extend that far into the future. In this chapter, we use the term sustainability in a narrower sense, adapting the definition of strong sustainability laid out by Daly (1991), which requires that both man-made and natural capital remain intact in the course of sustainable development or in a sustainable global economy. In this sense, a sustainable activity is one that leaves intact the ability of the atmosphere to support the present biota. In other words, for an activity to be sustainable, it should not diminish the ability of the atmosphere to perform the following essential services for the biota currently present:

- To regulate the global budget of energy and to redistribute energy between high and low latitudes and between oceans and continents.

- To establish surface temperature and moisture regimes, growing seasons, and so forth suitable for the biota that have previously adopted to such.

- To provide visible solar radiation at levels needed for photosynthesis by plants.

- To screen out harmful components of solar and cosmic radiation.

- To redistribute, remove, and eliminate gases and particles emitted by the biota that would be harmful if they were to accumulate in the atmosphere.

A workable definition of atmospheric sustainability must include reference to the present biota. Over longer time spans, living things can adapt to environmental change, initially by changing the community's structure and composition and eventually by evolving genetically. At issue here is the well-being of all the present biota and their descendants, reflecting the definition of sustainable development offered by the Brundtland Commission, as development that "meets the needs of the present without compromising the ability of future generations to meet their own needs" (World Commission on Environment and Development 1987).

From the point of view of the biosphere, the essential function of the atmosphere is to provide a reasonably stable climate. Climate in a broad sense encompasses the chemical and radiative properties of the atmosphere as well as the classical meteorological parameters. "Reasonably stable" requires that the rates of environmental change do not exceed those to which species and communities—or, in the human context, economies and societies—are adapted or can respond without serious negative consequences.

The effect of human activities on global climate in the narrower, meteorological sense is being intensely discussed both within the scientific community and within society at large. (The current state of the art on this topic is presented in the report of the Intergovernmental Panel on Climate Change—see Houghton, Callander, and Varney 1992; Houghton, Jenkins, and Ephraums 1990—and in a less technical, but scientifically accurate form by Nilsson 1992.) Human activities are altering the gaseous composition of the atmosphere in previously unknown ways and as a result are apparently warming global average temperatures to outside the envelope of the past million years. This can be achieved relatively easily, because the last 10,000 years have already been near the warm limits of this period. Furthermore, the atmosphere has a relatively small mass, and the addition of trace gases that make up only a small fraction of the atmosphere's total mass can significantly affect radiative or chemical balances. The old balances will not return within the next millennia. Can we achieve a new state that can still adequately maintain our natural systems, or will we continue to drift away from balance?

Changes in global climate over the last century by themselves do not seem particularly threatening; global temperatures have risen by fits and spurts, but by no more than 0.5 °C or so. There is no direct means of establishing that the warming we see is that expected from greenhouse gases. What we see unequivocally is the incessant year-to-year rise of CO_2 (carbon dioxide) and other atmospheric greenhouse gases. We can calculate with considerable confidence what the role of these gases, and of their increase, is in trapping thermal infrared radiation and so in warming the planet. We also are fairly confident that if the concentrations of CO_2 were orders of magnitude smaller than they are, Earth would be too cold to be habitable, perhaps completely covered with ice. However, present-day science reaches its limits in trying to determine precisely the change in climate expected from the present or future concentrations of greenhouse gases. The increases in temperature up to now, besides not being unequivocally a result of greenhouse gases, are at the low end of what might be expected. This may be either because the climate system is more stable to the greenhouse forcing than expected or,

perhaps more likely, because other changing processes have up to now countered the greenhouse warming.

There is a substantial reflection of solar radiation by tropospheric aerosols resulting from human activities; this reflection could have up to now partially countered the greenhouse gas warming (Charlson and others 1991). Due to increased atmospheric aerosol loading, cloud properties could be changing in such a way as to cool the planet. Natural phenomena can also act to slow greenhouse warming. For example, we know that a major volcano, Pinatubo, erupted last year and injected massive amounts of sulfate aerosol into the stratosphere, which should bring greenhouse warming to a halt for a year or two. Furthermore, some large-scale adjustment may have occurred in the internal dynamics of the oceans. However, all these possibilities for natural or inadvertent mitigation of greenhouse warming would be unlikely to continue to grow substantially with further increases in greenhouse gases. This is because carbon dioxide as well as the chlorofluorocarbons that also threaten the ozone layer once injected into the atmosphere remain there for a century or more. By contrast, stratospheric aerosols remain only a year or two, and tropospheric aerosols remain just a week or two.

The radiative climate on Earth is significantly different from pre-industrial times. Besides the effects of the greenhouse gases on infrared radiation, we are especially concerned with a very narrow band of wavelengths in the near ultraviolet. But other issues of harmful radiation might arise in the future. The inhabitants of the Earth are now flooded with electromagnetic radiation over a very broad spectrum, from the very low-frequency region of power transmission lines, through radio frequencies and microwaves, "light pollution" of the night sky, to ultraviolet and ionizing gamma radiation. It is usually assumed that the change in the radiative climate for photons less energetic than the ultraviolet has relatively little effect or is, at most, annoying. However, this has not been demonstrated convincingly even in the context of acute and chronic impact on humans, and studies on ecological effects are even less well investigated. Presently, the most threatening perturbation of radiative climate is the weakening of the stratospheric ozone layer, which shields the biosphere from ultraviolet radiation.

Characteristic patterns of temperature, winds, and so forth in the atmosphere define the physical climate. Similarly, the patterns of chemical composition of the atmosphere, which are subject to characteristic temporal and spatial variations, represent the chemical climate. Trace gases, for example, are distributed through the atmosphere in patterns of concentration reflecting their sources and sinks, and their concentrations are subject to diurnal, seasonal, and secular variations. Since many trace gases and aerosols have effects on organisms directly or through their influence on other atmospheric properties—for example, global temperatures—the perturbation of the chemical climate by human activities is of serious concern.

The atmosphere is closely connected to the biosphere. In fact, both the major and the trace gases that constitute the atmosphere are excreted from the biota: nitrogen from microbial denitrification, oxygen from plant photosynthesis, methane from bacterial fermentation, and so on. The atmosphere acts chemically to convert photochemically labile substances (such as hydrocarbons and reduced sulfur compounds) into photochemically inert compounds (such as CO_2, sulfate, and nitrogen, N_2), which are then taken up again by the biosphere. In this context, the atmosphere has two crucial functions: first, to remove chemical emissions from their source and prevent accumulation to toxic levels, and second, to combust trace gases photochemically so that they can be removed again from the atmosphere. Without this combustion, the biosphere would very soon choke on its own gaseous emissions.

Human activity has placed an additional burden on this system, releasing new kinds of emissions into the atmosphere and increasing many of the fluxes already emitted by natural processes. If the removal rates for these compounds could speed up at the same time as emissions increase, this change could in principle be sustainable. However, the atmosphere is apparently not able to accommodate this increased burden. In some respects, the increasing input of trace gases into the atmosphere even reduces the rate at which they can be removed, providing a situation both unstable and with unpredictable consequences.

In assessing sustainability, there are two substantial advantages to monitoring atmospheric properties: (1) the relatively rapid mixing of the atmosphere results in an intrinsic averaging and integrating effect, and (2) the low mass of the atmosphere makes it a sensitive indicator of chemical and physical change. The study of the time record of atmospheric CO_2 provides a clear example: the atmospheric concentration of this gas reflects the balance of inputs and outputs of CO_2 from respiration, photosynthesis, weathering, fossil fuel burning, deforestation, and so forth. It would be impossible to measure all of these processes individually to account for the overall balance with the accuracy required to deduce global trends. Yet the increase of atmospheric CO_2 is readily measured, and its magnitude provides a benchmark against which any model of the carbon cycle must be matched. Other compounds exist in the atmosphere that can serve as indicators of a changing chemical climate; these will be discussed in detail below.

Changing physical climate and carbon dioxide

Over the lifetime of our planet, life has flourished over a very wide range of climatic and chemical conditions. However, that would not have been possible if the planet had become too cold or too hot to maintain liquid oceans. Geophysical and biological processes have provided carbon dioxide and other greenhouse gases at concentrations suitable for maintaining a habitat for the unicellular life that existed over most of the history of the planet. Advanced life forms have only been present over a considerably narrower range of conditions, after development of the ozone shield and temperatures not dissimilar to those of today. Periods with temperatures warmer by as much as 10°C over the present ones occurred in the Cretaceous and earlier periods (1 to several hundred million years ago).

The extreme warmth of past geological periods is now generally explained as a consequence of CO_2 concentrations up to ten times higher than present levels. Geophysical processes are capable of providing such changes over tens of millions of years, and no other mechanism has been found capable of giving such drastically different climates. The correlation between temperature and atmospheric CO_2 is clearly seen in the analysis of Antarctic ice

Figure 8-1: Analysis of Air Trapped in Antarctic Ice Cores

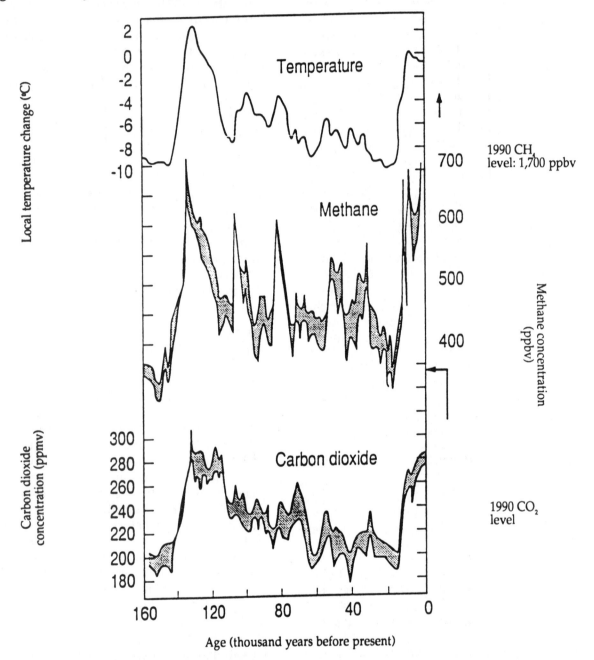

Note: Concentrations of methane and carbon dioxide were closely correlated with the local temperature over the last 160,000 years.
Source: Adapted from Houghton, Jenkins, and Ephraums 1990.

cores (see figure 8-1). Human cultures evolved over the last million years of Pleistocene climate and have therefore experienced a much narrower range of conditions. Civilization has evolved within the last 10,000 years; much of the technological development happened only in the last century.

The Pleistocene climate has been one of ice ages; large ice sheets have formed many times over the continents of the Northern Hemisphere as global temperatures dropped by several degrees from interglacial conditions. The extreme cold of ice ages is now explained in part by the low concentrations of carbon dioxide during these periods, not much more than half of present concentrations. Current temperatures are near or at the upper limit of that which has occurred over the last million years (see figures 8-2 and 8-3).

Present interpretations of the history of our planet thus show that it has experienced and survived large but slow fluctuations in carbon dioxide and temperature and that life has survived these fluctuations. The fiery temperatures of Venus, which are the result of a massive atmosphere comprised almost entirely of carbon dioxide, demonstrate that planetary habitability is not inevitable. Furthermore, even if we were not to distinguish habitats of humans from those of dinosaurs, it is remarkable that the current rates of change are hundreds to thousands of times faster than those of past geological changes.

Humans began to affect atmospheric chemistry when they learned to control fire, some 1.5 million to 2 million years ago, and began to use it on a large scale in Africa (James 1989). The use of fire by indigenous populations evidently changed the landscape quite dramatically, and on a nearly continental scale, an activity that might not be sustainable by our definition. This led to a new equilibrium based on fire-managed landscapes in the African savannas (Schüle 1990). But once this transformation had occurred, the new balance between ecology and human activity could probably have been sustainable indefinitely. Since the fires only short-circuited an otherwise balanced carbon cycle, and the emission of long-lived trace gases from the fires was small compared to that from natural sources, chemical climate probably did not undergo a dramatic change at this time.

The industrial revolution, based on the availability of abundant and cheap energy from the combustion of fossil fuels, has resulted in a very different situation. Carbon is now being mobilized into the atmosphere from a very large geological reservoir (coal, petroleum, gas; see figure 8-4). There is about ten times as much carbon readily accessible in fossil fuel deposits as there is in atmospheric CO_2, suggesting the potential for a major change in atmospheric composition when a significant fraction of the fossil fuel deposits are combusted (see figure 8-5).

From the beginning of the industrial revolution until now, concentrations of carbon dioxide in the atmosphere have increased from 280 to 360 parts per million, due to the combined influence of the burning of fossil fuels and deforestation.

Figure 8–2: Schematic Diagrams of Variations in Global Temperature since the Pleistocene Period on Three Time Scales

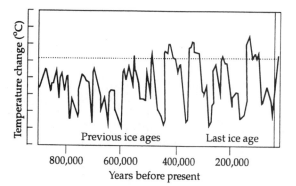

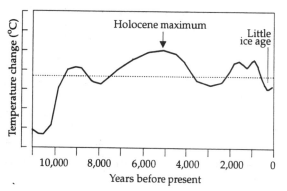

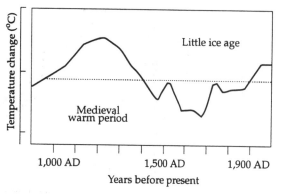

Source: Houghton, Jenkins and Ephraums 1990.

Carbon dioxide is a nearly inert gas. Its major path of removal is the ocean, mixing into deeper ocean layers and eventually being expelled as carbonate sediment. Also significant is the deposition of organic materials in sediments, the initial source of our fossil fuels. About half of the incremental carbon dioxide supplied to the atmosphere mixes into the upper layers of the oceans within a decade or two, and the remainder requires a century or more before its removal. High-precision measurements of the atmospheric con-

Figure 8–3: Global Mean Combined Land-Air and Sea-Surface Temperatures, 1861–89, Compared with the Average for 1951-80

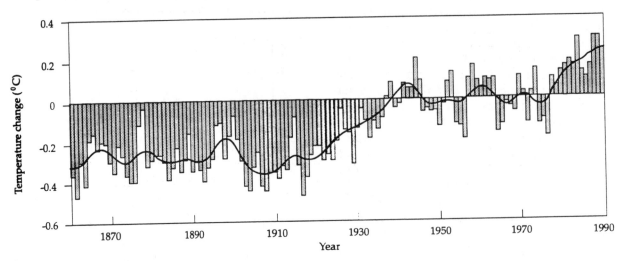

Source: Houghton, Jenkins, and Ephraums 1990.

Figure 8–4: Global Annual Emissions of CO$_2$ from Fossil Fuel Combustion and Cement Manufacturing, 1860–1990

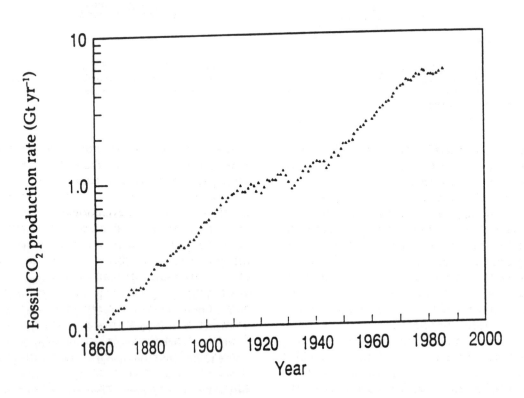

Note: The average rate of increase in emissions between 1860 and 1910 and between 1950 and 1970 is about 4 percent a year.
Source: Houghton, Jenkins, and Ephraums 1990.

Figure 8–5: Global Carbon Reservoirs and Fluxes

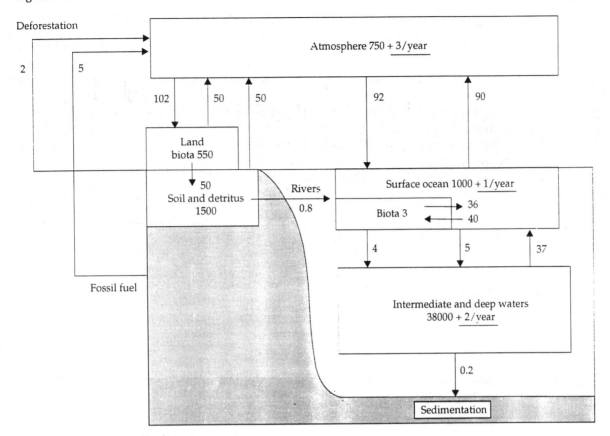

Note: Numbers apply to the pesent-day situation and represent typical values in the literature. Fluxes between atmosphere and surface ocean are gross annual exchanges. Numbers in italics indicate net annual accumulation of CO^2 due to the actions of humans. Units are gigatons of carbon (GtC; 1 gigaton = 10^9 metric tons = 10^{12} kilograms) for reservoir sizes and GtC yr^{-1} for fluxes.
Source: Houghton, Jenkins, and Ephraums 1990.

centration of oxygen (O_2) may help resolve some of the remaining uncertainties in the atmospheric balance of CO_2. Initial results show a decrease in atmospheric O_2 consistent with the increase in CO_2 (R. F. Keeling, personal communication, 1992).

Because of this very long atmospheric lifetime of the remaining fraction of the fossil fuel CO_2, we can only prevent further increase of carbon dioxide in the long run by nearly stopping our use of fossil fuels. However, because some of the current atmospheric excess will still move into the oceans within a few decades, it is presently possible to limit further growth by restricting the use of fossil fuels to about one-third of its present rate, and less ambitious limitations would still be able to reduce significantly the rates of future increases.

About 35 to 40 percent of the direct increase of greenhouse warming over the last century comes from gases other than CO_2: about 21 percent from methane (CH_4), 4 percent from nitrous oxide (N_2O), and the rest from various chlorinated compounds. The ozone loss from chlorinated compounds apparently largely compensates for its greenhouse warming (ozone being another important greenhouse gas), and the most important chlorinated contributors to greenhouse warming are being phased out because of their proven destruction of the ozone layer. Furthermore, methane has a relatively short decadal lifetime, so that its increases might be relatively reversible. Hence, controlling future increases of CO_2 is the primary question that needs to be addressed as a means of retarding future rates of increase in greenhouse warming.

At present, decisions to curtail further growth of the use of fossil fuels cannot be made and are not made on the basis of accurate detailed projections of future changes in climate. Rather, guidance is derived from the general magnitude and probable nature of changes inferred by the research community on the basis of three-dimensional models of climate. These models provide considerable detail as to possible climates in the future, but these are not validated. Many aspects of the models are based on well-established physical laws, the large-scale hydrodynamics, thermodynamics, and radiative transfer of the atmosphere. However, other aspects, such as those involving the formation of clouds and their interaction with radiation, processes of convection, and vertical transport of water vapor, are based on oversimplified and largely unverified assumptions.

Added to the uncertainties in the predictions of the climate models are the uncertainties in the further growth of greenhouse gases and uncertainties resulting from ignorance of details of the carbon cycle, future national economies, and possible restraints on the use of carbon because of concerns about the changes in climate (see figure 8-6).

Thus, only somewhat general and simple quantitative statements can be made about changes in climate that can be expected in the future. With the present enormous use of fossil fuels, the incremental greenhouse warming that has accumulated over the last century will at least double in the next thirty years. Global temperatures should be warmer than the average of the twentieth century by 1 °C to 3 °C over land. Smaller increases are anticipated over the ocean because the large mass of the ocean's surface waters requires decades to warm. It is also because of the oceanic mass that temperature increases would be only very slowly reversible even if all the excess greenhouse gases were removed.

Changes in temperature will be somewhat smaller in the tropics and somewhat larger during winter in high-latitude areas than the global average change. Models suggest significant mid-

Figure 8-6: Global Emissions of Carbon Dioxide from Energy, Cement Production, and Deforestation

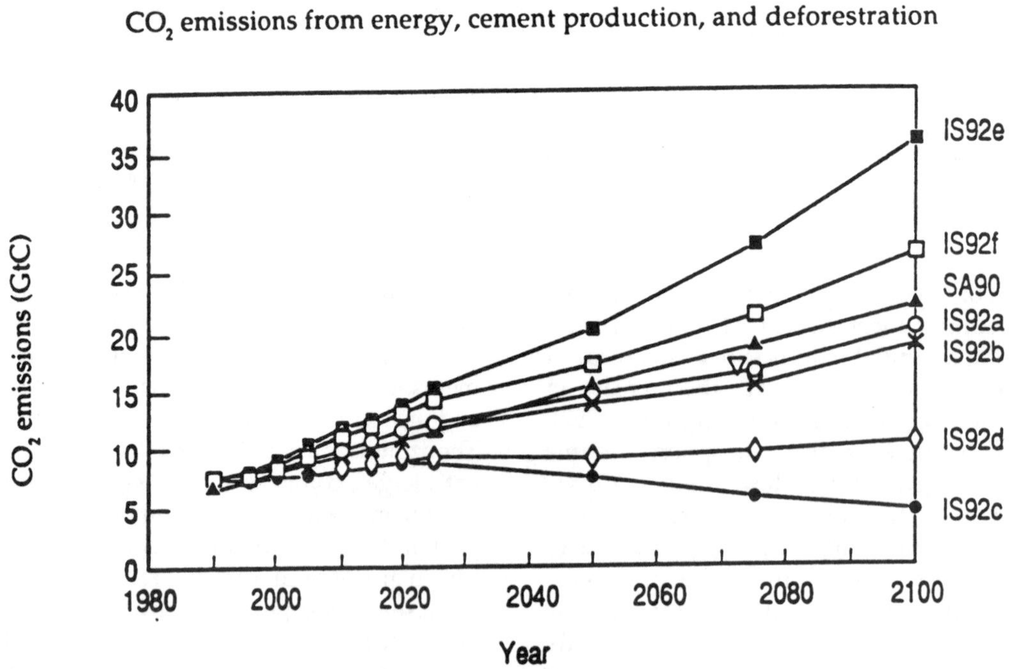

CO_2 emissions from energy, cement production, and deforestration

Note: In a 1992 supplement, the IPCC presented six different scenarios of carbon dioxide emissions instead of the one business-as-usual scenario in the original report (called SA90 in the figure). The major difference from previous estimates is that higher population forecasts increase the emission estimates, while phase-out of halocarbons and more optimistic costs of renewable energy reduce them. The small difference between a and b is mainly accounted for by the commitment that many OECD countries have made to stabilize or reduce carbon dioxide emissions.

Source: Adapted from Houghton, Callander, and Varney 1992; Nilsson 1992.

continental drought. Some large shifts in supplies of water from the atmosphere are fairly likely. A further doubling of the incremental greenhouse warming is likely by the end of the twenty-first century unless society acts to restrain this increase long before then (see figure 8-7). Without such restraints, the rate of increase of greenhouse warming will be considerably greater than it is today.

The increasing temperatures will be accompanied by rises in sea level, most likely primarily from thermal expansion of the oceans and from melting of small glaciers. It is not known whether the Greenland and Antarctic ice caps will grow or shrink over the next century, and this question contributes considerable uncertainty to the overall projection of future sea levels given by the report of the Intergovernmental Panel on Climate Change as between 0.3 and 1.1 meters by the year 2100 for the business-as-usual scenario (Houghton, Jenkins, and Ephraums 1990). Sea level rises of as much as a meter represent a serious threat to many coastal areas of the world.

Future global warming will be closely linked to the world's vegetation. Over moist land regions, vegetation is a dominant control on the flux of water between soil and atmosphere, and its productivity in turn depends on the availability of water. Of special concern are the possible effects of increased temperatures and accompanying shifts in rainfall patterns on the viability of natural forest ecosystems. The converse question, concerning the effects of forests on temperature and rainfall, also warrants attention. Climate modelers (for example, Nobre, Sellers, and Shukla 1991) have been addressing the possible consequences of converting the Amazon forest to grassland; these studies indicate that this conversion would be accompanied by substantial decreases in rainfall that extend the duration of the dry season, and by somewhat larger daytime temperatures. The implied changes could be irreversible on the southern margins of the forest. Additional effects would be expected from the large volumes of smoke in the atmosphere during tropical dry seasons.

Figure 8-7: Change in Temperature under Scenario IS92a

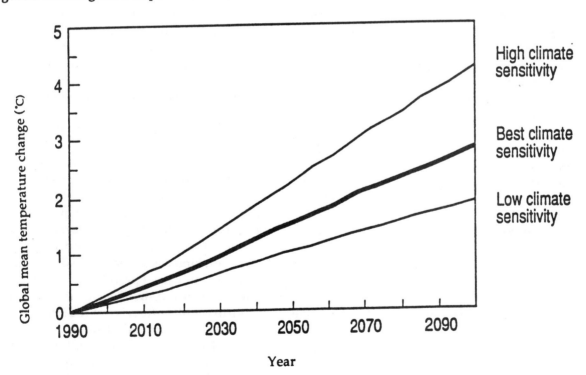

Note: Estimates of global mean temperature change IS92a using high (4.5 °C), best-estimate (2.5 °C), and low (1.5 °C) values of climate sensitivity. The effects of sulphate aerosol and ozone depletion have not been taken into account.
Source: Houghton, Callander, and Varney 1992.

A world 5°C to 10°C warmer than today by the middle of the twenty-second century is marvelous to contemplate for a climate scientist as a natural experiment, but it is not a world he would likely want to live in or bequeath to his great-grandchildren. Long before then, many of the world's species would have been stressed to extinction. We hope that reality will be more benign than our best estimates, but a prudent world cannot afford to wait to see if we are wrong; the only sensible path to a climate that will most probably support natural systems is to proceed toward as much restraint in our use of fossil fuels as the world can afford. Economic analyses show that initial reductions in the use of fossil fuels through conservation would be beneficial (Lovins 1991), but that beyond some point, further reduction could be prohibitively expensive. Taking the first easy steps today may allow us to avoid being forced to make impossible decisions in the future. The possibility of a much-accelerated rate of warming is more threatening than a slow continuation of the present warming trends.

Besides the uncertainty of present models of climate, the difficulty of interpreting global temperature records up to now in terms of greenhouse warming is used in arguments against efforts to restrict further use of fossil fuels. Indeed, the 0.5°C rise in temperature experienced over the last century is at the lower limit of that expected. If it is furthermore imagined that this rise is partially or largely a result of other climatic processes, it might be inferred that climate is much less responsive to changes in energy inputs than has been inferred. However, such a conclusion would fly in the face of past geological evidence that indicates a major role for greenhouse warming in forcing changes larger than what we now face. A more plausible interpretation of the up-to-now modest rise in temperature is that some other aspect of atmospheric radiation has also been changing and in part canceling the greenhouse warming. Increases in sulfate and smoke aerosols are one current suggestion for this factor. Most such interpretations would not be expected to buffer future greenhouse warming to the extent they may have in the past, so at best they might give us a little more breathing room.

Changing chemical climate

As already indicated, the chemistry of the atmosphere has co-evolved with the biota. This includes the chemical composition of the atmosphere, the spatial and temporal distribution of major and trace gases, and the chemical reactions that influence the formation and destruction of gases and aerosol particles. Biological organisms were and still are major sources and sinks of the constituents of the atmosphere.

However, over the last century, the use of fossil fuel has grown to a magnitude where it not only influences the CO_2 content of the atmosphere but also supplies much of the trace gas emissions that are changing our chemical climate. At the same time, cheap and abundant energy made possible the worldwide expansion of industrial and agricultural activity, which results in further emissions to the atmosphere and increasing concentrations of trace gases (see figure 8-8). The degree to which human society has taken over control of the biosphere is reflected in the estimate by Vitousek and others (1986, p. 368) that "nearly 40 percent of potential terrestrial net primary productivity is used directly, co-opted, or forgone because of human activities." Human activities now dominate the atmospheric cycle of many trace substances, resulting in widespread air pollution and a change of chemical climate not reversible on time scales of tens to hundreds of years.

The relationships between the sources of atmospheric trace gases and aerosols and the environmental consequences of these emissions can be represented in the form of a matrix (see figure 8-9). In this figure, the drivers of atmospheric change (agriculture, animal husbandry, fisheries, biomass burning, fossil fuel combustion, and industrial processes) are represented as one dimension, the effects on the atmospheric environment (ultraviolet radiation, global warming, photochemical smog, global oxidation efficiency, acid rain, visibility, and corrosion) as the other dimension. In the following sections, we discuss these threats to the health of the atmospheric environment and the ways in which human activity changes chemical climate.

Figure 8-8: Concentrations of Carbon Dioxide and Methane, 1750–1995

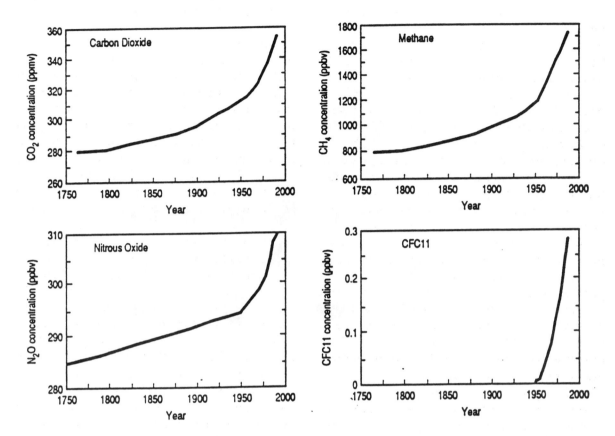

Note: Concentrations of carbon dioxide and methane remained relatively constant up to the eighteenth century and have risen sharply since then, due to the activities of humans. Concentrations of nitrous oxide have increased since the mid-eighteenth century, especially in the last few decades. Chlorofluorocarbons were not present in the atmosphere before the 1930s.
Source: Houghton, Jenkins, and Ephraums 1990.

Stratospheric ozone and ultraviolet radiation

The solar radiation spectrum contains wavelength regions energetic enough to cause chemical reactions in biological tissue. Much of this damaging radiation is filtered out by the atmosphere. Of particular concern at present is the observation that stratospheric ozone, which serves to remove a part of the spectrum called UV-B, is decreasing globally (see figure 8-10; World Meteorological Organization 1992). The present rate of decrease is estimated to be on the order of 5 percent a decade. In the polar regions, ozone becomes greatly depleted during the polar spring (the "ozone hole"), with effects extending to the higher mid-latitudes (for example, Australia and northern Europe). Present consensus attributes this decrease to

increasing inputs of chlorine and bromine species into the stratosphere. These species and their sources are as follows: chlorofluorocarbons are used as foaming agents, propellants, and refrigerants; methyl chloroform and carbon tetrachloride are used as industrial solvents; halons, which contain both bromine and chlorine, are used as fire suppressants. Methyl chloride and methyl bromide both have large natural sources, but anthropogenic emissions may also be important: methyl chloride is emitted in great amounts from biomass burning; methyl bromide is used as a pesticide in households and agriculture and may also have a substantial source in biomass burning. Other trace gases that play a role in regulating stratospheric ozone are nitrous oxide (N_2O), carbonyl sulfide (COS), methane (CH_4), hydrogen (H_2), carbon monoxide (CO), and the nonmethane hydrocar-

Figure 8-9: Atmospheric Life Support System

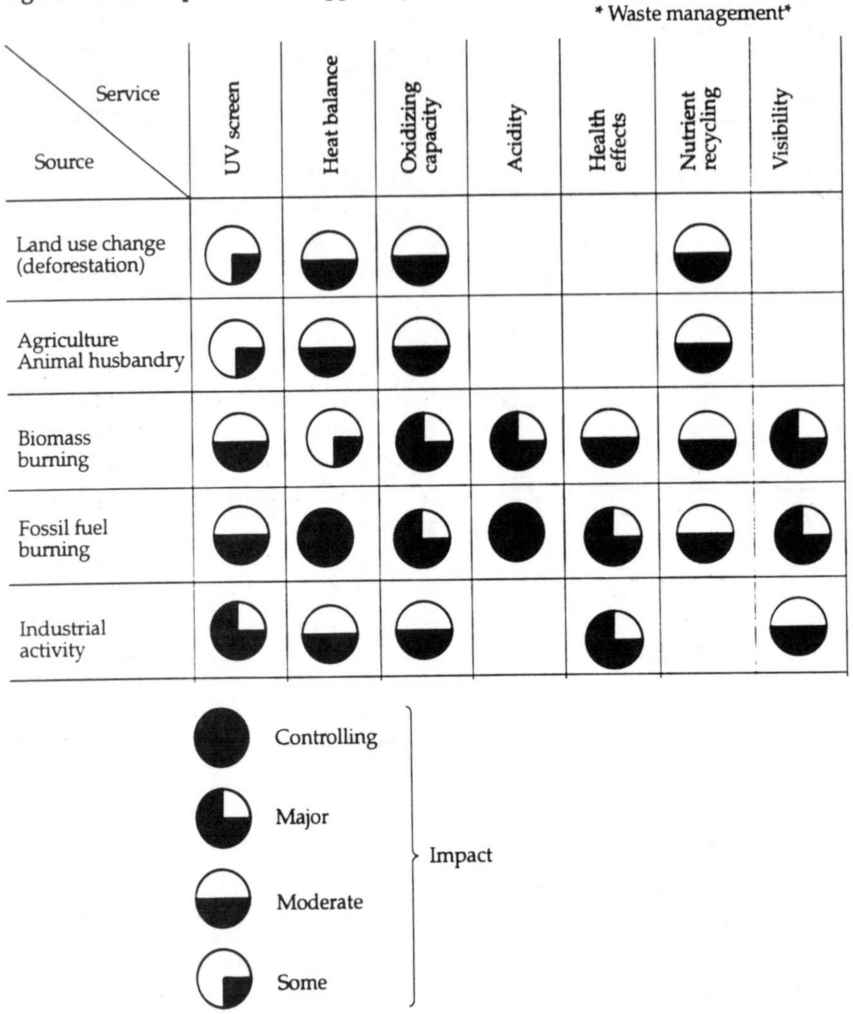

* Waste management*

Source \ Service	UV screen	Heat balance	Oxidizing capacity	Acidity	Health effects	Nutrient recycling	Visibility
Land use change (deforestation)	Some	Moderate	Moderate			Moderate	
Agriculture Animal husbandry	Some	Moderate	Moderate			Moderate	
Biomass burning	Moderate	Major	Major	Major	Moderate	Moderate	Major
Fossil fuel burning	Moderate	Controlling	Major	Controlling	Major	Moderate	Major
Industrial activity	Moderate	Moderate	Moderate		Major		Moderate

Impact:
- Controlling (full filled circle)
- Major (three-quarter filled circle)
- Moderate (half filled circle)
- Some (quarter filled circle)

Note: Service functions provided by the atmosphere are shown in the columns, human activities that influence the viability of these functions are shown in the rows. Symbols indicate the level of impact that human activities have on the various functions.
Source: Crutzen and Graedel 1986.

bons (NMHC). All of these gases have natural sources, but their anthropogenic emissions have now become so great that their atmospheric cycles are significantly perturbed. This perturbation is clearly evident in the form of continuously increasing atmospheric concentrations of N_2O, CH_4, H_2, and CO (see table 8-1).

Photochemical smog and acid rain

In contrast to the problems related to the depletion of stratospheric ozone, photochemical smog and acid rain are felt most seriously on the local and regional scales. Smog arises from photochemical reactions between hydrocarbons, nitrogen oxides, and a number of oxygen-containing molecules, most importantly the hydroxyl radical, OH. These reactions are a normal part of the photochemical cycles in the atmosphere and act even in unpolluted environments to remove biogenic hydrocarbons and nitrogen oxides emitted from soils by transforming them into less volatile and more water-soluble substances, which then are removed by precipitation or dry deposition. The environmental problems associated with photochemical smog and acid deposition are the result of an overloading of the self-cleaning ca-

Figure 8-10: Total Ozone Mapping Spectrometer Trends in Zonal Mean and Latitude, by Season, 1978–91

Trends in percentage per decade

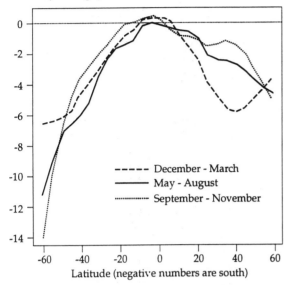

Latitude (negative numbers are south)

---- December - March
—— May - August
·········· September - November

Note: Covers the period from November 1978 through March 1991.

Source: World Meteorological Organization 1992.

pacity of the atmosphere. This overloading occurs either as the result of fossil fuel burning and industrial activities in the industrial countries, or as a consequence of biomass burning in its many forms (savanna fires, deforestation burns, domestic production of biomass energy, and agricultural burning of wastes) in the developing world. Recent studies suggest that biomass burning worldwide produces amounts of photochemical smog comparable to those resulting from the combustion of fossil fuels (Andreae 1991). Once the capacity of the atmosphere to dissipate and remove the emissions is exceeded, products like ozone and nitric acid are formed at concentrations that are toxic to biological organisms, corrosive to man-made and natural structures, and ecologically damaging through physicochemical changes in the environment (for example, lake and soil acidification). Sulfuric acid is produced from the sulfur contained in fossil fuels, especially coal, and also contributes to acid deposition. The environmental impact of photochemical smog and acid deposition has been discussed in many publications (see, for example, Andreae 1991; Crutzen and Graedel 1986; NAPAP 1991).

Table 8-1: Climatically and Chemically Active Atmospheric Trace Substances

Substance	Tropospheric concentration, 1989	Annual growth (percent)	Ocean	Plant and soil	Agriculture	Biomass burning	Fossil fuel	Industry	Photochemical	Function affected
CFCs	5–500 ppt	3–10	—	—	—	—	—	+++	—	UV
CH_3CCl_3	135 ppt	3.7	—	—	—	—	—	+++	—	UV
CCl_4	107 ppt	1.2	—	—	—	—	—	+++	—	UV
CH_3Cl	600 ppt	?	+	—	—	++	—	+	—	UV
CH_3Br	10–15 ppt	?	++	—	+	+	—	+	—	UV
N_2O	308 ppb	0.25	+	++	++	+	+	+	—	UV, GE
CH_4	1.69 ppm	0.8	+	+	+	+	+	+	—	GE, UV, OX
H_2	515 ppb	0.6	(+)	(+)	(+)	++	(+)	(+)	++	UV
COS	≈500 ppt	?	++	+	?	+	+	—	++	UV
CO	50–150 ppb	≈0.3	+	—	—	++	+	+	++	OX
NO_x	ppt-ppb	↑	—	+	+	+	++	+	—	OX, PL
SO_2	ppt-ppb	↑	(++)	(+)	—	+	+++	+	++	GE, PL
NMHC	ppt-ppb	↑	+	+	—	+	+	+	—	OX, PL
Aerosols	ppt-ppb	↑	++	+	+	++	++	+	++	GE, PL
CO_2	352 ppm	0.5	—	—	++	—	+++	—	+	GE
Tropospheric O_3	ppb range	≈1	—	(+)	(+)	(++)	(++)	(+)	+++	OX, PL, GE

— None.

Note: ppt, parts per trillion; ppb, parts per billion; ppm, parts per million; CFCs, chlorofluorocarbons; NMHC, non-methane hydrocarbons; UV ultraviolet radiation; GE, greenhouse effect; OX, oxidizing capacity of the atmosphere; PL, pollution. +, ++, and +++ indicate relative resource strength. Parentheses indicate that the source is indirect, that is, through release of a precursor photochemically converted to the substance in question.

129

Global oxidation capacity

Photochemical reactions in the atmosphere are responsible for the removal of gaseous emissions from the biosphere and from human activities. As an example of these processes, we will outline the atmospheric oxidation of methane. In the first step, methane reacts with the hydroxyl radical to form a methyl radical, CH_3:

$$CH_4 + OH => CH_3 + H_2O. \qquad (8-1)$$

The subsequent reaction sequence depends on the ambient concentration of nitric oxide, NO. In an NO-rich environment, a reaction sequence occurs that has the net consequence of producing ozone:

$$CH_4 + 4 O_2 => CH_2O + H_2O + 2 O_3. \qquad (8-2)$$

The OH consumed in the initial reaction is produced again within this reaction sequence. In NO-poor environments, a different reaction chain is followed, which consumes the radicals OH and HO_2 according to:

$$CH_4 + OH + HO_2 => CH_2O + 2 H_2O. \qquad (8-3)$$

The further oxidation of formaldehyde (CH_2O) to CO and finally to CO_2 has similar consequences for the budget of ozone and the OH and HO_2 radicals: in NO-poor environments, the oxidants are used up; in NO-rich environments, more oxidants are produced (Crutzen and Zimmermann 1991).

The effect of anthropogenic emissions of CO, hydrocarbons, and nitrogen oxides on the oxidation state of the atmosphere thus depends on the relative amounts of these pollutants. Here we need to look at effects at different scales as well. Since nitrogen oxides have a much shorter lifetime in the atmosphere than CO and CH_4, the relative amounts of NO, CO, and CH_4 will change with time (and therefore distance) following emission. Near the sources—that is, in polluted regions—the system will be NO-rich, and ozone and other oxidants will be produced (see figure 8-11). But in the remote atmosphere, the NO will have been removed, while much of the CO and CH_4 is still left, and therefore oxidants, particularly OH radical, will be consumed (see figure 8-12). The effect on the global atmosphere depends thus on the details of the three-dimensional distribution of the various trace gases and can only be simulated with fairly sophisticated models.

One of the most disquieting aspects of this issue is that it constitutes a potentially unstable system due to a positive feedback. Since the oxidation of CH_4 and CO consumes OH, increasing amounts of these trace gases in the atmosphere will consume even more OH. This would lead to

Figure 8-11: Surface Volume Mixing Ratios of O_3 for the Industrial and Preindustrial Periods

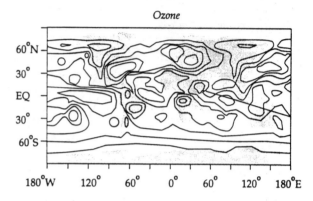

Ozone

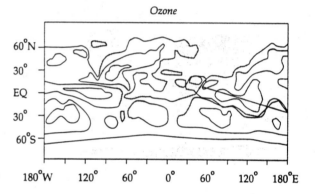

Ozone

Note: The figures for the industrial period are for 1980. Ratios were calculated using our three-dimensional tropospheric photochemical model. Surface is measured in 1,000 hectoPascal; units are parts per villion by volume.

Source: Crutzen and Zimmerman 1991.

Figure 8-12: Percentage Change in the Calculated Daytime, Zonal Average, and Annual Average Concentrations of Oxyl Radical since Preindustrial Times

Oxyl Radical

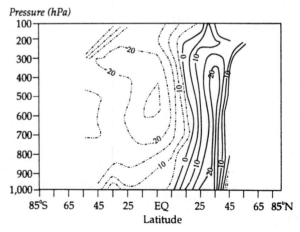

Source: Crutzen and Zimmermann 1991.

a decrease in the concentration of OH, so that CO and CH_4 would be oxidized less rapidly and would build up to a higher concentration. This would further suppress OH, and so on. The final result of this scenario would be an atmosphere very different from the present one; in fact so different that no models at present could predict its composition with any reliability. For further details, see the paper by Crutzen and Zimmermann (1991).

Detecting change

The chemical composition of the atmosphere is one of the most sensitive and unambiguous indicators of global change. Although there is an active discussion about the details of the processes defining the rate of increase of CO_2 in the atmosphere, there can be no argument that the atmospheric levels of CO_2 are changing and that they are higher than at any time within the last 160,000 years (the time covered by the oldest samples of Antarctic ice obtained so far). As table 8-2 shows, many other gases are also increasing in the Earth's atmosphere. The change in their global mean concentration tells us about changes in the budget of their sources and sinks, while their spatial distribution around the globe gives us information on the location of their most important sources. Seasonal variations in their concentrations can be used further to identify sources and sinks, because biogenic sources vary with the growth cycle and photochemical sinks change with the seasonal flux of solar radiation (Prinn and others 1992).

As pointed out in the section on global oxidizing capacity, changing OH levels in the atmosphere are one of the most fundamental perturbations of atmospheric chemistry. Yet, there are at present no reliable methods to measure OH on the time and space scales required to validate our current concepts and to detect a change in atmospheric abundance and distribution. At present, we have to rely on models (which use measurements of the distribution of chemicals that react with OH) to estimate the atmospheric concentration of OH (see, for example, Crutzen and Zimmermann 1991; Prinn and others 1992). The

Table 8-2: Emissions of Carbon Dioxide and Other Trace Gases and Aerosols from Deforestation and Biomass Burning

Species	Emission ratio (X 10,000)	Biomass burning (tg per year)	All sources (tg per year)	Fraction (percentage)
Carbon dioxide				
Net from deforestation	—	2,400	7,600	32
Gross from combustion	880	3,590	8,790	41
Carbon burned	—	4,080	—	—
Gases				
CO	80	290	1,100	26
CH_4	8	29	380	8
NMHC	10	36	100	36
N_2	4.7	39	150	26
N_2O	0.1	0.8	6	14
NO_x	2.3	9.6	40	24
NH_3	1.3	5.5	44	12
SO_x	0.25	2.4	200	1.2
COS	0.011	0.11	1.4	8
CH_3Cl	0.12	1.3	2.3	55
H_2	27	16	36	45
O_3	30	430	1,100	39
Aerosols				
Organic carbon	25	90	1,500	6
Black carbon	17	59	180	33
Total	2.5	9	22	40

Note: Tg, teragram (1 trillion grams).

development of more direct measurement approaches is highly desirable but may still require substantial technological advances.

Monitoring change

In order to apply measurements of atmospheric properties to the assessment of sustainable development, we have to address two problems: (1) What level of atmospheric change is consistent with sustainable development? (2) How must a monitoring program be designed to detect this critical level of change?

It appears that, fundamentally, any secular change of chemically or climatically important atmospheric properties is not sustainable. But a rate of change so slow that it would cause environmental damage only in thousands of years is clearly irrelevant, since the processes or human activities causing this change cannot be forecast over this time period. In order to be practicable, a time frame over which this change is of concern and a rate of change that is acceptable to the present biota and human society will have to be selected. The selection of this time frame is as much a social and political issue as a scientific one.

At present, several activities are under way to assess and monitor global change. Under the auspices of the World Meteorological Organization, a network of monitoring stations has been set up at remote oceanic sites to measure atmospheric CO_2, CH_4, and a number of meteorological and radiation parameters. The GAGE (Global Atmospheric Gas Experiment) monitors the concentrations of N_2O, CH_4, and a series of halogenated compounds at a number of remote marine sites. A large variety of regional networks monitor local and regional pollution. In connection with the Global Change/International Geosphere-Biosphere Program, especially its International Global Atmospheric Chemistry (IGAC) core project, new networks for detecting and monitoring the changing composition of the atmosphere are being planned. Site selection is now moving away from the remote marine locations, which are highly suitable for detecting highly averaged, global trends, and toward more continental locations more suitable for identifying sources and processes. Attempts to monitor sustainable development will have to take into account these present and projected networks, and specific requirements will have to be formulated for future networks.

Conclusions

In the preceding sections, we have outlined the major problems currently known to threaten the life support functions provided by the Earth's atmosphere: the greenhouse effect from gases and aerosols, the weakening ozone shield, the increase in local and regional pollution, and the decreasing capability of the atmosphere to oxidize biogenic and anthropogenic emissions. The symptoms that document the progressive, nonsustainable deterioration of the atmospheric environment are readily detected by chemical analysis of the levels of trace gases in the atmosphere. The increase in temperature observed over the last century, and particularly in the last decade, is not as unambiguous as the chemical record, but it points in the same direction.

The presently observed changes in physical and chemical climate appear still rather small: some percentages to tens of percentages of the original level. This, however, may lull us into a false sense of security. One of the bewildering characteristics of climate and weather (both chemical and physical) is its nonlinearity. For example, when air rises, it does not slowly become more and more turbid and gradually turn into a cloud; rather, the onset of cloud condensation is very sudden, and clear air turns into cloud over a distance of just a few meters. A less commonplace, but much more dramatic, nonlinear phenomenon is the Antarctic ozone hole. When Molina and Rowland (1974) predicted a loss of stratospheric ozone from the input of chlorofluorocarbons, they projected a slow, incremental decrease in ozone, on the order of a few percentages a decade. The appearance in the late 1970s of the hole in the polar ozone, where some 50 percent of stratospheric ozone disappears within a few weeks, was totally unpredicted in spite of the fact that the brightest minds in the community of atmospheric chemists had been studying the loss of stratospheric ozone for more than a decade. The most important lesson to be learned here is that, in physical and chemical climate, small changes in the driving forces can sometimes lead to very large and unpredictable effects.

Another reason why the linkages between causes and effects are often so difficult to establish in the system of physical and chemical climate is the fact that the relevant phenomena cross several scientific disciplines. Processes that encompass meteorology, photochemistry, oceanography, microbiology, and other scientific disciplines are beyond the grasp of individual scientists and can only be investigated by collaborative, cross-disciplinary efforts. There is only a short history of this type of collaborative approach in science; only a decade or two ago, fields like biogeochemistry were considered irrelevant by most of the scientific community. And while the multidisciplinary approach is now accepted in the sciences dealing with the Earth system, actually implementing this new way of thinking will take considerable time. Progress is urgently needed in the development of linked models that represent the inherent linkages among the atmosphere, the oceans, and the biosphere.

In order to establish the scientific foundation for sustainable development, an even more daunting task lies ahead: we will have to analyze the interactions between the natural sciences and the social and economic sciences. At present, these interactions are widely ignored by the practitioners on either side. At best, they are given lip service (as is, admittedly, done here), but little actual research is being undertaken. The ongoing efforts to put into action the International Geosphere-Biosphere Program and the Sustainable Biosphere Initiative should include the investigation of these interactions as central objectives. For example, research is urgently needed in the development of accounting techniques to represent the economic value of natural resources. This will have to include evaluation of the economic benefits of "services" such as protection from ultraviolet radiation by stratospheric ozone, fertilization of crops by atmospheric sulfate, and removal of pollutants by the oxidation power of the troposphere. Conversely, the economic cost of CO_2 emissions and the resulting rise in temperature will have to be quantified.

Although this chapter cannot provide detailed policy recommendations, some fundamental directions are evident. We must curtail emissions of gases that lead to progressive and accelerating deterioration of the fundamental life support system of the Earth. This is clearly the case for the chlorofluorocarbons, and the Montreal Protocols are an important step in the right direction. In the case of CO_2, current evidence is also strong enough that a prudent approach would clearly demand a reduction in emissions. Because of the multiple sources and sinks for many of the other gases and aerosols, an action to reduce one source will often lead to increased emission of the same or another gas from a different source. These complex interactions require that a detailed analysis of policy options and consequences be made before mitigation efforts are undertaken.

References

Andreae, Meinrat O. 1991. "Biomass Burning in the Tropics: Impact on Environmental Quality and Global Climate." In K. Davis and M. S. Bernstam, eds., *Resources, Environment, and Population: Present Knowledge, Future Options*, pp. 268–91. New York: Oxford University Press.

Charlson, R. J., J. Langner, H. Rodhe, C. B. Leovy, and S. G. Warren. 1991. "Perturbation of the Northern Hemisphere Radiative Balance by Backscattering from Anthropogenic Sulfate Aerosols." *Tellus* 43AB, pp. 152–63.

Crutzen, P. J., and T. E. Graedel. 1986. "The Role of Atmospheric Chemistry in Environment-Development Interactions." In W. C. Clark and R. E. Munn, eds., *Sustainable Development of the Biosphere*, pp. 213–50. Cambridge, England: Cambridge University Press.

Crutzen, P. J., and P. H. Zimmermann. 1991. "The Changing Photochemistry of the Troposphere." *Tellus* 43AB, pp. 136–51.

Daly, Herman E. 1991. "Sustainable Development: From Concepts and Theory to Operational Principles." In K. Davis and M. S. Bernstam, eds., *Resources, Environment, and Population: Present Knowledge, Future Options*, pp. 25–43. New York: Oxford University Press.

Houghton, J. T., G. J. Jenkins, and J. J. Ephraums. 1990. *Climate Change: The IPCC Assessment*. Cambridge, England: Cambridge University Press.

Houghton, J. T., B. A. Callander, and S. K. Varney. 1992. *Climate Change 1992. The Supplementary Report to the IPCC Scientific Assessment*. Cambridge, England: Cambridge University Press.

James, S. R. 1989. "Hominid Use of Fire in the Lower and Middle Pleistocene: A Review of the Evidence." *Current Anthropology* 30, pp. 1–26.

Lovins, A. B. 1991. "Energy, People, and Industrialization." In K. Davis and M. S. Bernstam, eds., *Resources, Environment, and Population: Present Knowledge, Future Options*, pp. 95–124. New York: Oxford University Press.

Molina, M. J., and F. S. Rowland. 1974. Stratospheric Sink for Chlorofluoromethanes: Chlorine Atom Catalyzed Destruction of Ozone." *Nature* 249, pp. 810–14.

NAPAP (National Acid Precipitation Assessment Program). 1991. *National Acid Precipitation Assessment Program: 1990 Integrated Assessment Report*. Washington, D.C.

Nilsson, A. 1992. *Greenhouse Earth*. Chichester, England: John Wiley.

Nobre, C. A., P. J. Sellers, and J. Shukla. 1991. "Amazonian Deforestation and Regional Climate Change." *Journal of Climate* 4, pp. 957–88.

Prinn, R., D. Cunnold, P. Simmonds, F. Alyea, R. Boldi, A. Crawford, P. Fraser, D. Gutzler, D. Hartley, R. Rosen, and R. Rasmussen. 1992. "Global Average Concentration and Trend for Hydroxyl Radicals Deduced from ALE/GAGE Trichloroethane (Methyl Chloroform) Data for 1978–1990." *Journal of Geophysical Research* 97, pp. 2445–61.

Schüle, W. 1990. "Landscapes and Climate in Prehistory: Interactions of Wildlife, Man, and Fire." In J. Goldammer, ed., *Fire in the Tropical Biota: Ecosystem Processes and Global Challenges*, pp. 273–318. Berlin: Springer-Verlag.

Vitousek, Peter M., Paul R. Ehrlich, A. H. Ehrlich, and P. A. Matson. 1986. "Human Appropriation of the Products of Photosynthesis." *BioScience* 36, pp. 368–73.

World Meteorological Organization. 1992. *Scientific Assessment of Ozone Depletion, 1991.* Geneva, Switzerland.

World Commission on Environment and Development (The Brundtland Commission). 1987. *Our Common Future.* Oxford, England: Oxford University Press.

Comments

Eneas Salati and Reynaldo Luiz Victoria

The chapter by Andreae and Dickinson is an excellent review of state-of-the-art knowledge of the role that the atmosphere's chemical composition plays in the global climate. It clearly shows the importance of the increase in the concentration of greenhouse gases, which could jeopardize both the sustainability of the Earth's productive system, and the interactions between the biosphere and atmosphere. Our comments are intended as contributions to, not critiques of, this excellent report. They are also relevant to discussions of the sustainability of the Earth's climate system. Being Brazilians, and also because tropical forests are at the center of discussions of global changes in climate, we offer examples mostly from the Brazilian Amazon. Recent deforestation in that region is now altering the ecosystem structure of certain subbasins, where potential regional impacts include changes in hydrology and the transport of sediments and nutrients. Developing the capability to predict such changes would provide a robust basis for developing sustainable alternatives.

The present chemical composition of the Earth's atmosphere would not be the same if living organisms did not exist, especially those that can synthesize organic compounds through photosynthesis and those that mediate and maintain the biogeochemical cycles. Therefore, the present chemical composition of the Earth's atmosphere is a consequence of physicochemical activities associated with living organisms throughout the history of our planet.

Although we can also say that humans have played a role since they first dominated fire, the average chemical composition of the Earth's atmosphere was largely controlled by natural processes until the beginning of the nineteenth century. From there on, with the onset of the industrial revolution and the deforestation associated with development, the concentration of greenhouse gases in the atmosphere has increased considerably. This is especially true for the last few decades. The emission rates of greenhouse gases has reached a point at which the natural regulatory systems can no longer prevent the increase of these gases in the atmosphere.

If we want to relate sustainability to climate, we should be aware of the global dimension, which was thoroughly reviewed in Andreae and Dickinson's work, and the regional dimension, which should be analyzed considering:

- Natural ecosystems, either undisturbed or subjected to very little human intervention
- Agricultural ecosystems
- Human activity, including large, medium, and small cities.

The natural ecosystems reached equilibrium through continuous interactions between the biosphere and the atmosphere. In some areas, the Amazon forest for instance, the present dynamic equilibrium of the atmosphere depends on the forest; in other words, the present climate depends on the forest (Salati 1985). Therefore, any change in the parameters that define the climate, either produced by deforestation or global changes in climate, may alter the present ecological equilibrium of the region and consequently its sustainability.

The following climate parameters may bear relation to sustainability and should therefore be measured:

(a) *Temperature, precipitation, solar radiation, wind, cloudiness, and so forth.* It is important to analyze not only their average values but also extremes events. In Manaus, for instance, measurements of temperature for the last three decades do not show any trend for variation in the average, either maximum or minimum, temperature (Ribeiro 1991), but they do show an increasing trend for the absolute maximum temperature (Villa Nova and Salati, unpublished data).

(b) *Parameters that integrate several factors, like river discharges and balance of water in watersheds.* Another important variable is the chemical characterization of surface waters, since it reflects the interrelations between the biogeochemical and hydrological cycles.

(c) *Isotopic composition of rainfall.* The ^{18}O and D concentration of rainfall water is directly related to the history of the water vapor from which it originates. It depends on previous occurrence of precipitation, temperature of evaporation and condensation, type of cloud, and so forth. Based on the isotopic composition of rainfall in the Amazon region, Salati and others (1979) estimated that roughly 50 percent of the precipitation is water recycled through evapotranspiration. More recently, Gat and Matsui (1991) and Victoria and others (1991) showed that there is as yet no clear distinction between the relative contribution of evaporational and transpirational processes to the total evapotranspirational flux. There is, however, a strong indication that evaporation may contribute up to 40 percent of total evapotranspiration during the dry season. The loci of evaporation, whether from floodplain, canopy, or open bodies of water (lakes and rivers), cannot yet be defined with the available data. Whether the isotopic features found for the Amazon are common to all other tropical areas is not yet known, merely for lack of data, but we are certain that, in the event of global or regional changes, the isotopic concentration of rainwater will be one of the first to change.

(d) *Biological indicators.* In addition to the climatological parameters, several biological indicators may also be used. For instance, some organisms living on the canopy of trees in humid regions may have their population altered by changes in the hydrological regime. Some fish species or other aquatic organisms may also be used as indicators of loss of sustainability of natural ecosystems.

(e) *Change in the flux of water vapor.* Another fingerprint for change in climate is the change in the flux of water vapor measured by rawinsondes.

For agroecosystems, the relationship between possible changes in climate and sustainability is more complex. The sustainability in this case might be maintained at a certain level with the use of technology. For instance, in the *cerrados* of central Brazil, a change in climate leading to a decrease in precipitation may be overcome with the use of irrigation techniques, therefore maintaining agricultural productivity, as long as care is taken to maintain the underground water reservoir of the region. It is evident that the use of technology to overcome possible changes in climate has limits, which are generally dictated by its economic or social sustainability. Thus, sustainable agricultural production that is developed in a region as a function of its previous climate may become unsustainable with a change in climate.

For urban ecosystems, it is also difficult to use a simple concept of sustainability. In this case, technological development and improvement of economic conditions may also permit different levels of sustainability. Thus, the sustainability of a way of life is dependent on both climatic and economic conditions; human comfort may be improved by artificially controlling the climate (temperature, humidity, and light). In general, the standard of living in cities of industrial countries is well above that of developing countries. If the later is to be improved, new projects of architecture and urban planning will be necessary, which will certainly require an increase in energy usage and consequently have a positive feedback on changes in climate.

It is, and will be, difficult to find parameters to measure the sustainability of urban planning; several might be useful: per capita income, use of potable water, energy consumption per capita, soil erosion, crime level, education level, and so forth. Change in climate may have a relation to such indexes.

The use of climate resources to increase the production of biomass in the tropics represents an excellent opportunity to transfer carbon from the atmosphere to the biosphere. In this region, the net primary production rate is among the highest in the planet for forests, aquatic plants, and crop stands. The limiting factor for biomass production is generally associated with the fertility of both terrestrial and aquatic systems.

One way to solve the problem, and which is already showing positive results (Salati 1987), is the recycling of urban and industrial sewage into production systems. The DHS system (Manfrinato, Salati Filho, and Salati 1990, 1993; Salati Filho 1991) is being used to produce biomass from rice and aquatic plants, decreasing the level of pollution of waters contaminated by urban sewage at the same time. To extend the concept to other systems, including forestry, is relatively simple. The technology to produce charcoal or biogas from biomass is readily available. This is an important field for scientific and technological development that could bring a better and longer sustainability to tropical regions, increasing the standard of living (social sustainability) at the same time.

References

Gat, J. R., and E. Matsui. 1991. "Atmospheric Water Balance in the Amazon Basin: An Isotopic Evapo-Transpiration Model." *Journal of Geophysical Research* 96:D7, pp. 13, 179–88.

Manfrinato, E. S., E. Salati Filho, and E. Salati. 1990. "Water Supply Systems Utilizing the Edaphic-Phytodepuration Technique." In P. F. Cooper and B. Findlater, eds., *Constructed Wetlands in Water Pollution Control.* Oxford, England: Pergamon Press.

———. 1993. "Water Supply Systems Utilizing the Edaphic-Phytodepuration Technique." In *Constructed Wetlands for Water Quality Improvement: An International Symposium.* Proceedings of a conference held in Pensacola, FL, October 21–24. Lewis Publishers.

Ribeiro, A. 1991. "Análises das variações climáticas observadas na região de Manaus (AM)." Master's thesis, University of São Paulo, Piracicaba.

Salati, Eneas. 1985. "The Climatology and Hydrology of the Amazonia." In G. Prance and T. Lovejoy, eds., *Amazonia: Key Environments,* pp. 18–48. Oxford, England: Pergamon Press.

———. 1987. "Edaphic-Phytodepuration: A New Approach to Wastewater Treatment." In K. R. Reddy and W. H. Smith, eds., *Aquatic Plants for Water Treatment and Resource Recovery.* Orlando, FL: Magnolia Publishing.

Salati, Eneas, A. Dal'Ollio, J. R. Gat, and E. Matsui. 1979. "Recycling of Water in the Amazon Basin: An Isotope Study." *Water Resources Research* 15, pp. 1250–58.

Salati Filho, Eneas. 1991. "HDS System: Utilization in the Treatment of Secondary Water Flow in the Cellulose and Paper Industries." In *Constructed Wetlands for Water Quality Improvement: An International Symposium.* Proceedings of a conference held in Pensacola, FL, October 21–24. University of West Florida.

Victoria, R. L., L. A. Martinelli, J. E. Richey, and J. Mortatti. 1991. "Mechanisms of Water Recycling in the Amazon: Isotopic Insights." *Ambio* 20:8, pp. 384–87.

9

Sustainability at Landscape and Regional Scales

R. V. O'Neill, C. T. Hunsaker, D. Jones, J. M. Klopatek, V. H. Dale, M. G. Turner, R. H. Gardner, and R. Graham

Many of the important threats to sustainability of the biosphere involve changes in patterns of land use as a result of an expanding human population. Loss of habitat, decreased biodiversity, tropical deforestation, and desertification all involve changes in the extent and patterning of natural systems on the landscape. Reversing current trends requires a new emphasis on the interaction between spatial patterning and ecological function. This chapter recommends a number of measures of landscape pattern, based primarily on remote sensing, and suggests critical research areas needed to address sustainability of heterogeneous spatial systems.

For decades, ecology has focused on paradigms that assume spatial homogeneity. Heterogeneity and pattern were invariably observed in field studies, but results were nevertheless averaged across space. The dominant paradigms held that the critical regularities were contained in the means. Heterogeneity was the "nasty bit" left over and relegated to unexplained variance.

Today, as we discuss the sustainable biosphere, it is impossible to ignore spatial pattern: 5.5 billion humans are carving the terrestrial biosphere into a mosaic of land uses that threaten the subsidies provided by intact ecosystems on intact landscapes.[1] For purposes of this chapter, we define the landscape scale as involving 10,000 to 10 million hectares, with each spatial unit or pixel involving 1 to perhaps 100 hectares.

Landscape and regional changes are implicated in all of the problems identified in the Sustainable Biosphere Initiative (Lubchenco and others 1991). The primary terrestrial contributor to global change in atmospheric carbon is the disruption of tropical forest landscapes (Dale 1990a, forthcoming; Dale, Houghton, and Hall 1991). The primary risk to biodiversity comes from landscape fragmentation and loss (Wilson 1988). An important threat to sustainable ecologi-

cal systems is the isolation of natural systems on the landscape, which affects the spread of and ability to recover from disturbances (Turner and others 1989, 1991). In fact, most of the phenomena we label as disturbance—from the eruption of Mount St. Helens, to invasions of the Gypsy Moth, to damage from hurricanes in the Everglades, to fires in Yellowstone—are spatial disruptions at the landscape and regional scale.

Tropical deforestation provides a strong motivation for considering landscape and regional scales. The Brazilian Amazon has the largest tract of moist tropical rain forest in the world (Molofosky, Hall, and Myers 1986). Remotely sensed imagery reveals that by 1987, 41,000 square kilometers had been cleared in Rondonia for colonization (Booth 1989; Malingreau and Tucker 1988; Stone, Brown, and Woodwell 1989). At current rates, the forest in Rondonia will be gone by 2000. The ecological effects of changing tropical forest landscapes include decreased biodiversity (Wilson 1988), disruption of hydrological regimes (Shukla, Nobre, and Sellers 1990), degradation of soil (Hecht 1981), and changes in greenhouse gases that could induce changes in climate (Houghton and others 1983; Post and others 1990).

Problems such as deforestation lead us to ask how sustainability is related to the mosaic of ecological systems at landscape and regional scales. Basically, these large scales are relevant to sustainability insofar as the arrangement of systems in space influences (1) the intrinsic stability of ecosystems and (2) the ability of ecosystems to provide a variety of human subsidies, including food, fiber, water, and recreation. Factors influencing intrinsic stability include increase in the frequency or extent of disturbances, significant loss of species, and decreased ability to recover from disturbances. Factors influencing sustained services to humans include erosion, water quality, and loss of wildlife.

Given the importance of changes in land use, it is providential that three technological breakthroughs have made the study of large-scale spatial changes practical. First, advances in satellite imagery (Dale 1990b; Tucker and others 1986) provide large-scale data sets. Second, developments in geographic information systems facilitate manipulation of data (Dearstone and others, forthcoming). Third, rapid developments in landscape ecology are providing the theory (Graham and others 1991; Hunsaker and others 1990) and models (Dale and others 1993; Southworth, Dale, and O'Neill 1991a, 1991b) for regional applications.

The purpose of this chapter is to suggest how landscape ecology can be applied to monitoring large geographic areas for sustainability. We offer a variety of elementary measures of landscape pattern that are both practical (based on current technology) and interpretable (based on current ecological understanding). We also recommend areas of research that must be addressed if we are to assure the sustainability of heterogeneous spatial systems.

Measuring pattern at landscape scales

Measurements at the landscape scale must satisfy four criteria. They must (1) be practical, (2) capture significant aspects of pattern, (3) be sensitive to changes through time or across systems, and (4) be interpretable in terms of ecological processes (O'Neill, Hunsaker, and Levine 1992).

Habitat coverage

The simplest landscape measure is the number of pixels (the smallest spatial units on the map) that change land use. Changes in natural vegetative cover, for example, reflect loss of habitat and can be directly translated into increased risk to wildlife species. O'Neill, Gardner, and Turner (1992) present a list of rare and endangered species in southeastern United States that are uniquely dependent on a particular type of habitat. In specific regions, such as the sandy scrub of central Florida, the list permits an immediate interpretation of habitat loss.

Attention can also be focused on specific transitions from one land cover to another. These include loss of rare land covers (such as wetlands), loss of windbreaks, or formation of contiguous agriculture adjacent to a stream or lake. We would also be concerned with connectivity between landscapes as reflected in corridors between patches of natural habitat (Forman and Godron 1986; Harris and Scheck 1991).

Ecotones

The length of ecotones or edges can also be related to suitability of the landscape for wildlife (Gardner and others 1991). In general, loss of edge can be related to decreased biodiversity since ecotones normally have higher species diversity. Ecotones often form unique habitats that are associated with rare and endangered species (O'Neill, Gardner, Turner, and Romme 1992).

It is also relevant to examine the relationship of edges to sizes of patches. For example, cowbirds on forest edges are nest predators on warblers. Forest patches have to be sufficiently large so that nest sites are far enough away from edges that cowbirds cannot find them. If patches get too small, warbler populations start to decline.

Patch configurations

Much of what we understand about the influence of landscape pattern on ecological processes is based on the configuration of patches. For example, the frequency distribution of patches by size can be important because some species require a minimal size of patch. The largest patch may also serve as a reservoir that maintains a population on the landscape. Fragmentation of a landscape into many isolated patches has been shown to reduce biodiversity (Bierregard 1990; Lovejoy, Bierregard, and Rylands 1986; Saunders, Hobbs, and Margules 1991).

It would also be possible to consider the frequency distribution of distances between patches. These nearest-neighbor distances are related to the difficulty experienced by wildlife moving across the landscape. Some spatial arrangements of patches are particularly vulnerable to fragmentation. Isolated habitat is often configured in a longitudinal pattern, like a string of pearls. Examples include alpine tundra along ridge tops of the Rockies, dune vegetation along beaches, and granite outcrops. Removing a single patch from this configuration may split the entire habitat in two if the gap exceeds the ability of the populations to disperse.

Attention does not need to be limited to patches of natural vegetation. It is also possible to interpret changes in the extent and pattern of clearing relative to risk of erosion. Erosion is significantly increased on long slopes of uninterrupted, unvegetated surfaces. On this basis, clearings might be weighted by slope, size, and proximity to other clearings.

Weighting change in habitat

Interpretations of change in landscape can be enhanced by weighting the transition of individual pixels. For example, a transition to agriculture might be weighted by distance to water to evaluate the impact on water quality. Greater weight might be given to a transition that fragments a large patch. Similarly, a transition could be weighted by the probability of forming a barrier to the movement of animals or the break up of a corridor. It would be important to distinguish between 100 pixels scattered randomly and 100 pixels in a line, forming a new barrier to the movement of animals.

Individual transitions can also be weighted by characteristics of the entire landscape. In an area with very little wetland (or riparian or critical habitat), loss of a pixel is more important than in a region where the habitat is abundant.

Many possibilities emerge through the use of ancillary data, such as agricultural censuses, human population numbers, or forest surveys. As an example, loss of a pixel of forest with recreational value would be weighted more heavily in regions with large urban populations.

Calculated landscape indexes

Dealing with changes in all types of land cover can be a daunting task, and some consideration must be given to reducing the amount of data. For example, the "U" index (O'Neill and others 1988a) is a simple measure of overall impact of humans. The index is calculated as the number of pixels in types of natural land cover divided by the pixels in human land uses, such as agriculture and urbanization.

Percolation theory (Gardner and others 1987) provides a framework for relating pattern of landscape to the ability of an organism to move across the landscape. Rates of diffusion can be calculated and interpreted in terms of wildlife use or spread of fires. The percolation backbone defines the fewest steps needed to traverse the landscape.

Percolation theory also defines critical values of habitat coverage (Gardner and O'Neill 1991). On a random square lattice, the critical value is 59.28 percent. If the percentage of cover for habitat is less than this value, the landscape becomes dissected into isolated patches. The resource utilization scale measures the scale at which an organism must operate to use the resources on a landscape (O'Neill and others 1988b). Similarly, epidemiology theory can be combined with percolation theory to calculate the probability that a disturbance or pest will spread or become endemic (O'Neill, Gardner, Turner, and Romme 1992).

Several other landscape indexes have been developed in recent studies. Dominance is an information theoretic index that indicates the extent to which the landscape is dominated by a single land use (O'Neill and others 1988a). Empirical studies confirm that the fractional dimension of patches indicates the extent to which humans have reshaped the structure of the landscape (Krummel and others 1987; O'Neill and others 1988a). Humans prefer simple shapes; nature generates complex configurations. Contagion (Haban Li and Reynolds, forthcoming; O'Neill and others 1988a) expresses the probability that land uses are more clumped than the random expectation.

One method to assess a land cover would be to ask, "How well is the land being used, compared with its potential?" This suggests an index that compares each pixel with an overlying map of potential vegetative cover and calculates the percentage difference. Another index might compare present land use with suitability for various human applications, such as agriculture.

Similarly, it should be possible to devise a measure of landscape suitability for animals. Consider a square "window" of pixels, the size of an organism's home range. Within the window, we could consider a variety of habitat requirements, such as mixture of vegetation and availability of water. We could then place the window over a corner of the map and calculate a correlation between the existing landscape and the habitat requirements. The window could then be moved systematically over the map to obtain an overall score that indicates the suitability of the landscape for this organism. We could design a suite of windows for insects, birds, mammals, and so forth. This approach provides a simple, easily interpreted method to compare two landscapes or to evaluate the impact on animals of a change in landscape pattern.

Indicators of economic activity

We must be careful not to miss obvious measures of potential human impact. One of these is simply the number of miles of roads. Vehicles that use roads kill wildlife. Road surfaces alter hydrologic pathways and, when they intersect streams, affect the quality of water. Roads also provide pathways that accelerate the dispersal of pests.

It is well established in economic theory that the number of miles of new roads (and their quality) indicates future development and economic activity (Jones and O'Neill n.d.). In simplest terms, products must be transported to market. As the distance to market increases, transportation costs eat into profits. At some distance, profits reach zero, and there is no motivation for farming, logging, or mining (Jones and O'Neill 1993a, 1993b, and forthcoming). Distance to market can also determine the motivation of farmers to employ conservation measures in their farming activities (Jones and O'Neill n.d.).

It would also be of interest to evaluate landscapes by distance to the nearest urban pixel. One could calculate the average distance for a scene or just draw an area of urban influence. Given global trends toward urban sprawl, this could be taken as a measure of risk for development or overuse.

Hierarchical scales of landscape pattern

Empirical studies (O'Neill and others 1991a, 1991b) have confirmed the prediction from hierarchy theory (O'Neill and others 1986; O'Neill 1988, 1989; O'Neill, Johnson, and King 1989) that landscapes should show pattern at distinct scales. This approach uses statistical analysis of transect data to identify multiple scales of pattern (Turner and others 1991). The number of scales is a unique index that focuses on the ecological processes that influence landscape pattern.

Disruptions of this scaled structure mean that ecological processes determining a particular scale have been disrupted. Although the detailed relationship between processes and scaled patterns is still a matter of research, we have hierarchical neutral models that are suitable for testing hypotheses in the field (O'Neill, Hunsaker, and Levine 1992).

Landscape pattern and water quality

It is also possible to assess the risk of water quality degradation due to changes in terrestrial landscapes (Hunsaker and others, forthcoming). Across a region, increase in agricultural and urban land uses or decreases in natural vegetation indicate a risk of future problems with water quality. The changes in basic cover could be weighted by distance to water, soil type, and slope calculated from digital elevation models. Essentially, the same data set can be used with the Universal Soil Loss Equation to estimate erosion. A second type of indicator might focus on the risks of undesirable hydrologic events. For example, a flood indicator could include vegetative cover, wetlands that modify peak flows, and surficial geology.

Riparian zones are important buffers for maintaining the quality of water in streams. Changes in the width of buffers, weighted by slope, are an important indicator. The actual index might be average width or miles of riparian zone that are narrower than desirable. The *Canadian Timber Management Guide* (Ontario Ministry of Natural Resources 1988) sets standards for the width of buffer zones that range from 30 meters on slopes of 0°–15° to 90 meters on slopes above 45°. This standard could be applied by counting pixels that encroach on the recommended buffers.

Research needs in landscape and regional studies

The research agenda for landscape studies can be stated simply: How do ecological processes interact with the environment to create patterns, and how do the patterns influence ecological function? Basically, there is a need to develop measures of spatial pattern and to correlate pattern with ecological processes in field studies. Without attempting to be all-inclusive, several areas of research seem particularly relevant.

To what extent does spatial pattern affect the ability of systems to recover from disturbance? We know that northern hardwoods may take sixty to eighty years to replace biomass and nutrients lost in harvesting (Likens and others 1978). How would this recovery time change if distances to seed sources were increased or if erosion set in?

To what extent is spatial pattern critical to the sustainability of plant and animal communities? For example, pollinators and nectar feeders fly, which permits them to cover large areas and explicitly integrate across spatial heterogeneity.

They require something to be blooming somewhere throughout the season. If the spatial scale of the heterogeneity is increased to exceed their ability to integrate, the result could be important changes in the plant community.

We need to identify ecological systems that are particularly sensitive to spatial disturbances. The proverbial erosion effects of tire tracks in the Arctic tundra are well known, but arid lands may be equally sensitive. Even the casual observer can see how small alterations in natural land forms result in major changes in the vegetation of arid lands.

The potential sensitivity of arid lands also alerts us to the need to identify critical thresholds in landscape pattern. Percolation theory indicates that small changes in land cover can critically alter connectivity between landscapes. But we also know from tragic experience in the American plains and the African Sahel that other critical thresholds exist. Beyond these thresholds, cascading effects or positive feedbacks cause bifurcations that move the system into new modes of operation (Schlesinger and others 1990).

To address sustainability at large scales, we need to integrate socioeconomic theory with ecology. Landscapes change because of human decisions. To predict such change requires an understanding of the economic forces that determine land tenure and land use (Jones and O'Neill 1993a, 1993b, and forthcoming). To reverse current trends requires that ecological consequences be translated into feedbacks, into the real cost of supplying environmental subsidies. The development of this interdisciplinary theory is critical, yet almost no support is available for this research.

Conclusions

The analysis presented in this chapter seems to justify three conclusions. First, an emphasis on landscape ecology is required since most threats to a sustainable biosphere involve changes in land use at large scales. Second, the combination of remote sensing, geographic information systems, and landscape theory permits us to define a significant number of new metrics that are both practical and interpretable. Third, continued progress involves difficult new areas of research. New research, particularly interdisciplinary socioeconomic-ecological studies, requires new sources of funding that currently do not exist.

Note

1. A billion is 1,000 million.

References

Bierregard, R. O. 1990. "Avian Communities in the Understory of Amazonian Forest Fragments." In A. Keast, ed., *Biogeography and Ecology of Forest Bird Communities*, pp. 333–43. The Hague, the Netherlands: SPB Academic Publishing.

Booth, W. 1989. "Monitoring the Fate of Forests from Space." *Science* 243, pp. 1428–29.

Dale, V. H. 1990a. "Strategy for Monitoring the Effects of Land Use Change on Atmospheric Carbon Dioxide Concentrations." In *Proceedings of Global Natural Resources Monitoring and Assessments.* Vol. 1, pp. 422–31. Bethesda, Md.: American Society for Photogrammetry and Remote Sensing.

Dale, V. H., ed. 1990b. "Report of a Workshop on Using Remote Sensing to Estimate Land Use Change." ORNL/TM-11502. Oak Ridge, Tenn.

———. Forthcoming. *Effects of Land-use Change on Atmospheric Carbon Dioxide Concentrations: Southeast Asia as a Case Study.* New York: Springer-Verlag.

Dale, V. H., R. A. Houghton, and C. A. S. Hall. 1991. "Estimating the Effects of Land Use Change on Global Atmospheric Carbon Dioxide Concentrations." *Canadian Journal of Forest Research* 21, pp. 87–90.

Dale, V. H., F. Southworth, R. V. O'Neill, and A. Rosen. 1993. "Simulating Spatial Patterns and Socioeconomic and Ecologic Effects of Land-use Change in Rondonia, Brazil." In R. H. Gardner, ed., *Some Mathematical Questions in Biology.* Providence, R.I.: American Mathematical Society.

Dearstone, K. C., V. H. Dale, R. H. Frohn, F. Southworth, R. V. O'Neill. Forthcoming. "Linking Spatial Data to a Model of Colonization and Deforestation of Rondonia, Brazil." *Geocarto International.*

Forman, R. T. T., and M. Godron. 1986. *Landscape Ecology.* New York: Wiley and Sons.

Gardner, R. H., B. T. Milne, M. G. Turner, and R. V. O'Neill. 1987. "Neutral Models for the Analysis of Broad-scale Landscape Pattern." *Landscape Ecology* 1, pp. 19–28.

Gardner, R. H., and R. V. O'Neill. 1991. "Pattern, Process, and Predictability: The Use of Neutral Models for Landscape Analysis." In M. G. Turner and R. H. Gardner, eds., *Quantitative Methods in Landscape Ecology*, pp. 289–307. New York: Springer-Verlag.

Gardner, R. H., M. G. Turner, R. V. O'Neill, and S. Lavorel. 1991. "Simulation of the Scale-dependent Effects of Landscape Boundaries on Species Persistence and Dispersal." In M. M. Holland, P. G. Risser, and R. J. Naiman, eds., *Ecotones: The Role of Landscape Boundaries in the Management and Restoration of Changing Environments*, pp. 76–89. New York: Chapman and Hall.

Graham, R. L., C. T. Hunsaker, R. V. O'Neill, and B. L. Jackson. 1991. "Ecological Risk Assessment at the Regional Scale." *Ecological Applications* 1, pp. 196–206.

Haban Li, and J. F. Reynolds. Forthcoming. "A New Contagion Index to Quantify Spatial Patterns of Landscapes." *Landscape Ecology.*

Harris, L. D., and J. Scheck. 1991. "From Implication to Applications: The Dispersal Corridor Principle Applied to the Conservation of Biological Diversity." In D. A. Saunders and R. J. Hobbs, eds., *Nature Conservation 2: The Role of Corridors*, pp. 189–220. London: Surrey Beatty and Sons.

Hecht, S. B. 1981. "Deforestation in the Amazon Basin: Magnitude, Dynamics, and Soil Resource Effects." *Studies in Third World Societies* 13, pp. 61–110.

Houghton, R. A., J. E. Hobbie, J. M. Melillo, B. Moore, B. J. Peterson, G. R. Shavers, and G. M. Woodwell. 1983. "Changes in the Carbon Content of Terrestrial Biota and Soils between 1860 and 1980: Net Release of Carbon Dioxide to the Atmosphere." *Ecological Monographs* 53, pp. 235–62.

Hunsaker, C. T., R. L. Graham, G. W. Suter, R. V. O'Neill, L. W. Barnthouse, and R. H. Gardner. 1990. "Assessing Ecological Risk on a Regional Scale." *Environmental Management* 14, pp. 325–32.

Hunsaker, C. T., D. A. Levine, S. P. Timmins, B. L. Jackson, and R. V. O'Neill. 1992. "Landscape Characterization for Assessing Regional Water Quality." In D. H. McKenzie, D. E. Hyatt, and V. J. McDonald, eds., *Ecological Indicators*, pp. 997–1006. New York: Elsevier.

Jones, D. W., and R. V. O'Neill. 1992. "Endogenous Environmental Degradation and Land Conservation: Agricultural Land Use in a Large Region." *Ecological Economics* 6, pp. 79–101.

————. 1993a. "Human-environmental Influences and Interactions in Shifting Agriculture." In T. R. Lakshmanan and P. Nijkamp, eds., *Essays on Space and Time*, pp. 297–307. New York: Springer-Verlag.

————. 1993b. "Human-environmental Influences and Interactions in Shifting Agriculture When Farmers Form Expectations Rationally." *Environment and Planning* 25, pp. 121–36.

————. Forthcoming. "Land Use with Endogenous Environmental Degradation and Conservation." *Resources and Energy.*

————. n.d. "Rural Land Use and Deforestation with Costly Investment in Transportation Infrastructure." Mss.

Krummel, J. R., R. H. Gardner, G. Sugihara, R. V. O'Neill, and P. R. Coleman. 1987. "Landscape Patterns in a Disturbed Environment." *Oikos* 48, pp. 321–24.

Likens, G. E., F. H. Bormann, R. S. Pierce, and W. A. Reiners. 1978. "Recovery of a Deforested Ecosystem." *Science* 199, pp. 492–96.

Lovejoy, T. E., R. O. Bierregard, and A. B. Rylands. 1986. "Edge and Other Effects of Isolation on Amazon Forest Fragments." In M. E. Soule, ed., *Conservation Biology: The Science of Scarcity and Diversity*, pp. 275–85. Sunderland, Mass.: Sinauer Associates.

Lubchenco, J., A. M. Olson, L. B. Brubaker, S. R. Carpenter, M. M. Holland, S. P. Hubbell, S. A. Levin, J. A. MacMahon, P. A. Matson, J. M. Melillo, H. A. Mooney, C. H. Peterson, H. R. Pulliam, L. A. Real, P. J. Regal, and P. G. Risser. 1991. "The Sustainable Biosphere Initiative: An Ecological Research Agenda." *Ecology* 72, pp. 371–412.

Malingreau, J. P., and C. J. Tucker. 1988. "Large-scale Deforestation in the Southeastern Amazon Basin of Brazil." *Ambio* 17:1, pp. 49–55.

Molofosky, J., C. A. S. Hall, and N. Myers. 1986. "A Comparison of Tropical Forest Surveys." DOE/NB-0078. Department of Energy, Washington, D.C.

Ontario Ministry of Natural Resources. 1988. "Timber Management Guidelines for the Protection of Fish Habitat." Toronto, Canada.

O'Neill, R. V. 1988. "Hierarchy Theory and Global Change." In T. Rosswall, R. G. Woodmansee, and P. G. Risser, eds., *Spatial and*

Temporal Variability in Biospheric and Geospheric Processes, pp. 29–45. New York: John Wiley and Sons.

———. 1989. "Perspectives in Hierarchy and Scale." In J. Roughgarden, R. M. May, and Simon A. Levin, eds., *Perspectives in Ecological Theory*, pp. 140–56. Princeton, N.J.: Princeton University Press.

O'Neill, R. V., D. L. DeAngelis, J. B. Waide, and T. F. H. Allen. 1986. *A Hierarchical Concept of Ecosystems*. Princeton, N.J.: Princeton University Press.

O'Neill, R. V., R. H. Gardner, B. T. Milne, M. G. Turner, and B. Jackson. 1991a. "Heterogeneity and Spatial Hierarchies." In J. Kolasa and S. T. A. Pickett, eds., *Ecological Heterogeneity*, pp. 85–96. New York: Springer-Verlag.

O'Neill, R. V., S. J. Turner, V. I. Cullinen, D. P. Coffin, T. Cook, W. Conley, J. Brunt, J. M. Thomas, M. R. Conley, and J. Gosz. 1991b. "Multiple Landscape Scales: An Intersite Comparison." *Landscape Ecology* 5, pp. 137–44.

O'Neill, R. V., R. H. Gardner, and M. G. Turner. 1992. "A Hierarchical Neutral Model for Landscape Analysis." *Landscape Ecology* 7, pp. 55–61.

O'Neill, R. V., R. H. Gardner, M. G. Turner, and W. H. Romme. 1992. "Epidemiology Theory and Disturbance Spread on Landscapes." *Landscape Ecology* 7, pp. 19–26.

O'Neill, R. V., C. Hunsaker, and D. Levine. 1992. "Monitoring Challenges and Innovative Ideas." In D. H. McKenzie, D. E. Hyatt, and V. J. McDonald, eds., *Ecological Indicators*, pp. 1443–60. New York: Elsevier.

O'Neill, R. V., A. R. Johnson, and A. W. King. 1989. "A Hierarchical Framework for the Analysis of Scale." *Landscape Ecology* 3, pp. 193–205.

O'Neill, R. V., J. R. Krummel, R. H. Gardner, G. Sugihara, B. Jackson, D. L. DeAngelis, B. T. Milne, M. G. Turner, B. Zygmunt, S. Christensen, V. H. Dale, and R. L. Graham. 1988a. "Indices of Landscape Pattern." *Landscape Ecology* 1, pp. 153–62.

O'Neill, R. V., B. T. Milne, M. G. Turner, and R. H. Gardner. 1988b. "Resource Utilization Scales and Landscape Pattern. *Landscape Ecology* 2, pp. 63–69.

Post, W. M., T.-H. Peng, W. Emanuel, A. W. King, and D. L. DeAngelis. 1990. "The Global Carbon Cycle." *American Scientist* 78, pp. 310–326.

Saunders, D. A., R. J. Hobbs, and C. R. Margules. 1991. "Biological Consequences of Ecosystem Fragmentation: A Review." *Conservation Biology* 5:1, pp. 18–32.

Schlesinger, W. H., J. F. Reynolds, G. L. Cunningham, L. F. Huenneke, W. M. Jarrell, R. A. Virginia, and W. G. Whitford. 1990. "Biological Feedbacks in Global Desertification." *Science* 247, pp. 1043–48.

Shukla, J., C. Nobre, and P. Sellers. 1990. "Amazon Deforestation and Climate Change." *Science* 247, pp. 1322–25.

Southworth, F., V. H. Dale, and R. V. O'Neill. 1991a. "Contrasting Patterns of Land Use in Rondonia, Brazil: Simulating the Effects on Carbon Release." *International Social Science Journal* 43, pp. 681–98.

———. 1991b. "Modes opposés d'occupation des sols au Rondonia, Brésil: Simulation de leurs effets sur les émissions de carbone." *Revue Internationale des Sciences Sociales* 130, pp. 729–46.

Stone, T. A., F. Brown, and G. M. Woodwell. 1989. "Estimates of Land Use Change in Central Rondonia, Brazil, by Remote Sensing." *Forest Ecology and Management* 38, pp. 291–304.

Tucker, C. J., J. R. G. Townsend, T. E. Goff, and B. N. Holben. 1986. "Continental and Global Scale Remote Sensing of Land Cover." In J. Trabalka and D. E. Reichle, eds., *The Changing Carbon Cycle: A Global Analysis*, pp. 221–41. New York: Springer-Verlag.

Turner, M. G., R. H. Gardner, V. H. Dale, and R. V. O'Neill. 1989. "Predicting the Spread of Disturbances across Heterogeneous Landscapes." *Oikos* 55, pp. 121–29.

Turner, M. G., R. H. Gardner, and R. V. O'Neill. 1991. "Potential Responses of Landscape Structure to Global Environmental Change." In M. M. Holland, P. G. Risser, and R. J. Naiman, eds., *Ecotones: The Role of Landscape Boundaries in the Management and Restoration of Changing Environments*, pp. 52–75. New York: Chapman and Hall.

Turner, S. J., R. V. O'Neill, W. Conley, M. R. Conley, and H. C. Humphries. 1991. "Pattern and Scale: Statistics for Landscape Ecology." In M. G. Turner and R. H. Gardner, eds., *Quantitative Methods in Landscape Ecology*, pp. 17–41. New York: Springer-Verlag.

Wilson, E. O., ed. 1988. *Biodiversity*. Washington, D.C.: National Academy Press.

Part B

Case Studies

10

Indicators of Biophysical Sustainability: Case Study of the Chaco Savannas of South America

Enríque H. Bucher

Even lacking a precise definition (Sarachchandra 1991), sustainable development obviously implies the management of at least three basic components: the biological machinery that provides resources and services, the human beings who use those resources and services, and the socioeconomic scenario in which the development process takes place. This chapter concentrates on possible indicators of sustainability related to the first component (biophysical machinery) and applicable to savannas in general and to the Gran Chaco region of South America in particular. It also tests the proposed criteria by applying them to different styles of land use common in the region. This restriction in scope does not mean that I ignore the critical importance of the other components, nor that I am fully convinced of the advantages of discussing each one of them in isolation. Unless we start dealing with the specifics, we run the permanent risk of being lost in endless and fruitless debates on vaguely defined concepts. To translate abstract concepts into management, economists and ecologists clearly need a common language and common criteria. This need includes the development of indicators of sustainability that can be collected easily and frequently and can be used to monitor the sustainability of large regions and even entire continents.

This issue is particularly important in the semi-arid savanna ecosystems of the world. Conversion of productive savanna land into barren wasteland has been taking place since humans first domesticated hooved mammals and began to control the movement and size of their herds. Many areas have been lost to production entirely, whereas much larger areas have had their productivity seriously impaired and continue on a downward trend. Although not as diverse as the tropical rain forests, semi-arid savannas are still very important in terms of their biodiversity. In these regions, human populations are dependent on the continued productivity of natural resources such as livestock, fuelwood, and wildlife, but the natural environment also directly affects individual well-being via parasites, diseases, and the like. These linkages influence human social and cultural systems, which in turn affect patterns of land use (Ellis and Swift 1988; Schofield and Bucher 1986).

The Gran Chaco

The vast plain known as the Gran Chaco is a natural region of about 1 million square kilometers extending over parts of Argentina, Bolivia, and Paraguay. The climax vegetation is a subtropical savanna (Bucher 1982). The eastern part is characterized by the presence of abundant swamps, reed beds, and gallery forests, whereas the predominant vegetation in the western Chaco is a medium-tall, xerophilous subtropical forest with a ground layer of grasses and many cacti and terrestrial bromeliads. Rainfall decreases westward from a maximum of around 1,200 millimeters along the Paraguay-Paraná rivers to a minimum of 450 millimeters in the southwest. This decrease in rainfall is accompanied by the lengthening of the winter dry season from two to seven months.

The Chaco supports considerable biological diversity (Bucher 1982). Its floristic richness includes eighty-three genera in the east, fifty-six in the center, and sixty-five in the west (Sarmiento 1972). Grass diversity is especially important: more than fifty species have been found in Joaquín V. González, Salta Province (C. Saravia Toledo, unpublished data). The vertebrate fauna includes about thirty-five species of amphibians, twenty of lizards, and at least twenty-five of snakes (Bucher 1982). The Chaco avifauna includes 408 species (Capurro and Bucher 1988; Short 1975). Invertebrate diversity is also great, although it is incompletely known. Overall, ants are extremely important in the Chaco, particularly leaf-cutting ants, which are significant as herbivores, detritus-reducers, and soil-modifying agents (Bucher 1982).

The impact of the European colonization in Argentina

The Chaco's primeval landscape was a parkland with patches of hardwood intermingled with grasslands (Bucher 1982). This mosaic of vegetation was kept stable by occasional flooding of low-lying areas in the east, but more importantly by periodic fires caused by lightning or set by Indians, in a kind of pulse equilibrium common to many semi-arid savannas throughout the world (Huntley and Walker 1982). After Europeans colonized the area, the frequency and intensity of fires decreased, particularly in the dry western Chaco, as the Indians withdrew and domestic cattle grazed the fuel needed by fires. Consequently, woody vegetation rapidly invaded grassland patches throughout western Chaco, to the point at which grasslands disappeared completely (Bucher 1982; Bucher and Schofield 1981; Morello and Saravia Toledo 1959).

A second stage in the alteration of landscape started in the 1880s when railways expanded into the Chaco. This expansion not only allowed intensive forest cutting but also helped the Chaco campesinos (*puesteros*) expand into the intervening areas between rivers. Crucial to this expansion was the introduction of railway transportation and new technologies, particularly the tools for digging the artesian wells that allowed campesinos to maintain cattle around watering points throughout the year.

Recent occupation of the Paraguayan Chaco

Because of lack of access and the war between Bolivia and Paraguay during the 1930s, the Paraguayan Chaco remained almost empty until the 1980s, when construction of the trans-Chaco road between Asunción and Santa Cruz de la Sierra began. Occupation of the area has been based on large-scale ranching in the west and mixed agriculture and ranching in the center (Mennonite colonies), where annual rainfall is more than 700 millimeters. In both cases, development is based on capital-intensive technology, usually financed by loans from multinational agencies. It follows the Brazilian model of occupation of the Amazon forest, in which nearly all native vegetation is eliminated and replaced with introduced pastures or crops according to rainfall. As a result, a large portion of the original biodiversity has been lost. Encroachment of the woody vegetation resulting from land clearing is a serious problem. Removal of all palatable native grass and shrubs may result in lack of availability of proteins and green material during the dry season, affecting the condition of cattle, particularly in years when frost damages the introduced pastures (Saravia and Bucher, personal communication).

Sustainable management of the Chaco: The Salta Project

In the Argentine province of Salta, a group of researchers and landowners have proved the feasibility of managing the Chaco in a sustainable way by restoring and maintaining the native forest and grasslands in a productive cycle. The Salta Project, started more than twenty-five years ago, is based on 300,000 hectares of public land and 60,000 hectares of private land located near Joaquín V. González, Salta (Bucher and Schofield 1981; Saravia Toledo 1987). The scheme preserves the natural vegetation and dedicates a small portion of the exploited area (less than 10 percent) to introduced pastures. The process includes two consecutive steps: first, restoration of the degraded vegetation, and second, institution of a multiple-species ranching system based on the sustainable exploitation of cattle, forest products (charcoal, fuelwood, and timber), and (possibly) wildlife.

The scheme is organized around the management of large units of land under a system of rest rotation of grazing by cattle, cutting of shrubs for charcoal and fuelwood, and felling of trees for fence posts and railroad ties. The smallest unit is around 5,000 hectares. Each unit is fenced to keep out cattle and goats. Then, in progressive sectors of about 100 hectares, all fallen wood is removed, and almost all the trees and scrubs are harvested to provide hardwood timber and fuel for the charcoal ovens. The forest is then exploited sequentially for timber and charcoal in cycles of about twenty to forty years allowing adequate time for the habitat and the grass cover to recover. Seeds of wild grasses are added where regrowth is poor, and the area is left undisturbed and protected from cattle until the young hardwood saplings are large enough to be immune to grazing, although limited grazing may be allowed to help disperse grass seeds. Once recovery is complete, cattle is reintroduced to carrying capacity density under a controlled grazing regime based on rest rotation (Saravia Toledo 1987). This careful level of stocking improves substantially on the present capacity of the western Chaco, which in its degraded form now rarely supports more than one cow per 15 to 30 hectares.

After about five years, when the young trees are about 2 meters tall, the saplings are thinned, and all undesirable woody plants are removed to relieve competition with the young hardwoods and then used to produce charcoal. At intervals of about twenty to forty years, the mature hardwoods can be harvested.

Thus, the whole area is composed of sectors each in a different stage of exploitation. While some sectors are producing good-quality hardwood timber, other areas are producing beef and charcoal. This management model has important consequences at the landscape level. Instead of having a homogeneous cover of secondary shrubland with isolated areas of highly degraded soil, a much greater degree of heterogeneity develops, which in turn has the potential for supporting greater biodiversity, since each management unit is interspersed with others in an irregular pattern that creates a complex mosaic of land-scape fragmentation patterns, edge configurations, and patch-boundary characteristics (Wiens, Crawford, and Gosz 1985).

Results after twenty-five years of management indicate that the productivity of both forage and beef increase dramatically in managed areas (see table 10-1). After eight years, 75 percent of the original productivity can be reached (Saravia Toledo 1987). By this careful management, the productive cycle can be maintained, providing profit and employment for people living in rural areas.

During the last decade, it became evident that wildlife could be incorporated in this production system. For example, exports of Tupinambis lizards and parrots have increased steadily. At present, more than 2.5 million lizard skins are exported annually from Argentina, and 141,000 parrots were exported in 1987, mostly from the Chaco (Traffic Uruguay, unpublished data). As a result, wildlife has become an important source of income for the campesinos, and the possibility of integrating its exploitation into the existing projects under a sustainable, multispecies scheme is being explored (Beissinger and Bucher 1992; Bucher 1989).

The Salta approach to managing the Chaco has the potential to enhance the social, medical, and economic well-being of human populations in a sustainable fashion, while preserving a very high proportion of the region's original biodiversity. Moreover, the scheme may have very important effects on social welfare and public health. The cycle of overexploited land, poverty, disease, and urban migration has been interrupted, not just by treating the disease or by alleviating poverty with charity but by using the land in an ecologically and economically sustainable manner (Bucher and Schofield 1981; Solbrig 1988). Moreover, increased prosperity and the construction of new wooden housing appear to be responsible for reducing Chagas disease. That is, rather than treating the problems of natural resource degra-

Table 10-1: Productivity of Cattle Ranching under Different Management Systems in Salta, Argentina

Parameter	Traditional system	Chaco del Norte
Carrying capacity (number of cattle per 100 hectares)	4.35	20.00
Productivity (kilograms per hectare a year)	1.21	21.78
Profit (U.S. dollars per hectare a year)	0.36	8.00

Source: Saravia Toledo 1987.

dation, poverty, and disease as separate problems, it may be more effective to deal with them simultaneously as interrelated problems (Bucher and Schofield 1981).

Indicators of sustainability

For any model of development, biophysical indicators of sustainability should deal with different scales of environmental health and cover at least the following broad aspects.

At the global scale,

- Contributions to the balance of atmospheric gases and impact on climatic stability
- Contributions to pollution of air, water, and soil.

At the regional scale,

- Sustainability of freshwater resources
- Preservation of soil integrity
- Preservation of biodiversity.

PRESERVATION OF THE ATMOSPHERIC BALANCE
Emissions of carbon dioxide (CO_2) and other greenhouse gases in the Chaco relate mostly to the burning of vegetation. Fire is an important ecological factor in all semi-arid savannas, and it cannot be easily eliminated. Fuelwood is a cheap and sustainable source of energy that may help to decrease the consumption of fossil fuels: during World War II, the Argentine railroad system ran its steam engines exclusively on fuelwood. Finally, the restoration of vegetation may be important in increasing CO_2 fixation and in reducing albedo from bare soil.

POLLUTION OF AIR, WATER, AND SOIL
Pastoral land use produces, on average, a limited amount of pollutants.

SUSTAINABILITY OF FRESHWATER RESOURCES
As in every region of the world, availability of fresh water is limited. Campesinos obtain water from shallow artesian wells that are replenished by rainfall. Large-scale ranching programs like those developed in Paraguay and Salta may require larger amounts of water, which has to be obtained from deeper groundwater sources. At least some of these sources may not be sustainable since they come from past geological times and are not replenished fast enough. Adequate evaluation of the sustainability of water resources should be an important prerequisite for any development program in the Chaco.

SOIL CONSERVATION
Pastoral activities may affect soil mostly through erosion and loss of nutrients in overgrazed areas. This process is very serious in areas occupied by campesinos, whereas it should be negligible in well-managed natural pastures, like in the Salta model.

PRESERVATION OF BIODIVERSITY
Loss of biodiversity is high (although generally slow) under the campesino model. However, at least some portion of the original biodiversity is preserved. Losses are still higher in the Brazilian model, which also implies the introduction of alien species of plants. On the contrary, the Salta model preserves a very high proportion of the original biodiversity (see table 10-2 for a description of the impact of different management models).

Synthetic indicators of sustainability

Measurement techniques and recommended limits for these indicators are already available and easy to use. However, a set of synthetic indicators of rangeland sustainability can provide a more reliable and comprehensive indication of sustainability. This set includes two well-known concepts among range managers: condition and

Table 10-2: Impact of Different Management Systems on Biophysical Sustainability in the Chaco

Subsystem	Campesino	Paraguay	Salta
Climate	Low	Medium	Low
Pollution	None	Low	Low to none
Water resources	None	Low	Low
Soil	High	Medium	Low
Biodiversity loss	High	Very high	Very low

trend. Both have been widely tested in many semi-arid ecosystems of the world with an annual rainfall of around 300 millimeters and apply perfectly well to the Chaco.

CONDITION

This term covers the assessment of the status of a particular area of savanna in relation to its potential, classifying its condition as excellent, good, fair, and poor (Dasmann 1951). In areas where savanna is considered the climax vegetation, range condition is measured as the degree of departure from the stable, climax mixture of grass, forb, and woody species, along a gradient of increasing grazing pressure.

TREND

A companion measurement that must accompany the assessment of condition concerns trend. This states whether a particular area is deteriorating, improving, or stable, under current management, which requires successive measurements of condition along time. For example, an area in excellent condition showing a deteriorating trend indicates inadequate management, whereas another in fair condition but showing an improving trend indicates good management.

Measurements of condition are based on an assessment of change in vegetation and rely on the presence or absence of indicator species that occur only in a well-defined range along the condition axis (Dasmann 1951). Indicator species may include not only plant but also wildlife species if suitable. For example, medium-size rodents like the Chaco cavy (*Pediolagus salinicola*) and the vizcacha (*Lagostomus maximus*) increase in degraded areas (Bucher 1982); whereas the blue-fronted Amazon parrot (*Amazona aestiva*) breeds only in old-growth forests where snags and old trees provide holes suitable for nesting (Beissinger and Bucher 1992).

The advantage of using synthetic indicators such as condition and trend is that they are simple and reliable. Even if the techniques for assessing them for a given region need to be developed by specialists, the resulting guidelines can be used by nonspecialists. Of course, the only prerequisite would be the ability to recognize the indicator species of the various successional stages. At the same time, evaluation of condition and trend provides a much better and more reliable synthesis of the sustainability of any management system than many specific measurements taken in isolation.

References

Beissinger, S. R., and Enríque H. Bucher. 1992. "Can Parrots Be Conserved through Sustainable Harvesting?" *Bioscience* 42, pp. 164–73.

Bucher, Enríque H. 1982. "Chaco and Caatinga-South American Arid Savannas, Woodlands, and Thickets." In B. Huntley and B. Walker, eds., *Ecology of Tropical Savannas*, pp. 47–79. Berlin: Springer-Verlag.

———. 1989. "Conservación y desarrollo en el neotrópico: En búsqueda de alternativas." *Vida Silvestre Neotropical* 2, pp. 3–6.

Bucher, Enríque H., and C. J. Schofield. 1981. "Economic Assault on Chagas Disease." *New Scientist* 92, pp. 320–24.

Capurro, H. A., and Enríque H. Bucher. 1988. "Lista comentada de las aves del bosque chaqueño de Joaquín V. González, Salta, Argentina." *Hornero* 13, pp. 39–46.

Dasmann, W. P. 1951. "Some Deer Range Survey Methods." *California Fish and Game* 37, pp. 43–52.

Ellis, J. E., and D. M. Swift. 1988. "Stability of African Pastoral Ecosystems: Alternate Paradigms and Implications for Development." *Journal of Range Management* 41, pp. 450–59.

Huntley, B., and B. Walker, eds. 1982. *Ecology of Tropical Savannas*. Berlin: Springer-Verlag.

Morello, J., and C. Saravia Toledo. 1959. "El bosque chaqueño I. Paisaje primitivo, paisaje natural y paisaje cultural en el oriente de Salta." *Revista Agronómica del Noroeste Argentino* 3, pp. 5–81.

Sarachchandra, M. L. 1991. "Sustainable Development: A Critical Review." *World Development* 19, pp. 607–21.

Saravia Toledo, C. 1987. "Restoration of Degraded Pastures in the Semi-arid Chaco Region of Argentina." In *Proceedings of the UNESCO International Symposium on Ecosystem Redevelopment: Ecological, Economic, and Social Aspects, April 1987*, pp. 25–37. Budapest: UNESCO.

Sarmiento, G. 1972. "Ecological and Floristic Convergences between Seasonal Plant Formations of Tropical and Subtropical South America." *Journal of Ecology* 60, pp. 367–410.

Schofield, C., and Enríque H. Bucher. 1986. "Industrial Contributions to Desertification in South America." *Trends in Ecology and Evolution* 1, pp. 78–80.

Short, L. L. 1975. "A Zoogeographic Analysis of the South American Chaco Avifauna." *Bulletin of the American Museum of Natural History* 154, pp. 163–352.

Solbrig, O. 1988. "Destrucción o transformación del paisaje tropical sudamericano?" *Interciencia* 13, pp. 79–82.

Wiens, J. A., C. S. Crawford, and J. R. Gosz. 1985. "Boundary Dynamics: A Conceptual Framework for Studying Landscape Ecosystems." *Oikos* 45, pp. 421–27.

11

The Sustainability of Natural Renewable Resources as Viewed by an Ecologist and Exemplified by the Fishery of the Mollusc Concholepas concholepas in Chile

Juan Carlos Castilla

I wish to acknowledge financial support from FONDECYT-CHILE and from the International Development Research Center-Canada. I benefited enormously from presentations given during the fourth Cary Conference at the Institute for Ecosystem Studies held in Millbrook, N.Y., in 1991, and from the symposium on the resource known as loco, Comité de las Ciencias del Mar, held in Santiago, Chile, in May 1992. Discussions with Dr. Jane V. Hall, Department of Economics, California State University, Fullerton, and Dr. Michael Berg, Department of Zoology, University of Cape Town, South Africa, enriched my understanding of economic theory and strategies for managing natural resources. I sincerely appreciate their contributions.

To sustain, to support, or to uphold are verbs commonly used in the catchphrases permeating the diverse documents dealing with development issues, the ecological basis of human life, environmental problems, or the future of the Earth (see, for example, Tolba 1984a, 1984b; WCED 1987; Brundtland 1989; McNeill 1990; Goodland and El Serafy 1991; IUCN 1991; Meadows, Meadows, and Randers 1992; see also chapter 1 of this volume). Moreover, the concept of sustainable development itself has become pervasive. Lele (1991) published a critical review on the concept of sustainable development, showing that this new paradigm harbors weaknesses, inadequacies, contradictions, and in some cases inconsistencies. Intellectual accuracy and rigor are needed in its use.

Indeed, there is a need to attach real substance to the definition of sustainable development as the development that meets the needs of the present without compromising the ability of the future generations to meet their own needs. Since the concept cannot be applied equally well under different economic and social realities, questions such as the following should be addressed in every case: (a) what is to be sustained? (b) for whom? (c) under which circumstances? (d) for how long? and, perhaps more critically, (e) is development synonymous with growth in the consumption of materials? (Lele 1991; see also Goodland and El Serafy 1991).

These questions should not be addressed exclusively by economists, because the answers should consider the available knowledge derived from disciplines such as biology, chemistry, sociology, physics, and so forth. In the same vein, the lack of research across disciplines leads to (a) undervalorization of the current knowledge, (b) failure to identify the critical issues to be tackled in future research, and (c) inadequate use of the deeply rooted perceptions of scientists working in different disciplines and using different paradigms.

Therefore, this chapter addresses, first, the basic tenets that form part of the paradigm of the Western mechanistic price system (as understood by an ecologist), confronting them with those that we, as ecologists, use frequently when dealing with natural renewable resources. Second, it focuses—perhaps simplistically, but as a way to illustrate some of the main conflicting issues—on two basic and contrasting models of growth: one relating to the mechanistic price system and another commonly used in fishery management strategies. Third, it describes the history of Chilean fishery of an economically extremely important mollusc, *Concholepas concholepas*, which is found exclusively in the southeastern Pacific coast. This example illustrates the biological knowledge and economic perceptions developed by a marine ecologist who has followed the ups and downs of this mollusc's fishery. Indeed, this example properly illustrates the saga of many marine resources exploited in developing countries, where economic pressure generated by the external debt and social problems, use of the Western mechanistic price system, and lack of integration of the peculiar characteristics of natural resources to such models have led to the overexploitation of many unique marine resources. The concept of equity, which is also at the center of sustainable development paradigm, is not addressed.

The mechanistic price system and the main tenets of natural renewable resources

The Western economic mechanistic price system, the related models, and their main assumptions and tenets have been discussed by numerous authors. This discussion summarizes the views of Hall and Hall (1984), Hall (1993), and Hall, Btajer, and Rowe (1991), which enables me to extract the main principles of the present mechanistic price system scheme operating in most Western societies (Chile included) and, furthermore, to relate them to the main tenets characterizing the natural

renewable resource complexes. Both, the mechanistic price system scheme and the natural renewable resource complexes can be extremely controversial issues. I take full responsibility for their interpretation. This is an important exercise because it highlights the major assumptions, rules, and articles of faith involved in these paradigms.

According to Hall (1993), humans react mechanistically and in predictable ways to economic signals, and therefore, understanding of the human factor is based on assumptions that individual maximization optimizes the system, that the past is the past (and does not count), that very simple signal (prices) encapsulating extraordinary complex information are captured in such signals (and are adequate measures of value), that each economic actor knows what they are doing and that growth is inevitable, unlimited, and desirable.

The main tenets of the mechanistic price system scheme can be simplified in six major concepts:

- Optimization, which takes place totally at a personal level
- Rationality, which takes place also at a personal level
- Values, which means that all values are monetized
- Marginalism, which indicates that the optimization process takes place at the margin (past is past)
- Impersonality, which means that transactions happen to be distant (few peoples buy fish directly from fishermen at the cove)
- Continuing and unlimited growth, which is highly desirable (Costanza 1989), and avoidance of the issues of equity and anthropocentric values, which are difficult to resolve (Hall 1993).

Table 11-1: Economic Tenets of Natural Renewable Resource Complexes Compared with the Price System Scheme Paradigm

Price system scheme	Natural renewable resources complexes
Optimization: personal	Externalities: personal and collective (pollution, overexploitation)
Rationality: personal	Rationality: personal and public goods
Values: monetized	Value: monetized and unpriced or underpriced (ecosystems, aesthetics)
Marginal: past is past	Holistic: past, present, and future are important
Impersonal transactions: distant	Perceptions: direct and indirect; distant and close
Growth: continuous, unlimited, and desirable	Growth: limited, not continuous, oscillating (carrying capacity of environment, energy flow scarcity)

Table 11-1 shows the major tenets of the mechanistic price system scheme compared with those operating in natural renewable resource complexes. The list is selective rather than exhaustive, but the differences are striking. Indeed it can be said that the tenets referring to the natural renewable resource complexes (at the level of population, community, or ecosystem) are basically the opposite of those ruling mechanistic price system schemes.

Hence, externalities are important tenets in natural renewable resource complexes, both at personal and at collective levels. For instance, pollution, overexploitation, or aesthetic values are externalities of natural renewable resource complexes. The rational approach, being personal, also includes public goods. Value includes both monetized and unpriced or underpriced values of the system, for example, aesthetics or unpriced values of the ecosystems or communities to which the monetized natural renewable resource complexes belong. In natural populations, communities, or ecosystems, the history in evolutionary or ecological time matters. The resilience capabilities and stability of natural renewable resource complexes are key factors: the perception of the observer (actor) is both direct or indirect and close or distant. Furthermore, interactions are extremely important as are the feedback mechanisms and the transitive or intransitive interactions. The most dramatic differences between mechanistic price system schemes and natural renewable resource complexes are related to growth. In natural populations, growth is limited and never totally continuous. There are different growth rates at particular stages, and population growth can follow a sigmoid model tending to reach a carrying capacity (K) or can follow a J model. Energy flow is a critical factor, and both scarcity and abundance can be spotted, which could be related to resource oscillations along time. Biological interactions, perturbations, and environmental heterogeneity can modulate population growth.

Two simple contrasting models

Figure 11-1 shows two contrasting models. In the case of the mechanistic price system scheme paradigm, the model exemplifies the relationship between capital and growth (monetary growth) in a bank account. There is a direct relationship resulting in an ever-increasing growth of capital and better interest rates if money is not drawn. In

Figure 11–1: Two Contrasting Models: Capital versus Interest and Stock Size versus Harvest

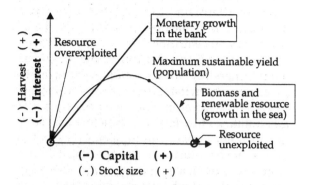

Note: Capital versus interest represents monetary growth in a bank. Stock size (or biomass) versus harvest represents a renewable resource in the sea.

Source: Taken from a conference given by M. Berg of the University of Cape Town, South Africa, in Santiago, Chile, May 1992.

the case of natural renewable resource complexes paradigm the model features the relationship between stock size or biomass and harvest of a natural resource at a given level of population. In this case—as for instance in the basic Gordon-Schaefer model (Gordon 1954; Schaefer 1954; see also Ricker 1975) and the maximum sustainable yield harvesting model—the argument of critical biomass harvesting around the greater excess above maintenance requirements is used. This excess (surplus production) is the maximum sustainable yield, and the exploitation rate that produces maximum sustainable yield is likely to be near a cliff edge. Slightly higher exploitation rates could drive the stock toward extinction.

This illustrates the deep conceptual differences that can arise around the main tenets of both mechanistic price system schemes and natural renewable resource complexes paradigms. This is not to say that alternative economic approaches regarding the exploitation of natural resources cannot be worked out. For instance, Gómez-Lobo and Jiles (1991) have addressed the use of the Gordon-Schaefer growth model (Gordon 1954; Schaefer 1954), in conjunction with models of economic return, to achieve a bioeconomic equilibrium for a given renewable population. Notwithstanding, past experience (particularly in the developing world) has shown specifically that the management of marine resources is not done on a sustainable basis, but according to the main philosophical tenets of the mechanistic price system scheme paradigm, such as continuous and unlimited growth (see Goodland and El Serafy 1991).

The Gordon-Schaefer (1954) model has been used to manage pelagic fisheries for more than twenty-five years (for a review of economic modeling see Clark 1985). Because it is simple and static rather than complex, the model is attractive to managers and, as demonstrated by Clark (1985), has a general theoretical validity. Nonetheless, there are numerous instances around the world in which pelagic fisheries have collapsed even when this or other related dynamic bioeconomic fishery models have been used: the collapse of the Peruvian anchovy fishery in the 1960s, the Norwegian overexploitation of marine resources in the 1960s, the capital overinversion and foreign fleets affecting island fisheries, and so forth. In most of these instances, negative externalities, lack of adequate biological knowledge, environmental perturbations, and probably the use of single-species modeling, in conjunction with economic pressures, should be blamed for the collapse. It must be remembered that in the mechanistic price system scheme paradigm, such externalities do not exist.

Furthermore, it must be kept in mind that models such as the one described above and the lateral bioeconomic models attached to them focus exclusively on the resource of interest. It is not a community approach. In fact, the community and ecosystem approach, wherein the species of interest is located, is considered to be an externality.

The example: The fishery of the mollusc *Concholepas concholepas* in Chile

Concholepas concholepas, known in Chile as loco, is a unique muricid mollusc found along the entire Chilean and Southern Peruvian coastline. It is fished exclusively by divers operating from small-scale artisanal boats. The life history, biology, and fishery of this valuable resource is described in numerous papers (for example, see reviews by Castilla 1982; Bustamante and Castilla 1987; Castilla 1988; Geaghan and Castilla 1988).

In 1987 the Chilean loco fishery operated only forty-five days, and more than 21,000 metric tons were landed. The total exportation value amounted to more than $42 million (all dollars are U.S. dollars). For the same year, the total exportation value of the Chilean shellfish fishery—based on several dozen species—amounted to more than $120 million. Figure 11-2 shows the landings and exportation values of the loco in

Chile between 1960 and 1992. As is true of most artisanal fisheries, information related to effort is not available. Nevertheless, four periods can be distinguished.

The first is a period of internal or local (Chilean) consumption between 1960 and 1974 in which landings fluctuated around 3,000 to 5,000 metric tons. The fishery operated on a free-entry basis and was unlicensed. No closed seasons occurred during this period, and external markets were nonexistent. During this period, Chileans consumed locos as they have done since pre-Columbian times (Ramírez and others 1991; Jerardino and others 1992), and nobody thought that by doing so, they were jeopardizing the ability of future generations to consume this prized mollusc. The general perception was that the resource could be sustained a long time.

The second is a period of local consumption plus heavy exportation of the resource between 1975 and 1981. In a very short period, landings increased to 25,000 metric tons a year (in 1980). The fishery still operated on a free-entry basis and was unlicensed; no closed seasons occurred; external markets opened mainly in Southeast Asia (Hong Kong, Japan, and Korea). Moreover, as a matter of policy, the Chilean government encouraged exports of all sorts of natural renewable and nonrenewable resources (Castilla 1990). Particularly strong economic incentives (signals) operated with regards to the exportation of nontraditional resources (see Bustamante and Castilla 1987). Chileans continued to have local access to the loco, until fishery authorities realized that the rate of exploitation was unsustainable: during 1981 landings dropped from about 25,000 to about 18,000 metric tons. Right or wrong, it was estimated that the future capability to export locos was being jeopardized. At that time, the value of the loco in international markets reached around $20 million.

The third is a period of regulatory measures as an answer to probable (though never verified) overexploitation. Hence, during 1982, 1983, and 1984 reproductive closed seasons—several months a year—were established. Landings were about 16,000 to 19,000 metric tons, and the external market values were around $18 million to $25 million. From the beginning of May 1985 to the end of May 1987, the loco fishery was closed, and, for the first time, a global quota of 4,000 metric tons was established (and greatly exceeded during 1985 and 1986).

Figure 11-2: Landings of *Concholepas concholepas* in Metric Tons and Exportation Values in Millions of U.S. Dollars, 1960-92

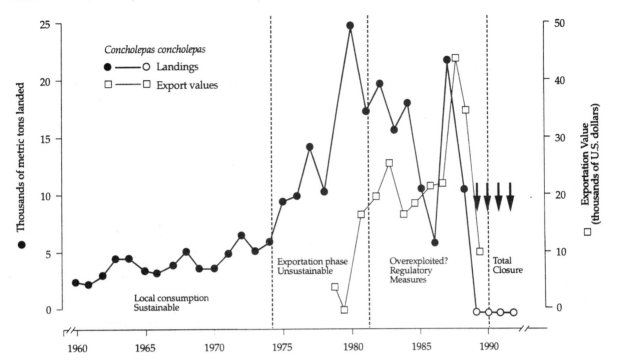

In 1987, at the end of the closure, the loco fishery was opened for only forty-five days. More than 21,000 metric tons were fished during that short period of time, with a market value of $42 million. Moreover, during 1988 the fishery was opened for only fifteen days with a maximum total quota of 4,000 metric tons for the whole country. The fishery effort was so elevated and centered in the most productive fishing grounds that more than 11,000 metric tons were fished in a few days, with a total export value of more than $35 million. Gómez-Lobo and Jiles (1991) have used this example to illustrate economic inefficiency. The global-quota strategy used in this case was not appropriated.

The fourth period—1990, 1991, and 1992—represents the total closure of the loco fishery, at least legally and in theory. Actually, the amount of illegal fishing of locos amounted to around 5,000 to 7,000 metric tons a year (see the arrows in figure 11-2). The loco resource has such an elevated value in the international market that illegal actors have devised and used all sorts of tricks to continue exploitation and exportation. The losses to the country in taxes forgone are extremely high (probably several millions of dol-

lars). In fact, this fourth period can be identified as the illegal or chaotic period. Indeed, it is not known whether or not this period can be considered sustainable or unsustainable from the fishery's point of view. Since no legal fishery is taking place, it is impossible to evaluate the actual condition of the resource. Moreover, not enough research is being conducted to evaluate the stocks of loco in the country.

The tragedy of the locos

"Each man is locked into a system (economic system) that compels him to increase his herd without limit—in a world that is limited" (Harding 1968, p. 1243). The example of the Chilean loco fishery portrays extremely well the so-called tragedy of the commons, which in this case was clearly forced by an economic vector. The questions addressed earlier in this chapter are particularly relevant here:

- What is to be sustained? If only the population of locos is to be sustained, then, sustainability has not been achieved in Chile in the past thirty years.

- For whom is it to be sustained? For the small-scale fishermen? For the country? For the industry? For the whole Chilean population that has consumed locos since ancient times?

- For how long is it to be sustained? For a decade? For the next generation?

- How do we know or assess the damage already inflicted on the loco population? Or perhaps there is no such a damage?

- What are the social, environmental, or ecological consequences?

Indeed, so far this chapter has only focused on this resource at the level of population. Nevertheless, the loco belongs to a rich and unique coastal community and ecosystem. In a series of papers, Castilla and co-authors (Castilla and Durán 1985; Castilla 1988; Durán and Castilla 1989) have highlighted several singularities or ecological externalities of this mollusc, which must be considered a keystone species (Paine 1966) in coastal benthic ecosystems of Chile. Its presence or absence is critical to the future structure and dynamics of these ecosystems. This is an unpriced aspect that cannot be fed into bioeconomic models. Last, but not least, the species is unique and present only along the coasts of Chile and Peru. What is the price of such externality?

The case of the loco fishery in Chile is only one among many examples of dramatically affected stocks of autochthonous species of invertebrates and marine algae in the country. The concepts of growth and development have both been wrongly equated with economic growth. Undoubtedly, a strong policy focusing on the economic exploitation of natural renewable resources—containing tenets of both economic and renewable resource models—is urgently needed. This is particularly imperative in the developing world.

Note

Since June 1992, the date of the conference on which this volume is based, the fishery of the mollusc *Concholepas concholepas* in Chile has experienced several changes. The most important refers to three experimental openings of the fishery (following nearly four years of total closure) for short periods: January and July 1993 for approximately seven days in each case and August 1994 for thirty days. New regulations based on the 1991 Chilean Fishery and Aquaculture Law have

been applied. In each case, the mollusc extractions have been tightly regulated, and the policy of allowing free entry to the fishery of *Concholepas* has been abandoned in the country.

References

Brundtland, G. H. 1989. "Global Change and Our Common Future, Washington, D.C., Benjamin Franklin Lecture (May 2)." *Environment* 31, pp. 16–20, 40–43.

Bustamante, R., and Juan C. Castilla. 1987. "The Shell Fishery in Chile: An Analysis of Twenty-six Years of Landings (1960–1985)." *Biología Pesquera* 16, pp. 79–97.

Castilla, Juan C. 1982. "Pesquerías de moluscos gastrópodos en Chile: *Concholepas concholepas*, un caso de estudio." In Juan C. Castilla, ed., *Segundo seminario-taller, bases biológicas para el uso y manejo de recursos naturales renovables: Recursos biológicos marinos*, pp. 199–212. Monografías Biológicas 2. Santiago de Chile: Pontificia Universidad Católica de Chile, Vicerectoría Académica.

———. 1988. "Una revisión bibliográfica (1980–1988) sobre *Concholepas concholepas* (Bruguiere, 1789) (Gastropoda, Muricidae): Problemas pesqueros y experiencias en repoblación." *Biología Pesquera* 17, pp. 9–19.

———. 1990. "Clase magistral: Importancia y proyección de la investigación en Ciencias del Mar en Chile." *Revista de Biología Marina, Valparaíso* 25:2, pp. 1–18.

Castilla, Juan C., and L. R. Durán. 1985. "Human Exclusion from the Rocky Intertidal Zone of Central Chile: The Effects on *Concholepas concholepas* (Gastropoda)." *Oikos* 45, pp. 391–99.

Clark, C. W. 1985. *Bioeconomic Modeling and Fisheries Modeling*. New York: Wiley-Interscience.

Costanza, R. 1989. "What Is Ecological Economics?" *Ecological Economics* 1, pp. 1–7.

Durán, R. L., and Juan C. Castilla. 1989. "Variation and Persistence of the Middle Rocky Intertidal Community of Central Chile with and without Human Harvesting." *Marine Biology* 103, pp. 555–62.

Geaghan, J. P., and Juan C. Castilla. 1988. "Assessment of the Present Capacity for Management of the 'Loco' *Concholepas concholepas* (Bruguiere, 1789) (Gastropoda, Muricidae) in Chile." *Biología Pesquera* 17, pp. 57–72.

Gómez-Lobo, A., and J. Jiles. 1991. "Regulación pesquera: Aspectos teóricos y experiencia mundial." Notas Técnicas 142. Corporación de Investigaciones Económicas para Latinoamérica (CIEPLAN), Santiago, Chile. August.

Goodland, R., and S. El Serafy, eds. 1991. "Environmentally Sustainable Economic Development Building on Brundtland." Working Paper 46. Environment Department, World Bank, Washington, D.C.

Gordon, H. S. 1954. "The Economic Theory of a Common Property Resource: The Fishery." *Journal of Political Economy* 62:2, pp. 124–42.

Hall, J. V. 1993. "The Iceberg and the Titanic: Human Economics Behavior in Ecological Models." In M. J. McDonnell and S. T. A. Pickett, eds., *Humans as Components of Ecosystems: The Ecology of Subtle Human Effects and Populated Areas*, pp. 51–60. New York: Springer-Verlag.

Hall, D., and J. V. Hall. 1984. "Concepts and Measures of Natural Resources Scarcity with a Summary of Recent Trends." *Journal of Environmental Economics and Management* 11, pp. 363–79.

Hall, J., V. Btajer, and R. Rowe. 1991. "The Values of Cleaner Air: An Integrated Approach." *Contemporary Policy Issues* 9, pp. 81–91.

Harding, G. 1968. "The Tragedy of the Commons." *Science* 162, pp. 1243–48.

IUCN (International Union for the Conservation of Nature). 1991. *Caring for the Earth: A Strategy for the Future of Life.* Gland, Switzerland.

Jerardino, A., Juan C. Castilla, J. M. Ramírez, and N. Hermosilla. 1992. "Early Coastal Subsistence Patterns in Central Chile: A Systematic Study of the Marine-Invertebrate Fauna from the Site of Curaumilla-1." *Latin American Antiquity* 3:1, pp. 43–62.

Lele, S. 1991. "Sustainable Development: A Critical Review." *World Development* 19:6, pp. 607–21.

McNeill, J. 1990. "On the Economics of Sustainable Development." Paper prepared for the USAID workshop, Washington, D.C., January 23–26.

Meadows, D. H., D. L. Meadows, and J. Randers, eds. 1992. *Beyond the Limits: Global Collapse or a Sustainable Future.* London: Earthscan Publications.

Paine, R. T. 1966. "Food Web Complexity and Species Diversity." *American Naturalist* 100, pp. 65–75.

Ramírez, J. M., N. Hermosilla, A. Jerardino, and Juan C. Castilla. 1991. "Análisis bio-arqueológico preliminar de un sitio de cazadores recolectores costeros: Punta Curaumilla-1, Valparaíso." In H. Niemeyer, ed., *Actas del XI Congreso Nacional de Arqueología Chilena.* Vol. 2, pp. 81–93. Santiago, Chile: Museo Nacional de Historia Natural y Sociedad Chilena de Arqueología.

Ricker, W. E. 1975. "Computation and Interpretation of Biological Statistics of Fish Populations." *Bulletin of the Fisheries Research Board of Canada* 191, pp. 382.

Schaefer, M. B. 1954. "Some Aspects of the Dynamics of Populations Important to the Management of Commercial Marine Fisheries." *Bulletin of the Inter-American Tropical Tuna Commission* 1, pp. 25–56.

Tolba, M. K. 1984a. "The Premises for Building a Sustainable Society." Address to the World Commission on Environment and Development, October. United Nations Environment Program, Nairobi, Kenya.

———. 1984b. "Sustainable Development in a Developing Economy." Address to the International Institute, Lagos, Nigeria, May. United Nations Environment Program, Nairobi, Kenya.

WCED (World Commission on Environment and Development). The Brundtland Commission. 1987. *Our Common Future.* Oxford, England: Oxford University Press.

Sustainable Development and the Chesapeake Bay: A Case Study

Christopher F. D'Elia

Jack Greer, director of the Coastal and Environmental Policy Program, made helpful comments on the manuscript. Charles Spooner of the U.S. Environmental Protection Agency, Chesapeake Bay Program, provided data on population growth in the Chesapeake watershed; Robert Summers and Darcy Austin of the Maryland Department of the Environment provided the three-dimensional figures of nitrate concentration from the Chesapeake Bay Monitoring Program; and Eric Itsweire of the National Science Foundation and Lawrence W. Harding, Jr. of UMCEES provided the Ocean Data Acquisition System image showing levels of phytoplankton biomass in the Chesapeake Bay.

The Chesapeake Bay stretches nearly 200 nautical miles and has a drainage basin of more than 160,000 square kilometers that includes large parts of Maryland, New York, Pennsylvania, and Virginia, small parts of Delaware and West Virginia, and all of the District of Columbia (see figure 12-1). Approximately one in twenty-five Americans lives in its watershed. Because it is the largest estuary in the forty-eight contiguous U.S. states and is located near the nation's capital, it has long garnered attention from the public and the nation's leaders. Because the earliest European colonists settled on its shores, human activities have had varying effects for nearly four centuries. Over that period, agricultural yields have been high, and the bounty of the bay has been rich harvests of oysters, finfish, and crabs. Unfortunately, this productive estuary no longer yields such rich harvests, and fewer and fewer people earn their keep as watermen. Instead, this land of pleasant living now attracts more and more people and, with them, rampant development.

No other U.S. estuary serves as a better model for assessing the prospects of sustainability in ecological, sociological, or economic terms. This chapter has several goals. The first is to provide some background information about current environmental and demographic concerns relevant to the Chesapeake Bay, viewed from the context of management activities and governance. The second is to consider how sustainability has been defined by others and to use the bay as a case study for defining and measuring sustainability, in ecological terms, for a land-margin ecosystem. The third is to address the role of monitoring and research in defining and measuring sustainability. The final goal is to raise crucial questions that will bear on our ultimate success in defining and achieving sustainability for the bay. Although I mainly focus here on the role of science in obtaining an understanding of how the Chesapeake Bay system functions or changes ecologically, I take some polemical liberty in commenting about issues that must be addressed if we are to be truly able to achieve sustainability in the Chesapeake system.

Figure 12-1: Map Showing the Chesapeake Bay and Its Watershed

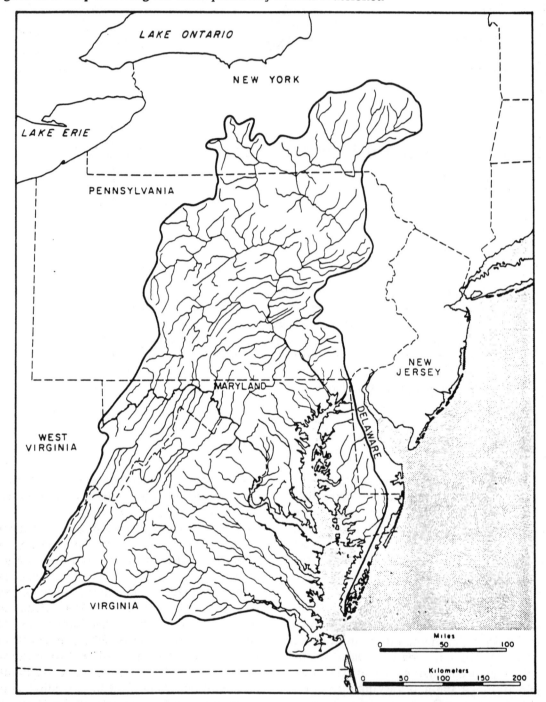

If you ask an ecologist, a sociologist, an economist, a public official, a waterman, a recreational fisherman, or for that matter a suffering wage earner and taxpayer to define sustainability, you are likely to get seven different definitions, probably sharing some common aspects. If you ask any of them whether we have achieved sustainable development for the Chesapeake Bay, you will inevitably get a single answer: no, although probably for different reasons. In effect, we all know that the Chesapeake is not a sustainable system, even though to each of us sustainability means something slightly different. Before offering my own definition of sustainability in the context of the Chesapeake, I first provide a brief history and description of the effects of human activity on that system.

Brief description and history of the Chesapeake Bay

The Chesapeake Bay is considered on average to be a partially mixed estuary, owing to its basin morphology and flow regimes (Pritchard 1955). Much of the bay is stratified, particularly in the warmer months. A current topic of interest for the Chesapeake is nutrient enrichment and its ultimate effect of promoting oxygen depletion in deep waters. The process by which enrichment occurs is outlined in figure 12-2. In brief, nutrient inputs from point sources (sewage treatment facilities) and nonpoint sources (runoff, groundwater, atmospheric deposition) increase the nutrient concentrations in the estuary. These elevated concentrations, in effect, fertilize and promote the growth of phytoplankton, which produces organic matter and increases turbidity of the water column. When freshwater flows are strong, the bay is most prone to stratification in which denser and more saline water moving from the sea is overlain by fresher water moving down the estuary. This, in turn, isolates deep waters from reaeration at the surface, and when organic material from primary producers moves to deep waters where it is consumed by microbes, oxygen is depleted. There is a direct relationship between the amount of organic material produced in surface waters and the expression of oxygen depletion in deep waters (Malone 1991, 1992), and it is clear that nutrient inputs from point and nonpoint sources, in turn, control the production of organic material by phytoplankton.

Paleostratigraphic analysis of sediment cores representing depositions from the first European colonization verifies the bay's natural susceptibility to the effects of nutrient enrichment and oxygen depletion (Cooper and Brush 1991). A relatively small colonial population caused pronounced ecological changes, principally through its land use practices. When land clearance and attendant erosion were greatest–during the late eighteenth through the late nineteenth century–sedimentation rates and the preservation of total organic carbon, nitrogen, and sulfur accelerated accordingly. During that period, more than 80 percent of the arable land in the Chesapeake Bay region was cleared of forests and used for agricultural purposes (Mackiernan 1990). Since then, increases in nutrient inputs associated with changes in land use have been further supplemented by inputs from industrial and domestic sources. Although reforestation has occurred in

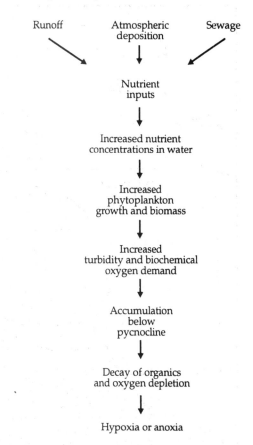

Figure 12-2: Typical Effects of Nutrient Additions to the Chesapeake Bay

Runoff   Atmospheric deposition   Sewage

Nutrient inputs

Increased nutrient concentrations in water

Increased phytoplankton growth and biomass

Increased turbidity and biochemical oxygen demand

Accumulation below pycnocline

Decay of organics and oxygen depletion

Hypoxia or anoxia

many areas since the turn of the last century, the application of nutrients to agricultural lands, in the form of fertilizers, has increased nutrient loadings from agricultural runoff.

The degradation of water quality appears to have accelerated in the last half century, as inferred from the elevated iron pyrite content in surficial sediments, an indicator of increasingly reduced conditions attendant to severe oxygen depletion (Cooper and Brush 1991). Beginning in the nineteenth century, this change was accompanied by an accelerated shift in the species composition of microalgae preserved in the sediments (Cooper and Brush 1991): centric, pelagic diatoms are now more abundant than benthic, pennate diatoms. The increased use of fertilizer has increased the production of algae in the water column and decreased production of algal species associated with the surface of benthic sediments. In addition, vascular plants rooted in the benthos have declined severely (Orth and Moore 1983). Such changes are characteristic of enriched water bodies in which nutrients stimulate the production of phytoplankton to the detriment of benthic plants.

The Chesapeake as a management case study

In many ways, the Chesapeake Bay is an ideal case study for the analysis of both sustainability and environmental management policy in the United States. For the better part of two centuries, it has played an important role in policy development, legislation, and litigation (Capper, Power, and Shrivers 1983; D'Elia 1987; Malone and others 1993). Of the present major environmental concerns for the bay (see, for example, Mackiernan 1990 for more details)–effects of nutrient enrichment, loss of living resources, destruction of habitats, and toxification–the effects of nutrient enrichment have received the most attention because they loom the largest in terms of degradation of environmental quality.

Hypoxia is the most significant ramification of nutrient enrichment. Newcombe and Horne (1938) first documented hypoxia in the deep channel of the Chesapeake Bay's main stem during the summer. In 1938, fisheries yields in the estuary were still high, and the public was not concerned about water quality. However, by the early 1970s, burgeoning population, urbanization in the watershed, and apparent declines in water quality and fishery yields raised concern over the bay's environmental quality. Problems related to nutrient enrichment in freshwater reaches of the bay's tributaries, such as the Potomac River, had resulted in an earlier focus on the construction of a sewage treatment plant in the Washington, D.C., metropolitan area, but the early 1970s marked the first serious public outcry for attention to issues affecting estuarine portions of the Chesapeake system. Accordingly, the U.S. Congress directed the U.S. Environmental Protection Agency (EPA) to initiate a study focusing on the main stem of the bay, and the Chesapeake Bay Program was established with an executive council composed of the governors of Maryland, Pennsylvania, and Virginia, the mayor of the District of Columbia, the administrator of the U.S. Environmental Protection Agency, and, beginning in 1987, the chair of the Chesapeake Bay Commission.

The EPA study had several early goals: (1) to document historical changes in water quality in the bay, (2) to understand the cause of the disappearance of submerged vascular plants, and (3) to estimate nutrient inputs from point and nonpoint sources. With respect to the first goal, unfortunately, even for such a well-studied body of water, the data recorded were too sparse and inconsistent to prove a bay-wide change in water quality (although recent study of the sedimentary record by Cooper and Brush 1991 has led to more clear-cut conclusions). However, in certain areas, such as the mesohaline region of the Patuxent River, changes were dramatic enough to raise substantial concern (Heinle and others 1980). With respect to the second goal, the disappearance of benthic vascular plants was generally attributed to the effects of nutrient enrichment. Finally, with respect to the third goal, it was readily apparent that most phosphorus came from point sources, at a reasonably constant rate year-round, while nitrogen came from nonpoint sources, especially during the high-flow period of the spring.

Increases in nutrient loadings derived from effluent and runoff were typically considered to have affected the duration and extent of estuarine hypoxia, but specific mechanisms were not well described or understood. Accordingly, considerable argument arose about appropriate strategies for reducing nutrients and, in particular, over whether nitrogen or phosphorus or both should be controlled (D'Elia, Sanders, and Boynton 1986). Since most nitrogen came from nonpoint sources, and most phosphorus came from sewage effluent, and considering EPA's policy to avoid advanced wastewater treatment other than the removal of chemical phosphorus, initial management plans emphasized control of the point source and phosphorus. Most agencies did not recognize the importance of understanding nutrient cycles or estuarine trophic dynamics. Especially unrecognized was the role of benthic sediments as a site for denitrification and seasonally variable regeneration of phosphorus and nitrogen (see, for example, Boynton and Kemp 1985).

Nonetheless, scientific progress was rapid, and studies of nutrients and trophic dynamics soon improved our understanding of the ecological function of the bay and suggested that the inputs of both nitrogen and phosphorus should be reduced substantially. (Two recent summaries of key scientific findings relating to nutrient enrichment and hypoxia provide additional details regarding the basic understanding of system function achieved in the 1980s: D'Elia and others 1992; Harding, Leffler, and Mackiernan 1992.) In 1987, the executive council of the Chesapeake Bay Program established a goal of a 40 percent reduction in the inputs of both nitrogen and phosphorus to the bay, a decision based as much on instinct as on early results of a complex mathematical model.

Few doubt the boldness of the executive committee's goal, for it has huge economic ramifications. However, recent EPA calculations on nutrient inputs are sobering in their suggestion that more than 80 percent of the nutrient inputs to the bay may ultimately be considered anthropogenic (D'Elia and others 1992; Thomann and others 1994; U.S. Environmental Protection Agency 1992). For purposes of this chapter, which seeks to understand ecological sustainability from a biophysical perspective, however, it is an interesting exercise to consider how this decision relates to sustainability for the Chesapeake Bay.

Sustainability and the Chesapeake

In considering sustainability from a biophysical perspective, this chapter focuses primarily on the ecological aspects of the Chesapeake, while stressing that virtually any vision of ecological sustainability has human dimensions and is inevitably related to human uses of ecological systems. Accordingly, thinking of sustainability in strictly scientific terms is merely an academic exercise, for clearly the issue of sustainability is related primarily to managing local impacts of humans rather than global impacts or those of natural events. Inevitably, decisions about what system states should be sustained must be made by public consensus, which one hopes occurs with the advice and counsel of scientists. One also hopes that scientists are willing to play an active role in this process.

The tendency even for scientists to view sustainability in terms of human uses is immediately evident to anyone who reviews definitions that have been used. Fisheries scientists have for years used sustained yield to indicate *maintaining constant harvests without depleting the breeding stocks necessary to replenish what is removed*. Within a larger context, numerous papers have offered definitions of sustainability (for example, Shearman 1990). In formulating its Sustainable Biosphere Initiative, the Ecological Society of America (Lubchenco and others 1991) has used sustainability "to imply management practices that will not degrade the exploited systems or any adjacent systems" (after Turner 1988, p. 394).

From an even more human-use perspective, the World Commission on Environment and Development has defined a sustainable society as one that "meets the needs of the present without compromising the ability of future generations to meet their own needs" (WCED 1987, p. 8). Meadows, Meadows, and Randers (1992, p. 209) have defined a sustainable society as "one that can persist over generations [and is wise enough] not to undermine either its physical or social systems of support." A recent bill before the U.S. Congress referred to sustainable use simply as "using resources at rates within their capacity for renewal."

Regardless of whatever definitional criteria might be used, clearly neither the scientific community nor the lay public regards the present condition of the Chesapeake system as something that one desires to sustain. In fact, the public will is to remediate and restore the bay to a previous idyllic (and not well-defined) condition that is beautiful to observe, bountiful in its seafood harvests, and well oxygenated, while being totally accessible to anyone who wants to use it for any purpose. This is what people really want to sustain–in effect, an oxymoron!

A very worrisome aspect of sustainability is that, in general, many people appear to want sustainability to pertain to a previous ecological condition that may or may not have existed and for which we have relatively little quantitative information to describe. A goal of ecologists should be to help the public understand (1) what are reasonable possibilities given competing uses, (2) what measures (and costs) will be required to achieve those states, and (3) what limitations exist on exploitation. This is largely beyond the present state of the art.

Sustainability and growth

The Chesapeake and its watershed have benefited from having generally enlightened leaders who consider the consequences of population growth and development. The executive council of the Chesapeake Bay Program commissioned a study of population growth and development in the Chesapeake watershed for thirty years hence (Year 2020 Panel 1988). The report did not address sustainability per se or attempt to identify a human carrying capacity for the watershed, but it did reach conclusions that undoubtedly apply to these issues. The U.S. EPA Chesapeake Bay Program (C. Spooner, personal communication) estimated that population will continue to grow at a substantial rate in the next three decades (see figure 12-3). Similar estimates by the National Oceanic and Atmospheric Administration (Culliton and others 1990) project comparable increases.

Figure 12–3: Population in Chesapeake Bay Watershed, 1950–90 and Projected until 2020

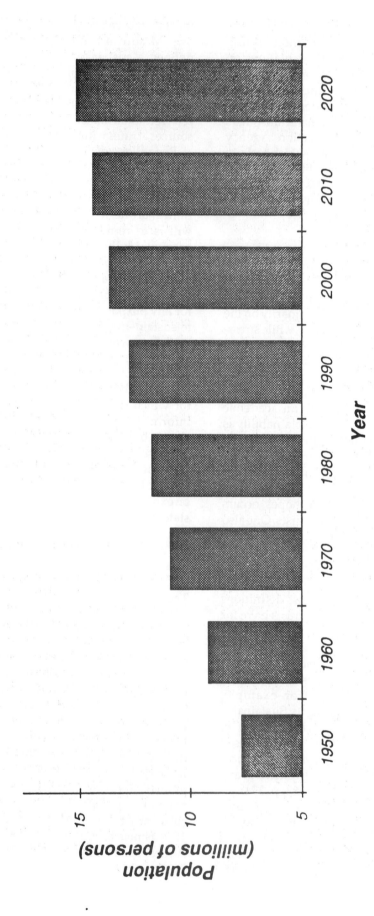

Note: Population includes residents of the District of Columbia, Maryland, Pennsylvania, and Virginia.

Two things especially caught my attention as I reread the report of the Year 2020 Panel. First was the acknowledgment that how the land is used is a basic factor in the ecological health of the Chesapeake Bay. This observation is important because it provides an implicit rationale for applying the analytical tools and principles of landscape ecology to understanding the bay's response to its watershed. Second was the recognition that with 2.6 million new people by the year 2020, the states and their local governments need to adopt a more highly integrated approach to planning and to directing and managing growth. This is important because it connects growth of the human population with environmental decline and because it implies that the result of such growth must inevitably lead to increased government regulation and control.

For the Chesapeake, two phases of human uses of the land apparently affect the water quality of the bay. In the early colonial era, *the activities of relatively few individuals had large impacts*, primarily in the form of substantial deforestation and clear-cutting for agricultural purposes. While the changes are observable in the sedimentary record, the impacts then were much less severe than one might expect today for the same changes in land use because fertilizer application, among other things, was not then the factor it is now.

With significant reforestation in the basin from the late nineteenth century until recently, some improvements occurred in the quality of the bay's water. This reforestation came not because of concern for environmental quality or appreciation of the effect of land use on water quality, but instead because of industrialization and urbanization. That the early effects of industrialization were manifested in improved environmental quality of the bay is somewhat ironic.

Recent trends toward degradation of water quality are probably more insidious and difficult to reverse. Present concerns over the quality of water relate more to the *cumulative impact of many individuals*, which will be much more difficult to reverse because of the sociological complexity involved with changing the behavior of a large number of people.

The 2020 report explicitly recognizes the consequences of human demographic change and land use. It also recognizes that the only rational response for government is to plan land use more wisely and to develop regulations and controls that will cause development to affect the watershed less. It is important for everyone to recognize the implications of this in microcosm, for it applies more broadly to our global situation. In essence, human population growth and uncontrolled development have disrupted our natural systems to the point where increasingly draconian controls are necessary to mitigate what humans do to the environment. In essence, if we do not check our rate of population growth, and we cannot individually undertake our social responsibility to live in concert with nature, we will have to preempt our own freedom through increased government regulation. Even if we were able to adapt our institutions and technology to obviate the effects of population growth, this will have to be done at the expense of individual freedoms and increased government regulations.

While sympathetic with concerns about excessive government regulation, I am truly amazed that certain political elements of society, who ostensibly cherish individual freedom so greatly, have such a difficult time coming to grips with the effect that uncontrolled population growth is having on individual freedom by promoting more stringent regulation. On the other side of the political spectrum, although I appreciate that the distribution and use of resources are both inequitable and unfair, I cannot imagine how, even in a fairer world, we can sustain exponential increase in population at the same time that we reduce our use of resources and our impact on the environment.

Monitoring and understanding sustainability

From a scientist's point of view, what might be said about the present status of the bay? What particular measurements are helpful in understanding the status quo and thus bear on sustainability? How, in fact, can one consider the issue of sustainability without addressing the status quo or understanding how the system functions?

In scientific terms, we must at least understand the basics of the system, its processes, and its reactions to perturbations before we can say anything about sustainability. I know of no quick indexes to measure ecological sustainability in land-margin ecosystems: no substitute exists for proper research and monitoring. This section first explains briefly why such research and monitoring are necessary and then describes several aspects of the Chesapeake Bay Program's monitoring effort that contribute to the program's potential success in assessing sustainability.

Scientifically designed monitoring

Programs such as the Long-Term Ecological Research (LTER) program (Callahan 1984) have provided more than a decade of long-term data on selected ecosystems. The particular advantages of such programs derive from their continuous, long-term, and scientifically oriented design. Data are scrutinized as they are collected and considered in perspective with other relevant information. These management features assure that the quality of the data is high and that the monitoring done is coupled with process-oriented research and is driven by questions about ecological function and about change. Although programs such as LTER are generally hailed as high-quality scientific programs, they are also roundly criticized because they appear to eschew issues of practical importance to managers. In contrast, monitoring programs conducted by governmental agencies are often criticized because they lack a scientific approach. The Chesapeake Bay Program's monitoring effort has achieved a successful balance between scientific quality and practical problem orientation (although scientists are always concerned that not enough process-oriented work is being done).

SEPARATING NATURAL AND ANTHROPOGENIC EFFECTS
Scientifically driven monitoring and research programs seek to differentiate different causative agents of ecological effects (for example, change in climate, anthropogenic effects, and local or regional perturbations). Few people outside the scientific community understand the difficulties scientists face in differentiating natural, large-scale (usually climatic) effects and anthropogenic, local effects. This is somewhat ironic, since personal experience provides enough evidence to the contrary: everyone experiences the variability inherent in weather, for example. We are all susceptible to being surprised by heat waves, cold spells, droughts, floods, and storms, and we tend to view every event as unusual or as the harbinger of a global change in climate. This sort of inherent human myopia challenges the scientific community continually to remind policymakers and the public (if not ourselves, too) not only of the nature of variability but also of the inherent difficulties in distinguishing natural from anthropogenic causes of change. It also requires us to recognize the value of and promote the gathering and analysis of long-term data.

IMPORTANCE OF LONG-TERM DATA
Among the many ironies raised in this chapter, none is more perplexing than the fact that so little of the huge amount of environmental data collected is applicable to or useful for determining long-term trends. Ecologists are accustomed to understanding the need for long-term modeling and research (Magnuson 1990); environmental managers and policymakers often are not. Monitoring is rarely oriented toward solving problems or asking questions, and this causes two problems: the persons or agencies who collect data feel no sense of responsibility or ownership, and they do not assess the quality of the data produced.

Other problems with monitoring also prevent the acquisition of reliable long-term data. Standard procedures are not applied, or they are misapplied (D'Elia, Sanders, and Capone 1989). Little attention is paid to improving methodologies or to understanding matrix effects. Quality assurance and quality control procedures are often disregarded or, in the other extreme, are arbitrary and bureaucratic. The uses of data and the quality or grade of data are rarely considered. We have research-grade chemicals and technical-grade chemicals–each useful for a particular application–yet paradoxically, we do not have grades for data. Far too much of our data has been collected in such mindless exercises as Section 302e (Clean Water Act) reporting.

PROCESS-ORIENTED MEASUREMENTS
Understanding system variability alone, although necessary, is not sufficient. Rates of ecological processes must also be understood, for these processes control state variables. For many ecosystems, studies of the regulation of primary production, of the transfer of carbon through the trophic system, and of the cycling and assimilation of nutrients have proven especially valuable. In the case of the Chesapeake, in addition to research studies supported by state regulatory agencies and federal agencies such as the National Science Foundation, National Oceanic and Atmospheric Administration (Sea Grant and the Coastal Ocean Program), Fish and Wildlife Service, and EPA, the basic monitoring program includes process-oriented monitoring for sediment nutrient fluxes, primary productivity, and other key functions of the system.

Major indexes in monitoring

Monitoring programs have typically focused on collecting information on a variety of standard topics. These programs have met with mixed success, often for institutional reasons. Management agencies have for years pursued the Holy Grail of a single general index of ecological health or condition that can be used to assess human impacts. Although I do not arbitrarily exclude the possibility that this can work, in a realistic sense, I do think such a goal is unnecessary and impractical. However, some practical indicators of human impact do exist that require some understanding of ecosystem function, and several of these are discussed next.

LIVING RESOURCES (ESPECIALLY FISHERIES AND HABITAT)
We are notoriously poor at managing fisheries worldwide, and the Chesapeake is no exception. Fisheries are extremely variable, and statistical reporting of catch is often inconsistent or unreliable. Figure 12-4 provides examples of data from catches of oysters, blue crabs, and striped bass that illustrate this. Landings of oysters are at historical lows. There is considerable debate over whether yields are down because of degrading habitat and water quality or overfishing. Striped bass, too, have exhibited serious declines, although there is recent evidence that stringent management actions have been dramatically successful. Similar debate exists about the cause (in this case overharvesting and destruction of habitat). Blue crabs have not shown serious declines as yet, but landings are extremely variable.

To complicate the issue, it is also proving particularly difficult to manage fisheries data. Jurisdictional boundaries, problems in obtaining accurate catch statistics from commercial and recreational fishing interests, and political interests cause further complications. Accordingly, even though public pressures to do so may be strong, managers should resist using harvestable species as key indicators of sustainability, because they are not, as a practical matter, sustainable and because fishery recruitment, natural mortality, and so forth are intrinsically highly variable.

Living resources such as habitats are another issue, however, and indexes of quality and extent of habitat such as marsh, nontidal wetlands, sea grass cover, and so forth are potentially important indicators of sustainability that integrate over at least several years of time. The most difficult problem in using habitat as an index is determining the rate and extent of change in habitat types. Until recently, this had to be done by exhaustive in situ sampling and observation. Recent advances in remote sensing and data management using geographic information systems offer substantial promise in providing both real-time and long-term information on changes in habitat.

TROPHIC STATE AND WATER QUALITY
Probably the best overall indicator of sustainability for the Chesapeake is trophic state (Harding, Leffler, and Mackiernan 1992; Smith, Leffler, and Mackiernan 1992; Taft and others 1980). The expression of trophic state is determined by nutrient inputs, freshwater flow, tidal height, basin morphology, and physical oceanographic conditions (Sanford, Sellner, and Breitburg 1990; Seliger, Bogg, and Biggley 1985; Webb and D'Elia 1980). Present evidence suggests that higher nutrient inputs have led to higher levels and growth rates of phytoplankton biomass (Malone 1991, 1992; Officer and others 1984; Seliger, Bogg, and Biggley 1985), a shift to a microbially dominated decomposer food web (Jonas 1992), and loss of living resource and habitat (Breitburg 1992). Certain components of estuarine and coastal systems, such as the benthos, provide help in integrating time-variable responses and thus can provide an important clue to a system's trophic state. Moreover, new mathematical approaches to understanding trophic interactions (Baird and Ulanowicz 1989) offer promise for analysis of trophic webs that may prove to be useful for assessing sustainability.

Chesapeake Bay program monitoring

Monitoring approaches in which oxygen, chlorophyll, nutrients, and other traditional, related variables for trophic state are determined within a specified temporal and spatial matrix have proven enormously useful for attaining a basic understanding of how the Chesapeake system functions. Four factors, in particular, account for the success of this approach. First, the methods used are by and large reliable, sensitive, and appropriate for the saltwater sample matrix. Second, quality assurance and quality control are appropriately applied to ensure that samples are collected and analyzed properly and that data are recorded correctly and without error. Third, professional-level staff at state and federal agencies review the data continually and analytically to

Figure 12–4: Landings of Oyster, Crab, and Striped Bass in the Chesapeake Bay, 1940–90

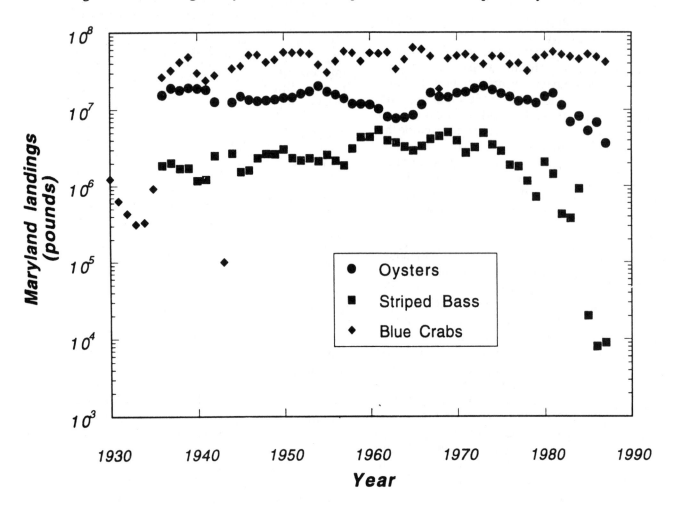

assess their meaning (see, for example, Magnien, Austin, and Michael 1991). Fourth, monitoring is complemented by process-oriented research that helps to put monitoring data in perspective of functional aspects of the system. In many regards, this approach is embodied also in the National Science Foundation–supported Long-Term Ecological Research Program (Callahan 1984). Because most monitoring programs do not combine these essential elements, and because they are not sustained for long periods of time, their utility is limited for understanding how a system functions and for differentiating natural from anthropogenic effects.

With respect to the kinds of comprehensive data now collected for the Chesapeake Bay, figure 12-5 provides an example of a time-space plot

for concentrations of nitrate in surface and deep waters in the bay over a seven-year period. It is obvious even to the relatively uninitiated observer that patterns exist in the availability of nitrate with time and location on the bay. These patterns vary considerably. When combined with data for other key parameters, when viewed in context with research on nutrient cycling and input, and when used critically to verify mathematical models based on realistic conceptual models, such data offer powerful opportunities to understand variability in the ecosystem's state variables: clearly, if one is to understand sustainability, one must also understand variability. Practical problems exist, however, in sustaining the funding and effort necessary to obtain this sort of information.

New approaches to monitoring

Monitoring is expensive and requires many personnel. One must consider not only the costs of monitoring but also the human resources available to collect and analyze information. It is therefore extremely important to develop monitoring techniques that are cost-effective and offer rapid and facile assessments of wide geographical areas, in as close to real time as possible.

Remote sensing is becoming an increasingly important tool for monitoring. Although it operates primarily at the experimental level at present, it will inevitably become a major tool for environmental monitoring in the next several decades. For example, remote color sensing of estuaries and coastal regions by satellite- and aircraft-borne instrumentation has already demonstrated its potential for understanding temporal and spatial variations in primary productivity. Although in situ sampling from ships has the capability of providing depth-integrated estimates of chlorophyll biomass at selected sites, spatial and temporal coverage is poor and cost is high. Satellite-borne sensors such as Landsat Thematic Mapper, Spot, and the proposed SeaWiFS and Modis instruments offer opportunities for obtaining excellent estimates of primary productivity with wide spatial and temporal coverage. In the absence of satellite-borne sensors, which is likely to occur with continuing emphasis on manned missions to space, excellent sampling coverage can also be obtained using aircraft-borne sensors such as ODAS (Ocean Data Acquisition System). Figure 12-6 shows an example of the estimation of phytoplankton biomass obtained for the Chesapeake Bay using the ODAS sensor. This type of information, when obtained routinely and managed using new computer techniques such as geographic information systems, offers enormous promise for determining the response of phytoplankton both to nutrient inputs and physical factors and for assessing changes in habitat (Harding, Itsweire, and Esaias 1992).

Satellite, aircraft, and shipboard measurements, although capable of offering wide spatial coverage, are necessarily limited in temporal coverage. Clearly, for ships, only so many stations can be occupied per cruise, and continuous operation at any single station is extremely costly when the daily costs of a ship start at a minimum of $1,500 a day. For satellites using passive methods to collect color data, coverage is limited to light periods, when satellites pass over the area of interest. Geostationary satellites are constrained to high orbits, so in any case, orbiting satellites are typically employed for high-resolution color-sensing coverage. Accordingly, for detailed temporal coverage, or when depth profiling is desirable, remote sensing using instrumented buoys is the alternative. The state of the art is developing well for this method of remote sensing, given our present capabilities to develop detectors for numerous parameters such as oxygen and chlorophyll fluorescence and our ability to store data using microelectronic technology or, better yet, to telemeter data back to the laboratory. Since sampling is seldom done over a twenty-four-hour period, and we are often remiss in considering factors that occur at night, instrumented buoys do offer particular opportunities.

Crucial questions

I would like to conclude by presenting a series of questions that will be of considerable importance if sustainability, by virtually any definition, is to be achieved. Some of these questions are rhetorical; some will require additional research and study; and some will depend on the ability of scientists, policymakers, and others to provide education and leadership to the public.

Is sustainability realistic in the face of population growth? This is a question that few dare to ask. The issue of population growth is a political hot potato. Few politicians on either side of the political spectrum want to confront this issue head on. Meadows and others (1992) have reevaluated their original *Limits to Growth* scenario because some of the dire predictions made did not come true in the 1980s. Even though it is difficult to put limits on results of models developed to estimate sustainability in the face of population growth, it seems obvious that the ultimate test of accuracy of the most dire predictions–an environmental Armageddon–is the last thing the modelers want to see. But exponential growth has inexorable consequences: the worst is that accelerating change occurs and that negative effects can thus be expected to occur at an accelerating pace. Must we wait to verify the most dire predictions of models by experience?

Can technology always provide the solutions? The public has an inordinate trust in technology and human inventiveness as a countermeasure to bad judgment or intemperate use of resources.

Figure 12–5: Time-Space Plots of Nitrate Concentration in Chesapeake Bay Program Monitoring Study, 1984–91

SURFACE LAYER NITRATE + NITRITE (mg/l)

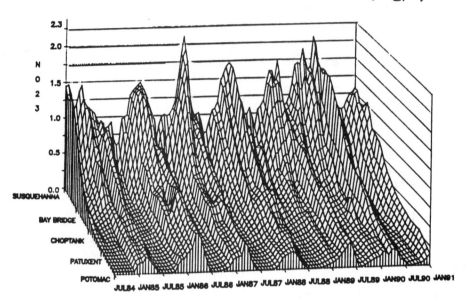

BOTTOM LAYER NITRATE + NITRITE (mg/l)

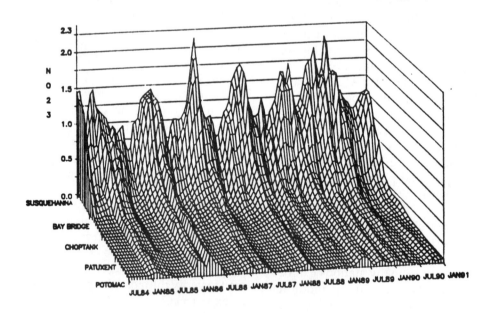

Source: Data from the Maryland Department of the Environment, Chesapeake Bay Program, Water Quality Monitoring Program.

Figure 12–6: Concentration of Chlorophyll in the Chesapeake Bay, April 23, 1990, as an Indicator of Phytoplankton Abundance

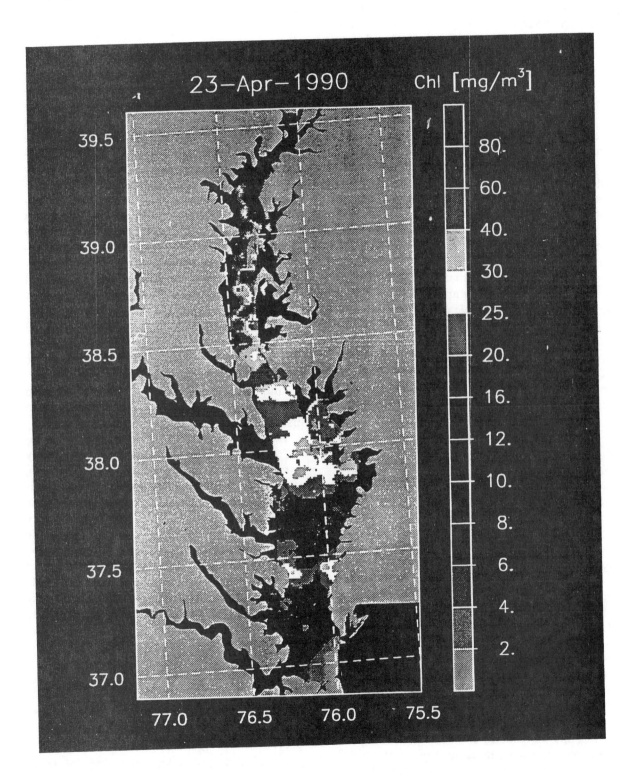

Source: Data were collected by Harding, Jr., Itsweire, and Esias (1992) using aircraft remote sensing with the National Aeronautics and Space Administration's Ocean Data Acquisition System.

Is there adequate political will? (Or better, are there sufficient economic resources?) If technology is the answer to our sustainability problems, we must also have the economic wherewithal to afford to use it. In the next two decades, federal and state governments in the United States will be sorely pressed by demographic changes that will put great demands on social spending, even if there is a political will to deal with the effects of human impact on such resources as the bay and its watershed. Clearly, other coastal waters besides the Chesapeake Bay are subject to rapidly increasing population and its effects (Culliton and others 1990). Tertiary treatment of sewage, for example, is expensive in terms of initial capital investment but also in terms of operation and management. If sustainability of environmental quality in the face of growth requires technology, then will the requisite funding be there to sustain technology? We may need to think of management solutions in terms of sustainable (or appropriate) technology (Schumacker 1973). We will have to be careful not to buy what will be too expensive to sustain in the future. We must find ways of setting priorities for environmental mitigation that prove most cost-effective. Are we even close to being able to provide the economic analysis necessary to do this, much less to see wise decisions implemented through the public process?

Can the public be educated adequately? Many of the pollution abatement issues we must deal with will require a cooperative and educated populace. Land use, refuse and sewage disposal, and other issues will require enthusiastic public support.

Can we improve the links between science and management? Science is considered by many to be superfluous to the public process of environmental management. Many scientists are reluctant to enter what they see primarily as a political arena. Yet, as never before, science must be part of the problem-solving process. Our ability to sustain ourselves as a human race will ultimately require a better interaction between science and management.

Will we accept more control and tighter regulation? With more people and more impact, tighter control and regulation seem inevitable. At what point do fundamental constitutional issues relating to individual freedoms (life, liberty, and the pursuit of happiness) come in conflict with the regulations necessary to sustain a healthy environment? This is ultimately the most difficult question to answer and the one that argues most strongly for humanity's need to self-limit its population growth and its use of natural resources. I see no easy answers at present and am not optimistic that this situation can improve in a more populous world.

Conclusions

Considerable and long-term interest in the Chesapeake Bay and its watershed have provided opportunities for in-depth scientific research and scientifically oriented monitoring. From these activities, we are obtaining a comprehensive understanding of the ecological functions of the bay and its natural variation and anthropogenic perturbations. Such activities are essential for enlightened understanding and management of a complicated system. Many would view sustainability for the bay in terms of a few ecological indicators: (1) reduced nutrient enrichment and hypoxia, (2) improved and bountiful fishery yields, and (3) improved habitat, primarily for rooted aquatic vegetation.

For the Chesapeake, how we use the land appears to hold the secret to sustaining a desirable ecological state in the bay itself. Although we may, with difficulty, have some success in sustaining the trophic state and yields of the system as a whole, it is hard to see how we can sustain historic yields on a per capita basis.

Without a public will to understand and reconcile the issue of what is sustainable by almost any criteria in the face of human population growth, all speculation about sustainability (by any definition) amounts to little more than an academic exercise. Leaders in science and public policy must redouble their efforts to promote public understanding of this problem and to find ways for controlling population that are effective and acceptable to the largest percentage of people possible. The challenge is awesome and the topic controversial—it is also the core issue relating to sustainability on Earth.

References

Baird, D., and R. E. Ulanowicz. 1989. "The Seasonal Dynamics of the Chesapeake Bay Ecosystem." *Ecological Monographs* 59, pp. 329–64.

Boynton, W. R., and W. M. Kemp. 1985. "Nutrient Regeneration and Oxygen Consumption by Sediments along an Estuarine Salinity Gradient." *Marine Ecology Program Series* 23, pp. 45–55.

Breitburg, D. L. 1992. "Episodic Hypoxia in the Chesapeake Bay: Interacting Effects of Recruitment, Behavior, and Physical Disturbance." *Ecological Monographs* 62, pp. 525–46.

Callahan, J. T. 1984. "Long-term Ecological Research." *BioScience* 34, pp. 363–67.

Capper, J., G. Power, and F. R. Shrivers, Jr. 1983. *Chesapeake Waters: Pollution, Public Health, and Opinion, 1602–1972.* Centreville, Md.: Tidewater Publishers.

Cooper, S. R., and G. S. Brush. 1991. "Long-term History of Chesapeake Bay Anoxia." *Science* 254, pp. 992–96.

Culliton, T. J., M. A. Warren, T. R. Goodspeed, D. G. Remer, C. M. Blackwell, and J. J. McDonough III. 1990. "Fifty Years of Population Change along the Nation's Coasts." National Ocean Service, National Oceanic and Atmospheric Administration, U.S. Department of Commerce, Rockville, Md.

D'Elia, C. F. 1987. "Nutrient Enrichment of the Chesapeake Bay: Too Much of a Good Thing." *Environment* 29, pp. 6–11, 30–33.

D'Elia, C. F., L. W. Harding, Jr., M. Leffler, and G. Mackiernan. 1992. "The Role and Control of Nutrients in Chesapeake Bay." *Water Science and Technology* 26, pp. 2635–44.

D'Elia, C. F., J. G. Sanders, and W. R. Boynton. 1986. "Nutrient Enrichment Studies in a Coastal Plain Estuary: Phytoplankton Growth in Large-scale, Continuous Cultures." *Canadian Journal of Fisheries and Aquatic Sciences* 43, pp. 397–406.

D'Elia, C. F., J. G. Sanders, and D. G. Capone. 1989. "Analytical Chemistry for Environmental Sciences: A Question of Confidence." *Environmental Science Technology* 23, pp. 768–74.

Harding, L. W., Jr., E. C. Itsweire, and W. E. Esaias. 1992. "Determination of Phytoplankton Chlorophyll Concentrations in the Chesapeake Bay with Aircraft Remote Sensing." *Remote Sensing and the Environment* 40, pp. 79–100.

Harding, L. W., Jr., M. Leffler, and G. B. Mackiernan. 1992. *Dissolved Oxygen in the Chesapeake Bay: A Scientific Consensus.* Technical Report. Maryland Sea Grant College, College Park, Md.

Heinle, D. R., C. F. D'Elia, J. L. Taft, J. S. Wilson, M. Cole-Jones, A. B. Caplins, and L. E. Cronin. 1980. "Historical Review of Water Quality and Climatic Data from Chesapeake Bay with Emphasis on Effects of Enrichment." U.S. Environmental Protection Agency, Chesapeake Bay Program Final Report, Grant R806189010. Publication 84. Chesapeake Research Consortium, Inc., Annapolis, Md.

Jonas, R. 1992. "Microbial Processes, Organic Matter, and Oxygen Demand in the Water Column." In David E. Smith, Merrill Leffler, and Gail Mackiernan, eds., *Oxygen Dynamics in the Chesapeake Bay*, pp. 113–48. College Park, Md.: Maryland Sea Grant College.

Lubchenco, J., A. M. Olson, L. B. Brubaker, S. R. Carpenter, M. M. Holland, S. P. Hubbell, S. A. Levin, J. A. MacMahon, P. A. Matson, J. M. Melillo, H. A. Mooney, C. A. Peterson, H. R. Pulliam, L. A. Real, P. J. Regal, and P. G. Risser. 1991. "The Sustainable Biosphere Initiative: An Ecological Research Agenda." *Ecology* 72, pp. 371–412.

Mackiernan, G. B. 1990. "State of the Chesapeake Bay." *Water Environment and Technology* 9, pp. 60–67.

Magnien, R. E., D. K. Austin, and B. D. Michael. 1991. "Chemical/Physical Properties Component: Level 1 Data Report." Maryland Department of the Environment, Special Projects Program Report. Annapolis, Md.

Magnuson, J. J. 1990. "Long-term Ecological Research and the Invisible Present." *BioScience* 40, pp. 495–508.

Malone, T. C. 1991. "River Flow, Phytoplankton Production, and Oxygen Depletion in Chesapeake Bay." In R. V. Tyson and T. H. Pearson, eds., *Modern and Ancient Continental Shelf Anoxia*, pp. 83–93. Special Publication 58 of the *Journal of the Geological Society* (London).

——. 1992. "Effects of Water Column Processes on Dissolved Oxygen, Nutrients, Phytoplankton, and Zooplankton." In David E. Smith, Merrill Leffler, and Gail Mackiernan, eds., *Oxygen Dynamics in the Chesapeake Bay*, pp. 61–112. College Park, Md.: Maryland Sea Grant College.

Malone, T. C., W. Boynton, T. Horton, and C. Stevenson. 1993. "Nutrient Loadings to Surface Waters: Chesapeake Bay Case Study." In T. C. Malone, ed., *Keeping Pace with Science and Engineering*, pp. 8–38. Washington, D.C.: National Academy Press.

Meadows, D. H., D. L. Meadows, and J. Randers. 1992. *Beyond the Limits.* Post Mills, Vt.: Chelsea Green Publishing Co.

Newcombe, C. L., and W. A. Horne. 1938. "Oxygen-poor Waters of the Chesapeake Bay." *Science* 88, pp. 80–81.

Officer, C. G., R. B. Biggs, J. L. Taft, L. E. Cronin, M. A. Tyler, and W. R. Boynton. 1984. "Chesapeake Bay Anoxia: Origin, Development, and Significance." *Science* 23, pp. 22–27.

Orth, R. J., and K. A. Moore. 1983. "Chesapeake Bay: An Unprecedented Decline in Submerged Aquatic Vegetation." *Science* 222, pp. 51–53.

Pritchard, D. W. 1955. "Estuarine Circulation Patterns." *Proceedings of the American Society of Civil Engineers* 81, pp. 1–11.

Sanford, L. P., K. G. Sellner, and D. L. Breitburg. 1990. "Covariability of Dissolved Oxygen with Physical Processes in the Summertime Chesapeake Bay." *Journal of Marine Research* 48, pp. 567–90.

Schumacker, E. F. 1973. *Small Is Beautiful.* London: Blond and Riggs.

Seliger, H. H., J. A. Bogg, and W. H. Biggley. 1985. "Catastrophic Anoxia in the Chesapeake Bay in 1984." *Science* 228, pp. 70–73.

Shearman, R. 1990. "The Meaning and Ethics of Sustainability." *Environmental Management* 14, pp. 1–8.

Smith, D. E., M. Leffler, and G. Mackiernan, eds. 1992. *Oxygen Dynamics in the Chesapeake Bay.* College Park, Md.: Maryland Sea Grant College.

Taft, J. L., W. R. Taylor, E. O. Hartwig, and R. Loftus. 1980. "Seasonal Oxygen Depletion in Chesapeake Bay." *Estuaries* 3, pp. 242–47.

Thomann, R. V., J. R. Collier, A. Butt, E. Casman, and L. C. Linker. 1994. "Response of the Chesapeake Bay Water Quality Model to Loading Scenarios." Chesapeake Bay Program Office, U.S. Environmental Protection Agency, Annapolis, Md.

Turner, M. G., ed. 1988. *Sustainable Environmental Management: Principles and Practice.* Boulder, Colo.: Westview Press.

U.S. Environmental Protection Agency. 1992. "Progress Report of the Baywide Nutrient Reduction Reevaluation." Chesapeake Bay Program, Annapolis, Md.

Webb, K. L., and D'Elia, C. F. 1980. "Nutrient and Oxygen Redistribution during a Spring/neap Tidal Cycle in a Temperate Estuary." *Science* 207, pp. 983–85.

WCED (World Commission on Environment and Development). 1987. *Our Common Future.* Oxford, England: Oxford University Press.

Year 2020 Panel. 1988. "Population Growth and Development in the Chesapeake Bay Watershed to the Year 2020." Chesapeake Executive Council, Chesapeake Bay Commission, Annapolis, Md.

13

Restoration of Arid Lands

G. Pickup and S. R. Morton

People of European origins began settling in Australia 200 years ago, and they quickly realized that the vast grasslands and shrublands of the interior could be used for pasturing stock. Today, most of the arid zone is classed as rangeland, where the dominant land use is pastoralism. This chapter provides an overview of recent research designed to assist sustainable management of the natural resources of arid Australia.

General characteristics of Australia's arid zone

As well as supporting an extensive pastoral industry, the Australian arid zone has high value as a tourist destination and is a unique biogeographical region of substantial importance for nature conservation. In addition, it is home to a large proportion of the Australian aboriginal population, and many of these people live on their traditional lands and continue many of their original land management practices. Of the total area of the rangelands (5.6 million square kilometers), 66 percent is pastoral land, 14 percent is aboriginal land, 4 percent is in conservation reserves, and 16 percent remains unallocated (see figure 13-1).

The principal feature of the arid Australian environment is the highly unpredictable year-to-year fluctuation in rainfall. Since plant growth is largely determined by available moisture, the production of biomass can vary by a factor of 10 between years. Plant establishment occurs intermittently, perhaps once every five years or more, and drought is a natural part of the unpredictability. Above all else, sustainable management involves coming to terms with this variability.

In general, rangeland soils are highly weathered and very infertile compared with soils of arid regions elsewhere on the globe (see Stafford Smith and Morton 1990). Soil fertility is predominantly linked to the underlying rock, but within any particular type of rock, the redistribution of

soil and nutrients by wind and water also creates areas of better soils. Even in a landscape that may appear flat and featureless, water and nutrients concentrate around bushes and trees or in gentle depressions. These sites of accumulation are key to the productivity of an area and are therefore important for the persistence of many native plants and animals as well as for the pastoral industry. Because these productive areas are easily overgrazed and eroded, special emphasis must be placed on their management.

The Australian rangelands are of low productivity, and pastoralism is conducted at low densities of human population. Properties in Australia (stations) typically range from 10,000 hectares up to 30,000 square kilometers and carry free-ranging sheep or cattle within five to forty fenced paddocks. A single property frequently supports only one family and rarely more than ten. Land is leased from state or territory governments; in some cases, the leases are perpetual, but even where they are not, they apply for decades. Often the lessee is also the manager, although particularly in the northern subtropical rangelands companies often own leases and employ managers. In all areas, land use is governed by covenants written into the leases under legislation.

Despite the arrangements for use of land under leasehold covenants in arid Australia, poor understanding of management requirements in the region has led to overgrazing by both domestic and wild animals. This overgrazing has been

Figure 13-1: Map of Australia Showing the Extent of the Rangelands and the Areas Devoted Principally to Grazing Sheep or Cattle

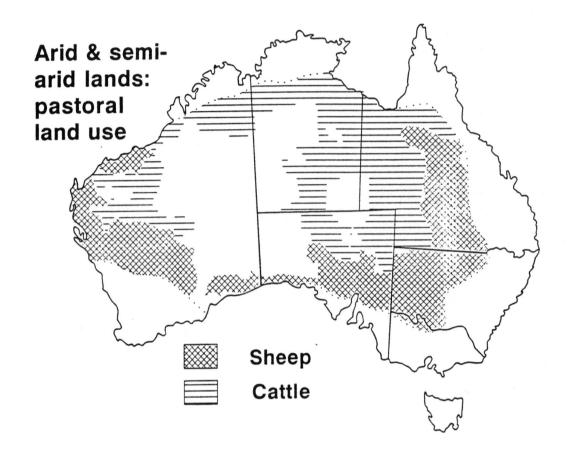

the most extensive contributor to land degradation. Intensive management and restoration of degraded land in the arid zone is frequently uneconomic due to the vastness of the region and low land values per unit of area. Further degradation needs to be avoided; thus, sustainable land management is more a matter of prevention than of cure. Our examination of sustainability begins with pastoralism because it is the most extensive use of land; later in the chapter we discuss land management approaches that might be necessary when conservation of biodiversity is incorporated into the definition of sustainability.

Sustainable pastoral management

Although sustainability has entered the popular political jargon in Australia, a precise definition remains elusive (Commonwealth of Australia 1990; Hamblin 1991). Problems arise because sustainability must be defined for a particular type of operation and also for particular scales in time and space. For example, sustainable management for pastoral purposes may have different objectives from those of management for fauna and flora conservation. Further, goals for sustainable management of a region will almost certainly differ from those for individual properties or paddocks, and activities that are sustainable over a few years may not result in century-long sustainability. We believe that the term should be used at the scales at which land is managed and should consider periods at least as long as a decade (and usually longer).

Given specific spatial and temporal scales, sustainable management involves using a natural system so that it can produce output at the end of a specific time similar to what it produced at the beginning. This definition avoids issues such as whether the output is economic or biological, whether management inputs change over time, and whether the type of production can vary. If land is managed basically to produce livestock, then a relatively narrow definition of sustainability may be used. For example, Pickup and Stafford Smith (1993) define sustainable pastoral use of land as the commercial production of livestock on rangelands that, at a minimum, seeks to:

- Maintain the long-term capacity of the ecosystem to produce forage from rainfall (although the composition of that forage may change, as may the short-term capacity to produce it).

- Produce acceptable financial as well as nonfinancial returns for the manager and dependents (the preferred standard of living may include intangibles such as lifestyle).

To make these principles operational, we must now determine how the natural system behaves and how management can operate sympathetically with that behavior. It may then become possible to put current pastoral activity on a more sustainable basis and, through conservative management, to restore many of our grazed ecosystems to a more productive condition (for examples, see Bastin 1991; Friedel, Foran, and Stafford Smith 1990; Lange, Nicolson, and Nicolson 1984; Purvis 1986).

Functioning of pastoral ecosystems

Two theoretical approaches to the functioning of grazed rangeland ecosystems have been developed, but a range of intermediate possibilities lies between these two extremes (DeAngelis and Waterhouse 1987; Ellis and Swift 1988). The equilibrium approach assumes that the system exists in some form of homeostatic state that is maintained by interactions among its components. In

equilibrium conditions, the system experiences negative feedback that dampens the effects of disturbance within a limited domain of attraction. In practical terms, this may mean that high grazing pressure reduces the production of forage, which, in turn, reduces attractiveness for grazing. However, this situation occurs where forage is largely produced continuously and is therefore more typical of areas with high rainfall than of arid rangelands.

The alternative nonequilibrium approach assumes that ecosystem behavior is stochastic but that an element of persistence is maintained. In a rangeland ecosystem, persistence implies a continuing ability to grow plants even after the longest drought or the heaviest grazing. Several mechanisms have been proposed to explain persistence in the face of the high probability of extinction that is inherent to stochastic domination (DeAngelis and Waterhouse 1987). These include the setting of upper and lower limits on process rates by factors such as limited water and nutrients or disproportionately large reductions in grazing in areas where only a few palatable plants survive. They also include the fact that landscape variability, and the larger range of conditions present at greater spatial scales, reduces the risk of extinction in a whole system even though that risk is high at individual points within it. Recolonization from adjacent areas may also offset local extinctions. Table 13-1 summarizes the main differences between the equilibrium and nonequilibrium views of how rangeland ecosystems function.

Until recently, arid rangelands were treated as equilibrium systems. More recently, non-equilibrium concepts that allow for highly stochastic behavior have gained favor (Behnke, Scoones, and Kerven 1993; Ellis and Swift 1988; Westoby, Walker, and Noy-Meir 1989). The stochastic element results from the fact that these ecosystems are driven by rainfall and therefore dominated by highly discontinuous abiotic processes. This approach is something of an abstraction, because rangeland ecosystems can display elements of both biotic and abiotically controlled behavior, depending on the time scale (Stafford Smith and Pickup 1993). At the short-term scale of the individual rainfall event or sequence of events, system behavior is dominated by abiotic processes and is highly stochastic. In the longer term, biotic factors may change the response of the system to short-term abiotic forces such as rainfall. For example, erosion induced by grazing may reduce

Table 13-1: Characteristics of Equilibrium and Nonequilibrium-based Grazing Systems

Characteristics	Equilibrium-based systems	Nonequilibrium-based systems
Abiotic patterns	Abiotic conditions relatively constant Plant-growing conditions relatively invariant	Stochastic/variable conditions Variable plant-growing conditions
Plant-herbivore interactions	Tight coupling of interactions Feedback control Herbivore control of plant biomass	Weak coupling of interactions Abiotic control Plant biomass abiotically controlled
Population patterns	Density dependence Populations track carrying capacity Limit cycles	Density independence Carrying capacity too dynamic for close population tracking Abiotically driven cycles
Community/ecosystem	Competitive structuring of communities	Competition not expressed
Characteristics	Self-controlled systems	External forces critical to system dynamics

Source: Ellis and Swift 1988.

the soil's capacity to store moisture and thereby limit the amount of vegetation that grows as a result of subsequent rainfalls. The short-term response of vegetation is then increasingly dominated by antecedent biotic conditions, and the stochastic element associated with abiotic control is reduced. In resilient systems, these biotic effects may be short-lived, and the system will recover. However, where resilience is biotically reduced, systems may lose their capacity to recover.

Traditional approaches to assessing sustainability of use employ the mix of plant species present as an indicator (Lauenroth and Laycock 1989). However, species composition can be relatively insensitive to a range of ecological processes such as soil erosion and can vary extensively with climatic factors (Friedel, Pickup, and Nelson 1993; Westoby 1980). Recent work also shows that the performance of grazing animals may be largely unrelated to the pasture's composition of species and that animal production in nonequilibrium systems is overwhelmingly influenced by total production of grass (Ellis and Swift 1988; Hodgkinson 1992; Mentis and others 1989; Wilson and MacLeod 1991). Under these circumstances, the continuing ability of a landscape to produce a large quantity of forage from rainfall may be the best measure of sustainable pastoral use.

In moisture-limited arid ecosystems, vegetation grows in a series of rainfall-generated pulses as production and reproduction occur (Friedel 1984; Noy-Meir 1973; Westoby 1980). After the growth period, moisture becomes limiting and plant activity is reduced. Much of the biomass produced during the growth period is then lost as plants die, are consumed by grazers, are converted to litter, and decay. During the period when moisture is available, plants grow faster than they are consumed by grazers, so growth and herbivory do not occur at the same rate or at the same time.

Vegetation pulse and decay behavior can be described by a time-series model with an input series (the rainfalls), a response function, a decay function (biomass consumption and decay), and an output series (the amount of biomass present at a particular time). The response function describes the magnitude of the plant growth response to a given rainfall and, eventually, the biological productivity of the system. It can vary through time in response to abiotic factors such as a sequence of rainfalls, each component of which offers particular opportunities for growth and changes the mix of species present (Westoby 1980). It can also be subject to biotically induced change, for example when heavy grazing after one vegetation pulse causes soil erosion and dampens the next pulse.

Some examples of the behavior of rainfall-driven systems are shown in figure 13-2. If the rainfall in the time-series model maintains its statistical characteristics over time and the response and decay functions do not change, the output series will maintain a given mean, variance, and autocorrelation structure. Thus, the state of the system varies in the short term, but its behavior in response to rainfall is persistent. Behavior is no longer persistent when the response function changes, producing a gradual or sudden change in the output series. If the output series continues to drift over time, the response function has become unstable. If the drift ceases, the response function is stable once more, but the productivity of the system has changed.

Changes in the characteristics of the rainfall response function through time are normal behavior in rainfall-dominated systems. If they result from the sequence of antecedent rainfalls, the associated change in the production of forage cannot be equated with a deterioration of or improvement in the condition of the rangeland. If the production of forage is reduced as a result of grazing, then there is a change in condition, but its seriousness depends on how easily the system can recover. For example, if grazing has resulted

in erosion or damaged the soil in other ways, it may take a very long time for the response function to shift back to previous conditions, even at high rainfalls. In some types of soil, it may even require the deposition of new soil transported from upslope or the addition of aeolian material for recovery to occur at all (Pickup 1985). Less serious changes in species composition may be reversed by a suitable sequence of rainfall (Westoby 1980). The type of change in response function that is most easily reversed occurs when grazing reduces cover but leaves the seed banks, store of moisture in the soil, and pool of soil nutrients relatively intact. The loss of soil moisture due to runoff associated with reduced vegetative cover will reduce the response of plants to rainfall, but good conditions for plant growth in wet years or a reduction in grazing will allow relatively quick recovery.

Figure 13-2: Changes in Biomass through Time in a Rainfall-driven System That is Initially Stable

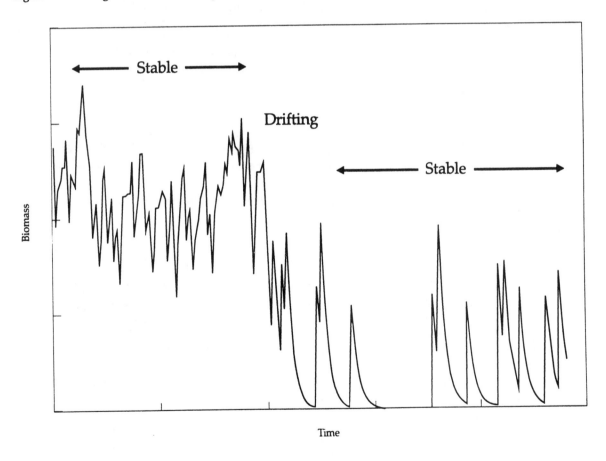

Note: The response function begins to drift and subsequently restabilizes at a lower level of productivity.

Measuring sustainability in the biological system

The short-term variations in biomass in a rainfall-driven system make it difficult to separate natural change from that induced by grazing. They also make it difficult to identify shifts in the vegetation response function, whether they be natural or induced by grazing. It is, however, possible to identify spatial patterns in the rate of vegetative growth and total biomass that are exclusively the result of grazing and thereby to separate change induced by grazing from other types of variability. Furthermore, when these patterns are examined in association with behavior of the system through time, they make it possible to separate short-term change in the productivity of vegetation from longer-term damage. These patterns are known as grazing gradients, and a technology for identifying and using them to assess range condition has been developed recently (Pickup 1989, 1992; Pickup and Chewings 1992). This technology uses data from satellites, which can readily be converted into measures of the amount of vegetative cover present (Graetz, Pech, and Davis 1988; McDaniel and Haas 1982). The use of satellite data also solves many of the logistical problems encountered in measuring grazing gradients with conventional ground-based techniques in highly diverse paddocks from tens to hundreds of square kilometers in size (Friedel 1990; Pickup 1989).

Grazing gradients develop because animals graze away from waterpoints and return to them at regular intervals to drink. The distance traveled varies with factors such as water salinity, availability of forage, meteorological conditions, and the species, breed, and condition of the animals themselves (Pickup and Chewings 1988a; Stafford Smith 1984). There is, however, a general decline in animal activity and impact on plants as the distance from water grows. Some grazing gradients may disappear with the next major rainfall. Others remain for longer periods and indicate that grazing has had a more lasting impact.

Grazing gradients resulting from the activities of either sheep or cattle can be detected by measuring differences in ground cover on satellite images acquired at different times (Pickup and Chewings 1988b; Cridland and Stafford Smith 1992). Simple examples of grazing gradients in a paddock with a uniform type of vegetation are shown in figure 13-3. When average cover is plotted against distance from water without any grazing, a straight line function should result, indicating no change across the landscape. Where grazing occurs, cover is reduced, but this effect is progressively smaller as the distance from water grows, until it is no longer discernible; this trend is shown by the line marked dry period. After rain, vegetation recovers, and the grazing gradient disappears. An increased level of cover then exists over the whole paddock, as the upper line in figure 13-3 shows. Thus, the previous level of grazing may be regarded as sustainable.

Figure 13-3: Schematic Diagram Showing Temporary and Permanent Normal Grazing Gradients

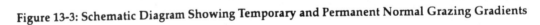

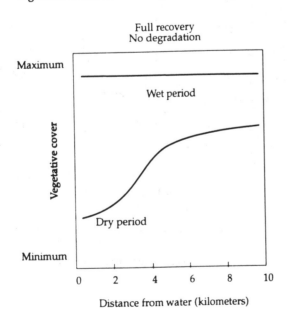

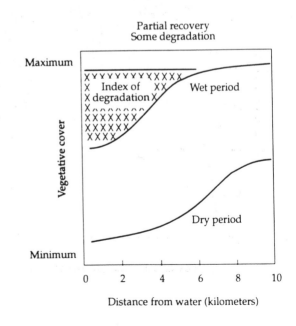

If a grazing gradient does not disappear, even after very large rainfalls, then the land has been damaged. Many landscapes are not damaged by grazing and recover fully after moderate rainfall. Others recover only partially and require a sequence of large rainfalls for the grazing gradient to disappear fully. They still retain a limited capacity for recovery, therefore, even though it may be many years before a suitable sequence of large rainfalls occurs. The distinction between a temporary grazing gradient and a permanent one is consequently somewhat arbitrary. Pickup and Chewings (1992) classified a permanent gradient as one that persisted during the best rainfalls of the past ten years, a period chosen because it represents the time for which archived Landsat MSS data are readily available in Australia.

Real grazing gradients can be very complex. Where several types of vegetation occur in a paddock, some may be particularly affected because animals prefer them over others (see Pickup and Chewings 1988b). The landscape must therefore be subdivided into types. Perhaps the biggest problem in detecting a grazing gradient occurs when it is superimposed on other types of spatial variability in the landscape such as an erosion cell mosaic (see Stafford Smith and Pickup 1993). This requires a set of special procedures in which the variance of plant cover is compared at different distances from water (Pickup and Chewings 1994).

Not all grazing gradients involve a simple increase in vegetative cover with distance from water. It is also possible to find inverse grazing gradients in which cover decreases with distance from water except in the immediate vicinity of the waterpoint (figure 13-4). These features indicate grazing-induced increases in the proportion of unpalatable herbage species or shrubs close to water. The inverse gradient develops because animals avoid the unpalatable cover and graze farther from water, where progressively more palatable forage is available. If this is the case, the inverse gradient should intensify with time since the last rain because grazing progressively reduces vegetative cover. The gradient may disappear partly or fully after the next rainfall. Where it does disappear, the capability of the landscape to produce vegetative cover in response to rainfall has not been reduced, but the ability to produce usable forage has.

Figure 13-4: Inverse Grazing Gradients Derived from a Landsat MSS Vegetation Cover Index for Two Land Systems in Central Australia

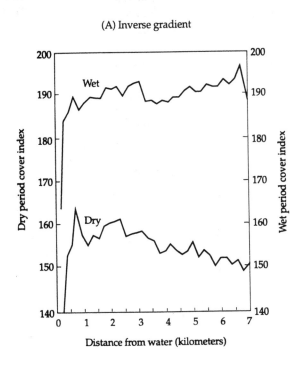

(A) Inverse gradient

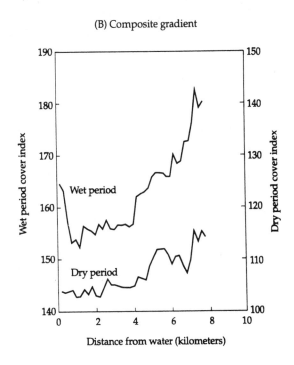

(B) Composite gradient

Normal and inverse grazing gradients are sometimes combined in the same type of landscape to produce a composite gradient. In this situation, cover decreases with distance from water up to a particular distance and then begins to increase (figure 13-4). Composite gradients that persist even in dry times usually develop where there is an increase in shrubs or a buildup of unpalatable species close to water. Composite gradients that persist for only a short time after rain indicate a flush of ephemeral species close to water that is quickly destroyed by trampling and, possibly, grazing. These effects displace the normal grazing gradient and push it farther from the waterpoint.

In short, the technology of grazing gradient provides a measure of the extent to which the capacity of an ecosystem to produce forage is being reduced by grazing. Variations on the procedure make it possible to determine whether quality as well as quantity of forage are affected (Pickup 1994), and large areas can be surveyed quickly and cheaply. Thus, changes in the indicator variables make it possible to determine whether pastoral management is sustainable or not.

Restoring and maintaining sustainability in grazing lands

The effects of grazing always involve some risk of land degradation, however small. Removal of vegetative cover can produce adverse changes in pasture species, increased runoff, and erosion of exposed soil. Trampling breaks down soil aggregates, making it easier for wind and water to transport them, encourages gullying by concentrating flow along paths and tracks, and reduces infiltration and capacity to hold moisture by compacting the soil. The risk of degradation is especially high where rainfall is unreliable because vegetation may not be restored to bare areas for long periods during droughts, thereby exacerbating erosion and further reducing the ability of the landscape to recover when it does rain.

The grazing management strategies adopted in Australia's rangelands may exaggerate the risk of degradation. Stafford Smith and Foran (1988), for example, have described two contrasting approaches for cattle properties: one buffers itself against land degradation and income fluctuation by low use of pasture and high rates of production per animal; the other involves high stocking rates but evades climatic downturns or droughts by early decisions on agistment or sale of animals. The second strategy is essentially one of gambling against short-term climatic variability and, if errors are made, can result in a property manager having too many sheep or cattle, which he cannot sell except at a loss. The temptation is then to retain them through a drought even though the pasture resource may not be adequate to support them. Land degradation can result.

If we accept that there is always some risk of land degradation, the best strategy is to manage landscapes and pastoral operations in such a way as to minimize it. This involves using monitoring data from satellites to identify the most vulnerable parts of the landscape and then designing paddocks with fence lines and waterpoints laid out to avoid heavy concentrations of animals in these areas. Two techniques have been developed recently in Australia to achieve this operation: erosion forecasting and grazing distribution modeling. Used together, they can provide low-risk farm layouts that will, in future, be coupled with herd economic and stocking strategy models to allow more sustainable use of land for pasture.

Erosion forecasting is based on changes in the statistical and spatial characteristics of landscapes that occur as they progressively degrade (Pickup and Chewings 1988b). The first step in making a forecast is to map erosion and deposition in the area of interest from satellite imagery. For central Australian landscapes, this may be done using a soil stability index whose value is low for eroded areas, high for deposition zones, and intermediate for stable or inactive parts of the landscape (Pickup and Nelson 1984). The frequency distribution and spatial autocorrelation function of this index change in a consistent manner as land degradation proceeds, reflecting changes in the behavior of erosion cells. Forecasting involves fitting a spatial interaction model whose parameters describe the variance and spatial autocorrelation function of the soil stability index in an area. An inverse filtering operation is then carried out with the parameters of the fitted model to obtain a noise or underlying pattern series. This series is filtered with the parameters of a similar spatial interaction model derived for a more eroded prototype area to produce a forecast. In effect, this procedure transfers the variance and spatial autocorrelation function properties of prototype areas to areas for which a forecast is required but does not change the location of erosion cells. This locational information is held in the underlying pattern series. The method appears to be reasonably accurate, and tests for a range of landscape types are presented by Pickup and Chewings (1988b).

Like erosion, grazing does not occur uniformly across a landscape. Instead, animals graze out from waterpoints and use gradually decreases as the distance from water grows in a broadly sigmoidal shape. This produces a concentric pattern around each waterpoint in paddocks with uniform vegetation (see figure 13-5). Where more than one type of vegetation is present, which is usually the case in the large paddocks used in Australia, the concentric pattern becomes distorted into a star-shaped one with distinct corridors of heavier grazing intensity where certain types of vegetation are more favored. Distortions can also result from the availability or otherwise of shade and, in the case of sheep, the presence of overnight camping sites and the prevailing direction of the wind. The corridors are areas of intense trampling in which the network of tracks leading to water can result in gullying.

Complex models of animal physiology have been used to derive models of the distribution of grazing and trampling under Australian conditions (Stafford Smith 1984). These models have substantial data requirements and are frequently not suitable for operational use. Simpler procedures based on linear regression models for sheep (Stafford Smith 1988) and convection-diffusion analogs for cattle (Pickup and Chewings 1988a) are now becoming available. These models have been successfully calibrated from remotely sensed data using spatial patterns of change over time in Landsat MSS Band 5 as a surrogate for the removal of vegetative cover by grazing.

The ability to calibrate grazing distribution models quickly for a range of different types of vegetation means that the effect of alternative waterpoint and fence line locations can be modeled. More even distribution of grazing may then be established to avoid the creation of grazing and trampling degradation hot spots. The modeled patterns may also be overlaid on erosion forecast maps to minimize use of the most erosion-prone areas and to reduce the movement of animals along the principal directions of water flow.

Figure 13-5: Predicted Patterns of Grazing around Four Waterpoints where Vegetation is Uniform

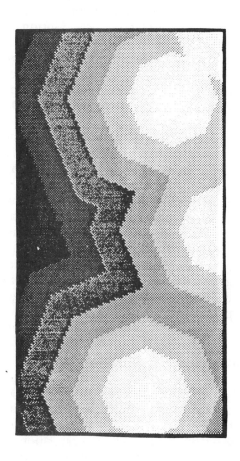

Note: Lighter shading indicates more-intense grazing.

Management for conservation

Some brief background is required to show why conservation management needs to be improved. Arid Australia exhibits a poor record of extinctions and contractions of range among its native mammals since European settlement: eleven species have become extinct, five have disappeared from the mainland and are now confined to off-shore islands, and fifteen more have declined dramatically and persist only in the semi-arid fringe (Morton 1990). This sorry chronicle represents the worst record of any continental region over the past 500 years (see Diamond 1984). The basic reason for these problems is damage caused by introduced animals. Domestic stock and feral

185

herbivores (particularly rabbits) ate out the best country and prevented native species from using their drought refuges, and introduced foxes and cats put further pressure on relict populations (Burbidge and McKenzie 1989; Morton 1990). Populations of remaining mammals and other animals are not universally declining (Curry and Hacker 1990), but there is still considerable concern that the ecological changes brought about by European settlement will continue to cause losses of biodiversity.

Our approach to sustaining and restoring the biodiversity of arid lands is less sophisticated than if we were only interested in maintaining pastoral values because much remains unknown about the functioning of natural ecosystems. We also lack the tools for measuring and forecasting system state under current or potential management regimes. This lack of technology cannot be used as an excuse for inaction given the rate of extinctions described above. We must therefore proceed on the basis of existing knowledge and accept that errors may be made.

Functioning of the natural ecosystem

Our approach to the problem of developing a system for conservation management in arid Australia is based on our understanding of the dominant ecological forces at work. Stafford Smith and Morton (1990) argue that two primary forces underlie ecological functioning in the arid zone: the supply of moisture and the availability of nutrients. At the most basic conceptual level, they suggest that two different types of landscape exist. One consists of relatively rich soils, such as those of the Mitchell grasslands and the chenopod shrublands. The other (and more common) is dominated by poor soils, such as the spinifex grasslands, but scattered throughout this vast expanse are run-on areas that tend, through the accumulation of water and nutrients, to be more productive. These patterns of resource richness may arise from nutrients, from water run-on, or from the accumulation of both, but from the perspective of ecological functioning, it is not especially important which is most influential at any one place. The contrasts drawn here are conceptual only; in real environments, these types of landscape are only points along a continuum (see figure 13-6).

Stafford Smith and Morton (1990) suggest that introduced herbivores preferentially select resource-rich areas because of their metabolic requirements. Because these herbivores have not been controlled by ecological forces in the way that native herbivores originally were, they have had a markedly degrading effect on the most productive country (Foran, Low, and Strong 1985; Griffin and Friedel 1985; Low, Muller, and Dudzinski 1980; Pickup and Chewings 1992; Purvis 1986). In areas of poorer soils, introduced herbivores focus almost entirely on resource-rich patches. In richer soils, use is more widespread, but patterning still occurs in relation to watering points (cattle and sheep) or suitability of substrate for burrowing (rabbits). This patterning has immense practical significance for conservation management.

Introduced grazing animals may affect native species in resource-rich areas in two ways. The first is that grazing frequently exaggerates the variability of plant production (Foran 1986; Friedel 1990; Pickup and Chewings 1992). The second is that the absolute rate of plant production is altered, usually downwards. These effects led to the extinction of many native mammals and continue to threaten the maintenance of biodiversity (see figure 13-7).

Measuring sustainability

Earlier we showed that it is possible to monitor the status of soil and vegetation on pastoral lands using remotely sensed grazing gradients and erosion forecasting, together with targeted ground-based techniques. Such monitoring techniques are vital to the development of an industry that is sustainable in economic terms. But how does one monitor for sustainability of land uses from the perspective of native plants and animals that live in these pastoral lands?

All the problems associated with creation of a monitoring system for vegetation and soil exist when native biota are considered, in particular the difficulties of identifying long-term trends in biotic populations in an environment characterized by capricious rainfall. These problems are compounded by lack of information about the determinants of distribution and abundance of organisms in arid Australia. Detailed understanding of all but a few groups of angiosperms is lacking. Distribution maps of higher vertebrates are available, but those of reptiles are unreliable and new species are discovered every year. Habitat requirements of only a few vertebrates have

Figure 13-6: An Area of Central Australia Showing Patterns of Moisture Run-on

Note: Pale areas shed water after rainfall, but darker areas receive run-on and thus are more productive and are described in the text as resource rich.

been analyzed quantitatively. A vast array of invertebrate species remains unstudied and usually undescribed. How can monitoring be conducted effectively under such conditions?

The short answer to this question is that most native species cannot be monitored effectively. Monitoring populations of just three kangaroo species in the southern, western, and eastern parts of the arid zone costs the various state and federal wildlife services in the vicinity of $A1 million a year (G.M. Maynes, personal communication). A few monitoring operations are under way to follow population trends in rare or endangered mammal and bird species, but these efforts are by their nature limited geographically. Even if the technical capacity existed to monitor the vast

mass of largely undescribed species apart from those isolated examples just mentioned, doing so would clearly be impossible on financial grounds. Every arid area around the globe would face identical problems. Thus, some form of surrogate must be found.

We recommend a twofold approach to this problem. The first principle of monitoring is to focus on those areas of land that have experienced regular use, most often pastoralism and to give lower priority to monitoring poorer and less frequently used land. This principle may be peculiar to the Australian arid zone, where substantial areas have been only mildly altered by human activity. Virtually all parts of the country that have been degraded are relatively rich in mois-

Figure 13-7: Suggested Chain of Events Leading to the Extinction of Native Australian Mammals Following Arrival in the Arid Zone of European Grazing Stock and Feral Animals

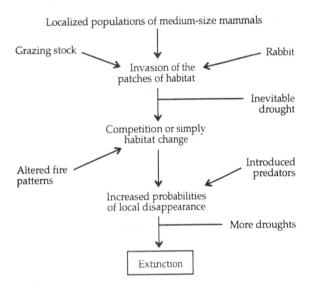

Source: Morton 1990.

ture and nutrients. Thus, to institute such monitoring, it is necessary first to identify patterning in the landscape that gives rise to the differential distribution of intensity in use. With techniques similar to those used to analyze grazing gradient, remotely sensed maps of the landscape can be produced showing the distribution of productive or vulnerable habitats. When this remotely sensed information is combined with digital data for the region from a geographic information system (such as data on geology and topography), the networks of such habitats can be examined at the regional scale, and decisions can be made about the most effective distribution of monitoring effort. We are currently building such a system for the Central Australian mountain ranges, an area of 120,000 square kilometers in the center of the arid zone.

The second requirement is to choose a surrogate to monitor. The recommended principle is to use a combination of remote sensing and ground monitoring to assess the status of perennial vegetation in the areas deemed of importance. The inherent assumption is that maintaining biological diversity is dependent on maintaining the full range of perennial vegetation; without this, biological diversity will inevitably decline. We do not assume that maintaining perennial vegetation is sufficient to guarantee the maintenance of

biological diversity. This recommendation is purely pragmatic, because focusing on perennial vegetation appears to be the only way to define adequate reserve networks and to search for measures of ecological sustainability in rangelands under human use. The monitoring that begins under this set of assumptions could subsequently be refined as further research improves our understanding of the relationship between spatial patterning of perennial vegetation and diversity of other organisms. This final point automatically highlights an area of research that should be of high priority.

Neither of the principles presented here has been fully instituted in arid Australia. Our research group is developing the remote-sensing and geographic information system tools necessary to test the suggestions, and plans are under way to test the techniques in our Central Australian study area.

Implementing a sustainable conservation management scheme

The management of sustainable conservation depends foremost on development of a representative network of conservation reserves; the techniques for doing so are relatively well understood in Australia (Margules, Pressey, and Nicholls 1991). The Australian government recognizes that the present reserve system does not adequately sample Australia's biological diversity (Commonwealth of Australia 1992). However, there are difficulties in achieving complete representation in the inland environment because unpredictable fluctuations from heavy rainfall to drought mean that no one place can be considered permanently secure for many plants and (especially) animals. It would be exceedingly hard to develop a suite of reserves that could take into account all possible climatic sequences and thereby guarantee the conservation of all species, across the vast landscape of outback Australia.

The solution to this dilemma is twofold. The first step is to develop a hierarchy of reserves, rather than to rely purely on national parks (or whatever term is used in a particular location). National parks would remain the most significant component of the system but would be complemented by a network of smaller reserves incorporating habitats that appear to be vital to the regional persistence of the biota but that cannot be declared as national parks because the areas concerned are too small or because the relevant authority has insufficient resources to manage them as parks. In this case, the current land manager, most often a pastoralist, could be paid an allowance to carry out the necessary conservation activities. In many instances it would not be necessary to remove the parcel of land permanently from other uses; only at key times (say during or at the break of drought) might conservation concerns take priority. Such an expanded but flexible reserve system would go a long way toward providing long-term conservation of biological diversity in the environment of arid Australia where rainfall is capricious and plant production temporally and spatially unpredictable (see Morton and others 1992 for a fuller development of these proposals).

A second element remains essential to the implementation of sustainable management: the development of sustainable grazing strategies in the country that lies between the various components of the reserve system. The requirements for maintaining sustainability in terms of continued production of plants and animals in the pastoral lands now need to be broadened to include maintenance of biological diversity under grazing. Apart from general investigations (Curry and Hacker 1990), no data have been published on the impact of different levels of grazing on any native animals except large kangaroos (Caughley, Shepherd, and Short 1987). Preliminary studies demonstrate that grazing indeed does affect a variety of animal taxa (C. D. James, personal communication), and analysis of these relationships through further research is of paramount importance.

A critical problem has so far been set aside: weeds and vertebrate pests. The principal plant invaders in arid Australia are *Acacia nilotica* (Mimosaceae), *Parkinsonia aculeata* (Caesalpiniaceae), *Cenchrus ciliaris* (Poaceae), *Prosopis spp.* (Fabaceae), and *Tamarix aphylla* (Tamaricaceae); a variety of strategies is required to control these species (Humphries, Groves, and Mitchell 1991). Of greater importance than all other weeds and pests, though, is the European rabbit. It is widespread, often phenomenally abundant, and a primary cause of land degradation and extinction of native species (Lange and Graham 1983; Morton 1990; Myers 1971). Several strategies for improving the control of rabbits are under investigation, including introduction of new diseases and development of immuno-sterilization vectors to limit reproduction (Cooke 1991; CSIRO Division of Wildlife and Ecology 1990).

Techniques for instituting sustainable grazing in the broader sense (including recognition of the necessity to consider the impact on biological diversity) are clearly much less advanced than those concerned with sustainability of an enterprise only on the basis of soil stability, palatable vegetation, and animal production. This disparity is not surprising, given the wider issues at stake when biological diversity is considered, and is undoubtedly characteristic of most arid environments around the world.

Conclusions

Our work on sustainability of land use in arid Australia, which is summarized in figure 13-8, has led us to four principal conclusions.

- Adequate monitoring systems are essential in the uncertain climate of all arid lands, particularly in Australia where rainfall is uncommonly difficult to predict. Remote sensing can now be used to monitor the effects of pastoral activity on soil and plant production, and we anticipate it becoming broadly accepted as a major tool in the Australian rangelands over the next few years.

- Control of weeds and mammalian pests remains a serious problem in arid Australia. Major research efforts are under way to improve control of the rabbit.

- A broader network of conservation reserves is necessary because the vegetation associations of arid Australia are inadequately sampled in the current system. The techniques for choosing representative areas of land are well developed, but research is necessary to determine the degree to which vegetation associations act as surrogates for the diversity of other groups of organisms.

- Wealth-generating uses of land are not yet meshed with ecological sustainability. A major research problem is to determine grazing levels that are consistent with maintaining regional biological diversity.

Figure 13-8: Some Major Requirements for Sustainable Land Management Flowing from the Biophysical Characteristics of Arid Australia

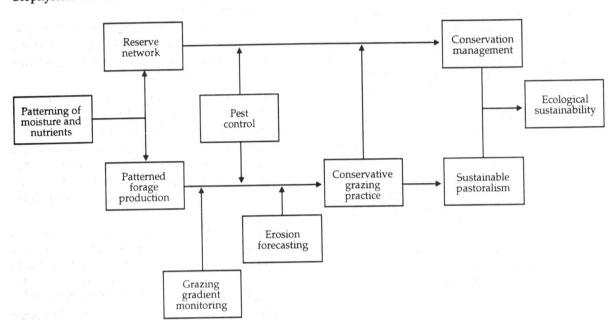

References

Bastin, G. 1991. "Rangeland Reclamation on Atartinga Station, Central Australia." *Australian Journal of Soil and Water Conservation* 4, pp. 18–25.

Behnke, R. H., I. Scoones, and C. Kerven, eds. 1993. *Range Ecology at Disequilibrium.* London: Overseas Development Institute, International Institute for Environment and Development, and Commonwealth Secretariat.

Burbidge, A. A., and N. L. McKenzie. 1989. "Patterns in the Modern Decline of Western Australia's Vertebrate Fauna: Causes and Conservation Implications." *Biological Conservation* 50, pp. 143–98.

Caughley, G., N. Shepherd, and J. Short, eds. 1987. *Kangaroos: Their Ecology and Management in the Sheep Rangelands of Australia.* Cambridge, England: Cambridge University Press.

Commonwealth of Australia. 1990. "Ecologically Sustainable Development." Commonwealth Discussion Paper. AGPS, Canberra.

———. 1992. "A National Strategy for the Conservation of Australia's Biological Diversity (Draft for Public Comment)." Department of the Arts, Sport, the Environment, and Territories, Canberra.

Cooke, B. 1991. "Rabbits: Indefensible on Any Grounds." *Search* 22, pp. 193–94.

Cridland, S., and M. Stafford Smith. 1992. "Development and Dissemination of Design Methods for Rangeland Paddocks Which Maximise Animal Production and Minimise Land Degradation." Technical Memo. Western Australian Department of Agriculture.

CSIRO Division of Wildlife and Ecology. 1990. *Biennial Report 1988–90.* Melbourne.

Curry, P. J., and R. B. Hacker. 1990. "Can Pastoral Grazing Management Satisfy Endorsed Conservation Objectives in Arid Western Australia?" *Journal of Environment Management* 30, pp. 295–320.

DeAngelis, D. L., and J. C. Waterhouse. 1987. "Equilibrium and Non-equilibrium Concepts in Ecological Models." *Ecological Monographs* 57, pp. 1–21.

Diamond, J. M. 1984. "Historic Extinctions: A Rosetta Stone for Understanding Prehistoric Extinctions." In P. S. Martin and R. G. Klein, eds., *Quaternary Extinctions*, pp. 824–62. Tucson: University of Arizona Press.

Ellis, J. E., and D. M. Swift. 1988. "Stability of African Pastoral Ecosystems: Alternate Paradigms and Implications for Development." *Journal of Range Management* 41, pp. 450–59.

Foran, B. D. 1986. "The Impact of Rabbits and Cattle on an Arid Calcareous Shrubby Grassland in Central Australia." *Vegetatio* 66, pp. 49–59.

Foran, B. D., W. A. Low, and B. W. Strong. 1985. "The Response of Rabbit Populations and Vegetation to Rabbit Control on a Calcareous Shrubby Grassland in Central Australia." *Australian Wildlife Research* 12, pp. 237–47.

Friedel, M. H. 1984. "Biomass and Nutrient Changes in the Herbaceous Layer of Two Central Australian Mulga Shrublands after Unusually High Rainfall." *Australian Journal of Ecology* 9, pp. 27–38.

———. 1990. "Some Key Concepts for Monitoring Australia's Arid and Semi-arid Rangelands." *Australian Rangeland Journal* 12, pp. 21–24.

Friedel, M. H., B. D. Foran, and D. M. Stafford Smith. 1990. "Where the Creeks Run Dry or Ten Feet High: Pastoral Management in Arid Australia." *Proceedings of the Ecological Society of Australia* 16, pp. 185–94.

Friedel, M. H., G. Pickup, and D. J. Nelson. 1993. "The Interpretation of Vegetation Change in a Spatially and Temporally Diverse Arid Australian Landscape." *Journal of Arid Environments* 24, pp. 241–60.

Graetz, R. D., R. P. Pech, and A. W. Davis. 1988. "The Assessment and Monitoring of Sparsely Vegetated Rangelands using Calibrated Landsat Data." *International Journal of Remote Sensing* 9, pp. 1201–22.

Griffin, G. F., and M. H. Friedel. 1985. "Discontinuous Change in Central Australia: Some Implications of Major Ecological Events for Land Management." *Journal of Arid Environments* 9, pp. 63–80.

Hamblin, A. 1991. "Sustainability: Physical and Biological Considerations for Australian Environments." Working Paper WP/19/89. Bureau of Rural Resources, Canberra.

Hodgkinson, K. C. 1992. "Elements of Grazing Strategies for Perennial Grass Management in Rangelands." In G. Chapman, ed., *Desertified Grasslands: Their Biology and Management*, pp. 77–94. London: Linnean Society of London.

Humphries, S. E., R. H. Groves, and D. S. Mitchell, eds. 1991. *Plant Invasions: The Incidence of Environmental Weeds in Australia*, vol. 2. Kowari: Australian National Parks and Wildlife Service.

Lange, R. T., and C. R. Graham. 1983. "Rabbits and the Failure of Regeneration in Australian Arid Zone Acacia." *Australian Journal of Ecology* 8, pp. 377–81.

Lange, R. T., A. D. Nicolson, and D. A. Nicolson. 1984. "Vegetation Management of Chenopod Rangelands in South Australia." *Australian Rangeland Journal* 6, pp. 46–54.

Lauenroth, W. K., and W. A. Laycock, eds. 1989. *Secondary Succession and the Evaluation of Rangeland Condition*. Boulder, Colo.: Westview Press.

Low, W. A., W. J. Muller, and M. L. Dudzinski. 1980. "Grazing Intensity of Cattle on a Complex of Rangeland Communities in Central Australia." *Australian Rangeland Journal* 2, pp. 76–82.

Margules, C. R., R. L. Pressey, and A. O. Nicholls. 1991. "Selecting Nature Reserves." In C. R. Margules and M. P. Austin, eds., *Nature Conservation: Cost Effective Biological Surveys and Data Analysis*, pp. 90–97. Melbourne: CSIRO.

McDaniel, K. C., and R. H. Haas. 1982. "Assessing Mesquite-grass Vegetation Condition from Landsat." *Photogrammetric Engineering and Remote Sensing* 48, pp. 441–50.

Mentis, M. T., D. Grossman, M. B. Hardy, T. G. O'Connor, and P. J. O'Reagain. 1989. "Paradigm Shifts in South African Range Science, Management, and Administration." *South African Journal of Science* 85, pp. 684–87.

Morton, S. R. 1990. "The Impact of European Settlement on the Vertebrate Animals of Arid Australia: A Conceptual Model." *Proceedings of the Ecological Society of Australia* 16, pp. 201–13.

Morton, S. R., D. M. Stafford Smith, M. H. Friedel, G. F. Griffin, G. Pickup, and A. S. Sparrow. 1992. "Sand-dune, Saltbush, and Stock: A Vision for the Stewardship of Arid Australia." Processed.

Myers, K. 1971. "The Rabbit in Australia." In P. J. den Boer and G. R. Gradwell, eds., *Dynamics of Populations*, pp. 478–503. Wageningen, the Netherlands: Centre for Agricultural Publishing and Documentation.

Noy-Meir, I. 1973. "Desert Ecosystems: Environment and Producers." *Annual Review of Ecology and Systematics* 4, pp. 25–51.

Pickup, G. 1985. "The Erosion Cell: A Geomorphic Approach to Landscape Classification in Range Assessment." *Australian Rangeland Journal* 7, pp. 114–21.

————. 1989. "New Land Degradation Survey Techniques for Arid Australia: Problems and Prospects." *Australian Rangeland Journal* 11, pp. 74–82.

————. 1992. "Modelling Patterns of Defoliation by Grazing Animals in Rangelands." *Journal of Applied Ecology* 31, pp. 231–46.

Pickup, G., and V. H. Chewings. 1988a. "Estimating the Distribution and Patterns of Cattle Movement in a Large Arid Zone Paddock: An Approach Using Animal Distribution Patterns and Landsat Imagery." *International Journal of Remote Sensing* 9, pp. 1469–90.

————. 1988b. "Forecasting Patterns of Erosion in Arid Lands from Landsat MSS Data." *International Journal of Remote Sensing* 9, pp. 69–84.

————. 1992. "A Grazing Gradient Approach to Land Degradation Assessment in Arid Areas from Remotely Sensed Data." *International Journal of Remote Sensing* 15, pp. 597–617.

Pickup, G., and D. J. Nelson. 1984. "Use of Landsat Radiance Parameters to Distinguish Soil Erosion, Stability, and Deposition in Arid Central Australia." *Remote Sensing of Environment* 16, pp. 195–209.

Pickup, G., and D. M. Stafford Smith. 1993. "Problems, Prospects, and Procedures for Assessing the Sustainability of Pastoral Land Management in Arid Australia." *Journal of Biogeography* 20, pp. 471–87.

Purvis, J. R. 1986. "Nurture the Land: My Philosophies of Pastoral Management in Central Australia." *Australian Rangeland Journal* 8, pp. 110–17.

Stafford Smith, D. M. 1984. "Behavioural Ecology of Sheep in the Australian Arid Zone." Ph.D. diss., Australian National University, Canberra.

————. 1988. "Modeling: Three Approaches to Predicting How Herbivore Impact Is Distributed in Rangelands." Research Report 628. New Mexico State University, Agricultural Experiment Station, Las Cruces, N.Mx.

Stafford Smith, D. M., and B. D. Foran. 1988. "Strategic Decisions in Pastoral Management." *Australian Rangeland Journal* 10, pp. 82–95.

Stafford Smith, D. M., and S. R. Morton. 1990. "A Framework for the Ecology of Arid Australia." *Journal of Arid Environments* 18, pp. 255–78.

Stafford Smith, D. M., and G. Pickup. 1993. "Out of Africa Looking in: Understanding Vegetation Change." In R. H. Behnke, I. Scoones, and C. Kerven, eds., *Range Ecology at Disequilibrium*, pp. 196–226. London: Overseas Development Institute, International Institute for Environment and Development, and Commonwealth Secretariat.

Westoby, M. 1980. "Elements of a Theory of Vegetation Dynamics in Arid Rangelands." *Israel Journal of Botany* 28, pp. 169–94.

Westoby, M., B. Walker, and I. Noy-Meir. 1989. "Opportunistic Management for Rangelands Not at Equilibrium." *Journal of Range Management* 42, pp. 266–74.

Wilson, A. D., and N. D. MacLeod. 1991. "Overgrazing: Present or Absent?" *Journal of Range Management* 44, pp. 475–82.

14

Currencies for Measuring Sustainability: Case Studies from Asian Highlands

P. S. Ramakrishnan

The concept of sustainability as generally understood implies the use of ecological systems in a manner that satisfies current needs without compromising the needs or options of future generations. Achieving such an objective involves a variety of choices. These choices stem from clearly defined ecological concepts and less obvious and highly variable social concerns.

In developing countries, population pressures are more intense than in the industrial world, and human societies are often strongly rooted to their traditional beliefs and influenced by socioeconomic, sociocultural, and sociopolitical considerations. In such a context, understanding the tradeoffs between meeting current needs and maintaining a variety of options for the future becomes increasingly complex. Ecological concepts are no doubt important, but social dimensions that are more elusive need to be given equal weight. Our understanding of the ecological processes that could form the basis for the sustainable use of a given ecosystem is far from adequate. Add to this the social dimensions, and we are left groping in the dark. It is in this context that some of the case studies considered here, and the northeast Indian case study in particular, become significant.

One of the important objectives of this chapter is to indicate the variety of routes that are available for developing the northeastern highlands in a sustainable way. While doing so, I evaluate a variety of parameters that may be considered for defining and measuring sustainability. The case study from northeastern India is a comprehensive multidisciplinary study, and the emphasis here is placed on work from the Asian highlands. However, a few scattered studies from elsewhere in the region are also considered to illustrate specific points under consideration.

Shifting agriculture, upland forests, and sustainable development: Case study of northeastern India

It is well recognized now that conservation and sustainable development are two sides of the same coin: one cannot be achieved at the expense of the other. From a human angle, such an integrated approach demands satisfying basic human needs in an equitable manner and maintaining and indeed promoting social, cultural, and biological diversity and ecological integrity of the system. The northeastern highlands of India, with a complex and large base of natural resources and a hilly terrain, provide the ecological diversity. The people of the region, comprising many tribes, provide the sociocultural diversity. To build on such a profile on a sustainable basis is a challenging opportunity. The following summarizes more than 200 publications arising from this case study.

The setting

Shifting agriculture (locally called *jhum*) is the chief land use system of the northeastern highlands in India. The forest farmer here and elsewhere in the humid tropics has managed his traditional shifting agriculture for centuries, achieving optimum yield on a long-term basis, rather than maximizing production for short-term considerations (Ramakrishnan 1984, 1992a; Ruthenberg 1971; Watters 1960). The farmer tries to capitalize on the soil fertility built up through natural processes during the forest fallow phase and the nutrients released in a single flush during the slash-and-burn operation. However, in the northeastern region and elsewhere, the jhum cycle (the length of the fallow phase during two successive croppings from the same site) has declined in recent years to become a short cycle of four to five years, reaching less than three years in places. This contrasts with the cycle of twenty years or more that was common in the not-too-distant past and that ensured that the system was in harmony with the environment. Shortening the cycle has resulted in poor recovery of soil fertility and the consequent problems of sustainability of the agricultural system, both in economic and ecological terms (Ramakrishnan 1985, 1992a). Further, shortened cycles do not permit the forest ecosystem to recover adequately, leading to loss of forest cover, its replacement by weed cover, and in extreme cases total desertification of the site (which means the decline in biological productivity of the ecosystem; see, for example, Ramakrishnan 1992b).

It is in this context that government agencies dealing with agriculture, forest, and soil conservation have attempted to replace the jhum system. For more than forty years, the attempt was to convince farmers to practice sedentary agriculture largely through the development of terrace farming. Incentives were provided in the form of monetary subsidies for terracing and establishing and maintaining terraces, for using high-yielding varieties of seed, and for applying fertilizers to sustain soil fertility. These subsidies were withdrawn after the initial introduction of alternate technology, however, and the farmer reverted back to his traditional jhum system. In more recent times, the Indian Council of Agricultural Research (ICAR) complex located in the northeastern region developed a model to replace jhum (Borthakur and others 1978). This model proposes a three-tier system for farming the hill slope. The upper third of the slope is designated for forestry, the middle portion for horticulture and plantation crops, and the lower third for terraced agriculture. This system demands inorganic fertilizer on the order of 60 kilograms of nitrogen, 30 kilograms of phosphorous, and 30 kilograms of potassium per hectare a year; this input obviously is a major deterrent to its acceptance. The system often also conflicts with the patterns of land tenure and with the social structure of tribal communities, adversely affecting the independence of the family unit. It cannot be sustained by a single family. In view of this and in view of the fact that it ignores traditional technologies of the tribal communities (Ramakrishnan 1984, 1992a), the ICAR model has not had a significant impact so far. Meanwhile, jhum has become even more untenable because of large-scale timber extraction, increasing population pressure, and simultaneous decline in land area for jhum, all of which contributed to the drastic decline in the cycle (Ramakrishnan 1992a). It is obvious that the jhum system as it is operating now in the northeast cannot be sustained. This prompted this effort to define sustainability and determine biophysical parameters for evaluating the sustainability of a forest-agroecosystem complex.

Traditional patterns of resource use

The northeastern hill region is inhabited by more than a hundred different tribes that are highly insulated, with their own language and cultural identities. The region is also characterized by extreme variations in ecology. Altitude varies widely from sea level to about 3,000 meters in Arunachal Pradesh. With an annual average rainfall of 200 centimeters for the region as a whole, rainfall may reach 12 meters in some areas or in an exceptional year even 24 meters, as it did in 1974 in Cherrapunji, one of the wettest spots in the world. The highly leached soils may be weakly to strongly acidic, supporting subtropical forests at lower elevations and subtemperate broadleaved or conifer forests at higher altitudes. A variety of degraded types of forests such as bamboo forests and grasslands also develop, depending on biotic disturbances (Ramakrishnan 1992a).

Tribal communities in the region engage in a variety of economic activities based on the availability of resources. In the more remote areas of Arunachal Pradesh, tribes such as the Sulungs are largely hunter gatherers, although they may also work in traditional agriculture and animal husbandry, particularly the raising of swine (Gangwar and Ramakrishnan 1987). The more advanced tribes such as the Apatanis of Arunachal Pradesh engage in sedentary agriculture on valley land and in traditional animal husbandry (Kumar and

Ramakrishnan 1990). All the tribal communities in the region depend on the forest for collecting wild food and extracting fuelwood and fodder for animal husbandry and for slash-and-burn agriculture, which is the traditional system of land use in the region.

THE JHUM SYSTEM

The jhum system is highly heterogeneous. This mixed cropping system follows a slash-and-burn operation and varies considerably in its cropping pattern, depending on the ecological conditions and socioeconomic and cultural background of each tribe. In the same region, cropping patterns also vary with the length of the jhum cycle. The number of species in the crop mixture may vary from eight to more than thirty-five, with much variation noted in the proportion of different species in the mixture. This makes the jhum system highly complex.

VALLEY LAND AGROECOSYSTEM

Agriculture is also practiced in valley land throughout the region. It is a sedentary form of wet rice (*Oryza sativa*) cultivation and is complementary to jhum. It is done wherever the terrain permits, on flat lands between hill slopes. Obviously, this system is restricted by topography. The soil in valley lands is fertile due to nutrient wash-out from the hilly slopes and therefore does not need added fertilizers. The main advantage is that the land gives sustained yield year after year. This land use also varies widely in the number of croppings a year, the mixture of crops used, the recycling of organic resources done to maintain soil fertility, and the inclusion or otherwise of pisciculture as an integral part of the cropping system. Thus, the Garos at lower elevations of Meghalaya may raise two crops, whereas the Mikirs in the same area or the Khasis at higher elevations may raise only one (Maikhuri and Ramakrishnan 1990; Patnaik and Ramakrishnan 1989). Apatanis of Arunachal Pradesh, who have one of the most efficient and advanced forms of valley cultivation, use late or early ripening varieties of rice depending on whether waste is recycled efficiently or not. The late varieties go with more fertile soils, and the early varieties go with less fertile soils. Since the organic waste is largely generated within the village, the late ripening variety is grown closer to the village. The early variety is sown farther away, where disturbance by wild animals and poor irrigation facilities can be major constraints (Kumar and Ramakrishnan

1990). Rice is supplemented by *Eleusine coracana* cultivated on elevated partition bunds between the rice plots. Pisciculture is done only with the late-maturing variety of rice, which improves the use of resources and the consequent efficiency of the system.

HOME GARDENS

An important agroforestry system of tribal communities is the home garden, variously termed the kitchen garden or forest garden. These gardens have highly diverse and stratified plant species, dominated by woody perennials. With a mixture of annuals and perennials forming a multiple-storeyed structure, they resemble a natural forest. From a plot of 0.5 to 2 hectares located close to the habitation, the farmer obtains food, fire wood, medicinal plants, spices, and ornamentals all year round. Apart from meeting the needs of the farmer, they also perform social or aesthetic functions, serving as an indicator of social status of the owner or improving environmental quality.

The cropping pattern in home gardens varies considerably. The Mikirs at lower elevations of Meghalaya, for example, emphasize the arecanut (betel nut, or *Areca catechu*) with betel (*Piper betel*), black pepper (*Piper nigrum*), and banana as cash crops (Maikhuri and Ramakrishnan 1990). The Khasis in the Cherrapunji region also grow cash crops such as the bay leaf (*Cinnamomum obtusifolium*), orange (*Citrus sinensis*), and jack fruit (*Artocarpus heterophylls*). A variety of ground-level species may be grown. Indeed, this land use system too varies from place to place, based on ecological and social considerations.

CASH CROP ECOSYSTEMS

A shift toward plantation and cash crops sometimes accompanies the rapid shortening of the jhum cycle (Ramakrishnan 1992a). Broom grass (*Thysanolalna maxima*) is collected from the wild and cultivated in many places, as for example, by the Khasis of Meghalaya (Gangwar and Ramakrishnan 1989). The grass used for making brooms may be part of a plantation crop such as *Cinnamomum obtusifolium*. Bamboo (*Dendrocalamus hamiltonii*) and thatch grass (*Imperata cylindrica*) are also grown or harvested from the wild. Ginger, banana, and pineapple are extensively cultivated in pure or mixed systems. Recently, government agencies have introduced rubber, tea, coffee, and cashew nut into the region.

FALLOW AND SEDENTARY SYSTEMS

As a result of increasing pressure placed on limited land by the growing population, more intensive systems of land use have developed recently in the northeastern region. Largely around urban growth centers, where the land is devoid of forest cover and often in a state of desertification, a semi-permanent bush-fallow system of agriculture is being practiced (FAO/SIDA 1974); this ultimately ends up in sedentary systems of agriculture, with appropriate crop rotation. At least two dozen cropping patterns are recognized in a 20-kilometer radius around the Shillong township in Meghalaya. Often lesser-known crop species such as *Flemingia vestita*, a legume, either intercropped or rotated every three or four years, improves soil fertility, apart from its value as a tuber during the lean season, when traditional food sources are scarce.

ANIMAL HUSBANDRY SUBSYSTEM

Animal husbandry is a low-cost subsystem because natural resources are relatively available and population pressure is minimal. Of all practices, swine husbandry is one of the cheapest to maintain, as it is based on efficient recycling of resources. The waste biomass from agriculture and domestic subsystems, including food unfit for human consumption, is recycled through swine husbandry. This detritus-based system is closely interlinked with shifting agriculture throughout the world (Ramakrishnan 1992a; Rappaport 1971).

Poultry is another important activity of tribal populations; goats and cattle are recent introductions into tribal societies and have not found acceptance, although they are sometimes raised for meat. However, the immigrant Nepalis and Biharis maintain cattle for milk. Many tribes maintain mithun (*Bos frontalis*), which are slaughtered during festivities. These semi-domesticated traditional animals are valuable for religion, for status, and for barter. Because the animals require large forested grazing lands, mithun husbandry has declined as deforestation has accelerated.

DOMESTIC SUBSYSTEM

Tribal communities depend on forests for obtaining fuelwood for cooking food and for heating their huts during winter months. They also collect a variety of plant and animal foods from the forests.

Currencies for measuring sustainability

A variety of currencies is used here to evaluate the land use systems as they operate now. These currencies also form the basis for devising sustainable development strategies. This section attempts to reconcile the different currencies for measuring sustainability.

CROP BIOMASS IN AGRICULTURE

A high diversity of species is characteristic of all traditional systems of agriculture—the home garden and the jhum system (with up to thirty-five species in a plot of 2 to 3 hectares)—and of many tropical agroecosystems (Ramakrishnan 1992a). High diversity contributes to stability of the ecosystem. With a multilayered canopy, a high leaf area index for capturing light efficiently, and a layered distribution of root mass in the soil profile for using nutrients optimally, crop productivity is high.

Indeed, the jhum farmer shifts his emphasis in the crop mixture depending on the jhum cycle. Under a short cycle of five years, for example, the emphasis is on tuber and rhizomatous crops since they use nutrients more efficiently and can maximize output under low-fertility soils. Under longer jhum cycles of twenty years, for example, the emphasis is on cereal crops such as rice and maize that use nutrients less efficiently. Such a shift in emphasis can also be seen under a given jhum cycle, with emphasis on cereals at the base of the slope (sites rich in nutrients) and emphasis in tuber and rhizomatous crops at the top of the slope (sites poor in nutrients). Therefore, the values for primary productivity under jhum compare with those of the secondary successional fallows up to twenty years (Toky and Ramakrishnan 1981, 1983a).

A characteristic feature of the jhum system is the high rate of biomass accumulation in relation to economic output. The high rates of organic matter produced under jhum (16 to 22 tons per hectare) are close to values obtained for natural plant communities (14.8 tons per hectare) of twenty-year-old forest fallow in the region. With higher crop diversity, it has been possible to combine the need for increasing the production of harvestable food with the need for maintaining a high content of organic biomass. Without this high production of organic matter, it would become necessary to import costly inorganic fertilizers, which are hard to come by and whose effectiveness in the face of high temperatures and heavy rainfall is questionable.

Sequential harvesting of crops is an effective way to recycle organic residues into the system over a period of time. Under the partial weeding done during jhum, even the weed biomass gets recycled into the plot in a phased manner so that a layer of humus is always present on the soil surface. About 20 percent of the weed biomass left in situ during cropping also contributes to biodiversity and helps conserve water and nutrients on the steep slope (Swamy and Ramakrishnan 1988). Sequential harvesting is an effective way to manage up to thirty-five or forty crop species over both space and time. Thus, after early maturing species such as maize and *Setaria italica* are harvested, more space is devoted to rice at the peak of its growth period. Successive harvests of cereals create additional space for the remaining perennial crops, which also receive humus and nutrients.

Mixed cropping also helps control biological pests (Litsinger and Moody 1976). The use of native varieties would probably ensure that a high degree of natural chemical defenses is maintained (Janzen 1973). Further, under mixed cropping, with 20 percent residual weed biomass, it is unlikely that any one of the populations of insects, bacteria, or nematodes would reach epidemic levels due to high genetic diversity.

The crop more than doubles soil cover between the ten- and thirty-year jhum cycle and increases it more than fivefold between the five- and thirty-year cycle (see table 14-1). In the ultimate analysis, mixed cropping maximizes production, minimizes losses, provides a wide base of food resources for tribal society by providing cereals, legumes, vegetables, and even fiber, and at the same time ensures leisure by effectively spreading out labor all the year round.

BIOMASS DURING THE FALLOW PHASE

In a series of studies, we have shown that the weed potential of a site is aggravated under jhum cycles shorter than ten years. The increased weed potential under cycles of four to six years is obviously due to the presence of the same weed species in the four- to six-year-old plots that are slashed, which helps to build up the soil seed bank. Long cycles of ten years or more, in contrast, may be sustainable since weeds decline naturally during long fallow periods.

Continuous cropping under terrace cultivation results in even higher weed potential than under short-cycle jhum. On old terraces, crop yield could be adversely affected because of intense competition with weeds. Indeed, this is one of the major difficulties of sustaining the terrace agroecosystem.

Large-scale deforestation for timber extraction and shortened jhum cycles of about five years have resulted in large-scale invasion of weeds, many of them exotic (Ramakrishnan 1991; Ramakrishnan and Vitousek 1989). This is a stage in site degradation. In the final stage, the landscape is totally bald and desertified (Ramakrishnan 1992a).

Table 14-1: Characteristics under Five-, Ten-, and Thirty-Year Cycles for the Garos at Burnihat in Meghalaya

Crop	Five year	Ten year	Thirty year
Economic yields (tons per hectare a year)			
Seeds	0.107	1.153	2.180
Leaf fruit	0.129	0.074	0.024
Tubers	0.320	0.613	0.192
Total	0.556	1.840	2.396
ANP	14.060	11.576	15.213
Growth rate (grams per square meter a day)	3.8	3.2	4.2
NPP	18.461	14.709	17.746
Growth rate (grams per square meter a day)	5.1	4.0	4.9
Number of cultivars	8	12	14
LAI	0.59	1.49	3.20
H.I.	0.030	0.125	0.135
H.I. (grain + seed)	0.184	0.230	0.182
Labor (days per hectare a year)	149	305	436

Note: H.I. = Crop yield / NPP; H.I. (grain + seed) = above-ground crop yield / ANP.
Source: Toky and Ramakrishnan 1981.

BIODIVERSITY

Perturbation of an ecosystem may promote or adversely affect biodiversity, depending on the intensity and frequency of the events (Chandrasekhara 1991; Ramakrishnan 1992a). In the northeastern hill region, a ten-year cycle seems to be the cutoff point for biodiversity in the rain forests. However, higher diversity values were obtained beyond a thirty-year cycle. Further, traditional agroecosystems are significant for conserving the biodiversity of crops (Ramakrishnan 1989b). The objective was to optimize biodiversity by conserving the keystone species that may have multiple uses or that may have possible value for the future. Biodiversity is a critical measure for sustainable development.

NUTRIENT CYCLING DURING CROPPING
AND FALLOW PHASES

During slash and burn involving low- or high-intensity burn, a variety of physicochemical changes occur in the soil (Ramakrishnan and Toky 1981). Carbon and nitrogen are volatilized. A rapid increase in soil pH occurs, with its implication for biological activities of the soil. Phosphorus and cations are released in a flush. Nitrogen buildup is soon initiated through microbial fixation. However, during the cropping phase nutrients are lost, partly through runoff and infiltration and partly through the removal of weeds and crops. One of the chief conclusions arising from a detailed study of soil fertility under the cropping phase is the generally poor level of nutrients under which the system has to operate (Ramakrishnan 1992a).

The jhum farmer tries to capitalize on the limited soil fertility that is highly transient, both in space and time. As already noted, he emphasizes crops that use nutrients efficiently under short jhum cycles of five years. He also places crops so that the more nutrient-efficient crops are largely on top of the slope and the less-efficient ones are at the base. By this he is able to achieve a high leaf area index for optimizing photosynthesis from a highly heterogeneous soil environment. Sequential harvesting and the consequent addition of humus through recycled crop and weed biomass ensures optimal use of nutrients for the succeeding crop species. A high level of synchrony between nutrients released by the organic residues and the pattern of use by the crops ensures optimal yield under the given situation.

The process by which nutrients are depleted from the soil through the cropping phase also continues through the fallow phase up to about ten years. The rapid transfer of nutrients from the soil to the living biomass during the early successional phase is reversed when litterfall occurs either through leaf drop or complete turnover of the early herbaceous vegetation, which happens only after about ten years of fallow regrowth (see figure 14-1). This implies that a ten-year jhum cycle is critical from the point of view of sustainable cropping under this system. Shorter cycles not only do not permit nutrient recovery in the soil but also accelerate a variety of losses from the system under frequent perturbations. More frequent losses under low levels of soil fertility under cycles of four to five years eventually lead to desertification. Indeed, traditional sys-

Figure 14-1: Economic Yield under Different Jhum Cycles of Thirty, Ten, and Five Years in Burnihat at Lower Elevations of Meghalaya

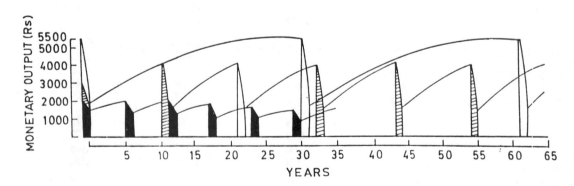

Source: Ramakrishnan 1985.

tems with cycles of ten years or more are closer to natural ecosystems where nutrient cycling and maintenance of soil fertility are based on efficient internal controls, thus contributing to their stability.

Detailed nutrient budget analysis throws further light on the value of using soil fertility as a currency for evaluating the jhum system. To take one example of such an analysis, during one cropping season it was shown that the system would lose up to about 600 kilograms of nitrogen per hectare (see table 14-2). It would take about ten years of fallow regrowth to recover this entire loss through a natural process of plant succession. However, under a short cycle of five years, the system is able to recover only half of what it had lost, that is, about 300 kilograms of nitrogen per hectare. In other words, under each cropping under a five-year cycle in a given plot, the system would lose about 300 kilograms of nitrogen per hectare, which is never put back into the system. This and similar losses of other elements from the system would lead to desertification (Ramakrishnan 1992a).

The link between the soil nutrient budget and cycling processes during the cropping and fallow phases has implications for sustainability of the jhum system under varied cycles. An obvious conclusion is that if the jhum could be done with a minimum cycle of at least ten years, it could be sustainable in the region. Under shorter cycles, the system obviously needs to be redeveloped through additional agroforestry inputs. An obvious choice that has found ready acceptance among the farmers of the northeast is *Alnus nepalensis* (the Nepalese alder). Growing at an altitudinal range of 500 to 1,900 meters in the northeast, this species could fix up to about 117 kilograms per hectare a year when young (Sharma and Ambasht 1988), and this species could recover all the nitrogen that the system loses during cropping under

a five-year cycle (Ramakrishnan 1992a). Therefore, it is not surprising to find many of the jhum plots in Nagaland being integrated with the Nepalese alder (Gokhale and others 1985). Indeed this species also provides cash income through wood biomass harvested every five or six years and regenerated through coppices.

Keystone species such as this are important for redeveloping jhum (Ramakrishnan 1989a). Thus, for example, the different species of bamboo (*Dendroclamus hamiltonii, Bamboosa tulda,* and *B. khasiana*) coming up in jhum fallows between ten to thirty years of fallow regrowth tend to conserve nitrogen, phosphorus, and potassium in the system (Rao and Ramakrishnan 1989; Toky and Ramakrishnan 1983b). Indeed, in younger fallows of less than five years, even the exotic weed *Mikania micrantha* conserves potassium under shorter cycles of five to six years (Swamy and Ramakrishnan 1987).

ECONOMIC EFFICIENCY
A series of studies done on jhum under cycles ranging from sixty-year cycles on one extreme to five-year cycles on the other suggests that from the point of view of economic yield and monetary analysis, a ten-year cycle should be the cutoff point (Ramakrishnan 1992a). The net economic returns to the farmer, after making allowances for a variety of labor inputs for slash and burn, is optimum under a ten-year cycle. The monetary output tends to decline under successive five-year cycles but remains stable under a ten-year cycle or longer (see figure 14-2). For the sustainability of the system as currently practiced, a minimal cycle of ten years is required. Indeed, the farmer is able to obtain a higher economic return under a ten-year jhum cycle than under terrace cropping on the same site (Ramakrishnan 1984).

Table 14–2: Net Change of Nitrogen in the Soil under Jhum at Shillong in Meghalaya at Five-, Ten-, and Fifteen-year Cycles
(thousands of kilograms per hectare a year)

Soil pool	Fifteen year	Ten year	Five year	
			First-year crop	Second-year crop
Before burning	7.68	7.74	6.40	5.98
At the end of cropping	7.04	7.15	5.98	5.60
Net difference	0.64	0.59	0.42	0.38

Source: Mishra and Ramakrishnan 1984.

The wide variety of jhum systems available in the northeast offers opportunity for manipulation so that the farmer can increase his returns. Thus the jhum system where potato is emphasized gives the farmer up to five times higher returns than another where the emphasis is on rice. Indeed wide variations in economic yield exist depending on the cropping pattern even under the same jhum cycle. Mere transfer of technology from one area to another could improve the returns.

ENERGY EFFICIENCY

The increasing agricultural yields of the last half century were made possible through the industrialization of agriculture involving large energy subsidies and high-yielding varieties of crops grown in pure stands. The drawbacks of such systems as models for development in an energy-limited world are obvious. Therefore, many traditional mixed cropping systems are held up as models of ecological efficiency. Under jhum, for every unit of energy input, which itself is chiefly in the form of human labor, fifty or more units of energy are harvested (Toky and Ramakrishnan 1982).

The jhum system is more efficient than sedentary terrace cultivation, which requires the subsidizing of fossil fuel energy in the form of fertilizers. The energy cost of establishing and maintaining terraces is high. Over a period of time, due to site degradation, the efficiency of fertilizer use under terraces declines drastically.

A comparison of jhum under different cycles suggests that if the cycle is long enough and the land is not a limiting factor, the input of solar

Figure 14-2: Changes in Cumulative Quantity of Available Phosphorus (A), Potassium (B), Calcium (C), and Magnesium (D) within a Soil Column of 40 Centimeters in Depth under Jhum Fallows of Various Ages

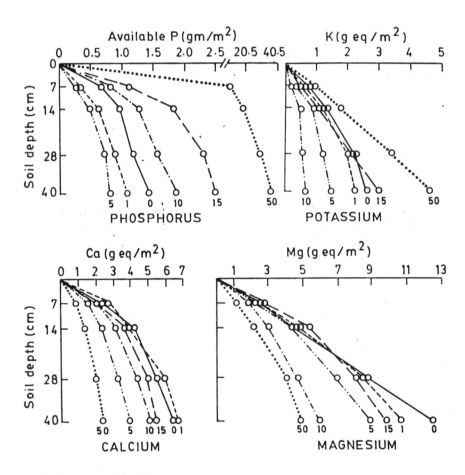

Source: Ramakrishnan and Toky 1981.

energy to a larger area of the jhum system could offset the need to import fossil fuel energy, which would ensure harmony of the system with the environment. Even when one uses a correction factor of 1/30, 1/10, or 1/5 for thirty-, ten-, and five-year cycles, one finds that a ten-year jhum cycle is the cutoff point for energy efficiency (output/input ratio) and land use (Ramakrishnan 1992a).

Keeping energy efficiency high, possibilities exist for increasing crop production by strengthening agroforestry, without departing too much from the traditional jhum system. In a wider context of Indian agriculture, it should be possible to replace imported fertilizers with local resources based on biofertilizers and small-scale watershed management projects and to have a stable system of production. With a large rural population of small and marginal farmers engaged in agriculture, emphasizing agricultural technology based on efficient recycling of natural resources seems to be more appropriate.

SOCIAL AND CULTURAL VALUE SYSTEM

Jhum has been a way of life for tribal communities along with other land uses such as valley and home garden systems. Therefore, basing sustainability on traditional technology and values and orienting sustainable development toward approaches with which these communities can relate become important. A variety of religious and cultural ceremonies are linked to the jhum calendar, starting with slash and burn and continuing through sowing and harvesting the crops (Ramakrishnan 1985). Indeed, the cultural link between traditional societies and their forest heritage—seen in the sacred grove forests maintained extensively in the past—is still found during the present (Khiewtam and Ramakrishnan 1989). Some plant species such as bamboos and the Nepalese alder are traditionally valued, and farmers have often been unable to relate to other tree species that are fast-growing and have the appropriate architectural form from a biological point of view (Ramakrishnan 1986). Nepalese alders and bamboos species are also ecologically significant keystone species for conserving nutrients, as discussed earlier. Indeed, a parallel is discernible between ecological and sociological keystone species. A technology, however effective, may not be relevant to a given society unless it is placed in the total social context. The human dimension of sustainability is critical to acceptance.

What is sustainability in the context of northeastern India?

The northeastern case study shows that sustainability can have a short- and long-term aspect to it. In the short-term context, two possibilities exist. The first is to sustain jhum in the present form at a minimal cycle of ten years since this is the cutoff point for efficiency. This could be done by strengthening the valley land and home garden ecosystems. Here, transfer of technology from one area to another is a possibility, since all these systems are highly heterogeneous and offer a wide variety of socioeconomic returns to the farmer. A valley land agroecosystem, such as that of the Apatanis whose complex agricultural system is integrated with pisciculture, is attractive for transfer to other areas. Land uses other than jhum and even the animal husbandry component such as swine husbandry and poultry could be further strengthened through appropriate technology inputs. This could take the pressure off the land devoted to jhum so that a minimal ten-year cycle could be ensured, at least in some areas.

Alternatively, as a short-term strategy, a jhum system with a short cycle of five years, for example, could be redeveloped based on alder technology. Nepalese alder is now extensively used to strengthen the agroforestry component of the jhum in places such as Nagaland (Gokhale and others 1985) so that the short-cycle system could be sustained and slash-and-burn operations eliminated or at least minimized.

On a long-term basis, a cooperative plantation economy involving coffee, tea, rubber, fruit trees, or even timber could be developed, based on the concept of the home garden. Such an economic initiative could be organized in small plots run by farmer cooperatives, which would ensure participation. An economy based on trees and forestry could be effectively done by an appropriate mix of species that are based on efficient recycling of nutrients. Appropriate rural technology could be introduced into the domestic sector. An integrated and holistic approach would ensure sustainability since it would involve people in the developmental process (see box 14-1).

Identifying the key social issue and building on it could be a sure way to ensure that farmers participate and that development is sustainable among rural communities. The case study of northeastern Indian illustrates this very effectively.

Box 14-1: Shifting Agriculture and Sustainable Development in Northeastern India

For improving the system of land use and resource management in northeastern India, the following strategies are based on a multidisciplinary analysis. Many of these proposals have already been put into practice.

- Employ a wide variation in the patterns of cropping and yield under jhum and transfer technology among tribes, areas, or ecosystems (emphasis on potato at higher elevations and rice at lower elevations has led to a manifold increase in economic yield despite low fertility of the more acidic soils at higher elevations).

- Maintain a jhum cycle of a minimum of ten years (which is critical for achieving sustainability) by emphasizing other systems of land use such as the traditional valley cultivation or home gardens.

- Speed up fallow regeneration after jhum by introducing fast-growing native shrubs and trees.

- Condense the time span of forest succession and accelerate restoration of degraded lands, based on an understanding of tree growth strategies and architecture, by adjusting the mix of species in time and space.

- Improve animal husbandry through improved breeds of swine and poultry.

- Redevelop village ecosystems through the introduction of appropriate technology to relieve drudgery and improve energy efficiency (such as cooking stoves, agricultural implements, biogas generation, small hydroelectric projects); promote crafts such as smithying and products based on leather, bamboo, and other woods.

- Strengthen conservation measures based on traditional knowledge and value system.

Source: Ramakrishnan 1992a.

Development of the Philippine highlands

A country of shifting agriculture, the Philippines experiences problems similar to those of the northeastern highlands of India (Fujisaka, Sajise, and del Castillo 1986). Methods of controlling soil erosion and conserving soil through tillage are less labor intensive and cost-effective than terracing. Redeveloping the agroforestry system using traditional knowledge is the starting point. Contour intercropping of nitrogen-fixing tree hedgerows and food and cash crops is one possibility for recycling nutrients efficiently. *Leucena leucocephala* and *Gliricidia sepium* tree hedgerows were found to be most appropriate and acceptable. Because the development of technology for appropriate land use is often based exogenously, acceptance has been limited. A major factor working against sustainable land use has been problems related to land tenure, which is often discriminatory. Several interactive factors need to be considered for the sustainable development of these highlands. These interactive integrative linkages are shown in Figure 14-3.

Figure 14-3. Integrative Diagram Linking the Three Major Issues and Many Sub-Issues Crucial for Rural Rehabilitation

Landscape as a unit
Site specific
Timeframe (short/long-term strategy)
Strengthen internal controls and reduce subsidies
Soil and water conservation/management
Traditional/appropriate technology
Enhance biodiversity
Resource optimization

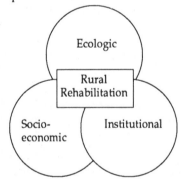

History and causes of degradation	Village-level organization
Cost/benefit sharing	Flexibility
Community participation	Monitoring
Role of women	Credit/marketing
Empowerment	Links with GOs/NGOs/
Tenurial rights	scientists
Value system	Incentives

Source: Ramakrishnan and others 1994.

Case studies of other shifting agricultural systems

Indonesia, Malaysia, and Thailand are among the countries in the region with highland shifting agriculture (UNESCO 1983). Social problems related to the transfer and implementation of technology have been a major impediment to sustainable development. In the Nabawan Project in Sabah, for instance, farmers were settled to wet rice cultivation, for which was not suitable for the ecological conditions of the area. The shortage of water was severe, and farmers were used to dry land rice cultivation. The project soon had to be abandoned. Problems often arise when alien crop species are introduced to replace upland rice because rice is culturally linked to the people's very existence.

Similar social and cultural issues stand in the way of sustainable land use development in the Thai highlands, too. With large-scale migration into the hills from the adjoining lowlands, social disruptions occur and are aggravated when technologies more suited to lowland social ethos are blindly imposed on the highlanders. Patterns of land ownership, for example, are quite different; the highlander has community-owned lands, whereas the low-lander has individually owned lands.

The Nepalese forestry project

The Nepal-Australia forestry program for the Nepalese Himalaya emphasized the people and the ecosystem as one resilient whole (Griffin 1988). Involving people in the early stages of the program, rather than at the end, was the key to the success of this forestry project.

The Indonesian transmigration program

In many case studies, demographic pressure hampers sustainable development. Ill-conceived agricultural activities often are responsible for site degradation and the consequent social disruptions. Before humans are moved to forest areas that are clear-cut, land use needs to be carefully planned. Such planning should take into consideration the social dimensions. The Indonesian transmigration is a telling example that has attracted considerable criticism from both within and outside the country (see box 14-2).

Case studies from the Himalayan region

In many hilly areas of the Himalaya, water is the key social issue. Land use development and restoration of forest ecosystems are often constrained by lack of adequate water outside the monsoon season. In a hilly terrain, uneven distribution of rainfall interacting with excessive land degradation aggravates the shortage of water.

In the village Sukhomajri located in the foothills of the Himalaya, called the Shiwalik ranges near Chandigarh in northwestern India, land was highly degraded with frequent crop failures. This compelled farmers to emphasize goat and sheep husbandry. Having identified water as the limiting factor, the Hill Resource Management Society (HRMS) of the local community, with scientific support, initiated a watershed management plan (Grewal, Mittal, and Singh 1990). Through a series of earthern dams and water management, in just about five years, annual household income increased an estimated Rs2,000 to Rs3,000, due to increased food production, better grass cover for

---

Box 14-2: The Indonesian Transmigration Program

This is the world's largest program for voluntary assisted migration, involving at least 2.5 million people since 1985. On the face of it, it is sensible to move people from overcrowded and degraded lands of Java, Madura Bali, and Lombok to sparsely populated outer islands. Although many settlers seem to be satisfied with their new environment, many settlements have been established on infertile soils and endangered ecosystems. Examples are the endangered heath forests (Kerangas) on infertile white sands of Bangka Island, south Sumatra, and the ultra basic soil in Southeast Sulawesi. Migration also causes social disruption: sponsored migrants are followed by perhaps twice as many unassisted migrants, who have caused considerable environmental damage and social problems. In particular, the interaction between migrants and local inhabitants has caused social disruption in the past, and this needs to be carefully analyzed to avoid repeating mistakes.

On the basis of a detailed analysis, Whitten and others (1987) conclude that transmigration is not the answer to Javas's demographic problems. They rightly point out that, though the program has slowed down, it will continue. What is important is to seek the means of eradicating the root cause of the population explosion in Java and to minimize social disruption by supporting sustainable development in the settlements.

cattle, and better forest cover for fodder and fuelwood. People's participation was the key to success, and other communities in the region initiated restoration programs based on the Sukhmajri model.

In the restoration study initiated in the central Himalayan Kumaon region, water was a limiting factor and bamboo was an economically important but declining natural resource. Many species of bamboo, *Thamnocalamus spathiflorus*, *T. falcuneri*, *T. jaunsarensis*, and *Chimnobambuse falcata*, were emphasized as agroforestry and social forestry species in private and common lands in a cluster of about fifty villages. Additional water was provided through rainwater and subsurface seepage harvesting tanks constructed cheaply using locally available resources (Kothyari and others 1991). This participatory research cum development program involved a few hundred people from the local community during a short period of six months!

Now a series of rainwater harvesting tanks are operating in the Himalayan belt, and water is the key factor catalyzing a variety of land use development and restoration activities such as the redevelopment of hill agroecosystems, management of forests for fodder and fuelwood, and development of integrated watersheds. Sustainable development is based on the participation of people and communities.

Building village-level organizations is critical in any effort to achieve sustainable development. Impressive social forestry programs have been carried out in China over some decades through collective units such as people's communes and production brigades on their own land; similarly, massive fuelwood plantations have been established and degraded forest lands rehabilitated in the Republic of Korea through village forestry associations (FAO 1979, 1982). In Bankura in West Bengal, India, tribal women organized themselves to restore the forest ecosystem using a three-tier societal framework starting at the village level; this effort has been an income-generating and ecologically valuable activity.

Forest protection committees created by the Bengal Forest Development in India involve villagers living along the periphery of forest dominated by *Shorea robusta* (Sal), with effective and profitable results (Malhotra and Poffenberger 1989). Conflicts arising at the village level because of social inequality and stratification are often resolved through local institutions created for ecodevelopment; these institutions often interact with nongovernmental voluntary groups and government agencies in diverse ecological situations (Agarwal and Narain 1989). The message that comes across loud and clear is that old social structures could form the basis for transforming the structure of societies where development is initiated. Participatory action-oriented research then could become meaningful. Some form of organization is, however, fundamental to achieving full participation.

Conclusions

The Asian highlands are characterized by a variety of traditional societies occupying distinct ecological niches. In such a context, sustainable development of local resources has to be based on a value system that people can understand and appreciate and therefore choose to participate in the process of development. Traditional knowledge and skills should be integrated. The unit for development may be a village, a cluster of villages, or a watershed. Location-specificity is important. Village-level institutions with participation from government and nongovernmental agencies and with special representation for women (who often play a key role in traditional societies) could form the basis for a bottom-up approach to institution building that scales up to the district level.

In the Asian highlands, land degradation due to improper use of forest resources is a priority for people-oriented sustainable development. Initiatives to promote the sustainable use of land should consider ecological processes and social concerns. A variety of currencies could be used to evaluate and monitor the system over a period of time and to allow possible and necessary reconciliations to be made, as illustrated by the northeast Indian case study. It is no longer possible to view ecology merely as a natural science, although natural science forms the foundation for studying ecological processes. One needs not only to draw parallels between studies of ecological and social processes but also to seek out cross connections (Ramakrishnan 1992a). We have very few comprehensive case studies on which to base our conclusions. The International Sustainable Biosphere Initiative (Huntley and others 1991) should help to catalyze studies in this direction.

References

Agarwal, A., and S. Narain. 1989. "Towards Green Villages." Centre for Science and Environment, New Delhi.

Borthakur, D. N., A. Singh, R. P. Awasthi, and R. N. Rai. 1978. "Shifting Cultivation in the North-eastern Region." In *Proceedings of the National Seminar Resources, Development, and Environment in the Himalayan Region*, pp. 330–42. New Delhi: Government of India, Department of Science and Technology.

Chandrasekhara, U. M. 1991. "Studies on the Gap Phase Dynamics of a Humid Tropical Forest." Ph.D. diss., Jawaharlal Nehru University, New Delhi.

FAO (Food and Agriculture Organization of the United Nations). 1979. *China: Mass Mobilization of Rural Communities for Reforestation.* Rome.

———. 1982. *Village Forestry Development in the Republic of Korea: A Case Study.* FAO/SIDA, Forestry for Local Community Development Programme, Rome.

FAO/SIDA (Food and Agriculture Organization of the United Nations/Swedish International Development Agency). 1974. *Report on Regional Seminar on Shifting Cultivation and Soil Conservation in Africa.* Rome.

Fujisaka, S., P. Sajise, and R. del Castillo, eds. 1986. *Man, Agriculture, and the Tropical Forest: Change and Development in the Philippine Uplands.* Bangkok: Winrock International.

Gangwar, A. K., and P. S. Ramakrishnan. 1987. "Agriculture and Animal Husbandry among the Sulungs and Nishis of Arunachal Pradesh." *Social Action* 37, pp. 345–72.

———. 1989. "Ecosystem Function in a Khasi Village of the Desertified Cherrapunji Area in Northeast India." *Proceedings of the Indian Academy of Science (Plant Science)* 99, pp. 199–210.

Gokhale, A. M., D. K. Zeliang, R. Kevichusa, and T. Angami. 1985. "Nagaland: The Use of Alder Trees." Education Department, Kohima, Nagaland.

Grewal, S. S., S. P. Mittal, and G. Singh. 1990. "Rehabilitation of Degraded Lands in the Himalayan Foothills: Peoples Participation." *Ambio* 19, pp. 45–48.

Griffin, D. M. 1988. *Innocents Abroad in the Forests of Nepal.* Canberra: Anutech Pty.

Huntley, B. J., E. Ezucurra, E. R. Fuentes, K. Fugii, P. J. Grubb, W. Haber, J. R. E. Harger, M. M. Holland, S. A. Levin, J. Lubchenco, H. A. Mooney, V. Neronov, I. Noble, H. Ronald Pulliam, P. S. Ramakrishnan, P. G. Risser, O. Sala, J. Sarukhan, and W. G. Sombrock. 1991. "A Sustainable Biosphere: The Global Imperative." *Ecology International* 20, pp. 5–14.

Janzen, D. H. 1973. "Tropical Agro-ecosystems." *Science* 182, pp. 1212–19.

Khiewtam, R. S., and P. S. Ramakrishnan. 1989. "Socio-cultural Studies of the Sacred Groves at Cherrapunji and Adjoining Areas in Northeastern India." *Man in India* 69, pp. 64–71.

Kothyari, B. P., K. S. Rao, K. G. Saxena, T. Kumar, and P. S. Ramakrishnan. 1991. "Institutional Approaches in Development and Transfer of Water Harvest Technology in the Himalaya." In G. Tsakiris, ed., *Advances in Water Resources Technology*, pp. 673–78. Rotterdam: ECOWARM A. A. Balkema.

Kumar, A., and P. S. Ramakrishnan. 1990. "Energy Flow through an Apatani Village Ecosystem of Arunachal Pradesh in Northeast India." *Human Ecology* 18, pp. 315–36.

Litsinger, J. A., and K. Moody. 1976. "Integrated Pest Management in Multiple Cropping Systems." In M. Stelly, ed., *Multiple Cropping*, pp. 293–316. Madison, Wisc.: American Society of Agronomy.

Maikhuri, R. K., and P. S. Ramakrishnan. 1990. "Ecological Analysis of a Cluster of Villages Emphasizing Land Use of Different Tribes in Meghalaya in Northeast India." *Agriculture Ecosystem and Environment* 31, pp. 17–37.

Malhotra, K. C., and M. Poffenberger. 1989. "Forest Regeneration through Community Protection." West Bengal Forest Department, Calcutta.

Mishra, B. K., and P. S. Ramakrishnan. 1984. "Nitrogen Budget under Rotational Bush Fallow Agriculture (Jhum) at Higher Elevations of Meghalaya in Northeastern India." *Plant and Soil* 81, pp. 37–46.

Patnaik, S., and P. S. Ramakrishnan. 1989. "Comparative Study of Energy Flow through Village Ecosystems of Two Co-existing Communities (the Khasis and the Nepalis) of Meghalaya in Northeast India." *Agricultural Systems* 30, pp. 245–67.

Ramakrishnan, P. S. 1984. "The Science behind Rotational Bush Fallow Agriculture System (Jhum)." *Proceedings of the Indian Academy of Science (Plant Science)* 93, pp. 397–400.

———. 1985. "Tribal Man in the Humid Tropics of the Northeast." *Man in India* 65, pp. 1–32.

———. 1986. "Morphometric Analysis of Growth and Architecture of Tropical Trees and Their Ecological Significance," pp. 209–22. Compte-rendu du Colloque International l'Arbre, September 9–14, 1985, Montpellier. Naturalia Monspeliensia, numero hors serie. Montpellier.

———. 1989a. "Conservation Strategies: An Agroecologist's Viewpoint." In M. L. Trivedi, B. S. Gill, and S. S. Saini, eds., *Plant Science Research in India*, pp. 25–38. New Delhi: Today and Tomorrow's Publications.

———. 1989b. "Nutrient Cycling in Forest Fallows in Northeastern India." In J. Proctor, ed., *Mineral Nutrients in Tropical Forest and Savanna Ecosystems*, pp. 337–52. Oxford, England: Blackwell Scientific Publications.

———. 1991. "Biological Invasion in the Tropics: An Overview." In P. S. Ramakrishnan, ed., *Ecology of Biological Invasion in the Tropics*, pp. 1–19. New Delhi: National Institute of Ecology.

———. 1992a. *Shifting Agriculture and Sustainable Development of Northeastern India.* UNESCO-MAB Series. Paris: Parthenon Publications.

———. 1992b. *Tropical Forest: Exploitation, Conservation, and Management Impact.* Paris: UNESCO.

Ramakrishnan, P. S., and O. P. Toky. 1981. "Soil Nutrient Status of Hill Agro-ecosystems and Recovery Pattern after Slash and Burn Agriculture (Jhum) in Northeastern India." *Plant and Soil* 60, pp. 41–64.

Ramakrishnan, P. S., and P. M. Vitousek. 1989. "Ecosystem Level Processes and the Consequences of Biological Invasions." In J. A. Drake, H. A. Mooney, F. di Castri, R. H. Groves, F. G. Kruger, M. Rejmanek, and M. Williamson, eds., *Biological Invasions: A Global Perspective*, pp. 281–300. SCOPE 37. Chichester, England: John Wiley and Sons.

Ramakrishnan, P. S., J. Campbell, L. Demierre, A. Gyi, K. C. Malhotra, S. Mehndiratta, S. N. Rai, and Sashidharan, E.M. 1994. *Ecosystem Rehabilitation of the Rural Landscape in South and Central Asia: An Analysis of Issues.* Special Publication, UNESCO, Regional Office of Science and Technology for South and Central Asia, New Delhi.

Rao, K. S., and P. S. Ramakrishnan. 1989. "Role of Bamboos in Nutrient Conservation during Secondary Succession following Slash and Burn Agriculture (Jhum) in Northeast India." *Journal of Applied Ecology* 26, pp. 625–33.

Rappaport, R. A. 1971. "The Flow of Energy in an Agricultural Society." *Scientific American* 225, pp. 117–32.

Ruthenberg, H. 1971. *Farming Systems in the Tropics.* Oxford, England: Clarendon Press.

Sharma, E., and R. S. Ambasht. 1988. "Nitrogen Accretion and Its Energetics in the Himalayan Alder." *Functional Ecology* 2, pp. 229–35.

Swamy, P. S., and P. S. Ramakrishnan. 1987. "Contribution of *Mikania micrantha* H.B.K. during Secondary Succession Following Slash and Burn Agriculture (Jhum) in Northeast India. I: Biomass, Litterfall, and Productivity." *Forest Ecology and Management* 22, pp. 229–37.

———. 1988. "Nutrient Budget under Slash and Burn Agriculture (Jhum) with Different Weeding Regimes in Northeastern India." *Acta Oecologica-Oecologia Applicata* 9, pp. 85–102.

Toky, O. P., and P. S. Ramakrishnan. 1981. "Cropping and Yields in Agricultural Systems of the Northeastern Hill Region of India." *Agro-Ecosystems* 7, pp. 11–25.

———. 1982. "A Comparative Study of the Energy Budget of Hill Agro-ecosystems with Emphasis on the Slash and Burn System (Jhum) at Lower Elevations of Northeastern India." *Agricultural Systems* 9, pp. 143–54.

———. 1983a. "Secondary Succession Following Slash and Burn Agriculture in Northeastern India. I. Biomass, Litterfall, and Productivity." *Journal of Ecology* 71, pp. 735–45.

———. 1983b. "Secondary Succession Following Slash and Burn Agriculture in Northeastern India. II. Nutrient cycling." *Journal of Ecology* 71, pp. 747–57.

UNESCO (United Nations Educational, Scientific, and Cultural Organization). 1983. *Swidden Cultivation in Asia.* Vol. 2: *Country Profiles.* Bangkok: UNESCO Regional Office.

Watters, R. F. 1960. "Some Forms of Shifting Cultivation in the Southwest Pacific." *Journal of Tropical Geography* 14, pp. 35–50.

Whitten, A. J., H. Haernman, H. S. Alikodra, and M. Thohari. 1987. *Transmigration and the Environment in Indonesia.* Gland, Switzerland: International Union for the Conservation of Nature.

15

Large Marine Ecosystems and Fisheries

Kenneth Sherman

"Environmental degradation is not inevitable; it is simply cheaper and easier for some in the short term. Environmental health also is not inconsistent with economic imperatives and political realities. In fact, a healthy environment is the basis for a healthy economy. Ecosystem ecology provides an important and useful approach both for assessing and for helping to restore the "health" of the biosphere." G. E. Likens 1992

Human intervention and changes in climate are sources of increasing variability in the natural productivity of the world's ocean. Overfishing has caused multimillion-metric-ton flips in biomass among the dominant pelagic components of the fish community off the northeastern United States (Fogarty and others 1991; Sherman 1991; Sissenwine 1986). The biomass flip, wherein a dominant species rapidly drops to a low level to be succeeded by another species, can generate cascading effects among other important components of the ecosystem, including marine birds (Powers and Brown 1987), marine mammals, and zooplankton (Overholtz and Nicolas 1979; Payne and others 1990). Other sources of perturbations to marine populations caused by the intervention of humans include incidental catches of marine mammals in fishing nets and the growing impacts of pollution. Efforts to reduce stress and mortality among marine mammals caught in fishing nets are being pursued (Bonner 1982; Loughlin and Nelson 1986; Waring and others 1990). Pollution at the continental margins of marine ecosystems that affects cycles of natural productivity, including eutrophication caused by high nitrogen and phosphorus effluent from estuaries, the presence of toxins in poorly treated sewage discharge, and loss of wetland nursery areas to coastal development, is also being addressed (GESAMP

1990). Recent studies implicate changes in climate and the natural environment as a prime driving force of variability in the level of fish populations (Alheit and Bernal 1992; Bakun 1992; Kawasaki and others 1991). The growing awareness that biomass yields are being influenced by multiple but different driving forces in marine ecosystems around the globe has accelerated efforts to broaden research strategies to encompass the effects of food chain dynamics, environmental perturbations, and pollution on living marine resources from an ecosystem perspective.

Mitigating actions to reduce stress on living resources within marine ecosystems are required to ensure the long-term sustainability of biomass yields. The principles adopted by coastal states under the terms of the United Nations Convention for the Law of the Sea have been interpreted as supporting the management of living marine resources from an ecosystem perspective (Belsky 1986, 1989). However, at present no single international institutional regime has been empowered to monitor the changing ecological states of large marine ecosystems and to reconcile the needs of individual nations with those of the community of nations (Myers 1990). In this regard, the need for a regional approach to implement research, monitoring, and the mitigation of stress in support of the development and sustainability of resources at less than the global level has been recognized from a strategic perspective (Malone 1991; Taylor and Groom 1989). From the ecological perspective, the concept that critical processes controlling the structure and function of biological communities can best be addressed on a regional basis (Ricklefs 1987) has been applied to ocean space in the use of marine ecosystems as distinct global units for marine research, monitoring, and management. The concept of monitoring and managing renewable resources from the perspective of a regional ecosystem was the topic of a series of symposia and workshops initiated in 1984 and continuing through 1992, wherein the geographic extent of each region was defined on the basis of ecological criteria. Under this approach, the regional units under consideration are referred to as large marine ecosystems (see table 15-1). These units are

extensive areas of ocean space of approximately 200,000 square kilometers or greater, characterized by distinct bathymetry, hydrography, productivity, and trophically dependent populations (Sherman and Alexander 1989; Sherman and others 1990). The concept of large marine ecosystems defines the unit of resource interest on the order of thousands of kilometers in scale with regard to fish and fisheries yields and represents an energy flow approach to factors determining variability in the ecosystem's productivity. In this approach, large-scale trophic, environmental, and climatic changes are examined in relation to the effects of fishery removals on the long-term sustainability of marine ecosystems.

Temporal and spatial scales influencing biological production in marine ecosystems have been the topic of a number of theoretical and empirical studies. The selection of scale in any

Table 15-1: Countries and Large Marine Ecosystems Accounting for 95 Percent of the Annual Global Catch, by Share of the Total, 1987

Country	Large marine ecosystem	Percentage of global catch
Japan	Oyashio Current, Kuroshio Current, Sea of Okhotsk, Sea of Japan, Yellow Sea, East China Sea, West Bering Sea, East Bering Sea, and Scotia Sea	14.43
Former Soviet Union	Sea of Okhotsk, Barents Sea, Norwegian Shelf, West Bering Sea, East Bering Sea, and Scotia Sea	12.63
United States	Northeast United States Shelf, Southeast United States Shelf, Gulf of Mexico, California Current, Gulf of Alaska, and East Bering Sea	7.03
China	West Bering Sea, Yellow Sea, East China Sea, and South China Sea	6.72
Chile	Humboldt Current	5.98
Peru	Humboldt Current	5.65
Subtotal		52.44
Korea, Federal Republic	Yellow Sea, Sea of Japan, East China Sea, and Kuroshio Current	3.50
Thailand	South China Sea and Indonesian Seas	2.48
Indonesia	Indonesian Seas	2.45
Norway	Norwegian Shelf and Barents Sea	2.40
India	Bay of Bengal and Arabian Sea	2.09
Denmark	Baltic Sea and North Sea	2.07
Iceland	Icelandic Shelf	2.02
Korea, Dem. People's Rep.	Sea of Japan and Yellow Sea	1.99
Philippines	South China Sea and Sulu-Celebes Sea	1.78
Canada	Scotian Shelf, Northeast United States Shelf, and Newfoundland Shelf	1.75
Subtotal		22.53
Cumulative total		74.97

(table continues on next page)

Spain	Iberian Coastal Current and Canary Current	1.69
Mexico	Gulf of California, Gulf of Mexico, and California Current	1.55
South Africa	Benguela Current and Agulhas Current	1.12
France	North Sea, Biscay-Celtic Shelf, and Mediterranean Sea	1.00
Subtotal		5.36
Cumulative total		80.33
Ecuador	Humboldt Current	0.84
United Kingdom & Scotland	North Sea	0.82
Poland	Baltic Sea	0.80
Viet Nam	South China Sea	0.77
Malaysia	Gulf of Thailand, Andaman Sea, Indonesian Seas, and South China Sea	0.74
Brazil	Patagonian Shelf and Brazil Current	0.72
Turkey	Black Sea and Mediterranean Sea	0.72
Argentina	Patagonian Shelf	0.69
Namibia	Benguela Current	0.64
Italy	Mediterranean Sea	0.62
Morocco	Canary Current	0.61
New Zealand	New Zealand Shelf Ecosystem	0.54
Netherlands	North Sea	0.53
Portugal	Iberian Shelf and Canary Current	0.49
Faeroe Islands	Faeroe Plateau	0.44
Subtotal		9.97
Cumulative total		90.30
Pakistan	Bay of Bengal	0.42
Ghana	Gulf of Guinea	0.40
Senegal	Gulf of Guinea and Canary Current	0.35
Venezuela	Caribbean Sea	0.34
Ireland	Biscay-Celtic Shelf	0.31
U.K., England, Wales	North Sea	0.30
Bangladesh	Bay of Bengal	0.29
Hong Kong	South China Sea	0.28
Sweden	Baltic Sea	0.26
Australia	North Australian Shelf and Great Barrier Reef	0.25
Cuba	Caribbean Sea	0.25
Romania	Black Sea	0.25
German Democratic Rep.	Baltic Sea and Scotia Sea	0.22
Panama	California Current and Caribbean Sea	0.21
Sri Lanka	Bay of Bengal	0.19
Nigeria	Gulf of Guinea	0.18
Uruguay	Patagonian Shelf	0.17
Finland	Baltic Sea	0.16
Subtotal		4.83
Cumulative total		95.13

Source: Based on fish catch statistics from FAO 1989.

study is related to the processes under investigation. An excellent treatment of this topic can be found in Steele (1988), which indicates that in relation to general ecology of the sea, the best-known work in the dynamics of fish populations are studies by Schaefer (1954) and Beverton and Holt (1957), following the earlier pioneering approach of Lindemann (1942). However, as Steele (1988) notes, this array of models is unsuitable for considering temporal or spatial variability in the ocean. The large marine ecosystem approach overcomes this difficulty by defining a spatial domain based on ecological principles and, thereby, providing a basis for focused scientific research and monitoring in support of the long-term productivity and sustainability of marine resources. Fish components have adapted reproductive, growth, and feeding strategies to the distinct environmental conditions within the ecosystem. Changes to the components of the system through the removal of fish can trigger a cascade effect involving higher trophic levels including birds and marine mammals and lower trophic levels including zooplankton and the economies dependent on the resources of the ecosystem. The theory and modeling relevant to measuring the changing states of large marine ecosystems are imbedded in contemporary studies of multistable ecosystems (Beddington 1986; Holling 1973, 1986; Pimm 1984) and pattern formation and spatial diffusion in ecosystems (Levin 1978, 1990).

Large marine ecosystems as global management units

Nearly 95 percent of the usable annual yield of the global biomass of fish and other living marine resources is produced in large marine ecosystems within, and adjacent to, the boundaries of the exclusive economic zones of coastal nations located around the margins of the ocean basins. The major biomass is caught within the geographic limits of forty-nine large marine ecosystems (whose boundaries are depicted in figure 15-1). Criteria used for defining the geographic limits of these ecosystems include distinct bathymetry, hydrography, productivity, and trophically dependent populations. Several occupy semi-enclosed seas, such as the Black Sea, the Mediterranean Sea, and the Caribbean Sea. Some can be divided into domains, or subsystems, such as the Adriatic Sea, which is a subsystem of the Mediter-

ranean Sea large marine ecosystem. In others, geographic limits are defined by the scope of continental margins. Among these are the U.S. Northeast Continental Shelf, the East Greenland Sea, and the Northwestern Australian Shelf. The seaward limit of large marine ecosystems extends beyond the physical outer limits of the shelves themselves to include all or a portion of the continental slopes as well. Care has been taken to limit the seaward boundaries to the areas affected by ocean currents, rather than relying simply on the limits of the 200-mile exclusive economic zone or fisheries zone. Among the ocean current's large marine ecosystems are the Humboldt Current, Canary Current, and Kuroshio Current. The large marine ecosystems that together produce approximately 95 percent of the annual yield of global fisheries biomass are listed in table 15-1.

Although the Food and Agriculture Organization's world fishery statistics show an upward trend in annual biomass yields for the past three decades, it is largely the clupeids that are increasing in abundance (FAO 1989). Large numbers of stocks have been and continue to be fished at levels above long-term sustainability. The variations in levels of abundance among species constituting the annual yield of global biomass are indicative of changing regional ecosystem states caused by natural environmental perturbations, overexploitation, and pollution. Although the spatial dimensions preclude a strictly controlled experimental approach to their study, large marine ecosystems are perfectly amenable to the comparative method of science as described by Mayr (1982). Since 1984, thirty case studies investigating the major causes of large-scale perturbations in biomass yields of large marine ecosystems have been completed (see table 15-2).

Historical perspective

For nearly seventy-five years, beginning around the turn of the century, fishery scientists were preoccupied with assessing single-species stock, although biological oceanographers did not achieve any great success in predicting fish yield based on food chain studies. As a result, through the mid-1970s, predictions of the levels of biomass yields for different regions of the world's ocean were open to disagreement (Alverson, Longhurst, and Gulland 1970; Lasker 1988; Ryther

Figure 15-1: World Map of Large Marine Ecosystems

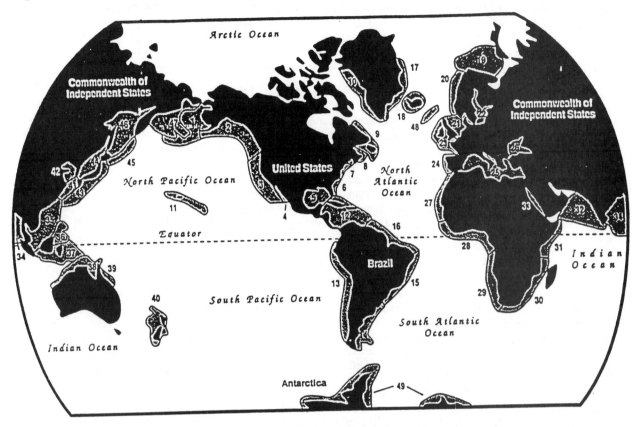

1.	Eastern Bering Sea	25.	Mediterranean Sea
2.	Gulf of Alaska	26.	Black Sea
3.	California Current	27.	Canary Current
4.	Gulf of California	28.	Guinea Current
5.	Gulf of Mexico	29.	Benguela Current
6.	Southeast U.S. Continental Shelf	30.	Agulhas Current
7.	Northeast U.S. Continental Shelf	31.	Somali Coastal Current
8.	Scotian Shelf	32.	Arabian Sea
9.	Newfoundland Shelf	33.	Red Sea
10.	West Greenland Shelf	34.	Bay of Bengal
11.	Insular Pacific--Hawaiian	35.	South China Sea
12.	Caribbean Sea	36.	Sulu-Celebes Seas
13.	Humboldt Current	37.	Indonesian Seas
14.	Patagonian Shelf	38.	Northern Australian Shelf
15.	Brazil Current	39.	Great Barrier Reef
16.	Northeast Brazil Shelf	40.	New Zealand Shelf
17.	East Greenland Shelf	41.	East China Sea
18.	Iceland Shelf	42.	Yellow Sea
19.	Barents Sea	43.	Kuroshio Current
20.	Norwegian Shelf	44.	Sea of Japan
21.	North Sea	45.	Oyashio Current
22.	Baltic Sea	46.	Sea of Okhotsk
23.	Celtic-Biscay Shelf	47.	West Bering Sea
24.	Iberian Coastal	48.	Faroe Plateau
		49.	Antarctic

Table 15-2: Twenty-Nine Large Marine Ecosystems and Subsystems for which Principal, Secondary, or Tertiary Driving Forces Controlling Variability in Biomass Yields Had Been Synthesized as of February 1991

Large marine ecosystem	*Author and reference*
U.S. Northeast Continental Shelf	Sissenwine (Sherman and Alexander 1986)
	Falkowski (Sherman, Alexander, and Gold 1991)
U.S. Southeast Continental Shelf	Yoder (Sherman, Alexander, and Gold 1991)
Gulf of Mexico	Richards and McGowan (Sherman and Alexander 1989)
	Brown and others (Sherman, Alexander, and Gold 1991)
California Current	MacCall (Sherman and Alexander 1986)
	Mullin (Sherman, Alexander, and Gold 1991)
	Bottom (Sherman, Alexander, and Gold 1993)
Eastern Bering Shelf	Incze and Schumacher (Sherman and Alexander 1986)
West Greenland Shelf	Hovgaard and Buch (Sherman, Alexander, and Gold 1990)
Norwegian Sea	Ellertsen and others (Sherman, Alexander, and Gold 1990)
Barents Sea	Skjoldal and Rey (Sherman and Alexander 1989)
	Borisov (Sherman, Alexander, and Gold 1991)
North Sea	Daan (Sherman and Alexander 1986)
Baltic Sea	Kullenberg (Sherman and Alexander 1986; Sherman, Alexander, and Gold 1993)
Iberian Coastal	Wyatt and Perez-Gandaras (Sherman and Alexander 1989)
Mediterranean-Adriatic Sea	Bombace (Sherman, Alexander, and Gold 1993)
Canary Current	Bas (Sherman, Alexander, and Gold 1993)
Gulf of Guinea	Binet and Marchal (Sherman, Alexander, and Gold 1993)
Benguela Current	Crawford and others (Sherman and Alexander 1989)
Patagonian Shelf	Bakun (Sherman, Alexander, and Gold 1993)
Caribbean Sea	Richards and Bohnsack (Sherman, Alexander, and Gold 1990)
South China Sea—Gulf of Thailand	Piyakarnchana (Sherman and Alexander 1989)
Yellow Sea	Tang (Sherman and Alexander 1989)
Sea of Okhotsk	Kusnetsov (Sherman, Alexander, and Gold 1993)
Humboldt Current	Alheit and Bernal (Sherman, Alexander, and Gold 1993)
Indonesia Seas—Banda Sea	Zijlstra and Baars (Sherman, Alexander, and Gold 1990)
Bay of Bengal	Dwivedi (Sherman, Alexander, and Gold 1993)
Antarctic Marine	Scully and others (Sherman and Alexander 1986; Sherman, Alexander, and Gold 1993)
Weddell Sea	Hempel (Sherman, Alexander, and Gold 1990)
Kuroshio Current	Terazaki (Sherman and Alexander 1989)
Oyashio Current	Minoda (Sherman and Alexander 1989)
Great Barrier Reef	Bradbury and Mundy (Sherman and Alexander 1989)
	Kelleher (Sherman, Alexander, and Gold 1993)
South China Sea	Pauly and Christensen (Sherman, Alexander, and Gold 1993)

1969). A milestone in fishery science was achieved in 1975 when the International Council for the Exploration of the Sea convened a symposium that focused on changes in the fish stocks of the North Sea and their causes. The symposium, which dealt with the North Sea as an ecosystem, following the lead of Steele (1974), Cushing (1975), Andersen and Ursin (1977), and others, was prompted by a rather dramatic shift in the dominance of the finfish species of the North Sea, which changed from a balanced pelagic and demersal finfish community before 1960 to become a dominant demersal community from the mid-1960s through the mid-1970s. Although no consensus on cause and effect was reached, the convener suggested that previous studies may have been too narrowly focused and that future studies should take into consideration, from an ecosystems perspective, fish stocks, their competitors, predators, and prey, and their interactions with the environment, fisheries, and pollution (Hempel 1978).

Perturbations and driving forces in large marine ecosystems

Marine scientists, geographers, economists, government representatives, and lawyers are becoming more and more aware of the utility of taking a more holistic ecosystem approach to resource management (Alexander 1989; Belsky 1989; Byrne 1986; Christy 1986; Crawford, Shannon, and Shelton 1989; Morgan 1989; Prescott 1989). The principal driving forces for changes in biomass vary among ecosystems (Sherman and others 1990). On a global scale, the loss of sustained biomass yields from large marine ecosystems as a result of mismanagement and overexploitation has not been fully investigated but is likely very large (Gulland 1984). It is clear that "experts" have been off the mark in earlier estimates of global yield of fisheries biomass. Projections given in *The Global 2000 Report* (U.S. Council on Environmental Quality 1980) expected the world's annual yield to rise little, if at all, by the year 2000 from the 60 million metric tons reached in the 1970s. In contrast, estimates given in *The Resourceful Earth* (Wise 1984) argue for an annual yield of 100 million to 120 million metric tons by the year 2000. The trend is upward; the 1988 yields of marine global fishery reached 86.8 million metric tons (FAO 1990). The lack of a clear definition of actual and potential global yield is not unexpected, given the limited efforts presently under way to improve the base of global information on yields of living marine resources.

More and more attention has been focused over the past few years on synthesizing biological and environmental information on the natural productivity of the fishery biomass within large marine ecosystems in an effort to identify the principal, secondary, and where important, the tertiary forces causing major shifts in the species composition of biomass yields. Effective management from an ecosystems perspective will be contingent on identifying these forces. Management of species responding to strong environmental signals will be enhanced by improving our understanding of the physical factors forcing biological changes, whereas in other large marine ecosystems when the prime driving force is predation—either by natural predators or by humans expressed as excessive fishing mortalities—options can be explored for implementing adaptive management strategies. Mitigation is required to ensure that the pollu-tion of the coastal zone of large marine ecosystems is reduced and does not become a principal driving force. Concerns remain regarding the socioeconomic and political difficulties in management across national boundaries, as in the case of the Sea of Japan ecosystem, where five countries share fishery resources (Morgan 1988), or the North Sea ecosystem, or the Caribbean Sea ecosystem, where thirty-eight nations share resources.

Some marine scientists consider changes in the ocean climate of the northern North Atlantic during the late 1960s and early 1970s as the dominant cause of change in the structure of the food chain and biomass yields of at least three northern North Atlantic large marine ecosystems. The population of important fish stocks (such as capelin and cod) has declined on a large scale within the Norwegian Sea, Barents Sea, and West Greenland Sea ecosystems. In the West Greenland Sea ecosystem, cod stocks have been displaced southward since 1980, attended by a decrease in their average size and abundance. Biomass yields declined from about 300,000 metric tons a year in the mid-1960s to less than 15,000 metric tons in 1985. Both changes appear to have been due to short-term cooling that influenced the stability of water masses and the dynamics of the plankton community, adversely affecting the growth and survival of early developmental stages of cod and reducing recruitment. Since the 1920s, the annual biomass yield of cod has been related to temperature, with catches increasing during warm periods and declining during cool periods. The effects of fishing mortality on the decline of the cod are secondary to the major influence of climatic conditions over the North Atlantic (Hovgaard and Buch 1990).

To the east, changes in the temperature structure of the Norwegian Sea ecosystem appear to be the major force controlling the recruitment of important cod stocks. Strong or medium production of cod biomass is related to warmer temperatures. The conditions for growth and survival of early developmental stages of cod are enhanced during warmer years, when the larval cod are maintained for longer periods within coastal nursery grounds, where their most important prey organism—the copepod, *Calanus finmarchicus*—swarms in high densities under conditions of well-defined thermocline structure and consequently under optimal conditions for feeding on the abundant phytoplankton.

The changes in biomass yields of the Barents Sea ecosystem have been attributed primarily to changes in hydrographic conditions and secondarily to excessive fishing mortality. The average annual biomass yield of the ecosystem in the 1970s was about 2 million metric tons (fish, crustaceans, molluscs, and algae). However, by the 1980s annual yields declined to approximately 350,000 metric tons. The decline of warm Atlantic water flowing into the Barents Sea ecosystem, coupled with excessive levels of fishing effort, led to (1) collapse of the major fisheries of the region (cod, capelin, haddock, herring, redfish, and shrimp), (2) subsequent disruption in the structure of the food chain, and (3) increase in the abundance of the shrimp-like euphausiids representing a significant amount of biomass that is underused in relation to the potential sustained yield of this ecosystem. Given the depressed state of the fish stocks, any restoration management would need to consider significantly reducing the fishing effort of the fishermen of Norway and the former Soviet Union, the coastal nations that share the resources of the Barents Sea ecosystem (Borisov 1991; Skjoldal and Rey 1989).

In the North Sea ecosystem, important species have flipped from a position of dominance to one of subordination. This biomass flip in the North Sea occurred over the decade of the 1960s. The finfish stocks of the North Sea ecosystem have been subjected to intensive fishing mortality. The yields of pelagic herring and mackerel decreased from 5 to 1.7 million metric tons, whereas small fast-growing and commercially less desirable sand lance, Norway pout, and sprat increased by 1.5 million metric tons along with an approximate 36 percent increase in gadoid yields. The causes for the biomass flips are poorly understood. Several arguments correlate the flip with changing oceanographic conditions. Others support overexploitation as the major cause. However, none of the arguments can be considered more than speculative at this time, pending rigorous analysis of more recent information (Hempel 1978; Postma and Zijlstra 1988).

Farther to the south, the Iberian Shelf ecosystem has been examined recently in relation to variability of biomass yield. Alternation in the abundance of horse mackerel and sardine within the Iberian Coastal ecosystem is attributed to changes in natural environmental perturbation of its thermal structure rather than to any density-dependent interaction between the two species. Similarly, in the Benguela Current ecosystem of the southwest coast of Africa, the long-term fluctuations in the abundance of pilchard, horse-mackerel, and hakes are attributed to changes in the oceanographic regime (see figure 15-2). The Benguela large marine ecosystem is bounded by warm water at both extremes: that toward the equator and that toward the South Pole. Cold, nutrient-rich water is upwelled with moderate intensity in the central section and more intensely in the northern and southern areas. Environmental conditions favor either the epipelagic or the demersal species, never both simultaneously, and have been the principal driving force for large-scale shifts in abundance among the fish species. The effects of the fisheries on changes in species abundance are secondary. Changes in abundance of pilchard stocks have led to detectable effects in the abundance of dependent predator species, particularly marine birds (Crawford, Shannon, and Shelton 1989).

The greatest increases in biomass yields in the Pacific have been reported at the area of confluence between the Oyashio and Kuroshio Current ecosystems off Japan (Minoda 1989; Terazaki 1989) and in the Humboldt Current ecosystem off Chile. In the Oyashio and Kuroshio Current ecosys-

Figure 15-2: Estimated Biomass of Pilchard (*Sardinops ocellatus*), Cape Horse-mackerel (*Trachurus capensis*), and Cape Hakes (*Merluccius capensis and paradoxus*) of the Benguela Current Ecosystem, 1950s–80s

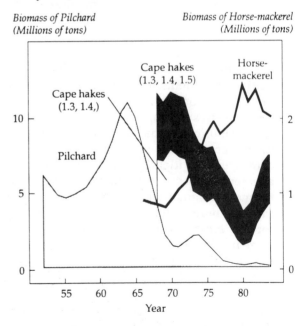

Source: Crawford, Shannon, and Shelton 1989.

tems, the yield of Japanese sardines increased from less than one-half million metric tons in 1975 to just over 4 million metric tons in 1984 (see figure 15-3). The yield of the Chilean sardine in the Humboldt Current ecosystem also increased from about 500,000 metric tons in 1974 to 4.3 million metric tons in 1986. The increased yields have been attributed to density-independent processes involving an increase in productivity of the lower food chain, made possible by coastward shifts in the boundary areas of the Oyashio and Kuroshio systems and shifts of the water mass in the Humboldt Current ecosystem. The effects of fishing on the sardines in both areas are of secondary importance compared with the enhanced productivity of the phytoplankton and zooplankton components of the ecosystems, which improved the environment for growth and recruitment. Studies are under way to determine the extent of the teleconnection between the Pacific-wide El Niño events of the past decade and both (1) the multimillion-metric-ton increases in yields of sardines occurring nearly simultaneously in

the northern and southern hemispheres and (2) the dramatic decline—from about 12 million metric tons in 1970 to less than 2 million metric tons by 1976—in the biomass yields of anchovy in the northern areas of the Humboldt Current ecosystem in the early 1970s (Canon 1986; see figure 15-4).

Although less dramatic, the long-term shifts in the abundance of both sardines and anchovies within the California Current ecosystem are considered the result primarily of natural environmental change and secondarily of intensive fishing, rather than of any density-dependent competition between the two species (see figure 15-5; MacCall 1986).

Changes in biomass yields of two other Pacific Rim large marine ecosystems have been the result of overexploitation. The introduction of highly efficient modern trawlers to the Gulf of Thailand ecosystem led to excessive fishing mortality and a marked reduction in annual yields of biomass of fish for human consumption between 1977 and 1982 (Piyakarnchana 1989; figure 15-6). Intensive fishery effort resulted in the depletion of the demersal fish stocks and dramatic reductions in the biomass yields of the Yellow Sea ecosystem. Between 1958 and 1968, fisheries yields declined

Figure 15-3: Catches of Japanese Sardines from the Area of Confluence between the Oyashio Current Ecosystem and the Kuroshio Current Ecosystem off the Coast of Japan, 1975-84

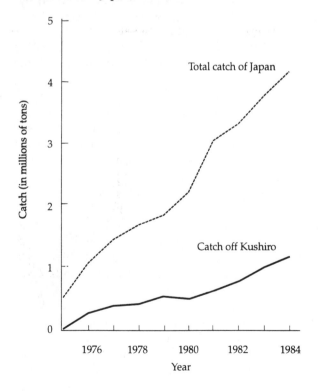

Source: Minoda 1989.

Figure 15-4: Catches of Anchovies and Sardines from the Waters of the Humboldt Current Ecosystem off the Coasts of Chile and Peru, 1964-83

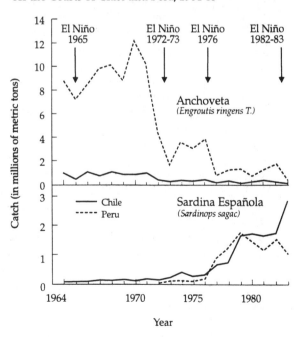

Source: Canon 1986.

Figure 15-5: Time Series of Sardine (Age 2+) and Anchovy Spawning Biomass (Log Scale) of the California Current Ecosystem, 1935-85

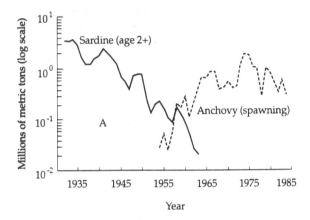

Note: The area denoted "A" indicates the approximate anchovy spawning biomass in 1940-41.
Source: MacCall 1986.

Figure 15-6: Total Catch of Carnivorous Feeding Species of Fish from the Gulf of Thailand Ecosystem, 1977-83

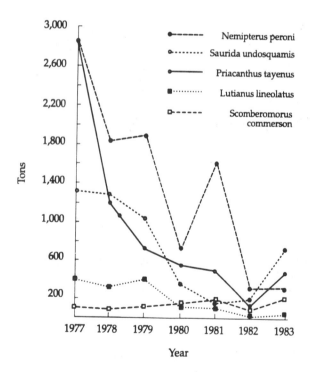

Source: Piyakarnchana 1989.

from 180,000 to less than 10,000 metric tons. The fishery then shifted to harvesting pelagic stocks, reaching a level of 200,000 metric tons in 1972, followed by a reduction to less than 20,000 metric tons in 1981. The fisheries of the Yellow Sea in 1982 shifted principally to anchovy and sardine, with a total annual yield of all species 40 percent lower than the 1958 level. The demersal fishery remains in a depleted state (Tang 1989; see figure 15-7).

The importance of a natural predator driving an ecosystem is evident in the large-scale changes in the community structure of the Great Barrier Reef ecosystem that extends over 230,000 square kilometers of the Queensland continental shelf. The predation by the crown-of-thorns starfish in the 1960s and 1970s resulted in a shift in the biomass of corals, community structure of the benthos, and a decoupling of energy transfer to several fish stocks.

To the north and west of Australia lies the relatively pristine Banda Sea ecosystem, where no large-scale fisheries are presently conducted. The ecosystem is under the influence of monsoon-induced seasonal periods of large-scale upwelling and downwelling. Biological feedback to these environmental signals is reflected in the changes in phytoplankton, mesozooplankton, micronekton, and fish. During upwelling events, productivity of the ecosystem is enhanced by a factor of 2 to 3. The biomass of pelagic fish resources is also higher during the upwelling period. The fish biomass of the ecosystem is estimated at between 600,000 and 900,000 metric tons in the peak upwelling season (August) and between 150,000 and 250,000 metric tons in the downwelling period (February). The estimated sustained annual biomass yield of the ecosystem is approximately 30,000 metric tons of pelagic fish.

Management considerations

Several ecologists have reviewed the empirical and theoretical aspects of yield models for large marine ecosystems. According to Beddington (1986), Daan (1986), Levin (1990), and Mangel (1991), published dynamic models of marine ecosystems offer little guidance on the detailed behavior of communities. However, these authors concur on the need for covering the common ground between observation and theory by implementing monitoring efforts on the large spatial and long temporal scales (decadal) of key components of the systems. Levin (1990) describes the

Figure 15-7: Annual Catch of Dominant Species of the Yellow Sea Ecosystem, 1953-84

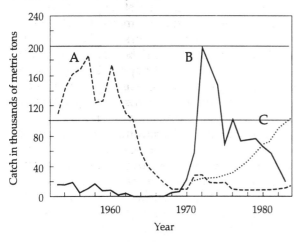

Note: A, small yellow croaker and hairtail; B, Pacific herring and Japanese mackerel; C, *Setipinna taty*, anchovy, and scaled sardine.
Source: Tang 1989.

sequence for improving our understanding of the possible mechanisms underlying observed patterns in large marine ecosystems as examination of (1) statistical analyses of observed distributional patterns of physical and biological variables, (2) construction of competing models of variability and patchiness based on statistical analyses and natural scales of variability of critical processes, (3) evaluation of competing models through experimental and theoretical studies of component systems, and (4) integration of validated component models to provide predictive models for population dynamics and redistribution. This approach is consistent with the recent observation by Mangel (1991) that empirical support for the currently used models of large marine ecosystems is relatively weak and that a new generation of models is needed to enhance the link between theory and empirical results.

Effective management strategies for large marine ecosystems will be contingent on identifying the major forces causing large-scale changes in biomass yields. Management of species responding to strong environmental signals will be enhanced by improving our understanding of the physical factors forcing biological changes; where the prime driving force is predation, options can be explored for implementing adaptive management strategies. Remedial actions are required to ensure that the pollution of the coastal zone is reduced and does not become a principal driving force in any large marine ecosystem. For at least one system, the Antarctic, a management regime has evolved that is based on an ecosystem perspective in the adoption and implementation of the Convention for the Conservation of Antarctic Marine Living Resources (Sherman and Ryan 1988). Efforts are also under way to manage the large marine ecosystems of the United States' exclusive economic zone, including the northern California Current ecosystem (Bottom and others 1989).

A systems approach to the management of large marine ecosystems is depicted in table 15-3. These ecosystems represent the link between local events (such as fishing, pollution, environ-

Table 15-3: Key Spatial and Temporal Scales and Principal Elements of a Systems Approach to the Research and Management of Large Marine Ecosystems

Scale or element	Description
Scale	
Spatial	Global (world's ocean), regional (exclusive economic zones), local
Temporal	Millennia-decadal, decadal-seasonal, seasonal-daily
Unit	Pelagic biogeographic, large marine ecosystems, subsystems
Element	
Research element	Spawning strategies; feeding strategies; productivity, trophodynamics; stock fluctuations, recruitment, and mortality; natural variability (hydrography, currents, water masses, weather); human perturbations (fishing, waste disposal, petrogenic hydrocarbon impacts, aerosol contaminants, eutrophication effects)
Management elements—options and advice—international, national, local	Bioenvironmental and socioeconomic models; management to optimize fisheries yields
Feedback loop	Evaluation of ecosystem status, fisheries status, and management practices

217

ment) occurring on the daily-to-seasonal temporal scale and their effects on living marine resources and the more ubiquitous global effects of climatic changes on the multidecadal time scale. The regional and temporal focus of season to decade is consistent with the evolved spawning and feeding migrations of fish, the keystone species of most large marine ecosystems. These seasonal migrations occur over hundreds to thousands of kilometers within the unique physical and biological characteristics of the regional large marine ecosystem to which the species have adapted. Because the fisheries represent most of the usable biomass yield of the large marine ecosystems and fish populations consist of several age classes, it follows that measures of variability in growth, recruitment, and mortality should be conducted over multiyear time scales. The naturally occurring environmental events and the human-induced perturbations that affect the demography of populations within the ecosystem should be considered. Management options from an ecosystems perspective should be based on scientific inferences of the principal causes of variability in abundance and should give due consideration to socioeconomic needs. The final element in the system, with regard to the concept of resource maintenance and sustained yield, is the feedback loop that allows the effects of management actions to be evaluated at the fisheries level (single species, multiple species) and the ecosystem level.

It will be necessary to conduct supportive research on the processes controlling sustained productivity of large marine ecosystems. Within several of these ecosystems, including the Northeast Shelf, Gulf of Mexico, California Current, and Eastern Bering Sea, important hypotheses concerned with the growing impacts of pollution, overexploitation, and environmental changes on sustained biomass yields are under investigation (see table 15-4). Comparing the results of research among systems should allow us to learn how the systems respond and recover from stress and to narrow the context of unresolved problems and capitalize on current research efforts. The list of reports describing the effects of biological and physical perturbations on the fisheries biomass yields of thirty large marine ecosystems given in table 15-3 addresses questions similar to those posed a few years ago by Beddington (1984, p. 209):

> There are a number of scientific questions which are central to the rational management of marine communities, but all revolve around the question of sustainability.

> What levels of mortality imposed by a fishery will permit a sustainable yield? Are there levels below which a fish population will not recover? Can judicious manipulation of the catch composition of the fishery alter the potential of the community to produce yields of a particular type, e.g., high value species? Can a community be depleted to a level where its potential for producing a harvestable resource is reduced?

> With the exception of the first question, these questions and others like them are rarely explicitly addressed in the scientific bodies of the various fisheries' organizations. Instead, such bodies concentrate on the estimation of stock abundance and the calculation of allowable catch levels, although often implicit in the advice given by these bodies to management are a set of beliefs about the answers to such questions.

Given the increasing number of responsibilities of government agencies for (1) managing fisheries, (2) mitigating pollution, (3) reducing environmental stress, and (4) restoring lost habitat, it is not surprising that interest in pursuing resource management problems from an ecosystem perspective is growing.

The topic of change and persistence in marine communities and the need for multispecies and ecosystem perspectives in fishery management relate to reports of changing states of marine ecosystems (Sugihara and others 1984). Collapses of the Pacific sardine in the California Current ecosystem, the pilchard in the Benguela Current ecosystem, and the anchovy in the Humboldt Current ecosystem are but a few examples of cascading effects on other components of the ecosystem, including marine birds (Burger 1988; Crawford, Shannon, and Shelton 1989; Croxall 1987; MacCall 1986).

Ecosystem assessment and monitoring

The National Marine Fisheries Service of the National Oceanic and Atmospheric Administration (NMFS; NOAA) has focused greater emphasis over the past decade on approaching fisheries research from a regional ecosystem perspective in large marine ecosystems within and adjacent

Table 15-4: Selected Hypotheses Concerning Variability in Biomass Yields of Large Marine Ecosystems

Ecosystem	*Predominant variables*	*Hypothesis*
Oyashio Current, Kuroshio Current, California Current, Humboldt Current, Benguela Current, Iberian Coastal	Density-independent natural environmental perturbations	*Increase in Clupeoid population:* Predominant variables influencing changes in biomass of clupeoids are increases in water-column productivity resulting from shifts in the direction and flow velocities of the currents and changes in upwelling within the ecosystem
Yellow Sea, U.S. Northeast Continental Shelf, Gulf of Thailand	Density-dependent predation	*Declines in fish stocks:* Precipitous decline in biomass of fish stocks is the result of excessive fishing mortality reducing the probability of reproductive success; losses in biomass are attributed to excesses of human predation expressed as overfishing
Great Barrier Reef	Density-dependent predation	*Change in ecosystem structure:* Extreme predation of crown-of-thorns starfish has disrupted normal links in the food chain between benthic primary production and the fish component of the reef ecosystem
East Greenland Sea, Barents Sea, Norwegian Sea	Density-independent natural environmental perturbations	*Shifts in the abundance of fish stock biomass:* Major shifts in the levels of fish stock biomass within the ecosystems are attributed to large-scale environmental changes in water movements and temperature structure
Baltic Sea	Density-independent pollution	*Changes in level of ecosystem productivity:* Apparent increases in level of productivity are attributed to the effects of nitrate enrichment resulting from elevated levels of agricultural contaminant inputs from the bordering land masses
Antarctic Marine	Density-dependent perturbations	*Status of krill stocks:* Annual natural production cycle of krill is in balance with food requirements of dependent predator populations; surplus production is available to support economically significant yields, but the sustainable level of fishing effort is not known
	Density-independent natural environmental perturbations	*Shifts in abundance in krill biomass:* Major shifts in abundance levels of krill biomass within the ecosystem are attributed to large-scale changes in water movements and productivity

to the exclusive economic zone of the United States: the Northeast Continental Shelf, the Southeast Continental Shelf, the Gulf of Mexico, the California Current, the Gulf of Alaska, the Eastern Bering Sea, and the Insular Pacific, including the Hawaiian Islands. These ecosystems, in 1989, yielded 9.0 billion pounds of fisheries biomass valued at approximately $17 billion to the economy of the United States (a billion is 1,000 million).

A description of the sampling programs providing the biomass assessments within the U. S. exclusive economic zone has been described in Folio Map 7 produced by the Office of Oceanography and Marine Assessment of NOAA's National Ocean Service. The map depicts the seven ecosystems under investigation (see figure 15-8). Sampling programs supporting biomass estimates in large marine ecosystems within and adjacent

to the exclusive economic zone of the United States are designed to (1) provide detailed statistical analyses of fish and invertebrate populations constituting the principal yield species of biomass, (2) estimate future trends in biomass yields, and (3) monitor changes in the principal populations. The information obtained by these programs helps managers understand the dynamics of marine ecosystems and how these dynamics affect harvestable stocks. Additionally, by tracking components of the ecosystems, these programs can detect changes, natural or induced by humans, and warn of events with possible economic repercussions. Although sampling schemes and efforts vary among programs (depending on habitats, species present, and specific regional concerns), they generally involve systematic collection and analysis of catch statistics; the use of NOAA vessels for fisheries-indepen-

Figure 15-8: Large Marine Ecosystems of the United States

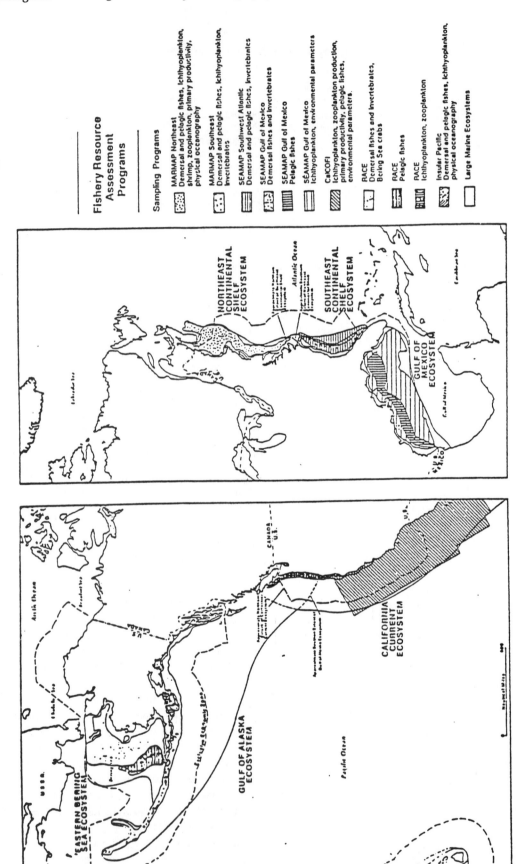

Source: Modified from U.S. Department of Commerce 1988, Folio Map no. 7.

dent bottom and midwater trawl surveys of adults and juveniles; ichthyoplankton surveys for larvae and eggs; measurements of zooplankton standing stock, primary productivity, nutrient concentrations, and important physical parameters (water temperature, salinity, density, current velocity and direction, air temperature, cloud cover, and light conditions); and, in some habitats, measurements of contaminants and their effects.

At the shoreward margin of large marine ecosystems, monitoring efforts include the use of mussels and other biological indicator species to measure the effects of pollution as part of NOAA's Status and Trends Program. The pilot EMAP Program of the U.S. Environmental Protection Agency, which focused on the estuarine and nearshore monitoring of contaminants in the water column, substrate, and selected groups of organisms, was extended to more open waters of large marine ecosystems in cooperation with NOAA during 1992 and 1993. In July 1991, a panel of international experts meeting at Cornell University recommended two methods for measuring the changing state of large marine ecosystems: (1) regular trawling using a stratified random sampling design and (2) plankton surveys (see table 15-5; Sherman and Laughlin 1992). Large-scale changes in the fisheries of the North Sea and the Northeast Continental Shelf of the United States have been successfully analyzed using trawling techniques for several decades (Azarovitz and Grosslein 1987). The surveys have been conducted by relatively large research vessels. However, standardized sampling procedures, when deployed from small calibrated trawlers, can provide important information on fish stocks. The fish catch provides biological samples for analyzing and comparing the contents of the stomach, age, growth, fecundity, and size (ICES 1991) and for clarifying and quantifying multispecies trophic relationships. Samples of fish caught by trawls can also be used to monitor the effect of gross pathological conditions that may be associated with coastal pollution.

The need for both biological and environmental monitoring in the North Sea ecosystem has been emphasized following the Symposium on Long-Term Changes in the Fish Stocks of the North Sea ecosystem (Hempel 1978). In this regard, physical measurements can be made from small trawlers or ships of opportunity, using readily available and relatively inexpensive systems for measuring temperature and salinity of the water column. Standard logs for observing weather—important in detecting global change—are an important component of the data-collecting effort. The monitoring of changes in fish stocks is ongoing in large marine ecosystems across the North Atlantic basin, including the Northeast U.S. Shelf, the Canadian Scotian Shelf, Newfoundland Shelf, the Greenland Shelf, Icelandic Shelf, Norwegian Shelf, Barents Sea Shelf, and the North Sea.

Table 15-5: Description of the Core Marine Ecosystem Monitoring Program

Focus	*Description*
Candidate parameters	Chlorophyll fluorescence,[a] copepod diversity,[a] diatom/flagllate ratio,[a] fisheries survey, nitrite, nitrate, nutrients,[a] photosynthetic active radiation,[a] pollution index (hydrocarbons, sewage), primary production,[b] rainfall or runoff, salinity structure,[a] stratification index,[a] temperature structure,[a] transparency and biomass,[a] wind strength and direction, zooplankton composition
Assessment	Changes in abundance and distribution
Biology	Age and growth, length, pathology, predator-prey
Acoustics for pelagics	Nets for demersals
Physical measurements	Salinity, temperature
Chemical measurements	Water samples (nutrients, productivity, pollutants)

a. Measurements derived from instrumented Continuous Plankton Recorder/Undulating Oceanographic Recorder sensors.
b. Based on inclusion of double-flash pump and probe system.
Note: The core program is based on transects sampled by UOR or instrumented CPR, supplemented by satellite oceanography and systematic trawl and acoustic surveys.
Source: Sherman and Laughlin 1992.

The plankton of large marine ecosystems can be measured at a relatively low cost by deploying continuous plankton recorder systems from commercial vessels of opportunity (Glover 1967). The advanced plankton recorders can be fitted with sensors for temperature, salinity, chlorophyll, nitrate/nitrite, light, bioluminescence, zooplankton, and ichthyoplankton (Aiken 1981), providing the means to monitor changes in phytoplankton, zooplankton, relative productivity, species composition and dominance, physical and nutrient characteristics, and biofeedback of the plankton to the stress of climatic change (Colebrook 1986; Dickson and others 1988; Jossi and Smith 1990; Sherman, Cohen, Langton 1990). Plankton monitoring using the continuous plankton recorder system is expanding in the North Atlantic (IOC 1992).

A critical feature of the strategy for monitoring large marine ecosystems is the development of a consistent long-term data base for understanding interannual changes and multi-year trends in biomass yields for each of the systems. For example, during the late 1960s and early 1970s, when foreign fishing was intense within the Northeast Continental Shelf ecosystem, marked alterations in the abundance of fish, and particularly among species of fish, were recorded. The finfish biomass of important species (cod, haddock, flounders, herring, and mackerel) declined by

Figure 15-10: Trends in Biomass of Mackerel (Age 1+) and Herring (Age 3+) and Trends in Relative Abundance of Sand Lance (Age 2+), 1970-86

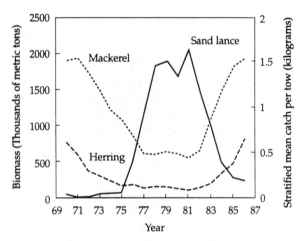

Source: Fogarty and others 1991. Trends in biomass are derived from virtual population analysis, and trends in relative abundance are based on research vessel surveys.

approximately 50 percent (see figure 15-9). This was followed by increases in the biomass of sand lance (see figure 15-10) and elasmobranchs (dogfish and skates; see figure 15-11) and led to the conclusion that the overall carrying capacity of the ecosystem for finfish had not changed, rather that excessive fishing of highly valued species allowed low-valued species to increase in abun-

Figure 15-9: Annual Catches and Estimated Biomass of Exploitable Fish and Squid of the Northeastern Continental Shelf Ecosystem, 1960-82

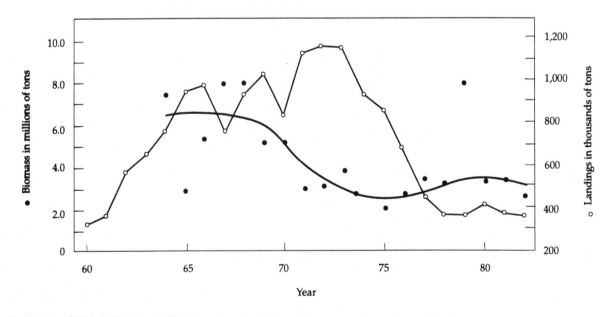

Note: Excludes menhaden and large pelagic species, such as large sharks and tuna.
Source: Sissenwine 1986.

Figure 15-11. Species Shift and Abundance of Small Elasmobranchs (Dogfish and Skates) on Georges Bank within the Northeast Continental Shelf Ecosystem of the United States, 1963 and 1986, and within the North Sea Ecosystem, 1977–85

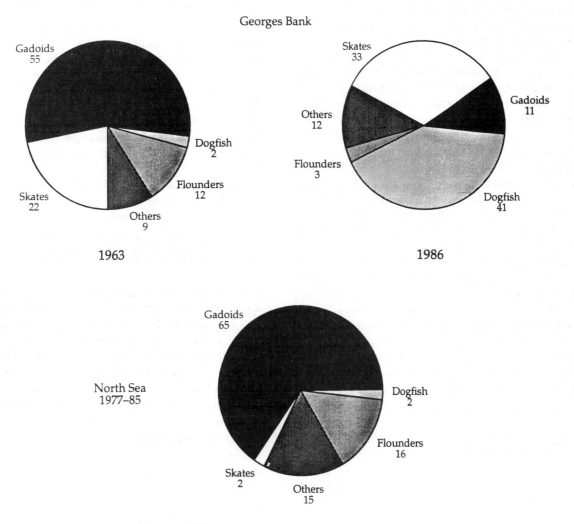

Source: Sherman, Cohen, and Langton 1990.

dance. Catch-per-unit-of-effort and fishery-independent bottom trawling survey data were critical sources of information in this case. However, the lower end of the food chain in the offshore waters of the ecosystem remained unchanged, as described earlier by Bigelow (1926) and Riley, Stommel, and Bumpus (1949), suggesting that the ecosystem remained highly productive during a period in which human intervention—fishing—caused the species dominance of fish to shift (Sherman and others 1983). The natural resilience of the ecosystem—its ability to recover from stress—can be documented in the recovery of mackerel to former (pre-1960) levels of abundance and the apparent recovery of herring to

1960s level of abundance on Georges Bank (Murawski 1991; Smith and Morse 1990).

Changing ecosystem states and health indexes

More and more effort has been directed over the past few years to synthesizing available information on factors influencing the natural productivity of fishery biomass and the changing states and health of large marine ecosystems. The goal has been to identify principal, secondary, and tertiary driving forces causing major changes in ecosystem states and biomass yields. Ecosystem health is a concept of wide interest for which a single precise scientific definition is problematic. Ecosystem health is used here to describe the resilience, stability, and productivity of the ecosystem in relation to its changing states. In present practice, assessing the health of large marine ecosystems relies on a series of indicators and indexes (Costanza 1992; Karr 1992; Norton and Ulanowicz 1992; Rapport 1992). The overriding objective is to monitor changes in health from an ecosystems perspective as a measure of the overall performance of a complex system (Costanza 1992). The health paradigm is an evolving concept based on the multiple-state comparisons of resilience and stability of the ecosystem (Costanza 1992; Holling 1986; Pimm 1984). Several variables important to the changing states and health of marine ecosystems are defined in table 15-6. Following the definition of Costanza (1992), to be healthy and sustainable, an ecosystem must maintain its level of metabolic activity and its internal structure and organization and it must be resistant to external stress over time and space (see table 15-7). Among the indexes being considered as experimental measures of changing ecosystem states and health are (1) diversity, (2) stability, (3) yields, (4) production, and (5) resilience.

The data from which to derive the experimental indexes are obtained from time-series monitoring of key ecosystem parameters. A prototype effort to validate their utility is being developed by NOAA at the Northeast Fisheries Science Center. The ecosystem sampling strategy is focused on parameters relating to the resources at risk from overexploitation, species protected by legislative authority (marine mammals), and other key biological and physical components at the lower end of the food chain (plankton, nutrients, hydrography; Sherman and Laughlin 1992). The parameters of interest depicted in figure 15-12 include the composition and biomass of zooplankton, marine mammals, and finfish; structure of the water column; photosynthetically active radiation; transparency; chlorophyll a; nitrite; nitrate; primary production; pollution; runoff; wind stress; community structure and counts of sea birds; domoic acid; saxitoxin; and paralytic shellfish poisoning. These experimental parameters incorporate the behavior of individuals, the resultant responses of populations and communities, as well as their interactions with the physical and chemical environment. The selected parameters, if measured in all large marine ecosystems, would permit us to compare the changing

states and health status among ecosystems. The interrelations between the data sets and the selected parameters are indicated by the arrows leading from column 1 to column 2 in figure 15-12. The measured components are depicted in relation to the structure in a diagrammatic conceptualization of patterns and activities within the large marine ecosystem at different levels of complexity (see figure 15-13). The broad-spectrum approach to research and monitoring of large marine ecosystems provides a conceptual framework for collaboration in process-oriented studies conducted by the National Science Foundation and NOAA on the Northeast Continental Shelf (GLOBEC 1991) and proposed for other large marine ecosystems (California Current, Antarctic marine ecosystems) and in the proposed study of the Indian Ocean–Somalia Current ecosystem planned as part of the Joint Global Ocean Flux Studies (JGOFS).

Initial efforts to examine changes in the state of ecosystems and relative health within a single ecosystem are under way for four areas of the Northeast Shelf ecosystem: Gulf of Maine, Georges Bank, Southern New England, and Mid-Atlantic Bight. Initial studies of the structure, function, and productivity of the system (Sherman and others 1988) report that the principal driving force affecting sustainable yield is fishing mortality expressed as predation on the fish stocks of the ecosystem and that long-term sustainability of high-economic-yield species depends on the application of adaptive management strategies (Murawski 1991; Sissenwine and Cohen 1991).

Several strategies for managing fish stocks of the Northeast Shelf ecosystem are under consideration by the New England Fishery Management Council and the Mid-Atlantic Fishery Management Council. In addition to issues related to the management of fisheries and significant biomass flips among dominant species, the Northeast Shelf ecosystem is also under stress from the increasing frequency of unusual plankton blooms and eutrophication within the near-shore coastal zone, which are the result of high levels of phosphate and nitrate discharges into drainage basins. Whether increases in the frequency and extent of near-shore plankton blooms are responsible for the rising incidence of biotoxin-related shellfish closures and deaths of marine mammals remains an open question that is of considerable concern to state and federal management agencies (Sherman, Jaworski, and Smayda 1992; Smayda 1991).

Table 15-6: Definitions of important variables

Variable	Definition	Units
Stability		
Homeostasis	Maintenance of a steady state in living organisms by the use of feedback control processes	
Stability	If, and only if, the variables all return to the initial equilibrium following their being perturbed from it; a system is locally stable if this return applies to small perturbations and is globally stable if it applies to all possible perturbations	Binary
Sustainable	A system that can maintain its structure and function indefinitely; all nonsuccessional (climax) ecosystems are sustainable, but they may not be stable (see resilience); sustainability is a policy goal for economic systems	Binary
Resilience	Speed with which variables return toward their equilibrium following a perturbation; not defined for unstable systems (Pimm 1984) or ability of a system to maintain its structure and patterns of behavior in the face of disturbance (Holling 1986)	Time
Resistance	The degree to which a variable is changed, following a perturbation	Nondimensional and continuous
Variability	Variance of population densities over time, or allied measures such as the standard deviation or coefficient of variation (standard deviation/mean)	
Complexity		
Species richness	Number of species in a system	Integer
Connectedness	Number of actual interspecific interactions divided by the possible interspecific interactions	Dimensionless
Interaction strength	Mean magnitude of interspecific interaction: size of the effect of one species' density on the growth rate of another species	
Evenness	Variance of the distribution of species abundance	
Diversity indexes	Measures that combine evenness and richness with a particular weighting for each; one important member of this family is the information theoretic index, H	Bits
Ascendancy	An information theoretic measure that combines the average mutual information (a measure of connectedness) and the total throughput of the system as a scaling factor (see Ulanowicz 1992)	
Other variables		
Perturbation	Change to a system's inputs or environment beyond the normal range of variation	Varies
Stress	A perturbation with a negative effect on a system	
Subsidy	A perturbation with a positive effect on a system	

Source: Adapted and expanded from Costanza 1992.

Present and future efforts

The topics of change and persistence in marine communities and the need for multispecies and ecosystem perspectives in fisheries management were reviewed at the Dahlem Conference on Exploitation of Marine Communities in 1984 (May 1984). The designation and management of large marine ecosystems are, at present, evolving scientific and geopolitical processes (Alexander 1989; Morgan 1988). Sufficient progress has been made to allow for useful comparisons among different processes influencing large-scale changes in the biomass yields of large marine ecosystems (Bax and Laevastu 1990).

Among the ecosystems being managed from a more holistic perspective are the Yellow Sea ecosystem, where the principal effort is being made by the Peoples Republic of China (Tang 1989); the multispecies fisheries of the Benguela Current ecosystem under management of the government of South Africa (Crawford, Shannon, and Shelton 1989);

Table 15-7: Indexes of Vigor, Organization, and Resilience in Various Fields

Component of health	Related concepts	Existing related measures	Field of origin	Probable method of solution
Vigor	Function Productivity System Throughput	GPP, NPP, GEP———> GNP————————> Metabolism—————>	Ecology Economics Biology	Measurement
Organization	Structure Biodiversity	Diversity index Average mutual information predictability————>	Ecology	Network analysis
Resilience		Scope for growth————>	Ecology	Simulation modeling
Combinations		Ascendancy—————>	Ecology	

Note: GPP, gross primary production; NPP, net primary production; GEP, gross ecosystem product; GNP, gross national product.
Source: Costanza 1992.

the Great Barrier Reef ecosystem (Bradbury and Mundy 1989) and the Northwest Australian Continental Shelf ecosystem (Sainsbury 1988), under management of the state and federal governments of Australia; and the Antarctic marine ecosystem, under the Commission for the Conservation of Antarctic Marine Living Resources and its twenty-one-nation membership (Scully, Brown, and Manheim 1986; Sherman and Ryan 1988). Within the exclusive economic zone of the United States, the state governments of Washington and Oregon have developed a comprehensive plan for managing marine resources within the Northern California Current ecosystem (Bottom and others 1989).

To improve the definition of ecosystem health so that it considers both natural environmental perturbation and the effects of human intervention on the changing states of ecosystems, future effort will focus on:

1. The development of ecosystem change and health indexes and indicators for large marine ecosystems.

2. The development of component models of large marine ecosystems incorporating measurements of changing states and health indicators rather than single, large models that generally have limited prediction capability.

3. The development and evaluation of models using health indicators that are directly applicable to management decisions; they should be simple in construction, allow for interaction with resource managers, and provide sufficient flexibility for testing hypotheses for a range of scenarios.

The NMFS-NOAA regional programs concerned with forecasting trends in biomass yields are being conducted in relation to the dynamics of large marine ecosystems. Results from several large-scale studies, including the GLOBEC and JGOFS efforts of the National Science Foundation, should provide important new insights on the structure and function of large marine ecosystems. Ongoing studies are now yielding information on changes in the productivity, habitat, and pollution stress of ecosystems. Future efforts will be needed to provide an improved, better-integrated base of information for assessing, understanding, and managing the nation's living marine resources within the boundary of large marine ecosystems, including wetlands and estuaries, as critical habitats of fishes and invertebrate (shrimp, shellfish) resources.

Figure 15–12: Schematic Representation of the Databases and Experimental Parameters for Indexing the Changing States of Large Marine Ecosystems

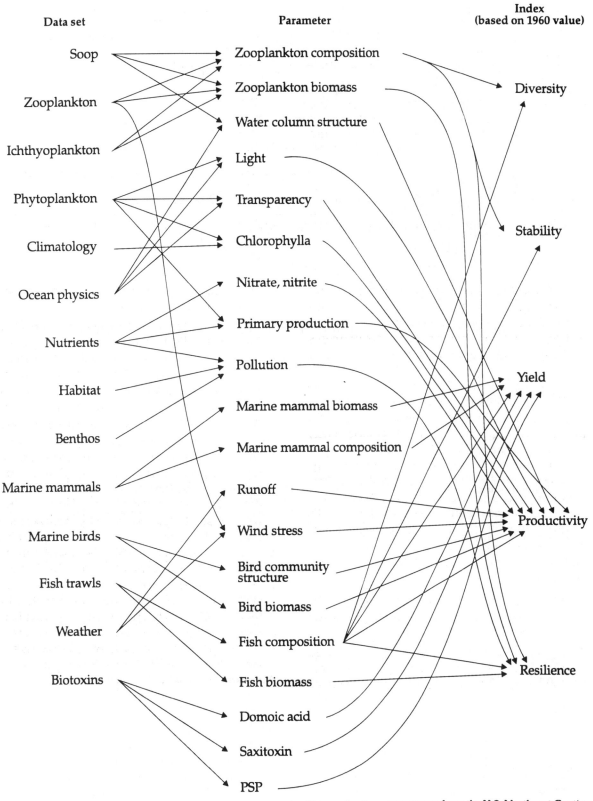

Note: The database represents time-series measurements of key ecosystem components from the U.S. Northeast Continental Shelf ecosystem. Indexes are based on changes compared with the state of the ecosystem in 1960.

Figure 15–13: Diagrammatic Conceptualization of Patterns and Activities at Different Levels of Complexity

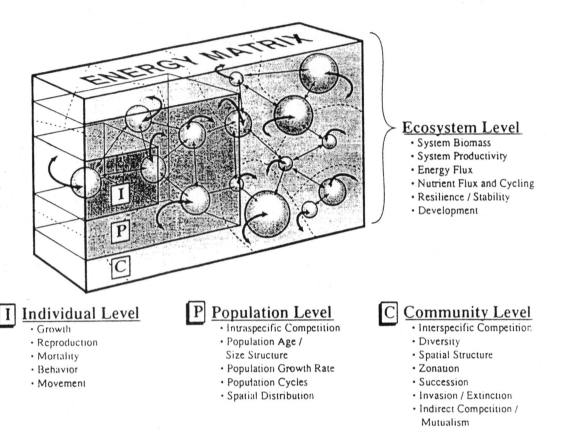

Ecosystem Level
- System Biomass
- System Productivity
- Energy Flux
- Nutrient Flux and Cycling
- Resilience / Stability
- Development

I Individual Level
- Growth
- Reproduction
- Mortality
- Behavior
- Movement

P Population Level
- Intraspecific Competition
- Population Age / Size Structure
- Population Growth Rate
- Population Cycles
- Spatial Distribution

C Community Level
- Interspecific Competition
- Diversity
- Spatial Structure
- Zonation
- Succession
- Invasion / Extinction
- Indirect Competition / Mutualism

Note: Each sphere represents an individual abiotic or biotic entry. Abiotic is defined as nonliving matter. Broad, double-headed arrows indicate feedback between entities and the energy matrix for the system. Thin arrows represent direct interactions between individual entities. Much of ecology is devoted to studying interactions between biotic and abiotic entities with a focus on how such interactions affect individuals (I), populations (P), or communities (C) of organisms. Ecosystem ecologists study these interactions from the viewpoint of their effect on both biotic and abiotic entities and within the context of the system. The boundaries of the system must be established to conduct quantitative studies of flux.

Source: Likens 1992.

References

Aiken, J. 1981. "The Undulating Oceanographic Recorder Mark 2." *Journal of Plankton Research* 3, pp. 551–60.

Alexander, L. M. 1989. "Large Marine Ecosystems as Global Management Units." In K. Sherman and L. M. Alexander, eds., *Biomass Yields and Geography of Large Marine Ecosystems*, pp. 339–44. AAAS Selected Symposium 111. Boulder, Colo.: Westview Press.

Alheit, J., and P. Bernal. 1992. "Effects of Physical and Biological Changes on the Biomass Yield of the Humboldt Current Ecosystem." In K.

Sherman, L. M. Alexander, and B. D. Gold, eds., *Large Marine Ecosystems: Stress, Mitigation, and Sustainability*, pp. 53–68. Washington, D.C.: American Association for the Advancement of Science Press.

Alverson, D. L., A. R. Longhurst, and J. A. Gulland. 1970. "How Much Food from the Sea?" *Science* 168, pp. 503–05.

Anderson, K. P., and E. Ursin. 1977. "A Multispecies Extension to the Beverton and Holt Theory of Fishing with Accounts of Phosphorus Circulation and Primary Production." *Meddelelser fra Danmarks fiskeri-og havundersøgelser* (Ny serie) 7, pp. 319–435.

Azarovitz, T. R., and M. D. Grosslein. 1987. "Fishes and Squids." In R. H. Backus, ed., *Georges Bank*, pp. 315–46. Cambridge, Mass.: M.I.T. Press.

Bakun, A. 1992. "The California Current, Benguela Current, and Southwestern Atlantic Shelf Ecosystems: A Comparative Approach to Identifying Factors Regulating Biomass Yields." In K. Sherman, L. M. Alexander, and B. D. Gold, eds., *Large Marine Ecosystems: Stress, Mitigation, and Sustainability*, pp. 199–221. Washington, D.C.: American Association for the Advancement of Science Press.

Bax, N. J., and T. Laevastu. 1990. "Biomass Potential of Large Marine Ecosystems: A Systems Approach." In K. Sherman, L. M. Alexander, and B. D. Gold, eds., *Large Marine Ecosystems: Patterns, Processes, and Yields*, pp. 188–205. Washington, D.C.: American Association for the Advancement of Science Press.

Beddington, J. R. 1984. "The Response of Multispecies Systems to Perturbations." In R. M. May, ed., *Exploitation of Marine Communities*, pp. 209–25. Berlin: Springer-Verlag.

————. 1986. "Shifts in Resource Populations in Large Marine Ecosystems." In K. Sherman and L. M. Alexander, eds., *Variability and Management of Large Marine Ecosystems*, pp. 9–18. AAAS Selected Symposium 99. Boulder, Colo.: Westview Press.

Belsky, M. H. 1986. "Legal Constraints and Options for Total Ecosystem Management of Large Marine Ecosystems." In K. Sherman and L. M. Alexander, eds., *Variability and Management of Large Marine Ecosystems*, pp. 241–61. AAAS Selected Symposium 99. Boulder, Colo.: Westview Press.

————. 1989. "The Ecosystem Model Mandate for a Comprehensive United States Ocean Policy and Law of the Sea." *San Diego Law Review* 26:3, pp. 417–95.

Beverton, R. J. H., and S. J. Holt. 1957. "On the Dynamics of Exploited Fish Populations." *Fishery Investigations* (U.K. Ministry of Agriculture, Fisheries, and Food) 2:19, pp. 1–533.

Bigelow, H. B. 1926. "Plankton of the Offshore Waters of the Gulf of Maine." *Bulletin of the Bureau of Fish and Wildlife* 40:2. Government Printing Office, Washington, D.C.

Bonner, W. N. 1982. *Seals and Man, A Study of Interactions*. Seattle: University of Washington Press.

Borisov, V. 1991. "The State of the Main Commercial Species of Fish in the Changeable Barents Sea Ecosystem." In K. Sherman, L. M. Alexander, and B. D. Gold, eds., *Food Chains, Yields, Models, and Management of Large Marine Ecosystems*, pp. 193–203. Boulder, Colo.: Westview Press.

Bottom, D. L., K. K. Jones, J. D. Rodgers, and R. F. Brown. 1989. "Management of Living Resources: A Research Plan for the Washington and Oregon Continental Margin." NCRI-T-89-004. National Coastal Resources Research Development Institute, Newport, Oreg.

Bradbury, R. H., and C. N. Mundy. 1989. "Large-scale Shifts in Biomass of the Great Barrier Reef Ecosystem." In K. Sherman and L. M. Alexander, eds., *Biomass Yields and Geography of Large Marine Ecosystems*, pp. 143–67. AAAS Selected Symposium 111. Boulder, Colo.: Westview Press.

Burger, J. 1988. "Interactions of Marine Birds with Other Marine Vertebrates in Marine Environments." In J. Burger, ed., *Seabirds and Other Marine Vertebrates*, pp. 2–28. New York: Columbia University Press.

Byrne, J. 1986. "Large Marine Ecosystems and the Future of Ocean Studies." In K. Sherman and L. M. Alexander, eds., *Variability and Management of Large Marine Ecosystems*, pp. 299–308. AAAS Selected Symposium 99. Boulder, Colo.: Westview Press.

Canon, J. R. 1986. "Variabilidad ambiental en relación con la pesqueria nerítica pelágica de la zona Norte de Chile." In P. Arana, ed., *La pesca en Chile*, pp. 195–205. Valparaiso: Escuela de Ciencias del Mar, Facultad de Recursos Naturales, Universidad Católica de Chile.

Christy, F. T., Jr. 1986. "Can Large Marine Ecosystems Be Managed for Optimum Yields?" In K. Sherman and L. M. Alexander, eds., *Variability and Management of Large Marine Ecosystems*, pp. 263–67. AAAS Selected Symposium 99. Boulder, Colo.: Westview Press.

Colebrook, J. M. 1986. "Environmental Influences on Long-term Variability in Marine Plankton." *Hydrobiologia* 142, pp. 309–25.

Costanza, R. 1992. "Toward an Operational Definition of Ecosystem Health." In R. Costanza, B. G. Norton, and B. D. Haskell, eds., *Ecosystem Health: New Goals for Environmental Management*. Washington, D.C.: Island Press.

Crawford, R. J. M., L. V. Shannon, and P. A. Shelton. 1989. "Characteristics and Management of the Benguela as a Large Marine Ecosystem." In K. Sherman and L. M. Alexander, eds., *Biomass Yields and Geography of Large Marine Ecosystems*, pp. 169–219. AAAS Selected Symposium 111. Boulder, Colo.: Westview Press.

Croxall, J. P., ed. 1987. *Seabirds: Feeding Ecology and Role in Marine Ecosystems.* London: Cambridge University Press.

Cushing, D. H. 1975. *Marine Ecology and Fisheries.* London: Cambridge University Press.

Daan, N. 1986. "Results of Recent Time-series Observations for Monitoring Trends in Large Marine Ecosystems with a Focus on the North Sea." In K. Sherman and L. M. Alexander, eds., *Variability and Management of Large Marine Ecosystems*, pp. 145–74. AAAS Selected Symposium 99. Boulder, Colo.: Westview Press.

Dickson, R. R., P. M. Kelly, J. M. Colebrook, W. S. Wooster, and D. H. Cushing. 1988. "North Winds and Production in the Eastern North Atlantic." *Journal of Plankton Research* 10, pp. 151–69.

FAO (Food and Agriculture Organization of the United Nations). 1989. *FAO Yearbook of Fishery Statistics: Catches and Landings.* Vol. 64 (for 1987). Rome.

————. 1990. *FAO Yearbook of Fishery Statistics.* Vol. 66 (for 1988) Rome.

Fogarty, M., E. B. Cohen, W. L. Michaels, and W. W. Morse. 1991. "Predation and the Regulation of Sand Lance Populations: An Exploratory Analysis." *ICES Marine Science Symposium* 193, pp. 120–24.

GESAMP (Group of Experts on the Scientific Aspects of Marine Pollution). 1990. "The State of the Marine Environment." Regional Seas Reports and Studies 115. United Nations Environment Program, Nairobi.

GLOBEC (Global Ocean Ecosystems Dynamics). 1991. "Initial Science Plan. February 1991." Report 1. Joint Oceanographic Institutions, Washington, D.C.

Glover, R. S. 1967. "The Continuous Plankton Recorder Survey of the North Atlantic." *Symposium of the Zoological Society of London* 19, pp. 189–210.

Gulland, J. A. 1984. "Epilogue." In R. M. May, ed., *Exploitation of Marine Communities*, pp. 335–37. Berlin: Springer-Verlag.

Hempel, G., ed. 1978. "Symposium on North Sea Fish Stocks: Recent Changes and Their Causes." *Rapport et Procès-Verbaux des Reunions* (Conseil International pour l'Exploration de la Mer) 172, p. 449.

Holling, C. S. 1973. "Resilience and Stability of Ecological Systems." Institute of Resource Ecology, University of British Columbia, Vancouver, Canada.

————. 1986. "The Resilience of Terrestrial Ecosystems Local Surprise and Global Change." In W. C. Clark and R. E. Munn, eds., *Sustainable Development of the Biosphere*, pp. 292–317. London: Cambridge University Press.

Hovgaard, H., and E. Buch. 1990. "Fluctuation in the Cod Biomass of the West Greenland Sea Ecosystem in Relation to Climate." In K. Sherman, L. M. Alexander, and B. D. Gold, eds., *Large Marine Ecosystems: Patterns, Processes, and Yields*, pp. 36–43. Washington, D.C.: American Association for the Advancement of Science Press.

ICES (International Council for the Exploration of the Sea). 1991. "Report of the Multispecies Working Group." ICES C.M. 1991/Assess:7. Copenhagen, Denmark.

IOC (International Oceanographic Commission of UNESCO). 1992. "The Use of Large Marine Ecosystem Concept in the Global Ocean Observing System (GOOS)." Prepared by K. Sherman for the twenty-fifth session of the IOC executive council, Paris, March 10–18. IOC/EC-XXV/Inf.7. Washington, D.C.

Jossi, J. W., and D. E. Smith. 1990. "Continuous Plankton Records: Massachusetts to Cape Sable, N.S., and New York to the Gulf Stream, 1989." NAFO Series Document 90/66:1-11. Northwest Atlantic Fisheries Organization.

Karr, J. 1992. "Ecological Integrity: Strategies for Protecting Earth's Life Support System." In R. Costanza, B. G. Norton, and B. D. Haskell, eds., *Ecosystem Health: New Goals for Environmental Management*, pp. 223–38. Washington, D.C.: Island Press.

Kawasaki, T., S. Tanaka, Y. Toba, and A. Taniguchi, eds. 1991. *Long-term Variability of Pelagic Fish Populations and Their Environment.* Proceedings of the International Symposium, Sendai, Japan, November 14–18, 1989. Tokyo: Pergamon Press.

Levin, S. A. 1978. "Pattern Formation in Ecological Communities." In J. A. Steele, ed., *Spatial*

Pattern in Plankton Communities, pp. 433–70. New York: Plenum Press.

————. 1990. "Physical and Biological Scales, and Modelling of Predator-prey Interactions in Large Marine Ecosystems." In K. Sherman, L. M. Alexander, and B. D. Gold, eds., *Large Marine Ecosystems: Patterns, Processes, and Yields*, pp. 179–87. Washington, D.C.: American Association for the Advancement of Science Press.

Likens, G. E. 1992. "The Ecosystem Approach: Its Use and Abuse." In O. Kinne, ed., *Excellence in Ecology* 3. W-2124. Oldendorf/Luhe, Germany: Ecology Institute.

Lindemann, R. L. 1942. "The Trophic Dynamic Aspect of Ecology." *Ecology* 23, pp. 399–418.

Loughlin, T. R., and R. Nelson, Jr. 1986. "Incidental Mortality of Northern Sea Lions in the Shelikof Strait, Alaska." *Marine Mammal Science* 1, pp. 14–33.

MacCall, A. D. 1986. "Changes in the Biomass of the California Current System." In K. Sherman and L. M. Alexander, eds., *Variability and Management of Large Marine Ecosystems*, pp. 33–54. AAAS Selected Symposium 99. Boulder, Colo.: Westview Press.

Malone, T. C. 1991. "River Flow, Phytoplankton Production, and Oxygen Depletion in Chesapeake Bay." In R. V. Tyson and T. H. Pearson, eds., *Modern and Ancient Continental Shelf Anoxia*, pp. 83–93. Special Publication 58. Boulder, Colo.: Geological Society.

Mangel, M. 1991. "Empirical and Theoretical Aspects of Fisheries Yield Models for Large Marine Ecosystems." In K. Sherman, L. M. Alexander, and B. D. Gold, eds., *Food Chains, Yields, Models, and Management of Large Marine Ecosystems*, pp. 243–61. Boulder, Colo.: Westview Press.

May, R. M., ed. 1984. *Exploitation of Marine Communities*. Berlin: Springer-Verlag.

Mayr, E. 1982. *The Growth of Biological Thought*. Cambridge, Mass.: Harvard University Press.

Minoda, T. 1989. "Oceanographic and Biomass Changes in the Oyashio Current Ecosystem." In K. Sherman and L. M. Alexander, eds., *Biomass Yields and Geography of Large Marine Ecosystems*, pp. 67–93. AAAS Selected Symposium 111. Boulder, Colo.: Westview Press.

Morgan, J. R. 1988. "Large Marine Ecosystems: An Emerging Concept of Regional Management." *Environment* 29:10, pp. 4–9, 26–34.

————. 1989. "Large Marine Ecosystems in the Pacific Ocean." In K. Sherman and L. M. Alexander, eds., *Biomass Yields and Geography of Large Marine Ecosystems*, pp. 377–94. AAAS Selected Symposium 111. Boulder, Colo.: Westview Press.

Myers, N. 1990. "Working towards One World. Book Review." *Nature* 344:6266, pp. 499–500.

Murawski, S. A. 1991. "Can We Manage Our Multispecies Fisheries?" *Fisheries* 16:5, pp. 5–13.

Norton, B. G., and R. E. Ulanowicz. 1992. "Scale and Biodiversity Policy: A Hierarchical Approach." *Ambio* 21:3, pp. 244–49.

Overholtz, W. J., and J. R. Nicolas. 1979. "Apparent Feeding by the Fin Whale, *Balaenoptera physalus*, and Humpback Whale, *Megoptera novaeangliae*, on the American Sand Lance, *Ammodytes americanus*, in the Northwest Atlantic." *Fishery Bulletin, U.S.* 77, pp. 285–87.

Payne, P. M., D. N. Wiley, S. B. Young, S. Pittman, P. J. Clapham, and J. W. Jossi. 1990. "Recent Fluctuations in the Abundance of Baleen Whales in the Southern Gulf of Maine in Relation to Changes in Selected Prey." *Fishery Bulletin, U.S.* 88, pp. 687–96.

Pimm, S. L. 1984. "The Complexity and Stability of Ecosystems." *Nature* 307, pp. 321–26.

Piyakarnchana, T. 1989. "Yield Dynamics as an Index of Biomass Shifts in the Gulf of Thailand Ecosystems." In K. Sherman and L. M. Alexander, eds., *Biomass Yields and Geography of Large Marine Ecosystems*, pp. 95–142. AAAS Selected Symposium 111. Boulder, Colo.: Westview Press.

Postma, H., and J. J. Zijlstra, eds. 1988. *Ecosystems of the World 27: Continental Shelves*. Amsterdam, Netherlands: Elsevier.

Powers, K. D., and R. G. B. Brown. 1987. "Seabirds." In R. H. Backus, ed., *Georges Bank*, pp. 359–71. Cambridge, Mass.: M.I.T. Press.

Prescott, J. R. V. 1989. "The Political Division of Large Marine Ecosystems in the Atlantic Ocean and Some Associated Seas." In K. Sherman and L. M. Alexander, eds., *Biomass Yields and Geography of Large Marine Ecosystems*, pp. 395–442. AAAS Selected Symposium 111. Boulder, Colo.: Westview Press.

Rapport, D. J. 1992. "What Is Clinical Ecology?" In R. Costanza, B. G. Norton, and B. D. Haskell, eds., *Ecosystem Health: New Goals for Environmental Management*, pp. 144–56. Washington, D.C.: Island Press.

Ricklefs, R. E. 1987. "Community Diversity: Relative Roles of Local and Regional Processes." *Science* 235:4785, pp. 167–71.

Riley, G. A., H. Stommel, and D. F. Bumpus. 1949. "Quantitative Ecology of the Plankton of the Western North Atlantic." *Bulletin of Bingham Oceanography College* 12:3, p. 169.

Ryther, J. H. 1969. "Relationship of Photosynthesis to Fish Production in the Sea." *Science* 166, pp. 72–76.

Sainsbury, K. J. 1988. "The Ecological Basis of Multispecies Fisheries and Management of a Demersal Fishery in Tropical Australia." In J. A. Gulland, ed., *Fish Population Dynamics,* 2d ed., pp. 349–82. New York: John Wiley and Sons.

Schaefer, M. B. 1954. "Some Aspects of the Dynamics of Populations Important to the Management of the Commercial Marine Fisheries." *Bulletin of the Inter-American Tropical Tuna Commission* 1:1, pp. 27–56.

Scully, R. T., W. Y. Brown, and B. S. Manheim. 1986. "The Convention for the Conservation of Antarctic Marine Living Resources: A Model for Large Marine Ecosystem Management." In K. Sherman and L. M. Alexander, eds., *Variability and Management of Large Marine Ecosystems,* pp. 281–86. AAAS Selected Symposium 99. Boulder, Colo.: Westview Press.

Sherman, K. 1991. "The Large Marine Ecosystem Concept: A Research and Management Strategy for Living Marine Resources." *Ecological Applications* 1:4, pp. 349–60.

Sherman, K., and L. M. Alexander, eds. 1986. *Variability and Management of Large Marine Ecosystems.* AAAS Selected Symposium 99. Boulder, Colo.: Westview Press.

————. eds. 1989. *Biomass and Geography of Large Marine Ecosystems.* Boulder, Colo.: Westview Press.

Sherman, K., L. M. Alexander, and B. D. Gold, eds. 1990. *Large Marine Ecosystems: Patterns, Processes, and Yields.* Washington, D.C.: American Association for the Advancement of Science Press.

————. eds. 1991. *Food Chains, Yields, Models, and Management of Large Marine Ecosystems.* Boulder, Colo.: Westview Press.

————. eds. 1993. *Large Marine Ecosystems: Stress, Mitigation, and Sustainability.* Washington, D.C.: American Association for the Advancement of Science Press.

Sherman, K., E. B. Cohen, and R. W. Langton. 1990. "The Northeast Continental Shelf: An Ecosystem at Risk." In V. Konrad, S. Ballard, R. Erb, and A. Morin, eds., *Gulf of Maine: Sustaining Our Common Heritage,* pp. 120–67. Proceedings of an international conference held at Portland, Maine, December 10–12, 1989. Maine State Planning Office and the Canadian-American Center of the University of Maine, Augusta.

Sherman, K., J. R. Green, J. R. Goulet, and L. Ejsymont. 1983. "Coherence in Zooplankton of a Large Northwest Atlantic Ecosystem." *Fishery Bulletin, U.S.* 81, pp. 855–62.

Sherman, K., M. Grosslein, D. Mountain, D. Busch, J. O'Reilly, and R. Theroux. 1988. "The Continental Shelf Ecosystem off the Northeast Coast of the United States." In H. Postma and J. J. Zilstra, eds., *Ecosystems of the World 27: Continental Shelves,* pp. 279–337. Amsterdam, Netherlands: Elsevier.

Sherman, K., N. Jaworski, and T. Smayda. 1992. "The Northeast Shelf Ecosystem: Stress, Mitigation, and Sustainability, 12–15 August 1991 Symposium Summary." Technical Memo NMFS-F/NEC-94. U.S. Department of Commerce, National Oceanic and Atmospheric Administration, Washington, D.C.

Sherman, K., and T. Laughlin, eds. 1992. "Large Marine Ecosystems Monitoring Workshop Report." Technical Memo NMFS-F/NEC-93. U.S. Department of Commerce, National Oceanic and Atmospheric Administration, Washington, D.C. Technical Memo NMFS-F/NEC-93.

Sherman, K., and A. F. Ryan. 1988. "Antarctic Marine Living Resources." *Oceanus* 31:2, pp. 59–63.

Sissenwine, M. P. 1986. "Perturbation of a Predator-controlled Continental Shelf Ecosystem." In K. Sherman and L. M. Alexander, eds., *Variability and Management of Large Marine Ecosystems,* pp. 55–85. AAAS Selected Symposium 99. Boulder, Colo.: Westview Press.

Sissenwine, M. P., and E. B. Cohen. 1991. "Resource Productivity and Fisheries Management of the Northeast Shelf Ecosystem." In K. Sherman, L. M. Alexander, and B. D. Gold, eds., *Food Chains, Yields, Models, and Management of Large Marine Ecosystems,* pp. 107–23. Boulder, Colo.: Westview Press.

Skjoldal, H. R., and F. Rey. 1989. "Pelagic Production and Variability of the Barents Sea Ecosystem." In K. Sherman and L. M. Alexander, eds., *Biomass Yields and Geography of Large Marine Eco-*

systems, pp. 241–86. AAAS Selected Symposium 111. Boulder, Colo.: Westview Press.

Smayda, T. 1991. "Global Epidemic of Noxious Phytoplankton Blooms and Food Chain Consequences in Large Ecosystems." In K. Sherman, L. M. Alexander, and B. D. Gold, eds., *Food Chains, Yields, Models, and Management of Large Marine Ecosystems.* Boulder, Colo.: Westview Press.

Smith, W. G., and W. W. Morse. 1990. "Larval Distribution Patterns: Evidence for the Collapse/ Recolonization of Atlantic Herring on Georges Bank." ICES C.M. 1990/H:17. Copenhagen, Denmark: International Council for the Exploration of the Sea.

Steele, J. H. 1974. *The Structure of Marine Ecosystems.* Cambridge, Mass.: Harvard University Press.

———. 1988. "Scale Selection for Biodynamic Theories." In B. J. Rothschild, ed., *Toward a Theory on Biological-physical Interactions in the World Ocean,* pp. 513–26. NATO ASI Series C: Mathematical and Physical Sciences, vol. 239. Boston, Mass.: Kluwer Academic Publishers.

Sugihara, G., S. Garcia, J. A. Gulland, J. H. Lawton, H. Maske, R. T. Paine, T. Platt, E. Rachor, B. J. Rothschild, E. A. Ursin, and B. F. K. Zeitzschel. 1984. "Ecosystem Dynamics: Group Report." In R. M. May, ed., *Exploitation of Marine Communities,* pp. 130–53. Berlin: Springer-Verlag.

Tang, Q. 1989. "Changes in the Biomass of the Yellow Sea Ecosystems." In K. Sherman and L. M. Alexander, eds., *Biomass Yields and Geography of Large Marine Ecosystems,* pp. 7–35. AAAS Selected Symposium 111. Boulder, Colo.: Westview Press.

Taylor, P., and A. J. R. Groom, eds. 1989. *Global Issues in the United Nation's Framework.* London: Macmillan.

Terazaki, M. 1989. "Recent Large-scale Changes in the Biomass of the Kuroshio Current Ecosystem." In K. Sherman and L. M. Alexander, eds., *Biomass Yields and Geography of Large Marine Ecosystems,* pp. 37–65. AAAS Selected Symposium 111. Boulder, Colo.: Westview Press.

Ulanowicz, R. E. 1992. "Ecosystem Health in Terms of Trophic Flow Networks." In R. Costanza, B. G. Norton, and B. D. Haskell, eds., *Ecosystem Health: New Goals for Environmental Management,* pp. 189–296. Washington, D.C.: Island Press.

U.S. Council on Environmental Quality. 1980. *The Global 2000 Report to the President: Entering the Twenty-first Century,* 3 vols. With the U.S. Department of State. Washington, D.C.: U.S. Government Printing Office.

U.S. Department of Commerce. 1988. "A National Atlas: Health and Use of Coastal Waters, United States of America." U.S. Department of Commerce, National Oceanic and Atmospheric Administration, National Ocean Service, Office of Oceanography and Marine Assessment, Washington, D.C.

Waring, G. T., P. M. Payne, B. L. Parry, and J. R. Nicolas. 1990. "Incidental Take of Marine Mammals in Foreign Fishery Activities off the Northeast United States, 1977–88." *Fishery Bulletin* (United States) 88, pp. 347–60.

Wise, J. P. 1984. "The Future of Food from the Sea." In J. L. Simon and H. Kahn, eds., *The Resourceful Earth,* pp. 113–27. New York: Basil Blackwell.

Part C

Managed Ecosystems

16

Sustainable Agriculture in the Tropics: Issues, Indicators, and Measurement

Nigel J. H. Smith and Donald L. Plucknett

Various definitions of sustainable agriculture have surfaced, often heavily flavored by the disciplinary backgrounds of the proponents. Nevertheless, a consensus has emerged that sustainable agricultural systems incorporate four main dimensions: the biophysical environment, the institutional and policy environment, social and cultural concerns, and economic viability. Unless all four components are addressed adequately, agricultural development goals can be thwarted, often with severe environmental and social repercussions.

Our intent here is not to add interpretations or nuances to the definition of sustainable agriculture. Considerable thought has already gone into analyzing the dimensions to sustainability in farming systems (Altieri, Letourneau, and Davis 1983; Brklacich, Bryant, and Smit 1991; CGIAR 1988; FAO 1991; Smith 1990; York 1988). Rather, our purpose is to focus on some of the major conceptual issues confronting efforts to improve the sustainability of agriculture as a framework for identifying ways to measure or ascertain sustainable systems.

Before exploring various dimensions to sustainable agriculture and their measurement, three overriding points are in order. First, sustainability does not mean keeping yields at their current levels. Yields must continue to rise for the major crops, and more work is needed to upgrade the productivity of the so-called minor crops that can be important in certain regions. If yields do not increase, it will be difficult to feed and improve incomes for the existing population in the tropics, let alone future generations. The world's population is expected to double before it stabi-

lizes sometime in the middle of the next century, and most of that growth will occur in the warmer climates. Second, intensifying production on existing cleared areas creates more options for development or preservation of remaining spaces.

Third, sustainable agriculture is not synonymous with low-input agriculture. Some low-input systems are not sustainable, from either the ecological or social perspectives. Conversely, some high-input systems can damage the environment. A broad spectrum of input intensity provides the flexibility needed for achieving sound agricultural development of the ecologically and culturally diverse tropics.

This survey of sustainability issues in tropical agriculture includes a discussion of the special challenge of marginal lands, the management of pests and diseases, the positive and negative contributions of weeds, the ecological and social role of tree crops, the interconnections among a mosaic of land uses, the intensification imperative, and the need for a blend of traditional knowledge and modern science. Finally, we explore some issues in a research agenda for sustainable agriculture.

In this discussion of salient issues in tropical agriculture, we examine the biophysical measurements required to monitor sustainability. Where appropriate, we assess existing measurements and methods for measuring and predicting sustainability on experiment stations and under actual conditions of production. A case is made for conducting both on-farm and on-station experiments and for protecting biodiversity in natural and moderately disturbed ecosystems.

The special challenge of marginal lands

As an overall strategy, it makes sense to concentrate food production on the optimal lands (Leonard 1989; Plucknett and Smith 1982). But a host of factors, ranging from inequitable land ownership to population pressure, often forces farmers to settle on marginal lands. Areas with erratic or excessive rainfall, poor soils, steep slopes, or inadequate drainage pose daunting challenges for agriculture.

It can be argued that rather than promote research on ways to improve agriculture on marginal lands, emphasis should be placed on the more productive environments. Although some scope may exist for encouraging people to leave marginal environments—thereby allowing degraded habitats to recuperate—political, economic, and demographic forces are likely to keep many people on marginal landscapes. By attempting to improve production on already disturbed environments, pressure could be reduced on even more fragile ecosystems.

Research strategies for achieving sustainable agriculture in marginal areas are similar in many regards to those suitable for the better-endowed lands. Increased emphasis can be placed, however, on developing crop varieties that withstand moisture stress, are adapted to poor soils, resist diseases and pests, and, in highland areas, tolerate cold. Marginal environments call for deployment of a range of practices that serve as insurance against late rains, lower than normal rainfall, or epidemics of pests and diseases. A "fruit basket" approach, for example, involves deploying a palate of different crops as well as several varieties of each crop that require different nutrients and have different abilities to tolerate environmental stresses. Farmers on marginal lands generally have fewer resources to combat such challenges, such as access to irrigation and pesticides. Genetic resistance, or tolerance, to environmental stresses is thus especially important in marginal areas.

Farmers in many parts of the lowland, humid tropics need varieties that tolerate acid conditions and aluminum toxicity. The repertoire of traditional varieties maintained by farmers in marginal areas often contains hardy land races: breeders need to tap this material when developing more productive varieties. Crops and varieties that produce reasonably well with low fertility, such as cassava and mango, should be promoted for marginal areas rather than genotypes that require heavy fertilization to achieve their potential yield.

Soil erosion can be particularly serious in marginal environments, where steep slopes or sparse vegetation facilitate rapid runoff and wind erosion. Many societies have confronted this problem, often with great success. Spectacular terraces adorn high mountains in many parts of the tropics and subtropics, including Java, Nepal, northern Luzon in the Philippines, the central Andes, Kenya (Davidson 1969, p. 35), and parts of Guatemala (Cook 1909). Most of these complex terrace systems were developed thousands of years ago for the dual purpose of irrigating the land and conserving the topsoil. Such long-term land improvements are expensive to build and are difficult to maintain.

In the case of the Great Lakes Region of Africa, classic bench terraces have been abandoned because they are associated with colonialism. Soil erosion accelerated markedly in Rwanda, Burundi, and eastern Zaire as such terraces were destroyed after independence. Soil erosion was exacerbated as the population continued to expand rapidly in the already densely settled region. Fortunately, some other soil conservation techniques have been promoted recently, including grass or tree strips to trap soil (Egger and Martens 1987). Other methods to check soil erosion on hillsides in the humid tropics include leaving bands of natural vegetation along contours, piling rocks and field debris in parallel strips, and building earthen bunds to create a sloping terrace (Plucknett 1976). Such relatively inexpensive methods of checking soil erosion can be introduced quickly to an area, particularly if the plant provides some uses, such as thatch or fodder.

Although ways to encourage building terraces in marginal environments should be pursued, abandoned terraces built in ancient times could be renovated. Between half and three-quarters of the Inca terraces are no longer used (Bray 1990). Peru and Bolivia import food for their rapidly growing populations and could meet at least some of their food needs by repairing old terraces.

An important indicator of sustainability in mountainous areas, therefore, is the degree to which the farmers strive to slow soil erosion. Soil conservation techniques should be one of the first priorities for any farming system (Adiningsih, Sudjadi, and Setyorini 1988). The notion that fertilizers can compensate for soil fertility lost due to erosion is an illusion, even in comparatively rich industrial countries. Subsoils often have different physical and chemical characteristics than more friable and fertile topsoils, and these properties can interfere with proper root development.

Some areas of the tropics can be regarded as marginal for agricultural development because of their low rates of photosynthesis. Year-round warm conditions do not necessarily translate into higher plant productivity. Many parts of the tropics that have high rainfall are cloudy most of the time, thereby reducing photosynthesis. In such cases, lands should never be cleared from forest for any other purpose, including crop production and grazing. Food production is more efficient in temperate or tropical areas that have abundant sunshine (Chang 1968).

In Amazonia, the largest remaining tract of tropical forest in the world, the lowest photosynthetic potential is found in the western region of the basin, precisely where the greatest biodiversity is generally found. The crumpled ranges of the towering Andes force westward-moving air to rise, thereby triggering increased precipitation and more overcast days than those experienced in other portions of the basin, except for an enclave of high rainfall around Belém. Areas of lower photosynthetic potential often coincide with zones of increased biodiversity and endemism. Plant diversity increases in western Amazonia, and the deeply cut valleys and rain-soaked ridges of the eastern Andes and associated lower, premontane slopes contain an unusual assortment of fruit trees and other plants (Clement 1991; Clement, Muller, and Chavez 1982; Myers 1990; Schultes 1991). The progenitor of the widely appreciated peach palm (*Bactris gasipaes*) arose in western Amazonia (Clement 1988), as well as a variety of other fruit crops, such as papaya (*Carica papaya*) and potential new domesticates (Smith and others 1992). Western Amazonia is also richer in mammalian species than other parts of the basin (Mares 1992; Pimm and Gittleman 1992). Areas with increased cloud cover, which are potentially less propitious for agricultural development, particularly for food crops, thus overlap with zones particularly important for conservation.

The pest and disease treadmill

Year-round warm temperatures are a double-edged sword for tropical farmers. Swidden fields, agroforestry plots, and dooryard gardens can provide a continual harvest of basic staples, fruits, and nuts, among other goods, yet arthropod pests and pathogens are not checked by cold winters and thus pose a ceaseless challenge for farmers and plantation owners (Janzen 1970, 1973). In addition to environmental concerns, pesticides are often too costly for most crops in the humid tropics. Pesticides may be economically viable for certain cash crops on a limited basis, but few farmers—large or small—can afford significant quantities of pesticides for basic staples. Furthermore, the number of arthropod species exhibiting resistance to pesticides doubled from 1970 to 1980, and some pests have even developed resistance to biopesticides, such as *Bacillus thuringiensis* (Anderson 1992; Brattsten and others 1986; Dover and Croft 1986).

Successful control of insects and pathogens in the tropics hinges on a better understanding of traditional methods of control and modern science. Traditional farmers employ a variety of techniques to control pests and pathogens, ranging from polyculture to the deployment of several cultivars for each crop. Breeders can help by screening traditional varieties, wild populations, and near relatives of crops for genetic resistance, then transferring such desirable traits to higher yielding material. In certain situations, particularly on islands and in some perennial crops, biocontrol methods can be effective in checking crop pests (Smith 1990).

Resistance to insects and disease has emerged as a major priority among breeders working with tropical crops. At the Mexico-based International Maize and Wheat Improvement Center (CIMMYT), an estimated 40 percent of the breeding effort is devoted to disease resistance (Winkelmann 1987). Near relatives of crops often contain the necessary genes for disease resistance, as in the case of rubber (Schultes 1977), oil palm (Gascon, Noiret, and Meunier 1989), coffee (Eskes 1989), sugarcane (Brandes and Sartoris 1936), cassava (Beck 1980; Hahn 1978; Hahn and others 1979; Hahn, Terry, and Leuschner 1980), and potato (Creech 1970).

Biotechnologies are being harnessed to develop and disseminate disease-resistant crop varieties. In Viet Nam, for example, "barefoot biotechnologists" have devised simple procedures so that farmers can readily multiply pest-resistant potatoes. European potato varieties fare poorly in Viet Nam, but a Viet Namese biotechnologist obtained more than 100 potato samples from the gene bank maintained by the International Potato Center (CIP) in Peru, selected those that fared well in Viet Nam, then developed an inexpensive method that farmers can use to multiply planting material using test tubes. CIP germ plasm coupled with innovative tissue culture techniques have allowed Viet Namese farmers to increase potato yields from about 10 tons per hectare to around 18 tons per hectare, without using pesticides (*Economist*, April 18, 1992, p. 87). Although gene banks have been criticized as "morgues and museums" (Buttel 1992), the better conceived and managed ones have made tangible and significant contributions to upgrading agricultural productivity around the world (Huamán and Schmiediche 1991; Plucknett and others 1987; Rick 1991).

Single-gene resistance against a disease rarely works for very long because of the evolution of new pathotypes. Many pathogenic fungi and bacteria have several races or strains that attack crops, even in the same area. Many disease-resistant genes are specific to certain races of a pathogen (Bennetzen and others 1988). A potpourri of genes is thus necessary to counteract most diseases; the appropriate gene for resistance needs to be inserted in the variety of crop to be released where that particular pathotype prevails. Carefully assembled and evaluated collections of germ plasm are thus essential to backstop breeding efforts, particularly in the tropics.

Given the increased number of insect generations possible in the tropics, access to, and deployment of, genetic resistance is critical to sustainability. Genetic resistance is cheaper in the long run for farmers, consumers, and the environment. Conservation of wilderness is essential for this dimension to sustainability, since resistance genes are sometimes only found in wild populations of crops or their near relatives. For example, resistance to nematode pests has been located ir. close relatives of the potato (Chavez and others 1988; Creech 1970; Hawkes 1977; Kahn 1984, p. 105).

An important measure of sustainability of agricultural systems in the tropics is the status of genetic resources of the crops involved. Comprehensive and well-managed gene banks supplemented by in situ conservation are key indicators of sustainability. Proper evaluation is essential if genetic resources are to contribute to sustainable agriculture. For the major crop plants, international nurseries have been set up to screen material for resistance to pests and diseases, among other traits. International nurseries serve as testing grounds to identify promising material for further crossing. The International Rice Research Institute (IRRI), for example, has helped organize a network of collaborators in dozens of countries to screen rice germ plasm; entries are supplied by IRRI and partners in the international rice nurseries. IRRI-coordinated nurseries have been responsible for developing various high-yielding varieties of rice that are resistant to evolving strains of brown plant hopper, a serious rice pest in Asia (IRRI 1983, p. 21).

Weeds as friend and foe

Year-round warmth in the tropics allows weeds to proliferate (Kamarck 1973). Dry seasons slow but do not halt the growth of volunteer plants in fields, pastures, and plantations. Weeds are often the major reason why farmers abandon their swidden fields and move on to clear a fresh patch of forest (Holm and others 1977; Joachim and Kandiah 1948; Plucknett 1976). In some cases, annual burning to control weeds leads to a buildup of perennial grasses, such as *Imperata cylindrica* in Southeast Asia (Kellman 1969). When invading perennial grasses attain almost pure stands, farmers have little hope of controlling them. Weed invasion is a major reason why some pastures degrade in Amazonia, thereby lowering the carrying capacity of ranches (Nepstad, Uhl, and Serrão 1991).

Every production system has it own problem with weeds, and various environmentally benign strategies can be employed to check them. Some of the more intensive agricultural systems may necessitate rigorous control of weeds. Herbicides can be appropriate in such cases, because chemicals used to control weeds appear to have minimal environmental impact and can be cheaper than manual labor or cutting with machinery.

One trick in weed control is to find intercrops that out-compete the weeds, while providing valuable fodder, mulch, or nitrogen fixation. Research is under way to find suitable nitrogen-fixing plants, such as species of *Centrosema*, that can withstand trampling and heavy grazing. Improving the productivity of pasture can relieve pressure on the remaining forests. Pasture improvement is an issue for both small- and large-scale operators in the Amazon. Cattle are an integral part of many small farms in Amazonia and other parts of the humid tropics, since they provide cash in emergencies, milk for children, and manure for crops (Lambourne 1937). A related tactic is to shade out weeds; for this reason, various perennial cropping systems, particularly agroforestry, can improve the sustainability of agricultural lands in the tropics.

Yet weeds are not all bad. Weed is a cultural term. So-called weeds help protect the soil from the erosive power of tropical downpours and may rapidly sequester nutrients that crop plants are unable to capture. In swidden systems, weeds are vanguard species that start the process of forest regeneration. Even the notorious alang-alang grass (*Imperata cylindrica*) in South and Southeast Asia has several uses. In southern Kalimantan, alang-alang forms part of the rice fallow system; in northeastern India and on Bali, the tough grass is employed for thatch (see chapter 14 of this volume); and on Sumbawa Island, game animals browse on succulent alang-alang shoots promoted by burns (Conway, Manwan, and McCauley 1983). Some pasture weeds in the Amazon fix nitrogen, such as species of *Cassia*.

Some of our crops started out as weeds, and uninvited plants in fields sometimes cross with crops, thereby enriching the domestic gene pool (Harlan 1965). In Mexico, for example, bees transfer pollen from wild field beans (*Phaseolus vulgaris*) to nearby planted beans. Farmers even recognize that the presence of "weedy" beans is a help to their fields, since it fortifies their crop. In parts of Mexico and Guatemala, maize (*Zea mays*) exchanges genes spontaneously with annual teosinte (*Zea mays mexicana*), a weedy relative (Doebley 1990; Galinat, Mangelsdorf, and Piersen 1956). Introgression of weeds with crops has also been recorded or suspected with pearl millet (Harlan 1971), finger millet (Hussaini, Goodman, and Timothy 1977), groundnut (Williams 1989), potato (Hawkes 1977), various squash species, and quinoa, a protein-rich crop of the high Andes now being sold by some health food stores in the United States (Wilson 1990).

Although weeds certainly need to be controlled as much as feasible within cultivated plots and plantations, a preoccupation with totally "clean" fields and borders is not only too costly in many cases, but also undesirable. Ruderal plant communities may provide havens for biocontrol agents that help suppress crop pests and may also provide food for pollinators of cultivated plants.

Tree crops as pillars of sustainability

In addition to weed control, tree crops can provide an array of other environmental services. With proper spacing and management, planted trees can help restore soil fertility and check erosion. Tree crops are well suited for most areas of the tropics, from jungles to desert fringes and from hot lowlands to the frost-prone slopes of high mountains. Tree crops are virtually synonymous with sustainable agriculture in many parts of the humid tropics, where multistory home gardens and polycultural swidden fields abound (Juo 1989).

Except for true deserts, any tropical landscape devoid of trees should be a warning signal that the landscape is degraded. Many tropical areas, now denuded of perennial cover, once supported woodlands, even in semi-arid regions. Several centuries ago, the Rajasthan School of artists in northwestern India depicted lush forests full of game; barren scrubland has now replaced these formerly rich woodlands (Roy 1987). Vast areas have been stripped of trees and shrubs by fuelwood gatherers, goats, timber traders, miners, farmers, and ranchers. Even areas lush with annual crops or pasture may mask ecological land mines created by the loss of tree cover. Soil erosion accelerated by wind and torrential downpours will eventually take their toll, and in dry areas, trees that formerly trapped precious moisture from fog or low clouds are often gone.

One measure of sustainability in tropical agriculture is the degree to which trees are incorporated in development plans. Ideally, some natural woodlands should be allowed to remain standing to secure supplies of a variety of goods, such as water, wood, game, medicinal plants, and fruits. For example, fruit pulp from the buriti (*Mauritia flexuosa*) palm and the açai (*Euterpe oleracea*) palm is readily sold in Brazilian cities. Buriti and açai grow in forest along streams and rivers and provide widely appreciated fruits and, in the case of açai, heart-of-palm as well.

Simply setting aside forest reserves is not enough; these areas must provide tangible benefits for the local population, and surrounding settlements need to be supported by viable agriculture. As part of this strategy, tree planting should be encouraged, but in practice this noble idea is often difficult to implement.

Two main considerations are necessary when promoting increased tree and bush cover in the tropics. First, the species involved must be suited to local ecological, cultural, and market conditions. Second, no one formula or blueprint will necessarily work over a broad area. A top-down approach to promoting perennial crops will not work; prescriptions must match the rich ecological and cultural heterogeneity of the target area.

Local people must be canvassed about their needs and aspirations, and market conditions need to be analyzed, for tree-planting schemes to be successful. Space is at a premium on most farms, ranches, and plantations, so selecting appropriate candidates for reforestation and for planting living fences in backyards, in orchards, and on ranches is critical. Also, varieties multiplied for distribution and sale should be able to withstand prevailing diseases and pests and be backed up by breeding and selection programs in case the situation of pathogens and insect pests changes. Mistakes made with the adoption of perennial crops are much more costly to rectify than those made with the adoption of annuals.

Trees and bushes can be planted in a wide array of cropping patterns, from polycultural plots to small, monocultural orchards and large-scale plantations. Agroforestry is already widely practiced, and further insights can be gained by studying indigenous systems. But agroforestry is no panacea: some species do not grow well under mixed-cropping conditions. Single-species stands can be sustainable. Diversity does not always mean greater stability or resiliency.

The land use mosaic

Just as a range of planting arrangements are appropriate for perennials, so a diverse array of land use systems can improve sustainability of agriculture. A farm, ranch, or plantation is embedded in a large socioeconomic and environmental arena, and a better understanding of the system's interactions and synergisms is critical to devising more productive and environmentally benign rural enterprises.

A single land use strategy for sustainable agriculture will not work in most tropical areas. Discussions on sustainability typically reflect the particular interests of their proponents, such as agroforestry or extractive reserves. Although agroforestry in its various forms and forest preserves where people harvest products certainly have their place, they are only pieces of a broader pattern of land use. A variety of interlocking annual and perennial cropping systems, orchards, ranches, and plantations is often found in the tropics. The relative area occupied by each and the crops involved are usually highly dynamic. Identifying and understanding such shifting relationships in land use are fundamental to sustainable development.

A clearer appreciation of the complementary interactions and antagonisms between land uses is a difficult task. Forces of change need to be elucidated and payoffs between land use systems pinpointed. Some land uses can be detrimental to sustainable agriculture, yet in some circumstances also beneficial. Although often controversial, raising cattle in rain forest areas often makes sense for smallholders, because manure is recycled to crops, biogas digesters provide lighting and cooking fuel, and cows provide milk for children. Larger ranches may degrade the environment but, if properly managed, can be sustainable and provide much-needed off-farm employment; such outside income often makes the difference between the survival or failure of a farm. Improved pasture management is essential, however, particularly on grazing lands cleared from forest.

A mosaic of land use systems has evolved in most areas of the tropics, particularly in wetter areas, in response to the rich cultural fabric and patchwork of biomes and ecosystems of the region. This rich quilt of farms, fields, and plantations is a heritage of in situ tradition supplemented by the diffusion of new technologies and ideas. Diversity in time and space, as exemplified by different uses of the land, can help provide a buffer against catastrophic disease and pest epidemics, among other environmental threats. Thus diversity of cropping and livestock systems on individual farms, as well as between different properties, is fundamental to the sustainability of tropical agriculture.

Development plans for a tropical region would do well to take into account the numerous ongoing experiments devised by operators of rural enterprises, from small to large scale. Successful analogs can often be found among some ranchers, farmers, and plantation owners, rather than on experiment stations. Although still needed on experiment stations, carefully controlled trials often investigate components of farming systems and are more likely to be successful if local experience is taken into account.

In addition to tapping local knowledge on successful cropping and livestock enterprises, scientists can enhance the impact of their work by conducting as much research on-farm as feasible. In this manner, extension work is built into the experiment, since farmers will more readily adopt technologies they see benefiting their neighbors. Progress toward sustainability will be quickened if both traditional knowledge and the frontiers of science are harnessed (Swaminathan 1990).

Researchers also need to be sensitive to the driving forces behind changes in land use. The waxing and waning of particular cropping patterns, the turnover of varieties, the encroachment of cattle ranching all need to be understood and this knowledge used to help set research priorities. A clearer understanding of the dynamics of changes in land use can also help fine-tune fiscal and socioeconomic policies.

Intensification: A pantropical imperative

At first glance, intensification, environmental health, and sustainability might seem incompatible. The notion of intensification often conjures up images of tractors causing plow pans, fertilizers causing eutrophication, herbicides destroying nontarget plant communities, and pesticides entering food chains. The case for intensification has been alluded to in our discussion of marginal lands and genetic resources. It also applies to the mosaic of land use systems: each system will have to be managed more efficiently and intensively to coax more goods and services for a given area.

An enormous research agenda lays ahead in this global imperative to intensify agriculture, including agroforestry, plantation systems, and livestock raising. How can this be done without destroying the resource base? This complex issue will require careful consideration by a range of disciplines, but a few indexes can be laid out here.

One consideration in intensification is the degree to which unanticipated outputs, which economists sometimes call externalities, might destroy the productive capacity of the land or damage the environments—and people who live in them—downstream from farming activities. Specifically, metabolic byproducts from farms and ranches, such as fertilizer not captured by plants and pesticides, can ruin water supplies for rural and urban folk, poison fish, or destroy aquatic environments so that game fish and turtle species are unable to survive.

More-intensive agricultural systems will necessitate greater use of energy. In the short term at least, the consumption of fossil fuel will thus increase in rural areas, and the implications of this for greenhouse gases warrant assessment. Some intensive agricultural systems, such as the cultivation of paddy rice, emit appreciable amounts of methane, one of the greenhouse gases. Intensification of agriculture thus entails careful monitoring for pollutants or gaseous emissions that may affect the local or even global climate.

Another critical dimension to intensification is monitoring the health of soil. Soil erosion is only one dimension to the productive capacity of the land. Intensification will entail a periodic report card on facets of soil such as organic matter, pH, level of phosphorus, salinity, and compaction. Inorganic fertilizers cannot correct for diminished levels of organic matter and compaction. Regular monitoring of soil conditions is expensive, but a necessary price to pay for more intensively managed systems. Several temperate-zone countries have recently established environmental monitoring systems to assess stresses created by various agricultural activities (see chapter 17 of this volume); determining how to adapt such systems, and bring down their costs, represents a major challenge for the tropics.

A blend of traditional knowledge and modern science

Answers to sustainability in tropical agriculture will be found among traditional farmers, field workers from such disciplines as anthropology, geography, and agricultural scientists, including biotechnologists. The appropriate mix of traditional knowledge and modern science will vary widely, depending on ecological constraints and market opportunities. In some highly intensive agricultural systems on the optimal farm lands, technologies to raise and sustain yields may come more from test tubes than from the crucible of folk experience. In other situations, such as marginal environments, traditional systems of resource management are likely to have much more to offer.

The imperative of tapping the frontiers of science and plumbing the depths of indigenous knowledge underscores the value of an interdisciplinary approach to sustainability. The ethnobotanist, anthropologist, and biotechnologist all have contributions to make in the search for sustainability.

An odyssey without end

Sustainability is a ceaseless journey, rather than a destination. Successful research for sustainable agriculture hinges on a multidisciplinary and highly flexible agenda, rather than a methodological straightjacket. It also hinges on continued investments in research, an important message to convey to governments.

As frustrating as this somewhat imprecise definition of sustainability may appear, dealing with peoples' cultures and economies, as well as the intricacies of ecosystems modified by humans, raises the task of identifying and measuring all the factors that impinge on raising sustainability to an even higher orbit. Resiliency is an important property in this quest for sustainability, both in human institutions as well as in the managed ecosystems that societies have created.

To find the paths to sustainable agriculture in the tropics, inputs from many disciplines need to be tapped, ranging from ecology to plant pathology and the social sciences. Sustainability is really an approach or a perspective, rather than a specific set of practices that can be easily measured and thus quantified.

Although more work is needed to improve our understanding of the dimensions to sustainability and how they can be measured, flexibility should always be paramount. Rigid definitions and compartmentalization, while making the task of modeling and prediction apparently easier, may lose some of the dynamism and complexity of tropical agriculture.

Satellite imagery and geographic information systems can help researchers obtain a better overview of land use systems in the tropics as well as identify early warning signals of environmental distress. Remote sensing can detect the early stages of a disease or pest epidemic and can alert policymakers to the spreading impact of a drought. Microcomputer-based systems have been developed for receiving satellite data that are small and inexpensive enough for use in the field. Such systems are already being used in Botswana to assist in land and water management and in Ethiopia to monitor droughts (Disney 1991). Geographic information systems can map spatial information on farm production, population clusters, and other socioeconomic and ecological data. Now a better integration of these two powerful tools is needed to further our efforts to build more sustainable agricultural systems in the tropics.

In spite of the difficulty of even gaining a firm grasp on all the facets of sustainability, certain conceptual features emerge from our discussion. Several key threads link the various facets of sustainable agriculture in the tropics. Soils need to be conserved, and methods of recycling nutrients need to be improved. Farmers, ranchers, and plantation owners need to be canvassed for their local knowledge as a prelude to introducing new technologies. Genetic resources need to be better conserved, both in situ and in collections of germ plasm, to uphold breeding efforts.

In regard to genetic resources, several points warrant emphasis. First, it is important to conserve wilderness, which sometimes contains wild populations of existing crops and domesticated animals, as well as their near relatives. Biodiversity is essential for the long-term success of agriculture (Pimentel and others 1992). Second, modified habitats can also be important for preserving genetic resources, as long as they are not destroyed. Third, existing crop gene banks need further support to improve their coverage, storage conditions, and evaluation of their accessions. More collections of germ plasm are needed, especially for the so-called minor crops, and collections should be duplicated to avoid irreversible losses. Development without concern for conservation will not work, nor will conservation without development that improves living conditions. Both are inescapably linked.

References

Adiningsih, G. S. A., M. Sudjadi, and D. Setyorini. 1988. "Overcoming Soil Fertility Constraints in Acid Upland Soils for Food Crop Based Farming Systems in Indonesia." *Indonesian Agricultural Research and Development Journal* 10:2, pp. 49–58.

Altieri, M. A., D. K. Letourneau, and J. R. Davis. 1983. "Developing Sustainable Agroecosystems." *BioScience* 33, pp. 45–49.

Anderson, C. 1992. "Researchers Ask for Help to Save Key Biopesticide." *Nature* 355, p. 661.

Beck, B. D. A. 1980. "Historical Perspectives of Cassava Breeding in Africa." In *Root Crops of Eastern Africa: Proceedings of a Workshop, 23 November 1980, Kigali, Rwanda*, pp. 13–18. Ottawa: IDRC.

Bennetzen, J. F., M. M. Qin, S. Ingels, and A. H. Ellingoe. 1988. "Allele-specific and Mutator-associated Instability at the Rp1 Disease-resistance Locus of Maize." *Nature* 332, pp. 369–70.

Brandes, E. W., and G. G. Sartoris. 1936. "Sugarcane: Its Origins and Improvement." In *Yearbook of Agriculture*, pp. 561–623. Washington, D.C.: U.S. Department of Agriculture.

Brattsten, L. B., C. W. Holyoke, J. R. Leeper, and K. F. Raffa. 1986. "Insecticide Resistance: Challenge to Pest Management and Basic Research." *Science* 231, pp. 1255–60.

Bray, W. 1990. "Agricultural Renaissance in the High Andes." *Nature* 345, pp. 385.

Brklacich, M., C. R. Bryant, and B. Smit. 1991. "Review and Appraisal of Concept of Sustainable Food Production Systems." *Environmental Management* 15:1, pp. 1–14.

Buttel, F. H. 1992. "The Environmentalization of Plant Genetic Resources: Possible Benefits, Possible Risks." *Diversity* 8:1, pp. 36–39.

CGIAR, Technical Advisory Committee (Consultative Group on International Agricultural Research). 1988. *Sustainable Agricultural Production: Implications for International Agricultural Research*. Rome.

Chang, J. 1968. "The Agricultural Potential of the Humid Tropics." *Geographical Review* 58:3, pp. 333–61.

Chavez, R., M. T. Jackson, P. E. Schiemidiche, and J. Franco. 1988. "The Importance of Wild Potato Species Resistant to the Potato Cyst Nematode, *Globodera pallida*, Pathotypes P4A and P5A in Potato Breeding. I. Resistance." *Euphytica* 37, pp. 9–14.

Clement, C. 1988. "Domestication of the Pejibaye Palm (*Bactris gasipaes*): Past and Present." *Advances in Economic Botany* 6, pp. 155–74.

———. 1991. "Amazonian Fruits: Neglected, Threatened, and Potentially Rich Resources Require Urgent Attention." *Diversity* 7:1–2, pp. 56–59.

Clement, C., C. H. Muller, and W. B. Chavez. 1982. "Recursos genéticos de espécies frutíferas nativas da Amazônia Brasileira." *Acta Amazonica* 12:4, pp. 677–95.

Conway, G. R., I. Manwan, and D. S. McCauley. 1983. "The Development of Marginal Lands in the Tropics." *Nature* 304, pp. 392.

Cook, O. F. 1909. "Vegetation Affected by Agriculture in Central America." Bureau of Plant Industry Bulletin 145. U.S. Department of Agriculture, Washington, D.C.

Creech, J. L. 1970. "Tactics of Exploration and Collection." In O. H. Frankel and E. Bennett, eds., *Genetic Resources in Plants: Their Exploration and Conservation*, pp. 221–29. Philadelphia, Penn.: F. A. Davis.

Davidson, B. 1969. *A History of East and Central Africa to the Late Nineteenth Century*. Garden City, N.Y.: Anchor Books.

Disney, J. 1991. "Resource Assessment and Farming Systems." *Resource* 4, p. 4.

Doebley, J. 1990. "Molecular Evidence for Gene Flow among *Zea* Species." *BioScience* 40, pp. 443–48.

Dover, M. J., and B. A. Croft. 1986. "Pesticide Resistance and Public Policy: Resistance Management Could Become the Key to Continuing Effective Pest Control." *BioScience* 36, pp. 78–85.

Egger, K., and B. Martens. 1987. "Theory and Methods of Ecofarming and Their Realization in Rwanda, East Africa." In B. Glaeser, ed., *The Green Revolution Revisited*, pp. 150–75. London: Allen and Unwin.

Eskes, A. B. 1989. "Resistance." In A. C. Kushalappa and A. B. Eskes, eds., *Coffee Rust*, pp. 171–291. Boca Raton, Fla.: CRC Press.

FAO (Food and Agriculture Organization of the United Nations). 1991. *Criteria, Instruments, and Tools for Sustainable Agriculture and Rural Development*. Proceedings of the Food and Agriculture Organization/Netherlands conference Agriculture and the Environment, 'S-Hertogenbosch, Netherlands, April 15–19. Rome.

Galinat, W. C., P. C. Mangelsdorf, and L. Piersen. 1956. "Estimates of Teosinte Introgression in Archaeological Maize." *Leaflets of the Botanical Museum of Harvard University* 17, pp. 101–24.

Gascon, J. P., J. M. Noiret, and J. Meunier. 1989. "Oil Palm." In G. Röbbelen, R. K. Downey, and A. Ashri, eds., *Oil Crops of the World: Their Breeding and Utilization*, pp. 475–93. New York: McGraw-Hill.

Hahn, S. K. 1978. "Breeding Cassava for Resistance to Bacterial Blight." *PANS* 24:4, pp. 480–85.

Hahn, S. K., E. R. Terry, and K. Leuschner. 1980. "Breeding Cassava for Resistance to Cassava Mosaic Disease." *Euphytica* 29, pp. 673–83.

Hahn, S. K., E. R. Terry, K. Leuschner, I. O. Akobundu, C. Okali, and R. Lal. 1979. "Cassava Improvement in Africa." *Field Crops Research* 2, pp. 193–226.

Harlan, J. R. 1965. "The Possible Role of Weed Races in the Evolution of Cultivated Plants." *Euphytica* 14, pp. 173–76.

———. 1971. "Agricultural Origins: Centres and Non-centres." *Science* 174, pp. 468–74.

Hawkes, J. G. 1977. "The Importance of Wild Germ Plasm in Plant Breeding." *Euphytica* 26, pp. 615–21.

Holm, L. G., D. L. Plucknett, J. V. Pancho, and J. P. Herberger. 1977. *The World's Worst Weeds:*

Distribution and Biology. Honolulu: University Press of Hawaii.

Huamán, Z., and P. Schmiediche. 1991. "The Importance of Ex Situ Conservation of Germ Plasm: A Case Study." *Diversity* 7:1–2, pp. 68–69.

Hussaini, S. H., M. M. Goodman, and D. H. Timothy. 1977. "Multivariate Analysis and the Geographical Distribution of the World Collection of Finger Millet." *Crop Science* 17, pp. 257–63.

IRRI (International Rice Research Institute). 1983. *Research Highlights for 1982.* Los Baños, Philippines.

Janzen, D. H. 1970. "Herbivores and the Number of Tree Species in Tropical Forests." *American Naturalist* 104, pp. 501–28.

———. 1973. "Tropical Agroecosystems: These Habitats Are Misunderstood by the Temperate Zones, Mismanaged by the Tropics." *Science* 182, pp. 1212–19.

Joachim, A. W. R., and S. Kandiah. 1948. "The Effect of Shifting (Chena) Cultivation and Subsequent Regeneration of Vegetation on Soil Composition and Structure." *Tropical Agriculture* 54:1, pp. 3–11.

Juo, A. S. R. 1989. "New Farming Systems Development in the Wetter Tropics." *Experimental Agriculture* 25, pp. 145–63.

Kahn, E. J. 1984. *The Staffs of Life.* Boston: Little, Brown, and Company.

Kamarck, A. M. 1973. "Climate and Economic Development." *Finance and Development* 10:2, pp. 2–8.

Kellman, M. 1969. "Some Environmental Components of Shifting Cultivation in Upland Mindanão." *Journal of Tropical Agriculture* 28, pp. 40–56.

Lambourne, J. 1937. "Experiments on the Economic Maintenance of Soil Fertility under Continuous Cropping with Tapioca." *Malayan Agricultural Journal* 25:4, pp. 134–45.

Leonard, H. J. 1989. "Environment and the Poor: Development Strategies for a Common Agenda." In H. J. Leonard, M. Yudelman, J. D. Stryker, J. O. Browder, A. J. De Boer, T. Campbell, and J. Allison, eds., *Environment and the Poor: Development Strategies for a Common Agenda,* pp. 3–45. U.S.–Third World Policy Perspectives 11. Brunswick, N.J.: Overseas Development Council.

Mares, M. A. 1992. "Neotropical Mammals and the Myth of Amazonian Biodiversity." *Science* 255, pp. 976–79.

Myers, N. 1990. "The Biodiversity Challenge: Expanded Hot-spots Analysis." *The Environmentalist* 10:4, pp. 243–56.

Nepstad, D. C., C. Uhl, and E. A. S. Serrão. 1991. "Recuperation of a Degraded Amazonian Landscape: Forest Recovery and Agricultural Restoration." *Ambio* 20:6, pp. 248–55.

Pimentel, D., U. Stachow, D. A. Takacs, H. W. Brubaker, A. R. Dumas, J. J. Meaney, J. A. S. O'Neil, D. E. Onsi, and D. B. Corzilius. 1992. "Conserving Biological Diversity in Agricultural/Forestry Systems." *BioScience* 42, pp. 354–62.

Pimm, S. L., and M. E. Gittleman. 1992. "Biological Diversity: Where Is It?" *Science* 255, p. 940.

Plucknett, D. L. 1976. "Hill Land Agriculture in the Humid Tropics." In *Hill Lands, Proceedings of International Symposium, 3–9 October, West Virginia University, Morgantown,* pp. 29–38. Journal Series 2074. Honolulu: Hawaii Agricultural Experiment Station.

Plucknett, Donald L., and Nigel J. H. Smith. 1982. "Agricultural Research and Third World Food Production." *Science* 217, pp. 215–20.

Plucknett, Donald L., Nigel J. H. Smith, J. T. Williams, and N. M. Anishetty. 1987. *Gene Banks and the World's Food.* Princeton, N.J.: Princeton University Press.

Rick, C. M. 1991. "Tomato Resources of South America Reveal Many Genetic Treasures." *Diversity* 7:1–2, pp. 54–56.

Roy, R. 1987. "Trees: Appropriate Tools for Water and Soil Management." In B. Glaeser, ed., *The Green Revolution Revisited,* pp. 111–25. London: Allen and Unwin.

Schultes, R. E. 1977. "Wild *Hevea*: An Untapped Source of Germ Plasm." *Journal of the Rubber Research Institute* (Sri Lanka) 54, pp. 227–57.

———. 1991. "Ethnobotanical Conservation and Plant Diversity in Northwest Amazon." *Diversity* 7:1–2, pp. 69–72.

Smith, Nigel J. H. 1990. "Strategies for Sustainable Agriculture in the Tropics." *Ecological Economics* 2, pp. 311–23.

Smith, Nigel J. H., J. T. Williams, Donald L. Plucknett, and J. P. Talbot. 1992. *Tropical Forests and Their Crops.* Ithaca, N.Y.: Cornell University Press.

Swaminathan, M. S. 1990. "Changing Nature of the Food Security Challenge: Implications for Agricultural Research and Policy." Sir John Crawford Memorial Lecture, Consultative Group on International Agricultural Research (CGIAR), World Bank, Washington, D.C.

Williams, D. E. 1989. "Exploration of Amazonian Bolivia Yields Rare Peanut Land Races." *Diversity* 5:4, pp. 12–13.

Wilson, H. D. 1990. "Gene Flow in Squash Species." *BioScience* 40, pp. 449–55.

Winkelmann, D. L. 1987. "Diversification, Sustainability, and Economics." In T. J. Davis and I. A. Schirmer, eds., *Sustainability Issues in Agricultural Development*, pp. 295–303. Washington, D.C.: World Bank.

York, E. T. 1988. "Improving Sustainability with Agricultural Research." *Environment* 30:9, pp. 18–20, 36–40.

Comments

R. Maria Saleth

A few critical issues need to be settled before pursuing the task of defining the concept of sustainable development. Just as defining the concept is a precondition for determining a measure of sustainable development, so is determining the context in and the level at which we need to define sustainable development. Although it is tempting to define sustainable development in a general fashion to cover everything from ozone to oysters, from a policy and operational point of view, we need to define the concept in the particular context of a given region or ecosystem or sector.

Still more important, in my view, is the choice of domain—whether physical or economic—in which the concept is to be defined. Many of us would agree that the concept of sustainability has ultimately to be defined and measured in the biophysical domain, but such a definition can never be independent of the economic, social, and even the cultural aspects. In other words, the economic, social, and cultural criteria will be the driving forces for the biophysical definition and measurement. It is well to keep in mind that our objective is to achieve the sustainability of the biophysical system not for its own sake but for the benefit of the people both in the present and in the future. Against this backdrop, Smith and Plucknett have made significant contributions to our understanding of the requirements for a proper definition and measurement of the sustainability of the agricultural systems in tropical regions.

Smith and Plucknett have viewed sustainable development in the context of the agricultural systems in the tropical regions as having four dimensions: biophysical, institutional and policy, sociocultural, and economic. They are careful to distinguish sustainability from the notions of stability, preservation, and low-cost production. Stability is a necessary, but not a sufficient, condition for sustainability because some apparently stable systems can actually be very brittle. Some of the sufficient conditions for sustainability include the resilience of the system and its ability to absorb and withstand stress and shocks.

Cross-country experience indicates that within the tropics, concerns about sustainability are critical for the agricultural systems based on marginal areas. Marginal areas do not always—or only—mean areas with eroded and unfertile soils, because even fertile land with a low rate of photosynthesis can be considered marginal in terms of net primary productivity even though it coincides with increased biodiversity and endemism. An implicit distinction exists between physically marginal areas and ecologically marginal areas, and this distinction has implications for sustainability indicators. In addition to the sustainability implications of marginal areas, pests and plant diseases and weeds also pose serious problems to the sustainability of tropical agriculture.

Smith and Plucknett have suggested a few important magnitudes or dimensions on which potential biophysical indicators of agricultural sustainability in the tropical regions should focus:

- The extent of farmers' efforts to slow soil erosion
- The status of genetic resources available
- The role of trees in development plans
- The extent to which land use is diverse (the land use mosaic)
- The magnitude of intensification imperative and
- The extent to which indigenous systems of knowledge can be blended with modern science.

The variables selected to reflect each of these dimensions may vary depending on the availability of data as well as the very appropriateness and capacity of the selected variable(s) for representing these magnitudes adequately. For instance, farmers' efforts to arrest soil erosion can be reflected by a host of variables both financial and technological in nature. These variables range from quantitative measures like the financial investment in soil control measures to mere qualitative measures like soil control practices or approaches adopted.

Similarly, the role of trees can be reflected by variables like the number and type of trees, the proportion of farm income—both monetary and real—derived from tree cultivation, the area under tree crops as a proportion of the total area under farms, and so forth. Likewise, a multiplicity of variables reflects both genetic capability and diversity of land use. Variables such as the extent of area affected or yield loss caused by pest and plant diseases can reflect indirectly the extent of genetic and land use uniformity present in the system besides indicating the presence of climatic and other factors conducive to the growth of pests. Further, the genetic diversity of the tropical system also depends on factors exogenous to the region to the extent that gene banks and genetic research institutions maintained elsewhere contribute to the genetic potential of tropical agriculture.

A few indirect indicators implicitly suggested by Smith and Plucknett, such as the rate of photosynthesis (and cloud cover) and biodiversity, are also evident. Since these two biological or biochemical factors determine biological productivity (or net primary productivity) essential for ensuring the ecological sustainability of any ecosystem, the measures that can reflect these two factors will necessarily form part of the set of sustainability indicators suitable for tropical agriculture. Given the authors' four-dimensional conception of agricultural sustainability, no single indicator can adequately reflect the sustainability status of agriculture (or other systems) either in tropical or temperate regions. Naturally, we need a set of indicators reflecting all four dimensions of sustainability noted by Smith and Plucknett.

These four magnitudes are related only to the ecological dimension of sustainability. Although it is true that the ecological system forms the foundation on which our economic and social systems are based, we also need to concentrate on the other two dimensions of sustainability, that is, economics and ethics. Although I agree with Smith and Plucknett that sustainability is not a destination but only a journey, I also note that sustainability is only a relative concept.

The chapter makes several important contributions. One of them is to note the potential possibility of turning certain problems into benefits. That is, sustainable development of agriculture depends on how apparent problems can be converted into potential benefits: for instance, by turning the ecologically marginal areas—regions with lower photosynthetic rates and cloud cover— into a zone for the conservation of biodiversity. Similarly, weeds can be exploited for their economic and genetic benefits. Although weeds allow gene flow across cultivated species, they are also used both as thatching materials and animal feed. One more fundamental input for improving the sustainability of the tropical agricultural systems, not appreciated enough so far, is the pool of indigenous knowledge for resource and genetic conservation. Further, biotechnological inputs should also be brought down to the village and farm levels through on-farm research trials that integrate both research and extension into a single process.

From a conceptual point of view, the authors' four-dimensional conception of sustainability can, in fact, be reduced to a three-dimensional one with ecology, economics, and equity dimensions insofar as the sociocultural aspects are fixed in the context of a given region or ecosystem and the institutional and policy aspects are manifested in the economic dimension. However, from a methodological point of view, Smith and Plucknett have correctly emphasized the contextual nature of the concept of sustainability both in time and space. That is, the definition and measurement of sustainability are specific to a sector or region since they take stock of the specific conditions and requirements of each sector (agriculture, industry, and so forth) as well as the requirement of different regions (also ecosystems), each differing in their endowment of resources. Likewise, the time factor also plays an important role because what is considered sustainable today may not be sustainable tomorrow. I earnestly believe that recognizing the contextual nature of the concept of sustainability is a critical first step toward developing efficient indicators for evaluating sustainability in any given context of time and space.

17

Biophysical Measurement of the Sustainability of Temperate Agriculture

C. Lee Campbell, Walter W. Heck, Deborah A. Neher, Michael J. Munster, and Dana L. Hoag

There is a growing awareness of the need to manage agroecosystems in such a way as to assure a continuing supply of agricultural commodities for human use without endangering our natural resources. The term sustainability is fairly recent, but there has long been a cadre of persons concerned with natural resources who have been prophets for the concept. In truth, many struggle to define sustainability for agroecosystems. One reason for this struggle may be that many people are driven more by their view of current agricultural practices as unsustainable and less by what they want to see as future practices in agricultural systems.

The challenges, then, are to define the desired nature or characteristics of a sustainable agroecosystem and to establish how to measure the level of sustainability of agroecosystems. The biophysical measurements that are chosen may reshape the definition of sustainability. Thus, the types and the spatial and temporal intensity of measurements must be determined carefully. Do we need comprehensive measurements taken at numerous times and over a preselected, limited geographic area, or do we need carefully selected measurements that can be taken at selected times over a growing season at a regional, national, or international spatial scale in order to assess the impact of stressors on the system? We have long obtained physical and chemical measurements of the environment around us to help interpret and predict the potential for agricultural production in the international community. However, we have done very little with biological (response) indicators that might better facilitate the interpretation of sustainability of ecosystems.

Thus, it is significant that the conference on which this volume is based gave focus to both sustainability and the development of biophysical measurements that can help interpret the sustainability of agricultural lands. This chapter addresses sustainability of agroecosystems and identifies biophysical measurements that are appropriate for monitoring programs to assess status and trends of agroecosystem health.

Sustainability, agroecosystems, and monitoring for status and trends

The concept of sustainability in temperate agriculture has many definitions. As a working definition, a sustainable agricultural system is "one that, over the long term, enhances environmental quality and the resource base on which agriculture depends, provides for basic human food and fiber needs, is economically viable, and enhances the quality of life for farmers and society as a whole" (Schaller 1990).

The agroecosystem must be considered as encompassing more than the cultivated crop and more than the part of the landscape that produces the food, fiber, and shelter normally associated with agricultural activities. *Agroecosystems* are a dynamic association among crops, pastures, livestock, and associated biota, atmosphere, soils, and water. Agroecosystems are part of a larger agricultural landscape that includes adjacent uncultivated land, drainage networks, and other vegetation and wildlife. Complementary to this definition is the concept that the agricultural landscape also contains farmers, farm workers, and rural communities. People are integral to the functioning of agroecosystems and agricultural landscapes; they make decisions concerning land use and selection of crops and livestock, and they impose social and economic values directly onto the agroecosystem and the agricultural landscape (Neher 1992).

This definition of agroecosystems recognizes their complexity and emphasizes a holistic approach that considers all components of agricultural landscapes. For an agroecosystem to be healthy, a balance must exist between the sustainable production of crops and livestock; maintenance of air, soil, and water quality; and assurance of diversity of wildlife and vegetation in the noncrop habitats. A change in any one component influences the other components in the agroecosystem and in adjacent, linked ecosystems.

The selection of measurements that could be used in a monitoring program to quantify or indicate sustainability in agroecosystems is critical. Societal values associated with sustainability must be determined, and assessment end points must be identified to reflect these social values. Societal values integrate independent, individual values. Therefore, no single answer exists about what is best for society, and these values or concepts will be very general. Nevertheless, any monitoring program must identify specific, quantifiable characteristics that indicate whether the perceived societal values are being maintained.

Assessment end points are "formal expressions of the actual environmental value that is to be protected, and as such should have unambiguous operational definitions, as well as social or biological relevance" (Knapp and others 1990). Assessment end points must be quantitative or quantifiable expressions (Suter 1990). These characteristics or assessment end points may be (1) single measurements, (2) indexes built from several measurements, or even (3) broader categories of concern (soil quality) that will be evaluated based on many measurements. Some end points relate to attributes that society wants to sustain, such as crop productivity. Others are attributes that may anticipate changes in the ecosystem (Marten 1988). For example, society may not be particularly interested in sustaining a certain level of chemical use, but if chemical use must be excessively high to maintain production, then it is likely that both production and resource quality will not be maintained in the long term.

The measurements that serve as the basis for quantification of assessment end points are indicators, or measurement end points. Thus, measurement end points are characteristics of the ecosystem and environment that, when measured, quantify the magnitude of stress, habitat characteristics, degree of exposure to stressors, or degree of ecological response to an exposure (Hunsaker and Carpenter 1990). Measurement end points, or indicators, can be divided into four classes: response, exposure, habitat, and stressor. Because of the multiple meanings of the word indicator in the ecological literature, we use the terms assessment end point and measurement end point.

A number of natural and human-induced stresses and activities could affect the sustainability of agroecosystems as well as other components of agricultural landscapes (see table 17-1). These include availability and use of water, cultivation and loss (erosion) of soil, salinization and alkalization of soil, use and accumulation of chemicals, air pollution, solid waste disposal on land, nutrient loss, water-logging, intensive animal production, fish farming, and climate. Each of these factors or issues should be addressed in a program to monitor the sustainability of agroecosystems. Several monitoring programs already incorporate some of the measurements.

Those factors and management strategies that serve to maintain agroecosystem health, as quantified by assessment end points, must be identified and encouraged. Many current practices may prove to be effective, but others may need to be changed if we are to maintain healthy ecological systems. One facet of a monitoring program designed to measure sustainability must be an assessment of environmental risk. It is expected that the assessment and measurement end points chosen would be useful in risk assessment. Additionally, risk assessment necessitates the assignment of statistical uncertainties to the data, indexes, and conclusions being reported.

Assessment and research monitoring programs

It is important to differentiate between assessment and research monitoring programs. Research

Table 17-1: Biophysical Measurements Available or Desired for Assessment of Sustainability of Temperate Agroecosystems

Issue and measurement	Current use	Key references
Water availability and use (applicable to irrigated, fed, flood-fed, arid, and humid agriculture)		
Soil moisture	EMAP, 26%[a]	Hillel 1982; Barnwell and others 1991
Water release curves	None	Hillel 1982
Area irrigated	EMAP	Heck and others 1992
Source of irrigation water used	EMAP, NRI	Heck and others 1992; Goebel and Schmude 1981
Efficiency of irrigation water used	None	None
Water infiltration rate	None	Hillel 1982
Hydraulic conductivity	None	Hillel 1982
Soil texture	EMAP, NRI	Heck and others 1991; Goebel and Schmude 1981
Soil cultivation and loss (methods of soil tillage, sedimentation, and erosion)		
Tillage methods employed	EMAP	Heck and others 1992
Crop residue on soil surface	52%	Barnwell and others 1991
Rates of erosion (USLE, WEPP)	EMAP, NRI	Foster and Lane 1987; Elliot, Foster, and Elliot 1991
Soil loss caused by wind erosion (WEE)	NRI	Goebel and Schmude 1981
Cesium-137 (retrospective; loss or accumulation)	Canada	Kiss, DeJong, and Rostad 1986; Ritchie and McHenry 1990
Depth of topsoil	None	None
Presence, quality, and diversity of filter strips	None	None
Outputs measured from drainage basin	None	None
Soil salinization and alkalization (increase in content of sodium and other salts in soils)		
Electrical conductivity	EMAP	Heck and others 1992
pH	EMAP, 7%	Heck and others 1992; Barnwell and others 1991
Exchangeable bases	EMAP, 7%	Heck and others 1992; Barnwell and others 1991
Aggregate stability	11%	Barnwell and others 1991
Land areas of saline and alkali soils	NRI	Goebel and Schmude 1981
Chemical use and accumulation (agricultural chemicals such as fertilizers, soil amendments, and pesticides)		
Use of agricultural chemicals	EMAP	Heck and others 1992
Soil biological health	EMAP	Heck and others 1992
Nitrates and toxic organics in drinking water	None	None
Number of applications during growing season	EMAP, IFS	Heck and others 1992; Wijnands and Vereijken 1992
Degree of resistance to pesticides	None	None
Weed populations and communities	None	Warcholinska 1978
Diversity of pests and beneficials	None	None
Leaching and movement of pesticides	None	None
Earthworm abundance	4%	Edwards and others 1990; Barnwell and others 1991
Air pollution (gaseous, solid, or liquid)		
Indicator plants for ozone (white clover)	EMAP	Heck and others 1992; Heagle and others 1991, 1992

(Table continues on next page)

Table 17–1: (continued)

Issue and measurement	Current use	Key references
Solid waste disposal on land (contaminants in the air or soil)		
Concentration of atmospheric pollutants	None	None
Symptoms of abiotic stress in plants	None	None
Heavy metal determinations (Hg, Cd, Pb)	EMAP	Heck and others 1992
Human health response (infections, exposures)	None	None
Nutrient loss (fertility, soil chemistry, and soil biology)		
Eutrophication in nearby surface water	None	None
Symptoms of nutrient deficiency in plants	None	None
Phosphorus and potassium status	IFS, EMAP, 11%	Brussaard and others 1988; Heck and others 1992
Leaching and movement of nutrients	IFS	Wijnands and Vereijken 1992
Soil nitrate	IFS, 4%	Wijnands and Vereijken 1992
Total nitrogen	89%	Barnwell and others 1991
Mineralizable nitrogen	EMAP, 22%	Cabrera and Kissel 1988; Stanford and Smith 1972
Total carbon	96%	Barnwell and others 1991
Organic carbon	None	Bornemisza and others 1979; Storer 1984, 1992
Organic matter	IFS, EMAP, 15 %	Brussaard and others 1988; Barnwell and others 1991
Microbial biomass	22%	Lodge and Ingham 1991; Babiuk and Paul 1970
Microbial activity	None	Schnurer and Rosswall 1982
Nematode communities	EMAP	Wasilewska 1979
Water-logging (soil tilth and structure)		
Water-holding capacity	EMAP	Heck and others 1992
Concentration of oxygen in soil	None	None
Bulk density	70%	Barnwell and other 1991
Soil compaction	None	None
Presence of plow layers	None	None
Permeability	None	Hillel 1982
Effectiveness of drainage systems	None	None
Earthworm abundance	4%	Edwards and others 1990; Barnwell and others 1991
Intensive animal production (livestock for market)		
Production of the herd (milk, meat, wool)	IFS	Hermans and Vereijken 1992
Size and composition of the herd	IFS	Hermans and Vereijken 1992
P-output in manure	IFS	Hermans and Vereijken 1992
Available grassland for grazing	IFS	Hermans and Vereijken 1992
Amount of purchased feedstuffs	IFS	Hermans and Vereijken 1992
Pests and diseases	None	None
Fish farming (aquaculture)		
Accumulation of fish biomass	None	None
Density of fish parasites and pathogens	None	None
Dissolved oxygen content of water	None	None
Turbidity of water	None	None
Aesthetic value of the rural landscape (spatial arrangement and area of agricultural landscape elements)		
Fragmentation (size, shape, edge, connectivity)	EMAP	Heck and others 1992
Presence of hedgerows or windbreaks	NRI	Goebel and Schmude 1981
Availability and quality of wildlife habitat	NRI	Goebel and Schmude 1981

Issue and measurement	Current use	Key references
Biodiversity of vegetation	NRI	Goebel and Schmude 1981
Diversity and vigor of wildlife populations	None	None
Habitat and vegetative cover (riparian, wetland)	NRI	Goebel and Schmude 1981
Enrollment in conservation reserve programs	EMAP, NRI	Heck and others 1992
Land use	EMAP, NRI	Heck and others 1992
Climate		
Air temperature	81 percent	Barnwell and others 1991
Radiation	52 percent	Barnwell and others 1991
Precipitation	81 percent	Barnwell and others 1991
Relative humidity	52 percent	Barnwell and others 1991
Wind speed	56 percent	Barnwell and others 1991
Pan evaporation	33 percent	Barnwell and others 1991
Soil temperature	33 percent	Barnwell and others 1991
Soil moisture	26 percent	Barnwell and others 1991

a. The agroecosystem component of the EMAP; the percentage of twenty-seven U.S. Corn Belt and Great Plains long-term research sites measuring the specified parameter (Barnwell and others 1991).

Note: EMAP, Environmental Monitoring and Assessment Program (United States); NRI, National Resources Inventory, conducted by the U.S. Department of Agriculture's Soil Conservation Service; USLE, Universal Soil Loss Equation; WEPP, Water Erosion Prediction Project; WEE, Wind Erosion Equation; IFS, Integrated Arable Farming Systems (the Netherlands).

monitoring programs are designed to monitor specific sites in great detail. Although often used for extrapolation to larger areas, research monitoring sites are not designed for that purpose, and extrapolation can lead to a biased interpretation of what is happening over a larger area. The monitoring done at a research site is usually continuous over a given period of time. It can be, and often is, done in conjunction with a modeling program so the data can be used to predict what might happen in an area under various conditions. Some research monitoring is done to help validate models.

Assessment monitoring is designed to determine the condition of resources within an area with either political (county, state, national, and so forth) or ecological (ecotone, ecosystem, watershed, and so forth) boundaries. The evaluation is based on the chosen assessment and measurement end points. Such a monitoring program should have a statistical sampling design with complete coverage of the area. Sampling intensity should be appropriate for the area being monitored and for meeting data quality objectives (desired ability to detect differences at a given level of statistical confidence). Monitoring is conducted from only one to several times during the year, so identifying the sample time or index period for monitoring is critical. Generally,

sampling should be done when the measurement of interest is most stable (lowest variance) and most representative of the condition of interest. Although assessment monitoring might be done over a span of only one to several years, this would provide information only for determining the status of the system. Assessment monitoring should be designed to monitor status and trends over a minimum of ten years. Where there is continuing interest in the sustainability of various ecological systems, such monitoring should become a permanent part of a country's heritage.

In the United States, the U.S. Environmental Protection Agency (EPA) has initiated the Environmental Monitoring and Assessment Program (EMAP), which monitors the status and trends of seven major ecological resources within the United States (Kutz and Linthurst 1990). The agroecosystem component of EMAP has used sustainability as a focus in developing a program to monitor the status and trends in agroecosystems of the United States (Heck and others 1991, 1992). This is perhaps the most intensive agroecological monitoring initiative ever proposed and includes a major research component to determine the feasibility of such a large-scale effort.

Although EMAP is the most developed monitoring program for implementation on an extensive geographic scale, several other national-scale monitoring programs have been proposed (see table 17-2). CSIRO in Australia is implementing the Land and Water Care Program to monitor changes in the extent and severity of land degradation and production from various systems of land use on a national, state, and territory level. Canada has proposed an Agroecosystem Health and Management Program to conduct a national survey on levels of organic matter, nutrients, and erosion of soils and to monitor cropping practices using remote-sensing technology and statistical information from the Canadian census of agriculture. This program and Environment Canada's Indicators Task Force are planning to develop indicators for application on a broad, national scale (Environment Canada 1991; Piekarz 1990). In the United Kingdom, the Terrestrial Initiative in Global Environmental Research plans to include research on the causes and consequences of climatic change across the United Kingdom. Planned activities include development of conti-

nental-scale models of the hydrological cycle, assessment of the sensitivity of plant and animal species to changes in climate, and application of remote-sensing and geographic information systems to predict national impacts of changes in climate. The European Community is discussing the possibility of initiating a large-scale, ecological monitoring program.

On an international scale, the United Nations Environment Program (UNEP) has initiated the World Soils and Terrain Project (SOTER; Baumgardner 1990) and the Global Assessment of Soil Degradation (GLASOD) Program in cooperation with the International Soil Reference and Information Center to map digitally and assess the degradation of global soils and terrain resources. The primary tasks are (1) to produce a general soil degradation map of the world and (2) to develop a soils and terrain digital data base. The SOTER Project has completed pilot studies in Latin America (Argentina, Brazil, and Uruguay),

Table 17-2: National-Scale Monitoring Programs for Temperate Agriculture

Contact person	Mailing address
C. Lee Campbell Technical director	EMAP-Agroecosystems, U.S. Department of Agriculture, Agricultural Research Service, 1509 Varsity Drive, Raleigh, NC 27606, United States
Anastasios Nychas General director	Commission of the European Community, Rue de la Loi 200, B-1049 Bruxelles, Belgium
David Smiles Chief	Division of Soils, CSIRO Land and Water Care Program, Canberra Laboratories, G.P.O. Box 639, Canberra ACT 2601, Australia
Geoff Pickup Officer in charge	Division of Wildlife and Ecology, CSIRO Land and Water Care Program, Centre for Arid Zone Research, P.O. Box 2111, Alice Springs NT 0871, Australia
John Haberern President	Soil Report Card, Rodale Research Institute, 222 Main Street, Emmaus, PA 18098, United States
M. Beran Program manager	TIGER Program, Institute of Hydrology, Wallingford, Oxon OX10 8BB, United Kingdom
David Waltner-Toews	Agroecosystem Health and Management Department of Population Medicine University of Guelph, Guelph, Ontario N1G 2W1, Canada
David Rapport	Agroecosystem Health and Management Institute for Research on Environment and Economy, University of Ottawa, Ottawa, Ontario K1N 6N5, Canada
G. Philip Robertson Principal investigator	LTER Sites, U.S. National Science Foundation, Kellogg Biological Station Michigan State University, Hickory Corners, MI 49060, United States
Gary Barrett	Association of Ecosystem Research Centers (AERC), Ecology Research Center Miami University, Oxford, OH 45056, United States
M. F. Baumgardner	SOTER Project, Agronomy Department, Purdue University Agricultural Experiment Station, West Lafayette, IN 47907, United States

North America (Montana in the United States and southern portions of the Canadian provinces of Alberta and Saskatchewan), and West Africa. The expected outcome of these programs is an operational world data base that can serve as a model for the design and construction of within-country data bases with sufficient detail and accuracy for local and provincial use. Other international programs that monitor aspects of agricultural systems include (1) the Food and Agriculture Organization of the United Nations, which compiles much of the global information on crop production and (2) the Famine Early Warning System of the U.S. Agency for International Development, which uses remote sensing to monitor changes in photosynthetic activity and then targets areas where crop production may be inadequate. An international data base of monitoring efforts is being compiled by the United Nations Global Environmental Monitoring System.

In the United States, the U.S. Geological Survey has established the National Water-Quality Assessment Program to monitor water quality and related biological end points within designated watersheds. The U.S. Department of Agriculture, Agricultural Research Service and the U.S. Geological Survey have established the joint Management Systems Evaluation Areas Program for research monitoring. The U.S. EPA has initiated the Midwest Agrichemical Surface/Subsurface Transport and Effects Research Program to monitor the quality of water, including groundwater.

Other monitoring programs within the United States include those initiated by the National Science Foundation in Michigan, the Leopold Center in Iowa (Benbrook 1991b), and the Rodale Institute in the state of Pennsylvania (Haberern 1991; Shirley 1991). The National Science Foundation has established some Long-Term Ecological Research sites that monitor indicators of agroecosystems at the Kellogg Biological Station in Michigan (table 17-2). The Leopold Center has outlined a list of benchmark indicators for monitoring the quality of soil, the function of hydrogeological cycles, the biotic community, and economic viability, all for the state of Iowa (Benbrook 1991b). In 1991, the Rodale Institute (1991) sponsored an international conference to identify indicators of soil quality and research needs for the production of a national soil report card (Shirley 1991). At the conference, measurable properties were identified for soil fertility, hydrology, toxicity, and temperature.

Measurements for monitoring sustainability

Three values are of primary importance to human society in determining the condition of agroecosystems. These values are (1) supply of agricultural commodities: the ability of an agroecosystem to provide adequate yield and quality of crops and livestock over the long term; (2) quality of natural resources: the freedom of natural resources from harmful levels of substances such as trace metals, pesticides, fertilizers, pathogens, salts, and pollutants in one or more component(s) of the agroecosystem; and (3) conservation of biological resources: the maintenance of the ecological soundness of crop and noncrop components of the agricultural landscape as habitat for plant, animal, and microbe species. These three values encompass human and ecological values for agroecosystems and encompass the concept of agroecosystem sustainability (see figure 17-1).

Assessment end points for use in a monitoring program

The selection and evaluation of assessment and measurement end points are critical to the success of a monitoring program. Clearly defined criteria for the identification, selection, and evaluation of end points encourage objectivity and an unbiased evaluation of all important characteristics prior to their acceptance or rejection for long-term use (Knapp and others 1990). Sets of critical and desirable criteria for the selection of assessment and measurement end points for an ecosystem monitoring program are given in table 17-3. In any monitoring program, the selection and evaluation of both assessment and measurement end points should be ongoing so that the most appropriate selections can be made to assess the health of the agroecosystem. As a monitoring program develops, the emphasis will shift from identification and evaluation of end points to their selection and implementation.

Biophysical measurements for use in temperate agriculture

Ideally, a monitoring program must have a suite or panel of such end points to address the identified societal values (see table 17-4; figure 17-1). The biophysical measurements presented in table 17-1 represent an extensive list of measurement end points that are candidates for agroecological

257

Table 17–3: Critical and Desirable Criteria for Selecting Measurement End Points for an Ecosystem Monitoring Program

Criteria	Characteristic of the measurement
Critical criteria	
Responsive	Must reflect changes in ecosystem condition and respond to stressors of concern or management strategy
Regional applicability	Must be applicable on a regional basis and to a broad range of regional ecosystems
Unambiguous	Must be related unambiguously to an end point or relevant exposure or habitat variable
Integrate effects	Must integrate ecosystem condition over time and space
Correlative	Must directly measure or correlate with changes in ecosystem processes, including unmeasured ecosystem processes
Important	Must reflect conditions that are important to overall ecological structure and function
Low measurement error	Must exhibit low natural temporal and spatial variability at the sampling site during the index period to be able to detect regional patterns and trends
Interpretability	Must have a clear interpretation or be related through conceptual models to meaningful changes in the ecosystem
Desirable criteria	
Simple quantification	Should be quantified by synoptic or cost-effective automated monitoring
Standardized method	Should have a generally accepted, standardized measurement method
Historical data	Should be generated from accessible data source
Retrospective	Should be related to past conditions by way of retrospective analyses
Anticipatory	Should provide an early warning of widespread changes in ecosystem condition or processes
Cost-effective	Should have low cost relative to its information value

Table 17-4: Association between Agroecosystem Assessment End Points and Societal Values

Assessment end point	Supply of agricultural commodities	Quality of natural resources[a]	Conservation of biological resources
Crop productivity	X		
Soil quality (physical and chemical)	X	X	
Water quality (ponds and existing wells)	X	X	
Land use and cover	X		X
Agrichemical use	X	X	X
Soil biological health (nematode indexes)	X		
Landscape structure		X	X
Groundwater and well comparisons	X	X	
Biological ozone indicator (clones of white clover)	X	X	X
Socioeconomic health	X	X	X
Pest density	X		X
Foliar symptoms	X	X	X
Beneficial insects	X		X
Genetic diversity	X		X
Habitat quality		X	X
Wildlife populations			X
Livestock productivity	X		
Nonpoint source loading		X	X
Water quantity (irrigation)	X		
Other biomonitor species	X	X	X

a. Air, soil, and water, including transport of contaminants into, within, and out of agroecosystems.

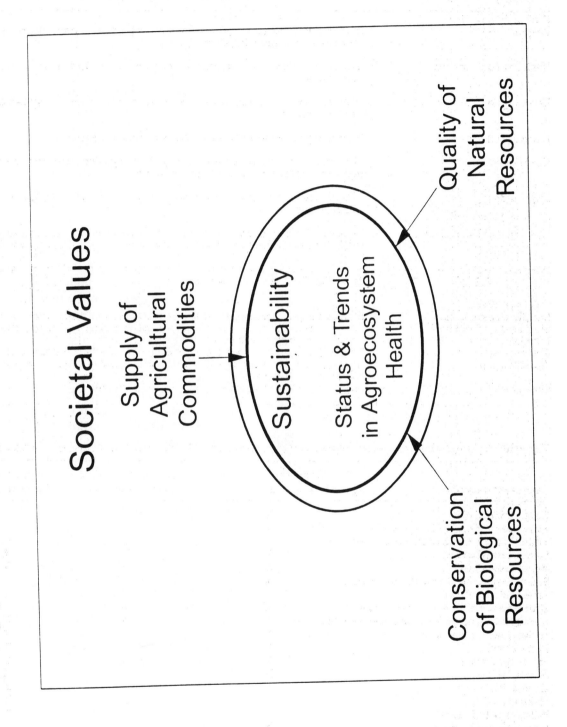

Figure 17-1: Societal Values to Be Addressed by a Series of Assessment End Points and Biophysical Measurements

monitoring programs. The actual measurement data can come from surveys; field sampling of soil, water, or air; remote sensing; and existing data sets. In practice, more than one societal value may be addressed by an individual assessment end point and its associated measurement end points. For example, assessment end points listed in table 17-4 could be monitored to describe collectively the condition of agroecosystems. Some of these assessment end points are physical or chemical measures, whereas others are biological. Some traditionally have been more directly associated with agronomic concerns (crop productivity), whereas others have been more broadly associated with ecological applications (landscape structure). Each assessment end point, however, is appropriately associated with agroecological concerns.

The diversity in assessment end points reflects the multicomponent and multipurpose nature of agroecosystems. The many-faceted character of agroecosystems makes it difficult to find a single measurement or index with which to answer the question, are the agroecosystems in this region healthy or unhealthy? A system might be socioeconomically viable but have low genetic diversity, for example. Or producers may substitute labor and capital inputs for lost productivity. Of course, the focus should be on long-term sustainability, which we can only surmise.

As mentioned above, measurement end points can be classified into four types: response, exposure, habitat, or stressor. These can be defined as follows (Messer 1990):

1. *Response measurement end point:* a biological or ecological characteristic measured to provide evidence of the condition of a resource at the organism, population, community, or ecosystem level of organization.

2. *Exposure measurement end point:* an environmental characteristic measured to provide evidence of the occurrence or magnitude of contact with a physical, chemical, or biological stressor.

3. *Habitat measurement end point:* a physical, chemical, or biological attribute measured to characterize the conditions necessary to support an organism, population, community, or ecosystem in the absence of stressors.

4. *Stressor measurement end point:* a characteristic measured to quantify a natural process, an environmental hazard, or a management action that results in changes in exposure or habitat.

All four types of measurement end points are useful in describing the condition of a natural resource, but the most important type is the response end point, which quantifies what is happening to the valued parts of the system. The other three end points serve supporting roles. The difference between an exposure or habitat measurement end point and a stressor measurement end point is that the former indicates how much stress is being experienced by a system (concentration of a heavy metal in soil), whereas the latter more directly measures the agent causing the stress (industrial emissions of a heavy metal). In this context, stressor includes both positive and negative influences. Precipitation is a natural stressor, because it influences plant growth, sometimes causing increases and sometimes decreases. Tillage is an example of an anthropogenic stressor. The relationships among the four types of measurement end points are diagramed in figure 17-2.

Any one assessment end point may involve one or more types of measurement end points (see table 17-5). For example, pest populations respond to the condition of an agroecosystem but also represent a stressor on other parts of the system (namely crops and livestock). Conversely, it may take several types of measurements to quantify a single assessment end point. To use crop productivity as an adequate assessment end point of ecosystem health, adjustments may be needed for habitat and stressors that influence crop growth (type of soil, weather, management inputs). The idea behind such an adjustment would be to account for known large effects so that the subtler aspects of a system's health are discernable.

Use of selected assessment end points in monitoring sustainability

Assessment and measurement end points were discussed above in very general terms. To illustrate these principles in more detail, two assessment end points will be discussed: soil quality and crop productivity. These are important components of agroecosystems and, therefore, ought to be considered when monitoring sustainability.

SOIL QUALITY (PHYSICAL AND CHEMICAL ATTRIBUTES)
Soils function as sinks and sources of biogeochemical elements, as filters for pollutants, and as an environment for growth and development of plants and other biological communities. Soils are liable to change, gradually or abruptly and

Figure 17–2: Relationship among Measurement End Points

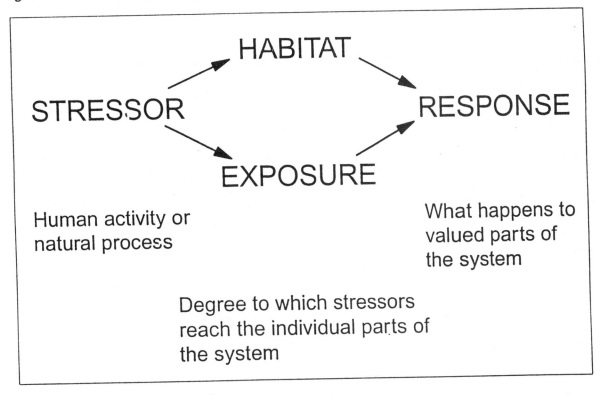

Note: The boundaries are not always clear

Table 17-5: Association between Agroecosystem Assessment End Points and Type of Measurement End Point

Assessment end point	Response	Exposure	Habitat	Stressor
Crop productivity	X			
Soil quality (physical and chemical)	X	X	X	X
Water quality (ponds and existing wells)		X	X	X
Land use and cover	X		X	X
Agrichemical use		X	X	X
Soil biological health (nematode indexes)	X			
Landscape structure			X	
Groundwater and well comparisons	X	X	X	X
Biological ozone indicator (clones of white clover)	X	X		
Socioeconomic health	X	X		X
Pest density	X	X		X
Foliar symptoms	X	X		
Beneficial insects	X	X	X	
Genetic diversity	X	X		
Habitat quality	X		X	
Wildlife populations	X		X	
Livestock productivity	X			
Nonpoint source loading		X		X
Water quantity (irrigation)			X	X
Other biomonitor species	X	X		

partly irreversibly, due to human use. The main activities affecting soils in agroecosystems include vehicular traffic, tillage, use of agricultural chemicals, waste disposal, and land use. The long-term goal of soil quality monitoring in agroecosystems is to provide a regional assessment of the cumulative response of the soil to these activities and to conservation efforts.

The focus of soil quality assessment in agroecosystems is on the presence, extent, and change in soil properties that (1) are important to the functioning of the soil system, (2) are known to be affected by agricultural land management, and (3) can be adequately measured in one annual sampling period at a regional scale. Although they should be sensitive enough to detect changes, these properties must also be stable enough that trends can be detected against their background variability. Some physical and chemical measurement end points associated with soil quality are defined in table 17-6.

An objective in the assessment of soil quality is to determine the range and frequency distribution (in proportion of land area) of individual measurements and to begin evaluating how well the chosen measurements and derived indexes reflect changing conditions. Because standards of soil quality vary with climate and soil, determining the *rate of change* of soil quality is one long-term objective. A second long-term objective is to combine indicator measurements into quantitative indexes so that general statements about soil quality on a regional basis can be made. Several possible indexes include structure, tilth, fertility, contamination, and productivity. For example, a tilth index might combine values of bulk density, available water capacity, porosity, organic carbon, and percentage clay content. Third, information on soil quality is combined with other monitoring data to produce a picture of overall agroecosystem health. A fourth long-term objective is to integrate information on the health of agricultural soils with information on soils in forests and arid lands to provide an overall picture of soil quality across terrestrial ecosystems.

Data for assessing soil quality can come from a number of sources. The best option is to collect soil from agricultural fields that have been selected from a statistically valid sampling frame. Care must be taken that the samples actually represent what they are intended to represent. Another source of data is information published by governmental soil conservation agencies, such as the U.S. Department of Agriculture's Soil Conservation Service, which provides the State Soil Survey Data Base and National Resources Inventory. To establish which published data are associated with the soil found at each sample site, the soil series at that location could be determined from soil survey maps or photographs.

Table 17-6: Description of Physical and Chemical Soil Quality Measurement End Points

Measure	Description
Organic carbon	Total organic carbon in first 20 centimeters of soil (plow layer)
Clay content	Percentage of clay content in plow layer
Available water capacity	Water retention between –33 and –1,500 kiloPascals matric potential
Porosity	Water retention at –5 and –10 kiloPascals matric potential
Soil pH	Measure of soil acidity
Potassium, magnesium, sodium, phosphorus	Exchangeable cations for nutrient availability
Base saturation	Extent to which the cation exchange capacity is occupied by base cations
Exchangeable acidity (humid regions)	Extent to which the cation exchange capacity is occupied by hydrogen and aluminum
Exchangeable sodium percentage (arid regions)	Extent to which the cation exchange capacity is occupied by sodium
Electrical conductivity	Soil salinity
Extractable aluminum (humid regions)	Extractable aluminum in the plow layer
Mercury	Total mercury in the plow layer
Bulk density (intact core)	Mass of dry soil per unit of volume
Hydraulic conductivity (intact core)	Rate at which soil transmits water while saturated

The data obtained can be used to evaluate how well the measurements and derived indexes truly reflect good, poor, or changing conditions. This is one of the greatest challenges in monitoring ecosystems: deciding which values are acceptable and which are unacceptable in the context of soil quality. These criteria are known for some soil parameters (exchangeable sodium percentage, conductivity). For other parameters, such as soil organic carbon or percentage clay content, it may be possible to determine if the *direction* of change is acceptable or unacceptable. Identified ranges for indicators and benchmark references of soil quality are generally lacking, and evaluation of soil quality measurements is made even more complex by the fact that what is a good or poor range or value varies with climate, soil, and management scenario.

CROP PRODUCTIVITY

People concerned about agriculture often focus on crop production. This concern is embodied in the question *Will There Be Enough Food?*—the title of the 1981 *Yearbook of Agriculture* (U.S. Department of Agriculture 1981). In addition to its crucial importance to human society, crop plants also provide food for soil microbes, plant-eating insects, and other organisms. Crop productivity is thus an important ecological parameter and an important assessment end point that is affected by many elements in agroecosystems (see figure 17-3).

Crop productivity as an assessment end point has four facets: (1) total production in a region, (2) yield (production per unit of land area), (3) yield as a biological response indicator adjusted for inputs, and (4) production efficiency (production per unit of input). Quantifying either of the last two requires a knowledge of inputs as well as yield, but the two perspectives are subtly different. To use yield as a biological response variable, one must adjust for those factors that contribute to yield but are considered extraneous to ecosystem health. These may include some natural inputs (such as rainfall), some human-produced inputs (such as pesticides), or both. The hope is that adjusted yield will reflect the subtle differences in productivity that may be obscured by large management effects. The fourth aspect, production efficiency, would quantify agroecosystem status by comparing production achieved with resources expended, whether or not those resources contribute directly to yield. This, of course, has implications for the ability of a society to

maintain production, and the overlap of ecological and socioeconomic issues in agroecosystems is apparent. Either of the last two aspects of crop productivity would be appropriate for a monitoring program. In either case, four unresolved issues are methods to (a) obtain data, (b) account for management inputs, (c) combine measures across different crops (if that is even desirable), and (d) interpret crop productivity in relation to sustainability.

The starting point for all measures is the yield of crops on the sampled field. There are methods of actually taking samples in the field to determine yield or production of dry matter, but it is usually simpler to obtain these data by asking the farmer. At the same time, information can be gathered about fertilizers, rotations, tillage systems, irrigation, conservation practices, and other management variables that may be affecting sustainability. Complementary material, such as conversion factors for standardizing inputs, multipliers for calculating primary productivity, weather data, and crop models, are needed from other sources. Variability and uncertainty of conversion factors are expected to make it difficult to assign statistical confidence to the final indexes.

Crop yields have, of course, been surveyed and reported for decades, but yield alone is not a sufficient indicator of health. If one field produces a greater yield than another because of additional fertilizer, is that first field healthier? To answer this, it is necessary to account for the effects of management inputs and perhaps for the influence of weather. One way to do this is to calculate ratios of output to input in which the numerator is some measure of production, and the denominator represents some input (water, nitrogen, and so forth) or combination of inputs. The traditional method has been to use prices as the scaling mechanism; however, this does not have the desired ecological orientation.

Various types of energy output to input ratios have also been used in agriculture (Fluck and Baird 1980), but the validity of the *energy ratio* (energy output per energy input) has been questioned, and *energy productivity* (kilogram of production per unit of input energy) has been suggested as a better measure (Fluck 1979). Energy conversions for the various inputs are often difficult to obtain. A slightly more sophisticated approach than output to input ratios tis o use monitoring data to determine the coefficients relating yield to inputs (Lin and others 1991).

Figure 17-3: Factors That Influence Crop Productivity

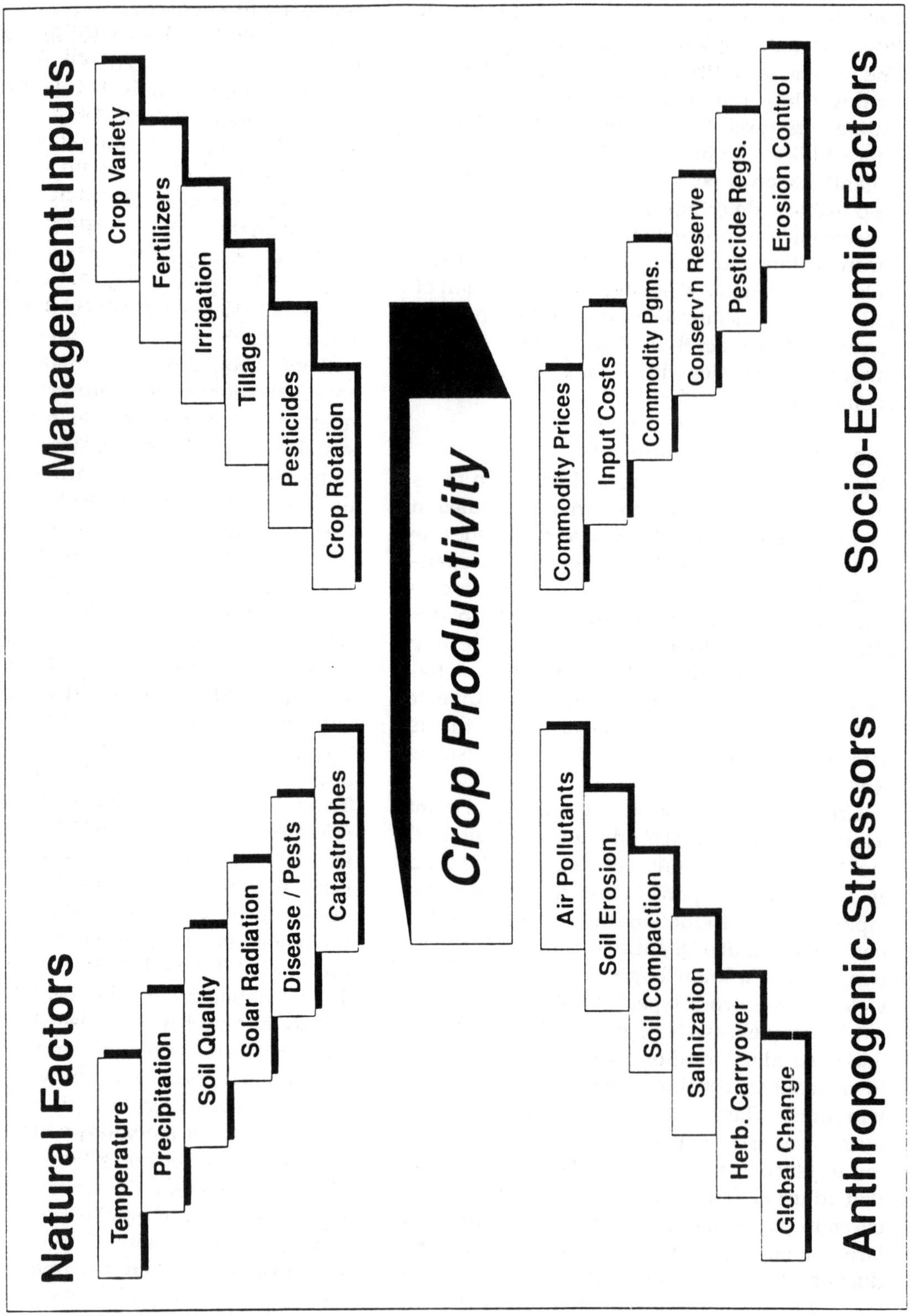

Figure 17-3: Factors That Influence Crop Productivity

Another way to account for inputs is to estimate what the yield on each field would have been if a standard set of inputs had been used. Such adjustments come from existing research findings on the response of yield to inputs or from models of crop growth. A similar method is to build a measurement end point from the difference or ratio between each field's yield and the yield predicted by a statistical or process model. Two critical steps are (1) deciding which inputs, natural and anthropogenic, should be accounted for and (2) finding the means to make those adjustments.

Whether to adjust quantifiers of yield for fluctuations in the weather is a major question. Such an adjustment may stabilize the variability inherent in yield data. If all weather variations were accounted for, however, it might be more difficult to detect changes caused by global changes in climate (except through shifts in land use).

A second major question facing a monitoring program for crop productivity is whether to report the productivity of individual crop species or to try to integrate values among crops. The latter approach may be a more appropriate biophysical measure at the ecosystem scale. A combined index does not, however, account for the fact that individual crops may respond differently to environmental changes.

Two ways in which a combined index might be calculated are normalized yield and net primary productivity. Normalized yield (Y') could be calculated for each field by using that field's yield per hectare (Y = production from field or area harvested), the average (Y_{ref}) over some meaningful region (such as a county) for an arbitrary reference period, and the standard deviation of that average yield (s). Similar to a standard normal variate, the calculation could be

$$Y' = [(Y - Y_{ref}) / s] + 5 \qquad (17\text{-}1)$$

The number 5 is added arbitrarily so that the distribution of Y' has a mean of 5. Because the standard deviation of Y' is 1 and its mean is 5, negative values will be conveniently rare. The values of Y' can be aggregated across crops. The advantage of this method of standardization is that both means and variances of different crops are put on a similar scale. For simplicity, s can be calculated from temporal (year-to-year) variation in the county means. The disadvantage comes in the interpretation, which must be done carefully. Trend detection would be an important application for such an index, since initial re-

gional differences are standardized out. In theory, this type of calculation can be made for any measurement, once baseline values have been established for each crop.

Net primary productivity provides another way of combining data from all crops into a single value. The net accumulation of plant biomass per unit of area per unit of time, it is a potentially useful measurement end point because it allows comparisons among different types of ecosystems, and it can be estimated from data on yield. The yield of each crop is expressed in kilograms per hectare and then converted from economic yield to production of dry matter, using conversion factors from the literature (Sharp and others 1976), along with standard moisture contents. If calculated this way, net primary productivity should not be reported for individual crops, because it is simply a multiple of the yield. Also, comparison among crop species is not meaningful because different crops would be expected to differ in net primary productivity. Regional productivity is a function of both the productivity of individual fields and the patterns of land use (Sharp and others 1976; Turner 1987).

A different, but complementary, approach to measuring plant productivity in agroecosystems is through the use of remote sensing. Greenness indexes derived from satellite data are related to the primary productivity of the vegetation (Roughgarden, Running, and Matson 1991). These allow larger scales to be considered than with field-based measures. Depending on the resolution of the scanner and the heterogeneity of the landscape, remotely sensed indexes may reflect not only crops but also pastures, idle land, woodland, roads, water, and so forth. Some information about land use or land cover may be needed in order for greenness indexes to be interpreted. Again, a primary challenge is to establish a range of healthy values for a landscape or region.

INTERPLAY OF SOIL QUALITY AND CROP PRODUCTIVITY
The physical and chemical properties of soils and the productivity of the crops that grow in them can be treated as two separate aspects of the condition of agroecosystems. In some ways, however, it may be useful to be explicit about the connection between these two assessment end points. One way to evaluate the overall condition of soil is to ask how healthy or unhealthy (or acceptable or unacceptable) each characteristic (or collection of characteristics) is for plant growth. Soil productivity indexes may be useful for this,

but they may be too crop-specific for implementation in national or international programs (Gersmehl and Brown 1990). Viewed another way, the soil serves as a habitat for crop growth, so it must be taken into consideration among all the other inputs. It can either be included explicitly (as with a crop model) or be intentionally left among those variables that crop productivity is intended to reflect.

The two assessment end points discussed here are simply illustrative and serve to represent the many other assessment end points that could have been discussed. Each one relates to a different aspect of the agroecosystem, yet each presents unique challenges in the collection of data, calculation of indexes, assurance of quality, and interpretation.

Statistical basis for a monitoring program for sustainability

Biophysical measurements intended to assess the sustainability of agroecosystems should be made with known statistical confidence and should be derived from a sampling frame that gives complete area coverage for the target populations of interest. The issue of statistical confidence is important in determining the quality of the measurements made, which then directly determines how much emphasis can be given to specific measurements in making policy and management decisions. Complete coverage of target populations is essential to avoid possible bias in sample selection (for example, finding a problem in a place that it is expected to occur), which could directly affect the interpretation of overall sustainability of the system.

A statistically valid sampling design should have the follow properties (Heck and others 1991):

- The sampling frame must cover the complete universe of interest; in agricultural surveys, an area frame is often used.

- A procedure must be available for dividing the frame into identifiable sampling units such that no part of the frame is omitted or included more than once.

- The number of sampling units required to achieve a specific level of precision at minimum cost must be known.

- Each sampling unit must be selected with a known probability.

- A procedure must be available for expanding

the sample into estimates of the measurements of interest over the domains of interest; this procedure is known as domain estimation.

- The design must permit the assessment of precision of the sample results.

Several examples of existing area frames that have been successfully implemented are those of the U.S. Department of Agriculture: the National Agricultural Statistics Service and the Soil Conservation Service, National Resources Inventory (Cotter and Nealon 1987; Nealon 1984; U.S. Department of Agriculture, Soil Conservation Service 1989). A new area-sampling frame has been proposed in conjunction with the U.S. Environmental Protection Agency's EMAP (Overton, White, and Stevens 1991) and is being evaluated for use in agroecosystems by the EMAP–Agroecosystems Resource Group (Heck and others 1992).

Ancillary information needed in a monitoring program

Biophysical measurements made in ecosystems are often insufficient alone to characterize present or future status and trends in that system. Information concerning processes derived from an understanding of the ecosystem's structure and function or from modeling efforts may aid in interpreting the meaning and relevance of specific measurements. Also, information on specific stressors may help to determine the forces (natural or anthropogenic) that are leading to change in the ecosystem's status. Equally important to measuring the current conditions or status of the ecosystem is predicting the future condition or trends of the system. Models or trend analysis can be used to predict future conditions; however, a discussion of the extensive literature on this topic is beyond the scope of this chapter.

ECOSYSTEM PROCESSES AND NATURAL VARIATION One of the keys to interpreting the results derived from biophysical measurements made as part of a monitoring program is to understand ecological processes in the overall agroecosystem. Such processes may include hydrologic cycles and nutrient cycles, as well as the life cycles of the plants and animals that constitute the agroecosystem. Understanding the structure and functions of the ecosystem, as indicated by specific processes and cycles, should allow us to determine the range of specific measurements that are expected as a result of natural variation. For example, for determining the assessment end point of crop productivity, one of the challenges in a national monitoring program for agricultural sustainability is to account for inherent natural variation in crop or pest populations. Measurements of soil parameters also have a certain degree of natural variation among regions, which also must be taken into account prior to determining whether a certain region has better agricultural health or sustainability than another region.

USE OF STRESS INDICATORS TO INTERPRET MONITORING RESULTS

As defined earlier, a stressor is an event, process, or activity that causes a change in exposure or habitat. Thus, stressor measurement end points are intimately linked to exposure and habitat measurement end points, as is evident from table 17-5. Much of the following discussion can be applied to all three types of measurement end points. Even in the strict sense, stressors are a diverse group: air and water pollution, agricultural chemical inputs, tillage, temperature, and rainfall, for example. Although the word stressors has negative connotations, stresses can have either positive or negative effects on the response indicators used to take the pulse of the agroecosystem.

Some data on stressors can be taken as part of an agroecosystem monitoring program. Obvious examples are management practices such as tillage and pesticide applications, which can be determined by surveys. Others include density of pests or quality of irrigation water. Exposure and habitat measures, such as concentration of contaminants in soil, would certainly be an appropriate part of the monitoring program. Even some of the response measurement end points can be designed to indicate certain stressors or classes of stress. A very specific example of this is the white clover system developed by Heagle and others (1991, 1992) as a biomonitor for ozone.

Other key information on stresses to the agroecosystem will most likely come from external sources. The best examples are data on weather conditions and pollutant concentrations. In the United States, for example, temperature and precipitation data are compiled from a network of cooperative weather stations (Cooter and others 1991). Use of such data presents several challenges (Cooter and others 1991; Peer 1990). Quality assurance can be difficult. Data may not be available at the monitoring sites themselves (al-

though this is not a problem when regional estimates are desired). Certain ecologically important parameters, such as solar radiation or evapotranspiration, may not be available or may need to be estimated from other data. Air pollution has been measured on networks such as the National Atmospheric Precipitation Assessment Program/National Trends Network and the National Dry Deposition Network in the United States (Bromberg 1990), the Canadian Air and Precipitation Monitoring Network (RMCC 1990), and the IMI/PMK network in Sweden (INFORMS 1990). Bromberg (1990) notes the uncertain future of the U.S. networks. He also identifies the high-priority research indicators for environmental monitoring: ozone, sulfur dioxide, nitric acid, and precipitation ions. Among the other research indicators are carbon dioxide and UV-B radiation.

Stressor information has at least three applications in monitoring agroecosystems. First, response and stressor measurement end points may give different pictures of the condition of the system (Messer 1990). Response end points may indicate the sum of past events in the system, whereas stressor information may suggest future responses of the system. Second, stressor (or exposure or habitat) data can be used to adjust certain response measurements. The idea behind such an adjustment is to account for known, large effects so that the subtler aspects of system health are discernable. An example given above is the use of models to account for the known effects of weather, physical and chemical characteristics of soil, and management on crop productivity, so that the effects of other ecosystem components can be discerned. Third, connections should be made between stressors and responses; for example, stressors may be associated with spatial and temporal changes in response measurements. Studies to identify such associations can be qualitative (for example, comparing maps of productivity to maps of ozone concentrations, comparing graphs of trends in crop productivity to graphs of specific climatic factors) or quantitative (correlation analysis). Geographic information systems may also be useful. Cooter and others (1991) give three examples of the use of these systems for coordinating weather data and for monitoring the health of forests: proximity analysis (to associate weather stations with monitoring sites), surface models, and overlay analysis. These same applications should be appropriate for agroecosystems.

If certain biological or ecological responses indicate a degraded ecosystem, we instinctively want to know why. Unfortunately, a monitoring program can take us only half-way to an answer. In order to attribute a problem to a certain stressor (or exposure or habitat variable), a reasonable mechanism is needed to explain the effect (Messer 1990). Even then, we can only talk about *associations*, not causes. Messer (1990) warns about several pitfalls in attributing ecological responses to stressors: correlation does not demonstrate a cause-and-effect relationship, degraded condition could be the result of multiple stresses, and degraded condition could be caused by one or more stresses that have not been monitored. In the end, associations must be interpreted carefully; they can be considered suggestive and may provide hypotheses for future research.

USE OF HISTORICAL OR OTHER DATA SETS IN A MONITORING PROGRAM

There are a number of reasons for a monitoring program to use data that have been collected in the past (or present) by other agencies and programs. The most tempting prospect is the hope of being able to make statements about trends, even when the monitoring effort is quite recent. Other reasons include avoiding duplication of effort among government agencies, supplementing sampling being done in the monitoring program, establishing expected values against which to check incoming data, and providing complementary data (on stressors) needed for interpreting the monitored data. We focus here on our experience in the United States in developing the agroecosystem component of EMAP, but the discussion illustrates two general observations.

First, other programs are already collecting information relevant to sustainability, but not in sufficient amounts or with sufficient breadth for a complete assessment (table 17-1). In general, a great deal of information exists on crop and livestock production in agroecosystems, but it tends to be economically oriented. Some data are available on inputs such as pesticides and fertilizer. Little information is available on the noncrop, nonlivestock components of agroecosystems, and little national-scale data exist on contaminants. Olson, Breckenridge, and Wiersma (1990) discuss several of the available data bases that are applicable to assessment of productivity. Olson and Breckenridge (1990) provide information on contaminant monitoring programs. Data on weather,

conversion factors, and so forth have been mentioned previously.

The best examples in the United States of historical data are (1) the land use and crop and livestock production estimates produced by the U.S. Department of Agriculture's National Agricultural Statistics Service, (2) the census of agriculture, which is conducted every five years, and (3) the National Resources Inventory of the U.S. Department of Agriculture's Soil Conservation Service. The National Resources Inventory provides information on land use, soil characteristics, soil erosion, irrigation, tillage, and so forth and has been conducted every five years since 1977 (U.S. Department of Agriculture, Soil Conservation Service 1989). Pesticide and fertilizer data are not as uniformly collected, but the U.S. Department of Agriculture, National Agricultural Statistics Service has recently (1990–91) begun an annual pesticide survey in the major states producing various field crops, vegetables, and fruits and nuts.

Some historical data exist in the form of aerial photography and satellite imagery, which can be used to evaluate land cover, landscape structure, and perhaps productivity. For example, the U.S. Department of Agriculture, Agricultural Stabilization and Conservation Service has low-altitude, true-color, 35-millimeter slides for North Carolina from 1984 to the present. There are limitations to this kind of data, such as the need for photointerpretation of aerial photographs. Additionally, acquisition of satellite imagery, such as from LANDSAT-V, can be expensive even before interpretational analyses are done.

Second, there are various points of view as to how these external data can and cannot be used in a monitoring program. Some people would like to be able to merge data sets from existing programs, at least in certain areas, with agroecosystem monitoring data. This requires that the data be comparable. Whether or not sampling designs must match is an issue that needs to be resolved. For some soils applications, the data need to come from the same site as the monitoring data, or, at least, the soils need to have been analyzed by comparable procedures. Certain kinds of data, such as weather data, can be used after interpolation between sample points (Messer 1990).

The comparability issue also applies to historical data. Methods of data acquisition and analyses must be comparable for connections to be made between the results of past and present monitoring efforts (Messer 1990). This is not a trivial matter. For example, because of advancing technology and a continued refinement of goals, even the 1977 National Resources Inventory is not directly comparable to subsequent years of the same program (U.S. Department of Agriculture, Soil Conservation Service 1989).

A less demanding way of using existing data is to use summaries about the condition of given regions, based on data from individual programs, and then to incorporate those summaries into the assessment of agroecosystem status and trends. In this case, samples do not have to be taken at the same locations used by the monitoring program, but certain other restrictions might apply. Again, sampling and analytical methods have to be comparable. If the main monitoring effort is based on a probability sample, different approaches are needed for data from programs that use a probability sample than for those that do not (Messer 1990).

At least three specific examples of the use of existing data have already been mentioned: the use of weather and other stressor data, the association of existing soils data with a sampled field (the soil series is first determined from a map or photo, and then its properties are obtained from a data base), and the use of yield data from the U.S. Department of Agriculture–National Agricultural Statistics Service as a baseline for calculating normalized yield. In the last example, the county averages could serve as constants for adjusting the mean and variance of incoming yield data. At this stage, then, there are several existing data sets of interest, several possible ways of using them, and several unresolved challenges (primarily statistical) in doing so.

Research needed to develop and implement biophysical measurements of sustainability in agroecosystems

The development and testing of assessment and measurement end points require (1) long-term studies to establish baseline variability, (2) field perturbation experiments of appropriate spatial scale, intensity, and duration to test the sensitivity and specificity of indicators, and (3) comparisons of systems exposed to stresses of different types and magnitudes (Lubchenco and others 1991). It is essential to know the baseline variability of the physical environment and the selected biological indicators in order to determine whether undesirable change has occurred.

Research is needed to identify, evaluate, interpret, and refine biophysical measurements that can be used for monitoring several important aspects of agroecosystem sustainability. Representative examples include the biological health of soil, density of pests and beneficial insects, quality of habitat for animals other than livestock, population density and diversity of wildlife, and quality of irrigation water. The development of measurements for these vital aspects of agroecosystems will permit a more complete and realistic assessment of their sustainability than is currently possible.

As a specific example, measurement end points that can be used to assess the biological health of soil and can be implemented in a monitoring program are generally lacking (Benbrook 1991a). Most research has focused on determining microbial biomass; however, no one standard method of quantifying microbial biomass yet exists that can satisfy all the critical and desirable criteria given in table 17-3 (Nannipieri, Grego, and Ceccanti 1990; Smith and Paul 1990). Another proposed measurement end point is the abundance of earthworms, in particular *Lumbricus terrestris*, which may help predict hydraulic properties of soil and potential for movement and transport of chemicals (Edwards and others 1990; Rodale Institute 1991). However, earthworms do not reside in all soil series and, therefore, are not a good choice for implementation and assessment on a national scale.

An alternative measurement that may serve to assess the biological health of soils in agroecosystems is the structure of the nematode community (Ingham and others 1985; Niblack 1989; Wasilewska 1979). Nematodes are ubiquitous, have short generation times allowing them to respond quickly to changes in food supply, are often the last organisms to die, and yet are responsive to disturbances in soil (Freckman 1988). Trophic, or functional, groups can be easily separated, primarily by anterior structures associated with various modes of feeding (Freckman 1988; Yeates and Coleman 1982), so identifying the species is not necessary. Their abundance and size make sampling easier and less costly than for other microflora and fauna (Freckman 1988). The EMAP's Agroecosystem Resource Group tested nematode communities as a biological indicator of soils in their 1992 pilot project (Heck and others 1992; Neher and others 1992).

Conclusions

The classification of an agroecosystem as healthy or unhealthy or as sustainable or unsustainable requires the establishment of specific, judgment criteria. To develop these criteria, states of ecological system health and properties or characteristics of each state must be compiled systematically and supported by experimental or descriptive diagnostic procedures (Schaeffer, Herricks, and Kerster 1988). The criteria on which judgments are based must also be established from a viewpoint that is ecologically, politically, socially, and economically acceptable to policymakers, citizens, scientists, and farmers.

The reference point for determining whether the status of a particular agroecosystem is acceptable or unacceptable remains a paramount question in the monitoring of agroecosystems. Because societal values are made up of the values of individuals who set varying priorities on maintaining the components of an agroecosystem, there may exist no single answer about what is best or most sustainable for a specific agroecosystem. However, through the presentation of clearly defined monitoring goals, scientifically sound and comprehensive monitoring data derived from a valid sampling frame, and clear interpretations of the agroecosystem's condition in relation to potential stressors, policymakers and the public can make informed decisions based on the biophysical measurements obtained for key assessment end points.

References

Babiuk, L. A., and E. A. Paul. 1970. "The Use of Fluorescein Isothiocyanate in the Determination of the Bacterial Biomass of a Grassland Soil." *Canadian Journal of Microbiology* 16, pp. 57–62.

Barnwell, T. O., Jr., E. T. Elliott, E. A. Paul, A. S. Donigian, and A. Rowell. 1991. "Assessment of Methods, Models, and Databases for Soil Carbon Sequestration Potential for U.S. Agroecosystems." Internal report. U.S. Environmental Protection Agency, Office of Research and Development, Environmental Research Laboratory, Athens, Ga.

Baumgardner, M. F. 1990. "A Global Soils and Terrain Database: A Tool to Quantify Global Change." In A. F. Brunman, ed., *Soil and the Greenhouse Effect*, pp. 179–95. New York: John Wiley and Sons.

Benbrook, C. M. 1991a. "Natural Resources Assessment and Policy." In R. Lal and F. J. Pierce, eds., *Soil Management for Sustainability*, pp. 145–66. Ankeny, Iowa: Soil and Water Conservation Society.

———. 1991b. "Protecting Iowa's Common Wealth: Challenges for the Leopold Center for Sustainable Agriculture." *Journal of Soil and Water Conservation* 46, pp. 89–95.

Bornemisza, E., M. Constenla, A. Alvarado, E. J. Ortega, and A. J. Vásquez. 1979. "Organic Carbon Determination by the Walkley-Black and Dry Combustion Methods in Surface Soils and Andept Profiles from Costa Rica." *Soil Science Society of America Journal* 43, pp. 78–83.

Bromberg, S. 1990. "Indicator Strategy for Atmospheric Stressors." In C. T. Hunsaker and D. E. Carpenter, eds., *Ecological Indicators for the Environmental Monitoring and Assessment Program*. EPA 600/3-90/060. Research Triangle Park, N.C.: U.S. Environmental Protection Agency, Office of Research and Development. September.

Brussaard, L., J. A. van Veen, M. J. Kooistra, and G. Lebbink. 1988. "The Dutch Programme on Soil Ecology of Arable Farming Systems. I. Objectives, Approach, and Some Preliminary Results." *Ecological Bulletins* 39, pp. 35–40.

Cabrera, M. L., and D. E. Kissel. 1988. "Potentially Mineralizable Nitrogen in Disturbed and Undisturbed Soil Samples." *Soil Science Society of America Journal* 52, pp. 1010–15.

Cooter, E. J., S. K. LeDuc, L. Truppi, and D. R. Block. 1991. "The Role of Climate in Forest Monitoring and Assessment: A New England Example." EPA 600/3-91/074. U.S. Environmental Protection Agency, Office of Research and Development, Atmospheric Research and Exposure Assessment Laboratory, Research Triangle Park, N.C. November.

Cotter, J., and J. Nealon. 1987. "Area Frame Design for Agricultural Surveys." U.S. Department of Agriculture, National Agricultural Statistics Service, Research and Applications Division, Area Frame Section, Washington, D.C.

Edwards, W. M., M. J. Shipitalo, L. B. Owens, and L. D. Norton. 1990. "Effect of *Lumbricus terrestris* L. Burrows on Hydrology of Continuous No-till Corn Fields." *Geoderma* 46, pp. 73–84.

Elliot, W. J., G. R. Foster, and A. V. Elliot. 1991. "Soil Erosion: Processes, Impacts, and Prediction." In R. Lal and F. J. Pierce, eds., *Soil Management for Sustainability*, pp. 25–34. Ankeny, Iowa: Soil and Water Conservation Society.

Environment Canada, Indicators Task Force. 1991. "A Report on Canada's Progress towards a National Set of Environmental Indicators." SOE Report 91-1. Ottawa, Canada.

Fluck, R. C. 1979. "Energy Productivity: A Measure of Energy Utilization in Agriculture Systems." *Agricultural Systems* 4, pp. 29–37.

Fluck, R. C., and C. D. Baird. 1980. *Agricultural Energetics*. Westport, Conn.: AVI Publishing Company.

Foster, G. R., and L. J. Lane. 1987. "User Requirements USDA-Water Erosion Prediction Project (WEPP)." Report 1. U.S. Department of Agriculture, Agricultural Research Service, National Soil Erosion Lab, West Lafayette, Ind.

Freckman, D. W. 1988. "Bacterivorous Nematodes and Organic-matter Decomposition." *Agriculture, Ecosystems, and Environment* 24, pp. 195–217.

Gersmehl, P. J., and D. A. Brown. 1990. "Geographic Differences in the Validity of a Linear Scale of Innate Soil Productivity." *Journal of Soil and Water Conservation* 45, pp. 379–82.

Goebel, J. J., and K. O. Schmude. 1981. "Planning the SCS National Resources Inventory," pp. 148–53. General Technical Report WO-28. Arid Land Resource Inventories Workshop, U.S. Department of Agriculture, Forest Service, Washington, D.C.

Haberern, J. 1991. "A Soil Health Index." *Journal of Soil and Water Conservation* 47, p. 6.

Heagle, A. S., M. R. McLaughlin, J. E. Miller, and R. L. Joyner. 1992. "Response of Two White Clover Clones to Peanut Stunt Virus and Ozone." *Phytopathology* 82, pp. 254–58.

Heagle, A. S., M. R. McLaughlin, J. E. Miller, R. E. Joyner, and S. E. Spruill. 1991. "Adaptation of a White Clover Population to Chronic Ozone Stress." *New Phytologist* 119, pp. 61–68.

Heck, W. W., C. L. Campbell, A. L. Finkner, C. R. Hayes, G. R. Hess, J. R. Meyer, M. J. Munster, D. A. Neher, S. L. Peck, J. O. Rawlings, C. N. Smith, and M. B. Tooley. 1992. "Environmental Monitoring and Assessment Program (EMAP): Agroecosystem 1992 Pilot Project Plan." EPA/620/R-93/010. U.S. Environmental Protection Agency, Washington, D.C.

Heck, W. W., C. L. Campbell, G. R. Hess, J. R. Meyer, T. J. Moser, S. L. Peck, J. O. Rawlings, and A. L. Finkner. 1991. "Environmental Monitoring and Assessment Program (EMAP): Agroecosystem Monitoring and Research Strategy." EPA/600/4-91. U.S. Environmental Protection Agency, Washington, D.C.

Hermans, C., and P. Vereijken. 1992. "Integration of Animal Husbandry and Nature Conservation on Grassland Farms." *Netherlands Journal of Agricultural Science* 40:3, pp. 301–07.

Hillel, D. 1982. *Introduction to Soil Physics*. New York: Academic Press.

Hunsaker, C. T., and D. E. Carpenter, eds. 1990. *Environmental Monitoring and Assessment Program: Ecological Indicators*. EPA/6–/3-90/060. Washington, D.C.: U.S. Environmental Protection Agency, Office of Research and Development.

INFORMS (Swedish Environmental Protection Agency). 1990. *Monitor 1990: Environmental Monitoring in Sweden*. Sweden: Ingvar Bingman. Available from Naturvårdsverket, Information Department S-171 85 Solna, Sweden.

Ingham, R. E., J. A. Trofymow, E. R. Ingham, and D. C. Coleman. 1985. "Interactions of Bacteria, Fungi, and Their Nematode Grazers: Effects on Nutrient Cycling and Plant Growth." *Ecological Monographs* 55, pp. 119–40.

Kiss, J. J., E. DeJong, and H. P. W. Rostad. 1986. "An Assessment of Soil Erosion in West-central Saskatchewan Using Cesium-137." *Canadian Journal of Soil Science* 66, pp. 591–600.

Knapp, C. M., D. R. Marmorek, J. P. Baker, K. W. Thornton, J. M. Klopatek, and D. P. Charles. 1990. "The Indicator Development Strategy for the Environmental Monitoring and Assessment Program." Draft report. Environmental Research Laboratory, Corvallis, Oreg.

Kutz, F. W., and R. A. Linthurst. 1990. "A Systems-level Approach to Environmental Assessment." *Toxicology and Environmental Chemistry* 28, pp. 105–14.

Lin, B-H, L. Hansen, S. Daberkow, and M. Dreitzer. 1991. "Substitutability of Crop Rotations for Agrichemicals: Preliminary Results." In *Agricultural Resources: Inputs Situation and Outlook Report*, pp. 24–29. AR-24. Washington, D.C.: U.S. Department of Agriculture, Economic Research Service, Resources and Technology Division. October.

Lodge, D. J., and E. R. Ingham. 1991. "A Comparison of Agar Film Techniques for Estimating Fungal Biovolumes in Litter and Soil." *Agriculture, Ecosystems, and Environment* 34, pp. 131–44.

Lubchenco, J., A. M. Olson, L. B. Brubaker, S. R. Carpenter, M. M. Holland, S. P. Hubbell, S. A. Levin, J. A. MacMahon, P. A. Matson, J. M. Melillo, H. A. Mooney, C. H. Peterson, H. Ronald Pulliam, L. A. Real, P. J. Regal, and P. G. Risser. 1991. "The Sustainable Biosphere Initiative: An Ecological Research Agenda." *Ecology* 72, pp. 371–412.

Marten, G. G. 1988. "Productivity, Stability, Sustainability, Equitability, and Autonomy as Properties for Agroecosystem Assessment." *Agricultural Systems* 26, pp. 291–316.

Messer, J. J. 1990. "EMAP Indicator Concepts." In C. T. Hunsaker and D. E. Carpenter, eds., *Ecological Indicators for the Environmental Monitoring and Assessment Program.* EPA 600/3-90/060. Research Triangle Park, N.C.: U.S. Environmental Protection Agency, Office of Research and Development. September.

Nannipieri, P., S. Grego, and B. Ceccanti. 1990. "Ecological Significance of the Biological Activity in Soil." In Jean-Mar Bollag and G. Stotzky, eds., *Soil Biochemistry,* vol. 6, pp. 293–355. New York: Marcel Dekker, Inc.

Nealon, J. P. 1984. "Review of Multiple and Area Frame Estimators." SF and SRB Report 80. U.S. Department of Agriculture, National Agricultural Statistics Service, Washington, D.C.

Neher, D. 1992. "Ecological Sustainability in Agricultural Systems: Definition and Measurement." *Journal of Sustainable Agriculture* 2:3, pp. 51–61.

Neher, D., J. R. Meyer, C. L. Campbell, and W. W. Heck. 1992. "Monitoring Sustainability in Agricultural Systems." Presented at the Organization for Economic Cooperation and Development workshop Sustainable Agriculture: Technology and Practices, Paris, France, February 11–13.

Niblack, T. L. 1989. "Applications of Nematode Community Structure Research to Agricultural Production and Habitat Disturbance." *Journal of Nematology* 21, pp. 437–43.

Olson, G. L., and R. P. Breckenridge. 1990. "Federal Contaminant Monitoring Programs and Databases: A Fish and Wildlife Perspective. No. 1990." Informal Report EGG-EST-9341. Center for Environmental Monitoring and Assessment, Idaho National Engineering Laboratory, Idaho Falls, Idaho.

Olson, G. L., R. P. Breckenridge, and G. B. Wiersma. 1990. "Assessment of Federal Databases to Evaluate Agroecosystem Productivity." EGG-CEMA-8924. Informal report. Center for Environmental Monitoring and Assessment, Idaho National Engineering Laboratory, Idaho Falls, Idaho. February.

Overton, S. O., D. White, and D. L. Stevens, Jr. 1991. "Design Report for the Environmental Monitoring and Assessment Program." Draft. U.S. EPA/600. U.S. Environmental Protection Agency, Washington, D.C.

Peer, R. L. 1990. "An Overview of Climate Information Needs for Ecological Effects Models." U.S. Environmental Protection Agency, Atmospheric Research and Exposure Assessment Laboratory, Research Triangle Park, N.C. June.

Piekarz, D. 1990. "Rapporteur's Report of Work Group: Indicators and Assessment of Agricultural Sustainability." *Environmental Monitoring and Assessment* 15, pp. 307–08.

Ritchie, J. C., and J. R. McHenry. 1990. "Application of Radioactive Fallout Cesium-137 for Measuring Soil Erosion and Sediment Accumulation Rates and Patterns: A Review." *Journal of Environmental Quality* 19, pp. 215–33.

RMCC (Federal/Provincial Research and Monitoring Coordinating Committee). 1990. *The 1990 Canadian Long-Range Transport of Air Pollutants and Acid Deposition Assessment Report. Part 3: Atmospheric Sciences.* Montreal, Canada.

Rodale Institute. 1991. "International Conference on the Assessment and Monitoring of Soil Quality, Emmaus, PA, July 11–13, 1991." Emmaus, Penn.

Roughgarden, J., S. W. Running, and P. A. Matson. 1991. "What Does Remote Sensing Do for Ecology?" *Ecology* 72, pp. 1918–22.

Schaeffer, D. J., E. E. Herricks, and H. W. Kerster. 1988. "Ecosystem Health. I: Measuring Ecosystem Health." *Environmental Management* 12, pp. 445–55.

Schaller, N. 1990. "Mainstreaming Low-input Agriculture." *Journal of Soil and Water Conservation* 45, pp. 9–12.

Schnurer, J., and T. Rosswall. 1982. "Fluorescein Diacetate Hydrolysis as a Measure of Total Microbial Activity in Soil and Litter." *Applied Environmental Microbiology* 43, pp. 1256–61.

Sharp, D. D., H. Lieth, G. R. Noggle, and H. D. Gross. 1976. "Agricultural and Forest Primary Productivity in North Carolina 1972–1973." Technical Bulletin 241. North Carolina Agricultural Experiment Station, Raleigh, N.C.

Shirley, C. 1991. "Experts to Issue `Soil Report Card.'" *The New Farm* 13, pp. 5–6.

Smith, J. L., and E. A. Paul. 1990. "The Significance of Soil Microbial Biomass Estimations." In Jean-Marc Bollag and G. Stotzky, eds., *Soil Biochemistry*, vol. 6, pp. 357–96. New York: Marcel Dekker.

Stanford, G., and S. J. Smith. 1972. "Nitrogen Mineralization Potentials of Soils." *Soil Science Society of America Proceedings* 36, pp. 465–72.

Storer, D. A. 1984. "A Simple High Sample Volume Ashing Procedure for Determination of Soil Organic Matter." *Communications in Soil Science Plant Analysis* 15, pp. 759–72.

———. 1992. "An Improved High Sample Volume Ashing Procedure for Determination of Soil Organic Matter." Processed.

Suter, G. W. II. 1990. "End Points for Regional Ecological Risk Assessment." *Environmental Management* 14, pp. 9–23.

Turner, M. G. 1987. "Land Use Changes and Net Primary Production in the Georgia, U.S.A., Landscape: 1935–1982." *Environmental Management* 11, pp. 237–47.

U. S. Department of Agriculture. 1981. *Will There Be Enough Food? The 1981 Yearbook of Agriculture*. O-354-445. Washington, D.C.: U.S. Government Printing Office.

U. S. Department of Agriculture, Soil Conservation Service. 1989. "Summary Report: 1987 National Resources Inventory." Statistical Bulletin 790. Iowa State University Statistical Laboratory, Ames, Iowa.

Warcholinska, A. U. 1978. "Studies on the Use of Weeds as Bioindicators of Habitat Conditions of Agroecosystems." *Ekol. Pol.* 26, pp. 391–408.

Wasilewska, L. 1979. "The Structure and Function of Soil Nematode Communities in Natural Ecosystems and Agrocenoses." *Polish Ecological Studies* 5, pp. 97–145.

Wijnands, F. G., and P. Vereijken. 1992. "Region-wise Development of Prototypes of Integrated Arable Farming and Outdoor Horticulture." *Netherlands Journal of Agricultural Science* 40:3, pp. 225–31.

Yeates, G. W., and D. C. Coleman. 1982. "Nematodes in Decomposition." In D. W. Freckman, eds., *Nematodes in Soil Ecosystems*, pp. 55–80. Austin: University of Texas Press.

Comments

D. W. Anderson

Campbell, Heck, Neher, Munster, and Hoag (henceforth referred to as the authors) have prepared a comprehensive report that discusses in a practical way the kinds of measurements that can be made to assess the sustainability of agroecosystems in temperate regions. A combination of text and tabular material has resulted in a concise presentation and discussion. There are, however, several points that I offer for consideration.

Does temperate agriculture have special properties that distinguish it from the agriculture of tropical regions, or grazing systems, and that warrant separate discussions? I think that it does. Temperate agriculture generally occurs in regions with more resilient, less weathered soils on more recent soil parent materials. Soils with reserves of nutrients in their parent materials can recover from major disturbance and be productive again, albeit at a lower level of productivity. These soil characteristics, particularly where combined with moderate climate, impart a high sustainability index to agriculture in comparison with many agricultural lands of tropical regions. Temperate agriculture is mostly, but not completely, the large-scale, intensive, high-yielding, high-input farming methods of the industrial countries, whereas tropical agriculture (as discussed elsewhere) is often on smaller scale, less mechanized farms.

The resources within agriculture and generally strong support for agricultural research and similar programs indicate that sustainability is more probable in temperate systems. The optimistic view is conditioned, however, by the knowledge that many of the agricultural practices are strongly driven by economics and that many agroecosystems in less favorable situations are highly dependent on high inputs of fertilizers and pesticides and often irrigation. Those conditions lead to enhanced environmental risk, plus the specter of collapse if external circumstances limit or remove the inputs.

The authors have differentiated between research monitoring, which is characterized by intensive, long-term measurements on a limited number of sites, and assessment monitoring that employs a sampling design with complete area coverage, which is statistically representative. The distinction is good, but one must question the statement that intensive, long-term monitoring on a few sites has a very limited role in monitoring sustainability. The problems of biased extrapolation to more general or larger-scale systems can largely be overcome by working within the structures of hierarchically based land classifications based on soil survey, climate, and other information (Anderson 1991). Actually, the Canadian effort to monitor soil quality (to be discussed later) relies heavily on research monitoring, with extrapolation to complete area coverage based on agricultural resource area maps assembled from soil survey and related sources and extrapolation to the future based on simulation models (Acton, MacDonald, and Pettapiece 1992). The authors state that some research monitoring is done to help validate models. Our experience, particularly in western Canada, is that long-term experimental sites such as crop rotation studies are essential sources of data to understand systems, develop conceptual and simulation models, and, with other sites, validate the models.

The authors have listed several national-scale monitoring programs for temperate agriculture, appearing to rely mainly on published reports and their own personal contacts. From a Canadian perspective, the list should include the national Soil Quality Evaluation Program that is led by the federal department, Agriculture Canada, and involves its own scientists in cooperative studies with universities and provincial agricultural departments. The monitoring is part of the National Soil Conservation Program and is a long-term project with the objective of monitoring soil quality in relation to agricultural sustainability (Acton, MacDonald, and Pettapiece 1992). The project involves assessments of soil organic matter, soil salinity, compaction, wind and water erosion, and pollution by organic chemicals and heavy metals. Canada is a large country with about 65 million hectares of agricultural land. The Canadian study involves detailed monitoring on a limited number of representative sites, the development and validation of process models, and the systematic extrapolation of findings within the framework of small-scale soil landscape maps or agricultural resource area maps. Agricultural resource area maps are generalized from larger scale, more detailed soil maps and recognize natural boundaries related to physiography and climate.

The authors have provided comprehensive lists of measurement end points for evaluating sustainability from the perspectives of societal values, agroecosystem health, and soil quality. What is lacking, quite understandably considering the scope of their task, is an appreciation of the relative value and applicability of the various measures. Soil quality, for example, remains poorly defined in a quantifiable sense but is a key element of agroecosystem sustainability. Soil organic carbon (or organic matter) is a measure reasonably responsive to the management of agroecosystems and often employed as an index of soil quality. The organic carbon content of the cultivated (Ap) horizon has generally declined since temperate soils were cultivated, often by 50 percent, to reach some new equilibrium consistent with relative inputs of organic residues and decomposition rates. Changes in organic carbon with cultivation are at first rapid, a consequence of the considerable stress on the system. With time, the rate of change slows as a new equilibrium is approached. The difficulty remains, however, of understanding the significance of a particular concentration of organic carbon (is organic carbon decreasing, relatively constant, or increasing?) and a baseline from which to make comparisons. Comparisons to virgin soils indicate a drastic reduction with cultivation, but comparisons of various management alternatives indicate that well-managed soils (good crop yields, applications of fertilizer or manure, rotation of crops, and minimal erosion) may have enough organic matter to provide nutrient reserves, good soil tilth, intake and storage of water, and so on, even though the organic carbon is well below the content of virgin soils. Here it is important not so much to know the carbon content in relation to a native control, but to know what has occurred in cultivated soils over the past years or decades.

The concentration of organic carbon in the plow layer is but one measure of agroecosystem sustainability. The mass of organic carbon on a soil profile basis is critical to evaluating absolute losses within the context of contribution to global concentrations of carbon dioxide. Several studies have indicated that measures of organic carbon that evaluate the more readily available energy and nutrient components (mineralizable carbon or nitrogen), biomass, or soluble carbon may be much more sensitive indicators of the health of soil ecosystems than total organic carbon (Anderson 1991). The attribute to be measured depends on the objectives of the assessment end points.

The authors refer several times to soil quality and mention the function of soils in the context of soil quality but do not present a coherent definition of it. Larson and Pierce (1991) define soil quality as the capacity of a soil to function within its ecosystem boundaries and interact positively with the environment external to that ecosystem. Soil quality cannot be defined, expressed, or evaluated in terms of a single use (yield of a particular crop, for example) and is a key factor in determining sustainability. In the words of Larson and Pierce (1991) soil quality describes how effectively soils:

- Accept, hold, and release nutrients and other chemical constituents

- Accept, store, and release water to plants, streams, and groundwater

- Promote and sustain root growth

- Maintain suitable soil biotic habitat, and

- Respond to management and resist degradation.

Soil quality can be evaluated and monitored by determining several soil attributes. Many of the attributes are highly correlated and related to the five functions listed above. Soil quality can be defined quantitatively as the state of existence of soil relative to a standard or qualitatively as degree of excellence (Larson and Pierce 1991). Soil quality expressed as the sum of individual soil properties permits comparisons among soils and can handle changes in quality with reference to time.

Another aspect of measuring soil attributes (or measurement end points) is that soil attributes vary in their rate of change or dynamic properties (Stewart and others 1990). Temporal variability varies with scale, in that small systems tend to be more dynamic or susceptible to change than large ones. Soil salinity indicates that well. The salt content of an A horizon varies on time scales of days to months, dependent on recent weather. The salt content of pedons (to a depth of, say, 1 meter) varies over the course of years or decades, whereas regional salinity is a longer-term phenomenon related to hydrogeology (Anderson 1991). In many cases, rather than monitoring a highly dynamic attribute such as soil salinity, it may be better to monitor the piezometric level of the groundwater system that produces the saline soils in a region.

The authors discuss the statistical basis for a monitoring program, particularly the need for statistical confidence and complete area coverage for the target population. Statistically representative and valid random sampling is a daunting task, particularly when areas of interest are large and soil or ecosystem attributes are many. The authors are correct in recommending the use of existing data sources, particularly census data, annual reports of yield, and so on. The Canadian effort in monitoring has related data from the agricultural census, done each decade, to agricultural resource areas rather than administrative divisions. Data based on natural rather than imposed boundaries are more relevant and easier to interpret.

Another chapter in this volume discusses evaluating changes in sustainability at the landscape scale (chapter 9). I consider that it will be difficult and expensive to obtain statistically valid, unbiased samplings. Goals of monitoring can best be achieved by sampling key ecosystems and attributes, as defined within a system such as that provided by the hierarchy (from specific to general) soil horizon, pedon-soil landscape (patch) soil region, or agricultural resource area, as defined by soil, physiographic, and climate maps. At middle to higher levels, the number, spatial arrangement, and health of the various patches (and associated biotic communities) become critical factors in sustainability. Odum (1989) recommends a top-down hierarchical approach.

Finally, the authors are to be commended for their comprehensive treatment of the topic and their multi-faceted view of the sustainability of temperate agroecosystems. I can recommend only a more careful discussion of the structure, spatial distribution, and regular temporal changes in the agroecosystems of interest.

References

Acton, D. F., K. B. MacDonald, and W. Pettapiece. 1992. "A Program to Assess and Monitor Soil Quality at Regional and National Scales: A Canadian Experience." Proceedings of the seventh International Soil Conservation conference, Sydney, Australia.

Anderson, D. W. 1991. "Long-term Ecological Research, A Pedological Perspective." In Paul G. Risser, ed., "Long-Term Ecological Research." *Scope* 47, pp. 115–34. New York: John Wiley and Sons.

Larson, W. E., and F. J. Pierce. 1991. "Conservation and Enhancement of Soil Quality." In *Evaluation for Sustainable Land Management in the Developing World.* Vol. 2: *Technical Papers*, pp. 175–204. IBSRAM Proceedings 12. Bangkok, Thailand: International Board for Soil Research and Management.

Odum, Eugene P. 1989. "Input Management of Production Systems." *Science* 243, pp. 177–82.

Stewart, J. W. B., D. W. Anderson, E. T. Elliott, and C. V. Cole. 1990. "The Use of Models of Soil Pedogenic Processes in Understanding Changing Land Use and Climatic Conditions." In H. W. Scharpenseel, M. Schomaker, and A. Ayoub, eds., *Soils on a Warmer Earth*, pp. 121–31. Proceedings of an international workshop on effects of expected climate change on soil processes in the tropics and subtropics, Nairobi, February 12–14. Amsterdam: Elsevier.

Measuring Sustainability in Tropical Rangelands: A Case Study from Northern Kenya

Walter J. Lusigi

Sustainability is not a new concept. It originated in man's quest to perpetuate life: each individual wants to survive as well as he can with his descendants. Eternity is, furthermore, an accepted religious concept separated from the concept of sustainability only by the means with which the permanence is achieved.

In natural resource management, sustainability has accompanied the use of resources by different societies. Hunter-gatherer societies lived in perfect harmony with the land, shifting cultivators abandoned their fields when their fertility declined and moved to other locations in order to allow the land to recover its viability, and pastoralists moved to balance pressure on resources as a biological necessity for survival in arid environments.

Modern concerns about sustainability in natural resource management seem to have started in Germany in the eighteenth century, when the principle of sustained yield was applied to forestry production. Since that time, the principle of sustained yield has been used in resource management under various labels like wise use, sustainable use, optimum sustainable yield, sustained regeneration, regenerative capacity, conservation, and so forth.

Recent attention to the issue of sustainability has been triggered largely by unprecedented irreversible resource degradation in many ecological systems through overexploitation causing depletion of nutrients and erosion of the top soil or pollution. Caring for the Earth (IUCN 1991) uses the word sustainable in several combinations, such as sustainable development, sustainable economy, sustainable society, and sustainable use. It is important for our understanding of sustainability to know what these terms presently mean. According to the authors of that work, if an activity is sustainable, for all practical purposes it can continue forever. When people define an activity as sustainable, however, they do so on the basis of what they know at the time. There can be no long-term guarantee of sustainability, because many factors remain unknown or unpredictable. The moral is to be conservative in actions that could affect the environment, to study the effects of such actions carefully, and to learn quickly from your mistakes.

The World Commission on Environment and Development (WCED 1987, p. 8) has defined sustainable development as "development that meets the needs of the present without compromising the ability of future generations to meet their own needs." The term has been criticized as ambiguous and open to a wide range of interpretations, many of which are contradictory. According to *Caring for the Earth*, the confusion has arisen because sustainable development, sustainable growth, and sustainable use have been used interchangeably, as if their meanings were the same. They are not. *Sustainable growth* is a contradiction in terms: nothing physical can grow indefinitely. *Sustainable use* is applicable only to renewable resources: it means using them at rates within their capacity for renewal.

In this chapter, we adopt the meaning of sustainable development defined in *Caring for the Earth*: sustainable development means improving the quality of human life while living within the carrying capacity of supporting ecosystems. The key word here is ecosystem, which brings in the concept of life renewal processes maintained by ecological systems. Likewise, a sustainable economy is the product of sustainable development. It maintains its base of natural resources. It can continue to develop through adaptations and through improvements in knowledge, organization, technical efficiency, and wisdom.

Natural resources are ecological systems that have structure and also function. Understanding the ecological basis of productivity in nature means understanding ecosystems. An ecosystem results from the integration of all of the living and nonliving factors of the environment for a defined segment of space and time. It is a complex of organisms and environment forming a functional whole. Stable ecological conditions are in a functional equilibrium that can be perpetuated indefinitely by the system's ability to overcome various disturbances. Ecologically stable—or persistent—systems are sometimes referred to as climax communities, differentiating them from secondary communities that are in a stage of succession toward climax after various disturbances or forms of use.

In order to manage ecological systems sustainably, resource managers have for a long time been preoccupied with trying to measure attributes of sustainability for various ecosystems. What would be the maximum the system could be used without damaging it? What is the threshold point, if one even exists? Measuring sustainability of an ecological system means measuring its resilience. This means that some measurable attributes of sustainability must exist.

The complexity of ecological systems dictates that a highly organized and integrated approach be applied to their study and management. This requires the use of multidisciplinary teams, because no one person can have all the expertise required.

Range management is the management of a renewable resource composed mainly of one or more ecosystems for optimum, sustained yield of the optimum combination of goods and services. Management means decisionmaking in the presence of uncertainty and involves the manipulation of one or more of the dependent or controlling factors. Composition mainly implies that range ecosystems may be mingled with other kinds of ecosystems, such as forests or cultivated lands, that also require manipulation by managers. Range ecosystems are natural pastures or derived pastures managed extensively on the basis of ecological principles. The optimum combination of goods and services is determined by the capabilities of the ecosystem, levels of technology, economic demands, and social pressures. The objective may include any of the values that the ecosystem is capable of producing. Management for optimum yield requires a selection of alternatives to maximize values and minimize costs or negative values. Sustained yield requires a continuous flow of energy with orderly cycling of matter. The restrictions imposed by the word sustained determine the maximum rate of usage under the constraints of the controlling factors (Van Dyne 1969). Range science is the organized body of knowledge on which the practice of range management is based. If we are to achieve overall sustainability of the range resource—or sustainable development of rangelands—we should seek to obtain a thorough understanding of their structure and functioning.

This chapter concentrates on the attributes of sustainability in tropical rangelands exploited by pastoralists and also inhabited by wildlife. It specifically looks at a case study of the arid and semi-arid rangelands of northern Kenya and how an attempt was made to measure sustainability of that ecosystem and to understand its functioning. A detailed discussion of the results of that study is outside the scope of this chapter, which examines what factors were taken into consideration, what questions were asked, and how the studies were designed to try to understand the functioning and sustainability of that ecological system. Although considerable progress has been achieved in the study of temperate rangelands, systematic studies of tropical rangeland are still at a relatively infant stage.

Tropical rangeland ecosystems

Tropical rangelands are part of the total system of land used by mankind. They are the areas of the world where wild and domestic animals graze or browse on natural vegetation. Rangeland vegetation includes grasslands, savannas or open scattered-tree forests, shrublands, and small grassy areas within forests. Range vegetation may never have been disturbed, or it may follow changes in land use, such as clearing brush or harvesting timber. Cultivation eliminates rangeland vegetation, but abandoned cropland returns to rangeland, especially in areas of shifting cultivation (Heady 1982). Varying demands for different kinds of products from rangelands cause frequent modification of land use. Therefore, boundaries between different areas of land use often change.

Rangeland covers nearly half the earth's land surface, 47 percent in all. Nearly half of this total area lies in the tropics and subtropics, between 23° north and south of the equator. For geographical convenience and because of irregular political boundaries, some areas that lie adjacent to, but outside, these zones are included (see figure 18-1). For instance, all of Mexico is included as well as parts of Australia, South America, India, and Saudi Arabia that are not located strictly within these boundaries.

The world's tropical rangelands support vast herds of domestic animals; cattle, sheep, goats, water buffaloes, camels, llamoids, donkeys, and horses. About one-third of the world's people live on these same rangelands both in cities and as producers on the land (see table 18-1). The tropical rangelands support nearly a billion domestic animals and almost as many people (a billion is 1,000 million). In some tropical lands, most notably Africa, great numbers of wild animals share the ranges with humans and their herds and flocks. Australian grasslands support kangaroos and varying numbers of feral rabbits.

Principal products from rangelands are meat, milk, fiber, and hides. Other rangeland values, which go far beyond grazing by animals, include water, recreation, fuel, and antiquities. Rangeland management has two sets of goals. (Child 1984). One is the protection, conservation, improvement, and continued use of the resources of the land, water, plants, and animals. The other is the increased well-being of the rangeland people

Figure 18-1: Zone of Tropical Rangelands

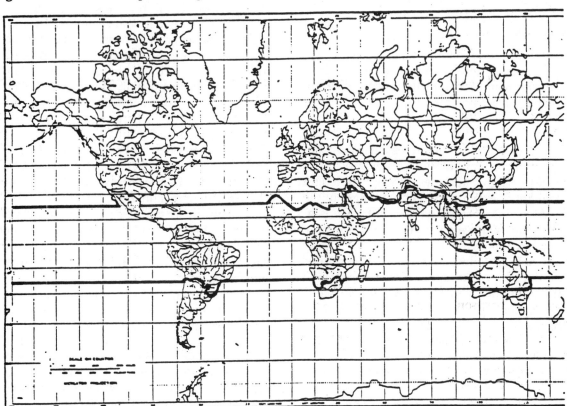

Note: The area between the two dark lines is the zone of tropical rangelands.
Source: Heady 1982.

Table 18-1: Human Population and Number of Domestic Livestock in the Tropical Rangeland Areas of the World
(in thousands)

Area	Humans	Cattle	Sheep and goats	Horses and donkeys	Buffaloes	Camels
Africa	206,795	128,484	65,521	8,175	2,150	9,410
Australia	12,755	27,357	162,937	450	—	2
India	547,950	176,750	4,300	1,930	60,000	1,130
Mexico and Central America	86,280	41,648	6,579	12,842	7	0
South America	149,035	56,114	68,694	22,362	150	0
Southeast Asia and Pacific islands	327,550	20,013	7,480	650	67,135	2,469
Total	1,330,365	450,366	315,513	46,429	129,442	13,011

— Unknown population of wild buffaloes.
Source: Heady 1982.

and others dependent on rangeland production. These aims may be global or local in scale, different in emphasis, and short or long term. They are inextricably mixed in complex systems that include human welfare, market economy, government, and conservation.

Structure of the tropical rangeland ecosystems

Climate, patterns of rainfall, topography, type of soil, and the relations among vegetation, animal life, and humans constitute the structure of tropical rangeland ecosystems.

CLIMATE

The functioning of any range ecosystem is dependent on climate. Tropical biotic communities must tolerate high light intensities, although the length of daylight does not vary much throughout the year. As a consequence, in the drier tropics, seasonal changes in range vegetation are mainly caused by changes in rainfall because the supply of radiant energy is more constant. Temperatures below freezing seldom or never occur except high on the mountains, which are inhabited by plants and animals adapted to the cold. There is considerable variation in the kinds of biotic community found on mountains since differences in rainfall give rise to environments varying from extremely dry deserts to the wettest of rain forests.

RAINFALL

Low rainfall limits the growth of plants and thus limits the population of animals that feed on the plants. In areas of light rainfall, 125 to 250 milli-

meters annually, plant growth is mostly desert scrub, grasses, cacti, and still or spiny shrubs.

An annual rainfall of 250 to 500 millimeters, with wet and dry seasons, produces a savanna characterized by widely spaced trees or shrubs with grasses covering the soil as an understory. An annual rainfall of 500 to 1,000 millimeters usually produces a dry forest ecosystem, with large trees and an abundance of scrubby undergrowth. Grasses grow in the scattered open spaces. In areas where the rainfall is more than 1,500 millimeters annually, in some places up to 4,000 millimeters, forest usually dominates the landscape. No open spaces remain for grass to grow. Grasslands prevail where man or fire has removed the trees and shrubs.

Time and frequency of rainfall affect both season and height of vegetational growth. Across much of central Africa and in South and Southeast Asia, the prevailing climatic influence is the monsoon rainy season. Rain results from the winds in Africa, India, Southeast Asia, and northern Australia when the low-pressure zone near the equator is invaded by cool air from the Pacific and Indian oceans.

As the monsoons advance inland from the coast, rainfall declines. Topographical features, such as mountains, interrupt the monsoonal clouds and cause them to drop rain on the windward side. On the Kenya coast of Africa, annual rainfall averages 1,250 millimeters, while 65 kilometers inland, near Tsavo National Park, it decreases to 500 millimeters. This occurs also in northern Australia, where the average annual coastal rainfall is 1,500 millimeters; 1,600 kilometers inland to the south, annual rainfall decreases to 130 millimeters.

Rain falls in varying amounts from one season to another. Rangelands are dry compared with forested areas and may suffer serious droughts, with lower than normal rainfall, which retard vegetational growth. If drought continues for a number of seasons, grasses, shrubs, and even small trees may die, leading to starvation of both wild and domestic animals and consequent suffering of the human populations dependent on these animals.

Rangelands in Central America, Australia, and the central Indian plains are subject to periodic and cyclic droughts, which complicate proper management. The dry rangelands of Africa, south of the Sahara, experience periods of drought lasting from three to seven years about three times in every century, when the effects of cumulative drying on rangelands become severe. In the dry tropics, the pattern of rainfall varies considerably. Where there are two rainy seasons each year, one may fail, while the other brings moisture; both may fail entirely or rain may fall in insufficient amounts for proper plant growth. Rain may fall in more than normal amounts for a number of successive seasons, increasing the plant cover dramatically.

TOPOGRAPHY

Elevation and slope exposure are the two critical elements in topography. The high plateau of East Africa—the highlands of Kenya, Uganda, and Tanzania—have almost temperate climates because of their high elevation, although they are near or on the equator. Rainfall patterns resemble those of the monsoonal tropics, but lower temperatures cause plants to grow at slower rates than in lower elevations.

In Mexico, Central America, and all tropical rangelands in the northern hemisphere, south-facing slopes get more sunlight and are warmer than north-facing slopes. Plants may grow earlier on these slopes, but since extra sunlight means greater evaporation of moisture, total growth of plants is less on the south-facing slopes. Steepness of the terrain also affects the density and vigor of plant growth largely due to the capacity of the slope to hold moisture and nutrients. The distance from oceans and other large water surfaces also affects plant growth because large bodies of water modify humidity and temperature.

TROPICAL SOILS

The variety of tropical soils stems from the variety of parent material, topography, climate, and vegetation. Soils associated with zones of climate and vegetation have distinctive properties related to the local climate and vegetation. Forest soils are usually very distinct from savanna soils of lower rainfall and sparser vegetation. However, in some cases, former forest areas have been burnt or otherwise changed so that they are now under savanna. In these cases, the original soil properties are modified, resulting in transitional soils between forest and savanna. On the basis of present knowledge, it is considered that vegetational zones match climatic zones more closely than do soil zones.

Red soils in the tropics vary widely in fertility, aridity, and permeability, but they are all characterized by the presence of iron oxides. Soil water in the humid tropics contains little organic matter and, in consequence, does not dissolve iron or aluminum hydroxides from the soil. Silica and other minerals are leached out, thus leaving a high concentration of iron and aluminum compounds.

Laterite is an extreme form of this kind of soil, often characterized by stony concentrations of iron ore. These soils contain very little organic matter and are infertile. Many tropical forests grow on laterite and support their growth by their own litter.

Black soils are moderately fertile soils of volcanic origin. They are rich in calcium carbonate and other minerals. They occur in semi-arid climates in an intermediate location between deserts and forests. These dark soils, found for example around Lake Chad and in the highlands of East Africa, support useful rangeland.

Vertisols occupy low-lying flat areas. High clay content and flatness impede their drainage, and many develop deep cracks during the dry season. The effective supply of moisture is less than on many other soils in the same climatic zone, and the natural vegetation thus tends to be more characteristic of drier areas than the amount of rainfall would suggest.

VEGETATION, ANIMAL LIFE, AND HUMANS

Many classification schemes have been proposed for the world's biotic communities. Perhaps the most important characteristic of the tropical rangelands is the close relationships among the vegetation, the animals, and human activities, which have to some extent maintained them the way they are. The broad range of animal species from browsers to grazers and the activities of humans through shifting cultivation, burning, and hunt-

Figure 18–2: Structure of a Basic Ecosystem

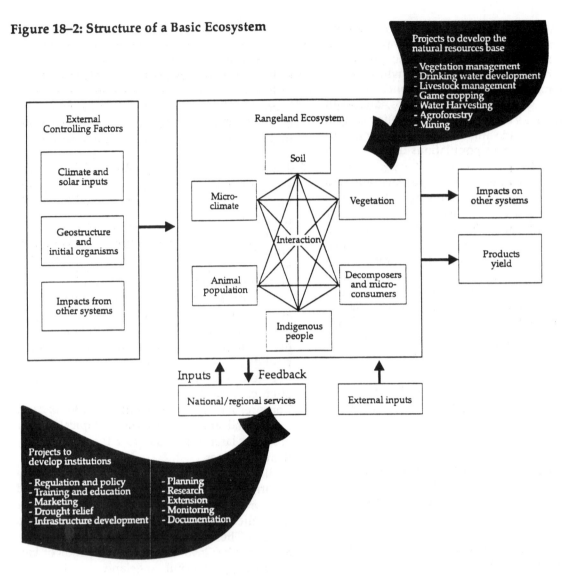

Note: Shaded areas constitute areas of potential focus for projects.
Source: Child and others 1984.

ing have been a major influence on the biotic structure of the tropical range ecosystem (see figure 18-2 and table 18-2). Although pastoralism and hunting are still a major use of rangelands in the tropics, cultivation is increasing to meet the demand for cereals from the world's growing human population. Tropical rangelands can be classified into six broad types: tropical grassland and savanna, tropical forest with seasonal rainfall, tropical rain forests, desert shrubs and grasses, seasonally flooded grasslands, and montane grasslands (Heady and Heady 1984).

Tropical grassland and savanna occur as broad expanses of grasslands without trees, savannas

with scattered trees, and woodlands with nearly complete canopies of deciduous trees. They are vast areas of country characterized by alternating wet and dry seasons and by periodic droughts of several years' duration. Frequent fires and repeated and often heavy browsing from animals reduce the density of woody plants but by no means eliminate them completely. There is a delicate balance between the effects of animals and fire on the growth of vegetation favoring different types of plants with different intensities of use.

High grass savanna occurs near dense forest and is dominated by *Pennisetum* and *Hyparrhenia spp*. The area is predominantly used by elephants

Table 18-2: Key Characteristics of Major Tropical Rangeland Systems

Systems	Length of dry season (months)	Type of grazing	Cattle per person	Animals per sq. kilometer	Site potential	Agroforestry
Savannas with tall grasses	6–9	Transhumance and village based	6–15	25, all domestic species	Low to high	Semi-arid trees, mostly legumes
Deciduous forests with high grasses	3–6	Transhumance and village based	1–4	25, all domestic species	High with seeded legumes	Wide range of possibilities
Desert shrub and grasslands	9–12	Nomadic	0–4	10, mostly camels and goats	Low except with water harvesting	Local leguminous shrubs and trees
Seasonally flooded and wetland vegetation	—	Seasonal use	—	—	High	Slight possibility
Tropical rain forests	< 3	Sedentary	± 1	< 5, all domestic species	High with legumes	Local species
Winter rainfall vegetation	5–7	Year-long	6–15	10, all domestic species	High with legumes	Coniferous trees
Montane forests	< 5	Year-long	—	> 25, on improved pastures of temperate species	High with legumes	Coniferous trees

— Not available.

Source: Child and others 1984.

and buffaloes, which can reach the tall grass. Tall grasses 1 to 3 meters in height and numerous trees, mainly *Acacia spp.* and *Combretum spp.*, constitute a narrow belt of savanna grassland across Africa from Senegal to the Sudan and from Kenya to Botswana. A third division of grassland savanna is more like desert than the other types of savanna covering most of West and East Africa.

Tropical forests with seasonal rainfall are usually partly deciduous and are commonly referred to as monsoon forests. They occur in Southeast Asia and from South Pacific to northern Australia. Seasonal forests also occupy large parts of Central America, the West Indies, and south of

the Amazon basin. Stands of tall deciduous trees in the seasonal forest zone occupy large areas across Zambia and Malawi. Fires are commonly used to maintain grassland in these areas.

Regions in the tropics with large amounts of rainfall and no lengthy dry periods grow dense forests and tall trees of many species. Luxurious growth of shrubs and herbs may occur beneath the canopy. Grazing resources for domestic animals depend on destruction of the forest by shifting cultivation and other practices that permit forage plants to grow on the vacated land for a few years. Desert shrubs and grasses occur in areas too dry for trees and support low-growing shrubs with few forage plants between them as in the deserts of Arabia, Pakistan, Northern Mexico, Somalia, Sahara, and Kalahari. Seasonally flooded grasslands are scattered throughout the tropical rangelands. These may be extensive, like the llanos of Colombia and Venezuela and the sudd in the Sudan. Black cotton soil areas found in Kenya, Tanzania, and Uganda also fall in this category. Montane tropical grasslands, found at high elevations in Africa, South America, and on some South Pacific islands, are important for grazing.

The human experience on tropical rangelands has a long history. This history has produced a wide variety of adjustments by rangeland vegetation and soil that are related to local environmental circumstances or human modifications of them and also to different and often changing cultural beliefs and values. In Saudi Arabia and the drier parts of East Africa, Sudan, Ethiopia, the Sahel region of Africa, parts of Asia, and other areas, pastoral nomadism is one of the normal ways of life. A pattern of transhumance—a combination of seasonal herd migrations with subsistence cropping, usually of cereals—may also be followed at a central or home location where the herds return for part of the year.

Functioning of the tropical rangeland ecosystem

Plants are the primary producers of the ecosystem, converting through photosynthesis the energy from the sun into energy usable by humans and animals. The flow of energy through an ecosystem is illustrated by Odum's classic drawing in figure 18-3 (Odum 1959). At each transfer of energy, great losses usually occur, and the only way to increase the efficiency of the system is to reduce the energy lost during these transfers.

The range ecosystem also functions through the recycling of nutrients. Unlike energy, which can be lost to the atmosphere, nutrients are recyclable, and the most important of these cycles are the nitrogen and the sulphur cycles, which are usually enhanced by the action of soil microorganisms. Soil nutrients can be lost through leaching. In order for the system to be sustainable, the above processes must be appropriately maintained, and this can only be done if we understand them properly. Measuring sustainability means to some extent measuring these processes.

Primary productivity and cycling of nutrients in every rangeland ecosystem are affected by human populations. People build their houses and even cities in rangelands. They, like the animals, walk on the soil, compacting it and trampling plants. Understanding the impact of humans on rangelands is important in understanding how these lands can sustainably be modified for their benefit.

Measurement and determination of sustainability in the rangelands of eastern Africa

The Integrated Project on Arid Lands (IPAL) study area (see figures 18-4 and 18-5), which is representative of rangelands in eastern Africa, covers approximately 22,500 square kilometers. It is sufficiently large and covers the major biotic communities found in the area, so that all processes being observed could be investigated. It is bounded, on the west, by Mt. Kulal, a major water catchment area, and to the east, by Mt. Marsabit. The study area partly covers the homes of the Rendille, Gabra, Boran, and Samburu, who are the major nomadic tribes in this area. With varying degrees of facility, the project was able to study the deterioration of arid land and the combination of causative factors: climatic fluctuation, the activities and attributes of the pastoralist societies and of their cattle, camel, sheep, and goat herds, including such important aspects as the increase in human population and the practice and effects of construction of *bomas* (night enclosures).

The greater part of the study area consists of a large central plain at less than 700 meters above sea level. The northern part of this plain is surrounded by volcanic mountain masses: the Huri Hills (1,301 meters) to the north; Mt. Marsabit (1,836 meters) to the east, and Mt. Kulal (2,295 meters) to the west. In the south and southwest, the area is bounded by the basement complex mountains, Mt. Nyiru (2,963 meters), Oldoinyo Mara (2,224 meters), the Ndoto Mountains (2,838 meters), and Baio Mountain (1,885 meters). To the west of Mt. Kulal lies Lake Turkana.

The main drainage lines originate in the hill masses and are mostly in the form of seasonal rivers, draining into the central plain where their water evaporates or sinks. Water from most of the land drains into the old saline lake bed of the Chalbi desert in the north of the area. There are four major desert plains, the Chalbi, the Koroli, the Hedad, and the Kaisut, each distinct in its degree of soil salinity and vegetation.

The soils are derived from the pre-Cambrian basement rocks or from more recent volcanoes, and they are estimated to be roughly equally divided in their area between these two parent

Figure 18–3: Energy-Flow Diagram of a Community Showing Large Respiratory Losses at Each Transfer

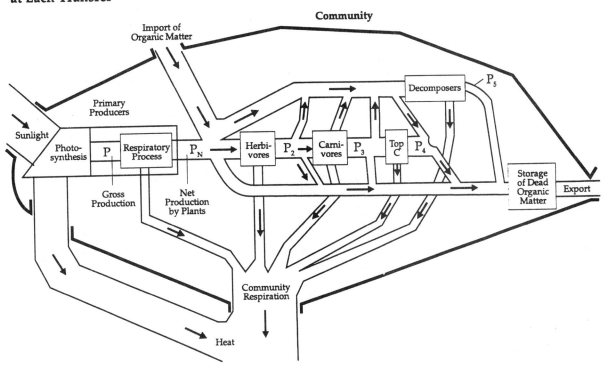

Note: P, gross primary production; P_N, net primary production; P_2, P_3, P_4, P_5, secondary production at the levels indicated.
Source: Adapted from Odum 1959.

types. The basaltic lavas, resulting from volcanic activity, surround the volcanic hills, and the sedimentary deposits, originating from the basement complex hills, occupy the central plains. The rains are unreliable and occur in two seasons, mainly in April/May (long rains) and November (short rains). The climate is discussed later in this chapter.

The special nature of threats to sustainable use of range resources in northern Kenya

Rangeland degradation has certain common characteristics wherever it occurs in the world. There is loss of vegetative cover, followed by soil degradation through various forms of erosion and compaction. These in turn lead to greatly reduced productivity in the ecosystems concerned. In the case of grazing systems, there is decreased forage for livestock and a consequent reduction in animal products for the subsistence of the human population. Although range degradation and its consequences can be attributed simply to the combined effects of climatic change and human impact, it is important to recognize that the na-

ture of the human influences varies from one region to another (as does the environment), which makes each local situation unique. Northern Kenya is no exception to this rule.

Three-quarters of Kenya's land surface is arid or semi-arid, and, across this region, several recent socioeconomic factors have been identified as contributing to the processes of range deterioration. Through the setting and realignment of political and administrative boundaries, the development of forest reserves and national parks, and the establishment of commercial ranches, and through the influence of missions and several other modern institutions, the movement of nomadic people has been restricted and the area they formerly occupied reduced.

Traditional antagonisms between tribes had compressed some tribal groups into a fraction of their former ranges until further encroachment was prevented some forty years ago. The antagonisms are still present, and the lack of security against inter-tribal livestock raiding and banditry further restricts the movement of people and the occupation of grazing lands. More than 25 percent of the project's study area is not used,

Figure 18–4: Location of the Study Area of the Integrated Project in Arid Land

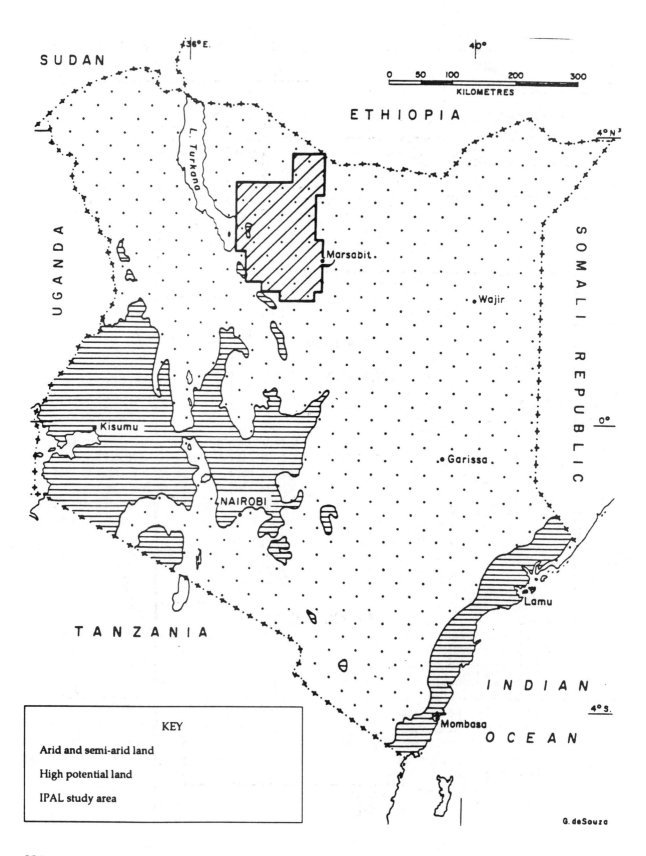

KEY

Arid and semi-arid land

High potential land

IPAL study area

G. deSouza

Figure 18–5: People of the Study Area of the Integrated Project in Arid Land

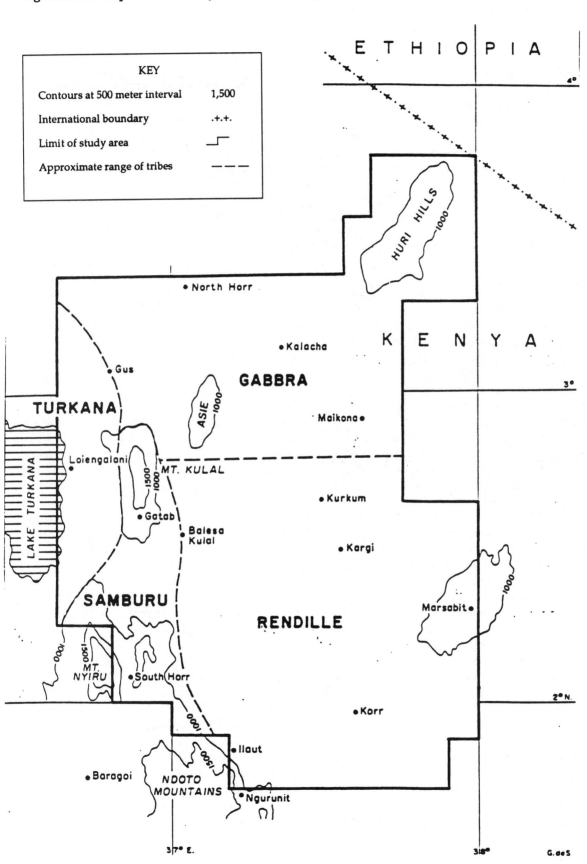

owing to fear of tribal raiding, and the additional pressure exerted on the more secure areas aggravates their overexploitation.

Another distinctive feature of the problem of use of the Kenyan range is the special nature of the pastoral economy. Although the people inhabiting northern Kenya have many similarities to other pastoralists living in the Sahelian zone, in Kenya, arid zone agriculture has never been practiced, and thus there is little of the close interaction and interdependence between agriculturalists and pastoralists that are an important feature of the Sahel.

The problem of accelerated human population growth in arid areas is perhaps not unique to Kenya, but it is certainly one of the key factors in the desertification processes occurring in the north of that country. Kenya's human population occupying arid land has doubled in the last twenty-five years and will, if present trends continue, double again in the next ten years. The pressure of human population is further aggravated by pressure from Kenya's high-potential areas, where population has exceeded its carrying capacity and is now moving to the marginal lands. With the alarming increase in the human population, there has come a corresponding increase in the numbers of domestic livestock.

A prominent factor in the deterioration of the arid lands of northern Kenya through overstocking is the drive to satisfy normal ambition for wealth (over and above subsistence needs), combined with a certain helplessness or fatalism about the consequences. In earlier times, when human requirements demanded only a moderate and transitory exploitation of grazing land, minor and localized damage could heal. More recently, the pressing, and at times desperate, needs of an overgrown and frequently hungry human population have imposed intolerable pressures on the arid lands, which, with their delicate balances and fluctuations, are experiencing, first, the erosion of their productive levels and, then, the disintegration of their ecological structures.

As a result of the rising human populations, there are increased demands on woody vegetation. In addition to the usual use of wood for building and for fuel, the pastoralist people in northern Kenya use large quantities in constructing bomas to keep their animals together at night and to prevent depredations by carnivores. These bomas are built at permanent and temporary camps. In temporary camps, they may be occupied for as short a time as a week before the

livestock are moved to a new area and a new boma is constructed. In the semi-permanent settlements, an accumulation of ticks and other parasites usually necessitates the periodic burning of the boma and the movement to a site that may be as little as 100 meters away. This practice appears to have the greatest impact on the woodlands of northern Kenya and is one of the most serious causes of desert encroachment in the region. In addition to the changing constraints on pastoralism noted earlier, such as reduced home ranges, another important trend of far-reaching consequences for land use is the increasing settlement of formerly nomadic people.

Centers of human and livestock concentration have arisen and recently have tended to expand rapidly, around a few springs and wells and especially around the boreholes that have been installed. Although the presence of fresh water is the most important factor in such concentrations, several other incentives contribute to their expansion. Many of them have become the sites for shops, schools, medical centers, and famine relief centers. However, of the greatest significance is the fact that these centers offer security from inter-tribal livestock raiding. Each of the concentration areas becomes a nucleus of denuded land that spreads in widening circles as the people are obliged to go farther for grazing and for the wood they need for fuel and for the fences to enclose their livestock at night. This accelerates the rate of localized range deterioration. As in many other arid regions of the world, the northern part of Kenya suffers from periodic droughts, which have occurred frequently in recent historical times. Formerly, the consequences of these droughts were not as serious as they are today, since the arid regions were sparsely populated. With the recent increases in population, droughts have become more serious, claiming the lives of large numbers of livestock and, where they shared the grazing lands, of wildlife as well. After periods of drought, the systems of production do not recover fully. Some families lose the bulk of their herds, which may have been small in the first place, and many become destitute and reliant on famine relief. The supply of famine relief food has become a permanent feature of the economy in Marsabit District. During serious droughts, such as that which occurred in northeastern Africa and the Sahel between 1968 and 1976, pastoralists become wholly dependent on the few perennial supplies of water, and the consequent concentrations of people and livestock destroy the vegetation.

Although it is a normal traditional practice to disperse from such areas of concentration when the rains come, there is a growing tendency for part of the population, especially women, children, and the older men, to remain behind, keeping with them the livestock they need for milk. The young men continue to take away into the surrounding country the unproductive animals (known as the *fora* herds)—males, castrates, and barren females—following largely traditional nomadic practices.

The problem of range deterioration in Kenya is therefore serious and complex. It concerns the plight of people who are using the only traditional means they have known to cope with a vast problem that has been caused to a great extent by modern influences. As yet, although these problems in northern Kenya are recognized by the government and are expected to receive considerable attention in development programs in the coming years, administrative and economic constraints have, until recently, militated against appropriate corrective measures. Among the most important have been the lack of funds and commitment for the development of low-potential areas, the insufficiency of suitable educational facilities, the migration of educated people out of the more remote and inhospitable regions to the towns, the lack of attraction of such regions for high-caliber civil servants, and above all, the lack of information on human and other resources that is essential for the rational development of the region.

Since the lives of people are at stake, no efforts should be spared to develop the resources of the arid lands of northern Kenya for the well-being of its people. However, development must take the form most suited to the sociological, economic, and ecological circumstances to which the region is best adapted. In northern Kenya, owing to the arid and variable climate and the present culture, the greater part of the land must remain rangeland to be used for grazing, and effective use will depend on maintaining considerable mobility in the livestock herds.

The IPAL study

The Integrated Project in Arid Lands (IPAL) was implemented from 1976 to 1987 in recognition of the importance of the arid lands of Kenya both because they support the indigenous people and the economy of the country as a whole and because they were gravely threatened by degradation through misuse. The project was originally set up as a pilot operation to investigate the processes and causes of environmental degradation in the arid and semi-arid region inhabited by pastoral nomads.

The IPAL was intended to contribute to the design of management activities directed toward achieving a sustained balance between production and consumption, taking into account the requirements of the growing and increasingly settled population. It was hoped, where possible, to demonstrate practical modifications and alternatives to the traditional livestock—based economy that could permit rehabilitation of already degraded lands. Equally important in this regard was the use of project findings in education and training and the dissemination of information on rational management.

Since most of the changes and processes being investigated needed continuous monitoring, one of the project's objectives was to provide the program basis for establishing an institution in Marsabit District for continued research, monitoring, and training relevant to the management of resources in the arid zone. The project developed and recommended the infrastructural basis for the required management.

Design of the IPAL study

IPAL's research activities in northern Kenya were based on the belief or hypothesis that a system of land use could be adopted in the near future that would reverse the present trends of degradation and establish a sustained production within the livestock economy in Marsabit District sufficient to support the growing population. Such a system would depend on appropriate management (in the widest sense) of human and natural resources, aided by suitable education at all levels.

The IPAL study was therefore designed to cover all the major components of the ecological system that have a bearing on its productivity for the welfare of humanity. The complexity of the problems to be tackled necessitated this multidisciplinary approach. Field work included research on the abiotic components of the ecosystem—climate, geomorphology, soils, hydrology, and the biotic components of the ecosystem—primary production (vegetation), and secondary production (livestock and wildlife). Humans and their livestock are one single dominant factor in the functioning of this ecosystem, and their activities were investigated under the human ecology and livestock components of the research program. IPAL investigations also included work on the contemporary problems of communication, education, and training and on the socioeconomic and political backgrounds. This case study of the IPAL project looks at how the design of each project component contributed to the understanding of that ecological system and how that understanding enhanced our ability to manage that system sustainably under the prevailing circumstances. In order to understand the functioning of the system, the correct elements and processes must be identified and the appropriate research questions formulated.

Human ecology

Notwithstanding the relevance of the ecological approach to development planning, a common failing, even among ecologically oriented planners, is the scant attention normally given to the so-called human factor. The existence of a human population presupposes complex ethnic, social, and biological influences and interactions. If these are not understood and adequately accommodated in resource management plans, the consequences can be serious, even disastrous. The failure of previous attempts to effect appropriate change in pastoral societies, which has been an important factor in the continuing deterioration of arid lands in Africa, has been due, at least partly, to an ignorance among planners of the biological and sociological bases of pastoralism. Little effort has been made to understand the values, the fears, and the aspirations of the people we intend to help.

Although ecologists have long recognized the dominant role of man as a cause of change in the biosphere, in practice they have been reluctant to alter the conventional view that man is the last link in the ecological chain and should therefore be considered last. This account of a study of an arid zone ecosystem in northern Kenya reverses the customary sequence, considering first the human populations as the main focus of the study and working outward to consider the human environment. The ecosystem approach remains the guiding principle.

Humans can justifiably be regarded as the dominant biotic element in the grazing land ecosystems by virtue of their overwhelming impact on them, exerted largely through domestic animals. However, the human-oriented approach is adopted in this account mainly because it re-

flects the primary objective of IPAL in seeking practical solutions to a critical human predicament. Expanding pastoral populations, responding to the impact of modern influences, occupy vulnerable habitats in which the production necessary for their support is being progressively reduced by overexploitation.

The measurement and interpretation of most ecological parameters are relatively straightforward. Similarly, the basic human biological requirements of food, fuel, and shelter can be assessed. Human populations are censused, and their structures and trends can be described. In the case of pastoralist societies, their fundamental resource requirements, met mainly by livestock production and woody vegetation, are calculable. Beyond these essentially measurable resources lies the relatively unquantifiable complex of human attitudes, characteristics, and requirements that are not so amenable to inclusion in ecosystem models, but that are, nevertheless, essential considerations in the integrated planning of land use programs. The project's additional function of advising the government of Kenya on the rational management of the arid grazing lands of Marsabit District necessitates understanding a wide range of local socioeconomic conditions and trends as well as knowledge of the ecological interactions of the pastoralists with their environment.

The work program of IPAL therefore included a program of research on human ecology in its broadest sense. In addition to augmenting the existing knowledge of the more purely ecological aspects of the human populations, it brought into focus the many socioeconomic factors that have a bearing on the process of desertification in northern Kenya. To do this necessitated adopting a frank and uncompromising approach to several unpalatable truths and the discussion of matters that are normally avoided because they embarrass authority. Nevertheless, unless the realities of the socioeconomic and the political background are squarely confronted, there appears to be little hope of implementing any land use policies of significance in the battle against desertification.

The following specific questions were addressed in this enquiry:

1. What were the basic elements of the pastoralist tradition that enabled the pastoralists to survive in this hostile environment?

2. What was the structure of the traditional pastoral economy, and how did it work?

3. How were their basic traditions being influenced by modern developments and the market economy?

4. How were the traditional pastoral economies functioning within the modern national monetary economy?

5. Are the traditional pastoral economies sustainable under the present circumstances?

6. How could pastoral economies be made to function better?

Livestock ecology studies

A few observations made in the human ecology studies are worth reiterating here because they form the background against which the IPAL livestock studies should be viewed. First, however much we may regret the past and the changes that have been forced on the peoples of northern Kenya, life for them will never be quite the same again. According to the charter of the Organization of African Unity, all territorial boundaries inherited from colonialism must be respected, and within Kenya itself the administrative boundaries have been reaffirmed. When this is coupled with population pressures from the outside, there is little hope that pastoral groups will ever regain their lost territories, and hence they are forced to accept their present reduced grazing areas. Second, because of the limited land potential coupled with the firm livestock cultures of the people, northern Kenya will remain largely rangeland, and a degree of mobility will continue to be a biological necessity for survival.

It was IPAL's intention, therefore, not to set the clock backwards but to assist in making the lives of the people of northern Kenya happy and meaningful under the changed circumstances. In their terms, this means making their land more productive through their livestock. The major objective of IPAL's livestock studies therefore was to develop management strategies for restoring and maintaining ecological stability. This specifically involved assessing the current importance and potential economics of livestock production systems for the people; determining livestock population parameters, including their likely trends and impact on ecological stability; developing livestock grazing and production strategies for controlled use of the range and long-term, sustained production.

IPAL's livestock studies concentrated on the four species culturally and economically most important to the people in the area: camels, cattle, sheep, and goats. Livestock are the principal link between people and primary production. Their efficiency in that process of energy transfer is an important factor in sustainability of the use of that system. This efficiency is determined by the number, class, distribution, density, location, disease, and offtake of livestock. All these attributes were the subject of intensive investigation.

SPECIFIC OBJECTIVES
The livestock studies surveyed the study area to determine the number and fluctuation of annual and seasonal livestock and wildlife and to estimate the rate and distribution of actual stocking in relation to a variety of environmental parameters. For the four main species of livestock (namely camels, cattle, sheep, and goats), it determined at regular intervals the key food plants in relation to their availability in the range and the seasonal fluctuations and nutritional value of the forage available for livestock. In different areas and under conditions of varying food availability, it monitored milk production and growth of the four main livestock species, measured the quantity and, where appropriate, the quality of food products, and identified inefficiencies and recommended solutions. The growth of herds was also determined to predict future offtake and expected returns.

The study also monitored the effects of disease on the production of livestock and determined whether treatment was cost-effective with respect to increased productivity. This information was used to recommend appropriate veterinary measures that may be applied to each species, sex, and age class of livestock. The relations between livestock and humans were studied to evaluate the present use to which livestock were put by their owners and to determine their effectiveness in meeting the needs of the society and to recommend appropriate adjustments to fulfill shortages and enable pastoralists to participate in the national economy.

Livestock offtake was examined to identify constraints to offtake, in particular marketing, and to recommend improvements. Finally, this information was used to develop an integrated management plan for livestock that would lead to (a) recovery of the range and (b) sustained yield of livestock food products to enable the Rendille people to be self-supporting in food and to participate more fully in the national economy.

291

METHODS USED

The principal method used involves systematic reconnaissance flights over a 6 percent sample of the study area. The method is described in Griffiths (1975) and Field (1981). The aircraft is used as an observatory from which the number of livestock, wildlife, and households is recorded and their distributions related to a variety of environmental parameters, which are monitored simultaneously.

The nutrition and intake of livestock were also studied in several types of range using the proportion of time spent on a given plant species or plant part as an index of the proportion of that plant in the diet (Field 1978: Schwartz 1980). This method is adequate for (a) detecting seasonal changes in food habits and (b) determining key food plants. It does not yield proportions of dry-matter intake. The range section is currently using oesophageally fistulated animals to check the method. The consumption of food was determined for cattle and goats, using the chromic oxide ration method. Intake by camels was determined by weighing their total fecal output over a twenty-four-hour period. Analyses of plants that camels use for food enabled the calculation of the digestibility of the diet, the indigestible fraction of which was represented by the feces. The digestible and indigestible fractions were summed to give total intake of food. Chemical analyses were carried out on forage plants, which comprise 80 percent of the diet. The analyses include dry matter, protein, energy, fiber, minerals, and digestibility. The chemical compositions of diets were reconstituted from these figures. The volume of water consumed was measured when livestock drink at wells.

Experimental animals consisting of camels, cattle, sheep, and goats contracted or owned by the project were intensively sampled to determine their production. The production of milk was monitored in the morning and evening when half of the udder was milked out and the volume measured. With camels, the time during which the calf is usually separated from its mother was recorded. Milk production was then calculated on a twenty-four-hour basis and estimated for the entire udder. The growth of animals was monitored at regular intervals by taking live weights. These were usually measured on the morning before the dehydrated animal was given water. In the case of camels and cattle, where weighing equipment is cumbersome, use is made of the relationship between live-weight and body size, in particular thoracic girth (Field 1979). Details of

the recruitment and mortality of livestock were recorded with information on matings and abortions to assist in interpretation of the gross data.

While general management of experimental flocks and herds followed the traditional pattern of the pastoral herds of the study area, each of the experimental flocks and herds was divided into two parts. To study disease, one was subjected to a package of inputs, mainly veterinary drugs, while the other acted as an untreated control. Differences in productivity between the herds receiving treatment and those receiving no treatment were compared with the costs of the supplementary inputs. The chief parameters of veterinary significance that were monitored included (a) monthly output of fecal worm eggs, comparing untreated animals with those subjected to regular anthelmintic treatment; (b) volume of blood-packed cells and the effects of regular anthelmintic, acaricidal, and ad hoc trypanocidal treatment; (c) monthly numbers and species of ticks feeding on the animals with and without weekly spraying with acaricide; (d) bimonthly levels of serum antibodies to trypanosomiasis in camels; and (e) causes of clinical disease and mortality as they occurred and the effects of therapy on disease, where appropriate.

Certain surveys periodically obtained information on the diseases in pastoral livestock. Some data were also acquired on the clinical conditions affecting pastoral herds through the operation of subsidized veterinary clinical services to the pastoral communities.

The main method used to investigate the interactions between livestock and humans was the household survey. In addition to asking questions, measurements were taken on-site of the numbers, weights, milk production, and occasionally blood of livestock. And, finally, the main method of studying livestock offtake was again the questionnaire survey, with emphasis on traders as well as households.

Vegetation studies

The project's first approach to investigating the problems of rangeland use in northern Kenya was to initiate a quantitative ecological study of the interactions and relationships between the livestock populations and the vegetation. It was envisaged that at least part of the solution to the most obvious problem—overgrazing—would depend on a firm factual basis relating to primary production and requirements for animal fodder in the region.

The program of research on vegetation maintained its main objectives; in the short term, it sought to identify and describe the processes contributing to land degradation and to determine the nature, rates, and causes of changes taking place in the vegetation. In the long term, the main objective was to provide, for the government of Kenya, recommendations on the sustainable management of the rangeland (within the context of a more comprehensive program of land and social reform), which would ensure the maximum sustainable productivity of the region, based on the rational and controlled use of the vegetation and appropriate rehabilitation measures. The urgency for such recommendations was evident from the rapid deterioration of the vegetation in the inhabited areas with the consequent reduction in livestock productivity, combined with the food requirements of the growing human population. The increase in the number of animals necessary to support the pastoralists, together with the continuing reduction in nomadic movement and the trend toward settlement, had resulted in the gross overstocking of the country within foraging range of the villages. The program of research on vegetation was designed to answer the following fundamental questions:

- What major plant communities occur in the region, and what are their botanical and physiognomic characteristics?

- What are their distributions and their relationships to altitude, topography, soils, climate, and human and animal influences?

- What are the characteristic biomass densities of the two main layers (herb and dwarf shrubs and trees) in each major community in relation to mean rainfall, drainage, soil conditions, and human and animal influences?

- What are the annual levels of primary production in each major plant community (in the herb and tree layers) in relation to recent rainfall under different conditions of soil, drainage, and use?

The answers to these questions constituted the baseline information on the vegetation of the region on which future ecological monitoring would depend. A further series of questions were posed, the answers to which related more directly to the management of the vegetation resources:

- What proportion of the annual primary production is available to livestock, and what proportion is consumed?

- What proportion of the biomass and annual production of wood is used by the pastoralists for building, fencing, and fuel, and what are their annual requirements?

- What is the spatial distribution of use of the vegetation?

- What are the tolerance levels of species and communities to exploitation?

- What are the rates of change in plant biomass and productivity in the different areas in the region in response to the impact of humans and animals?

Several of these questions, together with the final one, which concerns the estimation of carrying capacities and other aspects of management, had to be answered in collaboration with livestock ecologists.

RANGE MAPPING
The range mapping and classification done in collaboration with the woodland ecology work, which included aerial photo interpretation with ground truth checks, identified 144 types of ranges, which were mapped and described. A range type is a more or less distinct unit of vegetation, which may be delineated on the basis of aspect, composition, or density. Based on a minimum mappable size of 25 square kilometers, which was the average normal daily grazing range of livestock in the study area, and also taking into account similarities of plant composition and infertility of soils and land forms, the range types were grouped into twenty-four range units. The range types were mapped at 1:100,000 and the range units at 1:250,000. Each range unit was characterized by the three dominant species in the order of their importance.

DESCRIPTION OF TYPE OF RANGE
For any recommendation to be made on the use of a specific range type, it was important that all factors that influence the functioning of that system be understood. This was taken into account in the descriptions of each range unit, which included the following:

- A description of all the physical attributes: general topography, underlying rock, soil characteristics, drainage systems, erosion status, and various climatic factors such as temperature, precipitation and its reliability, and wind

- A description of all the vegetation factors, which includes species composition, cover, and biomass

293

- A description of past and present human influences through both livestock and settlement
- A subjective assessment of range condition and estimated carrying capacity for that site.

Both the range analysis method (U.S. Department of Agriculture 1970) and the concentric circle method of vegetation community analysis (Colorado State University 1970) were used in determining community structures and composition, while standing biomass was determined by clipped plots along the same paced transects through each type.

PRIMARY PRODUCTION

Knowledge of the primary production of a range site is essential in order to determine carrying capacity. Measuring plant production is a complex process involving the monitoring of plant materials produced by a system that is usually protected from most kinds of use, in protected enclosures over a period of many years, in order to reflect seasonal as well as yearly fluctuations. In the absence of such data, and in the urgent need of advice on which to base decisions on land management in this region, it was decided to use the aboveground standing crop biomass of the dwarf shrub and herb layer to estimate primary production. The data used were mainly based on two wet-season surveys.

RANGE CONDITION

Range condition is defined as the state of range health. Like health, condition is relative, and when a particular piece of range is said to be in good condition or poor condition, the description is always relative to a standard or ideal for that kind of range: its greatest potential lies in soil stability and in amount and quality of forage. A stable soil is basic to all range types. The primary objective in range management, then, is to maintain and improve those soils that are stable and to stabilize those that are now eroding.

A stable soil is a prerequisite to judging as satisfactory any area where a soil mantle has developed. This principle is applicable to ranges anywhere and relates to any normal vegetal cover; it does not change with site or with type of vegetation. If cover is lost, soil soon follows, and once the soil is gone, the resource is gone. The range condition for the range sites identified in our study area was determined by subjective judgment based on the following attributes: soil stability, composition of desirable and undesirable plants, bare ground and litter cover, and the state of erosion.

Range condition was based on four categories: excellent, good, fair, and poor. With the exception of one type of mountain range, none of the range types had in our judgment a condition better than fair, indicating the seriousness of the degradation of the grazing resource. For most of the study area, any management of the range resources would have to be preceded by effective range rehabilitation and improvement programs.

Determination of range condition is perhaps the weakest part of range science in the tropics. Most methods used were developed for temperate rangelands grazed by monospecies like sheep or cattle. The requirements of the broad array of animal species and habitats found in tropical rangelands have not yet been adequately investigated.

CARRYING CAPACITY

The concept of carrying capacity has arisen as a result of our recognition that plant communities have a limited tolerance to exploitation by animals. Exceeding this tolerance causes deleterious changes in vegetation, such as a reduction in productivity or diversity or both, and may be irreversible in practical terms. There are numerous difficulties in defining, estimating, and applying carrying capacity in actual land use situations. It is generally agreed that carrying capacity is the maximum biomass density of animal life (normally referring to livestock or wildlife) that can be maintained without detriment to the long-term productivity of the area. The concept defines the level of exploitation that will permit the survival of the ecosystem. It does not refer to a level of use in which the productivity of the ecosystem is maximized, such as a properly managed livestock ranch. In such circumstances, the maximum sustainable production of meat and milk will be achieved at a level of biomass density substantially lower than the carrying capacity and would be termed the maximal production or optimal stocking rate.

In the definition of carrying capacity given above, the term is taken to mean the long-term sustainable density of animal life. In arid environments, where climatic variability is high and is accompanied by proportional variability in plant production, the long-term carrying capacity is determined by the levels of plant production in drier years and not by the average years. Thus, although it is possible to speak of the short-term carrying capacity determined by the recent or current level of plant production, attempting to maintain stocking rates at this level will result in overstocking when dry years occur.

While production varies from year to year with variable rainfall, it also varies spatially according to recent distribution of rainfall, local drainage and soil conditions, and the history of land use. Carrying capacity estimates thus have to take into account local variation and are generally applied to relatively large areas in which the variability is accounted for in the averaging process. Despite the possibilities of estimating average carrying capacity across large areas of land, the interpretation of such estimates must allow for several qualifying factors, which tends to set the actual stocking rate attainable at a lower level than the theoretical carrying capacity. A discussion of these factors and their implication for determining final stocking rates in any particular site appears below.

Specific recommendations on proper stocking rates for the different range types of a region are an essential part of any range management plan. The recommendations can be based on long experience in range management under similar circumstances, or on published estimates for the ecoclimatic zone in question, or finally, in the absence of adequate prior information on the region, on actual measurements of the primary production of the area in relation to known fodder requirements of the livestock species.

In the IPAL study area the only available data to indicate levels of primary production are measurements from the clipping of the herb and dwarf layers of the vegetation, which were obtained in two range surveys in 1982 and 1983, and the biomass and production values for the tree and large shrub layer, obtained from the destructive sampling of the important tree species and transect observations made in each range type. These data were used as the basis for calculating carrying capacity. In order to arrive at realistic estimates of the forage available for livestock, several adjustments to the measured values of standing crop biomass were made. Since a large proportion of the foliage standing crop biomass in the herb and dwarf shrub layers is annual production, the distinction between standing crop and annual production has not been made here. Future measurements of these layers will be made to determine the relative dry weight values of standing crop biomass and annual production in the plant communities present in different ranges.

The following steps were taken to determine the carrying capacity of the herb and dwarf shrub layer obtained from clipping data. First, a *proper use* factor of 50 percent was deducted, following the standard practice in range science. From the figure thus obtained for available forage, a further deduction of 25 percent was made to allow for the errors associated with the use of small clipped plots. This gave the quantity of usable forage as 37.5 percent of the total standing crop biomass of the annual grasses and herbs, which was the value used in calculating the carrying capacity of these elements in the vegetation. For dwarf shrubs, since the foliage and production of new growth is low in relation to the standing crop biomass, especially in years and seasons of low rainfall, the estimated usable forage biomass was further reduced by half to 18.5 percent of the standing crop. In the special case of the large dwarf shrub Duosperma eremophilum, which is largely woody, 22 percent of the biomass was known from previous measurements to be available for forage, and therefore only 11 percent was used in the calculations of carrying capacity to allow for low production in dry years. Of the standing dead annual grass, only 18.5 percent was considered to be available.

Having estimated the available herb and dwarf shrub forage using the above adjustments to the standing crop biomass, the next step was to apportion this forage among the different livestock species. In consultation with the human ecologist, it was agreed that multiple use of the range by the four major livestock species—camels, goats, cattle, and sheep—would have to continue in the immediate future, until greater technical knowledge and a broader awareness enable the traditional pastoralists to accept any advantages to be gained by separating the species for the optimal use of the range. Camels overlap goats in their use of the herb layer, while cattle overlap sheep. This point was resolved by accepting the existing ratio of camel to goat biomass and cattle to sheep biomass, which, in both cases, was approximately 5:1. This ratio was determined from the average values of livestock biomass observed in eleven aerial census surveys carried out over four years. Indigofera spinosa, which is one of the most desirable plants for all the livestock species, was apportioned for use according to the proportions of biomass of the animal species.

The final estimates of carrying capacity based on the herb and dwarf shrub layers were deduced by using the average values of dry matter intake obtained by the livestock ecologist: camels, 4.81 kilograms a day; cattle, 4.45 kilograms a day; sheep, 0.76 kilograms a day; goats, 0.84 kilograms a day. Carrying capacity was, in all cases, expressed as the number of animals per square kilometer a year, and an estimated number of animals that could be supported by each range unit was also given based on its area. Until more data on primary production become available, these figures should be regarded with extreme caution. They represent the best estimate based on biomass data for the area.

The approach to estimating carrying capacities described above is somewhat traditional with respect to the tenets of range science and is based largely on the assumption that livestock carrying capacities are dependent on the productivity of the grass, herb, and dwarf shrub layers (the so-called range plants). This approach does not take into account two circumstances that are particularly characteristic of the range-livestock ecosystem of the arid zone in northeast Africa. First, trees and large shrubs constitute a substantial proportion of the range vegetation, and, second, camels and goats, which are browsers, obtain nearly 30 percent of their food from trees and large shrubs. Thus, in terms of biomass, 59 percent of the livestock are obtaining 30 percent of their diet from approximately 8 percent of the available forage in the region. It is, therefore, evident that considering the region as a whole, tree and large shrub forage is a greater limiting factor in determining the carrying capacity for camels and goats than are the herb and dwarf shrub layers. A further essential consideration in determining the carrying capacities of woodlands and shrublands is the impact that browsing animals, particularly goats, have on young trees. In heavily stocked areas, goats browse young trees and large shrubs so intensely that they may prevent their growth and eventually kill them. Under these circumstances, little or no recruitment to the larger size classes takes place, and an important tree or shrub species may be greatly reduced or eliminated in such an area. For this reason, the age class structure of tree and large shrub populations has been regarded as a critical criterion in determining the stocking rates of goats and, to a lesser extent, of camels. Poor structure, with few young trees present, may necessitate low stocking rates for goats and camels.

Woodland ecology studies

Trees have three important roles to play in the arid zone in northern Kenya, seen from the standpoint of the pastoralist populations. They pro-vide firewood, materials for the construction of houses and livestock enclosures, and browse for the livestock on which the pastoralists are almost wholly dependent for their subsistence. In addition to these three essential contributions of the pastoral economy, which are the main subjects discussed in this section, trees are valued for their shade (an important factor in the survival of cattle and small stock in the arid zone) and for their fruit and other useful products, such as fiber for rope and gum for the gum arabic industry. Their roles in the maintenance of soil fertility and in the reduction of soil erosion and desiccation, although of crucial importance, remain to be investigated systematically and are not discussed here.

The reduction and eventual loss of the tree layer in areas of exceptionally heavy livestock and direct human exploitation almost invariably take place several years after the destruction of the herb layer through overgrazing and trampling. Very large areas of rangeland, which are now in the intermediate stage of degradation, where the soil surface is almost totally denuded but where the tree populations are relatively unharmed, can be seen in the Samburu and Baringo districts of Kenya. Indeed, it appears that, in the process of degradation of the wooded grasslands of the arid and semi-arid zones of eastern Africa, a stage is passed through in which the reduction or removal of the grass results in vigorous growth of small trees, mainly Acacia species. This is due to the lack of root completion for the seedling trees and the absence of grass fires, which normally limit tree growth and effectively maintain the patterns of scattered trees, or of woodland and grassland mosaics, characteristic of undergraded rangelands in East Africa. In the semi-arid grasslands of Kenya, the destruction of the herb layer through overgrazing frequently leads to the growth of tree and shrub thickets, such as the *Acacia mellifera* thickets of Longido in northern Tanzania and Baringo and Samburu in Kenya. In the arid regions with less than 300 millimeters of mean annual rainfall, covering a large proportion of northern and eastern Kenya and also substantial areas in Somalia and southern Ethiopia, the low and erratic rainfall does not support a sufficient biomass density of trees to enable thickets to form, despite the absence of grass fires, except along some seasonal watercourses. The most extensive vegetation community across more than 200,000 square kilometers in northeastern Africa is the relatively open, dry shrublands (as defined by Dratt and Gwyne 1977) in which the small trees *Acacia reficiens* and *Acacia mellifera* are dominant or co-dominant. Within the IPAL study area, these communities constitute 26 percent of the area, while the two Acacia species, together with several others, occur as the dominant trees in a further 60 percent of the region, which is occupied by annual grassland and dwarf shrubland (Herlocker 1979).

Over the greater part of Marsabit District, in which the IPAL studies took place, the herb layer has been affected to varying degrees by overgrazing. In the vicinity of wells, spring, and boreholes, which provide perennial sources of water, the grasses have been greatly reduced or almost totally removed. In the southwest of the district, inhabited by the Rendille people, the denuded soils extending outward from the settlements for as much as 30 kilometers may coalesce, as they do between the villages of Korr and Ilaut. In such areas, the tree populations have also been greatly reduced but have not been totally destroyed. Nevertheless, the process of excessive tree felling and lopping is continuing, although apparently at a slower rate than the loss of the herb layer through overgrazing and trampling.

The direct causes of tree destruction are clear. Pastoralists need wood for fuel and also for the construction of livestock pens. In the areas of human and livestock concentration, tree felling is taking place faster than young trees can be recruited to the woodland populations. Although many young and repressed trees are normally available for recruitment to the mature tree populations in such areas, their growth above half a meter in height is normally prevented by the browsing of goats. The main indirect cause of excessive destruction of trees is the increasing settlement of formerly nomadic pastoralists, resulting in the growing impact of tree felling on woodlands close to the settlements. As the supplies of wood in and around the villages are exhausted, the people are obliged to travel farther each year to obtain it.

In great contrast to the overexploited woodlands near the settlements, as much as 40 percent of the IPAL study area is occupied by woodlands that are rarely used, mainly owing to the lack of security from inter-tribal raiding. Such unexploited regions show clearly the potential productivity of the ecoclimatic zones in which they are situated and provide standards against which the nature and degree of degradation in the inhabited areas can be assessed.

It is against this background of extremely uneven use of the land resources that the woodland research program was undertaken. Essentially, the research sought to discover how woodland exploitation can be managed to ensure the maximal sustained production of the tree populations for the benefit of the pastoralist people and the country as a whole. A second question concerned the size and disposition of the existing and potential productivity of the woodland and hence its potential contribution to the subsistence of pastoralist populations and to the wider economy. The management of the woodlands clearly had only been undertaken as an integral part of the coordinated management of the region's land and other resources. Detailed information was needed on the dynamics and productivity of woodlands, on the one hand, and on potential human use of the woodlands, on the other, to ensure rational management of this resource on a sustainable basis within the overall planning. The management of tree populations must be integrated with the regulation of land use in general, with water resource management, with settlement policy, with the provision of substitute building and fencing materials, and with tree planting, to help accelerate rehabilitation of the rangeland and the provision of fuel and building materials.

Geomorphology and soils studies

Soils with their parent material form the physical base of any ecological system. In general, soils of the IPAL study area reflect (a) climatic zones, (b) topography, (c) geology, and (d) geomorphological processes.

There is a broad correspondence between the major geological and geomorphic units within the study area. An extensive plain (Heda, Koroli, Kaisut) composed of quaternary sediments derived from pre-Cambrian gneiss occupies the center of the study area. Two major ecological units are present: piedmont plains at higher levels and sedimentary plains at lower levels. Soils are generally sandy loams but become more finely textured and saline to the northeast, especially in the lower drainage lines. An extensive system of old stabilized sand dunes fringes the northernmost edge of the plains. This central large plain drains gently north-northeastward into a large lacustrine plain system and eastward down the Milgis River drainage. The lacustrine plain system comprises three elevational levels, the lowermost of which lies within southern Ethiopia. This overlies the old Chalbi Lake bed and is characterized by poorly drained, excessively saline, clays that either crack or are puffy at the surface. The old lake bed remains uncovered along the perimeter of the Chalbi desert and represents the intermediate levels. These have shallow, well-drained, excessively calcareous, fine, sandy clay loams over massive hard pan. Higher levels may have stony desert pavement.

Floodplains and low terrace alluvial plains occur along the major seasonal drainages such as the Balesa Kulal and Milgis rivers and at the junction of the plains and lava footslope areas. Soils vary in texture as well as age. Much of the Milgis floodplain, for instance, is composed of relict soils formed by past river distribution systems. Large mountains rise on all sides of the central plain, at 1,500 to 3,000 meters elevation, and are principally volcanic (Marsabit, Kulal, Huri Hills), although those in the southwest are pre-Cambrian gneisses (Ndotos, Nyiru, Oldoinyo Mara), from which come the sediments forming the central plain.

The soils of volcanic mountains are related to the major geomorphological units that are elevationally defined. Well drained and friable throughout, they are deep red to dark brown clays at higher elevations, shallow dark reddish brown clay loams with stony and rocky components at middle levels, and very shallow to moderately deep dark brown calcareous stony clay loams with saline-sodic tendencies at lower elevations. Rocky and bouldery surfaces are also common; similar soils occur throughout the stony to bouldery olivine basalt plateau and step-faulted scarps.

The primary types of vegetation within the IPAL study area reflect a climatic zonation, such as the lack of a shrubland zone between bushland and dwarf shrubland in the southwest, and are often attributable to soils. Soils are also the principal determinants of the smaller, more localized types of tertiary vegetation within the context of a climatic zone. An example would be a topographically related sequence of different soil-vegetation units of a hillside catena.

Soil texture plays an important part in the distribution of vegetation within the study area. Soils developed from lavas tend to be loamy to clayey in texture, whereas those developed from gneissic materials tend to be sandier.

Maintenance of an appropriate soil stability is an important factor in the range condition and ecological stability of rangeland ecosystems. When induced, destabilizing factors like soil erosion contribute to the deterioration of the whole ecological system.

The different types of vegetation found in the IPAL study area have significant relationships to the present geomorphological processes that are also important in determining ecological stability in various ways. First, phenological changes in the course of the year follow the patterns of rainfall. During the dry season, the grasses dry up over the whole study area and are almost completely grazed off by animals. Transects sampling of the whole of the lowland portion of the study just before the beginning of the rains shows that bare ground covers more than 45 percent, while 20 percent is covered by woody or grass herb and litter, which means that at the beginning of the rainy season at least 65 percent of the ground has no vegetative cover. Results from these transects were used to develop a formula for estimating the risk of erosion in the study area, which was applied to different range types. The slope factor was not applied to the formula since it was only used on the lowland plains. When the first rains strike a surface without a closed vegetative cover, splash erosion occurs, destroying the upper layers of the surface. Morphodynamics are determined mostly by the density of the cover of grass and dwarf shrub and, to a much smaller extent, by large shrubs and trees.

From this observation, it can safely be concluded that the factors destroying the herb layer are far more significant in causing land degradation than in destroying the tree layer in the lowland portion of the study area. This does not apply to the forested areas, the mountains, and the riverine vegetation, where destruction of the tree layer could lead to serious land degradation.

Climate studies

Although drought may be accepted as a natural phenomenon in northern Kenya, its frequency and the seriousness of its effects on the lives of the pastoralists were main concerns of IPAL's investigations. Coetsee (1968) distinguished four types of drought: seasonal droughts, periodic droughts, disaster droughts, and droughts caused by man. Seasonal droughts are normal, regular phenomena at certain times of the year. During such seasons, rainfall is low, and there is a shortage of edible material for livestock. Periodic droughts are unpredictable and may occur at any time of the year. They are always a menace and require constant preparedness and continual planning. These droughts have neither a fixed pattern of occurrence nor regular duration. Disaster droughts are actually protected periodic droughts. All available feed is used up, and state assistance on a large scale is necessary to save livestock. Soil moisture falls to a very low point where it is not available to plants, and a large number of plants may die. Failure to provide for periodic droughts means that disaster droughts will assume even greater proportions. Droughts caused by humans occur when a shortage of feed is brought about by overgrazing or injudicious use of the range, even though climatic conditions may not be such as to cause drought. In areas where droughts are caused by humans, and this is the situation in northern Kenya now, even a seasonal drought is a disaster.

Although drought has been termed one of the clearest examples of humanity's hopelessness in the face of the broad-scale phenomena of nature, its effects could be lessened by adequate forward planning. The information for such planning could come from meteorological services and intensive weather monitoring, such as that carried out by IPAL.

The constant necessity of the pastoralists of northern Kenya to remain almost permanently on famine relief has clearly demonstrated the present inability of the traditional mechanisms to cope with the problem of drought. The traditional system must be improved and supplemented in such a way that the pastoralists are always ready to combat drought.

Water resources studies

Future development in Marsabit District depends on the availability of water, whether for extending the area available for grazing (when effective grazing control was instituted), for future settlement schemes, or for limited irrigation of crops. Consultants carried out two preliminary reconnaissance studies, one on surface water and the other on underground water. These are briefly summarized below.

SURFACE WATER

Over a period of four months in 1981, a preliminary survey was undertaken of the springs, seasonal watercourses, and dams in the catchment area of southwest Marsabit District; the results are now being analyzed. The work included the installation of equipment to monitor the quantity of water flowing in the major seasonal rivers and collected in the dams and to assess the chemical and bacteriological content of water bodies. The possible means for making maximal use of the surface water resources were also assessed. Simultaneously, the processes of land degradation through the movement of surface water were also assessed using suspended sediment data, chemical leaching data, bed-material data, and other information related to chemical weathering, soil erosion, and so forth. Preliminary results indicated very high seasonal variability in the flow of the river, with long periods with no surface flow. Data on total dissolved solids and suspended sediments and other attributes are similarly variable during times of flow.

GROUNDWATER

In the Chalbi basin, as in most regions of the world, groundwater occurs at some depth, but limitations in its quantity, quality, and the energy required to raise it to the surface may preclude its development. Initial results can be summarized as follows:

- Records, direct measurements, and resistivity measurements indicate that groundwater is fairly close to the surface in several areas but had not been developed to even a fraction of its full potential, that is, Hedad, Korante, and Balessa Kulal rivers. In some areas, the water was very deep and would be costly to develop, for example, southeast and southwest of the Huri Hills and the Segel and Bora areas.

- Most of the groundwater is suitable for livestock, but not for human consumption or for irrigation. However, in some areas, it is suitable for all uses, that is, Korr, Kalacha, some springs near Maikona, and much of the perched water in the river beds.

- The water in the perched or sporadic shallow aquifers (at Ngurunit) may be limited in quantity, and wells in the deeper aquifers may be limited in quality. In some areas (Korr), the low permeability of the aquifer makes it suitable for wells with only very low specific capacities.

Generally, the regional water tables are just above the bedrock or in the bedrock complex, whose general surface dips toward the Chalbi. However, in some areas, the bedrock is more than 300 meters below the ground surface, that is, beyond the capabilities of the resistivity instrument used. Resistivity measurements indicated that some groundwater must leak out of the Chalbi basin to the west of North Horr, but the movement elsewhere is toward the Chalbi.

Much groundwater is usable in the Chalbi basin. Any future studies could be useful if focused on the more usable shallow groundwater resources because capital and operational costs are relatively low, and these sources are more easily managed by local people.

Pastoral economy studies

The IPAL studies already discussed yielded valuable information on relationships between the various components of the ecosystem and the processes leading to environmental degradation. Although this information is valuable, it is difficult to translate into practical policy and management options to be implemented by planners and administrators. The information had to be transformed into management proposals. An economic analysis and assessment was initiated to show the amount of money to be spent, a monetary valuation of the expected returns, and a general assessment of the feasibility of the expected outputs and follow-up activities.

Many practices of animal husbandry and land use that seem to be grossly inefficient might be necessary adaptations to existing economic realities. These might be inherent in the pastoral system of production or be dictated by developments in other parts of the country or even on the world markets and therefore be outside the control of pastoralists.

Without a proper understanding of these economic conditions and a conscious attempt to change them for the better—or to adapt to them—any management proposals recommending changes to the existing patterns of behavior will be futile. This observation is in line with the conclusions of a recent evaluation by the U.S. Agency for International Development of their livestock sector projects in Africa. The evaluators reached a consensus that for those programs to have favorable and beneficial impacts on producer populations, national wealth, and environmental conditions, they had to be reoriented to make them more nearly compatible with the social, economic, and environmental realities of arid and semi-arid pastoral regions of Africa. This seemed to justify the creation of an economic studies component on the IPAL project.

Broadly, the study aimed to describe the economic relationships that exist within the Rendille nomadic pastoral ecosystem. The ways and means of improving the efficiency with which the production and distribution of goods and services

are provided were investigated. A methodology for analyzing the development potential for similar arid areas was also developed. The economic studies specifically undertook to:

- Estimate the annual production of livestock and livestock products available for satisfying human wants like food, shelter, clothing, and so forth
- Estimate the quantities of these commodities that were necessary at that time for satisfying subsistence needs when 70—90 percent of the diet consisted of milk, blood, and meat
- Estimate the amount of these commodities that was surplus to the people's subsistence needs and hence was available for marketing
- Estimate the quantities of livestock and livestock products that were marketed and the quantities of maize flour, sugar, and tea imported to the area in a given year
- Study the marketing channels through which livestock and livestock products (exports), foodstuffs, and consumer items (imports) were traded; suggest ways and means by which the existing system was to be made more efficient in regard to the quality of services rendered to communities and the quantity of goods moved in and out of the area
- Conduct, using data from ongoing IPAL studies, a cost-benefit analysis of experimental management interventions to determine whether they offered good returns for the money expended
- Investigate the potential for developing sources of income other than the sale of unprocessed livestock and livestock products, including the possibility of developing aloes and *Acacia senegal* as cash crops, the potential for expanding the collection and marketing of honey using modern hives instead of traditional methods, which destroy the bees, the possibility of locating a small-scale hides and skins tanning or curing factory in the area, the possibilities for developing tourism and fishing.

Education, training, and demonstration

"Lack of education and environmental consciousness was identified as a major cause of land degradation in Kenya. It was indicated that even though we have the technical know-how of the root causes of desertification, little effort has been made to educate the masses and particularly the young generation on preventive and remedial measures to fight against land degradation" (National Environmental Secretariat 1977). This quotation, taken from the recommendations of the

Kenya national seminar on desertification, underlines the importance of the role of education and training in the effort to improve and stabilize the production systems in arid lands.

IPAL's education and training activities were based on the belief that the results of scientific research are not useful in achieving the desired goals unless they are translated into a form usable by the population affected by land degradation. The aim was therefore to use the findings of the project in education and training for the dissemination of information on rational management.

At the local and national levels, the project was integrated into the Kenya government's development plans for northern Kenya, and the project was a member of the Marsabit District Development Committee, where all matters related to the development of the district were discussed.

In addition to making direct inputs at the district planning level, the project, in cooperation with the Kenya Institute of Education, investigated through consultants the best possible way of incorporating the project's results and arid land ecology in general into the school curricula for the pastoral areas. This effort was designed to cover primary and secondary schools and later to be extended to teacher training colleges and institutions of higher learning, like the university. Study grants enabled graduate students from the University of Nairobi and other institutions to be attached to the project and to conduct research on various components of the IPAL study using the project's facilities and advice.

On the basis of experience gained by the project staff and taking advantage of the established base for fieldwork, a series of seminars were offered to train decisionmakers, administrators, and local people. Training and orientation courses for all levels were offered at the project's new headquarters in Marsabit. These courses included instruction on all aspects of the project's work, especially observation techniques, lectures, and demonstrations in arid zone ecology, range management, arid zone forestry, and pastoral sociology. The facilities and experience of IPAL were also made available to visiting scientists and extension officials from other countries in the region.

Because communication in the arid areas is particularly difficult due to an inadequate road network and the inability of most of the pastoralists to read or write, the project investigated the most effective way of communicating information to pastoralists. Using the project as a test case, IPAL, in cooperation with the Kenya Ministry of Information and Broadcasting, broadcast a fifteen-minute radio program twice a week in the Rendille language.

Initial project findings

From the results of the fertility analyses of the soils, it would appear that none of the major mineral elements is lacking. Although the level of nitrogen in the soils is very low, with an average rainfall of only 225 millimeters a year, lack of water is the most important factor limiting the production of vegetation. After rainfall, the low nitrogen content is possibly the next limiting factor for vegetation other than legumes.

All the range types except the perennial grassland vegetation on the mountains are either in poor or fair condition. This is surprising since some of the areas have not been used for a long time due to problems of insecurity. A further investigation into the history of the use of this vegetation might reveal the reason for such a trend. As demonstrated by the vegetation exclosures, the recovery potential of the degraded vegetation is very high, particularly for areas with annual vegetation. In one of the less-grazed areas, for example, annual grass contributes to more than three-quarters of the standing crop biomass with substantive amounts of litter, which tend to exceed the standing crop biomass. These findings are important because they reflect the ecological limits of various plant communities due to factors of soil fertility and moisture. Annual grasslands cannot have a succession that leads to perennial vegetation, and they should be managed to achieve their optimal annual production.

Wood requirements in arid environments are known to vary greatly from one region to another, but the Rendille and Gabbra pastoralists, with their traditional diets of uncooked food—milk, meat, and blood—have a low annual requirement for firewood amounting to possibly 0.1 meter per person. This may be compared with an assumed annual consumption in agricultural areas of Africa of 1 meter per person. Now that the diet of the pastoralists of northern Kenya is increasing to include more grains, it can be concluded that their need for fuelwood will increase. In a study of relatively sedentary Rendille people in a degraded village environment at Korr, the annual consumption of wood for livestock night enclosures for a single family was approximately 432 kilograms. With four people per household, the annual consumption per head was estimated at 108 kilograms, and this too is bound to increase with the increase in the human population.

The main problem with the Rendille livestock is that, although in theory their numbers are adequate to supply basic human needs, they are not very productive. They suffer from numerous diseases, and their mortality is very high. For example, between 20 and 30 percent of all the cattle in Marsabit District died during the 1971–81 drought. Almost 400,000 ungulates were in the study area, of which all but 3 percent were domestic livestock. Although most of the livestock were sheep and goats—287,040—when expressed in terms of tropical livestock units, they contributed only 18 percent to the total animal biomass, while cattle contributed 40 percent and camels, 36 percent. Livestock were present at low densities in 1976 but increased in 1977 to more than three times their former densities. This was mainly due to the drought of 1976, which did not seem to affect wildlife, which are less dependent than livestock on fixed sources of water. Because of the fear of theft, livestock owners are obliged to keep their animals in night enclosures, which puts them at a disadvantage when compared with wildlife, which graze at night, benefit from moisture contained on plants, and retain moisture by staying in the shade during the day.

The results of the study, indeed, indicate that the IPAL study area is capable of supporting twice the present livestock densities. The key to rehabilitation of the area does not therefore seem to lie in the enforced sale of livestock but rather in achieving a better distribution of livestock. Such a solution would also be more acceptable to the people.

The nomadic community is expending exorbitantly high amounts of energy during the dry seasons in walking animals long distances, in digging and maintaining wells, and in drawing water for domestic use and for very young animals too weak to walk to water. Results of these studies reveal that there are sufficient water resources—both ground and surface—in the study area. The resistivity measurements carried out show that water can be obtained almost anywhere in the study area by the use of shallow hand-dug wells. This would probably be the best strategy to adopt since the people can maintain hand-dug wells better than they can the bore holes.

IPAL's socioeconomic studies have revealed that the Rendille and Gabra societies are gradually moving out of their isolation and are very slowly becoming integrated with the national economy and policy, in which they still possess marginal status. This trend is motivated by growing awareness that total reliance on pastoral nomadism will not provide sufficient insurance against drought nor the economic base necessary to improve living standards. The desire to improve the standards of living of the households, to diversify the region's economic base, and to become sedentary are three interrelated processes.

Conclusions

The problem of land degradation in the rangelands of northern Kenya and eastern Africa in general is serious and needs urgent attention, because not only does it involve the threatened survival of a people but because some of the processes of deterioration, if allowed to continue, may become irreversible.

Although livestock production will probably remain the best use of the arid lands of northern Kenya, the type of livestock operations carried out need to be considered carefully. Managing livestock for milk production does not seem practical in an arid environment. The efficiency of converting forage into livestock products for use by pastoralists might necessitate careful consideration of the suitability of present breeds of cattle.

In spite of common belief, the natural ecosystem is not always the most efficient for converting solar radiant energy in primary production or for transferring energy into secondary production. A manipulated system may produce more dry weight of plant material and frequently furnishes a diet more conducive to meeting nutritional requirements than does the native ecosystem. In view of reduced flexibility in the lives of the pastoralists of northern Kenya, range improvements, especially in already degraded areas where natural recovery would otherwise be too slow, should be considered seriously.

The Kenya Development Program focuses on ratifying the rights of pastoral people to their traditional grazing areas. This is seen as encouraging the social change necessary to translate subsistence pastoralism in part into commercial livestock production and to combat the present overgrazing and deterioration in range condition. Emphasis is placed now on the type of land ownership, not because of the moral issues involved but because without security of tenure people have little incentive to improve land resources. In Kenya today, most pastoral societies clearly feel the insecurity of their present position. The failure of previous attempts to effect change in pastoral societies is certainly due in part to ignorance of the biological basis of pastoralism, but there has also been little attempt to understand the sociological constraints on the fears and aspirations of the pastoralists.

Local conditions must be taken into account in physical, biological, and hydrological planning of the arid lands. For optimal productivity of the individual factors that have to be considered in development planning, priority probably should be given to human ecology and ecological approaches to land use. This does not imply that there is a limit beyond which ecological ideas should always prevail, but it does imply that there is a limit beyond which ecological compromise is impossible. In arid and semi-arid areas, for example, schemes are sometimes propounded for the settlement of nomadic populations, which, if permitted, not only would fail to realize any long-term social or economic benefit but also would destroy the grazing resource, especially during drought.

The initial results of IPAL discussed in this chapter will have some application elsewhere in the world. Whether or not pastoralism will change to meet the present demands of development depends on the pastoralist's attitude toward his own pastoral activities. A change in practice entails a far-reaching process of physical, mental, and spiritual adjustment—it actually amounts to a reorientation of the pastoralist as a person. But he will have to be helped through credible scientific advice to attain his aspirations.

References

Child, D., and others. 1984. *Arid and Semi Arid Lands*. Arkansas: Winrock International.

—————. 1987. *Arid and Semi-arid Lands: Guidelines for Development*. Arkansas: Winrock International.

Coetsee, M. J. A. 1968. "Droughts and the Farmer." *Farming in South Africa* 44:1, pp. 24–27.

Colorado State University. 1972. *Wildland Ecology Handbook*. Ft. Collins, Colo.

Dratt, D. J., and M. D. Gwyne. 1977. *Rangeland Management and Ecology in East Africa*. London: Hodder and Stoughton.

Field, A. C. 1978. "Preliminary Report on the Impact of Sheep and Goats on the Vegetation in Arid Zones of Northern Kenya." IPAL Technical Report E-19. UNESCO, Nairobi, Kenya.

Field, C. R. 1979. "A Preliminary Report on the Ecology and Management of Camels, Sheep, and Goats in Northern Kenya." IPAL Technical Report E-19. UNESCO, Nairobi, Kenya.

—————. 1981. "A Summary of Livestock Studies within the Mt. Kular Study Area." IPAL Technical Report A-3. UNESCO, Nairobi, Kenya.

Griffiths, Norton. 1975. "Aerial Survey Techniques." African Wildlife Leadership Foundation, Nairobi, Kenya.

Heady, H. F. 1982. *Range and Wildlife Management in the Tropics*. London: Longmans.

Heady, H. F., and E. B. Heady. 1984. *Range and Wildlife Management in the Tropics*. London: Longmans.

Herlocker, D. 1979. "Implementing Forestry Programmes for Local Community Development, South-Western Marsabit District, Kenya." IPAL Technical Report D-2a. United Nations Educational, Scientific, and Cultural Organization, Nairobi.

IUCN (International Union for the Conservation of Nature). 1991. *Caring for the Earth: A Strategy for Sustainable Living*. With the United Nations Environment Program and the World Wildlife Fund. Gland, Switzerland.

Lusigi, W. J. 1981. "Combating Desertification and Rehabilitating Degraded Ecosystems in Northern Kenya." IPAL Technical Report A-4. United Nations Educational, Scientific, and Cultural Organization, Nairobi.

Lusigi, W. J., ed. 1983. "Integrated Resource Assessment and Management Plan for Western Marsabit District, Northern Kenya." IPAL Technical Report A-6. United Nations Educational, Scientific, and Cultural Organization, Nairobi.

National Environmental Secretariat. 1977. "Working Paper on Soil Conservation." Paper presented at a seminar on desertification, Nairobi, Kenya.

Odum, H. T. 1959. *Fundamentals of Ecology*. U.S.A.: W. B. Sunders Co.

Schwartz, H. J. 1980. "An Introduction to the Livestock Ecology Program." IPAL Technical Report A-3. UNESCO, Nairobi, Kenya.

U.S. Department of Agriculture. 1970. *Range Analysis Handbook*. Region 2. Washington, D.C.

Van Dyne, G. M., ed. 1969. *The Ecosystem Concept in Natural Resource Management*. New York: Academic Press.

WCED (World Commission on Environment and Development). 1987. *Our Common Future*. Oxford, England: Oxford University Press.

Comments

Lee M. Talbot

By way of introduction, there is a need for some clarification in the focus of this discussion. Management is often considered to refer to conscious, intentional manipulation of some parts of the environment to achieve a particular objective. However, human use of these extensive parts of the globe ranges from casual exploitation by nomadic grazing and hunting to intensive manipulation. Most of these lands are not managed in the usual sense of conscious manipulation of some of the factors. Much of the past use of the northern Kenya rangelands, and some of the present use that Dr. Lusigi studied, is not in this sense managed.

However, rangelands cover vast areas of Africa and much of the rest of the world. These lands are used and they provide the resource base for the survival of a significant number of people worldwide. Our concern is with the sustainability of this use, so, clearly, our interpretation of management is broad.

Dr. Lusigi's chapter primarily describes a specific research project, the Integrated Project on Arid Lands (IPAL) in order to provide a specific, real-life example of measurement of sustainability. The purpose of IPAL was to understand the structure and functioning of the range resource involved as a foundation for understanding its sustainability and to identify the attributes of sustainability.

In his work, Dr. Lusigi describes the project and the attributes and measurements involved, that is, "how an attempt was made to measure sustainability of that ecosystem and to understand its functioning." A detailed discussion of the results of the study was outside the scope of his work.

A comprehensive research project such as IPAL can address one important part of the objectives of the conference that spawned this volume. Another part involves taking the knowledge from such a study and identifying from it indexes of sustainability, particularly in the form of attributes or parameters that can be monitored and that allow the ongoing measurement or determination of the sustainability of rangelands.

I will not comment on the specifics of the project or the description of them because Dr. Lusigi's work speaks for itself and does it very well indeed. Instead, my comments address the application of his project to the subject of managed ecosystems, and, in particular, I identify some of the questions that must be answered when we are seeking to design ways to identify and monitor the biophysical basis of sustainability.

Applications

The IPAL was a large project, a major undertaking. It involved many people and a broad range of research activities undertaken over a period of about twelve years. It provides a magnificent baseline for measuring the biophysical basis of sustainability in that area and that type of area.

The principle of the minimum

The IPAL has identified, defined, and measured a comprehensive series of biophysical factors or attributes. If we wish to determine the status and trends in sustainability of these or similar rangelands without duplicating this study, we need to identify which attributes we need to measure. From the standpoint of practicality and expense, we want to measure as few attributes as possible to achieve satisfactory results. Consequently, one key issue, from the standpoint of our concern with these measurements, is to determine what is the minimum number of these parameters and measurements that is needed to define sustainability and to identify changes or trends in the future.

This information would probably be most useful if it could be presented in the form of a model that encompasses these parameters, data, and measurements. Such a model would help us understand the system, but it could also be a practical tool that could be applied to this area but that would also apply to other comparable areas of the world's rangelands.

The question of periodicity and time scale

This study identified and measured parameters or attributes. One of the challenges we face in applying the results is to determine what should be the periodicity of these measurements in the future, particularly recognizing that these arid lands have great fluctuations in rainfall and related climatic conditions. Among the specific questions that come into play are:

- How often do you need to make specific measurements to determine sustainability?

- How do you recognize and take into account the radical differences in conditions from wet to dry periods? What is pertinent here is that the carrying capacity of these lands, for example for herbivores, may be several times higher in wet periods than in dry ones.

- Therefore, what is the time scale for sustainability?

In terms of time scale, what is sustainable in a wet year will not be sustainable in a dry one. Are we speaking of periods of one, three, five, or more years? For example, if one looks at sustainability over a long period, there will be periods of abundant growth (for example, of vegetation and animals) balanced by periods of stress, but in the long run, the system is sustainable.

In other words, what is sustainable over a multiyear period may involve severe die-offs during the dry periods. Maasai and other pastoralists in Kenya used to expect about a 15 percent die-off of their livestock during a drought year, and they sought to adjust the number of their livestock to provide insurance for that recurring situation. However, with increased human and livestock populations, the die-off in drought years becomes much more serious. Therefore, if sustainability is calculated on the basis of a long period, there will be losses in dry years, and livestock and people may die. From their particular points of view, such a situation is not sustainable. The sustainability issue for people is immediate. Yet from the standpoint of long-term sustainability, one year is not that important.

The special problem of arid areas: The vast differences between wet and dry periods

The world's arid or semi-arid zones are characterized by dramatic swings between wet and dry periods. These swings have profound effects on the ecosystems. There are both short-term and long-term irregular fluctuations in precipitation and associated climatic conditions. In my work in the Serengeti region of East Africa, I found that there had been two really dry periods in the past century. Superimposed on those long-term fluctuations were short-term ones. These were considered to be normal seven-to-fifteen-year shifts between wet and dry periods. There might be a period of several years where wet years alternated with dry ones, followed by several con-

secutive wet years or several consecutive dry ones.

These shifts caused profound differences in the composition, appearance, and functioning of the ecosystems involved. These changes involved the percentage composition and, to a large degree, the distribution of grasses and other rangeland plants. In the truly wet or dry periods, this was true for perennials as well as annuals. For example, during prolonged wet periods, some areas were characterized by dense stands of tall perennial red oats grass (*Themeda triandra*). Yet in extended dry periods, virtually no *Themeda* plans could be found in the area, and the nearest dense stands were more than ten miles away.

Changes in the seasonal and absolute availability of food and in its composition (for example, the percentage composition of nitrogen, fiber, and water) were reflected by marked changes in the food habits of the wild ungulates, with consequent changes in the dynamics and behavior of their population. For example, during wet periods, the impala in eastern Africa find optimum food most of the year and maintain harem herds virtually year-long, breeding throughout the year and producing herds that contain young of all ages. During dry periods when optimum food may only be available for one to three months, the impala maintain their harem herds and breed only during that wet period, and for some years the herds are characterized by even-aged groups of young. Further, the breeding success and survival of young are also markedly affected. During dry periods, about 15 percent of the young wildebeest in the Serengeti region survive to become yearlings, while during the prolonged wet periods, that figure may be close to 100 percent.

These climatic swings are also linked to another phenomenon that is often overlooked in considering sustainability. This is the fact that a relatively small number of people can exert a disproportionately heavy impact on the landscape during the rare periods of extreme climatic stress, such as prolonged dry periods when vegetation, soils, and wildlife are particularly vulnerable. For example, even though the population of Masai in the Serengeti region was relatively low, their normal pattern of burning and grazing had the effect of dramatically altering the vegetative cover, opening large areas that were formerly covered by forest or bush, during the two periods of extreme drought in the past century.

Therefore the usual one- or two-year study represents a view through a window showing conditions that may only be representative of one-tenth to one-twenty-fifth of what are normal conditions for the area involved. Where the conditions can be so radically different from wet to dry periods, a very long period of study is needed to give an adequate representation of overall conditions. There is the temptation—indeed the almost universal habit—of researchers to draw absolute conclusions based on their one- or two-year studies. Perhaps this is one of the reasons why our understanding of arid rangelands is still so incomplete.

This situation has profound implications for measurements of sustainability. When conditions vary so greatly from one year to the next, and from one decade to the next, how do you calibrate sustainability and for what period, and how do you determine the frequency and periodicity of measurements?

The boundaries of sustainability

The IPAL study chose representative sites for research within a large but carefully defined study area. However, when seeking to determine sustainability, how do you determine the boundaries of the area involved? The borders are often permeable. The markets for livestock often exist away from the rangelands proper. Equally, the sources of new livestock are outside the rangelands. In areas such as much of the Sahel, many of the pastoralists are also cultivators. To determine the sustainability of an area for humans, it is necessary to consider the agricultural lands as well as the rangelands. In the same way, both wildlife and pastoral herds and flocks are nomadic in arid areas. When trying to determine carrying capacity, or biomass per unit period, or sustainability, it is necessary to consider the entire area used by the animals. It is relatively meaningless to talk of the carrying capacity or sustainability of an area that is only a part of their annual range.

Maintenance mechanisms

Sustainability also implies concern with maintenance mechanisms, that is, the mechanisms or processes that maintain the system involved. Many rangelands, particularly those in areas with higher rainfall, are at a successional stage maintained by fire and grazing. Considerations and measurements of sustainability must take these mechanisms into account.

The human factor

Most areas, even remote ones on the edge of the deserts, are under continual and often profound human impact. In seeking to elucidate the ecological processes involved and to define the mechanisms of sustainability, and consequently, the parameters that must be measured, it is helpful to be able to separate the human impact from that of other factors. In practice, the best way to do this is to have control or benchmark areas where human influence is minimal. What does this imply for the design of measurements for sustainability?

How much of the human role needs to be measured? The IPAL study, quite correctly, focused strongly on identifying and measuring the human influences. But humans change, not only their numbers and their economic situations but their cultures, aspirations, and ways of life.

The myth of durability

In considering the sustainability of rangelands, there is a persistent problem in the form of the belief, I term it the myth, that savanna is an extremely durable ecosystem, which is sustainable regardless of human impacts and which, in its extreme form, denies that human-caused land degradation exists or is more than a transitory phenomenon. This myth has resurfaced recently in the form of papers based on the last twenty years of remote-sensing data for the Sahel, which show that the vegetated areas expand or contract in response to rainfall, but not necessarily in response to human use.

It is true that savanna or rangeland is *generically* durable. To the casual observer, the gross physiognomy appears much the same regardless the shape it is in. But the difference between a severely degraded rangeland and a highly productive one is great. The productivity of the rangelands is relatively fragile, involving the conditions of soils, vegetation, moisture, and animal life. We are concerned with sustainability of the conditions that permit such productivity, not merely the sustainability of land that has some form of minimal vegetation on it. Dr. Lusigi's chapter addresses well the issue of human impact on sustainability.

Application to other tropical areas

A major question that arises is the degree to which the results from the IPAL study apply to other tropical rangeland areas. First, the IPAL is in a particularly arid portion of the arid tropics. This study was in an area characterized by very low rainfall amounting to some 9 inches a year. One consequence is that fire plays little or no role in this grassland, unlike the situation in areas of higher precipitation. Fire characterizes most of the world's grasslands where rainfall is adequate, and indeed, fire—virtually entirely caused by humans—is a major factor causing and maintaining such grasslands. Second, IPAL is in an area where the pastoralists are not also agriculturalists. This is the situation in other areas of Kenya, as with the Masai, but in most of the rangelands of Africa, for example Somalia and most areas around the Sahel, the people are agropastoralists.

Therefore, the conditions are not exactly parallel with much, and probably with the greater part, of Africa's rangeland. However, the methodology and the definition of the factors involved in sustainability and the parameters that should be measured should, in general, apply to most rangelands. Additional measurements may be required for areas of higher precipitation and ones with different patterns of human activities.

Conclusions

A comprehensive research project such as IPAL can address one important part of the objectives of this volume. Another part involves taking the knowledge from such a study and identifying from it indexes of sustainability, particularly in the form of attributes or parameters that can be monitored, which allow the ongoing measurement or determination of the sustainability of rangelands.

The IPAL study provided information to help us understand the functioning and the factors that affect the sustainability of the rangeland ecosystem, and it identified and measured a series of attributes or parameters that describe or contribute to that sustainability. This review concentrates on questions that arise if one wishes to take those parameters and apply them to the study area or elsewhere, both to describe and to monitor the status and trends of sustainability of the system.

Among the key questions are those involving the minimum set of parameters needed, the periodicity of measurement, the boundaries of the area involved and the time scale for which sustainability is calibrated, and the applicability to other rangelands of the parameters derived from IPAL. Of particular importance is the need to understand and take account of the impact of short- and longer-term climatic fluctuations on the ecosystems involved and consequently on the sustainability of their characteristics under various types of human use.

Indicators of Grassland Sustainability: A First Approximation

Paul G. Risser

If ecosystems are to be managed in ways that ensure that the desirable characteristics are maintained indefinitely, then managers must know what to measure as indicators of the sustainability of the ecosystem. This objective of identifying biophysical indicators of ecosystem sustainability will necessarily contain some conjecture because humans have not managed ecosystems using rigorous criteria of sustainability for long periods of time. However, the argument presented here is that there is sufficient scientific information to offer a first approximation of a set of measurements that will predict the long-term sustainability of grassland ecosystems.

The seriousness of the need to predict sustainable ecosystems can be seen through observation of human history. This history is replete with examples of human populations who have mistreated ecosystems until sustenance support was no longer forthcoming. One example is the Anasazi (Navajo for "ancient ones") in the southwestern United States. This population, once thriving in such places as Chaco Canyon and Mesa Verde in 1100 A.D., had disappeared by 1300 A.D. due to various reasons: exploitation of the nutrients in the soil, the drought of 1272 to 1299 and a change toward a drier climate, and an increase in the size of cities beyond both the food sources and social structures necessary to support them (Smith 1988). Therefore, the measures of ecosystem sustainability must recognize not only the conventional ecological terms such as primary productivity and species diversity but also the requirements of human social systems. Moreover, any set of biophysical indicators must be sufficiently conservative to accommodate changes in the underlying physical conditions, such as a change in climate. The two lessons are that any proposed indicators of ecosystem sustainability must be cast in ways useful to society and that they must either accommodate or allow for changes in underlying physical conditions.

Grassland ecosystems

Grasslands are biological communities that contain few trees or shrubs, are characterized by mixed herbaceous vegetation, and are usually dominated by grasses. They cover about 46 million square kilometers and occur on every continent and large island throughout the world (Risser and others 1981; Whyte 1960). Although the climate of grasslands is characterized by at least one dry season, the presence and behavior of grasslands are controlled not simply by total annual precipitation, evaporation, or maximum or minimum temperatures but rather by complex relationships including the ratio of precipitation to evaporation and the seasonality of precipitation in relation to the temperature regime.

Grasslands are used and managed with various techniques, perhaps usefully arranged along a continuum from native rangeland to highly managed pastures and meadows. Throughout much of the world, many native mesic grasslands have been converted to other cropping systems. These mesic grasslands produce rich soils that are easily converted to cultivated crops or managed grasslands. Thus, any proposed indicators of ecosystem sustainability must depend on the desired outcomes of management and must also be specific to the type of ecosystem.

In summary, effective indicators of sustainability of a grassland ecosystem must be formulated to meet defined products, be described such that they are useful to society and to managers, be specific to the ecosystem, and allow for changes in the physical driving variables.

Indicators and end points

In the search for measurements that predict whether an ecosystem will maintain its essential properties over long periods of time, it is useful to distinguish two terms that are frequently encountered in the current literature. First, indicators refer to specific direct measurements that can be made on a property of the ecosystem, such as soil moisture. End points refer to synthetic terms that also can be measured but that encompass several processes or characteristics, such as species diversity. Both concepts are important; that is, indicators have the value of specificity but cannot directly measure more integrated processes; end points presumably capture more integrative processes of ecosystems, but interpreting the measurements is more difficult because of their inherently synthetic construction. Both concepts are included in this discussion, but for convenience indicators are used unless there is a special need to discuss the synthetic nature of an end point measurement.

Criteria

Several schemes have been suggested for criteria to be used in determining whether ecosystems are sustainable indefinitely (Karr and others 1986; Schaeffer, Herricks, and Kerster 1988) and in restoring grasslands (Jordan, Gilpin, and Aber 1987; Werner 1990). Some authors have proposed specific measurements that can be used in the field (Karr and others 1986), and others have offered more theoretical proposals (Shaeffer and others 1988). These more theoretical proposals are valuable because they can guide the development of approaches that can be applied in the field (see box 19-1). Since ecosystems undergo succession, either the guidelines for indicators must change with the successional status of the ecosystem or the indicators must be sufficiently general to accommodate successional changes. Also, since ecosystems are inherently complex, and this complexity may contribute to the feedback processes and the stability and resilience of ecosystems,

---

Box 19-1: System Characteristics Critical for Maintaining an Ecological System

- Habitat for desired diversity and reproduction of organisms
- Phenotypic and genotypic diversity among the organisms
- Robust food chain supporting the desired biota
- Adequate nutrient pool for desired organisms
- Adequate nutrient cycling to perpetuate the ecosystem
- Adequate energy flux to maintain the trophic structure
- Feedback mechanisms for damping undesirable oscillations
- Capacity to temper toxic effects, including the capacity to decompose, transfer, chelate or bind anthropogenic inputs to a degree that they are no longer toxic within the system.

Source: Schaeffer and others 1988.

---

there is a reasonable argument that some measure of complexity should be included in any indicator of ecosystem sustainability.

Ecosystem properties vary over time and across space. Indeed this temporal-spatial variability could be a component of measures of ecosystem sustainability. Therefore, sustainability indicators must have a variability component, either explicitly recognizing the variability expected in the indicator measurement itself or including variability as a measure per se.

In making recommendations for deciding if an ecosystem is sustainable, I am not proposing one more slate of characteristics to be included in a monitoring approach. These lists, included under the rubric of environmental audits, are certainly important for determining whether environmental deterioration is occurring and environmental standards are being met. A sample listing of such variables to be monitored, particularly at the global scale, is given in box 19-2 (Cairns 1991). In this discussion, indicators of ecosystem sustainability are designed as a few measurements that predict simply whether or not the ecosystem, and its essential characteristics and defined products, will continue indefinitely. These proposed indicators are designed to be relatively easy to measure and few in number.

Grassland indicators of ecosystem sustainability

The general concept of grassland sustainability is at the heart of range management, and particularly the concept of range condition (Lauenroth and Laycock 1989). Although the concept may have come from forestry, it has been used in rangeland management for more than half a century (Korstian 1919; Pendleton 1989). In range management, a range site is a landscape unit that is classified based on its relation to climax plant communities. These ideas have been modified over time to include climate and soil conditions more explicitly (Dyksterhuis 1949; Renner and Allred 1962). Range condition refers to the ecological or successional status of the vegetation on the range site as compared with the potential or climax plant community. Formally, the Society for Range Management defines range condition as "the current productivity of a range relative to what that range is naturally capable of producing" and range condition class as "one of a series of arbitrary categories used to classify range condition and [that] is usually expressed as excellent, good, fair, or poor."

A range in excellent condition would be productive and would be dominated by species of the climax or potential plant community; a range in poor condition would include few or no climax species and would be dominated by species unpalatable or of low value to livestock. The concepts of range condition have been criticized on a number of grounds (Risser 1989). The concerns include the difficulty of defining the climax or potential vegetation on all sites, the recognition that not all rangelands should be managed to approximate climax vegetation, that managed or tame pastures cannot be evaluated according to this method, and that the process tends to focus on plants and livestock and not on the broader array of organisms that might be included in a complete and sustainable grassland. There is ample discussion of these criticisms (Lauenroth and Laycock 1989), but for this discussion of sustainability, the concept remains important. Its importance rests on the assumption that climax vegetation is self-perpetuating and as such is sustainable.

Range condition is estimated on the percentage of herbaceous cover contributed by decreasers (species that are palatable and preferentially grazed by livestock), increasers (species that are

---

Box 19-2: Variables That Should Be Included in a Global Monitoring System

Species level
- Structural: for example, tissue or organ damage
- Functional: respiratory rates or behavior

Community level
- Structural: trophic relations
- Functional: colonization rate or rate of detritus processing

Ecosystem level
- Structural: trophic relationships characteristic of this particular type of ecosystem in this locale
- Functional: nutrient spiraling or energy cycling

Landscape level
- Structural: compatible with the landscape mosaic
- Functional: used with appropriate duration and frequency by species that regularly use the larger mosaic of which this is a part.

Source: Cairns 1991.

---

not so palatable and so increase as the decreasers are selectively grazed), and invaders (species that can only invade the grassland community when it has been disturbed by heavy grazing or some other event). A grassland in excellent to good condition has a high proportion of decreasers and few invaders. Table 19-1 demonstrates this response to grazing in the tallgrass prairie. In this case, big and little bluestem, switchgrass, and Indiangrass are decreasers, buffalograss and tall dropseed are increasers, and silver bluestem, tumble windmillgrass, and tumblegrass are invaders. If similar data were collected in the shortgrass plains, buffalograss and blue grama would be classified as decreasers. Similarly, because of differences in the potential or climax vegetation, in the mixed-grass plains between the tallgrass prairie and the western shortgrass plains, sideoats grama would be a decreaser species.

Despite these criticisms, this procedure for evaluating the condition of a range should be included as a measure of sustainability of grassland ecosystems. The species to be used in the analysis are well known for most classes of site and are certainly known for most regions of the

Table 19–1: Composition of Lightly and Heavily Grazed Areas in the Osage Hills in Northern Oklahoma and Eastern Kansas
(*percentage*)

Species	Lightly grazed	Heavily grazed
Little bluestem (*Schizachyrium scoparius*)	74.1	6.1
Big bluestem (*Andropogon gerardi*)	13.5	6.1
Indiangrass (*Sorghastrum nutans*)	4.8	—
Switchgrass (*Panicum virgatum*)	1.6	—
Buffalograss (*Buchloe dactyloides*)	1.6	21.6
Tall dropseed (*Sporobolus asper*)	0.4	23.4
Silver bluestem (*Andropogon saccharoides*)	—	12.9
Sideoats grama (*Bouteloua curtipendula*)	1.6	4.0
Scribner panicum (*Panicum scribnerianum*)	0.4	2.6
Blue grama (*Bouteloua gracilis*)	0.4	2.9
Purple lovegrass (*Eragrostis spectabilis*)	0.4	—
Fringeleaf paspalum (*Paspalum ciliatifolium*)	0.4	2.0
Tumble windmillgrass (*Chloris verticillata*)	—	6.1
Tumblegrass (*Schedonnardus paniculatus*)	—	0.9
Sedges		
Carex spp.	0.4	3.0
Other species	0.4	8.4

—Not available.

Source: Hazel 1967.

United States and in many parts of the world. Thus, the first of the five proposed sustainability indicators for grassland ecosystems is that the range condition be classified within the excellent to good categories. With the composition of the species of vegetation characterized as excellent to good, there is a strong expectation that the grassland will maintain itself even if the prevailing weather conditions are modified somewhat. As discussed below, this first indicator will be omitted when considering grassland ecosystems dominated by species other than native ones or when the species composition itself is being managed.

Aboveground primary production

Aboveground production of herbage is a function of several conditions, including the actual amount of material produced by the plants, the amount that is trampled and lost, the amount of regrowth after grazing and trampling, changes in species composition, whether the grassland has been burned, and the status of various abiotic variables such as soil depth and soil water (Abrams, Knapp, and Hulbert 1986; Risser and others 1981). In general, within natural grasslands, lowland sites produce more herbage than upland sites; deep soils produce more plant material than shallow sites; and with adequate amounts of available water in the soil, the burning of tallgrass prairie every few years increases the aboveground production (Abrams and Hulbert 1987; Abrams and others 1986).

Since production and loss of plant material occur throughout the growing season, the measurement of biomass at any one time underestimates the total amount of biomass produced throughout the season. For example, in northern Oklahoma in a rangeland dominated by warm-season species, measuring only the peak standing crop of the tallgrass prairie probably underestimates the total annual production by about 20 percent. Some grasslands have significant cool-season and warm-season species components, which produce maximum biomass early and late in the growing season, respectively. In these cases, a single estimate made at one time in the year will underestimate the total annual production of herbage even more.

In grassland ecosystems, the ratio of aboveground to belowground biomass ranges from about 1:1 in mesic grasslands to 1:6 or less in dry grasslands (Risser and others 1981). Thus, the aboveground biomass usually represents less than half the total biomass in the tallgrass prairie and far less than half in many drier grasslands. However, measuring belowground biomass accurately has proven to be difficult and extremely time-consuming (Kucera, Dahlman, and Koelling 1967). Studies demonstrate that heavy grazing apparently reduces belowground production (Weaver 1950), but insufficient data exist to draw firm conclusions about the relative reductions that might be expected from different levels of grazing intensity and from differences in weather conditions (Hayes and Seastedt 1987).

Peak standing crop has been measured from a number of grasslands. Table 19-2 summarizes data from twenty-three sites (see Risser and others 1981, p. 160, for the original citations). Abrams, Knapp, and Hulbert (1986) measured aboveground biomass from several sites in the Kansas tallgrass prairie over a ten-year period and obtained similar values. Averaged across upland and lowland sites, mid-season live biomass was 422 grams per square meter on annually burned and 364 grams per square meter on unburned sites for the ten years studied. During 1980, which was extremely dry, the comparable measurements were 185 on the lowland site and 299 on the upland site. Although there is considerable inter-year variability within measurements of peak standing crop, Risser and others (1981) found the variability in this ecosystem component far less than other common measures of ecosystem processes.

In summarizing aboveground biomass measurements of grasslands, the following points should be recognized:

- Standing biomass is only an estimate of total primary production and does not account for the material that has been consumed during the year.

- Belowground biomass is usually greater than aboveground biomass but is difficult to measure, and there are insufficient data from which to define specific relationships between grazing intensity and belowground productivity.

- The amount of biomass measured at the time of peak standing crop underestimates the total aboveground biomass produced throughout the year because not all species produce the greatest production at the same time.

Table 19–2: Summary of Peak Standing Crop Values from Several Tallgrass Prairies in the Central United States
(grams per square meter)

State	Peak standing crop
Illinois	302–489
Illinois	328
Illinois	280
Iowa	364
Iowa	369
Iowa	390
Kansas	180
Kansas	325–473
Michigan	238
Minnesota	447
Missouri	544
Missouri	508
Missouri	482–570
Nebraska	344–432
North Dakota	456
North Dakota	430
Oklahoma	316
Oklahoma	414
Oklahoma	348
Oklahoma	402
Oklahoma	592
Oklahoma	254–335
South Dakota	500–566

Source: Risser and others 1981, p. 160, for the complete citations.

- Aboveground biomass values demonstrate some variability among years because of different patterns of soil water, temperature, and other variables, although plant biomass values are less variable than virtually all other ecosystem processes.

Tallgrass prairies have peak standing crop values of about 400 grams per square meter. In drought conditions, the biomass measurements may decrease to below 200 grams per square meter, but over periods of nominal changes in climate conditions, the peak standing crop value remains above 300. Aboveground biomass does not respond to some types of disturbance (Schaeffer and others 1990), but it does represent an important estimate of ecosystem status, especially with respect to changes in climate. Therefore, as a first approximation, the second sustainability predictor for tallgrass prairie ecosystems is a seasonal peak standing crop of 300 grams per square meter or greater. This single predictor, however, can be made more accurate for grasslands in the north central Great Plains and the southeastern portions of the United States by referring to figure 19-1, taken from Parton and others (1987). The criterion for any site should be not less than 100 grams per square meter below the average value for the site being considered throughout the region, as depicted on this map of peak standing crops.

Figure 19–1: Regional Distribution of Peak Aboveground Standing Crop

Above ground plant production
(grams per square meter)

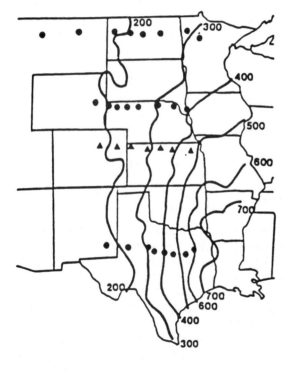

Source: Parton and others 1987.

Species diversity

Although numerous studies describe the plant and animal species composition of tallgrass prairies (Abrams and Hulbert 1987, see Risser and others 1981 for citations), relatively few have calculated species diversity. In those cases where such calculations have been made, the actual numerical terms have not always been consistent. Also, species diversity measurements are end points, as discussed previously, and it is difficult to provide biological interpretations to the numerical values.

Although species diversity in grasslands is expected to decrease with severe disturbances, in many cases less severe disturbances result in higher species diversity (Coffin and Lauenroth 1988). This pattern is true in the tallgrass prairie where light to moderate grazing pressure increases species diversity. Collins (1987) measured plant species diversity from an Oklahoma tallgrass prairie that had received different burning and grazing treatments. Diversity was calculated on the basis of relative plant cover (p_i), $H' = -$ sum (p_i ln p_i), and evenness as $E = (N_2 - 1) / (N_1 - 1)$, where $N_2 = \exp(H')$ and $N_1 = 1 / $ sum p_1^2.

As shown in table 19-3, plant species diversity ranged from 9.1 in the grazed and burned grassland to 5.0 in the ungrazed and burned grassland; ungrazed and unburned was 8.0, and grazed but the not burned was 8.5. The same values for evenness were 0.5, 0.5, 0.6, and 0.6, respectively. In these and other data, the evenness component does not appear to be particularly sensitive in grassland ecosystems.

Because of the uncertainty of interpreting indexes of species diversity, it is tempting to eliminate any measure of species diversity from consideration of indicators of grassland sustainability. However, since the final suite of indicators is small, and because the proposed measurements do not include any direct measurement of ecosystem complexity, plant species diversity is included. This term recognizes that the food and habitat requirements of many invertebrate and vertebrate species involve different and in some cases several plant species and communities. It also recognizes that some levels of disturbance actually increase plant species diversity; however, severe disturbance not only reduces species diversity but, because of the poverty of species, may restrict the ways in which the grassland can recover from disturbances or other stresses such as change in climate.

Table 19-3: Average Plant Species Diversity and Evenness Values from Oklahoma Tallgrass Prairie Subjected to Burning and Grazing Treatments

Treatment	Diversity	Evenness
No burning		
No grazing	8.0	0.6
Grazing	8.5	0.6
Burning		
No grazing	5.0	0.5
Grazing	9.1	0.5

Source: Collins 1987.

The recommended indicator of sustainability for tallgrass prairie ecosystems is that the plant species diversity [exp(H')] must not be less than 5.0. Since evenness is not particularly helpful, it is not included in the recommendation, although the term itself can be calculated from the same data set.

Soil organic carbon

Organic material accumulates in the soil from plant production and the activities of soil organisms. Thus, organic matter is usually highest in the soil nearest the surface and decreases as depth increases (Risser and others 1981). With reduced plant production, there is a decrease in the amount of organic material incorporated into the soil, either from decaying plant roots or from aboveground sources brought belowground by soil-dwelling invertebrates or vertebrates. Similarly, if the top horizons of the soil profile are lost by erosion, then the soil organic matter in the soil decreases. Finally, in the tallgrass prairie region, sandy soils generally produce less plant production than soils with more silt and clay materials. As a result, sandy soils have a lower content of organic material than heavier soils (Schimel, Coleman, and Horton 1985).

Soil organic material plays several important roles in grassland ecosystems. Specifically, it contains nutrients that are released on decomposition, thereby becoming available for plants and animals. In addition, it acts as a source of carbon for many soil organisms. Also, soil organic material contributes to the water-holding capacity and also to the desirable structural characteristics of the soil.

Because of its importance, soil organic matter is included as one of the five indicators of grass-land ecosystem sustainability. However, since the organic matter content is related to plant productivity, which varies across the region of the tallgrass prairie and the central United States, and because the organic matter is related to the soil texture, the specific criterion should be modified according to the location of the grassland. Therefore, the average soil organic matter sustainability indicator for the tallgrass prairie is 3.0 kilograms per square meter of carbon in the top 20 centimeters of the soil for sandy soils and 5.0 kilograms per square meter of carbon in silt-loam soils. However, this indicator should be modified to match figure 19-2, with the indicator value being no less than 500 grams less than the predicted carbon content at the site in question.

Nitrogen content of the vegetation

The nitrogen content of the vegetation is an indicator of the nutritional status of the plants (Harper, Daniel, and Murphy 1933; Spedding 1971). Since plants are the source of nutrition to herbivores, plant nitrogen content is a measure of forage quality. Also, the amount of nitrogen, and the ratio between carbon and nitrogen in the plant material, affects the rate at which the plant material decomposes in the soil (Pastor, Stillwell, and Tilman 1987). Therefore, nitrogen content of the plant material is important in determining not only the nutritional status of the plants themselves (Jaramillo and Detling 1988) but also the ways in which plants influence organisms that consume grass (including livestock) and the rates of carbon and nutrient cycling in the soils.

Nitrogen status in the grassland ecosystem is controlled by several variables, including graz-

Figure 19–2: Regional Distribution of Soil Carbon

Soil C
(kilograms per square meter)
(Sandy)

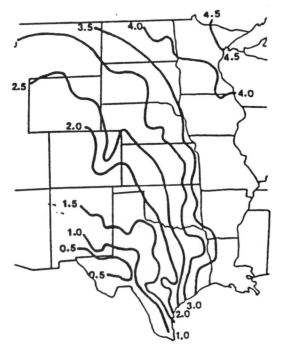

Soil C
(kilograms per square meter)
(Fine)

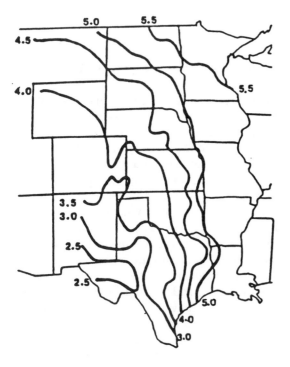

Source: Schimel, Coleman, and Horton 1985.

ing, burning, and nutrient status of the soils (Hobbs and others 1991; Parton and Risser 1980). In general, when grasslands are burned, a significant portion of the nitrogen in the vegetation is volatilized and lost to the ecosystem. Ungrazed grasslands frequently have higher concentrations of nitrogen in vegetation than those that are grazed. So, burning ungrazed or lightly grazed grasslands may result in more loss of nitrogen than burning more heavily grazed grasslands (Hobbs and others 1991).

Although several of these variables affect the nitrogen content of vegetation, the nitrogen content of tallgrass herbage is well known because it is frequently used as a measure of forage quality (Risser and others 1981; Spedding 1971). Overgrazing results in a decrease in nitrogen content of the vegetation based in part on changes in species composition. Also, decreased nutrient status of the soil results in lower nitrogen concentration in the vegetation. Since maintaining forage quality is important for the plants themselves, for consumers, and for nutrient cycling, nitrogen content of the vegetation forms the last of the five essential indicators of sustainability of a grassland ecosystem. From the available data, it is possible to propose that total nitrogen in the aboveground herbage must be maintained at a minimum of 0.6 gram per 100 grams of dry biomass (Harper, Daniel, and Murphy 1933; Hobbs and others 1991; Spedding 1971; and other references cited in Risser and others 1981).

Discussion

An almost infinite number of biophysical characteristics could be proposed as potential indicators of grassland ecosystem sustainability. However, as noted at the beginning of this chapter, the selected indicators should be small in number and relatively easy to measure, should reflect useful characteristics of the ecosystem as perceived by human values, and should be quantitatively conservative so as to accommodate changes in driving variables such as changing climate. Table 19-4 describes the five proposed biophysical measures for determining sustainability of a grassland ecosystem. In other words, if these five conditions are met, the essential grassland properties should persist indefinitely regardless of the use made of the grassland. The test of this proposal will require long-term measurements under many different types of grassland management and use.

Table 19–4: Proposed Biophysical Measures for Tallgrass Ecosystem Sustainability

Indicator	Measure
Range condition rating	Good to excellent
Peak standing crop of vegetation	More than 300 grams per square meter
Plant species diversity [exp (H′)]	More than 5.0
Soil organic material in top 20 centimeters of soil	
Sandy soils	More than 3.0 kilograms per square meter
Clay-loam soils	More than 5.0 kilograms per square meter
Nitrogen content in vegetation	More than 0.6% dry weight basis

Source: Collins 1987.

The numerical values proposed in table 19-4 are based on the tallgrass prairie of the central United States, although figures 19-1 and 19-2 demonstrate how these quantitative terms can be modified for conditions across the region. Similar values need to be developed for grassland ecosystems throughout the world; however, because the central United States includes a range of environments that encompasses conditions found in most grasslands worldwide, only small modifications should be required to make the proposed indicators useful elsewhere.

Since grassland ecosystems include both animals and microorganisms, it can be asked whether the proposed plant and soil indicators adequately represent these essential components. Both range condition and plant species diversity indicate that a variety of food materials is available for consumers and decomposers; these two indicators and the production of herbage indicate the quality of cover for animals; soil organic material and nitrogen content of plant material indicate both the quality of food materials aboveground and belowground as well as the potential rates of decomposition and nutrient cycling; and finally, the content of organic material in the soil and concentration of nitrogen in tissue are indirect measures of the ability of the ecosystem to retain nutrients. If these five indicators are sufficient to capture the essence of the entire ecosystem sustainability, the field measurements will be more easily accomplished than if animal census or soil sampling are required.

One component of grassland sustainability has been omitted from this analysis, namely, the upper trophic levels of birds and mammals. If these two components were included, the indicators would include the size of grasslands, heterogeneity of habitat, and, in the case of migratory species, characteristics of the entire range. There are data that could be used to estimate the habitat required to support a native avifauna (Graber and Graber 1963; Wiens 1974) and small and large mammal fauna (Coppock and others 1983; Grant and Birney 1979; McNaughton, Ruess, and Seagle 1988). Thus, if additional indicators were added to the five currently proposed, the most likely candidate would be a minimum size required to maintain a representative complement of bird species.

The focus of this discussion has been on grasslands that are used for their native species. In the management of tame grasslands or highly modified grasslands, the species composition is managed, in some cases for just a single plant species, such as bermudagrass (*Cynodon dactylon*; McMurphy and Tucker 1975). Under these conditions, the first and third indicators (range condition and plant species diversity) are not applicable. However, the other three criteria—production of herbage, amount of soil organic material, and concentration of nitrogen in the plant tissue—are important, and perhaps even adequate, indicators of grassland ecosystem sustainability.

References

Abrams, M. D., and L. C. Hulbert. 1987. "Effect of Topographic Position and Fire on Species Composition in Tallgrass Prairie in Northeast Kansas." *American Midland Naturalist* 117, pp. 442–45.

Abrams, M. D., A. K. Knapp, and L. C. Hulbert. 1986. "A Ten-year Record of Aboveground Biomass in a Kansas Tallgrass Prairie: Effects of Fire and Topographic Position." *American Journal of Botany* 73, pp. 1509–15.

Cairns, J., Jr. 1991. "Environmental Auditing for Global Effects." *Environmental Auditor* 2, pp. 187–95.

Coffin, D. P., and W. K. Lauenroth. 1988. "The Effects of Disturbance Size and Frequency on a Shortgrass Plant Community." *Ecology* 69, pp. 1609–17.

Collins, S. L. 1987. "Interaction of Disturbances in Tallgrass Prairie: A Field Experiment." *Ecology* 68, pp. 1243–50.

Coppock, D. L., J. K. Detling, J. E. Ellis, and M. I. Dyer. 1983. "Plant-herbivore Interactions in a North American Mixed-grass Prairie. II. Responses of Bison to Modification of Vegetation by Prairie Dogs." *Oecologia* (Berlin) 56, pp. 10–15.

Dyksterhuis, E. J. 1949. "Condition and Management of Rangeland Based on Quantitative Ecology." *Journal of Range Management* 2, pp. 104–15.

Graber, R. R., and J. W. Graber. 1963. "A Comparative Study of Bird Populations in Illinois, 1906–1909 and 1956–1958." *Illinois Natural History Survey Bulletin* 28, pp. 383–528.

Grant, W. E., and E. C. Birney. 1979. "Small Mammal Community Structure in North American Grasslands." *Journal of Mammalogy* 60, pp. 23–36.

Harper, H. J., H. A. Daniel, and H. F. Murphy. 1933. "The Total Nitrogen, Phosphorous, and Calcium Content of Common Weeds and Native Grasses of Oklahoma." *Proceedings of the Oklahoma Academy of Science* 14, pp. 36–44.

Hayes, D. C., and T. R. Seastedt. 1987. "Root Dynamics of Tallgrass Prairie in Wet and Dry Years." *Canadian Journal of Botany* 65, pp. 787–91.

Hazel, D. B. 1967. "Effect of Grazing Intensity on Plant Composition, Vigor, and Production." *Journal of Range Management* 20, pp. 249–53.

Hobbs, N. T., D. S. Schimel, C. E. Owensby, and D. S. Ojima. 1991. "Fire and Grazing in the Tallgrass Prairie: Contingent Effects on Nitrogen Budgets." *Ecology* 72, pp. 1374–82.

Jaramillo, J. V., and J. K. Detling. 1988. "Grazing History, Defoliation, and Competition: Effects on Shortgrass Production and Nitrogen Accumulation." *Ecology* 69, pp. 1599–1608.

Jordan, W. R., M. E. Gilpin, and J. D. Aber, eds. 1987. *Restoration Ecology: A Synthetic Approach to Ecological Research.* Cambridge, England: Cambridge University Press.

Karr, J. R., K. D. Fausch, P. L. Angermeier, P. R. Yant, and I. J. Schlosser. 1986. "Assessing Biological Integrity in Running Waters: A Method and Its Rationale." Special Publication 5. Illinois Natural History Survey, Champaign, Ill.

Korstian, C. F. 1919. "Native Vegetation as a Criterion of Site." *Plant World* 22, pp. 253–61.

Kucera, C. L., R. C. Dahlman, and M. R. Koelling. 1967. "Total Net Productivity and Turnover on an Energy Basis for Tallgrass Prairie." *Ecology* 48, pp. 536–41.

Lauenroth, W. K., and W. A. Laycock, eds. 1989. *Secondary Succession and the Evaluation of Rangeland Condition.* Boulder, Colo.: Westview Press.

McMurphy, W. E., and B. B. Tucker. 1975. "Midland Bermudagrass Pasture Research." Oklahoma Agricultural Station Progress Report 715, pp. 14–20. Oklahoma State University, Stillwater.

McNaughton, S. J., R. W. Ruess, and S. W. Seagle. 1988. "Large Mammals and Process Dynamics in African Ecosystems." *BioScience* 38, pp. 794–800.

Parton, W. J., and P. G. Risser. 1980. "Impact of Management Practices on the Tallgrass Prairie." *Oecologia* 46, pp. 223–34.

Parton, W. J., D. S. Schimel, C. V. Cole, and D. S. Ojima. 1987. "Analysis of Factors Controlling Soil Organic Matter Levels in Great Plains Grasslands." *Journal of the Soil Science Society of America* 51, pp. 1173–79.

Pastor, J., M. A. Stillwell, and D. Tilman. 1987. "Little Bluestem Dynamics in Minnesota Old Fields." *Oecologia* 72, pp. 327–30.

Pendleton, D. T. 1989. "Range Condition as Used in the Soil Conservation Service." In W. K. Lauenroth and W. A. Laycock, eds., *Secondary Succession and the Evaluation of Rangeland Condition*, pp. 17–34. Boulder, Colo.: Westview Press.

Renner, F. G., and B. W. Allred. 1962. "Classifying Rangeland for Conservation Planning." U.S. Department of Agriculture Handbook 253. Washington, D.C.

Risser, P. G. 1989. "Range Condition Analysis: Past, Present, and Future." In W. K. Lauenroth and W. A. Laycock, eds., *Secondary Succession and the Evaluation of Rangeland Condition*, pp. 143–56. Boulder, Colo.: Westview Press.

Risser, P. G., E. C. Birney, H. D. Blocker, S. W. May, W. J. Parton, and J. A. Wiens. 1981. *The True Prairie Ecosystem.* Stroudsburgh, Penn.: Hutchinson Ross Publishing Company.

Schaeffer, D. J., E. E. Herricks, and H. W. Kerster. 1988. "Ecosystem Health. I. Measuring Ecosystem Health. Environmental Audit. VI." *Environmental Management* 12, pp. 445–55.

Schaeffer, D. J., J. A. Perry, H. W. Kester, and D. K. Cox. 1988. "The Environmental Audit. I. Concepts." *Environmental Management* 9, pp. 191–98.

Schaeffer, D. J., T. R. Seastedt, D. J. Gibson, D. C. Hartnett, B. A. D. Hetrick, S. W. James, D. W. Kaufmann, A. P. Schwab, E. E. Herricks, and E. W. Novak. 1990. "Field Bioassessments for Selecting Test Systems to Evaluate Military Training Lands in Tallgrass Prairie. Ecosystem Health. V." *Environmental Management* 14, pp. 81–93.

Schimel, D. S., D. C. Coleman, and K. A. Horton. 1985. "Soil Organic Matter Dynamics in Paired Rangeland and Cropland Toposequences in North Dakota." *Geoderma* 36, pp. 201–14.

Smith, D. A. 1988. *Mesa Verde National Park: Shadows of the Centuries.* Lawrence: University of Kansas Press.

Spedding, C. R. W. 1971. *Grassland Ecology.* Oxford, England: Clarendon Press.

Weaver, J. E. 1950. "Effects of Different Intensities of Grazing on Depth and Quantity of Roots or Grasses." *Journal of Range Management* 2, pp. 100–13.

Werner, P. A. 1990. "Principles of Restoration Ecology Relevant to Degraded Rangelands." *Australian Rangeland Journal* 12, pp. 34–39.

Wiens, J. A. 1974. "Habitat Heterogeneity and Avian Community Structure in North American Grasslands." *American Midland Naturalist* 91, pp. 195–213.

Whyte, R. O. 1960. *Production and Environment.* London: Faber and Faber.

Sustainability in Tropical Inland Fisheries: The Manager's Dilemma and a Proposed Solution

Peter B. Bayley

The artisanal, multispecies fisheries typical in tropical lakes and river floodplains present unique problems for the manager. The manager's dilemma is to try to optimize yields for a few large, individual species or increase the total yield at the expense of some species that are more valuable. Many fisheries also require the resolution of conflicts between urban-based commercial operations and local, rural demands. Traditional management options are limited because of the high cost and complexity of enforcing regulations such as restricted types of gear, minimum size of fish, closed seasons, or limited entry. A progressive pulse fishing paradigm is proposed to aim for a sustainable multispecies yield consistent with local socioeconomic realities and persistence of species. This scheme permits high yields with compositions of diverse species near cities or major ports combined with increased control of exploitation through periodically closed areas as distance from markets increases. Increasing control lowers yields but permits optimal harvesting for larger, more valuable species. A long-term experimental management approach is essential, so that different levels of sustainability can be monitored at different points in the gradient of fishing restrictions. Other vital roles of the fishery manager are stressed, including the publicizing of the value of commercial and subsistence fisheries and, with the cooperation of other agencies, the maintenance or restoration of critical support factors (hydrology, water quality, higher vegetation) in the drainage basin.

The 1989 *FAO Yearbook* indicates that of the 99.5 million tons of nominal fish yield worldwide, 13.8 million tons (14 percent) were from freshwaters, which in turn mostly originated from capture fisheries in river floodplains and lakes in tropical Asia, Africa, and Latin America (FAO 1989).

In the past two decades, the published literature on freshwater tropical ecology has blossomed (see, for example, Lowe-McConnell 1975, 1987; Welcomme 1979, 1985), but the same cannot be said of publishable information on fish yields, fishing intensity, and socioeconomic factors. In view of these data limitations and the effects that rapidly increasing levels of human population have on exploitation rates, this chapter identifies the problems facing the managers of tropical fisheries and provides a management paradigm

appropriate for approaching levels of sustainable yields in extensive, multispecies fisheries. Broader issues of sustainability are addressed for these and other fisheries by Regier, Bocking, and Henderson (chapter 22 of this volume).

Approaches to predicting yield

Traditional fish population models explicitly or implicitly incorporate birth, death, recruitment, and growth rates on a stock of fish and can be used to predict yields given a constant environment (Beverton and Holt 1957; Graham 1935; Gulland 1969; Ricker 1975; Schaefer 1954). Data requirements are considerable even for the single-species temperate fisheries for which they were developed. Extensions of such models to multispecies fisheries are hampered by numerous theoretical and practical problems that will not be solved in a timely manner for most, if any, tropical freshwater systems (Pauly and Murphy 1982).

Studies that link production-related factors with fishery yield can be useful to obtain first-order estimates of yield (Henderson and Welcomme 1974; Melack 1976; Schlesinger and Regier 1982; Welcomme 1974, 1976) or to understand the environmental factors that support the fishery (Bayley 1989) but have limited predictive power (despite significant correlation coefficients).

Two empirical approaches offer more hope. First, comparative models based on ecologically and socioeconomically similar fisheries that account for fishing effort improve our ability to predict and assess the current state of multispecies yield (Bayley 1988; Henderson and Welcomme 1974). However, these are limited by the availability of data on yield and effort and the lack of additional explanatory variables, such as those describing the nature of the flood regime in large rivers (Junk, Bayley, and Sparks 1989; Welcomme 1985). Second, yield predictions based on the influence on recruitment, and hence future yield, of a key environmental variable such as flood stage have shown promise in river floodplains where time series are available (Welcomme 1985). Such models would be much improved if fishing effort and the effect of water level on catchability were known.

Results from these comparative models and descriptions of trends in the species composition of multispecies fisheries are currently the best points of departure to define, albeit approximately, what the manager can do and avoid in order to sustain a tropical fishery.

The multispecies fishery and the manager's dilemma

The diverse fish assemblages of tropical systems are reflected in most fishery yields, even though a few large species are typically the most valuable. The relationship between multispecies yield and fishing effort follows a unimodal relationship, such as the curves developed for tropical lakes, river floodplains, and coastal lagoons (Bayley 1988). The multispecies yield curve su-

perficially resembles the Graham-Schaefer logistic-derived parabola for a single-species fishery (see figure 20-1; Schaefer 1954). However, the generalized effort value appropriate for comparing fisheries (number of fishermen per unit of area) changes qualitatively at higher intensities, involving changes in gear and reductions in mesh size more appropriate for catching smaller species. Also, the drop in multispecies yield at high effort values reflects as much the technical or economic limitations of harvesting smaller but more productive fish or invertebrates as it does the overexploitation of some species.

Many managers and conservationists worry that overexploitation can cause biological extinction, and commercial extinction is often incorrectly reported to imply biological extinction. There is no evidence that an intensified fishery in a system unaltered by anthropogenic environmental change (of hydrology, water quality, or species introduction) has caused the biological extinction of a fish species. As a more extreme example, even with extensive degradation of the hydrologic regime and pollution in addition to exploitation, no fish species in the Upper Mississippi River has become extinct (Fremling and others 1989). However, it is conceivable that an intensive fishery on an isolated species in a small

Figure 20-1: Generalized Multispecies Yield and Effort Curve from a Single Fishery Based on a Model of Lake and River Floodplain Fisheries

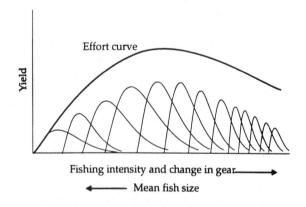

Note: The model predicted yields with 95 percent confidence ranges of 114–188 kilograms per hectare per year for fifteen river floodplains (on the basis of maximum flooded area) and 76–122 kilograms per hectare per year for thirty-one lakes. As effort (number of fishermen per unit of area) increases, methods change to exploit smaller, but usually more productive, species. Small curves indicate hypothesized single-species yield curves.

Source: Bayley 1988.

pond or stream could result in local extinction. Therefore, the following arguments refer to large lakes or river floodplains, which supply the bulk of the worldwide yield of tropical inland fish. I also assume that the multispecies curve approximates an equilibrium yield for a given fishing intensity, which has not yet been proven.

In economic terms, the multispecies yield curve corresponds to the Graham-Schaefer curve. Yield (income) increases with increasing investment or cost (effort) until the maximum sustainable yield is reached, but profitability (yield / effort = slope from origin to any point on the curve in figure 20-1) for individual fishermen usually decreases with increasing effort. Therefore, a fishery may become unprofitable at any point on the curve. Within the range of profitability lie considerations of employment and optimizing the supply of animal protein to the human population, both important factors in the socioeconomic circumstances of developing countries (Pauly, Silvestre, and Smith 1989).

Therefore, the manager of a multispecies fishery on a large lake or river floodplain has a range of options on the left side of the multispecies yield curve. Significant departures from this curve through the optimal harvesting of individual species (summing the maximum yields of individual species shown in figure 20-1 to exceed the predicted multispecies yield) are severely constrained by interactions between fishing gear and various species and by ecological interactions, of which predation is particularly prevalent in the tropics (Lowe-McConnell 1975).

The manager's dilemma is to try to optimize yields for a few large, individual species (left end of figure 20-1), thus making the fishery more profitable, but with less production of protein, or to increase the total yield at the expense of some species that are more valuable, but not necessarily profitable. It is difficult for a manager to admit that stocks of some species are being overexploited, that is, that increased effort is reducing the yield of those species, even though the multispecies yield is well below the maximum indicated by similar fisheries elsewhere. At the same time, it has proven to be economically, socially, and technically impossible to manage a multispecies fishery for a few large species under the conditions of most developing countries. Therefore, the typical manager implements regulations (close seasons, minimum sizes for mesh and fish) that are difficult to enforce, cause hard-

ship among some fishermen, and can deprive the human population of a sustained supply of protein. Therefore, in some fisheries it is fortunate that the regulations cannot be enforced. In others, some form of practical regulation is required.

The dilemma is made more acute when different socioeconomic interests are exploiting the same fishery resource, as exemplified by commercial operations supplying cities versus local fishermen satisfying subsistence requirements and local markets. For example, in the Amazon basin, migration from rural areas to cities has not decreased economic dependency on fish as the major source of animal protein but has resulted in a more capital-intensive system for preserving and marketing fish (Bayley and Petrere 1989). Although such fishermen travel hundreds of kilometers for valuable fish species, most fish are caught in a smaller radius around urban areas and comprise smaller, cheaper species that the majority of city dwellers can afford (Petrere 1978, 1985). Therefore, fisheries near cities usually yield more species and provide a higher yield than those far away. Conversely, rural, part-time fishermen are accustomed to higher catches per unit of effort, corresponding to the higher biomasses of lesser exploited areas (lower left limb in figure 20-1). Rural fishermen resent a competing fishery that requires them to spend more time fishing or to change to other fish species.

A proposed solution: Progressive pulse fishing

In large systems, it is possible to accommodate the interests of all groups of fishermen and consumers to some extent, if managers recognize that enforceable regulations should be adapted to socioeconomic realities in different parts of the system and if they accept that no single sustainable yield or species composition is optimum (Bayley and others 1992). An approach, termed here progressive pulse fishing, is proposed for large, dispersed, multispecies fisheries in which total yield per unit of area is allowed to remain relatively high near cities and is reduced by a combination of inherently higher fishing costs and regulation to optimize exploitation of progressively larger and more valuable species as distance from major markets increases (see figure 20-2). Therefore, higher yields based on more productive, cheaper fish can be maintained profitably to supply urban areas because the fisheries are closer to market. Conversely, lower yields of larger, high-valued species can be exploited profitably at greater distance, and through more extensive, periodic area closures such species will be conserved along with the rest of the fish community at a higher biomass. Except for national parks and areas close to urban centers, valuable species would always

Figure 20-2: Progressive Pulse Fishing Paradigm Proposed for Large River Floodplains and Some Lakes

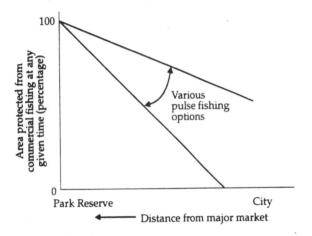

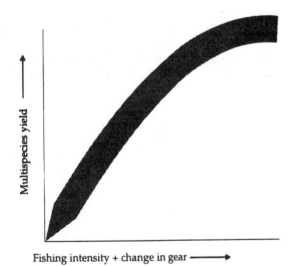

Note: Percentage of the area protected from pulse fishing versus distance from fish market (upper graph) is compared with the multispecies yield versus fishing intensity (lower graph). The multispecies yield is shown as a broad line to emphasize the uncertainty in sustainability until more data are generated by the experimental management process. The graphs are aligned to indicate that fishing intensity (and self-regulated changes in gear) should usually be inversely related to distance from market.

be exploitable somewhere. Many managers may find the proposed increase in restrictions farther from urban centers counterintuitive, because they are based in urban centers and are influenced by local information and fishermen.

Because the spatial distributions, dynamics, interactions, sustainability, and other ecological aspects of fish stocks are poorly known, the degree and size of area closures should be treated as a long-term management experiment, with a comparable amount of money spent on data collection and analysis as on enforcement. Frequency of closure should initially be at least twice the longest generation among the key species. Equilibrium levels (or approximations thereof) of multispecies yields and their compositions should be determined by monitoring their resilience following changes in fishing effort.

Gear regulations are impossible in dispersed fisheries (including many large lakes as well as rivers), and closed seasons are costly to enforce because they attempt to prohibit fishing everywhere. Neither approach guarantees the stocks against rapid depletion through recruitment overfishing. However, pulse fishing—in which easily controlled zones are periodically rested (except for local subsistence fishing) to allow stocks to recover—is a less-efficient but more feasible and safer approach. Specialized commercial operations that have to disembark at a limited number of ports, such as on some large lakes, may be amenable to regulations on gear, closed seasons, or catch quotas. Limited entry is rarely a practical option, except on the small scale of communal fishing property rights.

Discussion

Two elements of fishery management are implied but rarely stressed sufficiently: quality of data and stewardship of the environment. Poor quality of data is almost universal among artisanal fisheries and is also problematic in lakes with less-dispersed fisheries (Bailey 1992). Many managers and some scientists do not even recognize that their data may omit a large proportion of the yield attributed to subsistence or locally marketed fish. For example, 60 percent of Amazon yield is from subsistence or local markets, which cannot be effectively monitored using traditional survey techniques (Bayley and Petrere 1989). The official statistics on landings forwarded to the

Food and Agriculture Organization from Paraguay in 1984 totaled 5,000 tons, whereas a conservative estimate based largely on per capita consumption of local fish indicated 18,000 tons (Bayley 1985). Therefore, yield and effort from most tropical fisheries, in particular riverine ones, are underestimated by varying degrees. Catch per effort obtainable from part of the fishery cannot, on its own, be used to assess the status of the fishery. Also, demographic and social changes in developing countries result in changes in the contribution of different components of the fishery.

Stewardship of the environment is self-evident but is rarely within the purview of the fishery manager. Protection or restoration of the hydrology, soil, riparian or floodplain vegetation, and water quality of a drainage system is usually the responsibility of another agency or of no agency at all. Fishery managers can at least monitor and publicize the current or potential economic value of the fishery, and with the help of ecologists, publicize the probable consequences of alternative developments. Environmental degradation occurs gradually in concert with increasing human population but also can result from grandiose development plans, such as the proposal to convert the River Orinoco-Apuré into a shipping lane, remove the floodplains (which currently support 45,000 tons per year of fish yield), and introduce a variety of exotic fish known as tilapias (PROA 1991).

The issue of part-time rural versus large commercial fishermen introduced above has prompted many conservationists and anthropologists to take the side of rural fishermen and to promote property rights legislation in river floodplains (Chapman 1989). It is essential to foster the cooperation of fishermen in the management and data acquisition process in order to obtain acceptable rates of compliance with regulations. However, widespread granting of fishing property rights at the community level would heighten the conflict and deny essential supplies of protein to urban areas. Chapman's (1989) claim that property rights will remove the "tragedy of the commons" problem associated with a common property resource is incorrect, because she does not account for the fact that most of the fish catch derives from migratory fish populations that cover areas many orders of magnitude greater than those of proposed or traditional property boundaries (Welcomme 1985). This is true of river floodplains in general and also of some fish associated with lakes (Lowe-McConnell 1987).

Therefore, although in many socioeconomic situations exclusive rights to exploit a given area of water may be appropriate, many fish populations must remain as common property with management being applied on an appropriate scale. Such management, however, should take advantage of any communal regulatory traditions that serve levels of sustainable exploitation appropriate for the projected human population, which is increasing rapidly in rural as well as urban areas. The long-term responsibility of management agencies is to obtain the confidence and cooperation of all fishermen groups so that they can assist in enforcement and data collection and act as a constituency to defend the resource against harmful environmental change (Pinkerton 1989).

Data on yield versus effort obtained from lakes and river floodplains indicated significant ($P < 0.01$) modes, implying that some fisheries were at or beyond a maximum multispecies yield (Bayley 1988). Considering that those data are mostly from the 1970s and human population has typically grown 2.5 to 3.5 percent a year since then, more fisheries may now be beyond those maxima in the sense that increasing effort under current technology and socioeconomics is decreasing multispecies yield. The tragedy is that the collection of reliable data on yield and effort has deteriorated since the 1970s even though there was much room for improvement then. Also, major changes, such as the effect of introducing nile perch into Lake Victoria (Reynolds and Greboval 1988), require management decisions that are conjectural because of insufficient data on fisheries.

The definition of sustainability for a fishery is as illusive as that for any other resource, especially for single species (see chapter 4 of this volume). There is no single sustainable yield for a given multispecies fishery, and even optima should vary according to socioeconomic and ecological differences within an extensive fishery. Attempting to optimize the management of an extensive tropical fishery for a few, high-valued species may seem ecologically conservative but eventually leads to high-cost, engineering solutions (such as rearing in large-scale hatcheries to stabilize recruitment, which is highly variable in a natural system). There is growing evidence that such optimization increases the risk and cost of failure, at least in the socioeconomic sense (chapter 4 of this volume). Ironically, the current lack of money and efficiency in tropical fishery management is an advantage in this respect.

Conversely, the use of a variety of fish species offers more stability, because a more diverse, adaptable market will better accommodate natural fluctuations in population. The main question is whether an intensified multispecies fishery will cause an irreversible change—beyond such changes that occur naturally—such as the extinction of a species. This is unlikely in the large systems that currently supply most of the catch or have most potential, providing that the environment is maintained. Because the environment is often changed, the proposed gradient of protection within a fishery provides some assurance in the event of mismanagement or natural disruption (figure 20-2).

Conclusions: The fishery manager's responsibilities

The following list summarizes what the manager of a typical multispecies fishery should do.

- Invest sufficient resources in regular data collection (yield, effort, species composition, environmental variables) in cooperation with scientists.
- Devise regulations that can be enforced (progressive pulse fishing in extensive systems) and avoid legislation that causes widespread cheating.
- Recognize different socioeconomic circumstances and different management options that can aim for different levels of sustainability within extensive fisheries.
- Treat management decisions as long-term experiments.
- Beware of overcapitalization when subsidizing or promoting increased gear or processing capacity.
- Avoid concentrating management resources on a few high-valued species.
- Broaden the demand for different species by supporting product and market development (which is very limited in Asian and African fisheries).
- Obtain the confidence and cooperation of all fishermen groups so that they can assist in enforcement and data collection.
- Publicize the importance of the fishery to the region and, in cooperation with other agencies and fishermen, the importance of conservation or restoration of the environment.

To summarize, the manager of a multispecies fishery resource should realize that levels of sustainability are very poorly known and are probably not realistic for single species. Therefore, the management process must allow the resource to be tested and evaluated for sustainability while providing as much of it as possible to satisfy long-term demands for protein.

References

Bailey, R. G. 1992. "Inland Fishery Resources of Sub-Saharan Africa." In K. T. O'Grady, A. J. B. Butterworth, P. B. Spillett, and J. C. J. Domaniewski, eds., *Fisheries in the Year 2000*, pp. 21–28. Proceedings of the twenty-first anniversary conference of the Institute of Fisheries Management, September 10–14, 1990, Royal Holloway and Bedford New College, England Nottingham, England: Institute of Fisheries Management.

Bayley, P. B. 1985. "Fish Resources." In *Environmental Profile of Paraguay*, pp. 147–52. Washington, D.C.: International Institute for Environment and Development.

————. 1988. "Accounting for Effort When Comparing Tropical Fisheries in Lakes, River Floodplains, and Lagoons. *Limnology and Oceanography* 33, pp. 963–72.

————. 1989. "Aquatic Environments in the Amazon Basin, with an Analysis of Carbon Sources, Fish Production, and Yield." Special publication of the *Canadian Journal of Fisheries and Aquatic Sciences* 106, pp. 399–408.

Bayley, P. B., and M. Petrere Jr. 1989. "Amazon Fisheries: Assessment Methods, Current Status, and Management Options." Special publication of the *Canadian Journal of Fisheries and Aquatic Sciences* 106, pp. 385–98.

Bayley, P. B., P. Vázquez, F. Ghersi, P. Soini, and M. Pinedo. 1992. "Environmental Review of the Pacaya-Samiria National Reserve in Peru and Assessment of Project (527-0341)." Report for the Nature Conservancy. April.

Beverton, R. J. H., and S. J. Holt. 1957. "On the Dynamics of Exploited Fish Populations." *Fisheries Investigations* (United Kingdom Ministry of Agriculture and Fisheries) 2:19.

Chapman, M. D. 1989. "The Political Ecology of Fisheries in Amazonia." *Environmental Conservation* 16, pp. 331–37.

FAO (Food and Agriculture Organization). 1989. *FAO Yearbook.* Rome.

Fremling, C. R., J. L. Rasmussen, R. E. Sparks, S. P. Cobb, C. F. Bryan, and T. O. Caflin. 1989. "The Mississippi River Fisheries: A Case History." Special publication of the *Canadian Journal of Fisheries and Aquatic Sciences* 106, pp. 309–51.

Graham, M. 1935. "Modern Theory of Exploiting a Fishery and Application to North Sea Trawling." *Journal du Conseil International pour l'Exploration de la Mer* 10, pp. 264–74.

Gulland, J. A. 1969. "Manual of Methods for Fish Stock Assessment: Part 1. Fish Population Analysis." FAO Manuals in Fisheries Science 4. Food and Agriculture Organization of the United Nations, Rome.

Henderson, H. F., and R. L. Welcomme. 1974. "The Relationship of Yield to Morpho-edaphic Index and Numbers of Fishermen in African Inland Fisheries." CIFA Occasional Paper 1. Food and Agriculture Organization of the United Nations, Rome.

Junk, W. J., P. B. Bayley, and R. E. Sparks. 1989. "The Flood Pulse Concept in River Floodplain Systems." Special publication of the *Canadian Journal of Fisheries and Aquatic Sciences* 106, pp. 110–27.

Lowe-McConnell, R. H. 1975. *Fish Communities in Tropical Freshwaters: Their Distribution, Ecology, and Evolution.* London: Longmans.

———. 1987. *Ecological Studies in Tropical Fish Communities.* Cambridge Tropical Biology Series. Cambridge, England: Cambridge University Press.

Melack, J. M. 1976. "Primary Productivity and Fish Yields in Tropical Lakes." *Transactions of the American Fisheries Society* 105, pp. 575–80.

Pauly, D., and G. I. Murphy, eds. 1982. *Theory and Management of Tropical Fisheries.* Proceedings of the ICLARM/CSIRO Workshop on the Theory and Management of Tropical Fisheries, January 12–21, 1981. Manila, Philippines: International Center for Living Aquatic Resources Management; Cronulla, Australia: Commonwealth Scientific and Industrial Research Organization.

Pauly, D., G. Silvestre, and I. R. Smith. 1989. "On Development, Fisheries, and Dynamite: A Brief Review of Tropical Fisheries Management." *Natural Resource Modeling* 3, pp. 307–29.

Petrere, M., Jr. 1978. "Pesca e esforço da pesca no Estado do Amazonas. II. Locais, aparelhos de captura e estatísticas de desembarque." *Acta Amazonica* 8, pp. 1–54.

———. 1985. "A pesca comercial no Rio Solimões-Amazonas e seus afluentes: Análise dos informes do pescado desembarcado no Mercado Municipal de Manaus (1976–1978)." *Ciência e Cultura* 37:12, pp. 1987–99.

Pinkerton, E., ed. 1989. *Co-operative Management of Local Fisheries: New Directions for Improved Management and Community Development.* Vancouver, Canada: University of British Columbia Press.

PROA (Programa Orinoco-Apuré). 1991. "Programa Orinoco-Apuré." Publicación Especial DGSPROA/PE/01. Ministerio del Ambiente y de los Recursos Naturales Renovables, Caracas, Venezuela.

Reynolds, J. E., and D. F. Greboval. 1988. "Socioeconomic Effects of the Evolution of Nile Perch Fisheries in Lake Victoria: A Review." CIFA Technical Paper 17. Food and Agriculture Organization of the United Nations, Committee for Inland Fisheries of Africa, Rome.

Ricker, W. E. 1975. "Computation and Interpretation of Biological Statistics of Fish Populations." *Canadian Bulletin of Fisheries and Aquatic Sciences* 191, p. 382.

Schaefer, M. B. 1954. "Some Aspects of the Dynamics of Populations Important to the Management of the Commercial Marine Fisheries." *Bulletin of the Inter-American Tropical Tuna Commission* 1, pp. 27–56.

Schlesinger, D. A., and H. A. Regier. 1982. "Climatic and Morphoedaphic Indices of Fish Yields from Natural Lakes." *Transactions of the American Fisheries Society* 111, pp. 141–50.

Welcomme, R. L. 1974. "Some General and Theoretical Considerations on the Fish Production of African Rivers." CIFA Occasional Paper 3. Food and Agriculture Organization of the United Nations, Committee for Inland Fisheries of Africa, Rome.

———. 1976. "Some General and Theoretical Considerations on the Fish Yield of African Rivers." *Journal of Fish Biology* 8, pp. 351–64.

———. 1979. *The Fisheries Ecology of Floodplain Rivers.* London: Longmans.

———. 1985. "River Fisheries." FAO Fisheries Technical Paper 262. Food and Agriculture Organization of the United Nations, Rome.

21

Sustainable Development of Fisheries in Southeast Asia

Aprilani Soegiarto

The marine and coastal waters of the Southeast Asian region comprise one of the world's most productive areas, in which shallow-water marine plants and animals reach their peak of species diversity. This diversity is associated with very high production of organic matter, which in turn is converted into high fishery yields. Coastal ecosystems, such as upwelling areas, are capable of producing more than ten times as much organic matter per unit of area per unit of time as offshore waters. This very high production of organic matter is transformed into a tremendous variety of economically valuable products used by the people in the region.

The region produces about 8.4 million metric tons of fish. Due to the economic benefits that could be derived from these rich and diverse ecosystems, the coastal zones of Southeast Asia are densely populated. More than 70 percent of the population in the region lives in coastal areas, resulting in rather high levels of exploitation of the natural resources and degradation of the environment. Fish and other edible coastal products are consumed locally or exported. Beaches, such as coral reefs, attract tourists in growing numbers. Coastal habitats are more and more coveted for aquaculture of shrimps and fish, a booming industry of economic importance in the region.

The problem facing the nations of Southeast Asia is how to maintain the integrity of the base of marine and coastal resources for sustainable use. An overview has indicated that resources are being overused, and the basis of their production is eroded. If this trend continues, it will lead to a point of no return, and the countries of Southeast Asia will have to pay dearly in order to restore the base of resources that have been destroyed.

The physical setting

The waters and islands between Asia and Australia and between the Pacific and Indian oceans form one geographical unit. Geographically, the region consists of highly fragmented land area interspersed among wide stretches of sea surface and extremely long coastlines. Physically, it is divided into a continental part of mainland Asia, which consists of Myanmar, Thailand, and the Indo Chinese states of Laos, Kampuchea, and Viet Nam, and into the archipelago of Southeast Asia, including peninsular Malaysia, Brunei Darussalam, Singapore, Indonesia, and the Philippines (Chia Lin Sien and MacAndrews 1979).

In oceanographic terms, however, the waters of this region are part of the Pacific Ocean, which is separated from the Indian Ocean by the islands of Sumatra, Java, and the Lesser Sunda (Nusa Tenggara). The Southeast Asian waters consist of the Andaman Sea, the straits of Malacca, the Straits of Singapore, the South China Sea, the Gulf of Thailand, the Java Sea, the Florest Sea, the Banda Sea, the Arafuru Sea, the Timor Sea, the Celebes Sea, the Sulu Sea, and the Philippines Sea. The whole body of these waters covers approximately 8.94 million square kilometers, which represents about 2.5 percent of the world's ocean surface (Soegiarto 1978, 1985). Figure 21-1 and table 21-1 present geographic information on Southeast Asia, in particular the members of the Association of the Southeast Asian Nations (Soegiarto 1991).

Figure 21–1: Map of Southeast Asian Nations

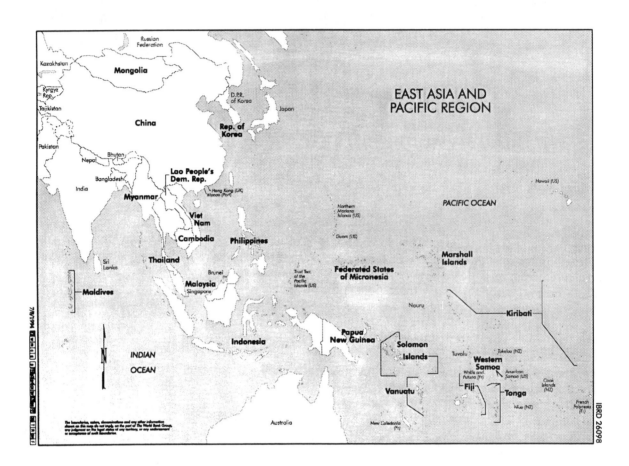

Fishery production

Fisheries are a valuable resource in the region. Indeed, the Southeast Asian seas support one of the world's most productive marine fisheries. Total annual catch from the region in recent years has been approximately 8 million metric tons, with certain fisheries capable of providing still greater yields. Table 21-2 illustrates annual catch, imports and exports, as well as consumption of fish in some countries in Southeast Asia for the year 1988 (FAO 1988).

Excluding the Gulf of Thailand, the Chinese and Vietnamese continental shelf in the South China Sea yields the greatest total annual catch in the region, nearly a million tons. Historically, these abundant fishery resources have been harvested in inshore and coastal waters with a variety of traditional fishing gears and have been an important source of food, animal protein, and employment for many of the region's coastal populations. Whole market and barter systems

with networks extending to the interior are based on these fisheries.

The early mechanized fishing efforts of Japan have been joined in recent years by fishing fleets from Taiwan (China) and South Korea. Modernization and expansion of the region's coastal fishing fleets began in earnest some twenty years ago with the introduction of trawl fishing in Thailand, followed by other countries. Coastal country trawling fleets have now become established in much of the region, fishing the inshore and coastal waters for demersal fish, crustaceans, and molluscs. Coastal countries have also established purse seining fleets in recent years, providing increased catches of coastal and oceanic pelagic fish. Mechanized fishing for export constitutes a significant source of foreign exchange, and the infrastructure supporting these fisheries is a further source of income and employment, for example, freezing, cold storage, processing, boat building, and net making and mending.

Table 21–1: Characteristics of the Marine and Coastal Zone of Members of the Association of the Southeast Asian Nations, 1988

Characteristic	Brunei Darussalam	Indonesia	Malaysia	Philippines	Singapore	Thailand
Land area (thousands of square kilometers)	5.8	1,904	303.8	297	0.6	513
Marine area, including 200 miles of extended jurisdiction (1,000 square kilometers)	0.7	6,841.7	138.7	551	0.1	94.7
Length of coastline (kilometers)	130	81,000	4,800	18,417	193	3,219
Area of mangrove (thousands of hectares)	18.4	4,250	113.3 (west) 538.9 (east)	106.1	1.8	287.3
Population (millions)	0.2	175	16.9	58.7	2.6	54.5
Percentage of the population living in the coastal zone	86	70	60	67	100[a]	60[a]
Gross national product per capita (U.S. dollars)	17,000	550	1,775	630	7,550	860

a. Approximate figure.
Source: Soegiarto 1991.

Table 21–2: Catch and Consumption of Fish in Southeast Asia, 1988

Country	Catch (metric tons)	Imports (millions of U.S. dollars)	Exports (millions of U.S. dollars)	Consumption (kilograms per capita)
Members of the Association of the Southeast Asian Nations				
Brunei Darussalam	3,279	8.50	0.30	42.7
Indonesia	2,703,260	19.38	664.48	13.6
Malaysia	604,128	146.98	190.28	36.6
Philippines	2,041,920	63.06	406.50	33.7
Singapore	15,240	370.31	356.19	40.7
Thailand	2,350,000	537.92	1,630.90	21.6
Nonmembers				
Kampuchea	70,000	—	—	9.3
Laos	20,000	—	—	5.6
Viet Nam	874,000	—	182.24	12.5

— Not available.
Source: FAO 1988; International Centre for Ocean Development 1988.

Problems of sustainable development

The marked increase in regional fishing effort during the past twenty years, encouraged by the rapidly increasing local and international demand for fishery products, has subjected many of the region's inshore and coastal fisheries to intense fishing pressure and has resulted in the overexploitation of several important fisheries. Concurrent with these events and adding to these difficulties has been the loss of important spawning and nursery grounds of many valued species due to increased coastal pollution and the widespread development of coastal lands.

Thus, many of the region's fisheries are already under stress. Spilled oil can have direct and indirect lethal and sublethal effects on eggs and juveniles of species as well as on adults. Important fish may be tainted, and fishing gear may be fouled by oil, depressing the fishing industry and thus indirectly affecting all those who depend on it for their food or livelihood.

The variability in fishing pressure is directly reflected in the total fishery catch of a given area. In general, the areas with the highest total catch are also the areas most intensely fished, such as those where the fish and invertebrate populations are under the greatest stress from fishing activities. Any additional stress on these intensely fished areas, such as oil pollution, may have an immediate, negative impact on existing fishery catches from the affected areas. In less intensely fished areas, the detrimental effects of marine pollution on catches is likely to be less obvious.

Very heavy fishing intensity (larger than 1,000 kilograms per square kilometer) is concentrated in the Gulf of Thailand, particularly in the Thai portion of the Gulf, the central Malacca Strait, in the Andaman Sea immediately west of the Isthmus of Kra and northwest through most of the Mergui Archipelago, off the mouths of the Mekong and Pasig rivers, and in the central Philippines.

Heavy fishing activities (100 to 999.9 kilograms per square kilometer) occur in the northern and southern Malacca Strait, along the east coast of the Malay Peninsula, in the southern Gulf of Thailand and over parts of the central Sunda Shelf, along the entire coast of Viet Nam, and northward along the entire Mainland Shelf, including around Taiwan (China), in most Philippine waters, off East Malaysia and Brunei, around southern Sulawesi and in the central and southern Makasar Strait, in the Bali Strait, along the north coast of Java, around the Riau archipelagoes off eastern Sumatra, and off northwest Sumatra.

The important ecosystems for consideration in the Southeast Asian region are

- Estuaries, common within the mouths of larger river systems.

- Mangroves, associated with low coastlines, estuaries, and rivers.

- Coral reefs, associated with most smaller islands and those coasts on larger islands lacking large inputs of freshwater or sediment from river systems.

Estuaries, mangroves, and coral reefs are among the most productive ecosystems known to humans, as measured by both primary productivity and biomass yields (Polunin and Soegiarto 1980). Production and export of organic materials in estuaries contribute to estuarine, coral reefs, and offshore fishery nutrition. The leaf litter production of mangroves is increasingly correlated with fisheries production within the mangrove system, represented by fish, bivalves, and crustaceans and by diverse fisheries production in the nearby estuaries and coral reef sea grass communities. Coral reefs, very efficient in recycling nutrients and using nutrients from adjacent systems, support sizable fisheries for numerous organisms that are harvested by and provide a significant portion of the protein consumed by coastal people (Gomez 1980; Murdy and Ferraris 1980).

The impact of oil on tropical estuaries is not yet well known, although it may be surmised that the most significant effect of high toxicity in the water column would be on shoreline fauna and flora. Since estuaries receive up to 50 percent of their organic matter from mangrove systems, the impact on mangroves is of importance. Mangroves (and coastal marshes) have been ranked as the ecosystem most sensitive, or vulnerable, to oil, owing to the persistence of oil in that environment and the slow recovery time of the ecosystem, estimated at twenty years or more (Odum and Johannes 1975). The vulnerability of coral reefs to oil depends on the level of toxicity in the water column (Ray 1980), presence and degree of mixing, and degree of direct exposure of corals and other organisms to the oil. Beach systems, although not too productive, provide habitat for certain organisms vulnerable to oil.

Conclusions

In conclusion, Southeast Asian marine and coastal waters are one of the most productive areas in the world. The fisheries are an important resource in the region, in particular for the livelihood of the traditional coastal communities. However, due to population pressures and the marked increase in regional fishing efforts in the past twenty years, coupled with the increase in pollution and environment degradation, these waters have experienced tremendous pressures. If this trend continues, countries of the Southeast Asian region will have to undertake heavy tasks and burdens in order to restore the destroyed resource base. It is probably not too late to make a concerted and coordinated effort for this purpose. Regional cooperation, such as that of the Association of the Southeast Asian Nations, Indo Pacific Fishery Council, or Southeast Asia Fishery Development Council, could serve as a vehicle for such an effort.

Note

This chapter was also published in 1993 by the Southeast Asia Programme on Ocean Law, Policy, and Management in the following collection of papers: *SEAPOL International Workshop on Challenges to Fishery Policy and Diplomacy in South East Asia,* edited by K. I. Matics and Ted L. McDormnan.

References

Chia Lin Sien and C. MacAndrews, eds. 1979. *Southeast Asian Seas: Frontiers for Development.* Southeast Asian Series. New York: McGraw-Hill.

FAO (Food and Agriculture Organization of the United Nations). 1988. *Fishery Statistics.* Vol. 66: *Catches and Landings;* vol. 67: *Commodities.* Rome.

Gomez, E. D. 1980. "Status Report on Research and Degradation Problems of the Coral Reefs of the East Asian Seas." South China Sea Fisheries Development and Coordinating Programme, Manila. May.

International Centre for Ocean Development. 1988. *World Fisheries: International Map.* Canada.

Murdy, F. O., and C. J. Ferraris. 1980. "The Contribution of Coral Reef Fisheries Production." *International Center for Living Aquatic Resources Research Newsletter,* 3:1, pp. 21–22.

Odum, W. E., and R. E. Johannes. 1975. "The Response of Mangroves to Man-induced Environmental Stress." In E. J. Ferguson-Wood and R. E. Johannes, eds., *Tropical Marine Pollution,* pp. 52–62. Elsevier Oceanographic Series 12. Amsterdam: Elsevier.

Polunin, N., and Aprilani Soegiarto. 1980. "Marine Ecosystems of Indonesia: A Basis for Conservation." Report of the International Union for the Conservation of Nature and World Wildlife Fund Indonesia Programme, Bogor.

Ray, J. P. 1980. "The Effects of Petroleum Hydrocarbon on Corals." Paper presented at the Petroleum and the Marine Environmental International Conference and Exhibition, Monaco, May 27–30.

Soegiarto, Aprilani. 1978. "Introduction to the Regional Oceanographic of the Southeast Asian Waters." Paper presented at the fifth FAO/SIDA Workshop on Aquatic Pollution in Relation to the Protection of Living Resources, Manila, the Philippines, January 17–February 27, 1977.

———. 1985. "Oceanographic Assessment of the East Asian Seas." In A. L. Dahl and J. Carew-Reid, eds., *Environment and Resources in the Pacific,* pp. 173–84. Regional Seas Program Studies 68. Nairobi, Kenya: United Nations Environment Program.

———. 1991. "The South China Sea: Its Ecological Features and Potentials for Developing Cooperation in Marine Scientific Research and Environmental Protection." *Jurnal Luar Negeri* (Department of Foreign Affairs, Indonesia) 18, pp. 28–47.

22

Sustainability of Temperate Zone Fisheries: Biophysical Foundations for Its Definition and Measurement

Henry A. Regier, Stephen A. Bocking, and H. Francis Henderson

With all of nature's renewable phenomena that have been used by humans, concern about sustainability must be about as old as any cultural husbandry practices. Many traditional cultures had effective systems for managing human uses of fish and their habitats. Empirical understanding of how technologically innovative humans threatened the biophysical foundations of these valued phenomena began to cumulate several centuries ago. We now understand something about the threats posed by numerous human causes to the sustainability of various kinds of fisheries.

In this review essay, the term fisheries is used in a broad sense to include finfish, shellfish, aquatic mammals such as whales and seals, and reptiles such as turtles. Our primary focus is on finfish; the story of other fisheries generally resembles that of finfish. For the scientific, technical, and policy aspects of the whole set of fisheries, there is effectively one collegial disciplinary domain with a number of major and many minor specializations. This applies particularly to the issue of biophysical foundations of sustainability.

Early concern about sustainability of fisheries focused on reproduction, apparently because of the belief that this was the major factor limiting the abundance of fish (see, for example, Milner 1874; Nettle 1857). As a result, attention focused on preventing interference with the reproductive process or on supplementing it artificially. The reproductive period of temperate fish stocks has long been known to be predictable, from other seasonal and ecological processes, from year to year in particular waters. During the reproductive process, many fish species enter waters where localized and species-specific spawning sites are found and where they are particularly vulnerable to capture by humans. Barring access to these sites, or disrupting the behavioral rituals that precede spawning, may curtail effective reproduction. An awareness of such biophysical foundations has long been part of fisheries traditions, especially with anadromous species in the temperate zones. In consequence, spawners were to be permitted unhindered, unmolested access to their preferred spawning area and to be left alone during their spawning activities. When the reproductive process was affected, attempts were made to mitigate the direct effects: fish hatcheries to compensate for sacrificed spawning grounds, fish ladders to bypass dams that barred spawners' migrations, and artificial spawning locations. These have seldom been fully successful.

The harmful effects on valued fish of the pollution of fish habitats were widely recognized in the nineteenth century. The evidence was sometimes quite compelling: for example, fish flesh smelled of phenols that were being released into the waters by early petroleum-based industry. By 1875 industrial wastes, sawdust from sawmills, and animal and human wastes from farms and cities were recognized as damaging to the Great Lakes fisheries (Pisani 1984). The human and industrial wastes generally came from settlements that were built near rivers and estuaries that in turn were ecologically quite productive of preferred fish.

Ecologically unsustainable practices of voiding human and industrial wastes into nearby waters have not yet been effectively corrected in many locales. Large-scale voiding into the atmosphere of acidic gases due to combustion has acidified vulnerable waters far downwind.

Informed observers have long recognized the harmful effects that destructive practices in the catchment basin—for example, clear-cutting in forestry, overgrazing of lands, hillside plowing in agriculture, and filling in of shallow waters—have on aquatic systems (Marsh 1857). Major effects on fish have been the result of increased variability of the water flow, with increased frequency of harmful episodes of abnormally high and low flows. Such abuses have been addressed repeatedly in many locales for many decades and still occur as new surprises for the ecologically innocent.

A fourth class of concerns about sustainability has related to overfishing. The story of the extinction of the passenger pigeon and American bison in North America in the nineteenth century alerted people interested in marine mammals and then in fish of the potential danger of uncontrolled exploitation. The earlier presupposition, often supported by respected scientists, was that oceans, large lakes, and large rivers as systems were simply too large to be threatened in any practical sense by humans. Eventually a risk of overfishing was perceived even with large stocks of marine finfish, perhaps mostly with respect to effective new methods of fishing by fishers who used less-effective older methods. The myth that the shelf seas and the open ocean could not be overfished, a myth that was under attack beginning in the late nineteenth century, was finally dispatched in 1972 (FAO 1973).

The introduction of foreign species occurred on a grand scale in the nineteenth century and has continued to the present. Many introductions were deliberate and others were accidental; many introductions of both types were eventually found to be undesirable. Some introductions, such as the entry of sea lamprey into the Great Lakes through ship canals, were disastrous: lamprey exhibited no prudence whatever in preying on fish species highly preferred by humans. Other introductions served useful roles in ecosystems that had been altered culturally in ways that could not be exploited efficiently by preferred native species, for example, European brown trout thrived in moderately altered cold-water streams in North America in which stocks of brook trout

had dwindled. Depending on which attributes of an ecosystem are used to specify a goal of sustainability, some introductions have threatened and some have fostered sustainability.

With hindsight, we note the beginnings a century ago of awareness of another type of threat: the globalization of harvest and trade, for example, with seal furs and whale oils. The nonadaptive dynamics of the commercial processes involved were such that it made good short-term economic sense to mine—that is, deliberately to overharvest—different stocks sequentially, starting with those nearest a commercial headquarters and then expanding farther along shore and offshore, and eventually reaching the most distant ocean. Limits on catches for the purpose of sustaining the resource made no economic sense to some commercial interests.

Some informed observers recognized these threats to sustainability of preferred fish species by late in the nineteenth century. Attempts to correct the more flagrant abuses are apparent in the nineteenth-century legislation of various countries. Some attempts proceeded to the international level; those that relate to fisheries interests included the 1892 Bregenzer Übereinkunft for the Bodensee (Regier and Applegate 1972), the 1902 International Council for the Exploration of the Seas (Went 1972), the 1909 Boundary Water Treaty between the United States and Canada (Rawson Academy of Aquatic Science 1989), and the Declaration of Principles of the 1908 North American Conservation Conference (Van Hise 1911).

Some piecemeal corrective measures then followed. But by the mid-twentieth century, it was widely apparent that abuses of all six classes were expanding in spite of earlier reform efforts. New rounds of emphasis on corrective measures followed; apparently none of these measures has been fully effective in addressing the root cause of an abuse.

The second half of the twentieth century brought with it a seventh threat to sustainability: hazardous contaminants produced through advanced technology. Nuclear bombs brought widespread contamination with radionuclides. The pesticide industry first produced persistent pesticides (such as DDT) and then persistent wastes (such as dioxins as by-products in the production of pesticides such as 2-4D). The threat that hazardous contaminants pose to sustainability of fish stocks relates to the risk of sterilization of the adults, mortality through poisoning of the embryos, or crippling of the surviving young.

An eighth class was predicted late in the nineteenth century but only taken seriously late in the twentieth century: widespread pollution of the atmosphere with radiatively active gases that cause the atmosphere to trap heat and thus increase average temperature (American Fisheries Society 1990).

Much of the second half of the twentieth century has involved see-saw-like oscillations between intensifying abuses and more effective, though piecemeal, counteractive measures, at least with respect to fish generally. On balance, the threats to sustainability of fish, worldwide, may still be expanding and intensifying, although they may be abating in some locales.

Husbandmen have known about harmful local effects from local abuses for centuries. The political activities that flowed from the relevant awareness of the 1890s show that people had come to recognize that humans were capable of adversely affecting regional phenomena that then had a bearing reflexively on the sustainability of preferred stocks in particular locales. During the second half of the twentieth century, we have become aware that we now affect the global biosphere and so risk the sustainability of some preferred regional and local phenomena of direct interest to some of us.

Six kinds of fisheries, with an emphasis on sustainability and equity

Distinctions are commonly drawn between several types of fisheries development. Six types are considered here: small-scale subsistence and commercial artisanal fisheries on wild stocks; commercial, industrial, and incidental fisheries on marine mammals; large-scale commercial and industrial fisheries on wild stocks of fish, other than marine mammals; moderate-size commercial fisheries on stocks of wild fish augmented by enhanced stock and habitat; commercial and subsistence husbandry of stocks of semi-domesticated species in artificial habitats under intensive culture; and recreational fisheries with variants that bear some resemblance to each of the other types. They are presented here in historical sequence, that is, in the order in which governance procedures related to sustainability were developed for each type.

We share the current consensus that to consider sustainability in the absence of other human values, such as equity, is largely to waste one's efforts (WCED 1987). Any measure related to the biophysical foundations of ecological sustainability must also make sense with respect to other major dimensions of the cultural mind-set, and especially to equity considerations. Our present emphasis on sustainability and equity should not be interpreted to imply that we dismiss as irrelevant other values, such as aesthetic and inherent values.

Small-scale artisanal fisheries

Throughout the world innumerable small-scale fisheries provide nutritious yields that are generally available even to the local poor people. About 40 million tons of fish—almost half of the total production—are taken annually by artisanal fisherfolk, mostly in warmer climates. An unknown but also large quantity is taken by occasional foragers, usually for food, but also for recreational purposes.

The rights and responsibilities of subsistence and artisanal fishers are ordered in different ways in different cultures. Under normal circumstances, these traditions relate in some appropriate way to the ecological sustainability of the yields and to social equity in the sharing of those yields. Externally imposed efforts to develop these fisheries have sometimes ignored the indigenous conventions, or suppressed them for no good reason, with adverse effects on sustainability.

Small-scale fishing may be the occupation of last resort in places and in times of poverty and social disorientation. Under the imperative of immediate survival, concern about sustainability and equity may not be apparent locally. The ecological degradation that then follows may be termed pollution due to poverty. An unusual connotation of pollution may be appropriate for such events in some cultures: to destroy the sanctity of the place.

Artisanal fisheries can and do intercept migratory stocks of interest to other groups in the broad fisheries sector. Migratory adult spawners and juvenile recruits to stocks may be removed from rivers and coastal areas to an unsustainable degree, in conditions of open access to such stocks. Some artisanal fishers remove large riparian trees for making boats, use firewood for smoking fish, and so forth, and thus create problems—the consequence of increased erosion—for other users of the forests and for themselves. But the great majority of artisanal fisheries do not pose this kind of threat to other fishery interests nor to other interests in society. In contrast, artisanal fisheries are often harmed by competition from politically powerful, large-scale commercial and intensive aquacultural fisheries, especially in the marine coastal zone. Also artisanal fisheries suffer adverse consequences of other practices in the river basins and along the coasts. These aquatic systems integrate environmental consequences of many developmental practices on land and in the water, for example in bioaccumulating hazardous contaminants. The harmful consequences of various abuses are particularly apparent with the large aquatic organisms, including fish, of the rivers, lakes, and estuaries.

Relatively few of the innumerable artisanal fisheries have been developed intensively through external political processes and funds. Fisheries in some large lakes and new reservoirs have been developed with motors for boats, synthetic fibers for nets, and so forth, but usually along artisanal lines.

Generally, artisanal fisheries do not now have much potential for increased yields and do not pose major direct threats to other developmental opportunities. Where the local system of governance is working well, it may be best to leave it be (Berkes 1989). Where the governance system has broken down, it might be fostered back to health rather than supplanted by an introduced system. Sometimes a hybrid between local communitarian and central bureaucratic or market-based governance works well (Pinkerton 1989).

Many subsistence or forage fisheries not only have been severely affected by the threats to sustainability outlined above, but have also been disturbed by the consequences of adopting modernization as the principal aim of development. This has been particularly serious among indigenous communities in the process of conversion from a subsistence to a market economy. Because a community often lacks the time to train its young people in the skills of foraging, and foraging itself is often regarded as backward, traditional knowledge is lost. Further, because the diet tends to become less diverse until a fully developed food supply and marketing system is reached, or because wild resources are less accessible during periods of adversity, both individual health and community resilience may suffer. Indeed, failure to address issues of short-term sustainability during the period of transition from traditional to modern economies and social struc-

tures is a fundamental defect of much formal development work and a threat to the eventual sustainable existence of such groups in a modern society.

What might be an appropriate measure for the biophysical foundations of finely dispersed small-scale fisheries in a region? Perhaps experts in integrated rural development have addressed this issue. The leakiness of locales with respect to limiting plant nutrients, such as phosphorus, may be an integrative measure.

Marine mammals: Whaling and sealing

Generally concerns about excessive levels of direct harvests and about significant incidental catches in other fisheries have been more apparent politically with marine mammals than with other fish. Intense concern about the sustainability of harvests of some seal and whale stocks emerged relatively early in the Northern Hemisphere, more than a century ago. Some populations and species had been suppressed to low levels. The international convention on the Pribilof fur seals of the North Pacific created important precedents. The total number to be taken and procedures for how the removals were to be allocated between countries were established. Thus sustainability and equity were both addressed in an operationally direct way. Good results followed from this convention, although further difficulties have had to be resolved from time to time.

Sustainability and equity issues were much more difficult to resolve with whales than with the Pribilof seals. The cost of achieving credible scientific information on which to base formal decisions was much higher. The dynamics of the marketplace, of commercial interests, and of international politics were not compatible with the ecological dynamics of the whale stocks. For example, the interest rate on money was higher than the growth rate of the whales, hence it was economically rational to mine the resource. Because the issue had become strongly politicized internationally, different nations were rarely willing to provide full and accurate information.

About a century after the issue of excessive direct harvests of some marine mammals was first raised, it was solved politically, at best temporarily, by the imposition of very severe constraints and some complete bans on commercial and industrial whaling and sealing. A long legacy of political concern about excessively intense whaling, which severely threatened the survival of some species, was combined with the new politics of animal protection to limit drastically the harvests of marine mammals generally.

More recently, some fisheries that use long drifting gill nets on the high seas for some species of finfish and shellfish (tuna and squid) expanded further within open oceanic waters. Marine mammals (and fish-eating birds) were quite vulnerable to capture in such nets, because of the manner in which the nets were actually fished in some waters. Because of widespread public concerns about the welfare of those mammals, political action has already included instances of a shift of onus in which the drift net fishers have to demonstrate that the fishing method to be used does not involve risks for the marine mammals (plus turtles and birds, perhaps) of those waters. Unless appropriate information is marshaled and found to be convincing, access to the fishery may be denied.

The example above is a case in which the process of technology assessment is a legal condition of access. For decades, the calculation of maximum sustainable yields or of total allowable catches of stocks has been a stock assessment process. A shift of onus in which fishermen have to demonstrate responsibility for the relevant measure of sustainability or performance has implications for the nature of information services useful with such a regime.

Marine mammals going about their business in coastal waters have become major tourist attractions in various parts of the world's oceans. Because tourist-related activities can and do interfere with the normal behavior of those mammals, progressively more restrictive constraints are also being placed on whale-watching and seal-watching activities.

The political successes of the animal protection interests have shifted the locus and type of commercial activities related to marine mammals. In some parts of the world, those animals are not now intercepted and killed for their skins, flesh, or fat but are rather intercepted and watched for personal pleasure. Enterprises and communities that serve tourists—often involving redirected fishing and whaling interests—have come to benefit economically.

Burgeoning populations of some marine mammals and birds are competing with fisheries for some finfish and shellfish stocks. Reduction in such supplies will presumably lead to a reduction in catches and an increase in price of the relevant fishery products. Control programs on some marine mammal populations may then come to

be more acceptable politically. The main countervailing argument advanced by animal protection interests may then be that people should generally change to vegetarian diets. (It may only be a matter of time until political interests related to plant rights become more prominent than they are currently.)

Large-scale fisheries for finfish and shellfish

The main general concepts and methods currently used in research and management related to capture fisheries were mostly developed first with respect to finfish populations. From here, they have often been adapted and applied to some of the other types of fisheries, such as shellfisheries, whaling, and sealing.

From relatively small beginnings in the late nineteenth century, large-scale fisheries (which no longer include whaling) have expanded progressively to all parts of the ocean. Inventiveness and ingenuity played key roles with respect to vessels, gear, processing, and marketing activities. The main emphasis has always been on appropriate, adaptive technology, at least to some general extent: large-scale, nonselective use of barriers, explosives, poisons, and entangling twine has seldom been condoned socially.

The main motivation for the expansion of modern, large-scale fisheries was to satisfy demands for fish (and fish meal) as reflected in the open markets, or in the bureaucratic processes of centrally planned economies, of the countries already well along the path of conventional development. Feeding the poor in any direct way was seldom a motivation, although less-favored or poor-quality fish did become available to the poor. Fisheries were intended to produce valuable commodities, directly and often in their eventual contribution of hard currency to a country's balance of accounts.

The overall process of large-scale fisheries development involved sequential cropping down of the more-valued stocks near a fishing port with a subsequent shift to less-valued stocks nearby and to more-valued stocks farther away. Some stocks were so plentiful, such as the cod of the Grand Banks, that they already attracted fishers from distant ports some five centuries ago.

The accumulated natural capital of valued fish stocks in a pristine fishery seldom yielded great profit to fishers, at least during the present century. The exploratory fishing process was costly. The rushed, disorderly competition in open-access situations generally led to overcapitalization, inefficient practices, and the dissipation of profits.

Because the fish and fisheries habitat of large waters were deemed to be unowned and access was effectively open, there was no rent to be paid for harvesting the fish. Unpaid rents that accrued to the fishers were eventually dissipated when the levels of fishing effort overshot what was necessary to achieve optimal yields. Rather than charge rent for use of such resources, countries often subsidized their fleets in a competitive international race for resources and thus contributed to the overfishing.

Over the past hundred years, most countries with large-scale international fisheries (and also whaling) have employed two often distinct groups of fisheries experts with contrasting commitments. A pro-growth group, closely affiliated with the commercial fishers and financial institutions, was committed to increasing landings progressively, usually with an emphasis on finding more effective ways to locate fish stocks and to catch fish. A pro-sustainability group was intent on preventing the overexploitation of the stocks. Greater political power in the short run usually lay with the pro-growth group, which often enjoyed direct access to senior politicians as patrons, while the pro-sustainability group served within a hierarchical bureaucracy or in an advisory role.

Starting in the 1950s, social scientists came to participate increasingly in the information services for fisheries. Through their bioeconomic model with its emphasis on efficiency, they crafted a partial synthesis to transcend the antithesis of the pro-growth and pro-sustainability factions. Eventually the social scientists—now including anthropologists, human ecologists, and political scientists—addressed issues of rights and responsibilities, hence social equity. In the abstract, it may be difficult to plan fishery practices so that economic efficiency and social equity are compatible. A two-stage process may be appropriate. The relevant government first specifies clearly the social equity considerations to be met: subject to those considerations, the issue of economic efficiency can then be addressed through the market, the bureaucracy, or other secondary institutional mechanisms. Sometimes a government does not possess the will to make the primary decisions and implicitly delegates this responsibility to the secondary institutions, generally with the result that the problem then worsens.

Networks of scientific researchers routinely shared information, sometimes even when such sharing was discouraged by a scientist's country. On occasion, pro-sustainability researchers informally provided relatively accurate data to their foreign peers for scientific purposes, while their countries were officially declaring the data to be inaccurate for political purposes.

The information collected and the publication services of the many fisheries commissions, together with the very extensive information services at the Food and Agriculture Organization of the United Nations (FAO) have played indispensable roles in the general, if slow, evolution of international cooperation toward sustainable and equitable fisheries regimes. Through moral suasion, the international agencies sought improvements in the relevance, accuracy, and precision of research and management data. Effective cooperation seldom came in time to prevent some degree of overfishing.

Pro-sustainability scientific researchers and advisers often assumed the responsibility of serving as stewards of sustainability and equity. This is to be expected with officials of international commissions and the FAO, which were set up for that purpose, among others. But it also frequently was the case with scientists of competing countries. In part, this may have been because scientists serving ostensibly quite different political ideologies shared scientific paradigms and mores; scientific collaboration became an indirect form of diplomacy.

In retrospect, informal and then formal commitments to sustainability and equity have acted to limit excesses within the pro-growth development of large-scale fisheries. The open-access feature was progressively constrained and superseded by regimes of limited or closed access, as in the 1984 United Nations Convention of the Law of the Sea (UNCLOS; United Nations 1984). Although most agreed that these regimes were a step in the right direction, closure of access at the national level was not necessarily accompanied by comparable measures within a country's fisheries. Many of the most valued large-scale stocks are now exploited too intensely.

From relatively small-scale beginnings several centuries ago, large-scale fisheries now land some 50 million tons a year. Of those, about 30 million tons are for human food and 20 million tons are for fish meal to be fed to domesticated animals, fish in aquacultural pens and ponds, and so forth.

No major new stocks of large-scale fisheries are likely to be found. As demand for fish for human food will rise, prices paid to fishers will rise. Progressively, the small pelagic fish that are now rendered into fish meal and the incidentally caught low-valued species that are now discarded offshore will be processed for human food, because it will pay to do so. Processing and marketing all small pelagic fish and all discarded by-catches for human food will not necessarily improve the lot of the poor consumer. The prices will likely be too high, in part because preventing those catches from spoiling in warm climates, which may occur in a matter of minutes in the absence of preservative means, will be expensive.

Appropriate changes in fishing technology, regulations, and practices will lead to a recovery of some stocks and an increase in the overall value of the landings, as has been demonstrated in some fisheries. It is clearly not technical knowledge, but rather the necessary political comprehension, that will remain illusive.

In summary, many international disputes, confrontations, and some occasional skirmishes (the Icelandic cod wars) have occurred in the large-scale fisheries. But progress has also been made toward regional and global regimes in which sustainability and equity appear as prominent guideposts. The positive achievements in fisheries and environmental (fish habitat) issues deserve to be celebrated.

Moderate-scale fisheries, with enhancement

Moderate-scale fish stocks of the coastal zone, large rivers, and large lakes have been subject to intense fisheries development, but their habitats have also been subject to many effects of other developments on land. With many stocks, some adverse effects of other developments have been corrected and some habitat factors have been deliberately enhanced to benefit particularly valued stocks, such as salmon species.

With anadromous species, many distinctive spawning runs or races have been extinguished due mostly to physical alteration and pollution of rivers. Attempts to create sustainable new runs in recent years have had some success.

Certain development uses of a river must be severely constrained or managed if the river is to be appropriate for spawning by valued species. If the costs of environmental husbandry were not incurred, the spawning stock would be depressed or even extinguished. The costs incurred in assuring appropriate spawning conditions justify the priority claimed by the countries sponsoring such husbandry to the recruits from it, as indicated in United Nations (1984).

In efforts to rehabilitate valued fisheries in degraded habitats or to enhance new fisheries in reservoirs, species not native to the aquatic system have often been introduced. Some introductions have proven successful—ecologically, economically, and socially—but some species behave differently and less desirably than expected in habitats new to them. Fish diseases and parasites may be inadvertently brought in with the introduced fish. Major problems of this sort have occurred in some waters. Prior impact assessments on any proposed introductions are coming to be expected, as in the Laurentian Great Lakes.

Coastal marine wetlands that are periodically inundated and floodplains bordering rivers and lakes are major spawning and nursery areas. These are being drained and diked to an increasing extent. What was once an interactive ecosystem of rivers, floodplain, estuary, and coastal plain becomes dismembered with commensurate losses in fish productivity. Often the value of the lost fish yields is unknown or ignored. Gradually, the importance of wetlands or wastelands to fish and other species has come to be recognized. Some areas are being granted protection, in the form of reserves, because of their ecological importance, which extends beyond the immediate locale in which they occur. Recently, issues relating to the protection of fisheries have emerged within the larger policy context of safeguarding biodiversity. Consequently, the focus is expanding from the sustainability of individual stocks to that of ecosystems.

Semi-domesticated species cultured in artificial habitats

Aquaculture resembles animal husbandry within agriculture more than it resembles capture fisheries on wild stocks. The size of the productive habitat and the environmental impact of a particular enterprise are usually quite small and local. In aquaculture, sustainability and equity considerations usually relate directly to the responsibilities that come with individual or community ownership rights. The relevant regime of rights and responsibilities is not well-developed in countries where aquaculture is not an old tradition; parts of Asia and Europe have old traditions.

As with small-scale artisanal fisheries, aquaculture should fit within a regime of integrated rural development. By comparison, moderate-scale fisheries such as those described in the preceding section tend to fit within river basin and coastal zone development. The oceanic regime for large-scale fishing is not yet as well articulated, but the 1984 UNCLOS has clarified major principles (United Nations 1984). At all three scales, the relevant institutions are designed to resolve problems of equity and sustainability, among others.

It is unlikely that small-scale artisanal and large-scale commercial fisheries—capture fisheries—can be developed further to increase sustained yields by more than a fraction of their current levels. Hopes that increased productive employment will produce greatly increased fish yields to help feed the vast growth in numbers of people are pinned mostly on intensive aquaculture. But even then, the costs of production will often put the price at a level too high for the poor. In the foreseeable future, if the poorest of the poor of the world will have some fish in their diets, much of it will come from protected and enhanced artisanal fisheries.

Intensive aquaculture, as with intensive agriculture, can be ecologically disruptive if practiced carelessly. Aquaculture ponds, as in a mangrove coastal zone, may interfere with the function of this zone as spawning and nursery areas for marine species. Pens in open waters lead to organic pollution through lost food and the physiological wastes of the cultured organisms.

Aquaculture, intensive and extensive, now uses fish meal and partially processed low-value species caught incidentally, for example, in fisheries targeted on shrimp. If the fish meal and incidental catches are processed for direct human consumption, the productivity of some types of aquaculture is reduced.

Fish-eating birds and mammals become serious pests with aquaculture enterprises. Attempts to control them may bring the fishers in conflict with animal protection interests. Introduced species that may have been artificially selected for particular genetic traits are often used in aquaculture. When some of these escape and become feral, they may become pests; for example, they may pollute the gene pool of the well-adapted natural stocks. If a natural stock is tuned genetically to particular spawning circumstances, then spawning may be disrupted by inappropriate features of hybrids of the wild and cultural stocks, that is, by gene pollution.

Aquaculturists are turning more and more to genetic enhancement for improved production. Access to wild gene pools is recognized as necessary for long-term success. Preservation of the natural biodiversity in appropriate nature reserves is therefore important to aquacultural interests.

Recreational fisheries

Recreational fishers (mostly males) may use very little equipment and resemble some artisanal subsistence fisheries in this respect. Or they may employ costly gear comparable to that of moderate-size commercial capture fisheries. Enterprises that cater to anglers' wishes may lease use of vessels, sell access to cultured fish in ponds or to wild fish in streams, and so forth.

Recreational anglers are often as interested in experiencing relatively wild, intact natural phenomena as they are in actually catching valued fish species. But there must be some reasonable likelihood of the latter. Many of the fish caught contribute to the diet of the angler's family.

In industrial countries, anglers, when organized, are often more powerful politically than small-scale to moderate-scale capture fisheries. Progressively, anglers limit the access of commercial fishermen from heavily angled water and eventually may have them excluded entirely. Not infrequently, commercial fishermen then transform their enterprises to serve anglers and tourists, as has also been the case with commercial whaling communities, which have adapted to serve tourists. To compensate displaced commercial fishers for the loss of access to fish, some governments purchase the fisheries, expunge the rights, and write off the assets.

Competition among anglers in turn leads to progressively severe limitations on the catch that a particular angler can land. Increasingly, more angler fisheries are now being managed, through mutual consent, so that few fish are killed, although many may be caught and released. Then the large fish of valued species remain in those waters for future angling opportunities. (In some waters individual fish that are caught repeatedly and relatively harmlessly are given distinctive names.) Anglers may help to protect healthy aquatic ecosystems and to rehabilitate degraded waters. These are ways in which sustainability and equity considerations are being addressed.

Angling is generally a sport for the more prosperous people of the more industrial parts of the world, although the progression from foraging and subsistence fishing to recreational angling appears to be a common means of legitimizing such activity even in developing countries. Anglers are usually prepared to pay the owners of the fish and their habitat for the opportunity to fish; wealthy anglers pay well for exceptional opportunities. Many anglers belong to clubs within which there is ritualized competition for relative status. Increasingly, practice of proper angler ethics (to safeguard sustainability) is a prerequisite for high status.

Sustainability concerns in marine fisheries: A case study

Concern about sustainability has long been apparent with the North Sea fishery. During the nineteenth century, fishermen spread north and west across the North Sea, as coastal stocks became depleted (Alward 1911). Technological change accompanied this movement. Instead of waiting for fish to school near shore or migrate into rivers, fishermen devised gear and vessels to catch the fish farther offshore. By approximately 1880, expansion had reached the limit of the sea, and catch rates in the more distant areas began to decline. This decline occurred as the British North Sea fisheries became more and more industrialized after 1880, as fishermen replaced sails with steam power, and passive with active gear. Plaice declined most, followed by haddock. With decline in yield, reduction in the size of individual fish, and changes in species composition, fishermen had to work harder for less gain (Cushing 1988; Meyer 1947).

In 1863 a British royal commission asked whether the supply of fish was increasing or decreasing (Commissioners Appointed to Inquire into the Sea Fisheries 1866). Although some evidence of overfishing was presented, most witnesses argued that fish remained abundant. The commission concluded that supply had not diminished and that further expansion was possible. Some felt that the oceans' living resources were inexhaustible (Huxley 1884). Others suggested that there were limits to the productivity of fish and warned of destructive exploitation and overfishing (Meyer 1947). Since 1875, empirical evidence accumulated that the stocks of flatfish were diminishing, probably due to destruction of immature fish. In 1893, a British committee considered measures to preserve and improve British sea fisheries; no action was taken on its recommended controls (Select Committee on Sea Fisheries 1893).

In the 1890s, Petersen examined plaice stocks in the Kattegat, focusing particularly on growth rates (Petersen 1903). He noted the possibility that fish were being taken before they had grown to full size and that this growth overfishing reduced the total value of catches. The best solution was education: fishermen could avoid growth overfishing themselves if the problem were explained to them. He also suggested a size limit for salable fish to remedy overfishing. He considered recruitment overfishing, which would reduce reproductive effectiveness and might threaten the survival of the stock, as only a distant prospect, because even if greatly depleted, there were still enough mature fish to provide sufficient eggs.

Garstang (1900) formulated catch per unit of effort as an index of stock and used it to show that between 1889 and 1898 stock density of the English North Sea fishery had declined almost 50 percent.

The International Council for the Exploration of the Sea was founded in 1902 to promote rational, scientific exploitation of the fisheries (Went 1972). Overfishing was of major concern from the start. From 1905 to 1914, the North Sea plaice dominated the debate over whether overfishing was primarily an economic problem, as Petersen and others believed, or a biological problem, in which fish stocks were actually being depleted, as Heincke argued. Petersen advised no controls on the fishery; Heincke argued that they were needed. No action was then taken.

Similar events occurred in Pacific Northwest halibut fisheries, including a shift to more distant fisheries as those closer were depleted and, between 1910 and 1930, a great decline in stock density and catches while effort rose three times. As in the North Sea, the fishery was marked by industrialization and technological innovation (Thompson and Freeman 1930). Beginning in 1917, Thompson proposed that the observed decline in stock density be corrected by restricting fishing effort. His objective was to ensure a stable, economically efficient fishery. Importantly, he proposed a limit on entry to the fishery, to permit stock density to recover and, eventually, catches to increase.

Russell (1931) used a mathematical mass balance expression as a basis for achieving a maximum sustainable yield and avoiding growth overfishing. He considered recruitment overfishing to be unlikely. Graham (1935), like Russell, pursued mesh regulations and developed a logistic model to predict the most profitable level of fishing effort. Before the 1939–45 war, empirical evidence became available showing that fish stocks heavily exploited before the 1914–18 war recovered when hostilities prevented fishing (Russell 1939). Catch statistics gathered in 1946 indicated a similar phenomenon had occurred in the 1939–45 war. At the 1946 Overfishing Convention in London, most European countries agreed to minimum landing sizes for demersal fishes and minimum mesh sizes for trawls, except those used for herring and shrimp, but did not agree to limit entry to a fishery. The major problem was seen as growth overfishing, and the solution was built on Russell and Graham's work.

In short, before the 1950s, in the North Sea (the most intensively studied marine fishery in the world), sustainability was defined as achieving maximum biological yield and maximum economic yield by avoiding the capture of young fish, that is, growth overfishing. Sustainability was not defined as maintaining the stocks themselves, that is, avoiding recruitment overfishing; given the scale of the fishery and the state of technology, recruitment overfishing was not considered likely (Cushing 1988). This reflected the biology of the dominant North Sea fisheries: being based on "r species," with little parental investment in offspring other than broadcasting large quantities of eggs, recruitment overfishing is unlikely. Influential work by Beverton and Holt (1957) was based on experience with such fisheries and was done before cases of recruitment overfishing had been convincingly documented with such stocks. Contemporary work by other researchers (Ricker 1954, 1958) that emphasized "K species" such as centrachids and salmonids, with strong parental involvement in caring for fewer eggs, inferred a greater risk of recruitment overfishing.

Simple equations describing the dynamics of fish populations, and relating stock density to fishing effort, were offered as a basis for management and international agreement. This required simple, understandable formulations emphasizing economic consequences. Ricker (1946) defined maximum sustained yield to express the principle that the maximum of the curve of yield in weight versus fishing mortality can be defined and that there is a greatest catch that can be safely taken for a long time. Such formulations could be explained and justified to persons who are not experts, could be translated into management advice, and could form the basis for negotiations and agreements. Their utility in arenas outside science is reflected in their use in areas beyond those originally intended (Holt and Talbot 1978); in part, it was the demands of negotiations and agreements that led to sustainability being defined in terms of maximum sustainable yield.

Changing definitions of sustainability may also be identified by comparing the objectives of international agreements. In 1946, the International Fisheries Convention defined the central concern as overfishing; in 1949, the International Convention for North-West Atlantic Fisheries sought, after Ricker (1946), to achieve a maximum sustained yield; the Permanent Commission in 1954 (which in 1959 became the North East Atlantic Fisheries Convention) sought to achieve conservation through rational exploitation; and in 1984, the Law of the Sea Conference defined conservation as optimum sustainable yield (Cushing 1988).

A major preoccupation of these international agreements was growth overfishing. Beverton and Holt (1957) justified dealing with growth overfishing by increasing mesh size. The Permanent Commission's first task was to extend the principle of mesh regulation, but during the 1950s and 1960s, larger fleets, new technology, and new markets, such as those for fish meal and frozen fish, led to a new stage of overfishing (Cushing 1988). Fish production increased from 22 million tons annually between 1948 and 1952 to 72 million tons between 1978 and 1983 (Gulland 1983).

Some scientists, on occasion, have resisted this emphasis on the conservation of existing fisheries solely through application of population dynamics. Kasahara (1961) argued that fisheries research should not focus on conservation but on development and exploitation of new resources (McHugh 1970). This reflected the interest in other countries, especially Japan and Russia, in the discovery and exploitation of distant resources. Some North American scientists also emphasized at that time that global production of fish was potentially almost unlimited; Larkin (1965), for example, noted that the then world catch of 50 million metric tons was "certainly less than one-tenth of the potential catch and perhaps as little as one-fortieth." This judgment was based on a notion that large fish were ecologically inefficient and could be sacrificed in favor of trophically more efficient small fish, or invertebrates, or even plankton; the greatly increased yield would more than compensate for the lower value per unit of mass of the catches. This notion is not now held in high regard, for reasons that, apparently, have not been fully explained.

In the 1960s, a different view of sustainability took hold. With the second industrialization of marine fisheries, and associated widespread evidence of recruitment overfishing, sustainability became defined not simply as avoiding growth overfishing, but as maintaining the viability of each valued stock, that is, avoiding recruitment overfishing. Markets sold many particular kinds of fish; they did not sell fish as homogeneous substance. Thus, different methods of control, in addition to mesh regulation, were needed. Only catch and effort quotas were politically feasible with large-scale fisheries; because effort statistics were poor, partly because effort measures could not be standardized sufficiently, the catch quota or total allowable catch became the focus of management (Cushing 1988).

Since the 1940s, the definition of sustainability has gradually become more complicated, as objectives other than maximum biological yield have become important. Graham (1943) argued that unlimited fishing must become unprofitable and inefficient; therefore, entry must be limited. There is a greatest yield, but he thought that to limit effort for greater value was much more important. In 1943, Herrington and Nesbit debated whether management should seek to achieve maximum biological yield or maximum economic yield. Nesbit, who argued for maximum economic yield, proposed reducing entry into the fishery to ensure healthy returns for those fishermen who remained (McHugh 1970); the tradeoff was between achieving maximum yield and avoiding loss of jobs. In summary, the objectives of large-scale commercial fisheries management became a combination of maximum yield, value, and jobs: in short, the greatest yield for the greatest value and the least loss of jobs (Cushing 1988).

By 1973, a consensus had emerged among fishery scientists that global production from capture fisheries with conventional types of fish could not increase far beyond its then current level because of the absence of large unexploited stocks and, consequently, that the chief task of fishery management was not to develop unexploited fish stocks, but to maintain sustainability of existing fisheries. There was also some consensus on a more complex view of sustained yield, going beyond maximum biological yield to include socioeconomic factors such as equity (allocation of resources) and a diversity of management objectives (FAO 1973). Critical reappraisal of assessments of stock-based maximum sustainable yield, as the primary kind of information on which to base decisions of total allowable catches to ensure sustainability, then followed, for example, by Larkin (1977) and Holt and Talbot (1978).

A tacit consensus was codified to some extent in United Nations (1984), which emphasized the conservation of existing living resources, not the development of new resources. Conservation within an exclusive economic zone came to be primarily the responsibility of the coastal state. Conservation requires ensuring that living resources are not endangered by overexploitation (avoiding recruitment overfishing) and that populations of harvested species are maintained or restored at a level that can produce the maximum sustainable yield (article 61.2, 61.3). All production in excess of that required to eliminate risk of overexploitation, and to maintain maximum sustainable yield, should be included within the allowable catch and harvested. If the coastal state cannot fully use the allowable catch, then it shall give other states access to the surplus (article 62.2).

The definition of maximum sustainable yield in UNCLOS is modified by consideration of several factors:

- Environmental factors, such as the interdependence of stocks (article 61.3) or the maintenance of species associated with harvested species (article 61.4).

- Economic factors, such as the needs of coastal fishing communities and developing states (article 61.3) and the needs of those who have habitually fished in areas to which other states are given access (article 62.3).

- Equity, such as the right of participation of land-locked states (article 69) and geographically disadvantaged states (article 70).

These considerations imply that indicators of sustainability limited to standard biophysical measures, or emphasizing only economic efficiency, are insufficient. Management must also be guided by the conditions particular to each coastal state, including the requirements of inshore artisanal fisheries traditionally neglected in resource development programs (Troadec 1983).

Management must relate to the sociopolitical behavior of individual fishers and aggregated fisheries. Individual transferable quotas have been introduced to give market forces and commercial management processes roles in sustaining economically efficient levels of production. But with such a reorientation of management, new inequities may arise, as in the initial assignment of quotas. Also entrepreneurship may be fostered at the expense of husbandry.

In retrospect, sustainability has always been a major concern of fisheries scientists and managers. That it has not been achieved in any major way may be partly because entrepreneurial progrowth interests enjoy political strength and have some scientific support on their side and partly because efforts to achieve stable fisheries have been focused too heavily on the short-term technical aspects of the problems as they are perceived at the time. As fisheries evolve along with many other societal changes, the issues change and earlier partial solutions become obsolete. Planning and management for sustainability in fisheries are coming to be focused more clearly on the processes of their development and practices and less on particular end states as defined in numerical measures of sustained yields of a few valued species.

The fisheries of the Great Lakes: Another case study

In the first section of this chapter, we sketched eight major kinds of threats to the sustainability of fisheries. By 1900, the first six had been recognized within the Great Lakes Basin (Bocking 1987). Although marine fisheries research was until recently based on single-species approaches, in the Great Lakes Basin (as in the Bodensee and Rhine River), awareness of the impact of ecosystem factors on fisheries, such as changes in the physical environment, developed relatively early. Throughout much of the twentieth century, however, efforts to cope with these threats were hindered by divergent views on which threat was most urgent (overfishing versus watershed modification; Egerton 1985). More recently, Great Lakes fisheries researchers, participating stakeholders, and government administrators have assumed a more comprehensive approach to these threats (American Fisheries Society 1990; Cairns, McCormick, and Niederlehner 1991; Edwards

and Regier 1990; Francis and others 1979; GLWQA 1978 with protocol of 1987; Loftus and Regier 1972). The general approach has been pragmatic.

The Great Lakes Water Quality Agreement of 1978, administered by the United States–Canada International Joint Commission, committed the parties to a goal of attaining ecosystem integrity in the basin (Regier 1992a). Soon after that, the United States–Canada Great Lakes Fishery Commission effectively committed itself to the same goal, consistent with the Strategic Great Lakes Fishery Management Plan of 1981, which was negotiated among all the states, the province, and the federal governments under the aegis of the commission. Subsequently, the states and province also committed themselves to this goal with respect to issues of the quantity and quality of water (Rawson Academy of Aquatic Science 1989). In recent years, various municipal and metropolitan governments have joined the consensus, for example, in the greater Toronto area (RCFTW 1992).

A quick study of the practical political consequences of commitments to ecosystem integrity in the Great Lakes Basin shows that a variety of objectives are now accepted as subsidiary to the goal, as indicated in table 22-1. All of these objectives, taken together, are intended to ensure the sustainability of the ecosystem's integrity. For currently degraded parts of the lakes, a satisfactory state of ecosystem integrity must first be attained and then sustained subsequently.

Only some of the key features of a vision of ecosystem integrity have as yet been specified for these lakes. The most comprehensive specification was included in the 1987 protocol to the 1978 Great Lakes Water Quality Agreement for Lake Superior. The shared vision was that Lake Superior should be rehabilitated to a state reasonably close to that of its pristine state. Implicitly, this meant that all the classes of threats or cultural stresses sketched above be relaxed and some active rehabilitative ecosystemic therapy be undertaken. All that is involved in the 1987 commitment is only gradually being made explicit.

A restoration to near-pristine states is unlikely to be undertaken with any of the other four Great Lakes or the four major rivers that thread the lakes to each other and to the Gulf of St. Lawrence. The preferred vision for each of these lakes has yet to be specified in any detail. The cultural stresses are to be relaxed and their adverse consequences to be remediated, but what the rehabilitated ecosystem's dominant structures and processes should be has not yet been agreed fully.

Table 22-1: Four Domains of Emphasis in the Current Politics in the Great Lakes Basin Concerning Sustainability and Integrity of the Environment

Focus of interest	Good features	Bad features	Relevant professionals
Quality of materials and substances	Valued abiotic resources, clean sand, pure water	Chemical and physical, pollutantsgarbage and wastes in dumps, hotspots in sediments	Engineers, geologists, environmental chemists, hydrologists
Abundance of species in their habitats	Valued living resources, naturalists' friends, rare species	Human pathogens, unwanted exotics, harmful pests	Forestry, fisheries, and wildlife managers, epidemiologists, public health officers
Local ecosystems in landscape networks	Healthy centers of ecological organization and connecting links in a dynamic network	Pathological centers of disorganization and proliferation channels	Parks and preserves remedial action planners, landscape designers
Natural and cultural interactions in bioregions	Caring healthy humans living with adapted nature in a regional mosaic of self-organizing ecosystems	Disoriented ailing humans degrading with debased nature in a regional self-reinforcing slum	The new regional planners, participation facilitators for redemocratization

Note: The normative distinction between good and bad is simplistic, of course.

Figure 22-1 shows three general states of ecosystem integrity that are currently being clarified. The vertical ovoid on the left denotes a reasonable approximation to the integrity of the primeval state, as with the formal commitments for the upper lake, Superior. The diagonal ovoid depicts degraded ecosystems, that is, states of disintegrity or self-reinforcing pathological integrity, which still persist in the two lower lakes, Erie and Ontario, and in large parts of the two middle lakes, Michigan and Huron. The horizontal ovoid relates to human-dominated ecosystems of the future that will exhibit an acceptable measure of partially designed cultural and natural integrity.

All the Great Lake Basin's jurisdictions at whatever level apparently concur that the parts of the basin ecosystem that now exist in a degraded, disintegrated state should be rehabilitated or restored to one of the two general domains that possess desirable integrity. Few of the degraded ecosystems, other than locales within Lake Superior, will likely be restored to approximate a primeval state. So they will be transformed into states with cultural and natural integrity, as in the horizontal ovoid. Comprehensive features of this kind of integrity are only now coming to be addressed explicitly in some parts of the basin. The Great Lakes Fishery Commission (1992) committed the various lake committees that serve

Figure 22-1: Three States of Ecosystem Integrity

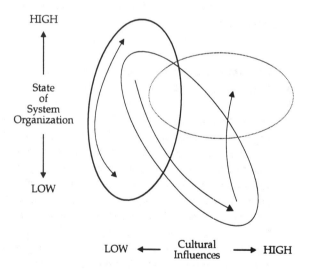

Note: Ovoids refer to three multidimensional ecosystemic domains; left ovoid reflects the fully natural state; the central slanting ovoid reflects different levels of ecosystemic degradation due to cultural abuse; the right ovoid reflects a healthy natural and cultural ecosystem or landscape mosaic. The state of healthy self-integration is high at the top of the figure and low at the bottom.

under its aegis to formulate by 1993 quantitative targets for the fish species associations in each of the lakes consistent with the quantitative environmental commitments under the Great Lakes Water Quality Agreement, as amended progressively.

For Lake Superior, the ecosystem objective was specified with respect to numerous water quality criteria, but also with respect to species that were deemed to be integratively or cumulatively vulnerable to the entire mix of cultural stresses being visited on that lake. The two species were the lake trout and an amphipod, *Pontoporeia affinis*. In this chapter, the suitability of the lake trout as an integrative indicator of the state of ecosystem integrity is sketched briefly, following Ryder and Edwards (1985) and Regier (1992b).

Lake trout thrive in appropriate natural waters that are not severely affected by moderate levels of any of the classes of stresses sketched above. Each stress triggers a diagnostic response and also contributes to an overall syndrome of harm of the population (Rapport, Regier, and Hutchinson 1985). The abundance of lake trout (a salmonid) as an integrative indicator may provide the best measure of sustainability of ecosystem integrity in the deep, cold, nutrient-poor parts of the Great Lakes waters. The necessary research has been completed to demonstrate that the walleye (a percid fish) could serve a similar role for moderately shallow, cool, nutrient-rich waters in the Great Lakes (Edwards and Ryder 1989). Although the necessary work has not been done, a similar case can presumably be made for smallmouth bass (a centrarchid fish) in shallow inshore waters of bays, at least where the degradation of such waters is minimal or has been remediated (GLSAB 1989).

The use of ecologically sensitive species of fish as integrative indicators of the state of integrity of the water and land ecosystem of a watershed has been applied to tributary basins to the Great Lakes, especially those in the Toronto area (Kauffman and others 1992). Both an index of biotic integrity and habitat suitability indexes—each of which is strongly rooted in ecological understanding (Karr and others 1986; Raleigh 1982)—have been tested for the streams in the Toronto area (Beak Consultants Ltd. 1991; Steedman 1988). They have been judged less useful, on balance, than the integrative indicator species approach (Kauffman and others 1992; Regier 1992b).

The accepted goal of ecosystem integrity in the Great Lakes Basin has not yet been specified sufficiently to address the question of what might be the best single measure related to the sustainability of a state of ecosystem integrity. A judiciously selected set of variables for a single integrative indicator species may be as close as we can get to a single measure of sustainability, but such a set would also be insufficient (Regier 1992b). It seems unlikely that any single measure, or some single numerical aggregation of interrelated measures, will suffice for all practical purposes. A particular measure of sustainability relates mainly to a subset of the pluralistic values of a democratic community of people. Different interests that focus on different legitimate values need information relevant to their various interests: this implies that sustainability will not likely be defined monistically nor measured in a single way.

Sustainability, science, and the environment

Definition and measurement of sustainability depend not solely on understanding its biophysical foundations. At least three aspects of the interaction among science, society, and the natural environment should also be considered: the diversity of forms of science considered relevant to sustainability, the divergent perspectives on the role of science in sustainability development, and the definition of a sustainable ecosystem in a state of desired integrity.

Science relevant to sustainability: Academic considerations

Maruyama (1974) has identified three kinds of mind-sets or broad predispositions that relate to contemporary science (see table 22-2). Each mind-set has mutually compatible elements from ontology (regarding the nature of reality or what is), epistemology (regarding ways of knowing or enquiry), ethics (regarding what ought to be done), and perhaps aesthetics (regarding what is beautiful or pleasing). Clearly the characterizations presented in table 22-2 are abstractions—presumably few people (except perhaps some disciplined academics!) would fit neatly into only one of the classes.

It is possible that the characterization of various features within a particular class—that is, the contents of a particular column in table 22-2—may be only one set of a number of possible sets

Table 22-2: Characteristics of Three Mind-sets Related to Sustainability of Renewable Resources and the Natural Environment

Characteristic	Unidirectional causal	Random process	Mutual causal
Science	Traditional cause-and-effect model	Classic thermodynamics, Shannon information theory	Open system thermodynamics, post-Shannon information theory
Information	Past and future inferable form	Information decays and gets lost, blueprint must contain more information than finished product	Information can be generated, nonredundant complexity can be generated without preestablished blueprint
Cosmology	Predetermined universe	Decaying universe	Self-generating and self-organizing universe
Social organization	Hierarchical	Individualistic	Nonhierarchical interactionist, holarchic
Social policy	Homogenistic	Decentralized	Heterogenistic coordination
Ideology	Authoritarian	Anarchistic	Cooperative
Philosophy	Universalism	Nominalism	Network
Ethics	Competitive	Isolationist	Symbiotic
Aesthetics	Unity by similarity and repetition	Haphazard	Harmony of diversity
Religion	Monotheism	Freedom of religion	Polytheistic harmonism
Decision process	Dictatorship, majority rule, or consensus	Do your own thing	Elimination of hardship on individuals, communitarian
Logic	Deductive, axiomatic	Inductive, empirical	Complementary
Perception	Categorical	Atomistic	Contextual
Knowledge	Believe in one truth, if people are informed, they will agree	Why bother to learn beyond one's own interest	Polyocular: learn different views and take them into consideration
Methodology	Classificational, taxonomic	Statistical	Relational, contextual analysis, network analysis
Research hypothesis and strategy	Dissimilar results must have been caused by dissimilar conditions; differences must be traced to conditions producing them	There is probability distribution; find out probability distribution	Dissimilar results may come from similar conditions due to mutually amplifying network; network analysis instead of tracing the difference back to initial conditions in such cases
Assessment	Impact analysis	What does it do to me?	Look for feedback loops for self-cancellation or self-reinforcement
Analysis	Preset categories used for all situations	Limited categories for one's own use	Changeable categories depending on the situation
View of community people as	Ignorant, poorly informed, lacking expertise, limited in scope	Egocentric	Most direct source of information, articulate in their own view, essential in determining relevance
Planning	By experts; either keep community people uninformed, or inform them so that they will agree	Laissez-faire	Generated by community people, learning by doing

Source: Maruyama 1974.

in each. Thus the mind-set of the second column may have a second variant relevant to bureaucratically dominated centralized economies that are (or were) managed primarily for the benefit of a favored class or nomenklatura. Also the third mind-set may have another variant besides the traditional communitarian approach shown in the table: the second may relate to regional (as opposed to local) systems of a type now emerging in the European Economic Community or in the Great Lakes Basin bioregion.

Maruyama's schema presupposes that the idea of fully objective science is an extreme abstraction. That sustainability could usefully be addressed objectively with respect only to its biophysical foundations is similarly unrealistic, as is implied in previous sections above. Generally it is now recognized that an ethics of improved equity must go hand-in-hand with an ethics of sustainability (WCED 1987) and that both will influence the selection of biophysical measures of sustainability. If Maruyama's schema has some relevance, then the epistemology (the dominant enquiry methods) and aesthetics (what people enjoy)—both relevant to a primary mind-set—will also influence the choice of measures of sustainability.

Decisionmaking in such issues in western countries is ostensibly quite pragmatic: a goal or vision that is widely shared in society is identified and endorsed through a participatory or representative political process, and means are then created to work toward achieving the goal or realizing the vision. Academic emphases on abstract features of different mind-sets within the policy may foster discord and hinder achievement of the shared purpose, at least in the short run (Norton 1991).

We grant Norton's pragmatic argument sketched above. Nevertheless scientists tend generally to be disciplined into particular mind-sets, paradigms, methodologies, rituals, and so forth. Scientists tend to ignore the advice of the oracle to know thyself! They tend to select items from within their received disciplinary mind-set, add a modicum of intellectual or practical value to the items, and then offer them to their peers or sell them to some client. This general process may be discernible within a quasi-competitive process such as a conference to identify appropriate biophysical measures of sustainability. Unless the process by which such measures are to be selected is intended to be entirely pragmatic, some further attention to these mind-sets may help to understand the proposals of different scientists.

Figure 22-2 is an attempt to show how three mind-sets, very approximately as expanded from the sketch by Maruyama (1974) given in table 22-2, relate currently to different academic disciplines that may have something to contribute to the issue of sustainability. Compared to physicists, on the one hand, and political scientists, on the other, ecologists as a set, at about the middle of the left-right spectrum, may comprise three subgroups of roughly equivalent strength. An ecological set, as it relates to sustainability in fisheries, is examined further in table 22-3.

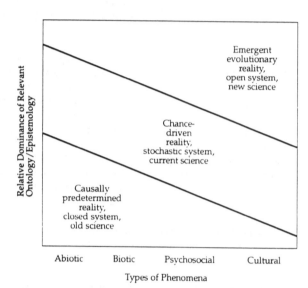

Note: Scientific and technical professionals commonly balance their work or iterate between three different mind-sets. Few have an explicit strategy or procedure for doing so. The ecosystem approach is just one of a variety of initiatives that involve some mixture of the three, with an emphasis on elaborating concepts and methods in the new science.

Presumably a set of measures of sustainability will need to serve all major interests as reflected in the contemporary political balance concerning the natural phenomenon to be sustained, for example, with respect to a particular fishery. Also if only one measure of sustainability is sought for a particular natural phenomenon, then that measure should be relevant within all the mind-sets, if a workable, pragmatic consensus is needed to realize sustainability. Further, the actions proposed to achieve sustainability of a particular natural feature must take into account, and perhaps help to modify, the evolving nature of human societies, that is, they must be oriented toward process.

It is obvious that the analysis sketched above does not lead directly to the identification of a particular measure of sustainability. But it may help to explain why different scientists prefer different measures or why particular interest groups in society favor one measure over another.

Table 22–3: Different Schools within Ecology, by Broad Mind-sets and Types of Fisheries

Mind-set	*Key concepts*	*Representative researchers*[a]	*Type of fisheries*
Causally predetermined reality, closed system	Environmental determinism with respect to spatial occurrence of particular species as fixed entities or ecological production at a particular trophic level	G. A. Gulland, M. B. Schaefer	Whaling and sealing; large finfisheries and shellfisheries in shelf seas
Chance-driven reality, stochastic system	Ecological association due entirely to the adaptive capabilities of individual organisms of species populations subject to natural selection through unpredictable environmental fluctuations	P. A. Larkin, C. J. Walters	Moderate-scale artisanal fisheries, especially on anadromous stocks; aquaculture
Emergent evolutionary reality, open system	Ecosystem integrity or harmony due to self-organizing capabilities of many living components of the holarchically nested open system	H. A. Regier, R. A. Ryder	Small-scale artisanal fisheries; regional fisheries and bays

a. Fisheries scientists do not usually limit their involvement to a particular paradigm, hence the authors listed here have been involved with, but are not limited to, the relevant mind-set.

Role of science in sustainable development

Friedmann (1987), as discussed by Dorcey (1991), has identified four traditions concerning the role of science (or more broadly, knowledge) on issues like sustainability. These include policy analysis, which envisages science as capable of providing the best solutions within existing social and economic structures; social reform, which envisages the application of science to making government action more effective, with planning as a preeminently scientific activity, and making conventional politics subordinate; social learning, in which science, and social experimentation, can contribute to incremental societal change; and social mobilization, which, in contrast to the preceding three, asserts the primacy of direct collective action from below to transform society, with science playing some supportive role in this transformation.

It is unlikely that any formulation of science in sustainable development fits neatly within a single of these traditions. Nevertheless, certain patterns are apparent. Strict reliance on a biophysical measure of sustainability, for example, incorporates elements of the traditions of policy analysis and social reform. Considerations of equity, and of the significant political and social factors within each of the six kinds of fisheries described above, may be grounded primarily within the tradition of social learning. This tradition became more prominent in the late 1960s and early 1970s, with efforts to reform reflected in the incorporation of a concept of integrity in legislation, such as the 1972 U.S. Water Pollution Control Amendments. Use of science for social mobilization is coming to involve science related to fisheries in bioregional contexts (Kauffman and others 1992; RCFTW 1992).

It is, at least, evident that views on appropriate measures of sustainability are affected by perceptions of the appropriate role of science in the interaction between society and the natural environment. Understanding these perceptions may also help explain why different scientists or interest groups prefer different measures of sustainability.

Sustainability, development, and integrity

The concept of sustainability presupposes that the living systems of interest can accommodate some use and abuse without collapsing or transforming into a less desirable kind of living system. Thus the living system is expected to have some adaptive capabilities to accommodate our interventions and presumably also some recuperative capabilities to reconstitute itself in some way following some interval of inevitable excess on our part. That there are limits and thresholds to such accommodation, in the sense of Holling (1986), has been explored briefly for the Great

Lakes (Steedman and Regier 1987), with an inference that such discontinuities can and do occur with these ecosystems and with fish populations in them.

We intervene with living phenomenon at many levels from the suborganismal to the biosphere. Presumably all levels contribute to the sustainability of each level, and all levels of such a holarchic system have roughly equivalent value for us and deserve the necessary protection and sustenance.

In all of the holarchic levels, a capability for normal self-organization is the essential biophysical foundation. But what is normal self-organization for the increasing proportion of ecosystems in which cultural forces rival in strength the natural forces? This question may deserve more attention before we try to decide what a sufficient set of measures of sustainability would be. For the Great Lakes, and especially for the fish and fisheries of the Great Lakes, it may now be timely to stipulate, through a trans-jurisdictional political process and to a practically sufficient degree, what and how much of it should and can be sustained following appropriate remediation and rehabilitation. A constraint to keep transactional costs within bounds would spur careful consideration of choices of measures. Then all the statistical questions related to sampling and estimation can be addressed effectively.

We cannot say what manifestations of sustainable states of fisheries will be considered most desirable by future generations and suspect that preferences will in any case continue to evolve with time. Currently the characteristics of fisheries that are seen to be desirable on a sustainable basis differ considerably from one societal group to another and from one culture to another, owing to differing economic and social conditions. Just as we expect component living systems to be able to accommodate some degree of external intervention, we also expect a range of states to exist in which fisheries might be sustained according to differing mixes of levels at which other human activities are being sustained. Achieving and managing sustainability are thus likely to continue to be a dynamic process and to evolve as human needs and values change, both locally and globally. It is in this sense that we view sustainability and development, however inconsistent they may appear to be with each other, as inextricably mixed.

References

Alward, G. L. 1911. *The Development of the British Fisheries during the Nineteenth Century with Special Reference to the North Sea*. Grimsby, England: Grimsby News.

American Fisheries Society. 1990. "Proceedings of the Symposium on Effects of Climate Change on Fish." *Transactions of the American Fisheries Society* 119:2, pp. 173–389.

Beak Consultants Ltd. 1991. *Duffin Creek Watershed Study: Fisheries Component (Phase I)*. Final report for the Metropolitan Toronto and Region Conservation Authority. Downsview, Ont. Beak Consultants, Ltd.

Berkes, F., ed. 1989. *Common Property Resources: Ecology and Community-Based Sustainable Development*. London: Bellhaven Press.

Beverton, R. J. H., and S. J. Holt. 1957. *On the Dynamics of Exploited Fish Populations*. London: Her Majesty's Stationery Office.

Bocking, S. 1987. "The Origins of Aquatic Ecological Research in the Great Lakes Region." M.A. thesis, University of Toronto, Toronto.

Cairns, J., Jr., P. McCormick, and B. Niederlehner. 1991. "A Proposed Framework for Developing Indicators of Ecosystem Health for the Great Lakes Region." Council of Great Lakes Research Managers, International Joint Commission, Ottawa, Canada, and Washington, D.C.

Commissioners Appointed to Inquire into the Sea Fisheries of the United Kingdom. 1866. *Report of the Commissioners Appointed to Inquire into the Sea Fisheries of the United Kingdom*. London: Her Majesty's Stationery Office.

Cushing, D. H. 1988. *The Provident Sea*. Cambridge, England: Cambridge University Press.

Dorcey, A. H. J. 1991. "Towards Agreement in Water Management: An Evolving Sustainable Development Model." In A. H. J. Dorsey, ed., *Perspectives on Sustainable Development in Water Management: Towards Agreement in the Fraser River Basin*, pp. 555–86. Vancouver, B.C.: Westwater Research Centre.

Edwards, C. J., and H. A. Regier, eds. 1990. *An Ecosystem Approach to the Integrity of the Great Lakes in Turbulent Times*. Special Publication 90-4. Ann Arbor, Mich.: Great Lakes Fishery Commission.

Edwards, C. J., and R. A. Ryder. 1989. "Biological Surrogates of Mesotrophic Ecosystem Health in the Laurentian Great Lakes." Great Lakes Science Advisory Board, International Joint Commission, Windsor, Ont.

Egerton, F. N. 1985. "Overfishing or Pollution? Case History of a Controversy on the Great Lakes." Technical Report 41. Ann Arbor, Mich.: Great Lakes Fishery Commission.

FAO (Food and Agriculture Organization of the United Nations). 1973. "Proceedings of the Food and Agriculture Organization of the United Nations, Technical Conference on Fishery Management, Vancouver, B.C., A. W. H. Needler (Chair)." *Journal of the Fisheries Research Board of Canada* 30:12 (part 2), pp. 1925–2537.

Francis, G. R., J. J. Magnusson, H. A. Regier, and D. R. Halhelm. 1979. "Rehabilitating Great Lakes Ecosystems." Technical Report 37. Great Lakes Fishery Commission, Ann Arbor, Mich.

Friedmann, J. 1987. *Planning in the Public Domain: From Knowledge to Action.* Princeton, N.J.: Princeton University Press.

Garstang, W. 1900. "The Impoverishment of the Sea." *Journal of Marine Biological Association* (United Kingdom) 6, pp. 1–69.

GLSAB (Great Lakes Science Advisory Board). 1989. *Report of the Great Lakes Science Advisory Board to the International Joint Commission.* Ottawa, Ont., and Washington, D.C.

GLWQA (Great Lakes Water Quality Agreement). 1987. "Revised Great Lakes Water Quality Agreement of 1978." International Joint Commission, Ottawa, Ont., and Washington, D.C.

Graham, M. 1935. "Modern Theory of Exploiting a Fishery and Application to North Sea Trawling." *Journal du Conseil International pour l'Exploration de la Mer* 10, pp. 264–74.

—————. 1943. *The Fish Gate.* London: Faber.

Great Lakes Fishery Commission. 1992. "Strategic Vision of the Great Lakes Fishery Commission for the Decade of the 1990s." Ann Arbor, Mich.

Gulland, J. A. 1983. "World Resources of Fisheries and Their Management." In O. Kinne, ed., *Marine Ecology,* vol. 5, part 2, pp. 839–1060. London: John Wiley and Sons.

Holling, C. S. 1986. "The Resilience of Terrestrial Ecosystems: Local Surprise and Global Change." In W. C. Clark and R. E. Munn, eds., *Sustainable Development of the Biosphere,* pp. 292–317. Cambridge, England: Cambridge University Press.

Holt, S. J., and L. M. Talbot. 1978. *New Principles for the Conservation of Wild Living Resources.* Wildlife Monographs 59. *Journal of Wildlife Management* 43 (supplement).

Huxley, T. H. 1884. "Inaugural Address of the Fishery Conferences." *Fisheries Exhibition Literature* 4, pp. 1–19.

Karr, J. R., K. D. Fausch, P. L. Angermeier, P. R. Yant, and I. J. Schlosser. 1986. "Assessing Biological Integrity of Running Waters: A Method and Its Rationale." Illinois Natural History Survey Special Publication 5. Champaign, Ill.

Kasahara, H. 1961. "Fisheries Resources of the North Pacific Ocean, Part 1." *H. R. MacMillan Lectures in Fisheries.* Vancouver, B.C.: University of British Columbia.

Kauffman, J., P. Rennick, H. A. Regier, J. A. Holmes, and G. A. Wichert. 1992. "Metro Waterfront Environmental Study." Metropolitan Toronto Planning Departments, Toronto, Ont.

Larkin, P. A. 1965. "North American Fishery Potential." In *The Fisheries of North America: The First North American Fisheries Conference, April 30–May 5, 1965.* Washington, D.C.: Government Printing Office.

—————. 1977. "An Epitaph for the Concept of Maximum Sustainable Yield." *Transactions of the American Fisheries Society* 106, pp. 1–11.

Loftus, K. H., and H. A. Regier, eds. 1972. "Proceedings of the 1971 Symposium on Salmonid Communities in Oligotrophic Lakes." *Journal of Fisheries Research Board of Canada* 29, pp. 613–986.

Marsh, G. P. 1857. "Report Made under Authority of the Legislature of Vermont on the Artificial Propagation of Fish." Free Press Print, Burlington, Vt.

Maruyama, M. 1974. "Paradigmatology and Its Application to Cross-disciplinary, Cross-professional, and Cross-cultural Communication." *Cybernetics* 17, pp. 136–56.

McHugh, J. L. 1970. "Trends in Fishery Research." In N. G. Benson, ed., *A Century of Fisheries in North America,* pp. 25–56. Bethesda, Md.: American Fisheries Society.

Meyer, P. F. 1947. "Raubbau in Meer? Ein Beitrag zur Überfischungsfrage unserer Meere." Hans A. Kuene Verlag, Hamburg, Germany.

Milner, J. W. 1874. "Report on the Fisheries of the Great Lakes: The Result of Inquiries Prosecuted in 1871 and 1872." In *Report, 1872—73 (U.S. Fish Commission).* Washington, D.C.: Government Printing Office.

Nettle, R. 1857. *The Salmon Fisheries of the St. Lawrence and Its Tributaries.* Montreal, Quebec: John Lovell.

Norton, B. G. 1991. *Toward Unity among Environmentalists.* New York: Oxford University Press.

Petersen, C. B. J. 1903. "What Is Overfishing?" *Journal of Marine Biological Association* (United Kingdom) 6, pp. 587—94.

Pinkerton, E., ed. 1989. *Co-Operative Management of Local Fisheries: New Directions for Improved Management and Community Development.* Vancouver, B.C.: University of British Columbia Press.

Pisani, D. 1984. "Fish Culture and the Dawn of Concern over Water Pollution in the United States." *Environmental Review* 8, pp. 117–31.

Raleigh, R. F. 1982. "Habitat Suitability Index Models: Brook Trout." FWS/OBS-82/10:24. U.S. Department of the Interior, Washington, D.C.

Rapport, D. J., H. A. Regier, and T. C. Hutchinson. 1985. "Ecosystem Behavior under Stress." *American Naturalist* 125, pp. 617–40.

Rawson Academy of Aquatic Science. 1989. *Towards an Ecosystem Charter for the Great Lakes–St. Lawrence.* Occasional Paper 1. Ottawa, Ont.

RCFTW (Royal Commission on the Future of the Toronto Waterfront). 1992. *Regeneration, Toronto's Waterfront and the Sustainable City: Final Report.* David Crombie, Commissioner. Toronto, Ont.

Regier, H. A. 1992a. "Ecosystem Integrity in the Great Lakes Basin and Historical Sketch of Ideas and Actions." *Journal of Aquatic Ecosystem Health* 1, pp. 25–37.

————. 1992b. "Indicators of Ecosystem Integrity." In D. Mackenzie, ed., *Proceedings of the International Symposium on Ecological Indicators, Ft. Lauderdale, Florida, September 1990,* pp. 183–200. Barking, England: Elsevier Applied Science Publishers.

Regier, H. A., and V. C. Applegate. 1972. "Historical Review of the Management Approach to Exploitation and Introduction in SCOL Lakes." *Journal of Fisheries Research Board of Canada* 29, pp. 183–692.

Ricker, W. E. 1946. "Production and Utilization of Fish Populations." *Ecological Monograph* 16, pp. 374–91.

————. 1954. "Stock and Recruitment." *Journal of Fisheries Research Board of Canada* 11, pp. 559–623.

————. 1958. "Handbook of Computations for Biological Statistics of Fish Populations." *Bulletin of the Fisheries Research Board of Canada* 119.

Russell, E. S. 1931. "Some Theoretical Considerations on the Overfishing Problem." *Journal du Conseil International pour l'Exploration de la Mer* 6, pp. 3–20.

————. 1939. "An Elementary Treatment of the Overfishing Problem." *Rapport Procès-Verbaux des Réunions* (Conseil International pour l'Exploration de la Mer) 110, pp. 5–14.

Ryder, R. A., and C. J. Edwards, eds. 1985. *A Conceptual Approach for the Application of Biological Indicators of Ecosystem Quality in the Great Lakes Basin.* International Joint Commission, Windsor, Ont., and Great Lakes Fishery Commission, Ann Arbor, Mich.

Select Committee on Sea Fisheries. 1893. *Report of the Select Committee on Sea Fisheries.* London: Her Majesty's Stationery Office.

Steedman, R. J. 1988. "Modification and Assessment of an Index of Biotic Integrity to Quantify Stream Quality in Southern Ontario." *Canadian Journal of Fisheries and Aquatic Sciences* 45, pp. 492–501.

Steedman, R. J., and H. A. Regier. 1987. "Ecosystem Science for the Great Lakes: Perspectives on Degradative Transformations." *Canadian Journal of Fisheries and Aquatic Sciences* 44 (supplement 2), pp. 95–103.

Thompson, W. F., and N. Freeman. 1930. "History of the Halibut Fishery." *Report of the International Fishery Commission* (Seattle, Wash.) 5.

Troadec, J. P. 1983. "Practices and Prospects for Fisheries Development and Management: The Case of Northwest African Fisheries." In B. J. Rothschild, ed., *Global Fisheries: Perspectives for the 1980s,* pp. 97–122. New York: Springer-Verlag.

United Nations. 1984. *United Nations Convention on the Law of the Sea.* New York: United Nations.

Van Hise, C. R. 1911. *The Conservation of Natural Resources in the United States.* New York: MacMillan Company.

WCED (World Commission on Environment and Development). 1987. *Our Common Future.* Report of the World Commission on Environment and Development, chaired by G. H. Brundtland. Oxford, England: Oxford University Press.

Went, A. E. J. 1972. "Seventy Years Agrowing: A History of the International Council for the Exploration of the Sea, 1902–1972." *Rapport Procès-Verbaux des Réunions* (Conseil International pour l'Exploration de la Mer) 165.

23

Sustainability of Managed Temperate Forest Ecosystems

Jerry F. Franklin

We would expect foresters to know a lot about sustainable management. Forests take long periods of time to develop, and foresters have been managing temperate forest ecosystems for several centuries. They are used to taking a long view, planning for forests and planting trees that are not likely to be harvested within their professional, and often personal, life span. At the same time, the concept of sustainability in forestry has often been narrow and limited to continued production of wood fiber. Similarly, our scientific understanding of the basis for forest productivity and techniques for assessing trends in productivity, especially of the entire ecosystem and over long periods of time, is not very robust.

This chapter reviews what we know about the sustainability of managed temperate forest ecosystems. Since this is such an immense topic, the review is primarily an overview with an emphasis on recent knowledge and emerging concepts of the productivity and maintenance of forest ecosystems rather than a comprehensive review of the last 100 years of forest science.

The chapter begins with a definition of sustainability, taking a broad view of forest productivity and sustainability rather than simply focusing on the production of wood products. The first major section considers the status of our knowledge of major ecosystem processes related to sustainability; it will be clear that much critical information on long-term productivity is lacking, particularly on the soil ecological subsystem, and other data, such as on respiration, are nearly impossible to gather. Next, biophysical measurements of sustainability are considered along with some suggestions for a minimal monitoring program. An extensive section on alternative management approaches follows; development and application of alternative silvicultural and landscape practices offer immense potential for integrating sustainable production of environmental goods and services with commodities. A section describing existing approaches, models, and data sets follows. The review concludes with a series of proposals for managed temperate forests to (a) develop critical scientific information, (b) implement and test new management systems, and (c) assess long-term productivity.

Definition of sustainability

Sustainability refers to the maintenance of the *potential* for our forest and associated aquatic ecosystems to produce the same quantity and quality of goods and services in perpetuity. Potential is emphasized since it makes implicit the option to return to alternative conditions rather than focusing exclusively on current conditions. This concept of sustainability considers a broad range of goods and services. It includes, for example, retaining the forest's capacity to provide functional services, such as regulating the flow of streams and minimizing the loss of nutrients and soil as a result of erosion. It means an ability to provide habitat, either currently or at some future time, for the full array of animal and plant organisms on the site. And, of course, sustainability means the continuing capacity to provide the same quantity and quality of products for human consumption.

The basis for sustainability lies in maintaining the physical and biological elements of productivity. Hence, sustainability requires that we prevent the following:

- Degradation of the productive capacity of our forest lands and the associated water bodies, that is, net loss of productivity, and

- Loss of genetic diversity, including extirpation of species, that is, net loss of genetic potential.

Each of these principles has both an ecological and an ethical basis; even though they are human constructs, they can be objectively defined in ecological terms. Principle two—no net loss of genetic potential—is probably the most fundamental, since we can sometimes restore productive capacity to degraded ecosystems but have only very limited capacity to restore lost genetic potential. No principle, in my view, is absolute or inviolate. There will be times when rational, even ecologically sensitive, human beings will violate either principle. But when such violations occur, they should be done with society's full knowledge of the act and its consequences, not as a result of ignorance and not in secrecy.

Sustainability absolutely should *not* be viewed exclusively or primarily in terms of the short-term production of specific commodities, such as sawlogs or trophy ungulates, although such concerns are an appropriate component of a concept of sustainable forestry. Assuming the above, sustainable practices for managed temperate forest ecosystems should place a very high priority on practices that meet the dual standards of maintaining (a) productive capacity and (b) genetic diversity. It is essential to maintain a broad view of productivity—goods and services—and of the spatial and temporal scales to which it is to be applied rather than to adopt a narrow construct that focuses solely on the production of wood fiber.

Status of knowledge of major ecosystem processes

There is a substantial base of knowledge on the components and processes that are the basis of productivity in temperate forest ecosystems. Foresters and forest scientists have contributed substantially to this base during the last century, although their contributions have tended to be narrowly focused on trees, wood production, and managed forests. Furthermore, the ecosystem paradigm is of relatively recent origin. Major boosts to our understanding of forests have come as a result of recent research programs that have focused on forests as ecosystems. The contributions of the International Biological Programme are particularly notable at both the international and national levels (Reichle 1981; Edmonds 1981). Programs centered on individual sites, such as Coweeta Hydrologic Laboratory (North Carolina; Swank and Crossley 1988), the Hubbard Brook (New Hampshire; Bormann and Likens 1981), and H. J. Andrews (Oregon; Edmonds 1981) experimental forests, have also contributed major advances to the knowledge of forest ecosystems.

A general review of the major components and processes of ecosystems that underline productivity is provided in this section, which considers the physical and biotic elements that are essential to the productivity of temperate forests. The physical variables that act directly on the biota (the operational environment) are distinguished from second- and third-order environmental variables, such as elevation and aspect, which are indirect influences. Although a secondary variable, soils are considered in some detail because of their influence on moisture and nutrient regimes, their importance to sustainability, and their susceptibility to human influences, both positive and negative. The biotic components of productivity, including the "ecosystem support staff" of smaller organisms, such as decomposers, are considered along with the photosynthetically active primary producers, such as trees.

Identification and discussion of important ecosystem processes, such as productivity and decomposition, are also covered. Ecological definitions of productivity are presented and contrasted with traditional forestry definitions. Natural variation in rates of ecosystem processes and recovery rates are also considered.

Physical components of productivity

Productivity comprises physical elements (the operational environment) and physical variables (such as soil and elevation).

THE OPERATIONAL ENVIRONMENT
At the most fundamental level, the biota respond to a relatively small set of physical factors: light, carbon dioxide, temperature, moisture, nutrients, mechanical forces, and toxic chemicals. This includes that part of the biota responsible for providing the energy base for the whole ecosystem,

for example, organisms with chlorophyll that are capable of photosynthetically capturing the sun's energy. These physical elements are sometimes referred to as the operational environment in an effort to distinguish them from physical variables, such as soil, elevation, or aspect, that indirectly influence biotic activity through their effect on these operational factors, the ones that the biota are actually sensing and to which they are responding (Waring and Major 1964).

Several of these variables can be quickly disposed of in this review since they are generally viewed as constants in temperate forest regions. Light, for example, is typically not a limiting factor in temperate forest regions. Sufficient light is generally available throughout the year even though the intensity is obviously greater in the summer than in the winter. Hence, light does not seriously constrain photosynthetic activity even during winter months, assuming that temperature and moisture conditions are suitable. Temperate forests in northwestern North America provide a good example of this, since mild, wet winters allow a substantial amount of the annual photosynthesis to occur outside the growing season (Edmonds 1981, chapter 10; Waring and Franklin 1979).

The carbon dioxide content of the atmosphere is, in contrast, often viewed as a limiting factor for productivity and, over the short term, as a constant. The atmospheric concentration of carbon dioxide is, of course, gradually increasing, and the potential impact of this increase on productivity of green plants is a controversial topic currently discussed and debated by scientists and participants attempting to assess impacts of global change on productivity. Predictions vary from little or no response to the increased levels of carbon dioxide to predictions of significant increases in plant productivity. An analysis of how productivity responds to increases in carbon dioxide is beyond the scope of this review and is not considered further here; the reader is referred to Adams and others 1990; Bazzaz 1990; Easmus and Jarvis 1989; and Jarvis 1989 for discussions of this topic.

Mechanical forces actually cover a variety of mechanical effects that can limit productivity through their direct impact on the green plants or other ecosystem processes. Examples include heavy snow or ice loads that damage or break trees; powerful winds that break twigs, branches, and boles of trees; and floods. Excluded from the endemic operational environment are catastrophic mechanical disturbances that essentially destroy the existing ecosystem and initiate a new one, such as an intense wildfire or volcanic eruption.

Toxic materials provide a chemical equivalent to the physical forces in the operational environment of the forest. These can be natural materials that are found in the soil or atmosphere of a region. For example, excessive magnesium levels in the ultrabasic metamorphosed type of rock known as serpentine effectively exclude many organisms and retard growth of many others. High atmospheric levels of sulphur compounds associated with hydrothermal vents might be another example of a natural chemical toxin. However, most of the toxic chemicals that are discussed today are of anthropogenic origin (Aber and others 1989), such as concentrations of atmospheric ozone and acid fogs. As with elevated levels of carbon dioxide, an analysis of the effects of various atmospheric and soil pollutants of anthropogenic origin is beyond the scope of this review and are not considered here.

MAJOR OPERATIONAL VARIABLES

The operational environmental elements of temperature, moisture, and nutrients stand out as variables responsible for most of the variability in productivity among temperate forest ecosystems. Levels of these variables vary widely among temperate forest sites on continental, regional, and even local scales. Multivariate analyses of the operational environment invariably identify some combination of temperature, moisture, and nutrients as major controllers of distribution and productivity of the forest community (see Gholz 1982; Zobel and others 1976).

Temperature is typically the primary operational physical factor controlling the distribution and productivity of forest ecosystems over regions and elevational gradients. Local variations in temperature regimes can also be substantial, however, such as on steep slopes of contrasting aspect or as a result of topographic conditions, such as a depression that accumulates and forms a frost pocket. Temperature directly controls various chemical and physical processes (such as photosynthesis, decomposition, and water uptake) and, indirectly, through its effects on moisture regime, controls potential evapotranspiration.

Moisture, as an operational element, is sensed by trees and other plants in terms of internal plant moisture stress (Waring and Schlesinger 1985).

The moisture regime is, however, the result of a complex interaction involving the balance between water uptake, which is generally from water stored in the soil, and water loss, which is primarily the result of loss to the atmosphere through stomata or openings in the leaves. Hence, daily and seasonal patterns in the intensity of the gradient from soil to plant to atmosphere are critical. Many indirect measures are used to provide an integrated index to overall moisture conditions of a forested site. Direct measurements typically mark internal plant moisture stress at selected times of year using pressurized chambers.

Nutrients are a third operational variable that typically controls forest productivity. Indeed, nutrients have received an extraordinary amount of attention from foresters because this is often the only environmental variable that is readily subject to human manipulation. Included here would be all of the macro- and micronutrients that green plants require, although some, such as nitrogen, have received much more attention than others. There is substantial regional variance in the relative importance of nutrients and moisture as limiting factors on productivity. In much of the world's temperate mesic forests, moisture is available throughout most of the summer; analyses of such areas, such as eastern North America and eastern Asia, including Japan, typically identify nutrients as a more important variable than moisture. In contrast, moisture is typically ranked as more important than nutrients in northwestern North America, where there is substantial moisture deficit in summer (Edmonds 1981; Waring and Franklin 1979; Zobel and others 1976).

In conclusion, the physical operational environment of a forest can be defined in terms of relatively few variables. The most important of these in influencing productivity are temperature, moisture, and nutrients.

SOIL AS AN ELEMENT OF PRODUCTIVITY

Foresters often focus on soil as the physical basis for productivity, which is reasonable given the direct relationship that soil has to two of the three operational variables: moisture and nutrients. It is the amount and condition of the soil that largely control the moisture and nutritional regime to which the tree is subjected. Consequently, human impacts on the soil's ability to provide water and nutrients can have a dramatic impact on forest productivity and may be either positive or negative (Grier and others 1989; Harvey and Neuenschwander 1991). Furthermore, impacts can be very long lasting.

As a physical medium, soils provide several functions: storage of moisture (a portion of which is available to plants), source and storage of nutrients, site for anchorage by plants, and habitat for critical plant symbionts, such as mycorrhizal-forming fungi and other organisms essential to ecosystem processes. Both physical and chemical aspects of the soil are important. Physical aspects include such variables as depth, drainage, bulk density, porosity (especially macropores), texture, and temperature; these variables, in turn, influence conditions critical to the biota, such as aeration (oxygen content), capacity to hold moisture, and availability of moisture. Important chemical aspects of the soil include quantities and qualities of the various macro- and micronutrients and the rates at which they are made available.

Biotic components of productivity

From a perusal of any soil textbook, it is clear that we know quite a bit about the chemical and physical processes of soil, but not nearly as much about their biota and biological functioning (Jenny 1980). Biota provide the other essential components of productivity. This includes the primary producers of the ecosystem—the organisms with chlorophyll that are capable of capturing the sun's energy through photosynthesis—and the most important of these in forest ecosystems are the trees. It also includes many other essential organisms that support the ecosystem: plants, animals, fungi, monera (such as bacteria), algae, and protozoa that decompose organic substances, make nutrients available, and assist the primary producers. Fungi that form mycorrhizae with vascular plants, thereby facilitating moisture and nutrient uptake from the soil, are a classic example of the latter, although other relationships may be of comparable importance, as in the case of the endophytic communities found on leaves and needles (Carroll 1980).

The importance of the biotic components to sustained productivity of the ecosystem should be obvious; nevertheless, it seems to be absent from many discussions of productivity and sustainability and is not made explicit in many others. The principle that sustainability requires maintenance of genetic diversity explicitly recognizes the importance of the biotic components and may be, in fact, the most important practical reason for conserving biological diversity in all of its forms.

PRIMARY PRODUCERS

Relatively little needs to be said about the importance of green plants to the productivity of our forest ecosystems. Green plants, and specifically trees, are the basic agents for capturing energy, the energetic base on which the entire ecosystem operates. Forest ecologists generally recognize that different species of trees, either singly or in combination, have different capabilities to capture the potential productive capacity of a site. The fact that different genotypes of the same species may differ markedly in their productivity on the same site is also generally understood and is the basis for various tree breeding programs to develop genotypes that have improved capabilities, such as more rapid growth or greater resistance to disease.

Nevertheless, there are many important gaps in our understanding of how species composition affects either short- or long-term forest productivity. For example, definitive theoretical and empirical information is still lacking on the relative yield of mixtures of species versus a single-species monoculture. This is also true of contrasting forest structures: yields from an even-aged stand with a single canopy layer versus an uneven-aged stand with multiple layers of canopy.

The fact that trees and their production are typically used to assess potential productivity of a forest site creates further complications. For example, trees and genotypes indigenous to a locality may not be as capable of exploiting the productive resources of a site as exotic species. New Zealand provides some outstanding examples of this phenomenon. *Pinus radiata*—a pine endemic to a small area in California—grows very rapidly in New Zealand and is highly productive of commercial wood products. Many of these exotic pine forests are grown on sites that were originally grasslands. Another North American pine, *Pinus contorta*, has escaped from cultivation in New Zealand and is forming forests at elevations substantially above the original timberline formed by native trees; this ability to grow at lower temperatures obviously has the potential to alter drastically the structure and function of these previously alpine habitats. Again, the point is that trees or other plants native to a habitat may not be the genotypes capable of achieving maximum short- or long-term productivity on the site. At the same time, local species or genotypes may well be optimal for other ecosystem functions, including the provision of habitat for native species.

Besides determining the rate of energy fixation or production for the site, primary producers also have the potential to alter significantly the soil's physical and chemical conditions. This can have either positive or negative effects on the long-term potential of a site and obviously should be considered in selecting genotypes, species, or combinations of species for management purposes. The ability of some families or genera of vascular plants to support nitrogen-fixing symbionts in root nodules is a well-known example; representative tree genera with this ability are *Acacia, Alnus*, and *Robinia*. Some tree species, such as members of the *Cupressaceae*, as well as many deciduous hardwoods, produce a base-rich litter that, among other things, reduces acidity, increases levels of nutrients, and results in richer and more active communities of organisms in the soil. Other tree species produce litter that increases soil acidity and decreases availability of soil nutrients. *Picea* and *Tsuga* are well-known coniferous examples. An extreme example of the negative effect of specific tree species on soil properties is *Eucalyptus*, which, over time, generates beneath it a bleached, nutrient-poor zone sometimes referred to as an eggcup podzol.

Clearly, we need to recognize explicitly (a) the importance of the genetic component of the primary producers at both the specific and intraspecific levels in influencing attainable short- and long-term productivity and (b) the circular problems inherent in using the productivity of trees as *the* measure of productivity of a site.

TREE SYMBIONTS AND DECOMPOSERS

The support staff of an ecosystem include many other organisms that carry out important functions, such as facilitating primary producers (the fungi that form mycorrhizae) or participating in the decomposition of organic materials and release of the nutrients they contain (many invertebrates, bacteria, and fungi). These organisms make up the bulk of the biological diversity found in forest ecosystems but are rarely explicitly recognized; hence, they are sometimes referred to as the invisible or hidden biodiversity of ecosystems (Franklin 1992).

Many of these groups are represented by several species, which may provide some functional redundancy, but also an array of genetic types that are closely adapted to specific niches. As a result, dominance among these organisms can shift seasonally or over longer periods in response to environmental changes and maintain a high level of functioning. For example, we know how fungi capable of forming mycorrhizae with trees shift dominance seasonally with soil moisture and temperature conditions, thereby maintaining optimal mycorrhizal function for the tree symbionts.

Although we have begun to appreciate the importance of such "lesser" organisms to ecosystem function, detailed knowledge of their distribution, community structure, ecology, functioning and, importantly, response to disturbances that disrupt or destroy the forest is not available. Developing this information is a high priority for scientists; in the meantime, applying management practices that are likely to conserve this functionally important diversity is a high priority for foresters.

HERBIVORES AND PATHOGENS
Herbivores and pathogens are a group of organisms that feed on and sometimes damage or kill the primary producers. Although foresters have tended to focus on the negative impacts that these organisms have on short-term productivity, herbivores and pathogens also make important functional contributions to the ecosystem.

Herbivores can have very important influences on productivity over either short- or long-term periods. For example, epidemic-level outbreaks of moths can defoliate forests for one or more seasons, drastically reducing tree growth and increasing mortality. Bark beetles are another common cause of death in trees. Grazing by ungulates, such as deer or elk, can alter the composition and structure of forests, significantly affecting their ability to regenerate and produce.

Disease organisms (rusts and various fungi capable of infecting living trees) as well as decomposers and herbivores can also reduce growth and cause the decay and death of trees and other plants. Yet many of the effects of herbivores and pathogens are essential to the long-term functioning of the ecosystem. They contribute to the natural thinning process, for example, by reducing vigor or killing individual trees. A continuing flow of dead trees is essential to provide the coarse woody debris essential to a variety of ecosystem functions (Franklin, Shugart, and Harmon 1987). Similarly, decay organisms may create cavities and other habitat niches in living trees. There is some suggestion that moderate levels of herbivory may actually contribute to overall productivity of an ecosystem by increasing the availability of nutrients and reducing competition.

Herbivores and pathogens are clearly important biotic elements that influence the productivity and sustainability of forest ecosystems. A substantial base of information exists on the negative impacts of pathogens and herbivores, and it is clear that, in some places and at some times, these may be a dominant influence. Very little quantitative data are available on the positive contributions these organisms may make to the productivity and sustainability of ecosystem.

Major ecosystem processes associated with productivity

A great deal of research has been conducted on the function and structure of forest ecosystems during the last three decades, with the International Biological Programme providing much of the impetus. Much of this work has dealt with the capture and fixation of energy through photosynthesis (primary productivity) and with cycles of material (carbon, nutrients, and water): pathways, rates, and controls. An important result of this research has been a new appreciation of the importance of structure and structural complexity to ecosystem function, including long-term productivity and the provision of habitat for a variety of forest-dwelling organisms. We now recognize, for example, that dead trees and tree parts are as important to the functioning of the forest as live trees (Franklin, Shugart, and Harmon 1987).

DEFINITION OF ECOSYSTEM PRODUCTIVITY
Various measures of ecosystem productivity and associated formulas are used by ecologists in assessing ecosystem productivity. These are substantially different from measures used by foresters, as will be discussed in a following section. Unrecognized, these differences are frequently the basis for significant, often public, disagreements among ecologists and foresters about the productivity of natural forests. Productivity is a rate and is typically measured on a yearly basis as mass per unit of area per year. In these formulas, autotrophs are organisms that capture energy from primary sources (primary producers or green plants), while heterotrophs are organisms that use organic compounds created by the primary producers as their source of energy (all animals).

The most common measures of productivity used by ecologists are gross primary productivity (GPP), net primary productivity (NPP), and net ecosystem productivity (NEP; Kimmins 1987). Gross primary productivity encompasses all of the productivity of (energy captured by) an ecosystem, forest or otherwise. The formula for GPP is

$$GPP = NPP + Ra$$

where Ra is the respiration of the autotrophs in the ecosystem. Net primary productivity is

$$NPP = {}^\wedge B + L + C$$

where $^\wedge B$ is the change in biomass, L is total litter production (including tree mortality), and C is consumption of green plants by herbivores. Net ecosystem productivity is calculated as

$$NEP = NPP - Re$$

where Re is the respiration of the entire ecosystem (both autotrophs and heterotrophs). Values for these formulas are typically reported as grams per square meter per year or metric tons per hectare per year.

These formulas contrast markedly with foresters' calculations of productivity, which typically involve only the production of bole or wood volume and are based on measures of tree growth, mortality, and, sometimes, birth (ingrowth). The differing viewpoints on productivity have profound consequences for examining older forest ecosystems where both GPP and NPP may remain high even though increments of additional wood mass have fallen to low or negative levels.

Although the concepts and formula may be quite clear, actually calculating the productivity of forest ecosystems is extremely difficult. Estimating respiration is one of the serious problems in determining either GPP or NEP; although respiration can be estimated for individual components, developing reasonable estimates for the entire ecosystem is impossible with existing technologies.

PRIMARY PRODUCTIVITY

The environmental factors controlling primary productivity in forest ecosystems have been extensively studied (Waring and Schlesinger 1985). As noted earlier, temperature, moisture, and availability of nutrients are the key variables.

Estimates of NPP have been calculated for numerous forest ecosystems (see, for example, Cannell 1982; Reichle 1981). The NPP variables of living biomass increment, litter production, and consumption by herbivores aboveground are all susceptible to measurement, albeit with some difficulty in the case of litter production and consumption. But perhaps the most difficult aspect of measuring NPP is the productivity that occurs belowground.

Most estimates of NPP for forest ecosystems are only for the aboveground portion because of the immense technical difficulties associated with estimating belowground productivity. Not only is there no easy method of observing and measuring belowground, but there is also considerable controversy about the accuracy of the labor-intensive approaches currently under use (Kimmins 1987).

The difficulty of measuring belowground productivity is extremely unfortunate because of the supposed overall importance of belowground productivity to the carbon budget of the forest. Recent research has shown that the belowground portion of the ecosystem is very dynamic, with high rates of turnover in fine roots and mycorrhizal fungal hyphae. Only 20 percent of the biomass is found belowground in a typical forest, and earlier studies assumed that belowground productivity was proportional to the mass. Unfortunately, energy demands may be as high as 50 to 70 percent of the photosynthate produced by the forest due to the high turnover of roots and hyphae.

It is also known that the energy requirements belowground increase on sites that are deficient in nutrients or water, because more fine roots and hyphae must be produced to exploit the soil mass for the required materials. One very important implication of this finding is that some or all of the increases in productivity associated with forest fertilization may represent shifts in the allocation of energy from belowground to aboveground; hence, the observed increases in aboveground productivity may not represent increases in total productivity of the ecosystem.

These discoveries about the energetic requirements and productivity of the belowground portions of terrestrial ecosystems, including forests, are forcing drastic reassessments. First, they have made clear that basing conclusions about total NPP only on aboveground measurements is highly questionable, if not dangerous. Today, any estimates of ecosystem productivity that do not include the belowground portion of the forest are open to challenge. This specifically includes any assessment of long-term trends in productivity and responses to experimental treatments, such as thinning and fertilization. Consequently, valid observational and experimental studies are relatively rare, and almost all of the older literature on productivity of the forest ecosystem is open to question.

A second important implication is that the trees and other green plants are critical sources of energy to sustain the extremely dynamic belowground ecosystem. In effect, the tree has been shown to be as important to the vitality of the soil as the soil has traditionally been viewed to be to the tree. Loss of this source of energy as a result of forest removal, even for short periods, is hypothesized to cause the failure of reforestation efforts and long-term loss of forestland to vegetation other than forests (Perry and others 1988).

Calculating NPP requires an estimation of litter production over the period of measurement. This is generally done by periodically collecting and weighing litterfall within the forest stand of interest. Numerous well-documented techniques involve litter traps placed on the forest floor that collect insect frass, flowering parts, leaves, twigs, and branches.

Few litterfall studies and calculations include the largest pieces of litter: dead trees. Current tree mortality is technically part of the litter factor in the NPP equation. Long-term studies of tree populations are necessary to obtain accurate data on annual rates of mortality because of high year-to-year variability, which often includes a major stochastic, or random, component (Franklin, Shugart, and Harmon 1987). For this reason, many studies of ecosystem productivity ignore tree mortality even though tree death may contribute as much organic material as the smaller, traditional components of litterfall (Sollins 1982).

Obtaining accurate measures of consumption by herbivores, the third element of the NPP equation, is very difficult although some techniques provide an approximation. Fortunately, aboveground herbivory is relatively insignificant in healthy forest ecosystems (Kimmins 1987). Hence, assumed values are unlikely to produce major errors in calculating NPP. Herbivory belowground is much more poorly understood, however, and could be a major factor in any calculation of NPP.

DECOMPOSITION AND SECONDARY PRODUCTIVITY
Decomposition is probably second only to primary production as the most important ecosystem process. Decomposition is carried out by a variety of organisms that break down organic materials to release energy and nutrients:

organic compounds + decomposition = energy
+ carbon dioxide + water + nutrients.

Most of the secondary producers (organisms that use existing organic carbon compounds as their base of energy) found in forest ecosystems are decomposers or detritivores (organisms that feed on organic litter), and most of the secondary productivity in forest ecosystems is associated with decomposition or detrivory. Much information has been developed on rates and pathways of and controls on decomposition during recent years. Important environmental variables include the moisture and temperate conditions found on the site; both can limit rates of decomposition. Chemical attributes of the detritus or litter have a major influence on rates of decomposition. Lignin and nitrogen contents of leaf litter, for example, both have been shown to be important variables and are used in general equations for predicting rates of decomposition. The available biota is another critical variable. For example, soil arthropods play critical roles in fragmenting larger organic materials while feeding on and consuming portions of them, providing large surface areas for colonization by other decomposer organisms. Consequently, excluding or eliminating segments of the soil fauna can have significant impacts on rates of decomposition.

Decomposition of large or coarse woody debris, such as large standing dead trees (known as snags) and logs on the forest floor, is particularly complex and has only recently become the subject of intensive study (see, for example, Harmon and others 1986; Harmon and Chen 1992).

OTHER CRITICAL ECOSYSTEM PROCESSES
Primary production and decomposition have been singled out for attention in this review because of their importance to the sustained productivity of all ecosystems, including forests. Many other ecosystem processes are important, however, some of which have already been identified, such as consumption by herbivores. The identification and elaboration of these processes alone could fill several pages.

Nitrogen fixation is one additional process that requires mention, however, because of its importance to fertility of the soil and site. It has also been the subject of important recent discoveries. Nitrogen fixation involves the conversion of elemental nitrogen in the atmosphere to the biologically useful forms of ammonia or nitrate. Although physical processes such as lightning discharges can produce this conversion, much, if not most, of the nitrogen is fixed biologically.

Relatively few organisms are capable of nitrogen fixation (cyanobacteria). Although some of these are free-living organisms, many of the most important nitrogen fixers live in association with other organisms. Well-known examples are nitrogen-fixing organisms that live in root nodules of legumes (the pea family) or in several other genera of vascular plants, such as alder, and as components of lichens.

Forest ecosystem studies during the last decade have identified at least four additional locales for nitrogen fixation. An early discovery during the International Biological Programme was fixation by large foliose lichens, primarily *Lobaria oregana*, living in canopies of old-growth Douglas fir trees (Carroll 1980; Denison 1979). Current estimates place annual nitrogen fixation at 5 to 9 kilograms per hectare in a typical 500-year-old forest. Rotting wood, particularly large logs, can also be the site of significant nitrogen fixation (Harmon and others 1986), as can areas of rot within living trees; current estimates of annual nitrogen fixation in intact, natural old-growth forests are typically 3 to 5 kilograms per hectare. Two other sites discovered to be sites of nitrogen fixation in intact forest stands are the rhizosphere (regions immediately adjacent to tree roots in the soil) and leaf litter (Heath and others 1987).

Rates of nitrogen fixation can be very high during early stages of succession on forest sites, when legumes or other trees and shrubs with nitrogen-fixing symbionts are dominant elements. For example, annual rates of nitrogen fixation in young *Alnus rubra* stands can exceed 200 kilograms per hectare (Trappe and others 1967).

This discussion of spatial and temporal locales for nitrogen fixation is essential to any analysis of forest sustainability because of nitrogen's importance as a nutrient. Although some forest systems may actually have an excess of nitrogen as a result of chemically enriched rainfall, this is not generally the case. Hence, in designing sustainable forest management systems, foresters must consider the need to maintain organisms, structures, and successional stages that contribute to nitrogen fixation.

Structural aspects of forest ecosystems related to sustainability

Structural complexity is the critical link in ecosystem function, whether the manager is concerned with productivity, maintenance of other ecosystem processes, such as nitrogen fixation, or provision of habitat for wildlife and other elements in biodiversity. Structure provides a surrogate for many processes and organisms that would otherwise be difficult to measure (Franklin and others 1981). Structure is also the major ecosystem attribute that foresters can manipulate directly.

Structural attributes of ecosystems involve both individual categories of structures, such as living trees and snags, and their collective arrangement, that is, structural attributes of the stand.

INDIVIDUAL STRUCTURES

Dominant trees are major structural components of forests, particularly in older stands (Franklin and others 1981). Shade-intolerant or pioneer species are often prominent in this role. Dominant trees carry out critical processes, such as much of the photosynthesis, as well as provide diverse and essential habitat for other organisms. In older natural forests, the dominant trees may attain very large sizes (for example, 1 to 2 meters in diameter and 50 to 90 meters in height in northwestern North America). Their canopies and boles provide habitat for a large number of epiphytic organisms, such as mosses and lichens, and habitat for a large and diverse community of invertebrates. Dominant trees are also the source of two other key structural components of the forest: large standing dead trees and large logs on the forest floor.

Intermediate-sized trees of shade-tolerant species are also important structural components of forests. They create a range of tree sizes and typically contribute to intermediate levels of canopy, producing a stand that has a many-layered canopy extending from the ground to the top of the crowns.

Large snags and fallen logs, typically larger than 10 to 15 centimeters in diameter and collectively known as coarse woody debris, represent two other important individual structures found in natural forests (Franklin and others 1981; Harmon and others 1986; Maser and others 1988). Biologists have recognized the importance of snags to many species of wildlife for some time (Hunter 1990) but only recently began to recognize the numerous ecological benefits of coarse woody debris on the forest floor and in associated streams. These benefits range from geomorphic functions, in influencing erosional processes, to biological diversity, in providing habitat for a broad array of animal and plant organisms, to providing sources of energy and nutrients for these systems.

The change in attitude toward coarse woody debris reflects a dramatic new recognition that dead trees are as important as live trees to ecological functioning in a forest (Franklin and others 1987). Moreover, the dead tree structures may perform terrestrial or aquatic functions for many centuries because they decay or disappear from ecosystems slowly (Harmon and others 1986). Furthermore, functions change throughout the lifetime or gradual decay of a snag or log.

OVERALL STAND STRUCTURE

Overall structural heterogeneity is an important feature of almost all natural forests. The forest as a whole cannot be reduced simply to individual structures and aggregated into a whole. Heterogeneity in both the horizontal and vertical dimensions is a hallmark of natural and, especially, older forests.

Variations in the density of the overstory canopy, including complete gaps in the canopy, are an important element in stand-level structural diversity. A natural stand typically has locales where levels of light are higher and vegetation on the forest floor is better developed than in other areas, where dense tree foliage, especially of shade-tolerant species, produces a heavily shaded environment from which understory plants may be absent or nearly so.

The variability in light conditions, as well as belowground competition for moisture and nutrients, contributes to the complexity and richness of understories in many late-successional forests. These diverse understories can be critical for some organisms; for example, the old-growth *Picea sitchensis–Tsuga heterophylla* forests of the Alaskan panhandle provide essential habitat for Sitka black-tailed deer (*Odocoileus hemionus sitkensis*; Alaback 1984; Schoen and Kirchoff 1990). Research throughout the temperate forest regions of the world is showing that developing and maintaining diverse understory plant communities in forest stands are an important and complex undertaking, not simply a matter of manipulating crown density or levels of light.

STRUCTURES IN TRADITIONAL MANAGED STANDS

Structural attributes of temperate forest stands subject to traditional management are typically very different from those of natural stands. The most common managerial system has been the creation of even-aged, even-sized stands using clear-cutting and artificial reforestation (Oliver and Larson 1990). Such stands are highly simplified and lack many structural components, such as snags and logs, as well as stand-level structural complexity, such as multiple levels of canopy, chaotic tree spacing, and gaps.

Managed stands have been simplified in response to economic criteria—efficient management and high productivity of target tree species—in the belief that much of the structural complexity found in natural stands is not essential to sustained productivity of the site. The recent research, briefly reported here, on the role of structural diversity in maintaining the processes and organisms essential to forest sustainability is a major challenge to those assumptions.

Disturbances and ecosystem recovery rates

Responses of forest ecosystems to disturbances, including the pattern and rate of recovery, are highly dependent on the intensity and type of disturbance, which, in turn, determine the carryover of biological materials from the old or disturbed to the new or recovering ecosystem. This section briefly reviews disturbances, biological legacies, and rates of ecosystem recovery. A great deal of literature is available on disturbances and their effects, including effects on at least some aspects of productivity.

DISTURBANCES

Forest ecosystems are subject to a wide variety of disturbances that influence both immediate and long-term productivity. The important variables in determining impacts on sustainability are the type, intensity, size, and frequency of disturbance. Among the important types of natural disturbances are fires, windstorms, floods, landslides, epidemic outbreaks of insects or disease, and volcanism. Forest cutting by humans is probably the most important single disturbance globally.

Each of these types of disturbance does, of course, display a range of intensities. For example, wildfires can be intense, stand-consuming crown fires, such as the 1989 fires in Yellowstone National Park, or low-intensity, creeping groundfires that leave most of the forest intact. Wind displays a similarly wide range of behaviors, often generating intense damage at a regional level in the form of a hurricane or typhoon or, at a more local level, in the form of a tornado; however, wind most often disturbs chronically and at the smaller spatial scale, blowing over or breaking individual or small groups of trees. Other natural disturbances illustrate a similar gradient from slight to intense effects on the forest ecosystem. This gradient is typically found within a single disturbance, such as a fire or windthrow, especially if it occurs on a larger scale.

Disturbances occur over a very wide spatial scale. Wildfires and windstorms can range from a few square meters to thousands of hectares. Some types of disturbances, such as floods and landslides, are constrained to certain scales by landforms; these may have an extensive linear (downstream) dimension, however, even if limited in width. Again, the larger the disturbance, the more heterogeneous it will be in terms of intensity; for example, larger wildfires almost always include areas of intense and very light burning.

Disturbances are sometimes characterized as being either stand regenerating or intrinsic to the within-stand dynamic of a forest. Such a categorization includes consideration of both size and intensity of a disturbance. A very low-intensity disturbance, such as a groundfire, is often considered to be an integral part of the environment of a forest stand, even if it is of large extent. Creation of a gap in a forest canopy by the uprooting of one or several trees is also typically considered to be part of a stand dynamic despite its intensity within a small area.

Frequency of disturbance is a fourth and extremely important variable. Many disturbances are highly episodic, occurring at infrequent intervals. In the case of some disturbances, such as wildfires, long intervals between occurrences tend to result in much more intense events than where short intervals are involved; this is typically related to the period available for fuels to accumulate. Frequent disturbances can also have very negative effects on productivity and the process of recovery, however, where they result in the loss of nutrients, soil organic matter, or organisms; repeated disturbances can, for example, eliminate or dramatically reduce the level of biological legacies, such as sources of mature tree seed, at each iteration. Hence, repeated intensive crown fires can produce large areas that are very slow to reforest. One of the reasons for the rapid recovery of ecosystems at Mount St. Helens (Washington State) in 1980 was the absence of a second major eruption over most of the area; therefore, the legacy of surviving organisms was not subject to further death and burial (Franklin, Frenzen, and Swanson 1988).

Human-induced disturbances exhibit all of the same variables as natural disturbances: type, size, intensity, and frequency. Indeed, forest harvest activities can be considered and scaled with regard to each of these. Types of activities can be as variable as felling and removal of timber and nondestructive removal of forest crops, such as rubber or nuts. Sizes can range from the small patch to thousands of hectares, as in the case of some forest cutting. Intensity, as noted later, can vary from intense clear-cutting followed by slash burning to selective cutting of individual trees. Finally, human disturbances can recur each year or after many decades or even centuries.

Disturbances do have contrasting impacts on the productivity of a site, and even a single type of disturbance can have either positive or negative effects, depending on the nature of the forest ecosystem and the intensity of the disturbance. For example, wildfire negatively affects ecosystem productivity by volatilizing significant amounts of nitrogen as the organic matter is consumed. Positive effects include short-term release of soil nutrients, particularly basic elements, as the organic matter is consumed; on some sites, accumulations of organic matter may be excessive from the standpoint of site nutrition. Wind-driven disturbances rarely result in short-term losses or gains in nutrients. Geomorphic disturbances, such as floods or landslides, can have positive or negative benefits, depending on whether nutrient-rich materials are removed, added, or buried by erosional or depositional processes.

BIOLOGICAL LEGACIES
Studies of early-successional recovery of ecosystems following disturbances generally give little attention to the influence of the ecosystem before the disturbance (Franklin 1990; Franklin, Frenzen, and Swanson 1988). The role of migration or reinvasion of organisms is typically emphasized, while surviving organisms and structures are largely ignored. However, disturbances are increasingly recognized as processes that leave behind varying levels of organisms, structures, and patterns. These biotically derived legacies from predisturbance ecosystems have important influences on the paths and rates of recovery.

As defined here, biological legacies are living organisms that survive a disturbance, particularly a catastrophic or stand-regenerating disturbance, organic debris, particularly the large organically derived structures, and biotically derived patterns in soils and understories. The living legacies may take a variety of forms, including intact plants and animals, perennating structures (rhizomes), and dormant spores and seeds. Important biotically derived structures include dead trees (snags) and fallen logs, large soil aggregates, and dense mats of fungal hyphae. These structures are appreciated more and more for their role in ecosystem functioning, such as the importance of large woody structures as wildlife habitat (Harmon and others 1986; Maser and others 1988). Pattern legacies include those created in soil properties—chemical, physical, and microbiological—through the action of plants and their litter, and patterns in understory vegetation associated with variations in the conditions of canopy light. These patterns can be either positive or negative; for example, patches of soil associated with some tree species may be enriched in nitrogen or various bases, while others may be leached of nutrients and acidified.

Disturbances of various types, intensities, spatial scales, and frequencies produce different types and levels of biological legacies. Some of the relationships are obvious. More intense or frequent disturbances tend to have lower levels of living legacies; however, disturbances vary widely in the types of living legacies they leave behind. For example, wildfires are most likely to kill smaller and thin-barked trees and spare large, thick-barked dominant trees. Windthrow, however, typically eliminates dominant trees, leaving behind the largely intact understory of tolerant tree seedlings and saplings. In northwestern North America, fire and wind differ dramatically in their compositional or successional consequences; wildfire favors the shade-intolerant pioneer, Douglas fir, while wind favors survival and subsequent dominance of the shade-tolerant western hemlock and western red cedar.

Almost all intense disturbances in forest ecosystems tend to leave behind large legacies of dead organic material, including structures (snags and logs); this is because most natural forest disturbances, such as wildfire and windthrow, kill trees but consume or remove relatively little of the material. This legacy provides a continuity of wildlife habitat, bridging the two generations of ecosystems as well as providing long-term transfer of organic material and nutrients.

Traditional intensive harvest of forests by humans has typically left a much smaller biological legacy than have natural disturbances. Although many of the original plant and animal species may survive, the intensity of management practices has a strongly negative influence on the level of living legacies (Halpern 1988, 1989). Legacies of large organic structures, such as snags and fallen logs, are also drastically reduced under most current silvicultural practices, which include both harvest and slash disposal operations.

As a result, the young forests that develop following traditional clear-cutting practices are typically much simpler in composition and structure than those that develop following natural disturbances.

The types and relative levels of biological legacies following a catastrophic disturbance, then, are extremely important in determining the rate at which the new forest ecosystem will recover and, perhaps even more important, the diversity of organisms, processes, and structures that it will contain. Many of these have direct significance for sustained levels of productivity. An outstanding example is the retention of organisms capable of fixing nitrogen and providing appropriate habitat for their propagation and functioning. In forest ecosystems, this retention may encompass a wide range of forms; in old-growth Douglas fir forests, for example, it includes canopy-dwelling lichens with cyanobacteria elements and microorganisms that live in decaying wood, such as fallen logs and snags (Franklin 1992).

The types and quantities of biologically derived materials persisting through a disturbance generated by either natural or human causes have a powerful influence on the levels of nutrients and organic matter present in the recovering ecosystem. Nature generally provides for high levels of legacies and for other mechanisms that retain nutrients. However, traditional forest harvest practices, such as clear-cutting, tend to minimize biological legacies and maximize nutrient losses, as in the volatilization of nitrogen that occurs during slash burning.

ECOSYSTEM RECOVERY TIMES

There have been numerous studies of succession in forest ecosystems, but very few actually investigate or predict compositional, structural, or functional recovery, except as it relates to production and standing crops of wood. Models and data related to production of wood are considered later in this report.

Recovery rates in forests are actually considered to be quite slow compared with other major types of ecosystems, such as grasslands, deserts, or tundra (MacMahon 1981). This relates in large measure to the structural complexity of forests and the long period of time required to reestablish a diverse and fully functional forest ecosystem.

Foresters have focused heavily on regeneration of trees and reestablishment of a forest canopy (forest dominance) on a site. Regeneration of trees can occur immediately under managed conditions as a result of planting but is highly variable under natural succession; it may be essentially instantaneous where an abundant source of tree seeds is present or may require many decades where environmental conditions are severe or seed sources are distant. Growth of the regenerated trees to the point where the tree canopy becomes continuous is also highly variable, depending on the productivity of the site. In the case of temperate hardwood forests, rapid growth of pioneers, such as *Prunus* or *Alnus*, may produce canopy closure in two or three years (Reiners 1992). Among the coniferous forests, moist and warm regions dominated by *Pinus* (such as the southeastern United States or the exotic plantations of New Zealand) are the fastest to return to tree dominance. In northwestern North America, closure of the forest canopy may require a decade for completion, even on productive sites; twenty to thirty years of succession may be required on typical sites following either logging or natural disturbance (Halpern 1988, 1989).

Much more is involved in ecosystem recovery, however, than simply tree dominance or even achievement of some level of biomass. A diverse array of structures, processes, and organisms must reestablish themselves at some level approximating the original forest. Significant biological legacies, such as snags and fallen logs, largely determine how rapidly recovery of the full functional ecosystem will take place. If such legacies are absent so that new structures have to be grown to desired sizes (and, in the case of dead wood structures, killed and decayed to particular states), the recovery process can be extremely slow, perhaps involving many centuries in some types of forest. If such legacies are retained on the disturbed sites, recovery can be much more rapid.

There is increasing evidence that some elements of the ecosystem are very slow to recover. One study in the Appalachian Mountains of eastern North America, for example, has shown that some understory plant species—mosses, herbs, and shrubs—may not have recovered to their natural levels even 100 years after logging. In the temperate rain forests of southeastern Alaska, development of a compositionally diverse understory of the type required as winter range by Sitka black-tailed deer (*Odocoileus hemionus sitkensis*) typically requires 200 years following logging (Alaback 1984).

If a late-successional forest is taken as the end point of successional recovery, it appears that several centuries are required for composition

and most structural and functional features to recover. In the temperate hardwood forests of northeastern North America, 150 to 200 years may suffice for recovery, but in the coniferous forests of northwestern North America, as many as 250 to 450 years appear to be necessary to fully achieve late-successional forest conditions (Franklin and others 1981; Franklin and Spies 1991).

RESTORATION OF SOIL PROPERTIES

Restoration of soil properties almost certainly requires even longer time periods than does recovery of the biological elements of the ecosystem (Grier and others 1989; Jenny 1980). Very little good information is available on the rates of soil formation, or even on the rate at which organic matter typically accumulates in the soil. Nevertheless, it is clear that soil typically develops at a very slow rate.

In fact, much (and possibly most) accumulation of soil parent material on a site results from episodic depositions of materials from adjacent sites and not the weathering of parent materials in place. The majority of deep forest soils are composed of alluvial, colluvial, glacial, aeolian, and volcanic materials that were moved to the site by water, gravity, ice, wind, or eruptions. Hence, the frequency and type of episodic events (primarily geomorphic) are extremely influential in determining both the depth of existing parent material and the probability for replenishment. This is an important point: replacement of soil parent materials on many sites may depend primarily on the recurrence of infrequent and highly episodic geomorphic process, such as a volcanic eruption; hence, soil conservation should have a high priority among forest management considerations.

Once in place, biological processes are critical in the evolution of the soil parent materials into an organically and nutritionally rich medium for growth. As noted earlier, this can be a slow process. It is probable that most forest soils are continuously and gradually accumulating soil organic matter under natural successional regimes. Although the available information is inconclusive, soil organic matter is probably not accumulating—and may be declining—under many forest management regimes currently in use (Kimmins 1987).

Perhaps the most difficult problem in soil restoration is the reintroduction and establishment of critical soil organisms, such as fungi, invertebrates, and bacteria, once they have been eliminated. There is good evidence that significant elements of the soil biota can be lost with the elimination of host tree species from the site (Perry and others 1989); this can lead, in turn, to serious problems in the reestablishment of forest cover.

Natural variation in ecosystem productivity

Significant variation in both space and time exists in the productivity of forest ecosystems. Spatial (site-to-site) variability has already been discussed and can effectively span two-and-a-half orders of magnitude in production of wood, from less than 10 to more than 250 square meters per hectare a year.

A forest ecosystem on a specific site can also experience substantial year-to-year variation in productivity, quite aside from long-term trends associated with successional development of the forest. The greatest variability—certainly in terms of percentages and, often, in absolute values as well—occurs on sites that are subject to major environmental stresses. These include marginal forests on hot, droughty sites, such as those found at lower timberline, and on cold arctic and alpine timberline. Productivity is typically low on these sites, and growth is responsive to variations (either positive or negative) in climatic conditions. Dendrochronology, the analysis and interpretation of tree rings, is based on the sensitivity of tree productivity to climatic fluxes, especially on severe sites. Productivity might easily span two orders of magnitude on sites with major environmental limitations. Although annual and periodic variability in the productivity of temperate forest ecosystems is present on moderate sites as well, it is smaller in magnitude than year-to-year variation.

Changes in local or global environmental and climatic conditions can be expected to produce major changes in the productivity of forest ecosystems. Effects of local pollutants, such as emissions from smelters, have been well documented. Effects of regional changes in pollutants or in climatic conditions are less clear but are currently the subject of intense scientific interest (Franklin and others 1991). Such changes clearly have the potential to produce major changes in the productivity of forest ecosystems; the direction of the change will, of course, depend on the current circumstance. If changes in environmental and climatic conditions produce additional drying in a forest ecosystem already moisture-limited, the resulting effect would probably be negative; conversely, increased levels of atmospheric carbon dioxide may result in increased productivity and more efficient use of available moisture.

Episodic and stochastic processes and thresholds

Forest ecosystems are subject to many important processes that are either episodic or stochastic or both. Some of these have already been discussed in earlier sections, particularly with regard to disturbances. Disturbances are among the most important of the processes that are, in the majority of cases, both episodic and stochastic, or random. Variation in environmental conditions (climate) is another example.

Two important aspects of the dynamics of tree populations central to forests and forest productivity—birth and death—can be episodic or stochastic processes or both. Birth, the successful establishment of new tree seedlings, may require a major (stand-regenerating) disturbance, which is typically both episodic and stochastic. It may also depend on the production of a bumper seed crop, another process that is at least episodic, and possibly stochastic. Finally, successful regeneration of trees on sites with severe environmental conditions may depend on the occurrence of one or two years with an unusually favorable climate. Regeneration of *Pinus ponderosa* forests in central Arizona, for example, requires the combination of two unusually moist springs and a bumper seed crop; these conditions occur only every two or three decades.

Scientific knowledge of tree death or mortality is surprisingly poor, considering its importance in forest ecology and productivity (Franklin, Shugart, and Harmon 1987). Some mortality is quite regular and predictable, particularly the natural thinning that occurs early in development of the stand. Much mortality, however, including such events as an outbreak of pests and pathogens or a major windstorm, is highly episodic. Generally, mortality of established trees (above the seedling and sapling stage) in forest stands is both episodic and stochastic, impeding our ability to predict rates, causes, and spatial patterns of mortality in mature and late-successional stands.

One of the major needs in forest management is to recognize the highly stochastic nature of most natural ecosystems. More management plans need to consider the potential for stochastic disturbances. More management decisions need to consider probabilities, such as in the potential for successful natural regeneration. Far too many management decisions are based on a deterministic view of forest ecosystem responses and an unwillingness to accept outcomes with less than 100 percent probability of success.

Thresholds have not been a major topic in considerations of the productivity of temperate forest ecosystems. Nevertheless, the occurrence of thresholds is implicit in many discussions, since so many processes fit the traditional logistic curve. However, few interpretations of physiological, population, community, or ecosystem phenomena have been explicitly made in terms of thresholds; they could be, however, and resource managers often assume that there are such points beyond which responses accelerate or decelerate. Threshold phenomena have been explicitly recognized in the area of landscape ecology. One example is the effect of dispersed patch clear-cutting on various landscape measures, such as mean patch size (see, for example, Franklin and Forman 1987).

Biophysical measurements for temperate forests

Many approaches to predicting the productivity of forests and forest sites have been developed over the last century. These include direct measurements of tree and stand growth and many indirect approaches, such as those using soils, landforms, and plant communities. Most of the approaches focus ultimately on the arboreal component as the measure of productivity and, often, only on bole (wood) production, rather than on all ecosystem components. This is acceptable to at least some degree, since many capabilities of a forested site (such as processes and organisms) are related to or indexed by the ability of the site to grow a tree to a maximum size at a particular rate. However, focusing exclusively on trees in assessing productivity ignores many elements essential to sustainable forestry.

Techniques for direct assessment or measurement of long-term trends in site productivity, as opposed to the modeling approaches discussed later, are not well advanced. Most of the existing measures show a high rate of error when applied to specific sites and stands. This natural variability makes it extremely difficult to identify long-term signals or trends in site productivity, a common problem with many ecological phenomena (Likens 1989).

Biological measurements

Biological measures used in assessing forest productivity include direct measures of forest yields and tree growth, measures of total ecosystem productivity, rates of key ecosystem processes, and vegetational associates or plant communities as indicators.

TREE PRODUCTIVITY AND WOOD PRODUCTION
The yield of a fully stocked forest stand over a given time period is the ultimate measure of arboreal productivity for a site (Daniel, Helms, and Baker 1979). Since such a measure is rarely possible, traditional approaches to predicting forest site potential and forest growth have been combined in a tree-based growth measurement called site index with yield tables of various types.

Site index is the height to which a tree of a given species will grow within a specific time period. Site index is typically based on height growth curves developed using empirical data on cumulative height attained by dominant and codominant trees over time. The index age varies with tree species; 50 years is a common age for fast-growing species, such as *Pinus sp.* in the southeastern United States, while 100 years is a common index age in western North America, where initial growth rates are slower. A site index is typically assessed by obtaining height and age on a sample of dominant and codominant trees from the site and projecting height to the index age using a set of site curves; the selected trees are typically assumed to have grown naturally.

Height growth rate of free-growing trees was selected and has been defended by foresters on the basis that it is relatively unaffected by stocking levels or tree density, whereas other measures of growth, such as diameter, are. Hence, it is considered to be a direct indicator of site potential, irrespective of stand conditions. Studies have shown significant effects of stand density on height growth, however, with considerable variability among species (Daniel, Helms, and Baker 1979). Furthermore, growth curves (patterns of height growth over time) may differ among sites for the same species and site index; that is, even where tree heights on two sites are identical at the index age, patterns of height growth both prior to and after the index age may differ. This has encouraged the development of more localized, or polymorphic, site curves as an alternative to the creation of a generalized set of site curves for a large region (Daniel, Helms, and Baker 1979).

Yield tables are the other half of the traditional approach to predicting forest productivity. Most yield tables, including all of the older ones, are constructed by sampling fully stocked stands of one (usually) or two or more (rarely) tree species that represent different ages and levels of productivity as measured by site index. The empirical data are used to develop comprehensive tables that predict the volumes of wood (cubic meters per hectare or board-feet per acre) to be expected from fully stocked stands of those species at various ages and on sites with different site indexes. Yield bulletins typically include much other tabular and graphical information as well, such as calculations of increment per unit of time and changes in tree density. Yield tables can be viewed fundamentally as tree population or demographic models. Early yield tables were almost entirely for stands of natural origin, but more recently, many have been developed for managed stands, such as plantations, and include effects of thinning and other management activities.

Yield tables have been superseded in many regions by computerized growth models that have the ability to incorporate substantially more variables, including effects of variable stand densities. These are discussed later, since they are not direct measurements of productivity. Most direct measurements of the productivity of a forest site are based on site index, which is then coupled with yield tables or yield models. Other techniques, such as projecting growth on the basis of recent patterns of tree growth, are occasionally used for estimating growth over the near future.

ECOSYSTEM PRODUCTIVITY
Ecological measures of productivity—gross primary productivity, net primary productivity, and net ecosystem productivity—are much more comprehensive than the traditional forestry measures. At least conceptually, they include all components of the ecosystem. Unfortunately, accurate estimates of total ecosystem productivity are extremely difficult, if not impossible, to obtain, particularly the respiration component and almost all measurements belowground. This calls

into doubt the accuracy of most available estimates of gross primary productivity and net ecosystem productivity for forest ecosystems.

Estimates of net primary productivity of forest ecosystems can and have been made for research sites. However, obtaining the necessary measurements requires heroic physical, as well as conceptual and financial efforts, so as a routine measure of ecosystem productivity, estimating net primary productivity is impractical. The conceptual contribution of ecosystem productivity is probably the aspect most relevant to this review. It recognizes explicitly the productivity of all parts of the ecosystem rather than focusing exclusively on trees and volume of wood. As a result, it provides us with a very different point of view on the health and productivity of an older forest ecosystem than do measures of productivity that are based on additional increments of wood or biomass.

PROCESSES AS INDEXES
Although not widely accepted, rates of key ecological processes, such as decomposition or mineralization of organic matter, are sometimes proposed as indexes to overall health or productivity of an ecosystem. One variable that seems to have a high level of sensitivity to pollutants and some other stresses is the time that evergreen trees retain needles or leaves.

SITE COMMUNITY CLASSIFICATIONS
Plant communities and vegetative indicator plants have been proposed and are sometimes used to assess the productivity of a forest site. Such approaches are based on the concept that specific plants—singly, in sets, or as communities—are indicative of specific environmental conditions, such as moisture, temperature, and nutrient regimes. Hence, inferences about site conditions and overall productivity can be drawn from their presence or abundance on a site.

The Finnish types of forest site represent the earliest development of this concept. These were based on the belief that empirical relationships exist between plant cover and tree growth. The presence of a certain plant species in the understory was assumed to indicate a particular quality of site.

Many vegetation-based approaches have been developed and are widely applied throughout the world. In Scandinavia, most vegetational approaches follow the original model pioneered by Cajander. The vegetation classification system developed by Braun-Blanquet dominates in central Europe and many other parts of the world. In western North America, Daubenmire pioneered the approach with his habitat-type concept, which is now widely applied to national forestlands.

Many other approaches have used plants as indicators of site environment and productivity, including the use of vegetative indicators to define the operational environment (see, for example, Waring and Major 1964). Most plant community or plant indicator approaches ultimately return to traditional forestry measures—site index and stand yields—to rate productivity of a site.

Physical measurements

Many scientists have proposed that measurements of physical site conditions, rather than trees or other biota, be used to rate potential productivity of a site. One advantage is that such approaches do not require the presence of any particular organism or stand condition in order to rate productivity; this also can (using some approaches) avoid biasing productivity estimates toward any particular genotype, species, or life-form. Biotic productivity is, however, the ultimate measure of sustainability, so that most physical measures are, in fact, referenced back to plant production.

ENVIRONMENTAL REGIME
Occasional proposals have been made to assess potential productivity of a forest site using direct measures of environmental variables, such as mean temperature, frost-free days, precipitation, and so forth. As noted earlier, there are strong correlations between overall productivity and environmental variables, such as moisture and temperature. Most of these studies are based on measures of the operational environment, however, and not on measurements of the regional climate.

Although climatological indexes have been developed for temperate regions, they are not currently used in assessing forest productivity. Indeed, the life zone approaches used in the United States early in this century might fall into this category. Holdridge's life zone concept is one environmental indexing scheme that is widely used for tropical forest areas.

SOIL PROPERTIES
Foresters have made considerable use of soils as a basis for predicting forest productivity (Daniel, Helms, and Baker 1979; Pritchett and Fisher 1987).

The need to predict yields on sites lacking the trees or the tree species of interest has been a particular stimulus to the use of soils. Soils are also viewed as a permanent feature of the site, in contrast to vegetative cover.

Soil taxonomic units or types have been one basis for predicting forest yields. Exclusive dependence on soil types has had limited success, however. This is related, in part, to variability in the soil mapping units. Site curves are typically used as a basis for rating soil productivity, but using inappropriate curves may create another problem, although one of the major uses of soil types has been in developing stratified management plans. Finally, soils are only one part of the environment to which the forest is responding.

Predictive equations based on combinations of soil properties—soil-site indexes—have been widely used. These are typically localized, empirical relationships. Data are collected on a variety of physical and chemical properties of soil and then subjected to multiple regression analysis with a site index as the response variable. Representative properties that have been used in equations include thickness of the A horizon, moisture-holding capacity, and total soil depth (Daniel, Helms, and Baker 1979). Currently, soil-site index approaches do not appear to be in wide use.

Site classification systems

Various site classification schemes attempt to combine elements of geology, physiography (landforms), soils, and vegetation for predicting the management potential, including productivity, of forest sites. These include the physiographic types of site developed in Ontario, Canada, by Hills, the classification of biogeocoenoses developed in British Columbia by Krajina, classifications developed for the Great Lakes region of the United States by Barnes and associates, and forest site classifications developed for New England by Leak and his associates.

Alternative management options

Traditional approaches to forest management in temperate regions focus on economically efficient production and harvest of wood products and reforestation of the site with a new generation of trees. The dominant paradigm is production of even-aged plantations of a single species with final harvest accomplished by clear-cutting.

Precommercial thinning and, in some cases, herbicide treatments are used to maintain rapid growth in crop trees and to free them from competing herbs, shrubs, or trees viewed as weeds. Some management regimes use fertilization to stimulate growth. Commercial thinnings may also be carried out. Rotation ages are determined primarily by economic analysis or, in the case of some government forests, by some biological criterion, such as culmination of mean annual increment. Levels of use vary but typically do not involve the removal of needles and twigs from the harvest site, although subsequent slash disposal activities, such as broadcast slash burning, may consume much of this material. Traditionally, all structural material that can be used is removed, and the remainder is disposed. The site is assumed to be capable of sustaining productivity levels under this regime.

Such an approach to forest management is fundamentally agricultural: it aims to maximize the desired output by simplifying the ecosystem of interest and subsidizing it with energy inputs, such as fertilizers. Implicit in this approach is a belief that what is good for wood production is good for other resource values. The tendency toward simplification is of particular concern because it traditionally occurs at many levels in temperate forest management in terms of genotype, species, product, stand structure, landscape pattern, and successional stage (Franklin and others 1986). Foresters sometimes persist in simplifying forest ecosystems even when doing so is not essential to management objectives and is done at substantial expense.

Development of alternative management paradigms is clearly appropriate, with the increased emphasis placed on the sustained production of all forest values, including wood products, and with our vastly greater knowledge of forest ecosystems and their functioning (Hopwood 1991). Traditional practices, which had their genesis 50 to 100 years ago, do not reflect either the broadened societal objectives for forest land or the scientific findings of the last twenty to thirty years. Returning to my initial commentary defining sustainability and its basis, it seems that sustainable forest management practices should emphasize the maintenance of the productive capacity of the forest land (principle 1) and of the biota that are the engines of the ecosystem (principle 2).

The question, then, is what form the new alternatives to traditional practices should take. The answer involves considerations and alternative approaches at the level of both the stand and the landscape. The stand level is considered first with the focus on management approaches in stands that are to be managed for some level of commodity production. A consideration follows of landscape-level approaches that involve both managed and reserved areas.

The central concept of alternative approaches for managed stands of temperate forest is to maintain or recreate stands that are structurally and compositionally diverse. That is, within the constraints of objectives and stand conditions, the effort is to maintain as much of the structural and compositional diversity as possible rather than to simplify the stand. Structural diversity is usually the goal, because structure is normally closely correlated to organisms and processes; that is, structure provides the necessary conditions or habitat for desired organisms and processes. The general principle of maintaining structural diversity should be kept in mind during the following discussion. The exact set of silvicultural practices—the treatments developed to create or maintain structural diversity—will vary with the type, condition, and environment of the forest and, of course, with the specific set of management objectives.

Creation of young stands

Young stands provide many opportunities for developing elements or attributes that are important in enhancing ecosystem processes and biodiversity. Aggressive efforts to create stands of mixed composition are one initial step. Plantings of single species and weeding by either chemical or mechanical means strongly direct the managed forest toward a monoculture. Plantings of multiple species and efforts to retain species mixtures in precommercial thinning or weeding exercises will, however, create compositionally diverse forests. Maintaining a mixture of species can greatly enhance a variety of ecological values, such as the ability to provide habitat for a broad array of organisms. For example, an occasional hardwood can add significant structural and species diversity (as host to a variety of plant epiphytes and animal species) to a conifer-dominated stand; this would include substantial heterogeneity in microclimatic and edaphic conditions. Hardwoods such as *Alnus sp.* and *Robinia* bring an additional benefit of nitrogen fixation.

Richer mixtures of conifers can also provide valuable diversity. For example, species belonging to the *Cupressaceae* (cypress or false cedar family), such as *Thuja* and *Chamaecyparis*, improve the quality of soil in addition to producing valuable wood products. All *Cupressaceae* accumulate calcium and other bases in their foliage, which produces high-quality litter (Kiilsgaard, Greene, and Stafford 1987). This litter contributes, in turn, to higher base saturation, higher rates of nitrogen mineralization, reduced acidity, and production of more biologically active mull humus conditions (Alban 1969; Turner and Franz 1985).

Delaying the process of canopy closure can also have environmental benefits in some young stands. Canopy closure is probably the most dramatic and, for some organisms and processes, the most traumatic single event in the life of the stand, other than its ultimate destruction by some catastrophe. Many aspects of the forest, including its composition and functioning, change rapidly and significantly at the time of canopy closure. Intensive forest management has traditionally sought to achieve rapid closure of the canopy (early full occupancy of the site by commercial trees) following a disturbance, such as clear-cutting. Yet the open conditions prior to closure of the tree canopy are important ecologically. The stage prior to canopy closure is rich in plant and animal species, including many game species, that are valued by humans (Hunter 1990; Thomas 1979). Vascular plant species with nitrogen-fixing symbionts are most common during this period. Hence, maintaining open conditions farther into the rotation—delaying full canopy closure—can provide ecological benefits.

Canopy closure can be delayed by maintaining wider spacings between trees. Reducing the planting densities between trees and undertaking heavy precommercial thinning achieve this objective. Furthermore, studies show that wide spacing can be maintained in young stands with little or no sacrifice in the volume of commercial wood produced (for example, Reukema 1979; Reukema and Smith 1987). Trees can be pruned to produce high-quality wood in the open-grown stands. Such prescriptions are used in management of *Pinus radiata* plantations in New Zealand.

Structural retention at harvest

Structural diversity is emerging from forest ecosystem research as a critical attribute in providing for a diversity of processes and organisms. Furthermore, it is some of the large structures—large living trees, large snags, and large fallen boles—that are typically absent from managed stands, since stands have traditionally been clear-cut. Retaining some of the structures from the old stand at the time of final harvest is one of the best ways to provide the new stand with a high level of structural diversity, including larger structures.

COARSE WOODY DEBRIS

Coarse woody debris, including large standing dead trees and fallen boles, are extremely important to ecosystem function. They provide habitat for many elements of biological diversity and essential processes. Rotting wood is also important to maintenance of site productivity by contributing nutrients and organic matter to the soil; even the identifiable wood fragments incorporated into the soil—soil wood—play a distinctive role (see, for example, several papers in Harvey and Neuenschwander 1991). Practices that contribute to maintenance of coarse woody debris include the retention of such material at the time of harvest cutting and the creation of snags and logs from trees reserved for that purpose.

Retention of snags and logs is particularly effective for maintaining coarse woody debris when harvesting trees in young and mature stands of natural origin and old-growth forests. Natural stands typically have significant amounts of coarse woody debris that can be used as a biological legacy. Retention of snags is more controversial and less effective than maintenance of logs for a variety of reasons. There are concerns for the safety of forest workers because of the potential for structural failure in snags. Retention of snags increases logging costs. Snags also create potential problems in fire protection because they tend to produce firebrands once ignited. Snags are a potential hazard to aircraft involved in management activities. Furthermore, many snags have relatively short life spans, especially if they are heavily rotted. Nevertheless, efforts to maintain snags on cutover forestlands are increasing because of their importance to many animal species. Two approaches used to reduce hazards associated with snag retention are (a) clustering of snags in small groups or patches and (b) creating snags from living trees following harvest cutting. Silvicultural prescriptions can be designed to maintain a given number and distribution of snags over the rotation. A common objective in *Pseudotsuga* forests in northwestern North America, for example, is the continuous availability of five large (more than 50 centimeters in diameter) snags per hectare.

Living trees can be used as sources for coarse woody debris in stands that lack either large snags or logs, as is the case for stands currently under intensive management. This is a particularly valuable practice for restoring structure to stands and landscapes that have been simplified by past practices.

Maintenance of appropriate quantities and qualities of coarse woody debris in managed stands is, of course, much more complex than simply providing periodically for a few dead trees. Different tree species provide snags and logs with substantially different characteristics and ecological potential. All tree species are not equal in terms of their behavior as coarse woody debris! Furthermore, coarse woody debris needs to be present in various stages of decay. Material of greater structural soundness may be important for geomorphic and some animal habitat roles, for example, while highly decayed wood is of greater value as a component of soil. Numerous questions exist as to the quantities and spatial distribution of coarse woody debris required to achieve specific management objectives; how much is enough? Developing the specific data ultimately needed for silvicultural prescriptions will be a challenge to scientists and managers for many years to come (Maser and others 1988).

RETENTION AND PARTIAL CUTTING OF GREEN TREES
Retention of green trees on cutover areas is another practice that can create higher levels of structural diversity on managed stands. This approach can be referred to as partial cutting, partial retention, or green tree retention, in an effort to distinguish it from both clear-cutting and selective cutting (Franklin 1990). Retention of green trees involves reserving a significant percentage of the living trees, typically including some of the larger or dominant individuals, at the time of harvest for retention through the next rotation. The density, composition, condition, and distribution of the reserved trees vary widely, depending on management objectives, initial stand conditions, and other constraints. The general objective is, however, to sustain a more structurally diverse stand than could be obtained through even-aged management. Partial cutting has not been widely used or recognized in forestry. Some silvicultural textbooks briefly discuss related concepts such as shelterwood with reserve, but these approaches have not been widely taught or applied in forestry.

Many ecological objectives, including several that contribute to sustainability, can be achieved by retaining living trees on harvested areas while simultaneously producing and removing wood products. First, living trees can be used as sources of coarse woody debris—snags and logs—especially where safety concerns or logging methods make retention of snags difficult. Living trees can also be retained to provide wildlife habitat.

Living trees can function as refugia and inocula for many of the smaller organisms or hidden diversity mentioned early in this review. For example, many species of the rich invertebrate fauna found in forests have poor dispersal capabilities (Lattin 1990). Such organisms typically do not recolonize areas once their habitat has been eliminated by clear-cutting. Refugia for these kinds of organisms can be provided by leaving host trees, which then become an inoculum or source of seeds for the new stand. The same concept is applicable to mycorrhizae-forming fungal species. At least some of these fungi can disappear from cutover areas if all potential host species are eliminated (Perry and others 1988). When some of their hosts are left behind, the fungal communities are conserved and can inoculate the young stands. This concept is a counterpoint to the forester's common complaint that living trees cannot be retained because they are sources of pests and pathogens, such as invertebrates and fungi. Most invertebrates and fungi in forest stands are, in fact, essential components that should be retained, and maintaining living trees on the site is one important tool for achieving this objective.

Retention of living trees, especially dominants, also alters the microclimate of the cutover area. That is what traditional shelterwood cutting is all about: the overstory moderates the microclimate, encouraging regeneration of trees where the environment on a clear-cut would be too severe due to heat or frost (Daniel, Helms, and Baker 1979). Obviously, what works for tree seedlings will work for other forest organisms as well: they would also be expected to survive better on partial cuttings than on clear-cuts. Perhaps as important, many organisms will move more readily through a patch or landscape that has at least some living trees than through a clear-cut environment because of the ameliorated climate or protective cover or both. Replacement of clear-cutting with partial cutting on a managed landscape matrix could dramatically improve overall connectivity and reduce the isolation of islands of natural habitat.

Retention of green trees can be used as a strategy to grow large, high-quality wood during the next rotation. For example, mature (80- to 250-year-old) *Pseudotsuga menziesii* are still capable of substantial growth (Williamson 1973). Hence, large living trees could provide both economic and ecologic benefits in scenarios involving management of a mixed stand with a low density of large, slower growing trees of one species on a long rotation, while simultaneously growing several rotations of a rapidly growing second species.

Partial cutting could be used to create mixed-structure stands that provide critical wildlife habitat. For example, in northwestern North America, numerous natural stands represent mixtures of young and old structures; the stand may be relatively young (for example, eighty years) but also contain a significant component of large, old trees, large snags, and large logs. Such stands are typically the consequence of wildfires or windstorms that left behind a large legacy from the original stand. Forests of this type often provide suitable habitat for animal species generally associated with old-growth forests (Ruggiero and others 1991). Partial cutting systems could be used to create comparable mixed-structure stands, which would provide late-successional forest habitat conditions in one-quarter to half of the time that would be required following traditional clear-cutting.

Partial cutting could also be used to reduce the impact that harvesting the forest has on hydrologic and geomorphic processes. For example, retention of living trees can reduce the potential for landslides by maintaining root strength, which is critical to maintaining the stability of soils on steep slopes. Retention could also be used to reduce the impact of cutting where harvesting the forest contributes to the frequency and intensity of flood flows. In northwestern North America, for example, maintaining a sufficient number of large trees to intercept snow and maintain the thermal balance on cutover areas will reduce the intensity of the rain-on-snow floods that are common in this region.

Prescriptions for partial cutting vary widely, depending on many factors, including management objectives and stand conditions. For example, providing a minimal number of snags and logs may require retention of as few as ten to eighteen trees per hectare. Creation of mixed-aged, mixed-structure forests suitable for late-successional forest species may require twenty to forty retained trees per hectare, depending on age of the forest.

The appropriate spatial distribution of retained living trees—whether to disperse them or con-centrate them in patches—is another important issue in partial cutting. The answer depends partially on objectives and constraints. For example, when small patches of living trees are retained, they may be more effective as refugia for invertebrates; aggregating them may also minimize impacts on logging and other forestry operations. At the same time, well-distributed snags and logs are desirable because they maintain productivity of the soil and provide habitat for some wildlife species.

SELECTIVE CUTTING

Selective cutting involves the removal of individual or small groups of trees at relatively frequent intervals (every ten years). This system is typically aimed at creating or perpetuating uneven-aged stands (more than three age classes) and always maintains a protective cover at the site. In the last several decades, large industrial forest landowners and government forest agencies have rarely used selective cutting as a major approach to forest management, although there have been exceptions. Its unpopularity is due to the high costs, inefficiency, technical difficulty in application, and potential damage to stands and sites when applied to large trees on steep mountainous topography.

Selective cutting can, however, be an effective technique for maintaining compositional and structural diversity in stands that are managed for low to moderate levels of wood production (Daniel, Helms, and Baker 1979). Of all the cutting systems, it provides the highest level of biological legacies of all types and, under some circumstances, minimizes impacts on the long-term productive potential of the site.

Selective cutting is not a panacea, however. It is a difficult system to apply and requires the forester to have a high level of technical competence, particularly if a high-grading approach, in which only the most valuable trees are removed, is to be avoided. It can be very difficult to apply when the preferred species of tree crop is intolerant of shading, and potential shade-tolerant competitors are present. The potential is also very high for damage to residual stands and for accelerated erosion and soil degradation when applied to stands on steep mountain topography; this is because selective cutting requires frequent entries to the stand, which, in turn, may necessitate creation and maintenance of a dense system of roads and skid trails. Use of aerial logging techniques can reduce some of these impacts, but their high cost may be prohibitive.

It also appears that selective cutting may not maintain conditions suitable for many interior or late-successional animal species, despite the high levels of structural retention. For example, at least some of the neotropical migrant songbirds that use the eastern North American deciduous forests respond negatively to the creation of even small openings within the large intact forest areas they require (Terborgh 1992). In another example from the tropics, selective logging has had significant and pervasive impacts on animal species of the interior forest. Hence, it is not safe to assume that selective cutting is the best approach to integrating forest harvest and environmental values, including sustainability.

Much more extensive use of selective cutting is appropriate in future efforts to develop forest management approaches that are more ecologically sensitive. It will be most applicable on areas where there is less emphasis on commodity production and where the species and topography are appropriate to frequent light-harvest entries. In contrast, partial cutting, as presented earlier, is typically designed around a single-harvest entry per rotation.

LONG ROTATIONS

The practice of using long rotations has a high potential as an alternative management approach that would reduce the impacts of harvest cutting on environmental values, including site productivity and biodiversity. This might involve increasing rotation ages by a factor of 1.5 to 2.0 over current rotations, which have been based on economic factors or biological maturity of crop trees (the culmination of mean annual increment). As a specific example, the rotation age (frequency of final harvest cut) on national forests in the northwestern United States might be shifted from the current 80 to 100 years to 160 to 200 years.

Such shifts in rotation age can have numerous environmental benefits, including reduced impacts on soils and biological diversity. They can drastically reduce the proportion of a managed landscape that is in a recently cutover condition, which, in turn, can reduce the risk to soils and water quality since, for example, recently cutover areas are much more subject to erosion and landslides. A higher percentage of the landscape would be in forest cover under long rotations, and some of this forest would include later stages of forest succession that would not be present in a landscape managed under short rota-

tions. Overall, long rotations help to maintain a greater diversity of organisms and processes.

Most large industrial forest landowners view long rotations as an anathema, but only from an economic standpoint. In their view, the return on their investment is simply not acceptable in managed forests with rotations longer than fifty to sixty years. Such strictly economic criteria are rarely applied to government forest lands, however.

Amelioration and restoration practices

The potential for restoring structures, organisms, and processes to forest stands that have been simplified or degraded warrants mention. There are many situations where silviculture can contribute to the restoration of degraded sites, the creation of habitat (such as snags and other structures), and the reintroduction of organisms. For example, in the Northwestern United States, workshops, experiments, and pilot tests are underway aimed at restoration of structural complexity in simplified young stands developed following earlier logging. Specific objectives typically include provision of habitat for species associated with mature and old-growth forests.

Existing materials for assessing sustained productivity

Productivity is a topic that has concerned foresters and forest scientists for several centuries. Numerous approaches have been developed to assess productivity and numerous datasets have been collected that vary widely in terms of their formality, levels of sophistication, effort, etc. Not surprisingly, there are great differences in approaches, both between different countries and regions within countries. In general, uniform approaches have not been developed and adopted, except in countries where a national forestry organization has had the ability to define and push adoption of a countrywide approach. There have been attemps through organizations like the International Union of Forest Research Organizations (IUFRO) to at least develop and adopt standardized terminology and explore common methodological approaches (AAAS 1967 and Newbould 1967). However, uniform methods do not generally exist even among adjoining regions, let alone countries.

Numerous other problems are associated with existing methodologies, predictive tools, and data sets in addition to this general lack of uniformity. For example, the vast majority deal only with the production of wood or biomass and do not address total productivity of the ecosystem. Further, even when a methodology purports to address productivity of the forest ecosystem, significant components, such as the productivity belowground, are ignored (Harris, Sanantonio, and Mc Ginty 1980). Hence, a wealth of material exists for assessing productivity of temperate forests, but little of it can be directly adapted to address the primary issue in this volume: measuring the productivity of ecosystems over long periods of time.

Measurement programs

Sample plots placed in forest stands have been a primary tool of foresters almost since the inception of the forestry profession. Although they vary widely in size, layout, permanence, and almost all other features, sampling plots have been around for a long time and have provided the bulk of the empirical data for estimating forest productivity.

Most countries, agencies, or corporations that are involved in management of significant forest properties have some kind of continuing forest inventory program that uses a system of sample plots. Continuous forest inventory is a central concept in forestry that generally involves the establishment of permanent sample plots over the forest property, usually using some systematic sampling design. The specifics of these plots vary widely with the organization, but the use of plot clusters is common. Measurement intervals also vary; however, five-year remeasurements are common.

In some countries, national organizations have responsibility for conducting forest inventories. In the United States, for example, the Department of Agriculture Forest Service takes periodic inventories of resources on all publicly owned forests. Regional experiment stations design and conduct this inventory, except on national forest lands, where it is carried out by the National Forest Management Organization. This inventory system, as with many directed to forest lands, is beginning to broaden its focus beyond the counting of standing live trees and calculation of wood volumes to the acknowledgment of other forest attributes (structures such as snags and fallen logs) and resources.

Such traditional inventories typically have numerous deficiencies that drastically limit their potential value as models for a system to assess long-term productivity. Foremost among these is that they are typically designed to provide a statistical sample of an entire forest ownership, state, region, or country. They do not provide estimates of standing crops (let alone productivity) at the level of an individual stand; the data cannot be related to some spatial data base. Hence, it is possible to infer that there are x hectares of stands of y age and z volume, but there is no way to determine where they are located within the sampling area.

Because forest sampling is conducted at very low densities and is not stand-specific, interpreting the causes of changes in stand volumes and growth rates between remeasurement periods is very difficult. The phenomenon of declining productivity in the third generation of forests in the southeastern United States provides an excellent example; in the 1970s and 1980s, growth rates appeared to have declined, leading to suggestions that site productivity might also be declining. Several alternative hypotheses were proposed, however, and resolution of this issue has been rendered difficult by the low density and geographical resolution of the sample.

Stand-based inventory systems do exist in some ownerships and provide a better opportunity to identify changes, and their causes, in the productivity of a forest over time. Clearly, none of these systems is designed to measure changes in the inherent productivity of a site. They are simply approaches to estimating standing volumes of wood or aboveground organic material and to calculating rates of accumulation or loss; that is, growth or productivity of the current stand.

A protocol or set of protocols to assess changes in long-term forest productivity has not yet been designed nor, obviously, implemented. The forestry organization that has gone the furthest in this direction, so far as I know, is the group in New Zealand concerned with management of the exotic *Pinus radiata* forests.

Long-term experiments are being developed and implemented by forest research and management organizations to address the specific issue of long-term forest ecosystem productivity under varying management regimes. Examples exist in many temperate forest regions. These are research projects, not routine operational activities; the investment in data collection is high, and the geographic scope is typically low. Nevertheless, these experiments will provide the most definitive information on long-term productivity and will almost certainly provide useful insights into the design of broader schemes for assessing the productivity of forest ecosystems.

Existing data sets

An immense number of data sets address the issue of forest productivity over a variety of spatial and temporal scales. The forestry literature is full of data on productivity, as are the files of forest research and management agencies. As noted earlier, the concept of continuous forest inventory is generally followed in most countries that have significant forestry programs.

It would be impossible to describe or list this immense body of data in a short review. Many reviews and directories are already available, several of which are cited below. Unfortunately, much of this information has limited value. As noted earlier, these data sets typically focus only on the tree and often only on the wood component. They do not address productivity of the ecosystem as it is currently defined.

The fact that these data sets consider only the aboveground portion of the tree or forest is a serious deficiency. When monitoring changes in forest productivity, this approach is unacceptable, particularly since shifts in the relative productivity of aboveground and belowground components can occur with changes in site conditions. In temperate regions, the proportion of photosynthate used belowground tends to increase substantially with increased nutrient or water stress (Kimmins 1987). Finally, these data sets have rarely been designed to assess long-term changes in productivity. Not only are essential elements missing, but the methods used have often been modified over decades of remeasurement, making comparisons of data difficult.

During the last few decades, various data sets on the productivity of temperate forest ecosystems have been developed that do attempt to address overall, rather than just wood, productivity. Even these are far too numerous to compile in this review. There are, however, some major references that provide access to many of these data sets and a great deal of the literature.

One of the best compilations of data on productivity of temperate forest ecosystems is the synthesis volume on forests generated by studies of the International Biological Programme (Reichle 1981). This volume summarizes most of the research on forest productivity conducted during a global ten-year effort. Included are numerous data sets from intensive study sites throughout (primarily, but not exclusively) the northern temperate region. Although incomplete for some variables, the focus is on ecosystem productivity.

Numerous research data sets have been generated since the 1960s, when studies of ecosystem productivity first became popular. Cannell (1982) has compiled many of these in a book, *World Forest Biomass and Primary Production Data*. Other important compilations and discussions of forest productivity are Eckardt (1968, a volume published as part of a UNESCO series), the proceedings of several conferences (International Union of Forest Research Organizations 1971, 1973), and a summary of research, *Productivity of the World Ecosystems* (Reichle, Franklin, and Goodall 1975). No list of major publications on forest productivity would be complete without mention of the Russian classic, *Productivity and Mineral Cycling in Terrestrial Vegetation*, by Rodin and Bazilevich (1967), which includes many tables of data on forests as well as other types of terrestrial ecosystems.

On an operational rather than a research level, the most comprehensive data sets on forest productivity are probably those associated with very intensive management of plantations. Examples include the exotic *Pinus radiata* plantations in New Zealand, Australia, and South Africa and hybrid *Populus* plantations worldwide. Forestry agencies in at least some of these locales have given substantial attention to long-term productivity and its measurement, including belowground components in a few cases.

As noted, innumerable data sets on forest productivity address the production of wood. Although essentially no data sets were designed specifically to address forest ecosystem productivity over long time periods, some major forest research projects have been or currently are being established throughout the northern temperate zone that should correct many of these deficiencies.

Predictive models

It is not surprising that many models of various types are aimed at predicting forest productivity; this is, after all, one of the major concerns of foresters and forest management organizations. Many approaches have been taken, including traditional forest yield tables and computerized growth and yield models of highly varied constructs. A growing number of forest succession models include predictions of overall changes in forest structure as well as biomass.

WOOD YIELD TABLES AND MODELS

Yield tables have been the most traditional form of forest production models (see, for example, Society of American Foresters, *Forestry Handbook*, 1984). These models typically have been developed using data collected from a large number of forest plots located in forest stands of relative species composition, stocking levels, geography, and so on. Through a variety of mathematical, statistical, and subjective analyses, such data are used as a basis for constructing tables that indicate the wood yields that should be expected at various time intervals on sites of varying productive potential. Productive potential is typically indexed by the site index criterion discussed earlier (heights achieved by dominant trees by some index age). Most yield table publications also include many other tables relating stocking density, periodic growth and mortality, and other stand variables to stand age.

Forest yield tables have most commonly been developed for well-stocked, even-aged stands of a single species. Such tables exist for almost every important species and type of forest in the northern temperate zone, and, typically, there are several yield tables (often representing different geographic regions or management intensities) for very important commercial tree species. As very general models to predict forest growth, yield models have major limitations, particularly in their ability to predict accurately the growth of specific stands.

The prediction of forest growth has shifted toward computer-based growth and yield models with the development of computer technologies. These tend to be much more sophisticated and deal with a larger set of variables than was possible with traditional yield tables. However, as with yield tables, they are normally based on empirical data sampled from some forest population.

Many such growth and yield models use a wide variety of approaches and assumptions. Early yield tables and growth simulation models focused on natural stands, but development of growth simulators for managed stands has been particularly popular with forestry agencies during the last several decades. This has allowed managers to consider the effects of various management regimes. ORGANON, a model developed at Oregon State University, is a good example of a state-of-the-art model of growth and yield (Hann, Olsen, and Hester 1992). FORTNITE is one of the few examples of a growth model designed to look at forest productivity as it is affected by various manipulations over long time periods (Kimmins 1987).

The limited empirical data bases from which yield tables and models have been constructed have been one of their major limitations. Mortality, the most difficult variable to estimate, creates the greatest degree of uncertainty in predicting yields.

ECOSYSTEM MODELS

During the last twenty years, a new class of forest growth model has emerged that focuses on predicting successional changes in forests over very long time periods. These models are based on the dynamics of tree populations, but they also provide output on stand-level attributes, such as accumulations of organic matter. Many of these forest ecosystem models are conceptually related and are sometimes referred to as the FORET family of forest growth models (Shugart 1984). The first of these models was JABOWA, which was developed for the Hubbard Brook Experimental Forest (New Hampshire). Its primary focus is on the processes of birth, growth, and death of the tree population. These processes are driven, in turn, by environmental conditions, including temperature and moisture at the site and light within the stand. The birth and death processes are based on probability functions. A variety of model outputs—tree density, biomass, leaf area, and so forth—is possible, depending on the interests of the scientist or manager.

Extensive work is under way to improve the capabilities of FORET-type models, including the development of spatially explicit versions, which keep track of the location of individual trees, incorporate the dynamics of coarse woody debris (standing dead trees, fallen logs, and so forth), and incorporate more realistic probability functions, such as for tree mortality. Versions have been developed that focus on the nutrient status of the site as well as forest structure.

Current models of this type have some limitations. Because they are designed to simulate changes in a variety of ecosystem attributes over very long time periods and for diverse sites, predictions of tree growth or wood production for specific stands may not be as good as for the traditional, and much more specific, growth and yield models.

An important attribute of these models is that they are stochastic or probabilistic rather than deterministic. Most forest growth and yield models are deterministic: only one solution is possible with an initial set of conditions. But, with the FORET family of models, an infinite number of solutions is possible. Hence, numerous, even hundreds of, simulations may be run for a given stand to produce an array of predicted outcomes: in effect, a probability distribution for future conditions of the stand.

Conclusions and recommendations

Assessing the long-term productivity or sustainability of temperate forest ecosystems represents a major challenge. Currently, this is not being adequately accomplished anywhere, nor does a suitable model or prototype exist for such a program. Hence, development of a protocol or, better still, a series of protocols for measuring the sustainability of forest ecosystems should have very high priority. Existing research and management programs can provide useful information and guidance in this effort.

The most important points in designing the assessment program are (a) recognizing the necessity of assessing several variables and (b) identifying those variables. Clearly, no single variable will adequately assess sustainability. Monitoring sustainability of forest lands and associated waters will require periodic assessments of a broad array of variables from the landscape to populations of specific organisms. Specifically, a monitoring program should assess the following:

- Forest cover and condition at the landscape level
- Flow and quality of water
- Structural conditions, including live and dead trees, of the forest stand
- Physical, chemical, and biological condition of the soil and
- Populations and trends in indicator organisms.

A program that covers such a broad range of parameters will require programs of highly varied spatial and temporal scale. An approach based on a single measurement, index, or sampling strategy is not going to be successful. Admittedly, giving up the notion of such a simple monitoring program creates greater complexities and much higher costs; nevertheless, it is an essential first step for a program that truly intends to monitor sustainability. Fortunately, such a strategy is consistent with the emerging interest in adaptive management of resources. This approach requires comprehensive monitoring to provide the resource management system with corrective feedback.

Once a decision has been made to proceed with a multi-factor monitoring program, the specific variables can be chosen and protocols developed by working with appropriate scientific teams. There will undoubtedly be substantial variation among forested regions, both in terms of variables and sampling techniques—another blow, unfortunately, to the notion of a singular global scheme. In the following sections, some candidate variables are proposed for a minimal monitoring program to assess productivity of the forest ecosystem.

Minimal program for monitoring sustainability of the forest ecosystem

A minimal program should incorporate the following measures: forest cover and condition at the landscape level, system losses and hydrologic controls, biological condition of the forest, condition of the soil, and biological diversity.

FOREST COVER AND CONDITION AT THE LANDSCAPE LEVEL Periodic assessments of the extent of forest cover, and some interpretation of its condition (age and stocking density), are the variables of interest in this segment of the monitoring program. These assessments would probably be made at five-year intervals and use various types of data obtained by remote imagery, satellites, or aircraft. The assessments would probably be made at the level of regions, in the case of large countries, or at the level of small countries.

SYSTEM LOSSES AND HYDROLOGIC CONTROL Aquatic systems—streams, rivers, and lakes—are probably the best integrators of the effects of human activities on terrestrial landscapes. The system losses referred to here are primarily losses of soil and nutrients that can be measured within aquatic systems as suspended or dissolved sediments and materials. Hence, a monitoring element that addresses the production or accumulation of sediments and the quality of water is important. Note that this monitoring occurs in the aquatic environment rather than in upland forest areas. The production of water—the total amount, seasonal distribution, and frequency and level of flood flows—is also extremely important, especially when water is recognized as one of the major products of a forest ecosystem. Both system losses and water production are probably best monitored by creating a system of benchmark watersheds in forested regions where the flow and quality of water are sampled on a more-or-less continuous basis. Techniques for such measurement programs are well known and should be easily adapted. The biggest problems are the initial cost of such installations and the continuing costs in funds and technical personnel of maintaining and analyzing data generated by such a monitoring program. However, government organizations such as the U.S. Geological Survey have extensive experience with these activities.

BIOLOGICAL CONDITION OF THE FOREST

The primary focus of this portion of the monitoring program is on some measure of productivity at the level of the individual forest stand. Tree growth per unit of time under some specified conditions, such as dominant free-grown individuals, still appears to be the best measure for integrating the overall effect of all variables influencing productivity. A direct measure of net primary productivity is beyond the scope of a routine monitoring program.

The use of tree growth per unit of time is conceptually the same approach that is used with the site index concept reviewed earlier. An alternative approach might be some measure of overall productivity of the stand; however, this can be very strongly influenced by stand conditions, so the problem of standardization is greater than where individual trees are used.

In addition to a measure of site productivity, it may also be important to monitor the structural diversity found within forest stands. Levels of standing dead trees (snags) and fallen logs on the forest floor are an example of an important structural element that has often been ignored in programs to monitor the condition of a forest. Because such material is extremely important as animal habitat, and can be important in maintaining site productivity, it should be an element of any scheme for monitoring forest ecosystems.

CONDITION OF THE SOIL

The soil is, in terms of human life spans, a largely nonrenewable resource. It is important, therefore, to monitor specifically the physical, chemical, and biological state of this basic resource. Although it can be argued that the use of some

biological measure of site productivity negates the need to monitor soil parameters directly, there is the possibility of doing irreversible harm to forest soils before that harm is reflected in declining productivity of the site. There is also the possibility of biological compensations for declining soil condition.

A soil monitoring program should include assessments of loss (due to erosional processes), physical conditions (bulk density and physical conditions), chemistry (primarily levels of critical nutrients with consideration of trace and toxic elements), and biota of the soil. One specific element of the soil biota that should receive attention in a monitoring program is the diversity of mycorrhizae-forming fungal species that are present.

BIOLOGICAL DIVERSITY

General measures of biological diversity, in terms of overall species richness, are probably not of much value in a monitoring program. Diversity indexes tend to assume that all species are of equal interest and that the richer the ecosystem, the better. This is clearly not the case with forested and, probably, most other natural or semi-natural ecosystems.

It will often be appropriate to include monitoring of selected organisms, however, because they have intrinsic importance to the ecosystem as indicator and keystone species or because they have high interest and significance to *Homo sapiens*. Species chosen for monitoring will have to be carefully selected based on scientific and societal considerations; however, monitoring at the level of individual species, guilds, functional groups, and so forth must almost inevitably be part of a comprehensive monitoring program.

This is probably the most difficult and, in terms of criteria for selecting organisms or organismal groups, the most poorly developed assessment approach. Although techniques exist for monitoring many vertebrate groups, such as birds, mammals, and amphibians, they may require high levels of technical expertise. More critical is the lack of developed approaches to the monitoring of functionally important groups such as invertebrates, including insects, and fungi.

Any monitoring program that purports to address sustainability of the forest ecosystem must, of necessity, address organisms as species or groups of species; it cannot be based totally on a single measure or integrated index of ecosystem function, such as productivity. Biodiversity is basic to long-term sustainability or productive potential.

Implementing a monitoring program

Generic plans for monitoring forest sustainability can be developed at the global and continental levels, but details of parameters and sampling techniques will have to be adapted to the particular conditions of regions and individual countries. Establishment of a global advisory body to develop general guidelines and assist in planning and implementing monitoring programs at the level of countries, regions, and continents would certainly be useful, so long as the equally critical elements of flexibility in design and scientific integrity and credibility are maintained.

Residents of rural environments in and around forests should be given special consideration for employment in the monitoring program. Traditionally, monitoring programs are assigned to professional and technical personnel within established agencies, who often live outside the affected region and are subject to frequent transfers. Resident populations have long-term familiarity with the region, including appropriate work experience, and they intend to reside in the locale. Necessary scientific and technical training could be provided for selected residents who could then be incorporated into the long-term monitoring program.

Accelerated research program

It should be clear from this review that research based on the productivity of forest ecosystems and their maintenance needs to be drastically expanded. Forest science, in particular, needs to broaden its view from the level of the tree (or just the bole) to that of the whole ecosystem. The following categories of research are critically in need of attention:

- Productivity of belowground portions of forest ecosystems
- Canopy architecture and its effect on productivity, particularly the relative effectiveness of multilayered and multispecies canopies
- Dynamics of soil organic matter and chemistry over long time periods, including rates of soil development under natural regimes
- Ecological role and dynamics of coarse woody debris across a full range of ecosystems and
- Improved understanding of causes and patterns of tree mortality and other stochastic processes in forest ecosystems.

For other suggestions on research programs, see *Forestry Research: A Mandate for Change* (National Research Council 1990).

References

AAAS (American Association for the Advancement of Science). 1967. *Primary Productivity and Mineral Cycling in Natural Ecosystems.* New York.

Aber, J. D., K. J. Nadelhoffer, P. Steudler, and J. M. Melillo. 1989. "Nitrogen Saturation in Northern Forest Ecosystems." *BioScience* 39, pp. 378–86.

Adams, R. M., C. Rosensweig, R. M. Peart, J. T. Ritchie, B. A. McCarl, J. D. Glyer, R. B. Curry, J. W. Fones, K. J. Boote, and L. H. Allen, Jr. 1990. "Global Climate Change and U.S. Agriculture." *Nature* 345, pp. 219–24.

Alaback, P. B. 1984. "A Comparison of Old-growth Forest Structure in the Western Hemlock-Sitka Spruce Forests of Southeast Alaska." In W. R. Meehan, T. R. Merrell, Jr., and T. A. Hanley, eds., *Fish and Wildlife Relationships in Old-Growth Forests*, pp. 219–25. Bronx, N.Y.: American Institute of Fisheries Research Biologists.

Alban, D. H. 1969. "The Influence of Western Hemlock and Western Red Cedar on Soil Properties." *Proceedings of the Soil Science Society of America* 33, pp. 453–57.

Bazzaz, F. A. 1990. "The Response of Natural Ecosystems to the Rising Global CO_2 Levels." *Annual Review of Ecology and Systematics* 21, pp. 167–96.

Bormann, F. H., and G. E. Likens. 1981. *Pattern and Process in a Forested Ecosystem.* New York: Springer-Verlag.

Cannell, M. G. R. 1982. *World Forest Biomass and Primary Production Data.* New York: Academic Press.

Carroll, G. C. 1980. "Forest Canopies: Complex and Independent Subsystems." In R. H. Waring, ed., *Forests: Fresh Perspectives from Ecosystem Analysis*, pp. 87–107. Proceedings of the fortieth annual Biological Colloquium. Corvallis, Oreg.: Oregon State University Press.

Daniel, T. W., J. A. Helms, and F. S. Baker. 1979. *Principles of Silviculture.* 2d ed. New York: McGraw-Hill Book Company.

Denison, W. C. 1979. *"Lobaria oregana*, A Nitrogen-fixing Lichen in Old-growth Douglas Fir Forests." In J. C. Gordon, C. T. Wheeler, and D. A. Perry, eds., *Symbiotic Nitrogen Fixation in the Management of Temperate Forests*, pp. 266–75. Corvallis, Oreg.: Oregon State University Forest Research Laboratory.

Easmus, D., and P. G. Jarvis. 1989. "The Direct Effects of Increase in the Global Atmospheric CO_2 Concentration on Natural and Commercial Temperate Trees and Forests." *Advances in Ecological Research* 19, pp. 1–55.

Eckardt, F. E., ed. 1968. *Functioning of Terrestrial Ecosystems at the Primary Production Level*. Proceedings of the Copenhagen Symposium. New York: United Nations Educational, Scientific, and Cultural Organization.

Edmonds, R. L., ed. 1981. *Analysis of Coniferous Forest Ecosystems in the Western United States*. United States/International Biosphere Program Synthesis Series 14. Stroudsburg, Penn.: Hutchinson Ross.

Franklin, J. F. 1990. "Biological Legacies: A Critical Management Concept from Mount St. Helens." In *Transactions of the Fifty-fifth North American Wildlife and Natural Resources Conference*, pp. 216–19. Washington, D.C.: Wildlife Management Institute.

———. 1992. "Scientific Basis for New Perspectives in Forests and Streams." In R. J. Naiman, ed., *Watershed Management: Balancing Sustainability and Environmental Change*, pp. 25–72. New York: Springer-Verlag.

Franklin, J. F., and R. T. T. Forman. 1987. "Creating Landscape Patterns by Forest Cutting: Ecological Consequences and Principals." *Landscape Ecology* 1, pp. 5–18.

Franklin, J. F., P. M. Frenzen, and F. J. Swanson. 1988. "Re-creation of Ecosystems at Mount St. Helens: Contrasts in Artificial and Natural Approaches." In J. Cairns, Jr., ed., *Rehabilitating Damaged Ecosystems*, vol. 2, pp. 1–37. Boca Raton, Fla.: CRC Press.

Franklin, J. F., H. H. Shugart, and M. E. Harmon. 1987. "Tree Death as an Ecological Process." *BioScience* 37, pp. 550–56.

Franklin, J. F., and T. A. Spies. 1991. "Composition, Function, and Structure of Old-growth Douglas Fir Forests." In L. F. Ruggerio, K. B. Aubry, A. B. Carey, and M. H. Huff, tech. coords., *Wildlife and Vegetation of Unmanaged Douglas Fir Forests*, pp. 71–80. PNW-GTR-185. Portland, Oreg.: U.S. Forest Service, Pacific Northwest Research Station.

Franklin, J. F., and others. 1981. "Ecological Characteristics of Old-growth Douglas Fir Forests." General Technical Report PNW-118. U.S. Department of Agriculture, Forest Service, Northwest Forest Range and Experiment Station, Portland, Oreg.

———. 1986. "Modifying Douglas Fir Management Regimes for Nontimber Objectives." In C. D. Oliver, D. P. Hanley, and J. A. Johnson, eds., *Douglas Fir: Stand Management for the Future*, pp. 373–79. Contribution 55. Seattle, Wash.: University of Washington, College of Forest Resources.

———. 1991. "Effects of Global Climate Change on Forests in Northwestern North America." *Northwest Environmental Journal* 7, pp. 233–54.

Gholz, H. L. 1982. "Environmental Limits on Aboveground Net Primary Production, Leaf Area, and Biomass in Vegetation Zones of the Pacific Northwest." *Ecology* 63:2, pp. 469–81.

Grier, G. C., and others. 1989. "Productivity of the Forests of the United States and Its Relation to Soil and Site Factors and Management Practices: A Review." General Technical Report PNW-222. U.S. Department of Agriculture, Forest Service, Pacific Northwest Research Station, Portland, Oreg.

Halpern, C. B. 1988. "Early Successional Pathways and the Resistance and Resilience of Forest Communities." *Ecology* 69, pp. 1703–15.

———. 1989. "Early Successional Patterns of Forest Species: Interactions of Life History Traits and Disturbance." *Ecology* 70:3, pp. 704–20.

Hann, D. W., C. L. Olsen, and A. S. Hester. 1992. *ORGANON User's Manual*. Oregon State University, Department of Forest Resources, Corvallis, Oreg.

Harmon, M. E., and H. Chen. 1992. "A Comparison of Coarse Woody Debris Dynamics in Two Old-growth Forest Ecosystems: Chanbai Mountain, PRC, and H. J. Andrews Experimental Forest, U.S.A." *BioScience* 41, pp. 604–10.

Harmon, M. E., and others. 1986. "Ecology of Coarse Woody Debris in Temperate Ecosystems." In A. MacFadyen and E. D. Ford, eds., *Advances in Ecological Research* 15, pp. 133–302. Academic Press.

Harris, W. F., D. Santantonio, and D. McGinty. 1980. "The Dynamic Belowground Ecosystem." In R. H. Waring, ed., *Forests: Fresh Perspectives from Ecosystem Analysis*, pp. 119–29. Corvallis, Oreg.: Oregon State University Press.

Harvey, A. E., and L. F. Neuenschwander, eds. 1991. "Proceedings: Management and Productivity of Western-montane Forest Soils." General Technical Report INT-280. U.S. Department of Agriculture, Forest Service, Intermountain Research Station, Ogden, Utah.

Heath, B., P. Sollins, D. A. Perry, and K. Cromack, Jr. 1987. "Asymbiotic Nitrogen Fixation in Litter from Pacific Northwest Forests." *Canadian Journal of Forest Research* 18, pp. 68–74.

Hopwood, D. 1991. *Principles and Practices of New Forestry*. Land Management Report 71. Victoria, B.C.: British Columbia Ministry of Forests.

Hunter, J. L., Jr. 1990. *Principles of Managing Forests for Biological Diversity*. Englewood Cliffs, N.J.: Prentice-Hall.

International Union of Forest Research Organizations. 1971. *Working Party on the Forest Biomass Studies. Section 25, Growth and Yield*. Gainesville, Fla.: University of Florida.

———. 1973. *Working Party on the Mensuration of Forest Biomass. 54.01 Mensuration, Growth, and Yield*. Vancouver, B.C., Canada.

Jarvis, P. G. 1989. "Atmospheric Carbon Dioxide and Forests." *Philosophical Transcripts of the Royal Society of London* B 324, pp. 369–92.

Jenny, H. 1980. *The Soil Resource Origin and Behavior*. New York: Springer-Verlag.

Kiilsgaard, C. W., S. E. Greene, and S. G. Stafford. 1987. "Nutrient Concentrations in Litterfall from Some Western Conifers with Special Reference to Calcium." *Plant and Soil* 102, pp. 223–27.

Kimmins, J. P. 1987. *Forest Ecology*. New York: Macmillan Publishing Company.

Lattin, J. D. 1990. "Arthropod Diversity in Northwest Old-growth Forests." *Wings* 15:2, pp. 7–10.

Likens, G. E., ed. 1989. *Long-Term Studies in Ecology: Approaches and Alternatives*. New York: Springer-Verlag.

MacMahon, J. A. 1981. "Successional Processes: Comparisons among Biomes with Special Reference to Probable Roles of and Influences on Animals." In D. C. West, H. H. Shugart, and D. B. Botkin, eds., *Forest Succession: Concepts and Application*, pp. 277–304. New York: Springer-Verlag.

Maser, C., R. F. Tarrant, J. M. Trappe, and J. F. Franklin, eds. 1988. "From the Forest to the Sea: A Story of Fallen Trees." General Technical Report PNW-GTR-229. U.S. Department of Agriculture, Forest Service, Pacific Northwest Research Station, Portland, Oreg.

National Research Council. 1990. *Forestry Research: A Mandate for Change*. Washington, D.C.

Newbould, P. J. 1967. *Methods for Estimating the Primary Production of Forests*. Oxford, England: Blackwell Scientific Publications.

Oliver, C. D., and B. C. Larson. 1990. *Forest Stand Dynamics*. New York: McGraw-Hill Book Company.

Perry, D. A., and others. 1988. *Maintaining the Long-Term Productivity of Pacific Northwest Forest Ecosystems*. Portland, Oreg.: Timber Press.

———. 1989. "Bootstrapping in Ecosystems." *BioScience* 39, pp. 230–37.

Pritchett, W. L., and R. F. Fisher. 1987. *Properties and Management of Forest Soils*. 2d ed. New York: John Wiley and Sons.

Reichle, D. E., ed. 1981. *Dynamic Properties of Forest Ecosystems*. International Biological Programme 23. Cambridge, England: Cambridge University Press.

Reichle, D. E., J. F. Franklin, and D. W. Goodall, eds. 1975. *Proceedings of a Symposium on Productivity of World Ecosystems*. Washington, D.C.: National Academy of Sciences.

Reiners, W. A. 1992. "Twenty Years of Ecosystem Reorganization Following Experimental Deforestation and Regrowth Suppression." *Ecological Monographs* 63:4, pp. 503–23.

Reukema, D. L. 1979. "Fifty-year Development of Douglas Fir Stands Planted at Various Spacings." Research Paper PNW-254. U.S. Department of Agriculture, Forest Service, Pacific Northwest Forest Range and Experiment Station, Portland, Oreg.

Reukema, D. L., and J. H. G. Smith. 1987. "Development over Twenty-five Years of Douglas Fir, Western Hemlock, and Western Red Cedar Planted at Various Spacings on a Very Good Site in British Columbia." Research Paper PNW-381. U.S. Department of Agriculture, Forest Service, Pacific Northwest Research Station, Portland, Oreg.

Rodin, L. E., and N. I. Bazilevich. 1967. *Production and Mineral Cycling in Terrestrial Vegetation*. London: Oliver and Boyd.

Ruggiero, L. F., K. B. Aubry, A. B. Carey, and M. H. Huff, eds. 1991. "Wildlife and Vegetation of Unmanaged Douglas Fir Forests." General Technical Report PNW-285. U.S. Department of Agriculture, Forest Service, Pacific Northwest Research Station, Portland, Oreg.

Schoen, J. W., and M. D. Kirchoff. 1990. "Seasonal Habitat Use by Sitka Black-tailed Deer on Admiralty Island, Alaska." *Journal of Wildlife Management* 54, pp. 371–78.

Shugart, H. H. 1984. *A Theory of Forest Dynamics: The Ecological Implications of Forest Succession Models.* New York: Springer-Verlag.

Society of American Foresters. 1984. *Forestry Handbook.* New York: John Wiley and Sons.

Sollins, P. 1982. "Input and Decay of Coarse Woody Debris in Coniferous Stands in Western Oregon and Washington." *Canadian Journal of Forest Research* 12, pp. 18–28.

Swank, W. T., and D. A. Crossley, Jr., eds. 1988. *Forest Hydrology and Ecology at Coweeta.* New York: Springer-Verlag.

Terborgh, J. W. 1992. *Diversity and the Tropical Rain Forest.* New York: Scientific American Library.

Thomas, J. W., ed. 1979. *Wildlife Habitats in Managed Forests: The Blue Mountains of Oregon and Washington.* USDA Agricultural Handbook 553. Washington, D.C.: U.S. Department of Agriculture.

Trappe, J. M., J. F. Franklin, R. F. Tarrant, and G. M. Hansen. 1967. *Biology of Alder.* U.S. Department of Agriculture, Forest Service, Pacific Northwest Forest and Range Experiment Station, Portland, Oreg.

Turner, D. P., and E. H. Franz. 1985. "The Influence of Western Hemlock and Western Red Cedar on Microbial Numbers, Nitrogen Mineralization, and Nitrification." *Plant and Soil* 88, pp. 259–67.

Waring, R. H., and J. F. Franklin. 1979. "Evergreen Coniferous Forests of the Pacific Northwest." *Science* 204:4400, pp. 1380–86.

Waring, R. H., and J. Major. 1964. "Some Vegetation of the California Coastal Redwood Region in Relation to Gradients of Moisture, Nutrients, Light, and Temperature." *Ecological Monographs* 34, pp. 167–215.

Waring, R. H., and W. H. Schlesinger. 1985. *Forest Ecosystems Concepts and Management.* Orlando, Fla.: Academic Press, Inc.

Williamson, R. L. 1973. "Results of Shelterwood Harvesting of Douglas Fir in the Cascades of Western Oregon." Research Paper PNW-161. U.S. Department of Agriculture, Forest Service, Pacific Northwest Forest and Range Experiment Station, Portland, Oreg.

Zobel, D. B., A. McKee, G. M. Hawk, and C. T. Dyrness. 1976. "Relationships of Environment to Composition, Structure, and Diversity of Forest Communities of the Central Western Cascades of Oregon." *Ecological Monographs* 46, pp. 135–56.

Comments

Ian J. Payton

The literature associated with the management of temperate forests is, as the author acknowledges, immense. In bringing together those elements that relate to sustainable management, Professor Franklin draws on his very extensive knowledge of forest management in its broadest sense. In this review, I offer comment on several aspects of the chapter, particularly as they relate to New Zealand's attempts to manage temperate forests in a sustainable manner.

The author comments that as temperate forests have been managed for several centuries, and because forestry crops have lengthy rotation periods, foresters are used to taking a long view. Although this may now be true of temperate forest management practices in those parts of the world with a long history of human settlement, elsewhere the emphasis continues to be placed on the harvesting of virgin old-growth forests with little thought for the longer term. Only when the finite nature of the resource is recognized are serious attempts made to manage it on a sustainable basis. Or to put it another way, moves toward sustainable forestry management practices appear to be born of necessity rather than an inherent desire for sustainability. In New Zealand, where European settlement during the nineteenth century was followed by large-scale clearance of forests for agriculture and timber production, it was recognition of the finite nature of the indigenous timber resource that led to the development of the exotic pine plantations that now supply much of the country's timber requirements. Even today, serious attempts to manage indigenous species for timber production are hampered by the perception that rotation periods are long, when compared with those of the exotic conifers, and the emphasis on short-term financial returns.

Implicit in our concepts of managing forest ecosystems for other than purely conservation purposes is the recognition that this involves the removal or harvesting of at least some parts of the ecosystem. Using the author's pragmatic definition that sustainability requires that there be no net loss of productivity or genetic potential, discussions on sustainable management center on the ability to replace that which has been removed from the ecosystem. For much of the biota, sustainable harvest is a viable option and may even improve productivity. Similarly, loss of nutrients through harvesting may be amenable to human manipulation.

Much more serious is the loss of soil or genetic resources. As the author notes, although soil may be restored in the longer term, loss of genetic potential is essentially permanent. What we frequently fail to realize is that the interdependent nature of much of the biota means that the loss of genetic diversity has ongoing and frequently unforeseen consequences. A recent New Zealand example is the discovery that a rare root parasite (*Dactylanthus taylori*), which is under threat from introduced herbivores and collectors, is pollinated by a species of endemic bat, which is also considered endangered. Simply protecting *Dactylanthus* against predators will not ensure its long-term survival.

Harvesting involves disturbance and can increase the risk of subsequent loss of nutrients and soil. Disturbance, however, is also a part of the natural forest cycle by which individuals and communities are replaced. Harvesting regimes, be they for timber or other forest products, need to take cognizance of the natural processes by which individuals and communities respond to disturbance. This needs to include consideration of whether replacement patterns are typically large or small scale and the processes by which nutrients are recycled. Management practices that do not mirror those of the natural forest ecosystem need to be closely examined for their potential to lead to a loss of net productivity. In this respect, timber harvesting systems that involve large-scale clear-cuts, particularly where these are followed by fire to remove the slash, create a huge potential for loss of not only soil and nutrients but also of genetic diversity.

The author makes the interesting assertion that indigenous genotypes may not be as capable as exotic species of exploiting the productive resources of a site. In support of this argument, he cites the rapid growth and high productivity of two North American pine species (*Pinus contorta* and *P. radiata*) in New Zealand. Although it is certainly true that in the short-term these exotic conifer species outperform their indigenous counterparts, the long-term sustainability of these fast-growing, short-rotation forests is still open to question. Few are past their second twenty-five- to forty-year rotation, and, particularly on nutrient-poor sites, fertilizer inputs are necessary to maintain growth rates. By contrast, the indigenous species they have replaced, by adopting a somewhat more conservative growth strategy, have weathered the vagaries of millenia of ecosystem change.

The treatment of herbivores and pathogens seeks to balance their negatively perceived impacts on forest productivity with their positive contribution to nutrient cycling and productivity within forest ecosystems. In addition we also need to distinguish between those herbivores and pathogens that have evolved with the particular forest ecosystem and are part of the natural cycle and those that have been deliberately or inadvertently introduced, frequently without their natural regulatory agents. While deer and elk species have evolved as part of many forest ecosystems in the northern hemisphere, forests in New Zealand evolved both in the absence of mammalian herbivores and their predators. Together with the Australian brushtail possum (*Trichosurus vulpecula*), which was introduced to establish a fur trade, introduced ungulate species have dramatically altered, and in some cases caused the collapse of, whole forest ecosystems in parts of New Zealand (King 1990). Once forest understory vegetation has been depleted, even low numbers of these introduced browsers are sufficient to maintain the depleted state (Allen, Payton, and Knowlton 1984). Similarly, fungal pathogens such as Dutch Elm disease and defoliating insects like the Asian gypsy moth threaten the sustainability of genetic potential in temperate forests of which they are not naturally a part.

Temperate forest management systems that focus on wood production have moved toward even-aged monocultures of the dominant tree species, with a clear-cut harvesting practice. New Zealand pine plantations are a prime example of this agricultural approach to forestry, with their single-canopy tree species, uniform single-layer canopy, and typically clear-cut harvest at intervals as short as twenty-five years. Yet even these forests retain a considerable indigenous biodiversity, and for some ground orchid species they are now the major strongholds (Johns and Molloy 1983). Even the kiwi, New Zealand's flightless ratite, can occasionally be found within pine plantation areas.

The author advances a range of potential benefits for moving away from the simplification of managed forest structures, all of which require forest managers to see the object of management in much broader terms than the efficient production of wood and the maximization of financial returns. Foresters, however, are not the only group who have championed the cause of single-purpose management of temperate forests. Of recent years, the conservation lobby has been equally forthright in its advocacy of locking up natural forests against most forms of harvesting. Changing these perceptions and gaining community sanction for multiple-use management will be critical to attempts to manage temperate forests in an ecologically sustainable manner that recognizes the need to retain both productive capacity and genetic potential.

When it comes to the measurement of sustainability, the author quite rightly points out that nowhere is this being adequately accomplished, nor are there suitable models or prototypes for such a program. However, most of the elements specified as necessary for assessing long-term sustainability are already available for at least some temperate forest ecosystems, albeit not in a coordinated fashion. Although we may not, at least in the short to medium term, be able to measure adequately all aspects of ecosystem productivity, keystone elements of productive capacity do exist and can be used to assess changes in ecosystem productivity. Similarly, although we cannot hope to measure the full spectrum of genetic diversity, we can identify keystone species as indicators of the continued presence of the guilds of organisms they depend on for their survival. Clearly a range of physical and biological variables needs to be measured in order to assess the sustainability of temperate forest management practices. The challenge is to get widespread agreement on the variables that are important for determining changes in productivity and genetic diversity and that are amenable to routine measurement. Any such program should seek to build on existing measurement programs, establish a minimum set of variables to be measured, and make full use of computer-based technologies to collate and analyze the data gathered.

Professor Franklin has put together a comprehensive and well-balanced account of ecosystem processes and management practices as they relate to the question of sustainability in temperate forests. The challenge of measuring sustainability and managing our temperate forests in a sustainable manner remains. Like many other fields of human endeavor, success will hinge as much on the commitment of people and the coordination of resources as on the technologies required to assess sustainability.

References

Allen, R. B., I. J. Payton, and J. E. Knowlton. 1984. "Effects of Ungulates on Structure and Species Composition in the Urewera Forests as Shown by Exclosures." *New Zealand Journal of Ecology 7*, pp. 119–30.

Johns, J., and B. Molloy. 1983. *Native Orchids of New Zealand.* Wellington, New Zealand: A. H. & A. W. Reed, Ltd.

King, C. M. 1990. *The Handbook of New Zealand Mammals.* Auckland, New Zealand: Oxford University Press.

24

Sustainable Management of Temperate Wildlife:
A Conceptual Model

Richard L. Knight

My thinking on this subject has benefited from discussions with D. R. Anderson, J. A. Bailey, T. L. George, H. A. L. Knight, and S. A. Temple.

"A thing is right when it tends to preserve the integrity, stability, and
beauty of the biotic community. It is not when it tends otherwise".
Aldo Leopold, *Sand County Almanac* (1949)

Aldo Leopold, who is credited with developing the discipline of wildlife management, and who originated the concept of the land ethic, most certainly had sustainability in mind when he penned these words. Landscapes that would allow people and wildlife to coexist in harmony were one of Professor Leganism" (Meine 1988). A half-century after he wrote these words, land managers are revisiting this arena and discovering the difficulties associated with sustainable wildlife management.

When defining sustainability, we need to identify what we are going to manage, for how long we are going to manage it, and for whom are we going to manage it. When discussing sustainable wildlife, some people think about sustaining ecosystems, while others think about sustaining populations of specific species. Historically, we could manage for maximum sustained yield of a particular species, almost always a game species (Leopold 1933). Today, in certain very specialized systems such as agriculture, this can still be done. This option, however, is becoming less viable when managing natural or semi-natural landscapes. Far too many publics are now interested in far too many diverse species or groups of species. Since today there is seldom unanimous agreement on what we are managing for, perhaps all we can aspire to is the vague goal of managing for biological diversity.

In addition to the taxonomic variation, there is great variation in spatial and temporal scales. The spatial dimensions shape the objectives of management. Certain publics of Colorado want to see wolves and grizzly bears reintroduced into Colorado mountains; others say that these areas are not large enough to support viable populations. When we talk about sustainable wildlife management, are we talking of time scales from 500 to 1,000 years or evolutionary time? The time scale will have profound impacts on the management approaches implemented. If we are not interested in evolutionary time, then we do not have to worry about allelic variation, a decision that could radically alter the approach followed.

When viewing temperate wildlife in terms of managing for sustainability, there are three categories into which most species will fall (see table 24-1). First, some temperate wildlife species are specifically managed for sport or commercial harvest (big game, fur bearers). Indeed, it was interest in these species that gave rise to the birth of wildlife management (Leopold 1933), and wildlife biologists have had great successes in managing them for sustained-yield harvests. These species are protected under a diverse array of state and federal statutes and treaties.

Second, some species are experiencing population declines. By their very designation, these species are presently unsustainable. Concern for

Table 24–1: A Conceptual Model Illustrating the Categories of Wildlife, the Various Approaches in Managing These Groups, and the Components of the Management Approach

Element	Single species	Multiple species
Categories	Game, endangered, pest	Mammals, birds, reptiles, amphibians, insects, plants, and so forth
Approach	Manipulate populations	Ecosystem processes, landscape mosaic
Components	Birth, death, dispersal	Fire, soil, tree gap, disease (ecosystem processes); area, isolation, juxtaposition (landscape mosaic)

them has been responsible for development of the Endangered Species Act and its goal of recovering species from impending extinction (see Rohlf 1991). Wildlife biologists have only recently focused attention on species facing extinction, and the list of species with declining populations is growing far faster than any organized effort to deal with it. For example, the United States government has placed more than 650 species on the list of endangered or threatened species, but another 600 just as vulnerable have yet to be included (Gibbons 1992).

The third category includes species that are neither game species nor endangered species. Concern for these species has generated interest in the maintenance of biological diversity and its resulting metadiscipline of conservation biology (Brussard 1985; Soule and Wilcox 1980; Temple and others 1988). Other than the U.S. Department of Agriculture's National Forest Management Act, which requires managing national forests and grasslands for viable populations of native vertebrates, the vast majority of wildlife species presently do not have adequate legislation to ensure their sustainability. It has been proposed that an Endangered Ecosystem Act is necessary to ensure the integrity and sustainability of these diverse species (Noss and Harris 1986).

Managing for sustainable wildlife

A classification system that places wildlife into one of two single-species categories (game or endangered) and all other species into wildlife communities will clearly necessitate different goals for sustainable populations and communities. The goal of managing harvested wildlife is to produce a sustainable surplus that can be cropped indefinitely, whereas the goal of managing de-

clining wildlife species is to recover the population's viability and thenceforth to sustain it indefinitely. Hence, when viewing species threatened with extinction, we are not interested, by and large, in recovering their populations so they can subsequently be harvested. The goal of managing wildlife communities is to "maintain or preserve the status of these species as members of the wildlife community of an area. Status is usually evaluated by the relative abundance of the species within the community" (Temple 1986).

Harvested wildlife

Wildlife management had its origins in the overexploitation of wildlife populations. The declines of many temperate bird and mammal species as a result of indiscriminate slaughter necessitated the creation of state and federal agencies with specific mandates for recovering overexploited populations of game species and producing sustainable harvests for sportsmen. The successes of these agencies are among the great conservation accomplishments of the twentieth century and were based on the theory of sustained-yield harvesting (U.S. Department of the Interior 1987).

The logistic growth curve is at the heart of managing a wildlife population for sustained-yield harvesting. Once a population has reached its carrying capacity, it is not necessarily productive because birth is balanced by mortality. The population can produce a sustainable harvest if some of the individuals are removed. If the yield is increased until it equals the number being recruited to the population by birth, the population is being harvested at its maximum sustainable level, and it will stabilize at about half its density at carrying capacity.

Although exploitation certainly reduces abundance, below certain levels of exploitation, populations can be sustained indefinitely. This involves the concept of density dependence. By reducing an animal's population, the impacts of predation, competition, and disease are also reduced. This results in higher survival rates and productivity of the exploited population, causing increased growth rates and producing more harvestable individuals. A number of population variables are necessary to monitor and predict sustainability for harvested species. This includes knowing birth rates and survival rates, each under various environmental conditions, and some estimate of population size.

The question of whether human exploitation is compensatory (for example, hunting replaces other kinds of mortality) is of fundamental importance in managing game species. That hunting is a compensatory form of mortality, rather than additive, is the unspoken assumption underlying the existence of game seasons and bag limits on North American wildlife. Wildlife managers assume there is a harvestable surplus of animals that are going to die from some cause (such as predation or starvation); hunting is an acceptable alternative to these other forms of mortality. If hunting were additive to these natural forms of mortality, then it would serve as a population depressant.

Exploitation can be compensated for only up to a point. At some level of harvest, hunting mortality adds to the total natural causes of mortality of a population. For populations that produce offspring that would be added to the subsequent breeding stock in the absence of exploitation, mortality from hunting is additive and will result in a population reduction.

Endangered wildlife

The perspective most relevant to today's concern for managing single-species populations focuses on nonharvested species that are experiencing declines in population. Although there are a number of sweeping explanations for population declines, important causes include chemical contaminants, overexploitation, and loss and fragmentation of habitat (Soule 1991). Habitat fragmentation disrupts dispersal between spatially isolated populations, which can result in declines in heterozygosity and allelic diversity, decreased viability of populations, and alterations in community assemblages with resultant disruptions in important interspecific interactions. Whereas populations of harvested species may require

focusing on birth and death rates, populations of declining species that are spatially isolated may require measuring these demographic parameters as well as other variables (dispersal rates and size, isolation, and shape of habitat fragments containing the population).

Whereas wildlife managers are relatively confident in their abilities to maintain sustainable populations of many game species, they are just now learning the correct approaches and requirements to restore declining animal populations to long-term viability. The approach used is to manipulate the species so that the population grows beyond the point of inflection on the logistic growth curve and reaches carrying capacity. For species threatened with extinction, the goal is to have the population close to carrying capacity so as to minimize the species experiencing the harmful effects of low population size (loss of heterozygosity, skewed sex ratios). This approach is especially relevant to endangered species because, unlike harvested species, species experiencing declines in population are often naturally rare and occur in low densities.

A problem associated with managing for declining species is how much change in a population must occur before one becomes alarmed and seeks a specific cause. Given the fact that population parameters normally vary from year to year, what sort of magnitude of change should occur to show alarm? The duration of a trend in a population parameter might be more important than the magnitude per se of the change. The geographic extent of a change in population parameters may determine its significance. A deviation in one local population may not be cause for concern, whereas a change that occurs over a large portion of the species' distribution might be cause for action.

When managing for endangered species, it is essential to identify both the proximate and ultimate causes responsible for declines in population. The proximate factor—or factors—is what causes the decline and usually relates to the species' demographics; the species is either experiencing a decrease in natality or an increase in mortality or both. The ultimate factor is the reason the species is declining and is almost always a severe change in environment (habitat fragmentation, environmental toxin).

Obviously, both proximate and ultimate factors need to be addressed when attempting to recover a species' population; however, the first priority is to deal with the proximate factor and then to address the ultimate factor. If curtailing the proximate factor can prevent a species from going extinct in the wild, restoring the species back to the wild once the ultimate factor has been corrected may not be necessary.

There are six general categories by which either birth or death rates of an endangered species can be manipulated to cause an increase in population. Three of these categories focus on increasing natality, while the remaining three concentrate on decreasing mortality (see table 24-2).

Dichotomy between harvested wildlife and endangered wildlife

A dichotomy between harvested wildlife and endangered wildlife relates to their evolutionary strategies. The reactions of a species to exploitation cannot be forecast without knowing the category of animal concerned. Some species live in a relatively stable environment and have not evolved a mechanism for responding rapidly to changes, while others live in relatively fluctuating habitats and are better able to adjust to rapid changes. In the one case, there has been selection toward population stability, and in the other, toward rapid reproduction, that is, the concept of r- and K-selection (MacArthur and Wilson 1967; Pianka 1970).

Game species, by and large, have great reproductive potential in that they tend to breed at an early age, have large clutch or litter sizes, and show reduced amounts of parental care (that is,

r-selected). In addition, they often have relatively broad ecological requirements and have increased fitness near ecological edges. In contrast, species experiencing declines in population are often incapable of responding to rapid changes in their environment and show a lower reproductive capacity. Instead, they defer breeding to an older age, have small litter or clutch sizes, and require a high degree of parental care. These species are often long-lived, leading to selection for large body size and repeated reproduction during the lifetime of the individual. In addition, these species may be habitat specialists, having a relatively narrow range of ecological conditions where they do best, or show an affinity for a type of habitat that is being destroyed or fragmented.

These distinctions, of course, are relative; a species may be r-selected relative to another but K-selected relative to a third. For example, a javelina is r-selected relative to a moose but is K-selected relative to a mouse. This is an important point, because r-selected species are more likely to withstand heavy cropping because they have greater recuperative powers.

Extreme K-strategists are unlikely to be suitable candidates for harvesting, yet the most extreme of all, the elephant, has often been recommended as such by conservationists anxious to show that the elephant could "pay its way." Alternatively, r-selected species may also decline as a result of overharvesting. Waterfowl have perhaps the richest history of sport hunting in North

Table 24–2: Six Approaches to Reversing Population Declines of Species Threatened with Extinction

Approach	Tactic	Example
Reduce mortality by stopping overexploitation	Enact legislation	Endangered Species Act
Reduce mortality by controlling predators, competitors, diseases, or parasites	Control exotic species	Feral pigs on Isla Santiago, Galapagos, Ecuador (Goblentz, and Baber 1987)
Reduce mortality by supplementing limiting factors	Provide supplemental food	White-tailed sea eagles in Sweden (Helander 1978)
Increase recruitment by increasing number of offspring per breeding	Double-clutching in birds	Peregrine falcon in eastern United States (Barclay and Cade 1983)
Increase recruitment by increasing number of breeding attempts	Provide additional nesting sites	Puerto Rican parrots (Snyder 1978)
Captive breeding and reintroduction	Captive breeding and hacking in birds	Guam rail (Haig, Ballou, and Derrickson 1990)

America yet are experiencing widespread declines. Most hunted duck species show all the characteristics of r-selected species in that they are short-lived, have large clutch sizes, breed early, and require a minimal amount of parental care. Loss and fragmentation of habitats are viewed as the greatest threats facing waterfowl: between the 1780s and the 1980s, a 53 percent loss in the original amount of wetlands has occurred within the United States (Dahl 1990).

Wildlife communities

Wildlife communities, although they comprise the vast majority of temperate wildlife, have received the least attention from wildlife managers. This may be due to the absence of any economic importance attributed to these species, although nature viewers would no doubt dispute that statement. It may also be due to the seemingly impossible task of simultaneously managing so many species. Whereas wildlife biologists are comfortable with the idea of managing single species, they were, until recently, largely unfamiliar with approaches to managing assemblages of species (Noss and Harris 1986). Indeed, the attempt of land managers to identify indicator species, keystone species, umbrella species, or guild-indicator species demonstrates their reluctance to leave the single-species approach behind.

When managing for wildlife communities, at least three approaches may be employed: (1) the species approach, (2) the ecosystem approach, and (3) the landscape approach. The species approach, as its name implies, focuses on one species that may be affecting a collection of species. This approach is similar to the single-species approach in that it concentrates on demographic variables, such as birth and death rates, and ecological concepts, such as predation, competition, diseases, and parasites. For example, this approach might attempt to increase productivity of a community of songbirds by controlling cowbird populations to reduce nest parasitism. A problem with this approach is that it focuses on species and, unless it is firmly embedded in management at the landscape level, exhausts the resources of any land management organization.

The second approach focuses on ecosystem processes and draws on ecosystem science for its inspiration. Land managers taking this approach are most concerned with ecological processes such as the formation of forest gaps, outbreaks of diseases caused by insects, and fire. This approach assumes that if ecosystems function properly, then the naturally occurring biological diversity is intact. A problem with this approach is that ecosystem function can become more important than species composition. Accordingly, the actual identity of a species is not as important as its functional role in the community (that is, as decomposer or consumer). This approach devalues the identity of species. An exotic species, if it performs the same function as a native species (that is, as pollinator) is no worse than the equivalent native species (see Lugo 1992).

A third approach in managing for wildlife communities is to manipulate habitat and landscapes in such a way as to influence groups of species collectively in the desired direction. For example, in order to maintain songbird communities of mature forests, land managers would want to minimize landscape and habitat characteristics associated with increasing edge and isolation, and decreasing size, of the stand.

Landscape and stand characteristics that influence wildlife communities include stand size, stand shape, connectivity of stands, amount and distribution of vegetative successional stages, and distribution and density of various habitat patches. These landscapes have to be viewed at different spatial scales, which necessitates management with two basic components (Saunders, Hobbs, and Margules 1991). First, the patches themselves have to be managed so as to maintain or simulate internal dynamics of natural systems. These internal dynamics include such diverse natural disturbances as tree gap formation, fire, epidemics of insects, flow of energy, and cycling of nutrients. Second, management has to focus on factors that are external to the patches but that influence internal patch dynamics. These include pollution, urbanization, spread of exotics, and alterations of water regimes. For larger fragments, emphasis should be placed on the internal dynamics; for smaller fragments, emphasis should concentrate on the external influences. External factors (such as acid rain or change in climate), however, can be important regardless of the remnant size.

Since most impacts on habitat fragments originate from the surrounding landscape, there is clearly a need to depart from traditional notions of management and to look instead toward integrated landscape management (Pickett, Parker, and Fiedler 1992; Saunders, Hobbs, and Margules

1991). Traditional management of natural resources stopped at the reserve boundary; fluxes of water, pollutants, and organisms do not. Placing the conservation reserves firmly within the context of the surrounding landscape and attempting to develop complementary management strategies seem to be the only way to ensure the long-term viability of temperate wildlife communities. Problems associated with a landscape approach include difficulty of acquiring enough protected areas to be able to manage effectively at an adequate spatial and temporal scale. In addition, parks and reserves are traditionally set aside for reasons other than their landscape configurations relative to biological diversity. Reserves are usually protected for their recreational or aesthetic purposes, not because of their productivity or unique vegetation. A sequence of steps that could be modified by land managers faced with the dilemma of managing landscapes for biological diversity is presented in box 24-1. This strategy incorporates aspects of the ecosystem and landscape approaches.

Box 24-1: Steps for Managing Temperate Wildlife Communities

Step 1. Set clear objectives (maximizing diversity of native wildlife, minimizing the number of species that fall below minimum populations).

Step 2. Associate wildlife communities with specific habitat configurations, using environmental suitability (vegetative structure, geomorphology, primary productivity, climate) as a surrogate for animal demography.

Step 3. Determine the minimum subsets of habitat fragments required to represent the diversity of a given area; know the distribution of species and types of ecosystems.

Step 4. Assess the potential sensitivity of groups of species to changes in landscape; this may be based on the life history strategies of the species or on the amount and distribution of suitable habitats.

Step 5. Manage the system to meet the predetermined objectives; management will have to be ongoing, and a monitoring system should be devised to measure responses of habitats and species.

Source: Modified from Hansen and others 1993; Saunders, Hobbs, and Margules 1991.

Dichotomy and conflict between single-species and wildlife community management

An important distinction between managing a single species and managing a wildlife community is that in the first case, the manager focuses on population variables such as birth, death, and dispersal, while in the second, the manager addresses ecosystem processes and landscape features in such a way that the wildlife community of interest shows collective population responses in the desired direction (such as increased birth rates).

A dilemma of considerable import when managing wildlife one species at a time is that the single-species approach inevitably results in management that contradicts other management. Put as a question, if sustainable management of one species or resource alters the population dynamics of another species, are we actually sustainable managers? Wildlife management tends to simplify wildlife communities by managing for a handful of harvested species. When managing for sustained yield of ungulates, what happens if the process entails altering populations of predators, competitors, diseases, or parasites or entails changing landscape patterns, which alters edge/ habitat interior ratios or connectivity? Following this, if the management practices are successful, what happens after the population increases and we begin to see alterations in ecological communities? For example, browsing by white-tailed deer can profoundly affect the abundance and population structure of several woody and herbaceous plant species. Because deer wander widely, the effects of high densities of deer can greatly modify the vegetation of an area (Alverson, Waller, and Solheim 1988). By reducing predators of white-tailed deer, we may be altering the naturally occurring vegetation of regions (Anderson and Loucks 1979).

This has, to a degree, occurred already. Wildlife managers have a long history of manipulating habitats to increase edge, because this generally results in higher species richness and greater populations of certain game species (cottontail rabbit, ruffed grouse; Leopold 1933). This increase in amount of edge habitat, along with the pervasive increase in habitat fragmentation by other types of human activities (such as road building), has been partly responsible for the decline in some North American songbird populations (Robbins, Dawson, and Dowell 1989; Terborg 1989).

Instead of accentuating the differences between single-species and multiple-species management, however, what is needed is a synthetic approach rather than the existing dualism. For example, the Hawaiian islands have an inordinate number of endangered species. We need to focus on particular aspects of the life history of each of these species in order to recover them while at the same time taking an ecosystem and landscape approach to ensure the integrity of the life support systems. One way of describing an ecosystem is to measure its productivity; another is to count the number of species it supports.

Use of models in managing for sustainable wildlife

Models are a collection of symbols that achieve a purposeful representation of reality by providing an abstraction that can be manipulated by changing the symbols or their relationships to each other (Jeffers 1982). Management decisions involve very complex living systems for which land managers frequently do not have the data necessary to make decisions. Thus models permit problem solving that would be too large and too expensive for experimental approaches. Although models can reduce the uncertainty of the consequences of management decisions, decisionmakers are all too eager to embrace poorly tested, poorly analyzed models.

Wildlife managers have used modeling for a variety of purposes, but its chief function has been to examine how populations change in size. This reflects back to the life table approach in population estimation (Caughley 1977). By using natality, mortality, and population age structure, wildlife biologists can look at the growth rate and determine how environmental variables may affect population size. Given a population estimate, for example, managers can then determine what effects different rates of harvest may have on the population and what different environmental factors might influence it.

Single-species models can be conveniently broken into those that focus on game species and those that do not. By and large, models for game species are deterministic and have been used for a wide variety of questions ranging from the influence of habitat, balance of energy, and importance of demographic changes (Gaudette and Stauffer 1988; Hobbs 1989; McCullough and others 1990; Medin and Anderson 1979).

Models for endangered species, historically, were very much like those for game species in that they were deterministic and yielded useful insights on the relative importance of topics such as birth and death rates (Grier 1988). In the ensuing years, alternative approaches have been developed. For example, the U.S. Fish and Wildlife Service developed habitat suitability index models, which assess the sensitivity of wildlife to habitat perturbations (Schroeder 1986; see Van Horn and Wiens 1991 for a critical review). In addition, population viability analysis and metapopulation models are being used for species experiencing declines in population (Gilpin and Hanski 1991; Soule 1987). Population viability analysis has been of immense importance for managing small populations that are particularly sensitive to stochastic phenomena such as loss of genetic diversity and catastrophic events (see Hedrick and Miller 1992). The metapopulation concept is equally applicable to harvested species and is the first attempt to integrate landscape ecology formally into the dynamics of a species' population (Murphy and Noon 1992).

The final frontier for wildlife modelers will focus on wildlife communities. Although only a few attempts have been made to model species communities, the models available have provided extremely important insights into how landscape configurations can influence wildlife assemblages (Temple 1986; Temple and Cary 1988).

Data sets used for monitoring and predicting sustainability of temperate wildlife

There are a number of well-established monitoring programs for terrestrial wildlife in North America. These projects generally cover large spatial scales and are organized by federal, state, or private organizations. They transcend the boundaries of protected areas and deal with both single-species and multiple-species assemblages, although with few exceptions, they focus on birds and mammals. These programs range from merely noting the presence or absence of a species within an area to collecting data that may be used to detect population trends. Data acquisition is often designed to serve the specific objectives of the agency or organization involved. Accordingly, many of the data bases are widely scattered, are often incompatible, and can be inaccessible to potential users.

In spite of limitations of some of the sampling methods and spatial and temporal scale of the data sets, the information available is considerable and could be used to monitor continent-wide trends for certain taxa. For instance, variations in bird populations, including information on reproductive success and mortality, could be monitored by using trends and density of winter bird populations from Christmas bird counts and winter bird population studies, monitoring nesting populations and densities from the breeding bird surveys and breeding bird censuses, determining reproductive success from the Nest Record Card Program, and determining mortality and dispersal from the Bird-Banding Laboratory. Although these data sets are tremendously valuable, they have seldom been integrated into nationwide appraisals of bird status (but see Robbins, Bystrak, and Geissler 1986; Root 1988). Presently, these data sets cannot be used to determine the cause of changes in population.

Some existing monitoring programs include the following:

- *The State Natural Heritage Program (Nature Conservancy)*, whose goal is to provide comprehensive information on both species and ecosystem diversity that can be used for acquiring, designating, and managing protected areas. Natural Heritage Data Centers exist in every state of the United States as well as in Latin America and elsewhere. The heritage program inventories are continually updated through a system for gathering and ranking information. They begin with broad information searches and are often supplemented with detailed field surveys. The data are stored in both manual and computer files (see Jenkins 1988).

- *Breeding Bird Survey (U.S. Fish and Wildlife Service and Canadian Wildlife Service)*, whose goal is to estimate population trends of birds that nest in North America north of Mexico and that migrate across international boundaries. The survey began in 1965 and provides information, both locally by ecological or political regions and on a continental scale, on short-term changes in populations that can be correlated with specific weather incidents, recovery periods following catastrophic declines, normal year-to-year variations, long-term population trends, and invasions of exotics. A sampling scheme is based on degree blocks of 1° latitude and 1° longitude. Each route con-

sists of fifty three-minute stops 0.8 kilometer apart and is run one morning each year, at the height of the breeding season, starting at a half hour before sunrise (see Robbins, Bystrak, and Geissler 1986).

- *Christmas Bird Count (National Audubon Society)*, whose goal is to determine continent-wide distribution and abundance patterns of most birds wintering in North America. First conducted in 1900 with twenty-seven people, the survey counted twenty-six localities, including two in Canada. In 1985–86, 38,346 people participated in 1,504 counts in the United States, Canada, Middle and South America, Bermuda, and the West Indies. Each count covers a circle 24 kilometers in diameter, and at least eight hours must be spent counting at each site. The survey takes place within a two-week period around Christmas (see Root 1988).

- *North American Nest Record Program*, whose goal is to record data on avian breeding biology such as the nesting season, clutch size, incubation period, nesting period, and nesting success; 300,000 nest records have been completed for 555 species, of which more than 150,000 have been computerized. This program would allow the reproductive success of North American birds to be monitored on an annual basis, but this has yet to be done for any species.

- *Breeding Bird Census and Winter Bird Population Study (Cornell Laboratory of Ornithology)*, whose goal is to estimate species density of nesting or wintering birds within particular types of habitat throughout the United States. Study plots of a fixed size and location are surveyed using the spot-mapping method (see Droege and Sauer 1989; Robbins 1981).

- *Bird Atlas Project*, whose goal is to provide an annual sample of changing abundance of bird species, primarily to determine the presence or absence of a species. The survey is usually based on blocks of land that cover 1° of latitude and 1° of longitude (see Laughlin, Kibgbe, and Eagles 1982).

- *Upland game bird call counts (U.S. Fish and Wildlife Service)*, whose goal is to discern population trends of upland game birds, particularly mourning doves and woodcock. Some states also conduct call counts for bobwhites, ring-necked pheasants, and other quail species (see Eng 1986a).

- *Waterfowl surveys (U.S. Fish and Wildlife Service, Canadian Wildlife Service, and state wildlife agencies)*, whose goal is to assess population trends in waterfowl. Annual trend data are gathered in May and June along aerial east-west transects distributed throughout breeding areas from the prairies to the boreal forest and into the tundra. Segments of transects are covered intensively by ground crews within twenty-four hours of the air counts, and a visibility index is applied to the aerial counts. These surveys are conducted over about 80,500 kilometers (about 2 percent of the breeding habitat). Brood counts are conducted to assess success of annual waterfowl breeding and are done from the air and from the ground. Finally, an annual winter inventory is conducted to determine the size and distribution of the mid-winter waterfowl population (see Eng 1986b).

- *Ungulates (state wildlife and conservation agencies)*, whose goal is to assess population trends from year to year in order to set hunting seasons and bag limits.

- *National Wetlands Inventory Project (U.S. Fish and Wildlife Service)*, whose goal is to collect information on the location, extent, status, and trends of U.S. wetlands. Maps are available for 51 percent of the lower forty-eight states, 14 percent of Alaska, and all of Hawaii. A national assessment of the status and recent trends in U.S. wetlands has been completed. The results are published in the Fish and Wildlife Service report, *Wetlands of the United States: Current Status and Recent Trends* (U.S. Department of the Interior 1992).

Measures of sustainability

Indicators of sustainable wildlife populations and communities are necessary to evaluate progress toward meeting management goals. For single-species populations, measurements that are necessary include changes in population sizes or densities, birth and death rates, and dispersal patterns. Specifically, for harvested species, managers need to monitor changes in populations and harvest rates, as well as changes in age and sex ratios. For endangered species, indicators of sustainability include reaching the minimum viable population estimates or being taken off the list of endangered species. It is essential to monitor population status after these events have occurred.

Measurements of sustainable wildlife communities may fall within either a species approach or an ecosystem/landscape approach. The use of particular species as surrogates to monitor the health of wildlife communities found early popularity (Code of Federal Regulations 1985; Severinghaus 1981; U.S. Department of the Interior 1980a, 1980b); however, it has recently received considerable criticism (Landres, Verner, and Thomas 1988; Mannan, Morrison, and Meslow 1984; Szaro 1986; Temple and Weins 1989; Verner 1984). There are two inherent assumptions when using indicator species as representative of relations between wildlife and habitat. First is the assumption that the indicator species is an appropriate agent for a larger suite of species of interest and that a change in the indicator species' population is reflective of widespread changes in habitat and environment. Second is the supposition that a change in the population of the indicator species can be used to predict the environmental variables responsible for these changes (Van Horne and Wiens 1991). These assumptions fail on both conceptual and empirical grounds (Landres, Verner, and Thomas 1988).

Alternatives do exist, however, for taking a species approach to monitor viable wildlife communities. For instance, a useful index might be ratios that reflect the number of species going extinct over the number of species extant, the number of species being listed or delisted as endangered over the number of species extant, or the total number of native species divided by the total number of species (both native and exotic) found in the area of concern (Anderson 1991). A landscape approach could include monitoring changes in patterns of land use (percentage of forest being converted to farmland), changes in patch characteristics and landscape mosaics (distribution of patch sizes, connectivity, shape, and so forth), or ratios reflecting the amount of an area of interest that is in a natural or disturbed condition. Ecosystem approaches could be measurements of human resources necessary to maintain functioning ecosystems or incidences of ecosystem processes such as formation of tree gaps, fires, or outbreaks of disease.

The challenge

How does a society complete the transition from a wildlife management paradigm that focuses on single-species management to a paradigm in which land stewards strive to preserve the integrity, stability, and beauty of the biotic community? This is clearly more than just a scientific dilemma, although natural resource managers are experimenting with new approaches and technologies. This challenge embraces the diverse and complex fabrics and colors of our society as a whole. Diverse publics find it easy to support efforts to save whooping cranes or grizzly bears, for here one can easily see the results of concerted efforts. For example, so many individuals of species *x* were alive in 1980, and, with the concerted efforts of agencies and environmental groups, this number had doubled by 1990.

The publics are not nearly as facile, however, with ecosystem and landscape approaches. Size, shape, and connectivity of habitat patches or natural fire regimes or forest gap formation are neither easily understood nor easily appreciated by a largely ecologically semi-literate citizenry. Other than the overwhelmingly important goal of increasing citizen ecological literacy, I suggest that scientists need to stress the values of ecosystem functions to society as a whole. When discussing the wealth of benefits accrued to society as a result of watershed management, flood control, soil formation, decrease in soil erosion, the proper balance of atmospheric gases, or the full spectrum of biological diversity, the scientific community needs to emphasize that these values are only fully realized when ecosystems are healthy. Once a society understands that ecosystem processes are more basic to an ecosystem than elements (read species) and that the processes create and ensure the maintenance of the elements, then perhaps we will truly begin to manage for sustainable wildlife communities.

References

Alverson, W. S., D. M. Waller, and S. I. Solheim. 1988. "Forests Too Deer: Edge Effects in Northern Wisconsin." *Conservation Biology* 2, pp. 348–58.

Anderson, J. E. 1991. "A Conceptual Framework for Evaluating and Quantifying Naturalness." *Conservation Biology* 5, pp. 347–52.

Anderson, R. C., and O. L. Loucks. 1979. "Whitetail Deer (*Odocoileus virginianus*) Influence on the Structure and Composition of *Tsuga canadensis* Forests." *Journal of Applied Ecology* 16, pp. 855–61.

Barclay, J. H., and T. J. Cade. 1983. "Restoration of the Peregrine Falcon in the Eastern United States." *Biological Conservation* 1, pp. 3–40.

Brussard, P. F. 1985. "The Current Status of Conservation Biology." *Bulletin of the Ecological Society of America* 66:1, pp. 9–11.

Caughley, G. 1977. *Analysis of Vertebrate Populations.* New York: John Wiley and Sons.

Coblentz, B. E., and D. W. Baber. 1987. "Biology and Control of Feral Pigs on Isla Santiago, Galapagos, Ecuador." *Journal of Applied Ecology* 24, pp. 404–18.

Dahl, T. E. 1990. "Wetlands Losses in the United States 1780's to 1980's." U.S. Department of the Interior, Fish and Wildlife Service, Washington, D.C.

Droege, S., and J. R. Sauer. 1989. "North American Breeding Bird Survey Annual Summary 1988." *U.S. Fish and Wildlife Service Biological Report* 89:13, pp. 1–16.

Eng, R. L. 1986a. "Upland Game Birds." In A. Y. Cooperrider, R. J. Boyd, and H. R. Stuart, eds., *Inventory and Monitoring of Wildlife Habitat*, pp. 407–28. Denver, Colo.: U.S. Department of the Interior, Bureau of Land Management Service Center.

————. 1986b. "Waterfowl." In A. Y. Cooperrider, R. J. Boyd, and H. R. Stuart, eds., *Inventory and Monitoring of Wildlife Habitat*, pp. 371–86. Denver, Colo.: U.S. Department of the Interior, Bureau of Land Management Service Center.

Gaudette, M. T., and D. F. Stauffer. 1988. "Assessing Habitat of White-tailed Deer in Southwestern Virginia." *Wildlife Society Bulletin* 16, pp. 284–90.

Gibbons, A. 1992. "Mission Impossible: Saving All Endangered Species." *Science* 256, pp. 1386.

Gilpin, M., and I. Hanski, eds. 1991. "Metapopulation Dynamics: Empirical and Theoretical Investigations." *Biological Journal of the Linnean Society* 42, pp. 1–336.

Grier, J. W. 1988. "Modeling Approaches to Bald Eagle Population Dynamics." *Wildlife Society Bulletin* 8, pp. 316–22.

Hansen, A. J., S. L. Garman, B. Marks, and D. L. Urban. 1993. "An Approach for Managing Vertebrate Diversity across Multiple-use Landscapes." *Ecological Applications* 3, pp. 481–96.

Hedrick, P. W., and P. S. Miller. 1992. "Conservation Genetics: Techniques and Fundamentals." *Ecological Applications* 2, pp. 30–46.

Helander, B. 1978. "Feeding White-tailed Sea Eagles." In S. A. Temple, ed., *Endangered Birds: Management Techniques for Preserving Threatened Species*, pp. 149–59. Madison, Wisc.: University of Wisconsin Press.

Hobbs, N. T. 1989. "Linking Energy Balance to Survival in Mule Deer: Development and Test of a Simulation Model." *Wildlife Monographs* 101, pp. 1–39.

Jeffers, J. N. R. 1982. *Modelling.* London: Chapman and Hall.

Jenkins, R. E., Jr. 1988. "Information Management for the Conservation of Biodiversity." In E. O. Wilson, ed., *Biodiversity*, pp. 231–39. Washington, D.C.: National Academy Press.

Landres, P. B., J. Verner, and J. W. Thomas. 1988. "Ecological Uses of Vertebrate Indicator Species: A Critique." *Conservation Biology* 2, pp. 316–28.

Laughlin, S. D., D. F. Kibgbe, and P. F. J. Eagles. 1982. "Atlasing the Distribution of the Breeding Birds of North America." *American Birds* 35, pp. 6–19.

Leopold, A. 1933. *Game Management.* New York: Charles Scribner's Sons.

————. 1949. *A Sand County Almanac.* New York: Oxford University Press.

Lugo, A. E. 1992. "More on Exotic Species." *Conservation Biology* 6, p. 6.

MacArthur, R. H., and E. O. Wilson. 1967. *The Theory of Island Biogeography.* Princeton, N.J.: Princeton University Press.

Mannan, R. W., M. L. Morrison, and E. C. Meslow. 1984. "The Use of Guilds in Forest Bird Management." *Wildlife Society Bulletin* 12, pp. 426–30.

McCullough, D. R., D. S. Pine, D. L. Whitmore, T. M. Mansfield, and R. H. Decker. 1990. "Linked Sex Harvest Strategy for Big Game Management with a Test Case on Black-tailed Deer." *Wildlife Monographs* 112, pp. 1–41.

Medin, D. E., and A. E. Anderson. 1979. "Modeling the Dynamics of a Colorado Mule Deer Population." *Wildlife Monographs* 68, pp. 1–77.

Meine, C. 1988. *Aldo Leopold: His Life and Work.* Madison, Wisc.: University of Wisconsin Press.

Murphy, D. D., and B. R. Noon. 1992. "Integrating Scientific Methods with Habitat Conservation Planning: Reserve Design for Northern Spotted Owls." *Ecological Applications* 2, pp. 3–17.

Noss, R. F., and L. D. Harris. 1986. "Nodes, Networks, and MUMs: Preserving Diversity at All Scales." *Environmental Management* 10, pp. 299–309.

Pianka, E. R. 1970. "On r- and K-selection." *American Naturalist* 104, pp. 592–97.

Pickett, S. T. A., V. T. Parker, and P. L. Fiedler. 1992. "The New Paradigm in Ecology: Implications for Conservation Biology above the Species Level." In P. L. Fiedler and S. K. Jain, eds., *Conservation Biology*, pp. 66–88. New York: Chapman and Hall.

Robbins, C. S. 1981. "Reappraisal of the Winter Bird Population Study Technique." In C. J. Ralph and J. M. Scott, eds., *Studies in Avian Biology*, vol. 6, pp. 62–57. Cooper Ornithological Society.

Robbins, C. S., D. Bystrak, and P. H. Geissler. 1986. *Breeding Bird Survey: Its First Fifteen Years, 1965–1979.* Research Publication 157. Washington, D.C.: U.S. Department of the Interior.

Robbins, C. S., D. K. Dawson, and B. A. Dowell. 1989. "Habitat Area Requirements of Breeding Forest Birds of the Middle Atlantic States." *Wildlife Monograph* 103.

Rohlf, D. J. 1991. "Six Biological Reasons Why the Endangered Species Act Doesn't Work–and What to Do about It." *Biological Conservation* 5, pp. 273–82.

Root, T. 1988. *Atlas of Wintering North American Birds: An Analysis of Christmas Bird Count Data.* Chicago, Ill.: University of Chicago Press.

Saunders, D. A., R. J. Hobbs, and C. R. Margules. 1991. "Biological Consequences of Ecosystem Fragmentation: A Review." *Conservation Biology* 5, pp. 18–32.

Schroeder, R. 1986. "Habitat Suitability Index Models: Wildlife Species Richness in Shelterbelts." FWS/OBS-82/10.28. U.S. Fish and Wildlife Service, Washington, D.C.

Severinghaus, W. D. 1981. "Guild Theory Development as a Mechanism for Assessing Environmental Impact." *Environmental Management* 5, pp. 187–90.

Snyder, N. F. R. 1978. "Puerto Rican Parrots and Nest-site Scarcity." In S. A. Temple, ed., *Endangered Birds: Management Techniques for Preserving Threatened Species*, pp. 47–53. Madison, Wisc.: University of Wisconsin Press.

Soule, M. E., ed. 1987. *Viable Populations for Conservation.* Cambridge, England: Cambridge University Press.

————. 1991. "Conservation: Tactics for a Constant Crisis." *Science* 253, pp. 744–50.

Soule, M. E., and B. A. Wilcox, eds. 1980. *Conservation Biology: An Evolutionary-Ecological Perspective.* Sunderland, Mass.: Sinauer Associates.

Szaro, R. C. 1986. "Guild Management: An Evaluation of Avian Guilds as a Predictive Tool." *Environmental Management* 10, pp. 681–88.

Temple, S. A. 1986. "Predicting Impacts of Habitat Fragmentation on Forest Birds: A Comparison of Two Models." In J. Verner, M. L. Morrison, and C. J. Ralph, eds., *Wildlife 2000: Modeling Habitat Relationships of Terrestrial Vertebrates,* pp. 301–04. Madison, Wisc.: University of Wisconsin Press.

Temple, S. A., E. G. Bolen, M. E. Soule, P. F. Brussard, H. Salwasser, and J. G. Teer. 1988. "What's So New about Conservation Biology?" *Transactions of the North American Wildlife and Natural Resources Conference* 53, pp. 609–12.

Temple, S. A., and J. R. Cary. 1988. "Modeling Dynamics of Habitat-interior Bird Populations in Fragmented Landscapes." *Conservation Biology* 2, pp. 340–47.

Temple, S. A., and J. A. Wiens. 1989. "Bird Populations and Environmental Changes: Can Birds Be Bio-indicators?" *American Birds* 43, pp. 260–70.

Terborg, J. W. 1989. *Where Have All the Birds Gone?* Princeton, N.J.: Princeton University Press.

U.S. Department of the Interior. 1980a. "Habitat Evaluation Procedures (HEP)." Ecological Services Manual 102. U.S. Department of the Interior, Fish and Wildlife Service, Division of Ecological Services, Washington, D.C.

————. 1980b. "Standards for the Development of Habitat Suitability Index Models." Ecological Services Manual 103. U.S. Department of the Interior, Fish and Wildlife Service, Division of Ecological Services, Washington, D.C.

————. 1987. *Restoring America's Wildlife: 1937–1987.* Washington, D.C.: U.S. Fish and Wildlife Service.

————. 1992. *Wetlands of the United States: Current Status and Recent Trends.* Washington, D.C.: U.S. Fish and Wildlife Service.

U.S. Government. 1985. Code of Federal Regulations. 36 CFR, chapter II 219, pp. 19–64. Washington, D.C.: Government Printing Office.

Van Horne, B., and J. A. Wiens. 1991. "Forest Bird Habitat Suitability Models and the Development of General Habitat Models." Fish Wildlife Research 8. U.S. Fish and Wildlife Service, Washington, D.C.

Verner, J. 1984. "The Guild Concept Applied to Management of Bird Populations." *Environmental Management* 8, pp. 1–14.

Sustainability of Wildlife and Natural Areas

Kent H. Redford and John G. Robinson

The term sustainability can be defined rather easily. It is a characteristic of some entity that lasts through time. The problem with the concept of sustainability, as used in conservation and development arenas, concerns the identity of that entity. What do we want to sustain? When this question is posed, there is a general agreement that it is some aspect of the biogeosphere. There is also agreement that the reason we want to sustain this aspect is to support human activities. But thereafter, the common ground is difficult to find. Do we want to sustain the environment, natural capital, or ecosystems? For which human groups do we want to sustain it: local communities, national states? At what level will these human activities be supported: at present levels or do we aspire to improve the quality of human life? And for how long will we sustainably use that resource? Answers to these questions reflect different understandings of what parts of the biogeosphere are important to human survival, different values that people place on preserving different parts of the biogeosphere, and different expectations and aspirations for human development.

Any discussion of sustainability must therefore define its universe of interest very precisely. In this chapter, we address the question of the sustainability of tropical wildlife and natural areas. Before moving on to a discussion of their sustainability, we need to examine these terms carefully and attempt to provide precise definitions.

First, we must consider the fact that the wildlife and natural areas under consideration are located in the tropics. Tropical wildlife differs from temperate wildlife in two major ways. First, the tropics are a long way from most international decisionmaking centers and therefore seem easier to deal with than temperate areas whose problems stare decisionmakers in the face. It is easier to promulgate facile solutions in areas rarely visited and poorly understood. Second, more people are living in areas termed natural in the tropics than in temperate areas; in all cases, they rely on wildlife, to a greater or lesser extent. The presence of these people in tropical areas, including indigenous, traditional, and colonist populations, creates a suite of problems, not generally regarded as relevant to temperate natural areas.

The second term to examine is wildlife. In temperate areas, particularly those in Europe and North America, there is a single-species tradition of wildlife management, which has largely defined the approaches taken to wildlife and its use. This tradition has given historically defined wildlife as those species of birds and mammals that hunters pursue for sport. This limited definition has begun to be modified, such that in many parts of the world, wildlife is now being defined as all wild plant and animal species.

The third term to examine is natural areas, which refers to areas in which natural rather than anthropogenic processes dominate. It is a category that includes landscapes and implicitly, therefore, processes of both a biotic as well as an abiotic nature. The degree to which an area is natural is the subject of much debate. Data from botany, archaeology, and anthropology collected in many parts of the world are showing that anthropogenic effects are ubiquitous in tropical areas and that the virgin habitat so sought after by ecologists may not exist. Despite this fact, most observers, on visiting an area, would agree on whether it is a natural area or not. This is to say that certain areas provide a gestalt of naturalness that corresponds to the lack of obvious, large-scale, human intervention.

Biodiversity

Combining the broader definition of wildlife—all wild plant and animal species—with the general definition of natural areas—landscapes including biotic and abiotic processes in which human actions are relatively insignificant—results in a term that, in this chapter, we define as biodiversity. In this context, the term serves as a useful replacement for wildlife and natural areas.

Biodiversity, one of the watchwords of the 1990s, is usually either not defined or defined in vague and highly variable ways (Noss 1990). Despite the imprecise ways in which the term is used, policymakers have taken what was an academic working concept (biodiversity) and put hundreds of millions of dollars into funded programs to conserve it (Redford and Sanderson 1992). Largely in response to this flush of funding, many interest groups have taken up the banner of biodiversity conservation, enlarging the definition to the point that the current global biodiversity strategy suggests that biodiversity be defined to include human cultural diversity, manifested in diversity in languages, religious beliefs, land management practices, art, and so forth (IUCN 1991). This definition allows Manhattan or São Paulo to be considered on equal footing with the Great Barrier Reef of Australia when it comes to levels of biodiversity and makes impossible any coherent discussion of biodiversity conservation.

In this chapter, we propose restricting the meaning of biodiversity, deliberately excluding human cultural diversity as well as the diversity represented in domesticated plants and animals. We have, in addition, divided the concept into various components and incorporated processes, a frequently neglected component of biodiversity (Franklin 1988; Noss 1990). In doing this, we provide a definition that closely approximates our charge, which is to examine wildlife and natural areas. We provide a formal definition, based on the Office of Technology Assistance definition (OTA 1987), generally regarded as being the most comprehensive of all definitions,

and certainly the one to which most frequent reference is made.

Biodiversity, then, refers to the variety and variability among living organisms, the ecological complexes in which they naturally occur, and the ways in which they interact with each other and with the geosphere. Biological diversity can be measured at different levels (genes, species, higher taxonomic levels, communities and biotic processes, and ecosystems and ecosystem processes) and at different scales (temporal and spatial). Biological diversity, at its different levels, can be measured in number or relative frequency.

Genetic diversity refers to the variability within a species, as measured by the variation in genes (chemical units of hereditary information that can be passed from one generation to another) within a particular species, population, variety, subspecies, or breed. All genetic diversity ultimately arises at the molecular level, based on the properties of nucleic acids. There is no single way to measure genetic diversity, but it can be assessed by DNA and protein polymorphism as well as by detection of polymorphism in quantitative morphological traits (Bawa and others 1991). Humans have affected the genetic diversity of plants and animals directly through the process of domestication, as well as indirectly through hunting, gathering, habitat alteration, and harvesting (see, for example, Ledig 1992; Ryman and others 1981). Very few people have investigated the ubiquitous effects of human activity on this component of biodiversity.

Species diversity refers to the variety of living species on earth and is measured at the local, regional, or global scale. It can be measured in a number of different ways, which differentially weight presence versus frequency of different species at a given locality. The species is the unit that biologists most commonly use to categorize the variation of life. It is also the unit best understood by lay people. As a result of this, and the pioneering efforts of taxonomists, much of the attention on biodiversity has been focused at the species level. There is, however, considerable disagreement on how to define a species and how to measure the diversity of species.

Diversity of higher taxonomic levels (genera, families, and so forth) refers to the variety of organisms within a given region at a taxonomic level higher than the species level. It is clear that the patterns of diversity manifested at the species level are by no means always the same as those demonstrated at the generic level and higher.

When the objective is to preserve the greatest genetic variation, species from different higher taxa should be selected; that is, the community that contains the most species may not contain the greatest amount of unique genetic information (Mares 1992; Platnick 1991). This component of biodiversity appears to be particularly important when comparing marine with terrestrial systems in that the patterns of genetic diversity within taxonomic groups may be different in these two systems (Thorne-Miller and Catena 1991).

Communities and biotic process diversity refers to the variety at the level of a group of organisms belonging to a number of different species that co-occur in the same habitat or area and interact through trophic and spatial relationships. Included in this level are communities of organisms, defined in a given time frame. This qualification is important because more and more ecologists are appreciating the dynamic nature of community composition (Hunter, Jacobson, and Webb 1988). Biotic processes include processes such as pollination, predation, and mutualism.

Ecosystems-level diversity refers to the variety of communities of organisms and their physical environment interacting as an ecological unit. The ecosystem level can be divided into ecosystem types and ecosystem processes. Ecosystem types are bounded communities interacting with the abiotic environment, such as gallery forest. One of the critical differences between this level and the community level is the inclusion of ecosystem processes, such as fire and nutrient cycling. Ecosystem processes can be classified on the basis of (1) functional attributes, that is, the capacity of the ecosystem to capture, store, and transfer energy, nutrients, and water; or (2) structural attributes, relating to abundance and distribution of species of various sizes and shapes, such as species as structural types; or (3) functional types, referring to the abundance and distribution of species with such functional attributes as the capacity to fix nitrogen and behave as predators, pollinators, and so forth (Anderson and others 1991).

Biodiversity conservation at the ecosystem level seeks to preserve the basic trophic structure of an ecosystem and the patterns of energy flow and nutrient cycling resulting from that structure (McNaughton 1989). Conservation of biodiversity at this level is in large part conservation of properties and processes, not of species or assemblages of species, because of the substitutability and redundancy of species within an ecosystem

(di Castri and Younes 1990; Ehrlich and Mooney 1983; Walker 1989).

Biodiversity can be measured in a variety of spatial and temporal scales. The time scale can vary from a few hours to decades or centuries. Biodiversity occurs at all spatial scales, from local through regional to global, and the forces responsible for observed patterns of biodiversity may vary according to such scales (see Auerbach and Shmida 1987). It is therefore important to specify both the temporal and spatial scale being considered as well as the level at which biodiversity is being discussed.

In addition to specifying temporal and spatial scales when defining biodiversity at a given locality, it is also important to specify whether or not the component in question is being measured in terms of presence/absence or relative frequency. The difference between these two is crucial, particularly when assessing the effects of human actions. For example, at a species level, large game mammals and birds at a given site may all be present but in relative frequencies greatly affected by hunting (Redford 1992). It is a much more difficult task to conserve the different components of biodiversity in their relative frequency than simply in terms of their presence or absence.

The sustainability of tropical biodiversity

In our discussion of tropical diversity, it is clear that biodiversity has different components. These are not vague, and they *can* be precisely defined. Now let us consider the sustainability of this diversity. Sustainability, as a concept, presupposes that this diversity will be used by people, *but* that the use—and the biodiversity—will not be lost in the process. These interdependent requirements are evident in all definitions that include sustainability, virtually all of which involve the concept of development. The World Commission on Environment and Development (otherwise known as the Brundtland Commission) in 1987 defined sustainable development as development that "seeks to meet the needs and aspirations of the present *without* compromising the ability to meet those of the future" (WCED 1987, p. 8; our italics). In *Caring for the Earth*, sustainable development is defined as "improving the quality of human life *while* living within the carrying capacity of supporting ecosystems (IUCN 1991, p. 10, our emphasis). The concept of sustainable development is widely accepted as bridging the need to conserve natural systems and the need to allow human beings the use of these systems. Many people would agree with the statement that the important questions facing the world community no longer have to do with the relationship between development and the environment but instead must now focus on how sustainable development can be achieved (Lele 1991).

However, when biodiversity is considered as an equal partner in sustainable development schemes, it is rarely possible to address adequately the dual requirements of use and conservation. Most authors who discuss sustainable development schemes use only vague, undefined terms when referring to the nonhuman, or natural, component:

- Natural capital, defined variously as "a stock that yields a flow of useful goods and services" (Daly 1991, p. 21) or "the soil and atmospheric structure, plant and animal biomass, etc. that, taken together, forms the basis of all ecosystems" (Costanza 1991 p. 76)

- "Essential ecological processes and life support systems" (IUCN 1980)

- The "Earth's vitality and diversity" (IUCN 1991).

These definitions obfuscate a fundamental contradiction between use and conservation: that is, any use tends to reduce the biodiversity of a system (Robinson 1993). When considering the natural world at the broad level of the ecosystem—as in these definitions—it appears to be possible to both use and conserve. When considering biodiversity, as defined here, it is obvious that there are real tradeoffs to consider.

Because use tends to decrease biodiversity, a consideration of sustainability must specify what degree of loss is acceptable. This is an arbitrary decision based on the specific components of biodiversity that one wishes to conserve and use, the needs of the human groups for which the system is being sustained, the quality of life to which these people aspire, and the time over which sustainability is desired. For example,

- If you are interested in the sustainability of a population of the white-lipped peccary (*Tayassu pecari*), you should not sanction use that would imperil the demographic sustainability of that population.

- If, however, you are interested in sustaining biological communities and biotic processes, then you should not sanction use that would threaten the ecological role of white-lipped peccaries, and you must address the question of minimum ecologically operational population sizes of the species.

- However, if you are interested in sustainability at the level of ecosystem processes, then you probably do not care about white-lipped peccaries per se but would settle for sustaining other species that interact with the rest of the biological community and the abiotic environment in a manner similar to the white-lipped peccary.

- And, at the level of landscapes or natural areas, questions of sustainability can be addressed using Munasinghe and McNeely's adaptation of Perring's definition: "Sustainability from a biophysical perspective is linked to the idea that the dynamic processes of the natural environment can become unstable as a result of stresses imposed by human activity. Sustainability in this scenario refers to the maintenance of system stability, which implies limiting the stress to sustainable levels on those ecosystems that are central to the stability of the global system" (chapter 2 of this volume). Of course, at this level, even more than at the previous one, a concern about peccaries has little relevance.

Only when it is possible to specify precisely the type of development, the objectives of that development, and the levels of biodiversity targeted for conservation will it be possible to assess a priori the costs of human action on tropical wildlife and natural areas. That there will be costs is clear. Proponents of sustainable development assure us that there are cost-free solutions to spring us from the trap of environmental degradation as a price for human development. They are wrong, and they are usually wrong because they define nature only in terms of what is required for human survival. As is clear from our definition of biodiversity, cost-free solutions are virtually impossible. If one only conserves those parts of the biosphere that are essential for human life, many elements of the natural tropical landscape will be lost.

Virtually every activity, be it sustainable agriculture, natural forest management, use of land by indigenous people, or hunting, has been said to be related to the conservation of biodiversity. In short, virtually nothing is said *not* to conserve biodiversity. Yet, it is clear to all intelligent observers that at all levels, biodiversity conservation has been dealt with in a monolithic fashion:

a given activity was said to either conserve biodiversity, or destroy it, with no intermediate possibilities allowed. This in turn is due to a lack of precise definitions combined with a desire to proffer cost-free solutions.

The detailed definition of biodiversity given above divides biodiversity into its various components. This division allows an assessment of the effects of different types of land use on the different components of biodiversity and therefore a priori acknowledgment of what components of biodiversity can be conserved under that system. This in turn allows establishment of criteria to select the version of system of land use that most effectively conserves these biodiversity components. It also allows an a priori acknowledgment of what biodiversity components will *not* be conserved in areas subjected to that type of land use. This recognition of the specific costs—biodiversity components—of a given type of habitat alteration is vital, for it allows the establishment of alternate areas where those biodiversity components can be maintained.

Using biodiversity cost-benefit calculus allows the creation of landscapes in which different systems of land use can be combined in such a fashion as to maintain every component of biodiversity under some type of land use, while maximizing sustainable human development at the *landscape* level. Under such a scheme, rehabilitated land could be coherently integrated with tree plantations, extractive reserves, and national parks, each system of land use conserving a different component of biodiversity. It is vital to point out that national parks with minimal human activity—the natural areas—are keystones in this scheme, for they are the only areas to conserve all components of biodiversity. Wildlife, in contrast, can be managed in a variety of land use settings, depending on the specific objectives.

References

Andersen, R., E. Fuentes, M. Gadgil, T. Lovejoy, H. Mooney, D. Ojima, and B. Woodmansee. 1991. "Biodiversity from Communities to Ecosystems." In O. T. Solbrig, ed., *From Genes to Ecosystems: A Research Agenda for Biodiversity*, pp. 73–82. Cambridge, Mass.: IUBS.

Auerbach, M., and A. Shmida. 1987. "Spatial Scale and the Determinants of Plant Species Richness." *TREE* 2:8, pp. 238–42.

Bawa, K., B. Schaal, O. T. Solbrig, S. Stearns, A. Templeton, and G. Vida. 1991. "Biodiversity from the Gene to the Species." In O. T. Solbrig, ed., *From Genes to Ecosystems: A Research Agenda for Biodiversity*, pp. 15–36. Cambridge, Mass.: IUBS.

Costanza, R. 1991. "The Ecological Effects of Sustainability: Investing in Natural Capital." In R. Goodland, H. Daly, and S. El Serafy, eds., "Environmentally Sustainable Economic Development: Building on Brundtland," pp. 72–79. Environment Working Paper 46. World Bank, Washington, D.C.

Daly, H. 1991. "From Empty-world to Full-world Economics: Recognizing an Historical Turning Point in Economic Development." In R. Goodland, H. Daly, and S. El Serafy, eds., "Environmentally Sustainable Economic Development: Building on Brundtland," pp. 18–26. Environment Working Paper 46. World Bank, Washington, D.C.

di Castri, F., and T. Younes. 1990. "Ecosystem Function of Biological Diversity." Summary report of an IUBS/SCOPE workshop, June 29–30, 1989. *Biology International*, special issue 22.

Ehrlich, P. R., and H. A. Mooney. 1983. "Extinction, Substitution, and Ecosystem Services." *BioScience* 33:4, pp. 248–54.

Franklin, J. F. 1988. "Structural and Functional Diversity in Temperate Forests." In E. O. Wilson, ed., *Biodiversity*, pp. 166–75. Washington, D.C.: National Academy Press.

Hunter, M. L., Jr., G. L. Jacobson, Jr., and T. Webb III. 1988. "Paleoecology and the Coarse-filter Approach to Maintaining Biological Diversity." *Conservation Biology* 2:4, pp. 375–85.

IUCN (International Union for the Conservation of Nature). 1980. *World Conservation Strategy*. With the United Nations Environment Program and the World Wildlife Fund. Gland, Switzerland.

————. 1991. *Caring for the Earth: A Strategy for Sustainable Development*. With the United Nations Environment Program and the World Wildlife Fund. Gland, Switzerland.

Ledig, F. T. 1992. "Human Impacts on Genetic Diversity in Forest Ecosystems." *Oikos* 63, pp. 87–108.

Lele, S. M. 1991. "Sustainable Development: A Critical Review." *World Development* 19, pp. 607–21.

Mares, M. A. 1992. "Neotropical Mammals and the Myth of Amazonian Biodiversity." *Science* 255, pp. 976–79.

McNaughton, S. J. 1989. "Ecosystems and Conservation in the Twenty-first Century." In D. Western and M. C. Pearl, eds., *Conservation for the Twenty-first Century*, pp. 109–20. New York: Oxford University Press.

Noss, R. F. 1990. "Indicators for Monitoring Biodiversity: A Hierarchical Approach." *Conservation Biology* 4:4, pp. 355–64.

OTA (Office of Technology Assessment). 1987. "Technologies to Maintain Biological Diversity." U.S. Government Printing Office, Washington, D.C.

Platnick, N. I. 1991. "Patterns of Biodiversity: Tropical vs Temperate." *Journal of Natural History* 25, pp. 1083–88.

Redford, K. H. 1992. "The Empty Forest." *BioScience* 42, pp. 412–22.

Redford, K. H., and S. E. Sanderson. 1992. "The Brief Barren Marriage of Biodiversity and Sustainability?" *Bulletin of the Ecological Society of America* 73:1, pp. 36–39.

Robinson, J. G. 1993. "The Limits of Caring: Sustainable Living and the Loss of Biodiversity." *Conservation Biology* 7, pp. 22–28.

Ryman, N., R. Baccus, C. Reuterwall, and M. H. Smith. 1981. "Effective Population Size, Generation Interval, and Potential for Loss of Genetic Variability in Game Species under Different Hunting Regimes." *Oikos* 36, pp. 257–66.

Thorne-Miller, B., and J. Catena. 1991. *The Living Ocean: Understanding and Protecting Marine Biodiversity*. Washington D.C.: Island Press.

Walker, G. 1989. "Diversity and Stability in Ecosystem Conservation." In D. Western and M. C. Pearl, eds., *Conservation for the Twenty-first Century*, pp. 121–30. New York: Oxford University Press.

(WCED) World Commission on Environment and Development. 1987. *Our Common Future*. New York: Oxford University Press.

WRI, IUCN, and UNEP (World Resources Institute, International Union for the Conservation of Nature, and United Nations Environment Program). 1992. *Global Biodiversity Strategy*. New York.

26

Tropical Water Resource Management:
The Biophysical Basis

Jeffrey Edward Richey, Eneas Salati, Reynaldo Luiz Victoria, and Luiz Antonio Martinelli

We would like to acknowledge the support of the U.S. National Science Foundation and the NASA Earth Observing System.

The tropics of the world—those regions between the tropics of Cancer and Capricorn—include environments ranging from the wettest on Earth to the driest. They include the great tropical rain forests of South and Central America, Africa, and southeast Asia and the Pacific rim. They include the deserts of Northern Africa and the cerrado of Brazil. They include the most dense populations on Earth and the most sparse.

Among the most publicized links between global change and the tropics are the emissions of greenhouse gases, particularly the carbon dioxide associated with burning vegetation, and the potential loss of biodiversity. At a more immediate management level, the tropics pose a different set of problems for water resources than do temperate zones. In temperate regions, management is a relatively clear-cut, if politically difficult, problem of the supply, allocation, and quality of water complicated by current and future vagaries in climate. Throughout the tropics, problems of water quality due to both natural disease vectors and pollution may be so severe as to imperil human health, and lack of flood control threatens millions. Loss of forest on the high-relief topography of Asia and Central America leads to massive erosion and loss of fertility.

These resource topics are symptomatic of the broader issues of the natural hydrological and biogeochemical cycles in the diverse tropical basins. One of the most significant challenges for defining the basis for sustainability is to determine how these cycles function on regional to continental scales; these cycles are of fundamental importance not only to the maintenance of natural systems but to any human occupation.

Then we have the problem of how to incorporate such knowledge into programs for development and resource management. Actually doing this requires a series of state-of-the-art advances in science and in communication. In fact, our understanding of the hydrological cycle at the relevant regional and continental scales is surprisingly rudimentary. The overall scientific and policy communities should recognize that there are new technologies and new ways of doing scientific business, each of which may be done by communities that rarely communicate with each other. There is the difficult problem of bridging the gap between those who purportedly know how the system functions (the environmental scientist), the maker or implementer (agency) of policy, not to mention the end user. In the case of projects in the developing nations, the development banks may play a key role, yet their capability to assimilate information about the physical basis of the problem may need to be enhanced. Yet scientists often take the position that their job is only to make information, usually just "their" information, available, not to be active in its dissemination.

In this chapter, we focus on how the biophysical basis for the sustainability of water resources for a representative area of the tropics, the Amazon basin of northern South America, might be defined. In terms of developing a biophysical model for tropical water resources, the basin is

- *Representative.* The Amazon consists of a variety of bioclimatic zones (rain forest, savannah, and cerrado) that could be considered representative of other tropical zones for purposes of an extended model and represents a series of hydrological and chemical regimes that are typical of the world's rivers.

- *Quantitatively significant.* The Amazon is a large area, accounting for a significant portion of the humid tropics and providing 20 percent of the world's river discharge to the oceans. The condensational energy released by convective precipitation within the basin has been shown to be of sufficient magnitude to affect global patterns of climate.

- *Qualitatively significant.* The Amazon is primarily undisturbed. It thus provides a unique natural laboratory as to how large-scale systems function in a natural state. This is a very important attribute for theoretical as well as practical purposes.

We will show that present knowledge, though sparse, reveals the key role of the forest in maintaining the dynamic equilibrium of the Amazonian ecosystem. In summary, the forest controls the dynamics of the basin, the balance of energy, the yield of sediment, the balance of nutrients, the diversity of species, the quality of surface water, the quality of soil, and the stock of soil in the biosphere. Potential consequences of deforestation include modifications in the basin's convective rainfall regime and downstream changes in the river's flow and transport of nutrients and sediments. In the Amazon, as elsewhere, natural oscillations in the hydrological cycle and the processes influencing those oscillations must be distinguished before possible anthropogenic impacts can be truly attributed. The lack of knowledge of the basic functioning mechanisms of the Amazonia ecosystem and of the most suitable methods for achieving a sustainable development of the region is the main reason that many of the agricultural and cattle ranching projects fail. Specific measurement, modeling, and remote-sensing programs can be identified that would dramatically improve the base of knowledge and management for the basin.

The synthesis represented in this chapter is based primarily on Martinelli and others (forthcoming), Victoria and others (1991), Salati (1987), and Salati and others (1989, 1991).

A definition of the biophysical basis of sustainability of the Amazon

Objective 1: To develop a biophysical definition of sustainability for both practical application and use in formulating a full definition of sustainable development in all its ramifications.

Definition and structure of sustainability

The sheer physical size and logistics of problems posed by tropical basins present challenges that must be resolved in order to develop a reasonable definition of a biophysical basis. At these scales, river basins are natural integrators of surficial processes. The water and dissolved and particulate materials observed in the main channel of the Amazon and other large floodplain rivers are the products of processes occurring in the drainage basin across widely varying temporal and spatial scales. An understanding of how these substances are routed from precipitation through their drainage systems to the oceans would yield important information on the processes controlling regional-scale hydrological and biogeochemical cycles. For example, the carbon measured in the main channel is a mixture of carbon originating from sources thousands of kilometers away in upland regions, as well as carbon introduced continuously (spiraled) from the adjacent floodplain. Organic matter of both sources has been subjected to transport and reactive processes within the channel. Of particular importance for biogeochemistry are the storage of water in various parts of the drainage system for periods of weeks and the transfer of this water between the various physiographic reservoirs.

Given these realities, the critical question that concerns the biophysical sustainability of the Amazon is the extent to which the land use of a particular region of the basin can be altered without affecting the overall regime of rainfall and runoff or of production and decomposition of organic matter. Further, the sustainability question can be defined on the basis of a set of interactive questions dealing with hydrological and biogeochemical cycles integrated across landscapes in the context of the phytogeography and physical structure of the basin (see figure 26-1).

The geological structure of the basin, including soil types, topography, and drainage networks establishes the overall physical matrix in which the biotic world can come to life. Within this overall framework, the relevant question for

Figure 26–1: Biophysical Synthesis

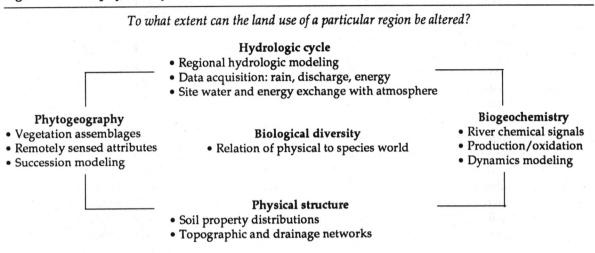

To what extent can the land use of a particular region be altered?

Hydrologic cycle
- Regional hydrologic modeling
- Data acquisition: rain, discharge, energy
- Site water and energy exchange with atmosphere

Phytogeography
- Vegetation assemblages
- Remotely sensed attributes
- Succession modeling

Biological diversity
- Relation of physical to species world

Biogeochemistry
- River chemical signals
- Production/oxidation
- Dynamics modeling

Physical structure
- Soil property distributions
- Topographic and drainage networks

the hydrology of the basin is how the climatic and surface features of the basin determine the temporal distribution of runoff and the spatial pattern of moisture storage.

It is convenient to think of basin-scale biogeochemical and water cycles as a combined problem in the regional balance and subsequent downstream routing of water. The balance of water at any site and time can be described by

$$R = P - ET \pm SM \qquad (26\text{-}1)$$

where P is precipitation, R is the effective runoff, ET is actual evapotranspiration, and SM is change in soil moisture and storage of groundwater. To provide overall constraints on fluxes of water and energy using data that are realistic to obtain, the plan starts at the regional scale, with river discharge (runoff). Given the heterogeneous nature of precipitation and collectors of precipitation, river discharge is a robust integrator of the long-term hydrologic properties of a drainage basin. Evapotranspiration can then be constrained annually as the difference between precipitation and runoff and examined in more spatial and temporal detail via regional applications by energy calculations. If the distributions of precipitation, runoff, and evapotranspiration can be calculated with sufficient precision, insight into the regional distributions of soil moisture is possible.

Phytogeography is one of the main links among the physical structure of the basin, hydrology, and the distribution of plant communities. As shown below, the hydrologic cycle depends intimately on the vegetation. Conversely, the very existence of communities depends on subtle variations in the moisture and temperature regime. An important question is how the distributions of vegetation communities (phytogeography) are influenced by hydrologic, geologic, and ultimately human factors.

The hypothesis can be posed that each vegetation community has characteristic soil properties and predictable seasonal patterns of moisture, net radiation, and evapotranspiration that can be established by (point) measurements at specific sites and extended by inference to similar communities. The first issue is to identify characteristic assemblages of vegetation over large areas, ultimately with regard to the physical differences between areas. The second issue is to bring these communities to life; that is, to discover what their successional patterns are and then how they are differentially fixing and transforming carbon and related elements.

The key to these questions is first to characterize assemblages of species and then to identify those properties that can be extrapolated to larger regions. A key output would be the definition of functional groups of vegetation, where a functional group is defined by attributes that are unifying (similar structure, function, and implicit taxonomy) and that can be determined (preferably by satellite). Then these groups can be coupled to landscape issues of short-term community succession: Why and how do existing functional groups grade from one type to another? How and at what rate does natural (short-term) succession operate dynamically (for example, filling gaps, blowing down, dying)? The physical attributes of the functional groups include biomass (nutrients, C) and structure (canopy architecture, *LAI*), which thus provides the bridge to the biogeochemistry.

The next major problem is to couple the hydrologic cycle and knowledge of the phytogeography with the biogeochemistry of the Amazon basin. For example, how does the structure and biological diversity of the Amazon ecosystem control the cycling of water, carbon, and nutrients under natural conditions and under different conditions of land use?

The hard question of linkage is in how the biogeochemical dynamics and community structure might respond to changes in the state of the system that occur abruptly (direct clearing or physical intervention) or more subtly (such as changes in ambient environment: moisture, temperature, carbon dioxide) either as propagating edge effects or regional effects.

With the above perspectives and information, it should then be possible to address the problem of how information on the biophysical perspective of the Amazon ecosystem can be used to address issues of biodiversity.

A toolbox

The degree of geographic variation of land surface properties in this continental-scale drainage basin and the variety of possible measurements and scientific and resource interests require a toolbox of models, both heuristic and mathematical, and of field measurements to force some discipline and cooperation on activities. A range of such models is necessary to handle processes at different scales, and some attention needs to be placed on consistency between the physics and chemistry represented at various scales. Within the guidance provided by such models, field programs must provide the pertinent data, if not the needed check on reality.

MODELING

Immediately, any such model must deal with the issue of scale; that is, we have to transfer our understanding from very small scales (where it is possible to do field research), to regional scales (a river basin), and ultimately to the Amazon as a whole and its interactions with the global atmosphere. The first problem for a large drainage basin such as the Amazon is to establish the hierarchy of time and space at which the processes that control the fluxes of interest are oper-

able. Hydrologic and ecological modelers have traditionally focused most of their attention at the very small to moderate spatial scales of square meters to several hectares. The integrated effect of small-scale cycling may or may not influence cycling at larger temporal or spatial scales. The question of how spatially to average the hydrologic parameters of mesoscale areas when their component parameters are spatially variable and poorly characterized at a smaller scale is one that has drawn the attention of many investigators. Heterogeneity of the environment with regard to mechanisms that produce runoff, measurement and logistic realities, and differences in response between smaller and larger catchments make it difficult to extrapolate from one site to larger areas.

Traditionally, large-scale hydrologic models have inferred the nature of hydrologic systems on the basis of input-output data; without considering microscale physics in their derivation. Most of them are "black box" in nature and some are highly conceptual, but all have lumped, physically meaningless parameters. These models need sufficiently long meteorologic and hydrologic records for their calibrations; they have not used such data as basin geomorphology, soils, and vegetation; their parameters are not measurable in the field or by remote sensing and are difficult to interpret. Furthermore, lumped parameter models do not provide space-time distributions of water within the basin and therefore are of little use for the study of biogeochemical processes. However, by representing a large-scale basin as a homogeneous one-dimensional system with uniform climate forcing, current physically based, one-dimensional models have also shown great uncertainties in their predictions. These uncertainties are primarily caused by spatial variabilities in the basin's physical characteristics and, for a large-scale basin, a lack of spatial uniformity in climate forcing, such as fractional coverage of rainstorms. Under changing climate and land use conditions, the uncertainties in the model predictions increase. Therefore, it is essential for large-scale models to incorporate these spatial variabilities.

Driven by the need to improve the representation of the land surface processes, general climate models have been developed recently that take into account morphological and physiological characteristics of the vegetation as well as physical characteristics of the soil. These include the Simple Biosphere Model (SiB; Sellers and others 1986). Given the properties of vegetation and soils and soil moisture, plus wind speed, air temperature and humidity at a reference level above the canopy, visible and near-infrared incoming solar radiation, and precipitation, these models can be used to calculate the fluxes of vapor more accurately than models using simple formulations of the balance of energy. For application to the Amazon, SiB-type models have to be calibrated with measurements of air temperature and humidity above the canopy, precipitation and downward fluxes of solar and near-infrared radiation, and wind speed for typical ecosystems (terra firme forests, igapó forest, campina forest, floodplain vegetation, and vegetation of areas under use, such as grass).

HYDROLOGIC NETWORK

As the backbone of large-scale hydrologic analyses, the Departamento Nacional de Águas e Energia Elétrica (DNAEE) maintains a gaging network of 600 precipitation, river stage, and meteorological (solar radiance, surface temperature, humidity, wind) stations throughout the basin. Daily records of at least a ten-year duration are available for most stations, and longer records exist for specific stations. These data constitute the primary data set available for the water resources of the Amazon. Specifically, precipitation patterns can be determined by analyzing the data from rain gage networks. Because of the well-known sparseness of precipitation data in these networks, it is necessary to improve the methods for obtaining such information from satellite data. Satellite observations can be related to the rain gage network by using proxy precipitation records derived from measurements of outgoing longwave radiation obtained from GOES or AVHRR. The proposed Tropical Rainfall Mission (TRMM) could provide valuable data on the distribution of rainfall.

River stage records, the data from which discharge is calculated, are among the most complete and the most accurate data available for remote basins. The DNAEE maintains stage stations at seven sites along the Amazon mainstem, at one to five sites along major tributaries (Rio Madeira, Japurá, and so forth), and more intermittently along subtributaries. The density is greatest in the most populated regions and in the areas with the greatest potential to generate hydropower.

Evapotranspiration is a much more stable process than precipitation (it is less variable over time, and variations occur over a longer period of time). Methods for determining evaporation lo-

cally at a point using micrometerologic data are available but have not been useful or practical for application at the basin scale. Most models of rainfall and runoff treat evaporation as a function of potential evaporation, which in turn is based on a bulk transfer coefficient and a reduction factor. These methods of calculating evaporation depend on knowledge of soil moisture, which can vary greatly over relatively small distances. A mesoscale representation of this process must, therefore, incorporate information about the spatial variability—and mean value—of soil moisture. Regional potential evapotranspiration can be calculated using the climatological data (insolation, humidity, temperature, wind speed) available from the meteorological network using the Monteith (1973) method adapted to a tropical forest (Villa Nova, Salati, and Matsui 1976). Based on detailed eddy correlation methods, Shuttlesworth (1988) has modified the empirical (bulk) formulation fitted for the micrometeorological data and shown that this model yields results within 15 to 20 percent of the actual fluxes and describes the seasonal cycle. Given the variability in the base climatological data, it is not always possible to calculate evapotranspiration even on a monthly basis for all years. Where data are limited, it may be necessary to calculate the monthly or annual means and to derive the distribution of these averages from theoretical considerations. Remote sensing of the radiances corresponding to these energy terms may be the best way to do this. Within the likely evolution of the capability for detecting these terms over remote basins, however, the challenge is large. For example, at the present time it is not possible to measure soil moisture under dense tropical forest canopies using remote sensing.

RESEARCH INSTITUTIONS OF THE AMAZON
AND PROCESS STUDIES

The complement to the network type of information are the detailed, generally more process-oriented studies carried out by individual scientists and research teams, usually in affiliation with a research institution involved in the region. In the Amazon, these include the following.

The Instituto Nacional de Pesquisas da Amazonia (INPA, Manaus) has a broad mandate in areas related to hydrology and ecology. The Museu Paraense Emilio Goeldi (MPEG, Belém) complements INPA, with strengths in anthropology and history. The Instituto de Pesquisas Espaciais (INPE, São Jose dos Campos) is the lead organization in Brazil for remote sensing of the Amazon, including a LANDSAT receiving station. It is also the base for many of the climatological studies in the Amazon, has impressive computer facilities, and is participating in field campaigns in the Amazon. The Centro de Energia Nuclear na Agricultura (CENA, Piracicaba) is a research branch of the University of São Paulo specializing in the application of sophisticated stable and radioactive isotope and analytical chemical techniques to environmental problems. With support from the International Atomic Energy Agency, it has pioneered the application of these techniques to the large-scale problems of hydrology in the Amazon. The University of Pará (Belém,) has a good geoscience department and has conducted studies in climate issues. The Empresa Brasileira de Pesquisa Agropequaria (EMBRAPA, Brasilia) maintains a number of field sites in the Amazon for studies of soil fertility.

Several large international projects are working in collaboration with these institutions. CAMREX, a multidisciplinary group from CENA, INPA, and the University of Washington have been working together since 1982 on the biogeochemistry and hydrology of the Amazon river system. EOSRAM, the group of CAMREX, together with INPE is working on a large-scale analysis of the Amazon basin through the NASA Earth Observing System mission. ABRACOS is a joint Anglo-Brazilian study on the effects of changes in land use on the micrometeorology of specific sites. The Max Plank Institute (Germany) has maintained a long-term interest in the Amazon, particularly in the area of limnology. ORSTOM (France) has had particular interests in fisheries, hydrology, and soil chemistry.

The Amazon hydrologic cycle: The biophysical basis of the intact system

Objective 2: To assess the state of the science of these measurements.

Physical structure

The physical structure of the Amazon has two components: the geomorphology and drainage network and the distribution and fertility of the soil.

GEOMORPHOLOGY AND DRAINAGE NETWORK
The Amazon is a classic river basin, with a central plain bordered by highlands and a terrestrial drainage network within which the mainstem and its extensive floodplain (*várzea*) receive inputs from a series of tributaries of different sizes (see figure 26-2). It is characterized topographically by a great plain at altitudes lower than 200 meters. This plain is more than 3,400 kilometers long from east to west and 2,000 kilometers wide from north to south. The great plain is bounded at the north by the Guyanan Shield (Guyana plateau), composed of ancient pre-Cambrian rocks. In this plateau, with altitudes averaging from 600 to 700 meters, the highest elevation in the Brazil–Fog Peak (Pico da Neblina) is 3,014 meters high. To the south, the plain is bounded by the Brazilian plateau, also composed of pre-Cambrian rocks, with average heights of 700 meters; to the west, it is bounded by the Andean mountain range, of tertiary origin, dividing the slopes of the Atlantic side from those of the Pacific. The Andean mountain range forms a semicircle, opening toward the east, and has altitudes above 4,000 meters. Since its emergence, the Andean mountain range has been the main source of sediments for the Amazon plain. Today, about 13.5 tons per second of material is eroded from the Andes. It is important to stress the small surface gradient along the main channel of the Amazon River; the vertical drop between Iquitos in Peru and the estuary 2,375 kilometers downstream is only 107 meters. Yet, although from a geomorphologic viewpoint the great plain exists, it is in fact divided by innumerable tributaries and streams that have cut deep furrows into the soil and created a complex microstructure of hills, gullies, and plains, with local slopes often exceeding 45°. In evaluating these lands for agriculture or cattle ranching, this fact is very important, since erosion can rapidly eliminate the fertile soil stratum after the forest cover is removed.

The Amazon mainstem has a total length of 6,771 kilometers, running from the Andes to the Atlantic Ocean. Formed by the Ucayali and Marañon in the Andes, it is first called the Rio Solimões in Brazilian territory, changing to the Amazon after the junction with the Rio Negro (for clarity, we refer to all sections as the Amazon River). Of the north-draining tributaries, the Içá and Japurá rivers have Andean origins but are mostly lowland drainages. The Rio Negro drains primarily the caatinga forest on the Guyana Shield, although its major tributary, the Rio Branco, drains a drier savannah region. Of the south-draining tributaries, the Jutaí, Juruá, and Purús rivers drain the sediments of the sub-Andean trough and of the central plain, while the Rio Madeira begins in

Figure 26–2: The Amazon Drainage Basin

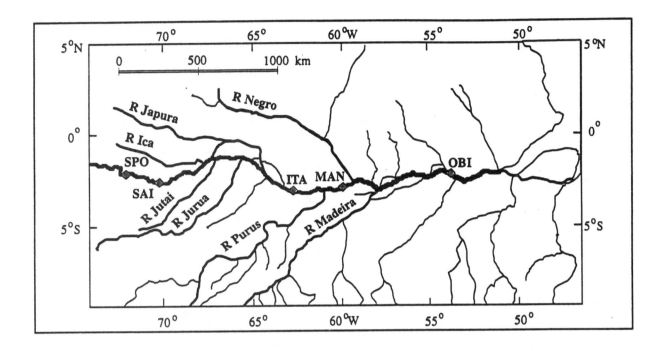

Note: DNAEE gaging stations include São Paulo de Olivença (SPO). Santo Antônio do Içá (SAI), Itapeua (Ita), Manacapurú (Man), and Obidos (Obi). Major tributaries are indicated by name.

the Bolivian Andes and passes across the Brazilian Shield and the central Amazon plain. The tributaries of the lower course of the Amazon, the Trombetas and Uatumã rivers, are shield-draining rivers that have large "mouth bays," where sediments are deposited. The main channel also receives input from smaller, ungaged tributaries and unchanneled várzea areas.

In the reach between São Paulo de Olivença and Obidos, floodwaters and direct precipitation regularly inundate about 40,000 square kilometers of várzea through an extensive network of drainage channels (*paranas*) and overbank flow during the 7 to 10 meter rise and fall of the river over the course of a year. Approximately 10,000 square kilometers are covered by thousands of permanent lakes that range in size from less than a hectare to more than 600 square kilometers and are typically 6 to 8 meters deep at high water. As the river falls, land is exposed again, and the lakes become isolated from the main channel, with depths decreasing to 1 to 2 meters. Determining the relative distribution of mainstem versus local

sources of water for the várzea is important for analyzing the nutrient cycling of the region and for estimating the extent of biogenic gas fluxes; floodplains are an important source of methane to the troposphere.

SOIL DISTRIBUTIONS AND FERTILITY

The majority of the soils are chemically poor, with kaolinite and iron and aluminum oxides dominating the clay mineral fraction. About 80 percent of the soils show low levels of exchangeable basic cations. The high rainfall regime is the main reason for the leaching processes and consequent loss of exchangeable bases and silica. The nutrients lost with the intense leaching cannot be replaced either by the poor geological substrate or by nutrients derived from the decomposition of organic matter that could be retained in the soil. In contrast, the physical properties of the Amazon soils are generally good. They are well drained, due to their very stable sand and silt granular structure, originating from the cementing action of iron oxides, aluminum, and organic matter.

413

As a consequence, due to their low natural fertility, the majority of the Amazon soils are not suitable for agriculture. Phosphorus is one of the most problematic nutrients in the Amazon. Although generally present at normal concentrations for soil samples, it is rarely available, due to its adsorption to the oxides, hydroxides, and kaolinite minerals. Another common problem is aluminum toxicity due to the characteristic acidity of many tropical soils. Deficiencies like that would normally be correctable by liming; tropical soils, however, have a high buffer capacity, which makes liming or any other amending difficult and expensive.

Phytogeography

Classification of types of vegetation for the whole of the Amazon basin has progressed little since the 1971 RADAMBRASIL project, which was based on SLAR images. In addition, the Amazon has a long history of botanical collecting. Much of what is known about Amazon flora is derived from approximately 290,000 herbarium specimens. Unfortunately, by far the majority of collected specimens are from "collecting islands," such as the Manaus area, and little is known about the regional distribution of the documented flora.

The vegetation in the Amazon basin has been described as different formations. The forest formation with the largest area is the terra firme forest. This type of forest has an area of 3.8 million square kilometers in the Brazilian Amazon. The terra firme forest can be divided in different formations. The most common is the dense forest, with the greatest biomass, occurring mainly in places where no major factors limit its growth.

Contrasting with the dense forest is the open forest, with lower trees and biomass and higher concentrations of shrub and liana species due to greater penetration of light. According to Pires and Prance (1985), the lower biomass of this type of forest is caused by a low water table, poor drainage, and long dry seasons with low relative humidity. The same authors divide the open forests into three types: open forest without palms, open forest with palms, and liana forest.

The third group within the general terra firme group is the dry forest, which is a transition forest found at the border between Amazonia and central Brazil. This region is characterized by long dry seasons with low relative humidity. Finally, there are the montane forests, generally occurring at higher altitudes, at the border of the basin.

Another type of forest is the inundated forest, which occurs in places periodically inundated by rivers. The two most important types are várzea and igapó forests. The first are found in the floodplains of white-water rivers, which are characterized by a rich soil. The second are found at the margins of black-water rivers, consequently with poorer soils than those of the floodplains of white-water rivers.

A second general type of vegetation, occupying a smaller area than the forest formations, is the savannah. There are also two main types of savannah: terra firme and inundated. The savannahs on terra firme are generally open grasslands, with or without woody vegetation. Inundated savannah occurs mainly in the lower Amazon, between the Negro and Xingu rivers. The typical vegetation of these areas are grasses, shrubs, small vines, and several floating species. Finally, there is the type of vegetation that grows over pure leached white sand, generally classified as campina, campinarana, or chavascal.

As reported by Nelson (1992), Gentry (1986) has shown a strong correlation between annual rainfall and diversity of woody plants in lowland neotropical forests: lowland dry forests generally have about 50 species greater than or equal to 2.5 centimeters DBH per 0.1-hectare plot, moist forests about 100 to 150 species, wet forests about 200 species, and pluvial forests about 250 species. Based on this correlation, diversity of edaphically similar sites should increase progressively from the dry transverse zone (dry forest) through Manaus (moist forest) to west of Iquitos (pluvial forest).

Land use may be considered as a special aspect of phytogeography, because, typically, the main effect of agricultural or industrial development is to change radically the type of vegetation. Although the regrowth differs from the original vegetation, it forms a new subset of the larger array of phytogeographic classes. Most of the clearing of the forest in the Amazon basin has been to establish pasture and to a lesser extent crops, timber, and charcoal fuel; clearing for whatever reason typically is followed within a decade by regrowth of shrubs and trees having low species diversity and biomass in comparison with the original forest. Cleared areas and areas of regrowth differ from the forest in important hydrologic parameters such as temperature, net radiation, soil moisture, and leaf area index. In the disturbed areas, these parameters can be measured on the ground and the measurements extrapolated regionally by remote sensing.

Hydrologic cycle

The first-order calculation of the water budget (equation 26-1) yields the following. The Amazon basin encompasses an area of 6.4 million square kilometers, with an average precipitation of 2,200 millimeters a year. These figures represent a flux of 14.1 trillion cubic meters a year of water into the basin. The ultimate discharge of water from the basin is about 200,000 cubic meters, or 6 trillion cubic meters a year. Therefore, approximately 60 percent of the yearly precipitation within the basin is returned to the atmosphere, where it may again become precipitation. These averaged calculations can be refined, as follows.

SOLAR ENERGY AND TEMPERATURE
The amount of solar energy reaching the upper atmosphere in the Amazon remains practically constant the year round. For instance, in the city of Manaus, situated in the central Amazon, the solar input varies from a maximum of 885 calories per square centimeter a day in January to a minimum of 767 calories per square centimeter a day in June. Solar radiation reaching the Earth varies primarily as a function of cloud cover. Data are available on the extent of variations in solar energy at selected sites in the cities of Belém, Manaus, and Rio Branco. The yearly (insolation ratio—m/n ratio—in the areas mentioned is below 50 percent and varies during the year. The solar energy reaching the upper canopy of the forest is around 425 calories per square centimeter a day (Ribeiro and others 1982; Villa Nova, Salati, and Matsui 1976). Villa Nova calculated that 210 calories per square centimeter a day are used in evapotranspiration processes and that 215 calories per square centimeter a day are consumed in heating the air and are diverted into other processes. These data indicate that evapotranspiration and water balance are of great importance for the energy balance of the region.

An important characteristic of the region's climate is the small variation in the monthly average temperature, especially in the central strip below an altitude of 200 meters (see figure 26-3). For instance, in the city of Belém, the highest monthly average temperature, 26.9 °C, occurs in November and the lowest, 24 °C, in March. In Manaus, the highest average monthly temperature, 27.9 °C, occurs in September and the lowest, 25.8 °C, between February and April, with a variation of only 2.1 °C. In the city of Iquitos, the highest average monthly temperature, 32 °C, occurs in

November and the lowest, 30 °C, occurs in July. Overall, September and November are the months with the highest temperature, coincident with the minimum precipitation. This pattern can be explained by the portioning of the solar energy. During the rainy months, a larger part of the energy is used as latent heat, promoting evaporation, while in the dry season a higher proportion is used as sensible heat, increasing the air temperature. This isothermy results from the great quantity of water vapor in the atmosphere.

WATER VAPOR FLUX
Water vapor of the Amazon region originates primarily in the Atlantic Ocean and enters the region with the trade winds, which blow year round from the east. Fluxes decrease from east to west across the basin. Precipitable water vapor in the region averages 35 millimeters or higher with a seasonal variation of 10 millimeters. Therefore, the average water vapor stored in the atmosphere above the Amazon basin is of the order of 0.2 trillion tons. The greenhouse absorption of outgoing longwave radiation by this significant mass of water vapor largely accounts for the remarkable isothermal behavior observed in the region (low fluctuation of surface temperature between day and night). Comparison of the seasonal cycle of the basinwide, vertically integrated divergence of atmospheric moisture and the Amazon streamflow at Obidos (500 kilometers from the mouth) show that the streamflow at Obidos lags the seasonal divergence of atmospheric moisture in the basin by approximately three months. Therefore, three months can be taken as a first-order estimate of the time that water resides in the Amazon hydrological system (Marques, Salati, and Santos 1980). At the southern boundary of Amazonia, the direction of water vapor fluxes is from north to south for almost the entire year. This shows that water vapor from Amazonia can influence the concentration of water vapor in the atmosphere above the Brazilian Highlands.

PRECIPITATION
Precipitation is more variable than temperature (figure 26-3). Fluctuations in the intertropical convergence zone induce wet and dry seasons alternating between the northern and southern sides of the basin. A pronounced difference in wet and dry seasons between the northern and southern sides is caused by the slow seasonal migration of

Figure 26–3: Precipitation and Temperature

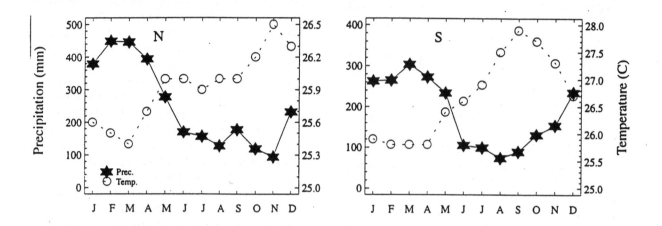

Months

the continental convective bands over tropical South America. The most important synoptic-scale (rain-producing) systems in the Amazon may be sea breeze lines that sometimes propagate inland all the way to the Andes. The secondary maximum of precipitation in the southern Amazon can likely be accounted for by the interaction of cold fronts with convective precipitation. Near the ocean, rainfall rates may reach up to 3,250 millimeters a year, and the same pattern is observed in the northwestern Amazon region. The highest precipitation in the basin is observed in the Andes, with values up to 7,000 millimeters a year; the minimum of 1,750 millimeters a year occurs in the central part of the basin. In Belém and Manaus, the rainy season goes roughly from December to June. It is interesting to note that the distribution of rainfall is different above and below the equator. There is a lag of six months in the maximum level of precipitation north and south of the equator. Salati and Marques (1984) estimated an average of 2,300 millimeters a year for the basin for the period 1972–75, while M. N. G. Ribeiro (personal communication) estimated an average of 2,100 millimeters a year for Manaus for the period 1911–85.

EVAPOTRANSPIRATION

As indicated by the mass balance in the basin, one of the most prominent features of the forest in the Amazon is its capacity to recycle a considerable amount of water through the process of evapo-

transpiration (Salati 1986; Salati and Marques 1984). Several independently used methods have indicated the importance of the Amazon forest in this process.

The first studies concerning the meteorology and hydrology of the Amazon measured fundamental climatological parameters like temperature, precipitation, solar radiation, and winds. With respect to the water balance in the region, studies were conducted at two scales. At the local scale, studies involved measurements made in small basins of a few square kilometers, while at the regional scale, studies involved measurements made over thousands of square kilometers. The first three studies encompassed large areas of the basin. Molion (1979) used the climatonomic method; Villa Nova, Salati, and Matsui (1976) used an adaptation of the classic Penman method; and Marques, Salati, and Santos (1980) used the aerological method. The others used small watersheds. For instance, Ribeiro and Villa Nova (1979), Leopoldo and others (1982) and Shuttlesworth and others (1984) all used the Reserva Ducke forest, a 1.3-square-kilometer ecological station near Manaus. Distinct methods were used for the estimations: Ribeiro and Villa Nova (1979) used both the Penman and the Thornthwaite methods, while Leopoldo and others (1982) and Jordan and Heuneldop (1981) used water balance, and finally Shuttlesworth and others (1984) used eddy correlation measurements over a period of approximately one year.

The overall results were variable but converged to a common conclusion. For instance, the studies carried out on the Reserva Ducke Forest revealed a difference of 1 millimeter a day between the smaller (3.7 millimeters a day; Shuttlesworth and others 1984) and the larger (4.6 millimeters a day; Leopoldo and others 1982) values. The relative contribution to rainfall ranged from 48 to 81 percent. Despite this variability, it is clear that a large amount of water, sufficient to contribute at least 48 percent of the rainfall, returned to the atmosphere through evapotranspiration.

A second independent type of analysis is possible, using the water stable isotopes (^{18}O and deuterium) as tracers of the precipitation/evapotranspiration sequence (for an explanation of isotope terminology, see Dall'Ollio 1976; Salati and others 1979). Evapotranspiration is an isotopically nonfractionating process, thus returning to the atmosphere water of isotopic composition similar to its source (rainwater), which in turn is isotopically heavier than the atmospheric water vapor. Therefore, as a mass of air moves inland, it receives an input of isotopically heavier water supplied by the forest evapotranspiration. This technology was used first in the Amazon by Dall'Ollio (1976), who divided the Amazon basin into different sectors and analyzed the evolution of the water vapor through the behavior of oxygen and deuterium isotopes in each. A model was developed based on the assumption that, as a mass of air moves inland and loses water through precipitation, rainfall becomes progressively depleted in heavy isotopes. The pattern of this depletion, assuming steady state conditions in the atmosphere, can be modeled by a Raleigh-type equation. For the Amazon however, the observed depletion in samples of rainfall water was much smaller than expected based on the amount of precipitation and the Raleigh law (Dall'Ollio 1976; Salati and others 1979). The discrepancy was credited to the recycling of water through the evapotranspiration of the forest. As a result, the actual depletion in the isotopic composition of the rainfall is smaller than the values predicted by the Raleigh equation.

Dall'Ollio's model was developed with a limited set of data, consisting of monthly rainwater samples of fifteen stations during the years 1972–73. The extension of this data base with continuing sampling did not change the trends and confirmed the importance of forest evapotranspiration in the Amazon water cycle (Victoria and others 1991). The same authors suggest that there is a substantial input of water from the evaporation of open water surfaces, mainly during the dry season. Evaporative process from open bodies of water may contribute up to 40 percent of the total flux of recycled water. Possible sources of free water available for evaporation are rivers, lakes, and water deposited on the surface of leaves of the canopy. In fact, the canopy intercepts 10 to 20 percent of water, as a function of the intensity and duration of rainfall (Franken and others 1982). Thus trees may play an additional role in the Amazon water cycle, where the water stored on their leaves after precipitation occurs provides an important source of water to the atmosphere. Victoria and others (1991) suggest that the interception process may be larger than thought before and consequently may be an important source of water evaporation to the atmosphere.

The most important fact is that the water vapor flux originating in the Atlantic Ocean is not of sufficient magnitude to explain the rainfall and the vapor outflux in the basin. As a direct consequence, it is necessary to assume that evapotranspired water recirculates in the basin.

DISCHARGE

The most striking features of Amazon River discharge are its magnitude and its highly damped hydrograph (see figure 26-4). Although differences in discharge of 7–10 meters are common along the main stem, there is only a twofold to threefold difference between low and high discharge. São Paulo de Olivença has average minimum and maximum discharges of 20,000 and 60,000 cubic meters a second, Manacapurú averages 70,000 and 130,000 cubic meters a second, and Obidos averages 100,000 and 220,000 cubic meters a second, respectively. The total Amazon input to the Atlantic includes the Tapajos, Xingu, and Tocantins rivers, for a mean annual input of about 200,000 to 220,000 cubic meters a second. The damped hydrograph of the main stem reflects in part the offset input from tributaries. The peak flows from the northern and southern tributaries are typically three months out of phase as a result of the seasonal differences in precipitation. Average tributary discharges range from about 3,000 cubic meters a second for the Jutai and Juruá rivers to about 30,000 cubic meters a second for the Negro and Madeira rivers.

For each reach of the river, inputs from the last reach upstream and from the large, gaged tributaries constitute major inputs. In addition, we

Figure 26–4: Discharge along Ordinate and Tributary Gaging Stations, 1972–84
(*thousands of square meters*)

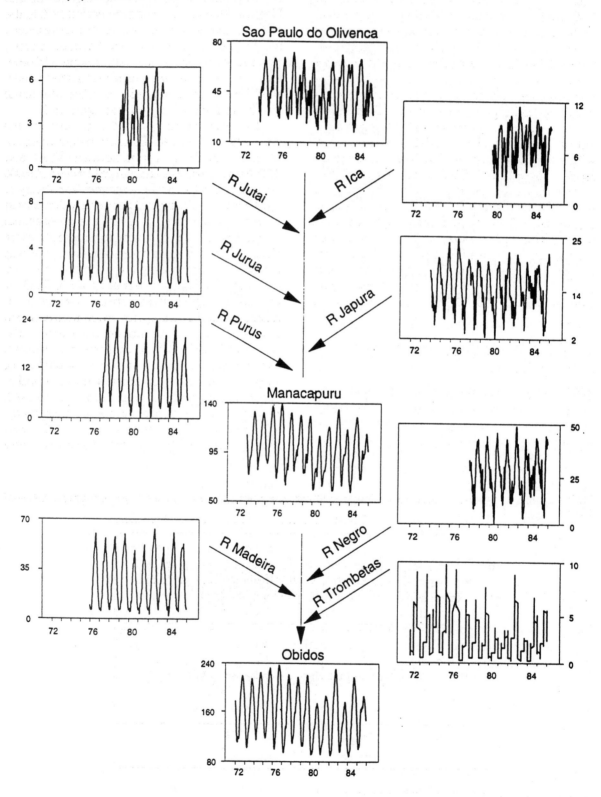

Note: Calculated from DNAEE stage records for main stem (Santo Antônio do Içá and Itapeua are not shown). Years indicated by abscissa are from September 1 through August 31 (the water year for São Paulo de Olivença).
   Source: After Richey, Nobre, and Deser 1989

must assess the other potential sources (and sinks) of water. These (ungaged) flows range from 3,000 cubic meters a second during the dry season to 7,000 cubic meters a second during the wet season in the upriver and downriver sections; midriver flows are about half of these values. These estimates of flow for individual paranas and ungaged tributaries from the calculations of area precipitation compare reasonably well to direct measurements of discharge on those rivers. Overall, exchange was greatest during early falling to midfalling water in the upriver and downriver reaches, with a net flow from the floodplain to the main stem of about 20,000 cubic meters a second. Net exchanges were generally lower in the midriver reach, where the area of the floodplain is relatively small. Therefore, water derived from local drainage through paranas and small tributaries constitutes a significant component of the water budget of the main stem. These flows correspond to about 30 percent of the flow at Itapeua and cumulatively to about 25 percent of the flow at Obidos.

Long-term variability in the climate/discharge record

The data from the DNAEE records represent a short period of time. In order to determine whether the data from the detailed discharge records starting in 1972 are representative of longer time periods, the discharge history must be considered. The only long-term discharge record available for the Amazon is a record of the stage of the Rio Negro at Manaus, covering the period 1903 to the present. That is, the Manaus record represents a ninety-year integration of runoff and, ultimately, climatic conditions over 3 million square kilometers of the Andean and western Amazon watershed. These data can be used to calculate a discharge time series for Manacapurú (see figure 26-5).

The mean discharge at Manacapurú for the period 1903–85 was 94,600 cubic meters a second. Minimum discharge varied between 48,000 and 84,000 and maximum discharge between 100,000 and 140,000 cubic meters a second. Variability of the Amazon hydrograph is obviously dominated by the annual cycle. To reveal the nonseasonal variability of the Amazon hydrograph more clearly, the long-term mean annual cycle was removed, producing a deseasonalized hydrograph (the lower part of figure 26-5). Over the period 1903–26, there were pronounced oscillations about the mean, with differences between minimum and maximum deseasonalized discharge of 30,000 to 40,000 cubic meters a second. The minimum anomaly on record, 45,000 cubic meters in 1926, has been attributed to a period of extensive drought and fires. From 1927 to 1962, the oscillations exhibited a comparable frequency, with reduced amplitude of 10,000 to 20,000 cubic meters a second. Near the end of a secular trend

Figure 26–5: Long-Term Discharge Record for Manacapuru and Deseasonalized Q'hydrograph, 1903–85

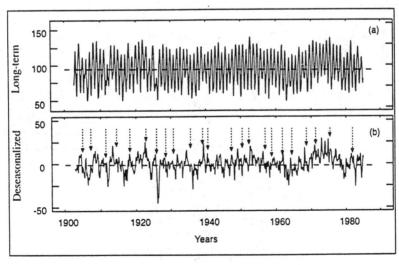

Note: Arrows indicate occurence of ENSO events.
Source: After Richey and others 1989.

of increasing discharge, which began around 1963, the maximum anomalies on record, 30,000 cubic meters a second in 1973 and again in 1976, were obtained. Thereafter, discharge returned to its long-term mean value. Power spectrum analysis of the deseasonalized hydrograph reveals a pronounced spectral peak at 2.4 years. The tendency for regular oscillations on the two- to three-year time scale is evident in the deseasonalized time series itself. Similarly, recurrence intervals are dominated by the two- to three-year flows. The deseasonalized hydrograph exhibits no significant linear trend over the period of record.

These data indicate that the period of 1972 to the present is indeed representative of the historical pattern, and results obtained from these data could be applied to the longer-term record. This conclusion, however, leads to the provocative problem of determining the factors influencing the interannual variability that is observed. The oscillations of river discharge predate significant human influences in the Amazon basin and reflect both extrabasin and local factors.

Climate records and general circulation model calculations suggest that interannual variations in the precipitation regime and hence discharge of the Amazon may be linked to changes in the general circulation of the atmosphere over the tropical Pacific Ocean associated with the El Niño–Southern Oscillation (ENSO) phenomenon. To test this hypothesis, the river discharge anomalies can be compared to atmospheric pressure anomalies at Darwin, Australia, a widely used index of the ENSO. Qualitatively, the months of maximum pressure anomalies (Southern Oscillation negative phase) corresponding to ENSO warm events preceded the negative flow anomalies in most cases. Major ENSO events, for example, in 1925–26 and 1982–83, are reflected in pronounced low discharges. The converse effect, high discharge associated with the Southern Oscillation positive phase, is also apparent. The unusually cold waters of the eastern Pacific in 1989 were accompanied by very high discharge in the Amazon. These observations can be corroborated statistically through cross-spectral analysis between the deseasonalized Amazon and Darwin records and between monthly mean sea surface temperature in the eastern and central equatorial Pacific, a key oceanic indicator of ENSO, and Amazon discharge for the period 1946–85. We conclude from these results that the variability in the Amazon hydrograph on two- to three-year time scales is coupled with the ENSO cycle.

This analysis demonstrates the long-term link between atmospheric circulations outside the basin and discharge within the basin, but it does not shed light on the actual physical mechanisms involved. It has been suggested that the descending branch of zonal circulation over the equatorial Pacific could be shifted eastward to over Amazonia during the Southern Oscillation negative phase, suppressing convection and hence precipitation, while the ascending motions associated with the Southern Oscillation positive phase would be strengthened, promoting increased precipitation over Amazonia and northeastern Brazil. However, only a portion of the variance in the discharge regime is linked to the ENSO phenomenon. Relations between runoff and precipitation are not straightforward, due in part to the carryover storage (basin memory effects) typical of large catchments. The influences of local climate, such as the boundary layer convergence mechanisms and the steady progression of individual fronts and air mass boundaries characteristic of the region, contribute to variability in discharge.

These patterns of interannual variability indicate that considerable caution must be exercised in determining anthropogenic impacts, particularly with the use of short-term records over large areas,. Conversely, it would be difficult to identify a unique deforestation effect in the highly damped discharge regime of the Amazon River mainstem. The likelihood of linkages between the Amazon basin and large-scale atmospheric circulations reinforces the importance of determining the factors controlling the hydrology of the basin in the face of extensive changes in land use. A rigorous analysis of the regional hydrology of the basin using field measurements and remote sensing integrated through realistic, physically based modeling must be considered as the long-range goal for assessing and managing sustainable development in the basin.

The implications for changes in land use

Patterns of land use in the Amazon basin are changing. As summarized by Nelson (1992), the total area deforested was about 400,000 square kilometers, as of August 1989, which corresponds to 8.1 percent of the area and 10.2 percent of the forests. For the 11.6-year period 1978–89 the rate was about 21,000 square kilometers a year (0.53 percent of the naturally forested area a year). Since the peak of 1987, rates have decreased, due to a number of possible factors, including weakening of the threat of agrarian reform by 1988, heavy rainfall in 1989, drastic reduction in the money supply for investments in 1990, and widespread popular sentiment opposed to deforestation in Brazil and abroad, spurring more effective law enforcement. In 1991, deforestation was about half the 1989 rate.

Although speculation is considerable, few data are available on the effects of disturbances on the hydrologic cycle of the Amazon. Several approaches have been taken to speculating on possible consequences.

INTUITION AND BACK-OF-THE-ENVELOPE CALCULATIONS

Salati and others (1979) postulated that a major alteration in vegetative cover of the region would lead to changes in the climate at the microscale and mesoscale. Changes would be felt particularly through variations in the albedo, in the rainwater residence time, increase in runoff, and decrease in evapotranspiration. Increases in maximum temperatures and daily thermal amplitudes, due to a decrease in precipitation, would also be expected. Such alterations would be felt not only in the Amazon region itself but also in other nearby regions, especially the Brazilian central plateau. Bearing such evidence in mind, it is clear that a major alteration in vegetative cover of the region would lead to changes in the climate at the microscale and mesoscale.

LARGE-SCALE MODEL SIMULATIONS

More recently, simulation models have been used to speculate as to what the consequences of turning the Amazon into pasture might be. Two of the most recent general climate model simulations of tropical deforestation were conducted by the United Kingdom Meteorological Office (Lean and Warrilow 1989) and by Shukla, Nobre, and Sellers (1990). In Lean and Warrilow, the model's horizontal resolution was 3.75° longitude by 2.5° latitude, and all the model's vegetation north of 30° South in South America was replaced by grass. Although the total area in which the model's vegetation changed was almost twice that used in DHS and in Shukla, Nobre, and Sellers, their results were similar to those in DHS: surface temperature increased by 2.5°C and evapotranspiration decreased for the pasture scenario compared to the forest one. Additionally, it was found that simulated precipitation was reduced over Amazonia. As in DHS, the increase on surface

temperature was attributed to the decrease in roughness length. In Shukla, Nobre, and Sellers, the COLLA General Climate Model, coupled with the Simple Biosphere Model (SiB) of Sellers and others (1986), was used with a horizontal resolution of 2.8° longitude by 2.8° latitude face roughness length. The annual mean budget of surface energy for Amazonia in the two simulations shows that absorbed solar radiation at the surface is reduced in the deforestation case (186 watts per square meter) relative to the control case (204 watts per square meter) because of the higher albedo for grassland compared to forest (21.6 and 12.5 percent, respectively). That plus the larger outgoing longwave radiation from the surface due to the higher surface temperature in the deforested case mean that the amount of net radiative energy available at the surface for partition into latent and sensible heat flux is smaller in the deforested case than in the control case (146 and 172 watts per square meter, respectively). Also, as remarked in Shukla, Nobre, and Sellers, less precipitation is intercepted and evaporated again because the surface roughness and the canopy water-holding capacity of the pasture are relatively small. Furthermore, the transpiration rates are reduced due to the reduced moisture-holding capacity of the soils under pasture.

An interesting result is that the reduction in calculated annual precipitation was larger than the reduction in evapotranspiration (642 and 496 millimeters, respectively), which suggests that changes in the circulation of atmosphere may act to reduce further the convergence of moisture flux in the region, a result that could not have been anticipated without the use of a dynamic model of the atmosphere, as noted in Shukla, Nobre, and Sellers (1990). This, in turn, implies that runoff also decreased for the deforested case, since the decrease in precipitation was larger than the decrease in evapotranspiration.

Taken together, the results of these studies seem to suggest that the regional climate is significantly sensitive to the removal of tropical forest. In general, the somewhat short period of integration in these studies precludes drawing conclusions about the significance of changes in global climate or even changes in regions adjacent to Amazonia.

The conversion of tropical forested areas into pastures and other types of short vegetation causes changes in the microclimate of the disturbed areas; if the size of the perturbed area is sufficiently large, even the regional climate may be altered.

Depending on their scale, these alterations may cause changes in climate at the global level and affect regions distant from the tropical forests.

LOCAL CHANGES IN CLIMATE

Changes also occur in albedo and in energy and water balances. There is a tendency toward less water infiltration, more runoff during rainy periods, and less runoff during prolonged dry periods. An important conclusion of the micrometeorological studies conducted at Ducke Reserve, near Manaus in central Amazonia (summarized in Shuttlesworth 1988), is that the annual flux of latent heat into the atmosphere is close to its potential value, that is, 20 percent smaller than the potential evapotranspiration during the dry season and about 10 percent above the evapotranspiration rate during the rainy season. Shuttlesworth suggests that there might be a reduction of between 10 and 20 percent in the evapotranspiration for pastures as compared to that for the rain forest, mostly because the albedo of grass is higher than the albedo of tropical forests (thus, the amount of available energy is smaller, other things being equal). That reduction, in turn, might cause rainfall to decrease by 10 percent, he suggested. Yet, this hypothetical scenario takes into account only changes in evapotranspiration due to changes in the availability of radiative energy. Important changes also occur due to the decrease in surface roughness at the soil level. Loss of organic matter in the top soil and fauna in the soil, compaction due to agricultural practices and overgrazing, and soil erosion may cause large changes in the physical and chemical characteristics of the predominantly clay soils of the Amazonian terra firme forest. Those changes likely combine to reduce infiltration rates drastically, increase surface runoff during rainy periods, and decrease soil moisture in the shallower rooting zone of the grass vegetation primarily during the dry season. Decreased availability of soil moisture also reduces evapotranspiration.

Comparative measurements of the diurnal cycle of canopy and subsurface temperature at cleared and forested sites in Ibadan, Nigeria, and in Surinam showed a large increase of soil and air temperatures (more than 5 °C and 3 °C, respectively) for the cleared areas compared to the forested ones. Not being in the shade of a tall canopy, the diurnal fluctuation of ground temperature and humidity deficit was much larger for the cleared sites in these two studies as well. Those changes in soil microclimate have a profound effect on the biological, chemical, and physical processes in the top soil. Plants, animals, and microorganisms living in that layer experience temperature, humidity deficit, and water stresses not present in the remarkably constant microclimate of the forest floor.

REGIONAL CHANGES IN CLIMATE

The summation of local changes in climate over a sufficiently large quasi-contiguous area (say, larger than 1 million square kilometers) might change the transport of water vapor and the water balance at a regional level with consequent changes in the energy balance. Climatic alterations and the scale at which they occur depend on the geographic location and its geomorphology. For instance, even small changes in the low-level wind regime on mountainous areas such as the Andean cordillera can cause a large change in the temporal and geographic distribution of rainfall. It is not possible yet to predict accurately, by means of model simulations of climate, regional changes in climate associated with the observed patterns of deforestation. An important reason for such a limitation is that when current climate models are integrated in a control model, such as attempting to mimic the observed climate, they commonly fail to represent important aspects of the regional climate. One problem is, of course, resolution. It is expected that only when model resolution becomes of the order of 100 kilometers (current climate model resolution is typically between 200 and 500 kilometers) will the models probably capture the finer details of the regional climate. Yet, the results of recent climate model simulations of Amazonian deforestation, reviewed in the previous section, suggest the following changes at the regional level to be likely following extensive deforestation of tropical forests: increase in surface and soil temperature, increase in the diurnal fluctuation of temperature and specific humidity deficit, and reduction in evapotranspiration and PBL moisture. In two of the three studies (Lean and Warrilow 1989; Shukla, Nobre, and Sellers 1990), yearly average precipitation and runoff decreased for Amazonia as a whole for pasture vegetation compared with forest. The annual reduction in rainfall in these two simulations was larger than the corresponding reduction in evapotranspiration, thus explaining the reduction in runoff. It is likely, however, that runoff will increase following rainy periods, that is, runoff (and river streamflow) will be higher after deforestation during the rainy season and will decrease during the dry season.

GLOBAL CHANGES

Tropical forests contribute in many ways to maintain the present dynamic and chemical equilibrium of the atmosphere. Forests represent a carbon reservoir, both through their areal and root systems as well as through organic matter in the soil. Estimates indicate that the Amazon region possesses a reserve of carbon at about 100 gigatons. Therefore, conversion of forests into pastures will release carbon dioxide from the biosphere into the atmosphere, likely enhancing the greenhouse warming.

The burning associated with the process of converting forests into pastures also releases great quantities of particles and compound gases into the atmosphere. These particles cause changes in the atmosphere, especially in its chemical composition and energy balance. To understand and predict any possible large-scale change in climate due to tropical deforestation, it is crucial to know the extent to which the patterns of rainfall change when rain forests are converted into grasslands. It is well known that the tropical regions function as atmospheric sources of heat through the release of latent heat by the condensation in convective clouds. The heat so released drives large-scale tropical circulations (of the Hadley-Walker type) with ascending motion over the tropical regions, mostly over Amazonia, tropical Africa, and the Indonesia–western Pacific region, and descending motion over the dry subtropics, primarily over the subtropical oceans. It is conceivable that a significant reduction in rainfall over Amazonia (say, greater than the 20 percent reduction suggested by the model simulations described in Lean and Warrilow 1989 and Shukla, Nobre, and Sellers 1990) might have an effect in these tropical circulations. However, it is unclear what these changes would be and how they would manifest themselves in terms of climatic changes in the tropics but away from the perturbed areas and in the extra-tropics. Regarding the extra-tropics, Paegle (1987) suggests a possible link between tropical convection and quasi-stationary features of the large-scale circulation over North America. He suggests that the westward shift of the subtropical jet stream from the east coast of North America in boreal winter to the west coast in spring and a concomitant westward shift of the North American longwave trough may be linked to the seasonal, northwestward migration of the area

of maximum rainfall over tropical South America from central Amazonia in January to February to Central America in June to July.

Tropical forest areas also have a characteristic energy balance that contributes to the transport of energy as latent heat (water vapor) from the equatorial regions to those of greater latitude. This is particularly conspicuous in central Brazil, southern Bolivia, Paraguay, and northern Argentina, where, due to the generally southward low-level circulation, most of the water vapor present comes from Amazonia. Therefore, changes in atmospheric moisture in Amazonia due to deforestation might affect the precipitation of the adjacent regions to the south.

Hydroelectric impoundments

Given the vastness of the Amazon hydrologic cycle, the desire to harness some fraction of the energy in the form of hydroelectric power is obvious. In 1987 the Brazilian Ministry of Energy presented the Plan 2010, with the main objective of transforming the Amazon into an energy-export region by that year. That plan was the center of debates about its potential environmental impacts and even the real energy needs of the country.

The first and by far the largest dam is the Tucuruí dam on the Rio Tocantins, 300 kilometers south of Belém, built primarily to supply power to the electrometallurgical industry of the Carajás region of the eastern Amazon. Tucuruí has a nominal capacity of 8,000 megawatts, with about half of that currently on line. Much less efficient are the other dams of the Amazon. The Balbina power plant, built at the Rio Uatuma, north of Manaus, generates only 110 megawatts from an inundated area 2,360 square kilometers, similar to the Tucuruí. Balbina thus generates only 0.1 megawatt per flooded square kilometer against 3.3 megawatts per flooded square kilometer in Tucuruí, and its estimated construction cost of US$3,000 per kilowatt is about four times higher than the cost of building Tucuruí. The Samuel dam, constructed 50 kilometers south of Porto Velho, Rondônia, is another example of the problems associated with hydropower dams in the Amazon. The flatness of the area is also a problem at Samuel. To keep water from spilling into adjacent drainage basins, a huge dike, of almost 60 kilometers in extension, had to be constructed. The nominal capacity of Samuel is 217 megawatts, but as in Balbina, availability of enough water will probably be a problem. The estimated size of the inundation area is 540 square kilometers, generating therefore 0.4 megawatt per square kilometer, a bit more than Balbina, but still much less than Tucuruí. The cost of constructing Samuel was US$5,000 per kilowatt, almost 1.5 time higher than Balbina.

These dams have had controversial effects on the environment and indigenous peoples. An interplay between changes in land use and hydroelectric potential is shown by the following example. The sedimentological studies done for the construction of the Samuel dam did not take into account the possible changes in land use and their effect on the sediment load of the Rio Jamari. Studies that are presently being carried out using the ^{210}Pb technique to calculate the sedimentation rate in a lake near the dam are showing increases in the rates that might be closely correlated to deforestation or tin mining activities in the basin (Forsberg and others 1989). These rates, if continued, will result in a drastically shortened life for the dam.

Future measurement protocols for maintaining sustainability

Objective 3: To assess proposals and suggest research for indicators and/or indexes of sustainability that can be collected easily and frequently used to monitor the sustainability of large regions composed of a mosaic of ecosystem types, up to continent size.

Indexes for monitoring and predicting sustainability

Indicators of sustainability encompass simple measures such as a sustainability index and complex measures such as modeling, prediction, and management. Once determined, a core set of measurements must be collected now and into the future.

SIMPLE INDICATORS: A SUSTAINABILITY INDEX
A sustainability index that somehow summarizes the health or integrity of ecological and human systems in a manner comparable to how the gross national product summarizes economic health is an attractive management target. To what use would such an index be put, and what information should it contain? Many resource-based sectors have their targets—for example, catch or crop yield—but what are the analogs for natural systems? A robust sustainability index

could be a useful means of tracking or monitoring a situation, where a full-blown field campaign would be impossibly expensive to maintain, and the results too complicated to explain. As such, it could provide a useful bridge between the complexities of the physical world and the complexities that managers must confront and sell. How inclusive and universal should such a sustainability index be? There is an elegance to the concept that it should be universally applicable, across all systems and all scales. Such a sustainability index would have to be something like an increase in carbon dioxide. Although perhaps indicative of the planet's health, such a sustainability index is by definition so broad that it carries little new information. Rather, it might make sense to explore more regionally based indexes that summarize the biophysical information of that region in a context as rich in information as possible.

In this spirit, we explore here a sustainability index based on the water cycling characteristics of the Amazon. Ultimately, the integrity of the Amazon ecosystem depends on a dynamic equilibrium between the vegetation and water cycle, such that about half of the rainfall can be derived from evapotranspiration. To reflect this, a simple sustainability index might be the ratio of evapotranspiration to precipitation, where a deviation from 0.5 induced by a change in land use would indicate a loss of sustainability. In practice, this would be difficult to monitor, and deviations from 0.5 could occur for other reasons. The inverse ratio, runoff to precipitation, would be easier to monitor but would suffer from the same lack of precision.

A more robust sustainability index would be the behavior of runoff to precipitation relative to the $\partial^{18}O$ content of precipitation by region (remember the previous discussion of stable isotopes; see figure 26-6). An intact system would be characterized by a runoff to precipitation ratio of about 0.5 and a $\partial^{18}O$ of about $-6°/_{\infty}$. In a system where the recycling of water is affected, runoff would increase (and evapotranspiration would decrease) relative to precipitation, while the relative amount of ^{18}O would decrease; for example, the $\partial^{18}O$ value of rain would become more negative.

MORE COMPLEX INDICATORS: MODELING, PREDICTION, AND MANAGEMENT
A more complex analysis of sustainability that would allow prediction of management options should be based on regional modeling. To simu-

Figure 26–6: Ratio of Runoff to Precipitation Relative to δ¹⁸O, by Region

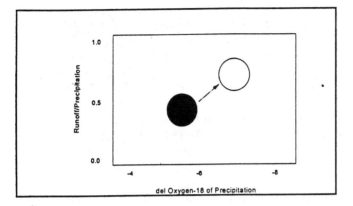

late the hydrologic and biogeochemical consequences of changes in land use, an Amazon tributary-scale (10,000 to 100,000 square kilometers) model for basin runoff and water balance dynamics coupled with the DNAEE data base is necessary. For the purpose of routing both water and its chemical load, the model must provide detailed information about dominant hydrologic processes arrayed in the horizontal, including the residence time of water within each flow pathway. The model must also recognize the constraints of this logistically difficult region.

For example, our research group is formulating a tributary-scale model (RAM) for storm runoff and water balance dynamics for the Amazon River basin (Zhang, Richey, and Dunne 1990). The model is based on the realistic parameterization of microscale physics concerning the production of runoff and the dynamics of soil moisture on hillslopes and flow routing through actual drainage networks. The model allows explicit incorporation of key vegetation, soil, and geomorphologic features of the basin and accepts realistic space-time rainstorms. The model is designed to make maximum and more direct use of the information about land surface and climate forcing, which have been and are to be obtained from the field and by current and anticipated remote-sensing technology. The model integrates several physically based submodels concerning the primary components of the land phase of the hydrologic cycles. The four submodels include the following:

(1) *Model for distributed rainstorms.* The basin area modeled here is larger than the area of rainstorm events that generate runoff and recharge soil moisture. Physically based models for storm runoff and water balance dynamics require spatially and temporally realistic inputs from rainstorms. Precipitation patterns have been observed to have a well-defined hierarchic structure. According to their areal extend, storms can be classified as synoptic area (larger than 10,000 square kilometers), large mesoscale area (1,000 to 10,000 square kilometers), or small-scale area (100 to 1,000 square kilometers). Within the large mesoscale area, either inside or outside a small mesoscale area, are areas made of several convective cells. Each cell ranges from 10 to 30 square kilometers in area. The life spans of these different scales of rainstorms are, respectively, days for synoptic storms, several hours for large mesoscale storms, and a few hours for small mesoscale storms and convective cells. In this hierarchic structure, rainfall intensity increases as the scale decreases. Rainstorms of the small mesoscale or cell clusters are considered significant to basin hydrology and are used as basic rainstorm input for the model.

(2) *Hillslope runoff production model.* Precipitation must then be partitioned through a model for the production of hillslope runoff and soil moisture dynamics. Storm runoff on hillslopes may be produced by three mechanisms: infiltration excess or Horton runoff, saturation excess runoff, and subsurface stormflow. Horton overland flow occurs when the rainfall intensity exceeds the infiltration capacity of soil. Saturation excess runoff occurs when the soil becomes saturated to the surface from below. This mechanism results in the partial areas of runoff production located adjacent to streams. The partial areas may expand or contract during and between storms. Subsurface stormflow occurs when there is significant downslope flow below the hillslope surface and soil saturation from below does not reach the surface. The response of any particular basin may be dominated by a single mechanism or may involve more mechanisms that occur at the same time in different parts of the basin. Hydrologic models for large areas should consider these different runoff production mechanisms. In the heavily vegetated Amazon River basin, it is also necessary to take into account the effects of vegetation on the production of runoff.

Given these processes, RAM will need to convert the rainstorms into hillslope runoff and soil moisture storage in time and space. The microscale processes will be parameterized and averaged within the large-scale model. Separate submodels must be developed for the interception and storage of moisture by land surface vegetation, soil infiltration and infiltration excess runoff, soil moisture dynamics, subsurface stormflow, and saturation excess runoff.

(3) *Model for evapotranspiration.* A model will be used to calculate moisture flux due to evapotranspiration during periods between storms or on "unwetted" lands between patches of storms. The model will determine the antecedent condition of soil moisture for the production of hillslope runoff. Evapotranspiration from land surface soil and layers of vegetation will be calculated using several of the detailed biophysics models being developed elsewhere (the Simple Biosphere Model, SiB) as nodes. These models are designed as a subgrid model of general climate models for calculating the transfer of surface energy, mass, and momentum between the atmosphere and the vegetated land surface. They are physically consistent with the hillslope submodel for runoff production and soil moisture dynamics. The hillslope model will provide realistic initial and boundary soil moisture conditions for SiB-type models, while SiB-type models will provide detailed information on moisture flux from layers of soil and vegetation to atmosphere and antecedent conditions of soil moisture for the hillslope model for runoff production and soil moisture recharge.

(4) *Geomorphologically based channel routing model.* Once runoff to the stream network has been generated, the model will integrate the parameterized and averaged microscale processes of hillslopes and route the hillslope hydrographs to the outlet of the basin. The model will be developed using a generalized basin geometric and stream network structure, to facilitate the integration and routing that occurs in a large drainage basin. In the model, structure and geometry of the basin network are quantified with a width and an area function. Hydrologic response of a basin is closely related to the generalized drainage network by the width function rather than by Horton or Strahler laws. With the generalized structure of the basin network, the flow is routed to the basin outlet by assuming a spatially constant velocity of travel. For routing flow within a drainage basin, the assumption of a spatially uniform velocity of travel has proved to be a reasonable approach.

MEASUREMENT SCHEMES

A core set of measurements must be made into the future. Precipitation, discharge, temperature, humidity, and wind fields must be measured as well as possible over as wide an area as possible. The DNAEE network is fundamental to this effort. It should be maintained and enhanced (including automatic weather stations). To tie to biogeochemical cycles, measurements of atmospheric gases indicative of ecosystem function (carbon dioxide, methane) should be monitored, preferably at selected "towers" coupled with measurements of atmospheric boundary layer. River chemistry at the mouths of key tributaries, with more in areas subject to a change in land use, should be monitored. The actual design of such sampling programs is controlled primarily by the pragmatic realities of what is economically and logistically feasible.

Management options for achieving sustainability of production of goods and services and of ecosystem integrity

The problem of how to preserve the Amazon is extremely complex. Use and preservation of the Amazon's resources have important social and political aspects. Pressure on the Amazon rain forest continues to increase, as the human population grows and the needs of the people outstrip the capacity of the forest to sustain them. For example, the recent decline of the Zona Franca (free trade zone) in Manaus may soon force 100,000 people out of work, many of whom will then turn to the interior if their needs cannot otherwise be met.

The application of science and technology combined with resource management must play a key role in addressing the sustainability of the Amazon. Specific technical issues include problems such as recovering degraded areas and identifying natural products from plants or animals that can be exploited sustainably. Conservation goals must include the preservation of biodiversity as well as maintenance of dynamic processes of the underlying hydrologic and biogeochemical cycles essential to the structure and function of the basin. How can scientific information (data, models) be used in political decisionmaking? How can demographic and economic information really be used for modifying current patterns of land use and developing the elusive target of self-sustaining development?

In summary, sustainability of the tropics should mean not only biodiversity but, in particular, the biophysical processes of the underlying hydrologic and biogeochemical cycles essential to the structure and function of these basins. Studies of these cycles in their natural state are important because they give mankind the time and the tools needed to learn how the necessities of inhabitants can be reconciled with the necessary preservation, in a truly self-sustained development. Such studies provide a basic data set, against which possible effects of changes in land use can be tested.

References

Dall'Ollio, A. 1976. "A composição isotópica das precipitações do Brasil: Modelos isotérmicos e a influência da evapotranspiração na bacia Amazônica." Master's thesis, Universidade de São Paulo, Piracicaba.

Forsberg, B. R., J. M. Godoy, R. L. Victoria, and L. A. Martinelli. 1989. "Development and Erosion in the Brazilian Amazon: A Geochronological Case Study." *GeoJournal* 19, pp. 402–05.

Franken, W., P. R. Leopoldo, E. Matsui, and M. N. G. Ribeiro. 1982. "Interceptação das precipitações em florestas Amazônica de Terra-Firme." *Acta Amazônica* 12, pp. 15–22.

Gentry, A. H. 1986. "An Overview of Neotropical Phytogeographic Patterns with an Emphasis on Amazonia." In M. Dantas, ed., *Proceedings*, Vol. 2, *Flora and Forest*, pp. 19–36. First symposium on the humid tropics. EMBRAPA-CPATU Documentos 36. Belém.

Jordan, C. F., and J. Heuneldop. 1981. "The Water Budget of an Amazonian Rain Forest." *Acta Amazônica* 11, pp. 87–92.

Lean, J., and D. Warrilow. 1989. *Nature* 342, pp. 411–13.

Leopoldo, P. R., W. Franken, E. Matsui, and E. Salati. 1982. "Estimativa da evapotranspiração de floresta Amazônica de Terra-Firme." *Acta Amazônica* 12, pp. 23–28.

Marques, J., Eneas Salati, and J. M. Santos. 1980. "Cálculo da evapotranspiração real na bacia Amazônica através do método aerológico." *Acta Amazônica* 10, pp. 357–61.

Martinelli, Luiz A., Reynaldo L. Victoria, Jeffrey E. Richey, J. Mortatti, and A. H. Devol. Forthcoming. "The Amazon Basin: Natural Cycles and Land Use Change."

Molion, L. C. 1979. "A Climatonomic Study of the Energy and Moisture Fluxes of the Amazon Basin with Considerations of Deforestation Effects." Ph.D. diss., University of Wisconsin, Madison.

Monteith, J. L. 1973. *Principles of Environmental Physics.* New York: Elsevier.

Nelson, B. W. 1992. "Classification of Amazon Vegetation by Satellite Remote Sensing. Uma Estratégia Latino-Americana para a Amazônia." Fundação Memorial de América Latina, São Paulo, Brazil.

Paegle, H. 1987. "Interactions between Convective and Large-scale Motions over Amazonia." In R. Dickinson, ed., *The Geophysiology of Amazonia*, pp. 347–87. New York: John Wiley.

Pires, J. M., and G. T. Prance. 1985. "The Vegetation Types of the Brazilian Amazon." In G. T. Prance and T. E. Lovejoy, eds., *Key Environments, Amazonia*, pp. 109–45. New York: Pergamon Press.

Ribeiro, M. N. G., E. Salati, N. A. Villa Nova, and C. G. B. Demetrio. 1982. "Radiação solar disponível em Manaus (AM) e sua duração com o brilho solar." *Acta Amazônica* 12, pp. 339–46.

Ribeiro, M. N. G, and N. A. Villa Nova. 1979. "Estudos climatológicos da Reserva Florestal Ducke, Manaus, AM. III. Evapotranspiração." *Acta Amazônica* 9, pp. 305–10.

Richey, Jeffrey E., J. B. Adams, and Reynaldo L. Victoria. 1990. "Synoptic-scale Hydrological and Biogeochemical Cycles in the Amazon River Basin: A Modeling and Remote-sensing Perspective." In H. Mooney and R. Hobbs, eds., *Remote Sensing of Biosphere Functioning*, pp. 249–68. Berlin: Springer-Verlag.

Richey, Jeffrey E., J. I. Hedges, A. H. Devol, P. D. Quay, Reynaldo L. Victoria, Luiz A. Martinelli, and B. R. Forsberg. 1990. "Biogeochemistry of Carbon in the Amazon River." *Limnology Oceanography* 35, pp. 352–71.

Richey, Jeffrey E., L. A. Mertes, Reynaldo L. Victoria, B. R. Forsberg, T. Dunne, E. Oliveira, and A. Tancredi. 1989. "Sources and Routing of the Amazon River Floodwave." *Global Biogeochemical Cycles* 3, pp. 191–04.

Richey, Jeffrey E., C. Nobre, and C. Deser. 1989. "Amazon River Discharge: 1903 to 1985." *Science* 246, pp. 101–03.

Richey, Jeffrey E., and Reynaldo L. Victoria. 1994. "C, N, and P Export Dynamics in the Amazon River." In R. Wollast, ed., *Interactions of C, N, P, and S Biogeochemical Cycles*. Berlin: Springer-Verlag.

Salati, Eneas. 1986. "The Climatology and Hydrology of Amazonia." In G. T. Prance and T. E. Lovejoy, eds., *Amazonia*. Oxford, England: Pergamon Press.

———. 1987. "The Forest and Its Hydrological Cycle." In R. Dickinson, ed., *The Geophysiology of Amazônia*, pp. 347–87. New York: John Wiley.

Salati, Eneas, A. Dall'Ollio, J. Gat, and E. Matsui. 1979. "Recycling of Water in the Amazon Basin: An Isotope Study." *Water Resources Research* 15, pp. 1250–58.

Salati, Eneas, and J. Marques. 1984. "Climatology of the Amazon Region." In H. Sioli, ed., *The Amazon Limnology and Landscape Ecology of a Mighty Tropical River and Its Basin*, pp. 87–126. Dordrecht: Dr. W. Junk Publishers.

Salati, Eneas, Reynaldo L. Victoria, Luiz A. Martinelli, and Jeffrey E. Richey. 1989. "Deforestation and Its Role in Possible Changes in the Brazilian Amazon." In R. DeFries and T. F. Malone, eds., *Global Change and Our Common Future: Papers from a Forum*, pp. 159–71. Washington, D.C.: National Academy Press.

Salati, Eneas, Reynaldo L. Victoria, Jeffrey E. Richey, and Luiz A. Martinelli. 1991. "Forests: Their Role in Global Change, with Special Reference to the Brazilian Amazon." *Proceedings of the Second World Climate Conference.* Cambridge, Mass.: Cambridge University Press.

Sellers, P. J., Y. Mintz, Y. C. Sud, and A. Dalcher. 1986. "A Simple Biosphere Model (SiB) for Use within General Circulation Models." *Journal of Atmospheric Science* 43, pp. 505–31.

Shukla, J., C. Nobre, and P. Sellers. 1990. "Amazon Deforestation and Climate Change." *Science* 247, pp. 1322–25.

Shuttlesworth, W. J. 1988. *Quarterly Journal of the Royal Meteorological Society.*

Shuttlesworth, W. J., J. H. C. Gash, C. Lloyd, C. J. Moore, J. Roberts, A. de Marques Filho, G. Fisch, V. de P. Silva Filho, M. N. G. Ribeiro, L. C. B. Molion, L. D. de A Sa, C. A. Nobre, O. M. R. Cabral, S. R. Patel, and J. C. de Moraes. 1984. "Eddy Correlation Measurements of Energy Partition for Amazonian Forest." *Quarterly Journal of the Royal Meteorological Society* 110, pp. 1143–62.

Victoria, Reynaldo L., Luiz A. Martinelli, J. Mortatti, and Jeffrey E. Richey. 1991. "Mechanisms of Water Recycling in the Amazon Basin: Isotopic Insights." *Ambio* 20, pp. 384–87.

Villa Nova, N., Eneas Salati, and E. Matsui. 1976. "Estimativa de evapotranspiracão na bacia Amazônica." *Acta Amazônica* 6, pp. 215–28.

Zhang, W., Jeffrey E. Richey, and T. Dunne. 1990. "Modeling Runoff and Water Balance Dynamics for Large Scale Tropical Drainage Basins." AGU Chapman Conference, Lake Chelan, June.

Comments

José G. Tundisi

The chapter deals with the fundamental question of sustainability in the largest basin on Earth: the Amazon. Some basic questions and problems are addressed, mainly related to the physical effects of the Amazon on the communities and the control of biogeochemical cycles by the large and diverse biomass of plants and animals.

Particularly for the long-term climatological and hydrologic cycles, the records are described and discussed. Of special interest is the analysis of long-term variability, the interannual variations in the precipitation regime, the discharge of water, and the conclusion that extrabasin atmospheric circulation interferes with discharge of the Amazon. The description of physical structure and type and distribution of soil provides the background for application of the sustainability concept.

The patterns of land use are presented; the possible changes that would occur in the water cycle with the change in vegetative cover are discussed. However, there seems to be a scarcity of data about this problem. This is a key issue: the extent to which a major change in the vegetative cover of the Amazon would produce changes at the micro, meso, and macroscale in the climate. What would be the implications for global changes in the planet? The sections on large-scale simulations and the local or regional changes in climate deal with this problem and try to give answers based on tendencies. The possible changes in the atmosphere produced by forest burning are discussed, particularly the effect of chemical composition and the energy balance on tropical circulations. More information is clearly needed before any realistic scenario can be made.

The hydroelectric power plant in Amazonia produces many changes because it is a source of methane and other gases to the atmosphere. It also has a considerable impact on the quality and regional cycle of water, mainly on the Balbina and Samuel reservoirs. Patterns of land use changed extensively after the Amazonian dams were filled.

Satellite imagery indicates that these dams have a short life cycle due to the increase of suspended material carried to the reservoir after intensive deforestation. It remains to be determined what would be the ideal pattern for construction of dams in the Amazon. Large dams such as Tucurui, Balbina, and Samuel undoubtedly produce a lot of changes in the water cycle, the quality of water, and the biota (Tundisi, Matsumura-Tundisi, and Calijuri 1992; Tundisi, forthcoming).

Finally, the authors discusse the design of a sustainability index and provide a basic idea for such an index based on the behavior of runoff and precipitation relative to ^{18}O content by region. The search for such indexes is vital for the future management of the system. The discussion of several types of models to be applied is also pertinent because such models help in the development of predictive capabilities.

The given suggestions for future measurements are interesting and pertinent but, probably, should be more emphatic. The construction of a permanent data bank is the key for the sustainability issue. A more complete analysis and detailed discussion of the sampling schemes and of the overall problem would fill an existing gap. Equally important is the discussion of the management options for the Amazon basin and the various alternatives. This was only slightly mentioned by the authors since this is not the main scope of the chapter, but management and management alternatives are undoubtedly one of the major questions to be considered in the Amazon region.

Two important conclusions can be drawn when analyzing this chapter. (a) First, a sustainability index for the whole region would be impossible, due to its size, diversity, and local and regional biogeophysical characteristics. (b) A much stronger data base is clearly needed. The bottleneck to any proposition about sustainability is clearly the scarcity of continuous data in sub-basins and small watersheds. Any efficient decision about the occupation and management of the Amazon basin has to be based on a reliable, continuous, and strong data bank.

Other remarks

There is no doubt that more research is needed on the hydrologic cycle, not only on a regional and continental scale in the tropics but also in selected representative local watersheds. The quantification of this cycle is an important problem, somewhat neglected in tropical regions. For example, the key role of forests in the water cycle needs to be known for selected watersheds, especially for different types of vegetation.

The integration of natural processes by the river basins is an important concept in the definition of sustainability. The question posed regarding land use and interference with the cycle of water and of carbon and organic matter is fundamental. One particular problem in this cycle is the storage and retention time of water in several subsystems (river, floodplain, lakes, wetlands).

The Amazonian region is very dynamic. One main forcing function is the fluctuation in the level of water that sets up seasonal patterns and to some extent regulates the chemical and biological response of the lotic and lentic systems. The biological diversity is dependent not only on the yearly, physical changes such as fluctuations in the level of water but also on periodic shifts of the river patterns and drainage, which produce patches of isolated forests and oxbow lakes, reminiscent of river meanders.

The definition of the main functional groups of vegetation is an important output, but on a finer scale, the physiological responses of the vegetation are also important. The physiology of the vegetation in the Amazon region is one of the important links among the physical processes, the biogeochemical dynamics, and the community structure.

References

Tundisi, José G. 1994. "Tropical South America: Present and Perspectives." In R. Margalef, ed., *Limnology Now: A Paradigm of Planetary Problems.*

Tundisi, José, T. Matsumura-Tundisi, and M. C. Calijuri. 1992. "Limnology and Management of Reservoirs in Brazil." In M. Straskraba, José G. Tundisi, and A. Duncan, eds., *A Comparative Reservoir Limnology and Water Quality Management.* Dordrech: Kluwer.

27

Limitations in Measuring Sustainability

Richard A. Carpenter

Sustainability, as in sustainable development, I take to mean the continuation of the potential for production from, and use of, managed ecosystems. Demand for food, fiber, and other natural products is increasing so that production and use of ecosystems everywhere are at a high level. Management practices to get the most out of these renewable natural resources (soil, water, plants, and animals) may overwhelm their resilience and self-maintenance capabilities. And yet, forgoing too great a margin of production in order to diminish risk of degradation may worsen the lot of poor, needy people.

It is urgently necessary to be able to measure and predict the sustainability of alternative strategies in agriculture, forestry, fisheries, and other managed ecosystems. Year-to-year data on harvests are obviously the most common and available measure. But yields may be maintained, and degradation obscured, by increasing inputs such as fertilizer, technology, and improved varieties of plants or animals. When decreasing yield is the first or only sign of unsustainability, then some damage to the fundamental potential of the ecosystem may already have occurred and may be difficult to repair.

Natural variations are often quite large compared with mean values of measured parameters. This means that the ratio of signal to noise is so low that it is difficult to detect whether some change in an ecosystem is due to human intervention or not.

These limitations in measuring sustainability are not well understood by many officials and policymakers in economic development, who assume a degree of certainty and understanding that is not justified by the state of the science. It is important to correct these expectations, particularly in international development assistance agencies, where sustainable development is now a catchphrase. These agencies should support research and monitoring to improve measurements of sustainability if their own projects are to be examples of sustainable development.

This chapter presents evidence of the limitations in measuring sustainability from a wide variety of managed ecosystems around the world. In sum, the following excerpts and abstracts convincingly document the severe limitations and inadequacy of biophysical measurements and indicators of sustainability, on which important decisions and econometric analysis must be based.

Relevance to policy and management

Asian Development Bank. 1990. *Economic Policies for Sustainable Development.* Manila: Asian Development Bank.

The Asian Development Bank recently sponsored studies in seven countries to determine how sustainable development might be implemented in practical programs.

- In the preparation of this report no task proved more daunting than the assembly of *reliable statistical indicators* of recent trends and the current state of the environment.

- Aside from the most glaring cases where officials and researchers are aware of what is happening and can describe conditions in general terms most eloquently, the lack of quantitative environmental information comparable with the statistics available regarding economic parameters is a major obstacle to integrated economic-cum-environmental planning.

- *Statistical information on the environment is scarce, often inaccurate, seldom comparable from country to country, and rarely available in a time series covering a sufficient number of years to indicate trends in a reliable way.* Thus, descriptions remain anecdotal and lack the hard edge of quantification which is necessary for analysis and policy formulation. . . .

- Without question one of the most important findings of this study is that while reliable data on conventional economic parameters are plentiful, statistical information on the condition of the environment is scarce and poorly organized [emphasis added] .

Brussard, P. F. 1991. "The Role of Ecology in Biological Conservation." *Ecological Applications* 1, pp. 6–12.

- It is usually taken as a sine qua non that sensible management begins with a solid, fundamental understanding of a species' ecological relations and natural history. Unfortunately we are woefully short on this information for most species of conservation concern. . . . Finally, the solid, underlying science necessary for developing appropriate conceptual models for biodiversity management is generally lacking; even worse, what is known is rarely applied.

Cairns, J. 1991. "The Need for Integrated Environmental Systems Management." In J. Cairns and T. V. Crawford, eds., *Integrated Environmental Management*. Chelsea, Mich.: Lewis Publishers, Inc.

Proactive or preventive measures are desirable to maintain the environment in good condition. Changes in management practice, however, are difficult to justify.

- The uncertainty of the outcome is often unacceptably high. Predicting the precise environmental benefits . . . is a very risky business. This is one of the reasons there is a reluctance to take any action. It is presumed that [making big management changes] would be very costly and the biological benefits not entirely clear. The same thing is true of efforts to restore the tropical rain forests. In both situations, the problem is that the science of ecology still does not have the robust predictive models needed to make the outcome of a particular course of action more certain. . . . Problems such as enormous loss of topsoil, prospects of global warming, and storage of hazardous waste materials, will very likely have such severe consequences that by the time the information base is adequate for the construction of a robust predictive model, it may be too late to take corrective action.

Carpenter, S. R. 1990. "Large-Scale Perturbations: Opportunities for Innovation?" *Ecology* 71, pp. 2038–43.

It is often impossible to replicate ecosystem experiments or otherwise to establish a normal range of variation.

- The variability of community and ecosystem variates may be so great that experiments with only two replicates cannot detect perturbation effects unless they are very large. . . . The intrinsic variability of ecosystems may be so large that rather powerful manipulations would be needed to detect responses even if experiments could be replicated.

Carter, G. C., and B. I. Diamondstone. 1990. *Directions for Internationally Compatible Environmental Data.* New York: Chemisphere Publishing Corporation.

Monitoring programs are poorly coordinated, according to this report of a recent workshop on environmental data measurement and use:

- This results in significant variations in sampling methods, measurement standards, quality control, and procedures to evaluate the quality of the documentation of the data, and often makes it impossible to assess the quality of the measurements. It is often impossible to integrate independently collected data sets for problem solving because of the great difficulties in reconciling one data set with another. Often, data sets may turn out to have little or no value, especially for third-party use in interdisciplinary problems.

- Quality control and data compatibility are required for all measurements, but these requirements are especially difficult to satisfy in biota, due to the intrinsic nonuniformity of intraspecific characteristics, the uncontrollable differences in test environments, and numerous difficulties related to the sampling process. . . .

- In trying to estimate total exposure, the largest uncertainties stem from the lack of good measurement systematics for biota, poorly controlled procedures for the analysis of biological tissues, as well as a dearth of relevant models. . . .

- To date, no single internationally adopted set of standards exists for statistical concepts such as "bias," "precision," and "limit of detection." Work must proceed towards agreement on these measures so that numerical data bases can be based on a single set of definitions.

Cocklin, C. R. 1989. "Methodological Problems in Evaluating Sustainability." *Environmental Conservation* 16, pp. 343–51.

New Zealand has embodied sustainability in its laws, according to Cocklin, but the evaluation of particular initiatives for sustainable development has not been adequately addressed.

- The problems are magnified in the context of sustainability. Most simply, how do we in fact measure whether a system is sustainable or not? In principle and in certain applied cases, it can be a relatively easy task to establish the sustainability of individual resources or systems. Harvesting models for renewable resources, such as fisheries, forests, and aquifers, bear testimony to this. But if we adopt the holistic interpretation of sustainability, it will almost certainly prove impossible to define any single measure of sustainability at a general-system level.

Consultative Group on International Agricultural Research (CGIAR). 1990. *Sustainable Agricultural Production: Implications for International Agricultural Research.* FAO Research and Technology Paper 4. Rome: Food and Agriculture Organization of the United Nations.

The Technical Advisory Committee of CGIAR has characterized the problems of sustainability in agricultural systems.

- At the level of the production system, measurements can be made on a continuing basis during the course of routine experimentation. The question arises, however, of the extent to which the wider aspects of sustainability might be quantified, using a judicious combination of theoretical considerations, experimentation, and modelling. TAC does not consider that Centres should be solely responsible for developing methodologies for this purpose, but they should collaborate with institutions and organizations that specialize in the assessment of agricultural change and environmental impact.

Liverman, D. M., M. E. Hanson, B. J. Brown, and R. W. Merideth, Jr. 1988. "Global Sustainability: Toward Measurement." *Environmental Management* 12, pp. 133–43.

Several organizations compile and publish extensive data bases on environmental and social measures, often as appendixes to documents that expand on or interpret the data: the World Bank's *World Development Report*; the World Resources Institute's series; the Organization for Economic Cooperation and Development's *State of the Environment*; the Worldwatch Institute's *State of the World*; and the Population Reference Bureau's *World Population Data Sheet*.

- Although these recent contributions imply that progress is being made in the development and critical analysis of sustainability indicators, in many cases the existing or proposed indicators are not the most sensitive or useful measures.

Magnuson, J. J. 1990. "Long-term Ecological Research and the Invisible Present. Uncovering the Processes Hidden Because They Occur Slowly or Because Effects Lag Years Behind Causes." *BioScience* 40, pp. 495–01.

- As with observational studies, field experiments also can be susceptible to serious misinterpretation if they are not conducted in the context of long-term ecological research.

For example, only with 132 years of records has the general warming trend been detected in the southern ocean oscillation index and correlated with ice cover.

Sawhill, John C. 1991. "Into the Future." *Nature Conservancy* (November-December), p. 9.

The Nature Conservancy acquires ecosystems, often of large scale, in order to protect them from anthropogenic impacts. But, is effective conservation on this scale practical or even possible?

- In short we need to learn enough about how ecosystems function to improve [and] preserve design and to intervene successfully in management. Similarly, we need to develop new ways of measuring success. No one's tried conservation on this scale before, and the methods for monitoring progress simply don't exist.

United Nations Economic Commission for Latin America and the Caribbean. 1991. *Sustainable Development: Changing Production Patterns, Social Equity, and the Environment.* Santiago, Chile.

Understanding, and even monitoring, of how natural systems function is so inadequate that environmental impacts go unrecognized in decisionmaking.

- There can be no policy of sustainable development without a more detailed knowledge of the acceptable limits of exploitation of ecosystems. The establishment of these standards is essential to development and is even more important in those cases where direct intervention is selected. However, one of the main problems in the region is the lack of sufficient information to establish adequate environmental standards. Incentives for scientific and technological research in all relevant fields are needed if this situation is to be improved. . . . There is substantial evidence that marine and coastal resources are being mismanaged and abused. All too often, the decisions taken in respect of these resources are dictated by narrow, short-term interests. Such decisions are usually taken without having a full scientific knowledge of the potential long-term adverse effects, or without even caring about those effects.

Health of ecosystems

Cairns, J., and B. R. Niederlehner. 1989. "Adaptation and Resistance of Ecosystems to Stress: A Major Knowledge Gap in Understanding Anthropogenic Perturbations." *Speculations in Science and Technology* 12, pp. 23–30.

- The capacity of ecosystems to adapt to anthropogenic stress is presently poorly understood. Unfortunately, there are few places in the world where human activities do not have a major influence on natural systems. The capacity of natural systems to generalize an adaptation from one stress to new stresses is virtually unknown. . . .

- Mechanisms of adaptation at the community level and the influence of the type of stress, either common in evolutionary history, such as organic enrichment, or unprecedented, such as synthetic pesticides, are only partially understood, and their reversibility is not assured once the stress is removed.

Ecological Society of America. 1991. "The Sustainable Biosphere Initiative: An Ecological Research Agenda." *Ecology* 72, pp. 371–412.

- Research programs exist to develop specific sustainable natural resources (e.g., sustainable forestry or sustainable agriculture). However, *current research efforts are inadequate for dealing with sustainable systems that involve multiple resources, multiple ecosystems, and large spatial scales.* Moreover, much of the current research focuses on commodity-based managed systems, with little attention paid to the sustainability of natural ecosystems whose goods and services currently lack a market value.

- [Current] efforts are not presently united in a comprehensive research framework. Such a framework is needed because ecological processes link natural and managed populations to ecosystems and because common ecological principles underlie effective management strategies.

Lovejoy, T. E. "Diverse Considerations." In E. O. Wilson, ed., *Biodiversity*, pp. 421–27. Washington, D.C.: National Academy Press.

- [There are major] limitations deriving from our relatively shallow knowledge of flora and fauna . . . we do not even know the extent of biological diversity on our planet to the nearest order of magnitude. . . . biologists can say relatively little about which species occur where, which are in danger of extinction, where protected areas should be established, and where heavy environmental modification for development is permissible. . . . If we want to perpetuate the dream that we are in charge of our destiny and that of our planet, it can only be [by] maintaining biological diversity—not by destroying it.

Mooney, H. A. 1991. "Emergence of the Study of Global Ecology: Is Terrestrial Ecology an Impediment to Progress?" *Ecological Applications* 1, pp. 2–5.
Terrestrial ecology lacks fundamental knowledge and even a plan to acquire such knowledge.

- Why is it that we are perceived to lack a coherent body of knowledge, and effort, that will readily interface with the current information on the physical drivers and responders to global change?

O'Neill, R. V., C. Hunsaker, and D. Levine. 1990. "Monitoring Challenges and Innovative Ideas." U.S. Environmental Protection Agency International Symposium on Ecological Indicators, October 15–19, 1990, Ft. Lauderdale, Florida.

- Ecosystems are complex, and it is difficult to predetermine what aspects of system structure of dynamics will respond to a specific insult. It is equally difficult to interpret whether a response is a stabilizing compensatory mechanism or a real loss of capacity to maintain the ecosystem. . . . The problems are compounded in broad monitoring programs designed to assess ecosystem "health" at regional and continental scales. It is challenging in the extreme to monitor ecosystem response, at any scale, to past insults as well as an unknown future array of impacts.

Agriculture

Carpenter, R. A., and D. E. Harper. 1989. "Towards a Science of Sustainable Upland Management in Developing Countries." *Environmental Management* 13, pp. 43–54.

- A . . . hypothesis is that statistically reliable data can be obtained from experiments in upland situations, although natural variations of soils, weather, and vegetation are great. . . . The objective of the work is to provide credible quantitative information to help policy and decision makers and resident farmers to plan and implement improved practices based on ecological principles . . . The signal-to-noise ratio in these field experiments is low, and the detection of changes due to human intervention in soil erosion, nutrient movement, and plant productivity is difficult.

Consultative Group on International Agricultural Research (CGIAR). 1990. "Report of the Committee on Sustainable Agriculture. Consultative Group Meeting May 21–25, 1990." The Hague, Netherlands.

- Absolute and universal measurement of sustainability is difficult and probably lies outside CGIARC responsibilities. No single indicator is likely to incorporate many normative judgments that are difficult to quantify—such as the reversibility of degradation, the critical threshold of decline, or the level of diversity necessary to protect the future genetic base of agriculture.
- Several quantifiable indicators taken over time can provide data along crucial dimensions that help to indicate the sustainability of most agricultural production systems. These include, especially, soil organic matter, soil acidity, crop yields or biomass yields per hectare, and net value added to production.

Henderson, C. 1987. "Famines, Droughts, and the 'Norm' in Arid Western Rajasthan: Problems of Modeling Environmental Variability." *Research in Economic Anthropology* 9, pp. 251–80.

- Despite its enormous impact on such populations, the problem of environmental variability has received little sustained attention in anthropology. . . . This situation reflects the fact that research is often carried out within a single year's time. Most descriptions of production outline the events of an "average" or "normal" year, under the assumption that the knowledge of a single annual cycle is sufficient to understand the relationships between local producers' activities and their environmental parameters.
- A key heuristic device assumed in many ecological models is that of cyclical resonance: resources vary around some mean or a state that is characterized as "normal." . . . Quite simply, there is no such thing as a cyclical pattern that can be identified by examining differences in annual rainfall totals.

Nickum, J. E. 1989. "Volatile Waters: Is China's Irrigation in Decline?" East-West Center Working Paper. East-West Center, Honolulu, Hawaii.

- More often than not messages from China's irrigation front this past decade have been dire reports of inadequate support, poor morale, and lost battles. Is China's irrigation sector in trouble, beset by hostile disbursers and myopically indifferent farmers? It is not at all clear that it is.
- What is clear is that the aggregate body counts of irrigated [land] must obscure more than they inform about a very complex, dynamic, and diverse set of conditions.

Rapport, D. J. 1990. *The Use of Indicators to Assess the State of Health of Ecosystems: An Historical Overview*. Notebook of the International Symposium on Ecological Indicators. Environmental Management Assessment Program, U.S. Environmental Protection Agency, Washington, D.C.

- Historical references to degradation of agricultural lands and forests can be found in the writings of Plato and even earlier. Yet many centuries later, we are far from consensus as to the identity of a minimal but sufficient set of indicators by which to measure changes in the state of nature.

Rerkasem, K., and A. T. Rambo. 1988. *Agroecosystem Research for Rural Development.* Chiang Mail, Thailand: Multiple Cropping Centre, Faculty of Agriculture, Chiang Mai University and SUAN.

Sustainability is an emergent property of agroecosystems and is not identical to sustainability as meant by ecologists in natural ecosystems.

• Unlike natural ecosystems, agricultural ecosystems are purposive; they are managed by people to achieve socially defined objectives and their emergent properties are defined in terms of their relationship to meeting these objectives.... Sustainability is not a measurement of the ability of the agroecosystem to persist over time on its own but instead refers to its ability to persist with an acceptable level of human inputs such as labor, fertilizer, or pesticides.

Walters, C. J., and C. S. Holling. 1990. "Large-scale Management Experiments and Learning by Doing." *Ecology* 71, pp. 2060–68.

• In no place can we claim to predict with certainty either the ecological effects of the activities, or the efficacy of most measures aimed at regulating or enhancing them.

• Every major change in harvesting rates and management policies is in fact a perturbation experiment with highly uncertain outcome, no matter how skillful the management agency is in marshalling evidence and arguments in support of the change.

Soil

Andrus, C. 1986. "Soil Erosion and Streamflow from Tropical Grasslands: How Much Do We Really Know?" East-West Center Working Paper. East-West Center, Honolulu, Hawaii.

• Land clearing and fire have transformed large areas of tropical forest in Asia and the Pacific into grassland.... Government agencies in a number of Asian and Pacific countries view ... grasslands as undesirable and have adopted measures to halt expansion of grasslands and convert portions of the area back to trees ... [C]onflicts have spawned a rash of statements concerning the relative merits or disadvantages of tropical grassland with respect to soil erosion and streamflow levels.... What do we really know about the hydrological properties of tropical grasslands? More specifically, how do these properties vary with different levels of burning and grazing, and how do these compare with properties of cultivated or forested land?

Binns, T. 1990. "Is Desertification a Myth?" *Geography* 15, pp. 106–13.

• Over the years the definition of desertification has moved from the "expansion of desert-like conditions" to "a process of sustained land (soil and vegetation) degradation in arid, semi-arid, and dry sub-humid areas, caused at least partly by man," and reducing productive potential to an extent which can neither be readily reversed by removing the cause nor easily reclaimed without substantial investment.... A further problem revealed by studies of drought, degradation, and desertification is a lack of reliable statistics over any considerable length of time ... data needed to classify land are available for very few areas and for very few years, and in most of Africa little is known about range condition, crop yield, or the extent of soil erosion.

Blaikie, P. 1989. "Environment and Access to Resources in Africa." *Africa* 59, pp. 18–40.

• In the area of understanding and evaluating environmental degradation in Africa, the following causes of uncertainty emerge. First, there is the problem of data—its scantiness, unreliability, irrelevance, and ambiguity. Statistics are seldom in the right form, are hard to come by, and even harder to believe let alone interpret.

Faeth, P., R. Repetto, K. Kroll, Q. Dai, and G. Helmers. 1991. "Paying the Farm Bill: U.S. Agricultural Policy and the Transition to Sustainable Agriculture." Washington, D.C.: World Resources Institute.

• In the field, erosion-induced productivity changes are almost impossible to isolate and measure accurately.... Because there is no satisfactory methodology for separating the interacting effects of many factors on crop yields, soil productivity declines due to soil erosion can be easily masked.

Forestry

Bruijnzeel, L. A. 1990. "Summary and Conclusions." In *Hydrology of Moist Tropical Forests and Effects of Conversion: A State of Knowledge Review*, pp. 175–84. Netherlands: IHP Committee.

• Of the two main components of ET [evapotranspiration], rainfall interception has frequently been overestimated because of inadequate sampling designs. The second major component (transpiration) is often only known indirectly and unreliably. . . . The information presented in this report leads to the observation that the adverse environmental conditions so often observed following "deforestation" in the humid tropics are not so much the result of deforestation per se but rather of poor land use practices after clearing of the forest.

Dover, M., and L. M. Talbot. 1987. "To Feed the Earth: Agro-Ecology for Sustainable Development." World Resources Institute, Washington, D.C.

• If diversity causes stability, the most species-rich communities—such as tropical rain forests and coral reefs—should be able to withstand the greatest disruption at human hands. In fact, these communities are among the most fragile.

Harris, L. D. 1984. *The Fragmented Forest: Island Biogeography Theory and the Preservation of Biotic Diversity*. Chicago, Ill.: University of Chicago Press.

• The actual requirements of individual species, populations, and communities have seldom been known, nor has the available information always been employed in site selection and planning for nature reserves. The use of lands surrounding nature preserves has typically been inimical to conservation, since it has usually involved heavy use of pesticides, industrial development, and the presence of human settlements in which fire, hunting, and firewood gathering feature as elements of the local economy.

• Thus, although a great deal of scientific information was available, it was not in a form readily usable for comprehensive planning, nor was it clear that the scheduling of timber operations in hundreds of districts and thousands of old-growth tracts would be greatly or immediately improved by increased knowledge of the internal functioning of the old-growth ecosystem.

Leopold, L. B. 1990. *Ethos, Equity, and the Water Resource*. Washington, D.C.: U.S. Forest Service.

• The Forest Service advertises its dedication to multiple use. But its research gives no assurance that its policy of clear-cutting followed by monoculture will result in sustainability. . . . To my knowledge no Forest Service research is aimed at evaluating over the long-term the effect of changing a multi-storied, mixed-species stand to an even-aged, single species forest. . . . There has been no attempt to make measurements to test the validity of this assumption.

McNitt, B. 1991. "Discussing Free Trade and Tropical Forests." *Conservation Exchange* 9, pp. 5–8.

• The problem is that no one knows what sustainable management of the tropical forest is. No one knows how to do it. Sustainable timber extraction from these forests is still a concept, not a reality (Guillermo Castilleja, resource specialist with the National Wildlife Federation's International Department).

Metz, J. J. 1991. "Vegetation Assessment and Research Methods for Community Forestry in Nepal." East-West Center Working Paper 27. East-West Center, Honolulu, Hawaii.

• A . . . reason to abandon the use of sustainable yield calculations is that the data on which such estimates can be based do not exist. Estimates of biomass and productivity are based on exhaustive, destructive samplings of representative examples of major forest types.

• Not only are the number of such studies completed in Nepal an inadequate data base, but this work is based on and hence only valid for forests with undamaged trees.

Talbot, L. M. 1990. "A Proposal for the World Bank's Policy and Strategy for Tropical Moist Forests in Africa." Draft for discussion. World Resources Institute, Washington, D.C.

• Increasingly, however, scientists are questioning whether sustainability of commercial logging in natural tropical moist forests has ever been demonstrated, and whether it is, indeed, ever possible in other than plantation type situations. . . . [Environmentalists] point to the unquestionable loss of tropical forests following lumbering operations and they say that the claim of "sustainability" is a smoke screen to cover destruction of irreplaceable forests for financial gain.

Water

Birkeland, C. 1990. "Caribbean and Pacific Coastal Marine Systems: Similarities and Differences." *Nature and Resources* 26, pp. 3–12.

- Productivity can be high in areas of low nutrient input because nutrients are perpetually recycled at several levels: microbiologically, physiologically (between the animal and the plant tissues of symbionts), ecologically (in the detrital foodweb and in other interactions between trophic levels), hydrodynamically (by eddies, gyres, high residence time of water in lagoons, and other enclosed coastal features), and through retention of nutrients from the water column to the reef surface by active current producing suspension-feeders such as sponges . . .

- As nutrient input increases on coral reefs up to a point, the growth of benthic vegetation and rates of primary productivity increase. This can sometimes lead to overgrowth and even mortality of corals. Pollution of shallow marine habitats by eutrophication (nutrient input) leads to dominance by benthic algae. Long-term users of the Great Barrier Reef have noted an increase in algal cover and a decrease in coral cover attributed to increased urbanization, industrialization, and agricultural development in relatively heavily populated areas on the Queensland coast. The mechanism by which this operates may be increased nutrient input by sewage or by terrestrial runoff from baring the soil and exposing the coast to erosion.

Group of Experts on the Scientific Aspects of Marine Pollution (GESAMP). 1990. "The State of the Marine Environment." Regional Seas Reports and Studies 115. United Nations Environment Program, Nairobi.

- The most recently reported [global fisheries catch], for 1987, achieved a new record of 92.7 million tonnes, and preliminary figures for 1988 indicate a further increase to 94 million tonnes. It is now expected that the figure of 100 million tonnes, which many believed to be the maximum sustainable global yield of conven-

tional fisheries, will be reached well before the end of the century. However, this progressive increase conceals great variability of natural resources and many problems.

- If environmental assessments are to be valid, the chemical measurements on which they are based must be reliable and adequate for their intended use. This is specially important where the information is to be used for decision making and the enforcement of regulations or for legal purposes.

- It has recently become clear that many chemical measurements in the sea made more than ten years ago are dubious, making it difficult to establish time trends. . . . There is a growing awareness of the need to validate measurements and to be confident of their reliability and adequacy for environmental assessment.

- There is a parallel and equally important need for similar quality control of biological data. However, as biological measurements are more diverse and inherently more variable than chemical measurements, it is more difficult to distinguish errors due to sampling from those due to analytical procedures. Some biological methods are well standardised, but others [are] rather idiosyncratic.

- In addition, the inherent variability of populations and communities leads to a diversity of techniques and many biological data are "snapshots" of dynamic and variable parameters rather than determinations aimed at absolute, or even relative, values of stable characteristics. This makes comparison between different data sets difficult, unless comparable methods have been used and statistical limits to the estimates obtained.

- At a stage where it is necessary to look for relationships between environmental factors and biological responses, this lack of systematic quality control for the biological components of an investigation is inconsistent with the critical scrutiny given to chemical observations, and detracts from the value of the derived relationships. Major efforts are needed to improve this situation.

- The collection of biological material for analysis of contaminant content is rarely undertaken with sufficient safeguards to ensure that the samples are representative of the population. . . . The accurate identification of species is still a significant problem in some biological samples, and there are contentious attributions and difficulties . . . [L]ow levels of contamination could build up insidiously in the sea with subtle effects causing damage to wide areas in the long term.

- Because of the difficulty of recognizing changes of this kind against the background of natural variability, they can be studied only indirectly through a combination of experimental approaches (both in the laboratory and in mesocosms), field surveys, and modelling of process dynamics.

Hofer, T. 1990. *Deforestation: Changing Discharge and Increasing Floods: Myth or Reality?* Berne, Switzerland: University of Berne.

- Climatological data are easily available. Hydrological information is restricted, not only for foreigners but also for Indian scientists. This data situation makes research in India very difficult. . . . [T]here is no evidence that the flooded area in the Gangetic Plain has been increasing over the last decades . . . The decisive statement of the Chenab investigation is representative for all the four analyzed river systems. . . . It is not possible to identify significant changes in the discharge characteristics caused by eventual man-induced ecological degradation of the watershed. . . . Either the trends are statistically not significant or they are parallel for precipitation and discharge.

Karr, J. R. 1991. "Biological Integrity: A Long-neglected Aspect of Water Resource Management." *Ecological Applications* 1, pp. 66–84.

- Although perception of biological degradation stimulated current state and federal legislation on the quality of water resources, that biological focus was lost in the search for easily measured physical and chemical surrogates. The "fishable and swimmable" goal for the Water Pollution Control Act of 1972 . . . and its charge to "restore and maintain" biotic integrity illustrate that law's biological underpinning. Further, the need for operational definitions of terms like "biological integrity" and "unreasonable degradation" and for ecologically sound tools to measure divergence from societal goals have increased interest in biological monitoring.

MacKay, Kenneth Tod. 1991. "Global Warming, Fisheries, and Policy for Sustainable Development." Presented at the International Conference on Global Warming and Sustainable Development, International Center for Living Aquatic Resources Management, Bangkok, June 10–12, 1990. International Center for Living Aquatic Resources Management, Manila, Philippines.

- Accurate catch data are probably severely underestimated as recent data from the Philippines suggest that even if accurate data are obtained on marketable catch (which is seldom the case) there is still another 67 percent of the catch that is consumed or processed locally. Furthermore, many different species are involved in reef fisheries, about sixty species in the Philippines. Accurate data on their capture and details on their interactions are not available. The underlying productive system in coral reef communities is also very complex. It is expected that global climate change will have adverse effects on coral reef systems through sea level rise, sea temperature increase, and increased ultraviolet radiation. ICLARM is working with Philippine researchers to model coral reef fisheries systems, but we concluded that there was little scope for research on the effect of global climate change on coral reefs. The data base is weak, and there is no strong environmental signal that links coral reefs and climate change. Furthermore, the current threat of siltation from terrestrial agriculture and forestry mismanagement and habitat destruction by harmful fishing methods (cyanide, pesticides, and dynamite) may destroy the coral areas well before the effects of global climate change are apparent. Current estimates suggest that 75 percent of the Philippine coral reef areas have been destroyed or severely degraded. Coral reefs are facing the same threats as tropical forests.

- Predictions on the consequences of global climate change for developing countries should only be undertaken where there are good data bases and strong signals between climate change and the production system. In most cases the first step to research the consequences of climate change on fisheries will be to develop suitable data on local production. There may be a need to set up a network of long-term benchmark sites to allow for an examination of changes in fish populations and in the aquatic environment over time.

Morrison, R. J. 1991. *Assessment and Control of Marine Pollution in the South Pacific Islands.* Proceedings of the Pacific Science Congress, Honolulu, Hawaii, May 27–June 1, 1991. Fiji: University of the South Pacific Suva.

- The knowledge gaps that have been identified include the following:

   a.   A lack of long-term data to facilitate the recognition of temporal and spatial trends. There are one or two notable exceptions which are discussed further below.

   b.   A knowledge of the behaviour of toxic contaminants (e.g., pesticides) in critical environments is unavailable.

   c.   There is no basis for estimating the health impacts of the microbiological contamination caused by uncontrolled sewage discharges.

   d.   Few baselines exist for the development of programmes studying ecosystem changes as pollution indicators.

   e.   Apart from certain fish species, information on the extent of use of marine resources is lacking.

National Research Council. 1990. *Managing Troubled Waters: The Role of Marine Environmental Monitoring*. Washington, D.C.: National Academy Press.

- [M]ore than 133 million is spent annually on monitoring programs in the U.S. to acquire information for environmental management decisions and ultimately to ensure protection . . . The general perception is that the costs of monitoring programs, as currently conducted, often exceed their utility and benefit.

- [Despite] three decades of intense activity of protection and restoration, monitoring, public health, measuring microbial indicators, . . . most environmental monitoring programs fail to provide the information needed to understand the condition of the marine environment or to assess the effects of human activity on it. Monitoring is generally not well coupled with research programs and designed to improve the appropriateness of routine measurements and allow interpretation of the implications of monitoring results.

- The marine environment is complex and variable, and it is often difficult to detect, identify, and measure anthropogenic impacts clearly. These factors, coupled with limitations to scientific knowledge, emphasize the need for realistic expectations.

- [R]isk-free decision making is not possible. When well developed, applied, and used, environmental monitoring can help quantify the magnitude of uncertainty, thereby reducing but not eliminating uncertainty in decision making.

Regier, H. A. 1992. "Indicators of Ecosystem Integrity." In D. Mackenzie, ed., *Proceedings of the International Symposium on Ecological Indicators, Ft. Lauderdale, Florida, September 1990*, pp. 183–200. Barking, England: Elsevier Applied Science Publishers.

- Our new indicators will begin to have practical consequences early in the next century since a data series is not likely to be invested with much credibility until it is at least ten years long.

Distributors of World Bank Publications

ARGENTINA
Carlos Hirsch, SRL
Galeria Guemes
Florida 165, 4th Floor-Ofc. 453/465
1333 Buenos Aires

Oficina del Libro Internacional
Alberti 40
1082 Buenos Aires

AUSTRALIA, PAPUA NEW GUINEA,
FIJI, SOLOMON ISLANDS,
VANUATU, AND WESTERN SAMOA
D.A. Information Services
648 Whitehorse Road
Mitcham 3132
Victoria

AUSTRIA
Gerold and Co.
Graben 31
A-1011 Wien

BANGLADESH
Micro Industries Development
Assistance Society (MIDAS)
House 5, Road 16
Dhanmondi R/Area
Dhaka 1209

BELGIUM
Jean De Lannoy
Av. du Roi 202
1060 Brussels

BRAZIL
Publicacoes Tecnicas Internacionais Ltda.
Rua Peixoto Gomide, 209
01409 Sao Paulo, SP

CANADA
Le Diffuseur
151A Boul. de Mortagne
Boucherville, Québec
J4B 5E6

Renouf Publishing Co.
1294 Algoma Road
Ottawa, Ontario
K1B 3W8

CHINA
China Financial & Economic
Publishing House
8, Da Fo Si Dong Jie
Beijing

COLOMBIA
Infoenlace Ltda.
Apartado Aereo 34270
Bogota D.E.

COTE D'IVOIRE
Centre d'Edition et de Diffusion
Africaines (CEDA)
04 B.P. 541
Abidjan 04 Plateau

CYPRUS
Center of Applied Research
Cyprus College
6, Diogenes Street, Engomi
P.O. Box 2006
Nicosia

CZECH REPUBLIC
National Information Center
P.O. Box 668
CS-11357 Prague 1

DENMARK
SamfundsLitteratur
Rosenoerns Allé 11
DK-1970 Frederiksberg C

DOMINICAN REPUBLIC
Editora Taller, C. por A.
Restauración e Isabel la Católica 309
Apartado de Correos 2190 Z-1
Santo Domingo

EGYPT, ARAB REPUBLIC OF
Al Ahram
Al Galaa Street
Cairo

The Middle East Observer
41, Sherif Street
Cairo

FINLAND
Akateeminen Kirjakauppa
P.O. Box 128
SF-00101 Helsinki 10

FRANCE
World Bank Publications
66, avenue d'Iéna
75116 Paris

GERMANY
UNO-Verlag
Poppelsdorfer Allee 55
53115 Bonn

GHANA
Greenwich Mag. and Books
Rivera Beach Hotle
PO Box 01198
Osu-Accra

GREECE
Papasotiriou S.A.
35, Stournara Str.
106 82 Athens

HONG KONG, MACAO
Asia 2000 Ltd.
46-48 Wyndham Street
Winning Centre
7th Floor
Central Hong Kong

HUNGARY
Foundation for Market Economy
Dombovari Ut 17-19
H-1117 Budapest

INDIA
Allied Publishers Private Ltd.
751 Mount Road
Madras - 600 002

INDONESIA
Pt. Indira Limited
Jalan Borobudur 20
P.O. Box 1181
Jakarta 10320

IRAN
Kowkab Publishers
P.O. Box 19575-511
Tehran

IRELAND
Government Supplies Agency
4-5 Harcourt Road
Dublin 2

ISRAEL
Yozmot Literature Ltd.
P.O. Box 56055
Tel Aviv 61560

R.O.Y. International
P.O.B. 13056
Tel Aviv 61130

ITALY
Licosa Commissionaria Sansoni SPA
Via Duca Di Calabria, 1/1
Casella Postale 552
50125 Firenze

JAMAICA
Ian Randle Publishers Ltd.
206 Old Hope Road
Kingston 6

JAPAN
Eastern Book Service
Hongo 3-Chome, Bunkyo-ku 113
Tokyo

KENYA
Africa Book Service (E.A.) Ltd.
Quaran House, Mfangano Street
P.O. Box 45245
Nairobi

KOREA, REPUBLIC OF
Pan Korea Book Corporation
P.O. Box 101, Kwangwhamun
Seoul

Korean Stock Book Centre
P.O. Box 34
Yeoeido
Seoul

MALAYSIA
University of Malaya Cooperative
Bookshop, Limited
P.O. Box 1127, Jalan Pantai Baru
59700 Kuala Lumpur

MEXICO
INFOTEC
Apartado Postal 22-860
14060 Tlalpan, Mexico D.F.

NETHERLANDS
De Lindeboom/InOr-Publikaties
P.O. Box 202
7480 AE Haaksbergen

NEW ZEALAND
EBSCO NZ Ltd.
Private Mail Bag 99914
New Market
Auckland

NIGERIA
University Press Limited
Three Crowns Building Jericho
Private Mail Bag 5095
Ibadan

NORWAY
Narvesen Information Center
Book Department
P.O. Box 6125 Etterstad
N-0602 Oslo 6

PAKISTAN
Mirza Book Agency
65, Shahrah-e-Quaid-e-Azam
P.O. Box No. 729
Lahore 54000

PERU
Editorial Desarrollo SA
Apartado 3824
Lima 1

PHILIPPINES
International Book Center
Suite 1703, Cityland 10
Condominium Tower 1
Ayala Avenue, H.V. dela
Costa Extension
Makati, Metro Manila

POLAND
International Publishing Service
Ul. Piekna 31/37
00-677 Warszawa

PORTUGAL
Livraria Portugal
Rua Do Carmo 70-74
1200 Lisbon

SAUDI ARABIA, QATAR
Jarir Book Store
P.O. Box 3196
Riyadh 11471

SLOVAK REPUBLIC
Slovart G.T.G Ltd.
Krupinska 4
P.O. Box 152
852 99 Bratislava 5

SINGAPORE, TAIWAN,
MYANMAR,BRUNEI
Gower Asia Pacific Pte Ltd.
Golden Wheel Building
41, Kallang Pudding, #04-03
Singapore 1334

SOUTH AFRICA, BOTSWANA
For single titles:
Oxford University Press
Southern Africa
P.O. Box 1141
Cape Town 8000

For subscription orders:
International Subscription Service
P.O. Box 41095
Craighall
Johannesburg 2024

SPAIN
Mundi-Prensa Libros, S.A.
Castello 37
28001 Madrid

Librería Internacional AEDOS
Consell de Cent, 391
08009 Barcelona

SRI LANKA AND THE MALDIVES
Lake House Bookshop
P.O. Box 244
100, Sir Chittampalam A.
Gardiner Mawatha
Colombo 2

SWEDEN
Fritzes Fackboksforetaget
Regeringsgatan 12, Box 16356
S-106 47 Stockholm

Wennergren-Williams AB
P. O. Box 1305
S-171 25 Solna

SWITZERLAND
Librairie Payot
Case postale 3212
CH 1002 Lausanne

Van Dierman Editions Techniques - ADECO
P.O. Box 465
CH 1211 Geneva 16

TANZANIA
Oxford University Press
Maktaba Street
P.O. Box 5299
Dar es Salaam

THAILAND
Central Department Store
306 Silom Road
Bangkok

TRINIDAD & TOBAGO
Systematics Studies Unit
#9 Watts Street
Curepe
Trinidad, West Indies

UGANDA
Gustro Ltd.
1st Floor, Room 4, Geogiadis Chambers
P.O. Box 9997
Plot (69) Kampala

UNITED KINGDOM
Microinfo Ltd.
P.O. Box 3
Alton, Hampshire GU34 2PG
England

ZAMBIA
University of Zambia Bookshop
Great East Road Campus
P.O. Box 32379
Lusaka

ZIMBABWE
Longman Zimbabwe (Pvt.) Ltd.
Tourle Road, Ardbennie
P.O. Box ST 125
Southerton
Harare